A Touchstone Book

A Heritage of Her Own

Toward a New Social History of American Women

edited, with an introduction, by

NANCY F. COTT
and
ELIZABETH H. PLECK

A Touchstone Book
Published by
SIMON AND SCHUSTER
NEW YORK

A Touchstone book
Published by Simon and Schuster
A Division of Gulf & Western Corporation
Simon & Schuster Building
Rockefeller Center
1230 Avenue of the Americas
New York, New York 10020

Designed by Libra Graphics, Inc.
Manufactured in the United States of America
1 2 3 4 5 6 7 8 9 10
1 2 3 4 5 6 7 8 9 10 Pbk.

Library of Congress Cataloging in Publication Data

Main entry under title:

A Heritage of her own.

(A Touchstone book)
Bibliography: p.
Includes index.
1. Women—United States—History—Addresses, essays, lectures. I. Cott, Nancy F. II. Pleck, Elizabeth H.
HQ1410.H47 301.41'2'0973 79-19565

ISBN 0-671-25068-X
0-671-25069-8 Pbk.

ACKNOWLEDGMENTS

Grateful acknowledgment is made to the following publishers and journals for permission to reprint this material:

"The Planter's Wife: The Experience of White Women in Seventeenth-Century Maryland," by Lois Green Carr and Lorena S. Walsh. Reprinted by permission of the authors and publisher from *William and Mary Quarterly*, 3d Ser., 34 (1977): 542–571.

"Vertuous Women Found: New England Ministerial Literature, 1668–1735," by Laurel Thatcher Ulrich. Reprinted by permission of the author and publisher from *American Quarterly* 28, Spring 1976, pp. 20–40. Copyright 1976, Trustees of the University of Pennsylvania.

"Quaker Marriage Patterns in a Colonial Perspective," by Robert V. Wells. Reprinted by permission of the author and publisher from *William and Mary Quarterly*, 3d Ser., 29 (1972): 415–442.

"Eighteenth-Century Family and Social Life Revealed in Massachusetts Divorce Records," by Nancy F. Cott. Copyright © 1976 by Peter N. Stearns. Reprinted with the permission of the author and publisher from the *Journal of Social History* 10 (Fall 1976): 20–43.

"Eighteenth-Century American Women in Peace and War: The Case of the Loyalists," by Mary Beth Norton. Reprinted by permission of the author and publisher from *William and Mary Quarterly*, 3d Ser., 33 (July 1976): 386–409.

"Passionlessness: An Interpretation of Victorian Sexual Ideology, 1790–1850," by Nancy F. Cott. Reprinted from *Signs: A Journal of Women in Culture and Society* 4 (1978): 219–236, by permission of the author and publisher, The University of Chicago Press. Copyright © 1978 by The University of Chicago. All rights reserved.

"The Lady and the Mill Girl: Changes in the Status of Women in the Age of Jackson, 1800–1840," by Gerda Lerner. Reprinted by permission of the author and publisher from *Midcontinent American Studies Journal* 10 (Spring 1969): 5–14. Copyright 1969 by American Studies, Inc., and copyright 1979 by Gerda Lerner.

"Beauty, the Beast, and the Militant Woman: A Case Study in Sex Roles and Social Stress in Jacksonian America," by Carroll Smith-Rosenberg. Reprinted by permission of the author and publisher from *American Quarterly* 23 (1971): 562–584. Copyright 1971, Trustees of the University of Pennsylvania.

Daniel Scott Smith: "Family Limitation, Sexual Control, and Domestic Feminism in Victorian America," *Feminist Studies* 1 (Winter–Spring 1973): 40–57. Reprinted by permission of the author and publisher, *Feminist Studies, Inc.*, % Women's Studies Program, University of Maryland, College Park, Maryland 20742.

Johnny Faragher and Christine Stansell, "Women and Their Families on the Overland Trail to California and Oregon, 1842–1867," *Feminist Studies* 2 (Fall 1975): 150–166. Reprinted by permission of the publisher, *Feminist Studies, Inc.*, % Women's Studies Program, University of Maryland, College Park, Maryland 20742.

"The Life Cycles and Household Structure of American Ethnic Groups: Irish, Germans, and Native-born Whites in Buffalo, New York, 1855," by Laurence A. Glasco. Reprinted by permission of the author and publisher from *Journal of Urban History* 1 (May 1975): 339–364. Copyright © 1975 by Sage Publications, Inc.

"Life in the Big House," from *Roll, Jordan, Roll: The World the Slaves Made*, pp. 343–346, 353–361, 737–739, by Eugene D. Genovese. Copyright © 1972, 1974 by Eugene D. Genovese. Reprinted by permission of Pantheon Books, a Division of Random House, Inc.

"Marital and Sexual Norms Among Slave Women," from *The Black Family in Slavery and Freedom, 1750–1925*, pp. 62–83, 557–561, by Herbert G. Gutman. Copyright © 1976 by Herbert G. Gutman. Reprinted by permission of Pantheon Books, a Division of Random House, Inc.

CONTENTS

INTRODUCTION

BY NANCY F. COTT AND ELIZABETH H. PLECK

THE RESURGENCE OF FEMINISM since the 1960s has sparked insistent questions about the origins of "woman's place." Throughout the contemporary women's movement scholars and others are asserting a feminist will to recover their past, as a means to envision and direct their future. Women now seek to conform the study of history to its traditional purpose *par excellence:* to let us know where we have been, so that we will know where we are going. An intent to renovate marks this search, undertaken by women who feel that their own past has been implicitly and mistakenly omitted in a history of humanity that is in fact the history of men. The endeavor of truth-telling begun by researchers, teachers, and writers of women's history in the past decade has served a "consciousness-raising" function: women who learn more fully about their own history often become more conscious of identification with their gender-group, more aware that their personal circumstances carry the legacy of a sex-specific historical experience, more determined to advance their position as women. Since the appearance of modern feminist thought, the rise of feminist activism and interest in women's history have been symbiotic.

Two tenets in particular of recent feminist thought have required a new look at history. First, the belief that women as a group have a point of view and experience certainly distinguishable from men's implies that all readings of the past (as well as perspectives on current culture) are fatally defective if lacking women's outlook or failing to treat women's position. Most written history can be so described, and so compels a thorough re-viewing. Second, the conviction that inequalities between the sexes are socially constructed rather than divinely or naturally ordained has an inherent historical significance. The proof of social rather than natural origins of women's roles must lie in examination of the past and discovery of social variation over time. It follows that a true history of society should refute natural determinism regarding women's roles; it should reveal the sources of and the purposes served by those social constructions which have hampered women's power and autonomy; it should point the way to change.

The dramatic intensification of scholarly work in women's history in the past decade has another source besides the contemporary women's movement. The rise of the "new social history," which concerns the affairs of ordinary people rather than affairs of state, and focuses on the continuous process of social experience rather than on discrete political events, has been a motivating and facilitating force. Appearing in the *Annales* school of French historical study in the 1920s, the approach of the new social history did not gain prominence in the United States until the 1960s, when scholars, especially those influenced by the New Left, were spurred by social reform and political protest to look at history "from the bottom up" rather than from the point of view of ruling elites. They began to give a voice to the unspoken past of ordinary Americans. In part their new interests reflected the changed composition of the historical profession. History, the oldest and most tradition-laden of scholarly pursuits, was for centuries an art patronized by the rulers of society to ensure their own immortality, and written by members of church and court circles, or learned gentlemen of leisure fascinated by the wars and reigns of the powerful. Its subject matter reflected those class affiliations and aspirations. When the practice of history became more "scientific" and professional in the late nineteenth century, its elite bearing still distinguished it fundamentally from the arriving social sciences. By the 1960s, however, the study of history was no longer the preserve of the gentleman scholar. Diverse immigrants had made their way into the academy. Sons—and daughters—of the working class, perhaps the first generation in their families to have an education, joined the ranks of historians. Their championing of the history of immigrants, peasants, blacks, and industrial workers arose (consciously or unconsciously) in part from their own identities.

To these new subjects came scholars influenced by the outlook of the social sciences and interested in taking the title "social history" from the superficial description of the manners and morals of high society and removing it to the comprehensive study of the history of society and social relations. Social historians began to employ social science methods of explicit conceptualization and hypothesis testing, systematic comparison, and analysis of long-term social trends, in preference to the narrative chronicle and the description of specific extraordinary events. Their attempts were facilitated by new sources of data and new methods for processing them. To unearth the lives of the "anonymous," traditional historical sources such as intellectual treatises, diplomatic correspondence, generals' strategic accounts, or autobiographies by the learned would not serve. Historians had to seek more popular sources, such as folktales, work songs, and oral histories, or documents which yielded mass data, such as registers of births and deaths, censuses, church lists, factory rolls, or records of tax collectors, courts, prisons, and hospitals. Historians of the 1960s used the quantitative methods and computer techniques pioneered in social science to deal with this data.

Although recent trends have precipitated the study of women's history, the field has historical precedent. For several centuries, recurring waves of feminist activism have generated inquiries into women's history, from records of accomplishments of "learned ladies" compiled in eighteenth-century France and England, to readings of history by feminist authors such as Kate Millett and Adrienne Rich today. In between stand out such examples as the surveys of women around the globe by early American feminists and abolitionists Sarah Grimké and Lydia Maria Child, the review of past triumphs and defeats by the activist authors of *A History of Woman Suffrage*, the anthropological-historical theses of Charlotte Perkins Gilman in the 1890s, and painstaking studies of women's work and institutions by social welfare reformers of the early twentieth century. Not professional historians pursuing their craft but women who sought to understand and to re-form the past, to find alternatives to the present, and to create stirring visions of the future have (until the present) made most of these investigations.[1]

The use of history by women trying to advance their sex has ranged, one might colloquially say, from "boosting" to "knocking." That is, some have emphasized women's strengths and accomplishments in the past; at the opposite end, others have promoted social change by stressing (and censuring) the disabilities and constraints suffered by women. Either view can be summoned to the pursuit of feminist (or, indeed, anti-feminist) goals. In American feminist thought the latter has generally dominated, but not without some light from the other end of the spectrum. Enlightenment author Mary Wollstonecraft, for instance, saw the oppression of women when she looked at their past. Mid-nineteenth-century Americans such as Elizabeth Cady Stanton followed that lead, but their polemic and organizing tactics also recognized special strengths in women. The *doyenne* of nineteenth-century manners, Sarah Josepha Hale, editor of *Godey's Lady's Book* and prime advocate of women's advancement within their own "domestic sphere," boosted women's record of accomplishments. Charlotte Perkins Gilman, on the contrary, more like Wollstonecraft a century earlier, searingly condemned the Victorian woman's position and blamed it on past centuries of women's restricted development. If feminists such as Wollstonecraft and Gilman often sounded unsympathetic to the creature called woman, it was not woman's essential character, nor woman as she might be, that they deprecated, but woman as she had become misshapen by gender-dictated constraints. Their social-historical perspective pointed out the possibility of change, since it removed woman's condition from the natural realm, but—unmitigated—it posed a challenge to feminist hopes: How can a sex so long disabled be competent to reclaim its rightful equality? Elizabeth Cady Stanton and Charlotte Perkins Gilman recognized and evaded that problem —as feminist revolutionists had to—by distinguishing woman's reserved potential from her prevalent character and emphasizing the rapidity of progressive change.

As more women joined the historical profession in the early twentieth century, research into women's history became more substantive, data more plentiful, interpretations less schematic. Following the trend of the "new history" of the time, scholars took a closer look at the relation of women's status to their role in economic production. During the 1920s and 1930s, three historians working on the colonial period significantly advanced the development of the field of women's history, discovering new sources as well as innovative uses for conventional ones. Mary Sumner Benson examined prevailing attitudes and expectations in *Women in Eighteenth-Century America* (1935). Focusing on ideology rather than behavior, she used prescriptive, religious, and periodical literature, diaries, travelers' accounts, and fiction. Elisabeth Anthony Dexter probed women's independent business pursuits and other economic contributions in *Colonial Women of Affairs* (1924). In legal records and colonial newspapers she found the evidence she sought of women's commercial activity. Julia Cherry Spruill ventured a comprehensive regional survey of the economic, familial, religious, social, and intellectual habits of white women in *Women's Life and Work in the Southern Colonies* (1938). She employed a wide range of sources, from sermons to wills to family letters, church records to account books to legal transactions. All these authors alluded to a shift occurring in the latter part of the eighteenth century. As the colonists (and then independent Americans) became more affluent, their cities more populous, and their commercial development more mature, the defining characteristics of women of the middle and upper classes began to center more on sentiment than industry. Elisabeth Dexter especially emphasized this. Her book showed that women during the colonial years pursued a variety of business occupations beyond their domestic obligations, and she found a higher proportion of "she-merchants" then than in 1910. Concluding her study with the year 1776, she advanced the hypothesis that acceptance of women's independence and initiative in occupations outside the home declined between 1776 and 1840, thus setting the stage for women's rights protests in the mid-nineteenth century.[2] By suggesting that kind of change, Dexter and the other scholars were affirming the social construction of women's roles. They showed that women's place was not always the same, nor inevitable, while refuting the nineteenth-century assumption that the path of history is one of linear progress. Their work also proposed that demands for wider opportunities for women were not so much a modern departure as a return to traditional prerogatives.

Historian Mary Ritter Beard, far more than her contemporaries Dexter, Benson, and Spruill, reinstated the perspective of the "booster" to inspire the reclamation of women's history that began in the 1960s. For forty years Beard tirelessly researched, spoke, and wrote toward her goal of bringing the world history of women to light, all the while opposing the "feminist" view which emphasized women's disabilities and subordination to men. Repeatedly in her works, which culminated in *Woman as Force in History* (1946), she took "the long view" and argued that women were makers and breakers of civilizations. Far from cowering in domestic dependence, women in Beard's view of history maintained diverse, productive, valorous lives. Beard saw women's care-giving role within the family as a source of female cultural strength. Her faith in woman as "force" forbade her probing into women's subjection, especially within the family. Current scholars share Beard's motivating belief that women's more complete knowledge of their past will foster their autonomy and self-esteem. Like Beard, they reject the assumption that the male is the measure of achievement and excellence, and seek to uncover the unique historical experience of women. Unlike Beard, however, many scholars now dare to impeach women's role within patriarchal family structure. The "new women's history" is more dialectical than Beard's version, acknowledging both strengths and constraints in women's family roles.

The new practice in women's history not only challenges conventional history as Mary Beard's lifework did, but also presses even farther. Women historians who reopened the field began by criticizing, rather than simply building upon the work of their predecessors. An important historiographical essay of 1971, "Women in American Society: An Historical Contribution," by Ann D. Gordon, Mari Jo Buhle, and Nancy E. Schrom, stated the new point of view. The authors divided earlier studies bearing on the history of women into three categories: institutional histories of women's organizations (principally organizations for woman suffrage), biographies of exceptional women, and studies of prescriptive or didactic literature on women's place, family purposes, and the like. They raised objections to the first type because its very focus implied that women deserved historical attention only when they acted like men, by appearing in political life. Moreover, they felt that these histories usually revealed only superficial agencies of social change (ignoring deep-lying economic or social conditions) and tended to gloss over the discrimination suffered by women outside the articulate white middle class. They found biographies wanting because the subjects were always women of wealth or special distinction, susceptible to characterizations of quaintness or psychological reductionism. The authors criticized works in the third category for mistaking image for reality, for insufficiently attending to the gap between ideals and behavior, and for assuming too much about societal norms from unreliable and always class-limited evidence. (People's behavior, social historians now generally agree, is more complex and various than prescriptive literature gives account, although the expectations and ideology it reveals may supply a context for behavior and clarify the boundaries between acceptable and deviant acts.) The essay propounded a new history, explicitly linked to present concerns: "Through a historical critique we can begin to transcend the imposition of contemporary institutions and values on our lives. Without such a critique our view of daily life remains at the level of individual reaction to what strikes us as intolerable." The authors' view was also explicitly dialectical, asserting both the long oppression of women and women's long tradition of struggle. They sought to apply to the case of women the black liberation movement's lesson that understanding history can promote group unity and reveal cultural strengths, as well as evoke past injustices. Opposing the notion that women's history was one of undifferentiated oppression, the authors asked for deeper and more inclusive investigations of ordinary women's lives, to distinguish individuals' varying experiences of womanhood. They asked also for more comprehensive appraisals of change, since they proposed that private as well as public life, familial as well as state constitutions, were subject to structural change.[3]

The characteristic approach of the new women's history is to extend to the past questions raised by and essential insights derived from the contemporary women's movement. Liberal, Marxist, and radical feminists have all raised questions that have stimulated historical research. When Betty Friedan published *The Feminine Mystique* in 1963 and defined "the problem that has no name" suffered by middle-class housewife-mothers, she not only sowed the seeds for the National Organization for Women, but also spurred historical investigation of the ideology and practice of domesticity. Friedan's revelatory assertion that "normal" American women were deprived of personal identity and achievement apart from their home and family roles made women ask about the origins of that all-powerful tie between woman and home and family. The initiation of historical research, especially with regard to nineteenth-century "woman's sphere," owed a great deal to Friedan's formulation and to its companion movement for equalization of women's rights and opportunities. Since liberal feminists saw alternatives to the homebound horizons of women in the world of paid work, their scrutiny of the home also raised the issue of women's employment.

Marxist feminists injected into the discussion queries about the effects of capitalism, particularly industrial capitalism, on women's familial role and economic participation. Broadening the characteristic Marxist emphasis on the determinative role of productive relations and class struggle, Marxist feminists created a new analysis from women's point of view. They pointed out that changes in the mode of reproduction (the process by which a society reproduces its people and its social relations) were as important as changes in the mode of production. They insisted that analysis of the relations between the sexes had to accompany analysis of the relations between the classes.[4] The transition from agrarian to industrial society, a focus of Marxist theory, also commanded historians' and feminists' interest, as the appearance of industrial wage work afforded women the new possibility of self-support, which had the dual potential of submitting them to the exploitation of the employer and of freeing them from their subordination in the patriarchal family. Early research in women's history often centered on the period and process of industrialization, not only because that was a unique social transformation, but also because Marxist feminists had designed a theoretical approach which demanded testing.

Radical feminists have, like the Marxists, pointed to capitalism's function in women's subordination, but they consider the central problem to be patriarchy—men's purposeful control of women, especially through the family unit. Radical-feminist ideas regarding women's oppression and economic dependence within the family, the feminine sex role, and the connections between social roles and sexuality have enormously influenced subject matter and approach in the new women's history. While the search for information about past sexual ideology and behavior would not have gone on without the generally more open discussion of sex which began in the 1960s, neither would it have taken its current path without theories of women's liberation asserting women's right to control their own bodies and sexual practices. Critiques of current sex-role conditioning have sustained research into historically shifting prescriptions of proper feminine demeanor and into role stress. Harking back to Charlotte Perkins Gilman's turn-of-the-century critique of domestic work and women's "sexuo-economic" dependence on men, radical-feminist thinking has frequently sparked, and at least been tacitly present in, analyses of women in the household and family of the past.

The new women's history seeks to bring the lives of ordinary women to the foreground and to understand them in the largest context. As well as criticizing the sexual selectiveness of most earlier historical writing, and attempting to restore women's presence in culture, recent scholars have been exploring women's creation of their own subculture, a way of life defined by language, tasks, and values peculiar to women. Women's history concerns not only what was done *to* women, but also what was done *by* women—often, exclusively *among* women. To see both the cultural and subcultural roles played by women is to understand the coexistence of strengths and subordination.

When they initiated this kind of study, feminists debated whether the position of women vis-à-vis men was analogous to that of a subordinate class, a caste, or a minority group in relation to the dominant power. From years of controversy a consensus has emerged that none of these analogies is wholly suitable. Women constitute a majority of the population. They do not (by and large) live separately from men. Indeed, like no minority group or subordinate class or caste, women live on intimate terms with those who claim superior rights over them, and, besides, bear and nourish and often educate the opposite sex. The personal distinctions and social relations compelled by the existence of two sexes require analysis in and for themselves, in no analogous terms. Recent scholarship has affirmed that sex is, in Joan Kelly-Gadol's words, "a category as fundamental to our analysis of the social order as other classifications, such as class and race."[5]

In establishing sex as a fundamental category, women's history goes beyond the rest of social history. Despite focusing on ordinary people, using new sources, adopting social science methods, and emphasizing social categories such as class, race, age, and family status, social history has often slighted gender differentiation. Urban history studies have given no special attention to women, despite the fact that urban populations as they grew in America had a uniquely high numerical surplus of women over men. Studies of religious change and denominationalism have taken little note that the sex ratio among Protestant converts and supporters was sharply skewed in women's favor. Histories of social reform movements such as abolitionism or progressivism have failed to distinguish the contributions of women. Studies of class mobility based on tax or census listings of the occupations of "household heads" have usually neglected women's economic contribution, thus impairing conclusions about the wealth levels of families.[6] Even studies in the history of the family—a growing component of the new social history—have given little recognition to women as such. Family history, which shares the concentration on ordinary rather than exceptional lives and on private rather than public events, sprang up contemporaneously with women's history, but from different roots, and has maintained a different orientation. The social origins of scholarship about family history are less in the women's movement than in public concerns voiced in the late 1960s about youth culture and the "breakdown of the family." Compared with the pursuit of women's history, explorations in family history have only implicit links to political questions and more explicit links to social science theory and method. Indeed, the development of the field of history of the family in the United States relies on demographers' invention of the technique of "family reconstitution" (pioneered by the French scholar Louis Henry after World War II), on the contribution by sociologists (most notably Talcott Parsons) of structural-functional analysis, on psychoanalytic and other psychological theories relating infant to adult behavior, and on the emphasis on the links between child rearing and culture in the "culture and personality" school of anthropology. Scholarship on the history of the family has most frequently named and dealt with categories such as "household," "parents," "children," "adolescents," and "the aged," without recognizing that each of these is fundamentally divided by sex. The result can be a history that either ignores women or gives the false impression that female and male experiences within the primary institution of the family are the same.

Oriented toward the analysis of sex in the social order, women's history works to encompass the diversity within the category "woman." Through the life cycle of the individual, "woman" has changing incarnations, tied to changes in biology and kinship. Women enter life as daughters. As they reach sexual maturity and attain reproductive capacity, some remain single but most marry and become mothers. Later, mothers see their children leave home; they become mothers-in-law, perhaps, and grandmothers; they reach menopause and become incapable of bearing children. Wives may become widows, and widows may remarry and become wives again. Through these changes in the life cycle, women's roles within their families and in society vary. The location of a woman's work inside or outside her home may depend on whether she is a mother or a daughter, a wife or a widow. Women at varying stages of life may experience historical change differently: in one instance, the industrialization of spinning more immediately affected daughters, whose primary occupation was home spinning, than it affected their own mothers, who were occupied with the other household tasks.

Furthermore, women are described by more than sex and age. They have racial, regional, ethnic, and class identities which they share with men of their group. Women's acts and thoughts come from these identities as well as from their sexual identity. Consider the white planter's wife and the black female slave in the antebellum South: sharing womanhood, they differed in virtually every other respect. Both the wife and the slave were the planter's property, but the white woman, before she was married or after she was widowed, could own the black, and at any time could command her. Which was more influential, the gender which united them or the racial, wealth, and status differences which set them apart? How the several determinants of a woman's identity compare in importance is a central issue in women's history. Current research has frequently pointed out that the common values within a given social grouping —within the planter class or the group of slaves, for instance—do not negate the different experiences that women and men within the group will have because of sex. Yet neither do the common dictates of gender overrule differences among women of divergent social groups. The questions of whether, when, and how far a shared sense of female identity and experience can bridge social differentiation among women have been asked principally in comparison of working-class with middle-class women but may be applied much more widely.

Women's history also disputes the conventional division of history into eras or periods. All such demarcations are arbitrary, in the last analysis, since historical change is constantly taking place. The time boundaries chosen mirror what historians think important in their subjects' lives. To most social historians it is irrelevant to define eras by the years of wars or rulers' reigns. Looser characterizations derived from political events are as often defective: for instance, neither historians investigating class stratification and mobility nor historians of women's lives can accept the substitution of the "era of the common man" for the "Jacksonian era." Since history has traditionally made man as its subject and measure, its periodization has little to do with changes in women's lives. Indeed, what have been known as periods of intellectual advance or political freedom may have been just the opposite from women's point of view.[7]

The most striking and characteristic advances in the new women's history have occurred in the intersection of the themes of women's experience in the family, women's roles as economic producers, and the development of women's consciousness. The emphases within our volume on family, work, and feminism reflect that pattern because of its inherent justification, as well as because of its currency. Women's history must refer to the history of the family, since women's activities have so largely been defined by household and family needs. Even women who have purposely evaded the domestic sphere or family ties, and have lived independently or sought public careers, find that social attitudes toward them are still shaped by the family norm. The "deviance" attributed to nondomestic women expresses how strong that norm is. We emphasize women's family roles since most women—daughters and adult single women as well as wives and mothers—have been situated in domestic life. Their history can only be understood accurately in that context; yet, the fact that history shows women's situation to be socially constructed rather than "in the nature of things" indicates that it is subject to change.

The view of women as members of families is balanced by views of women as workers, and as individuals aware, to greater or lesser degrees, of sharing a sex identity. "Work" here is construed broadly, for if only the monetary standard defining work in the modern world were used, most women's occupations would become invisible. What is most remarkable about women's work seen over time is the conjunction of tremendous change and tremendous stability. The former appears in women's increasing movement from the domestic arena into the paid labor force, in the shift of women's economic contributions from household production of basic commodities and domestic service to factory production and white-collar employment, and in the changing distribution of age and marital status among women in the labor force. Yet, there is overwhelming continuity in women's prevailing responsibility for housework and child care. The new women's history has paid special attention to women's work partly to redress the underestimation of women's economic contributions, as measured by men's standards. The new attention also derives from an assumption that a woman's occupations in the broadest sense—how and where she spends her time, what patterns of industriousness and social relationships her pursuits entail—have an important bearing on her self-perception and social identity. The investigation of women's work, like the investigation of women's family roles, should lead to the discovery of women's consciousness.

To call our third theme "feminism" is to use a shorthand to denote the complicated subject of how women thought about themselves, what drives for autonomy they had, and if and when and why some manifested and acted upon a sense of "we-consciousness," in Simone de Beauvoir's term. The questions for women's history raised by contemporary feminists all involve women's consciousness; that is, they ask not only how gender defines women's treatment, occupations, and so on, but also how women themselves perceive the personal, social, and political meanings of being female. The investigation of women's sense of their own womanhood adapts the Marxist concept of class consciousness to the analysis of gender. It is central to the new women's history because it is central to modern feminist theory, where it is most succinctly expressed in the claim "the personal is political," and enacted in the tactic of consciousness raising. Although the essays here are in social history, the majority, because of their concern with women's consciousness or inchoate feminism, tackle essentially political questions. A good part of the new social history, which began by rejecting political history in its narrative form, has been "political" history, now seen much more inclusively as the history of formal and informal struggles for power. Political questions have motivated major preoccupations in social history. For example, questions about the existence of slave revolts in the antebellum South and about the absence of a viable socialist party in the United States have sustained continuing study of the social condition of slaves and of workers. Women's history identifies an even broader range of political issues, because sexual politics extends from the national arena to the bedroom and nursery. Likewise, feminist issues are not limited to formal politics—the vote, legislation, and so on—but can be seen in all aspects of women's activities and relationships. When women's consciousness becomes an element in the inquiry, questions about women's social circumstances are equally questions about the allocation of power and resources between the sexes. Consideration of women's consciousness demands a model of women's experience more complex than either one of victimization or of triumphs. It weakens any presumption that women were acted upon, rather than actors, and goes beyond objective appraisal to analysis from women's subjective point of view.

Scholars can point to considerable advances in concept formation and data collection in women's history in the past ten years, but they also must acknowledge certain limitations to date. The greatest attention has been paid to the nineteenth century, to the middle class, to the more urban Northeast, to heterosexual relations, to WASPs, and to the age between sexual maturity and menopause. Our volume reflects those strengths (and corresponding gaps) while it attempts, so far as the quality of existing publications allows, to convey the true diversity of women in the United States. No doubt some incipient generalizations about women's historical experience in the United States will be revised as research energies diversify and the scope of scholarship broadens with respect to region, ethnicity, class, sexual preference, and age. What has been suggested thus far on the subject of gender consciousness and the conditions for emergence of feminist attitudes has been based on research on middle-class white women. Those women who constituted the leadership and most of the membership of organized feminism and the struggle for suffrage also have left the largest written record of their thoughts. The relative lack of knowledge of working-class and black women's sentiments is due in part to the kinds of sources used for the investigations: the diaries and letters of the literate evoke their writers' thoughts more effectively than do the vital statistics, census listings, factory rolls, or plantation records usually found to document the lives of workers or slaves. Yet, the gaps also stem from failures of conceptualization. Historians have too often assumed that the ideas and self-perceptions of black and working-class women follow the path of middle-class white women's thinking, or derive wholly from their class or ethnic or familial identity and not from gender.[8]

The investigation of women's history is necessarily comparative, and interdisciplinary. We must appraise comparatively the experiences of women of different cultures, social groups, ages, and so on in order to derive generalizations about womanhood. We must compare women's experience with men's. A complete analysis of the meaning of gender in the social order requires study of what happens among women and among men when each are by themselves, and comparison between these two worlds, as well as study of the social relations between men and women. Women's history is and will be increasingly an integrative study, since its authentic project is to portray not women's culture or experience in isolation, but the social relation of the sexes.[9] In order for current research and theorizing in women's history to affect other sorts of historical writing as they must, however, tremendous inertia has to be overcome. High school history textbooks, despite their constant updating, still barely show women in their pages.[10] But efforts are being made at every educational level, and progress is perceptible, if halting.

So far the writing of women's history has been more frequently and successfully interdisciplinary than it has been comparative, owing in great part to the appearance of women's studies, the fresh blossoming of scholarship about women instigated by feminist ideas and female participants in many disciplines. The constituents of women's studies share a common set of intents: to use sex as a category of analysis, to review existing knowledge and theory in order to criticize omissions and distortions respecting women, to expand sources of information and devise new concepts and paradigms more suitable to an inclusive humanism. Interdisciplinary communication has been a unique hallmark of and an advantage to scholars in women's studies. It has concrete representation in such journals as *Feminist Studies, Signs: A Journal of Women in Culture and Society*, and *Women's Studies*, which have provided an outlet for publication and a forum for discussion.

More challenges and promises of the field lie ahead. Initial questions about domesticity, women's work and industrialization, and sex roles and sexuality have hardly been answered but new questions and frameworks vie for recognition. Forthcoming, it appears, are a new awareness of intrafamily conflict, a greater reliance on analysis of age-groups, pairings such as mother and daughter and generations, an interest in biosocial issues, and a focus on joining and disengagement from social action. The history of feminism persists as an underlying theme. It remains to be answered why feminism, a universal ideology addressed to the condition of all women, has more than once risen and declined in its organized form. Its international links have been knit and raveled, while its constituency has been largely white and middle-class. Historical research on the suffrage movement suggests that the viability of political organization among women varies with the strength of the female subculture and degree of gender consciousness. But the history of feminism in even a broader sense is what is sought. Women have always acted politically; the forms and goals of their political action have varied through time. We know little of these developments in the conventional political arena—from eighteenth-century women's participation in urban crowd actions against unfaithful husbands, for example, to nineteenth-century women's organization of societies and petition campaigns for women's rights—but it is more than we can yet document about the internal growth of feminist consciousness. The fragmentation accompanying the wide diffusion of the women's movement in the 1970s especially calls attention to the relation between individual feminist consciousness and the organized public movement called feminism.

If it is to be faithful to its precedents, the endeavor of recreating women's history will continue to be stimulated by current questions of women's rights and responsibilities, and continue to proceed together with current efforts on behalf of progressive social change. The project of discovering universal, sex-inclusive history—the true history of society—is just beginning. We hold off for the future one of its most intriguing questions: whether in a society characterized by genuine equality of the sexes the distinctiveness of women's historical experience will persist or cease.

NOTES

1. Just as feminists have contributed significantly to women's history, professional women historians have contributed to the feminist movement. In an essay on the historians meriting inclusion in the biographical dictionary *Notable American Women*, Kathryn Kish Sklar points out that eleven of the twenty-two living between 1880 and 1950 were affiliated with some kind of feminist activism. Kathryn Kish Sklar, "American Female Historians in Context, 1770–1930." *Feminist Studies* 3 (1975): 173.

2. Dexter proposed several reasons for the change in the early national period: growing national wealth and the waning of pioneer exigencies on the East coast advanced aspirations to gentility and the image of "the lady"; the organization of work became more complex and the workplace became separate from the home, curtailing women's informal exposure to business activity; the institution of formal schooling requirements for certain lines of work ended women's entry through casual or apprenticeship training; and standardization of the common law and codification of professional requirements in some instances restricted women's access to business opportunities.

3. The essay appeared in *Radical America* 5 (July–August 1971). See Ellen DuBois, "Feminism and Women's History," a paper delivered at the Organization of American Historians meeting, April 20, 1978, San Francisco, California, for a recent critique extending the point of view of the earlier essay.

4. See Joan Kelly-Gadol, "The Social Relations of the Sexes: Methodological Implications of Women's History," *Signs: A Journal of Women in Culture and Society* 1 (1976): 817–823, for expansion of this theme.

5. *Ibid.*, p. 816. See also Gerda Lerner, "Placing Women in History: Definitions and Challenges," *Feminist Studies* 3 (1975): 5–14, and Hilda Smith, "Feminism and the Methodology of Women's History," in Berenice A. Carroll, ed., *Liberating Women's History: Theoretical and Critical Essays*, (Urbana: The University of Illinois Press, 1976), pp. 369–384.

6. See Mary P. Ryan, "Women and the New Social History," a paper delivered at the Organization of American Historians meeting, April 7, 1977, Atlanta, Georgia, for critical comparison of women's history with the new social history.

7. Kelly-Gadol, in "The Social Relations of the Sexes," pp. 810–812, stresses that the inclusion of women in history necessitates reviewing periodization. An interesting example of quite divergent trends in literacy occurring among men and among women can be found in Kenneth A. Lockridge, *Literacy in Colonial New England* (N.Y.: Norton, 1974), pp. 38–42, 57–58.

8. Linda Gordon comments on the problem of "objective" versus "subjective" data in "What Should Women's Historians Do? Politics, Social Theory, and Women's History," *Marxist Perspectives* 1 (Fall 1978): 131–132.

9. In addition to Kelly-Gadol, "Social Relations," see Lerner, "Placing

Women in History," p. 13, and Carroll Smith-Rosenberg, "The New Woman and the New History," *Feminist Studies* 3 (1975): 196.

10. See Frances Fitzgerald, "Rewriting American History, I and II," *The New Yorker*, Feb. 26, 1979, p. 59, and March 5, 1979, p. 49.

1

The Planter's Wife

The Experience of White Women in Seventeenth-Century Maryland

■

LOIS GREEN CARR and LORENA S. WALSH

Longheld assumptions or exaggerations about the British emigrants who colonized America—that they were all martyrs or saints, or all derelicts or convicts—are fast being exploded by social historians. Two historians of colonial Chesapeake society, Lois Green Carr and Lorena S. Walsh, find in passenger lists, court records, wills, and inventories of estates evidence of the peculiar demographic circumstances of early Maryland, and are able to draw a remarkably full portrait of the life experience of white women there. Since research and analysis on colonial women and the family to date have concentrated on the New England colonies, this essay is especially welcome. Its findings exhibit the importance of investigating regional differentiation within the British colonial settlements, no less in areas like family life which might be supposed to be unvarying.

FOUR FACTS WERE BASIC to all human experience in seventeenth-century Maryland. First, for most of the period the great majority of inhabitants had been born in what we now call Britain. Population increase in Maryland did not result primarily from births in the colony before the late 1680s and did not produce a predominantly native population of adults before the first decade of the eighteenth century. Second, immigrant men could not expect to live beyond age forty-three, and 70 percent would die before age fifty. Women may have had even shorter lives. Third, perhaps 85 percent of the immigrants, and practically all the unmarried immigrant women, arrived as indentured servants and consequently married late. Family groups were never predominant in the immigration to Maryland and were a significant part for only a brief time at mid-century. Fourth, many more men than women immigrated during the whole period.[1] These facts—immigrant predominance, early death, late marriage, and sexual imbalance—created circumstances of social and demographic disruption that deeply affected family and community life.

We need to assess the effects of this disruption on the experience of women in seventeenth-century Maryland. Were women degraded by the hazards of servitude in a society in which everyone had left community and kin behind and in which women were in short supply? Were traditional restraints on social conduct weakened? If so, were women more exploited or more independent and powerful than women who remained in England? Did any differences from English experience which we can observe in the experience of Maryland women survive the transformation from an immigrant to a predominantly native-born society with its own kinship networks and community traditions? The tentative argument put forward here is that the answer to all these questions is Yes. There were degrading aspects of servitude, although these probably did not characterize the lot of most women; there were fewer restraints on social conduct, especially in courtship, than in England; women were less protected but also more powerful than those who remained at home; and at least some of these changes survived the appearance in Maryland of New World creole communities. However, these issues are far from settled, and we shall offer some suggestions as to how they might be further pursued.

Maryland was settled in 1634, but in 1650 there were probably no more than six hundred persons and fewer than two hundred adult women in the province. After that time population growth was steady; in 1704 a census listed 30,437 white persons, of whom 7,163 were adult women.[2] Thus in discussing the experience of white women in seventeenth-century Maryland we are dealing basically with the second half of the century.

Marylanders of that period did not leave letters and diaries to record their New World experience or their relationships to one another. Nevertheless, they left trails in the public records that give us clues. Immigrant lists kept in England and documents of the Maryland courts offer quantifiable evidence about the kinds of people who came and some of the problems they faced in making a new life. Especially valuable are the probate court records. Estate inventories reveal the kinds of activities carried on in the house and on the farm, and wills, which are usually the only personal statements that remain for any man or woman, show something of personal attitudes. This essay relies on the most useful of the immigrant lists and all surviving Maryland court records, but concentrates especially on the surviving records of the lower Western Shore, an early-settled area highly suitable for tobacco. Most of this region comprised four counties: St. Mary's, Calvert, Charles, and Prince George's (formed in 1696 from Calvert and Charles). Inventories from all four counties, wills from St. Mary's and Charles, and court proceedings from Charles and Prince George's provide the major data.[3]

Because immigrants predominated, who they were determined much about the character of Maryland society. The best information so far available comes from lists of indentured servants who left the ports of London, Bristol, and Liverpool. These lists vary in quality, but at the very least they distinguish immigrants by sex and general destination. A place of residence in England is usually given, although it may not represent the emigrant's place of origin; and age and occupation are often noted. These lists reveal several characteristics of immigrants to the Chesapeake and, by inference, to Maryland.[4]

Servants who arrived under indenture included yeomen, husbandmen, farm laborers, artisans, and small tradesmen, as well as many untrained to any special skill. They were young: over half of the men on the London lists of 1683–1684 were aged eighteen to twenty-two. They were seldom under seventeen or over twenty-eight. The women were a little older; the great majority were between eighteen and twenty-five, and half were aged twenty to twenty-two. Most servants contracted for four or five years service, although those under fifteen were to serve at least seven years.[5] These youthful immigrants represented a wide range of English society. All were seeking opportunities they had not found at home.

However, many immigrants—perhaps about half[6]—did not leave England with indentures but paid for their passage by serving according to the custom of the country. Less is known about their social characteristics, but some inferences are possible. From 1661, customary service was set by Maryland laws that required four-year (later five-year) terms for men and women who were twenty-two years or over at arrival and longer terms for those who were younger. A requirement of these laws enables us to determine something about age at arrival of servants who came without indentures. A planter who wished to obtain more than four or five years of service had to take his servant before the county court to have his or her age judged and a written record made. Servants aged over twenty-one were not often registered, there being no incentive for a master to pay court fees for those who would serve the minimum term. Nevertheless, a comparison of the ages of servants under twenty-two recorded in Charles County, 1658–1689, with those under twenty-two on the London list is revealing. Of Charles County male servants (N = 363), 77.1 percent were aged seventeen or under, whereas on the London list (N = 196), 77.6 percent were eighteen or over.

Women registered in Charles County court were somewhat older than the men, but among those under twenty-two (N = 107), 5.5 percent were aged twenty-one, whereas on the London list (N = 69), 46.4 percent had reached this age. Evidently, some immigrants who served by custom were younger than those who came indentured, and this age difference probably characterized the two groups as a whole. Servants who were not only very young but had arrived without the protection of a written contract were possibly of lower social origins than were servants who came under indenture. The absence of skills among Charles County servants who served by custom supports this supposition.[7]

Whatever their status, one fact about immigrant women is certain: many fewer came than men. Immigrant lists, headright lists, and itemizations of servants in inventories show severe imbalance. On a London immigrant list of 1634–1635 men outnumbered women six to one. From the 1650s at least until the 1680s most sources show a ratio of three to one. From then on, all sources show some, but not great, improvement. Among immigrants from Liverpool over the years 1697–1707 the ratio was just under two and one half to one.[8]

Why did not more women come? Presumably, fewer wished to leave family and community to venture into a wilderness. But perhaps more important, women were not as desirable as men to merchants and planters who were making fortunes raising and marketing tobacco, a crop that requires large amounts of labor. The gradual improvement in the sex ratio among servants toward the end of the century may have been the result of a change in recruiting the needed labor. In the late 1660s the supply of young men willing to emigrate stopped increasing sufficiently to meet the labor demands of a growing Chesapeake population. Merchants who recruited servants for planters turned to other sources, and among these sources were women. They did not crowd the ships arriving in the Chesapeake, but their numbers did increase.[9]

To ask the question another way, why did women come? Doubtless, most came to get a husband, an objective virtually certain of success in a land where women were so far outnumbered. The promotional literature, furthermore, painted bright pictures of the life that awaited men and women once out of their time; and various studies suggest that for a while, at least, the promoters were not being entirely fanciful. Until the 1660s, and to a lesser degree the 1680s, the expanding economy of Maryland and Virginia offered opportunities well beyond those available in England to men without capital and to the women who became their wives.[10]

Nevertheless, the hazards were also great, and the greatest was untimely death. Newcomers promptly became ill, probably with malaria, and many died. What proportion survived is unclear; so far no one has devised a way of measuring it. Recurrent malaria made the woman who survived seasoning less able to withstand other diseases, especially dysentery and influenza. She was especially vulnerable when pregnant. Expectation of life for everyone was low in the Chesapeake, but especially so for women.[11] A woman who had immigrated to Maryland took an extra risk, though perhaps a risk not greater than she might have suffered by moving from her village to London instead.[12]

The majority of women who survived seasoning paid their transportation costs by working for a four- or five-year term of service. The kind of work depended on the status of the family they served. A female servant of a small planter—who through about the 1670s might have had a servant[13]—probably worked at the hoe. Such a man could not afford to buy labor that would not help with the cash crop. In wealthy families women probably were household servants, although some are occasionally listed in inventories of well-to-do planters as living on the quarters—that is, on plantations other than the dwelling plantation. Such women saved men the jobs of preparing food and washing linen but doubtless also worked in the fields.[14] In middling households experience must have varied. Where the number of people to feed and wash for was large, female servants would have had little time to tend the crops.

Tracts that promoted immigration to the Chesapeake region asserted that female servants did not labor in the fields, except "nasty" wenches not fit for other tasks. This implies that most immigrant women expected, or at least hoped, to avoid heavy field work, which English women—at least those above the cottager's status—did not do.[15] What proportion of female servants in Maryland found themselves demeaned by this unaccustomed labor is impossible to say, but this must have been the fate of some. A study of the distribution of female servants among wealth groups in Maryland might shed some light on this question. Nevertheless, we still would not know whether those purchased by the poor or sent to work on a quarter were women whose previous experience suited them for field labor.

An additional risk for the woman who came as a servant was the possibility of bearing a bastard. At least 20 percent of the female servants who came to Charles County between 1658 and 1705 were presented to the county court for this cause.[16] A servant woman could not marry unless someone was willing to pay her master for the term she had left to serve.[17] If a man made her pregnant, she could not marry him unless he could buy her time. Once a woman became free, however, marriage was clearly the usual solution. Only a handful of free women were presented in Charles County for bastardy between 1658 and 1705. Since few free women remained either single or widowed for long, not many were subject to the risk. The hazard of bearing a bastard was a hazard of being a servant.[18]

This high rate of illegitimate pregnancies among servants raises lurid questions. Did men import women for sexual exploitation? Does John Barth's Whore of Dorset have a basis outside his fertile imagination?[19] In our opinion, the answers are clearly No. Servants were economic investments on the part of planters who needed labor. A female servant in a household where there were unmarried men must have both provided and faced temptation, for the pressures were great in a society in which men outnumbered women by three to one. Nevertheless, the servant woman was in the household to work—to help feed and clothe the family and make tobacco. She was not primarily a concubine.

This point could be established more firmly if we knew more about the fathers of the bastards. Often the culprits were fellow servants or men recently freed but too poor to purchase the woman's remaining time. Sometimes the master was clearly at fault. But often the father is not identified. Some masters surely did exploit their female servants sexually. Nevertheless, masters were infrequently accused of fathering their servants' bastards, and those found guilty were punished as severely as were other men. Community mores did not sanction their misconduct.[20]

A female servant paid dearly for the fault of unmarried pregnancy. She was heavily fined, and if no one would pay her fine, she was whipped. Furthermore, she served an extra twelve to twenty-four months to repay her master for the "trouble of his house" and labor lost, and the fathers often did not share in this payment of damages. On top of all, she might lose the child after weaning unless by then she had become free, for the courts bound out bastard children at very early ages.[21]

English life probably did not offer a comparable hazard to young unmarried female servants. No figures are available to show rates of illegitimacy among those who were subject to the risk,[22] but the female servant was less restricted in England than in the Chesapeake. She did not owe anyone for passage across the Atlantic; hence it was easier for her to marry, supposing she happened to become pregnant while in service. Perhaps, furthermore, her temptations were fewer. She was not 3,000 miles from home and friends, and she lived in a society in which there was no shortage of women. Bastards were born in England in the seventeenth century, but surely not to as many as one-fifth of the female servants.

Some women escaped all or part of their servitude because prospective husbands purchased the remainder of their time. At least one promotional pamphlet published in the 1660s described such purchases as likely, but how often they actually occurred is difficult to determine.[23] Suggestive is a 20 percent difference between the sex ratios found in a Maryland headright sample, 1658–1681, and among servants listed in lower Western Shore inventories for 1658–1679.[24] Some of the discrepancy must reflect the fact that male servants were younger than female servants and therefore served longer terms; hence they had a greater chance of appearing in an inventory. But part of the discrepancy doubtless follows from the purchase of women for wives. Before 1660, when sex ratios were even more unbalanced and the expanding economy enabled men to establish themselves more quickly, even more women may have married before their terms were finished.[25]

Were women sold for wives against their wills? No record says so, but nothing restricted a man from selling his servant to whomever he wished. Perhaps some women were forced into such marriages or accepted them as the least evil. But the man who could afford to purchase a wife—especially a new arrival—was usually already an established landowner.[26] Probably most servant women saw an opportunity in such a marriage. In addition, the shortage of labor gave women some bargaining power. Many masters must have been ready to refuse to sell a woman who was unwilling to marry a would-be purchaser.

If a woman's time was not purchased by a prospective husband, she was virtually certain to find a husband once she was free. Those famous spinsters, Margaret and Mary Brent, were probably almost unique in seventeenth-century Maryland. In the four counties of the lower Western Shore only two of the women who left a probate inventory before the eighteenth century are known to have died single.[27] Comely or homely, strong or weak, any young woman was too valuable to be overlooked, and most could find a man with prospects.

The woman who immigrated to Maryland, survived seasoning and service, and gained her freedom became a planter's wife. She had considerable liberty in making her choice. There were men aplenty, and no fathers or brothers were hovering to monitor her behavior or disapprove her preference. This is the modern way of looking at her situation, of course. Perhaps she missed the protection of a father, a guardian, or kinfolk, and the participation in her decision of a community to which she felt ties. There is some evidence that the absence of kin and the pressures of the sex ratio created conditions of sexual freedom in courtship that were not customary in England. A register of marriages and births for seventeenth-century Somerset County shows that about one-third of the immigrant women whose marriages are recorded were pregnant at the time of the ceremony—nearly twice the rate in English parishes.[28] There is no indication of community objection to this freedom so long as marriage took place. No presentments for bridal pregnancy were made in any of the Maryland courts.[29]

The planter's wife was likely to be in her mid-twenties at marriage. An estimate of minimum age at marriage for servant women can be made from lists of indentured servants who left London over the years 1683–1684 and from age judgments in Maryland county court records. If we assume that the 112 female indentured servants going to Maryland and Virginia whose ages are given in the London lists served full four-year terms, then only 1.8 percent married before age twenty, but 68 percent after age twenty-four.[30] Similarly, if the 141 women whose ages were judged in Charles County between 1666 and 1705 served out their terms according to the custom of the country, none married before age twenty-two, and half were twenty-five or over.[31] When adjustments are made for the ages at which wives may have been purchased, the figures drop, but even so the majority of women waited until at least age twenty-four to marry.[32] Actual age at marriage in Maryland can be found for few seventeenth-century female immigrants, but observations for Charles and Somerset counties place the mean age at about twenty-five.[33]

Because of the age at which an immigrant woman married, the number of children she would bear her husband was small. She had lost up to ten years of her childbearing life[34]—the possibility of perhaps four or five children, given the usual rhythm of childbearing.[35] At the same time, high mortality would reduce both the number of children she would bear over the rest of her life and the number who would live. One partner to a marriage was likely to die within seven years, and the chances were only one in three that a marriage would last ten years.[36] In these circumstances, most women would not bear more than three or four children—not counting those stillborn—to any one husband, plus a posthumous child were she the survivor. The best estimates suggest that nearly a quarter, perhaps more, of the children born alive died during their first year and that 40 to 55 percent would not live to see age twenty.[37] Consequently, one of her children would probably die in infancy, and another one or two would fail to reach adulthood. Wills left in St. Mary's County during the seventeenth century show the results. In 105 families over the years 1660 to 1680 only twelve parents left more than three children behind them, including those conceived but not yet born. The average number was 2.3, nearly always minors, some of whom might die before reaching adulthood.[38]

For the immigrant woman, then, one of the major facts of life was that although she might bear a child about every two years, nearly half would not reach maturity. The social implications of this fact are far-reaching. Because she married late in her childbearing years and because so many of her children would die young, the number who would reach marriageable age might not replace, or might only barely replace, her and her husband or husbands as child-producing members of the society. Consequently, so long as immigrants were heavily predominant in the adult female population, Maryland could not grow much by natural increase.[39] It remained a land of newcomers.

This fact was fundamental to the character of seventeenth-century Maryland society, although its implications have yet to be fully explored. Settlers came from all parts of England and hence from differing traditions—in types of agriculture, forms of landholding and estate management, kinds of building construction, customary contributions to community needs, and family arrangements, including the role of women. The necessities of life in the Chesapeake required all immigrants to make adaptations. But until the native-born became predominant, a securely established Maryland tradition would not guide or restrict the newcomers.

If the immigrant woman had remained in England, she would probably have married at about the same age or perhaps a little later.[40] But the social consequences of marriage at these ages in most parts of England were probably different. More children may have lived to maturity, and even where mortality was as high newcomers are not likely to have been the main source of population growth.[41] The locally born would still dominate the community, its social organization, and its traditions. However, where there were exceptions, as perhaps in London, late age at marriage, combined with high mortality and heavy immigration, may have had consequences in some ways similar to those we have found in Maryland.

A hazard of marriage for seventeenth-century women everywhere was death in childbirth, but this hazard may have been greater than usual in the Chesapeake. Whereas in most societies women tend to outlive men, in this malaria-ridden area it is probable that men outlived women. Hazards of childbirth provide the likely reason that Chesapeake women died so young. Once a woman in the Chesapeake reached forty-five, she tended to outlive men who reached the same age. Darrett and Anita Rutman have found malaria a probable cause of an exceptionally high death rate among pregnant women, who are, it appears, peculiarly vulnerable to that disease.[42]

This argument, however, suggests that immigrant women may have lived longer than their native-born daughters, although among men the opposite was true. Life tables created for men in Maryland show that those native-born who survived to age twenty could expect a life span three to ten years longer than that of immigrants, depending upon the region where they lived. The reason for the improvement was doubtless immunities to local diseases developed in childhood.[43] A native woman developed these immunities, but, as we shall see, she also married earlier than immigrant women usually could and hence had more children.[44] Thus she was more exposed to the hazards of childbirth and may have died a little sooner. Unfortunately, the life tables for immigrant women that would settle this question have so far proved impossible to construct.

However long they lived, immigrant women in Maryland tended to outlive their husbands—in Charles County, for example, by a ratio of two to one. This was possible, despite the fact that women were younger than men at death, because women were also younger than men at marriage. Some women were widowed with no living children, but most were left responsible for two or three. These were often tiny, and nearly always not yet sixteen.[45]

This fact had drastic consequences, given the physical circumstances of life. People lived at a distance from one another, not even in villages, much less towns. The widow had left her kin 3,000 miles across an ocean, and her husband's family was also there. She would have to feed her children and make her own tobacco crop. Though neighbors might help, heavy labor would be required of her if she had no servants, until—what admittedly was usually not difficult—she acquired a new husband.

In this situation dying husbands were understandably anxious about the welfare of their families. Their wills reflected their feelings and tell something of how they regarded their wives. In St. Mary's and Charles counties during the seventeenth century, little more than one-quarter of the men left their widows with no more than the dower the law required—one-third of his land for her life, plus outright ownership of one-third of his personal property. (See Table I.) If there were no children, a man almost always left his widow his whole estate. Otherwise there were a variety of arrangements. (See Table II.)

During the 1660s, when testators begin to appear in quantity,

TABLE I
Bequests of Husbands to Wives, St. Mary's and Charles Counties, Maryland, 1640 to 1710

		Dower or Less	
	N	N	%
1640s	6	2	34
1650s	24	7	29
1660s	65	18	28
1670s	86	21	24
1680s	64	17	27
1690s	83	23	28
1700s	74	25	34
Totals	402	113	28

Source: Wills, I–XIV, Hall of Records, Annapolis, Md.

nearly a fifth of the men who had children left all to their wives, trusting them to see that the children received fair portions. Thus in 1663 John Shircliffe willed his whole estate to his wife "towards the maintenance of herself and my children into whose tender care I do Commend them Desireing to see them brought up in the fear of God and the Catholick Religion and Chargeing them to be Dutiful and obedient to her."[46] As the century progressed, husbands tended instead to give the wife all or a major part of the estate for her life, and to designate how it should be distributed after her death. Either way, the husband put great trust in his widow, considering that he knew she was bound to remarry. Only a handful of men left estates to their wives only for their term of widowhood or until the children came of age. When a man did not leave his wife a life estate, he often gave her land outright or more than her dower third of his movable property. Such bequests were at the expense of his children and showed his concern that his widow should have a maintenance which young children could not supply.

A husband usually made his wife his executor and thus responsible for paying his debts and preserving the estate. Only 11 percent deprived their wives of such powers.[47] In many instances, however, men also appointed overseers to assist their wives and to see that their children were not abused or their property embezzled. Danger lay in the fact that a second husband acquired control of all his wife's property, including her life estate in the property of his predecessor. Over half of the husbands who died in the 1650s and 1660s appointed overseers to ensure that their wills were followed. Some trusted to the overseers' "Care and good Conscience for the good of my widow

TABLE II
Bequests of Husbands to Wives with Children, St. Mary's and Charles Counties, Maryland, 1640 to 1710

	N	All Estate		All or Dwelling Plantation for Life		All or Dwelling Plantation for Widowhood		All or Dwelling Plantation for Minority of Child		More than Dower in Other Form		Dower or Less or Unknown	
		N	%	N	%	N	%	N	%	N	%	N	%
1640s	3	1	33									2	67
1650s	16	1	6	2	13	1	6	1	6	4	25	7	44
1660s	45	8	18	8	18	2	4	3	7	9	20	15	33
1670s	61	4	7	21	34	2	3	3	5	13	21	18	30
1680s	52	5	10	19	37	2	4	2	4	11	21	13	25
1690s	69	1	1	31	45	7	10	2	3	10	14	18	26
1700s	62			20	32	6	10	2	3	14	23	20	32
Totals	308	20	6	101	33	20	6	13	4	61	20	93	30

Source: Wills, I–XIV.

and fatherless children." Others more explicitly made overseers responsible for seeing that "my said child . . . and the other [expected child] (when pleases God to send it) may have their right Proportion of my Said Estate and that the said Children may be bred up Chiefly in the fear of God."[48] A few men—but remarkably few—authorized overseers to remove children from households of stepfathers who abused them or wasted their property.[49] On the whole, the absence of such provisions for the protection of the children points to the husband's overriding concern for the welfare of his widow and to his confidence in her management, regardless of the certainty of her remarriage. Evidently, in the politics of family life women enjoyed great respect.[50]

We have implied that this respect was a product of the experience of immigrants in the Chesapeake. Might it have been instead a reflection of English culture? Little work is yet in print that allows comparison of the provisions for Maryland widows with those made for the widows of English farmers. Possibly, Maryland husbands were making traditional wills which could have been written in the communities they left behind. However, Margaret Spufford's recent study of three Cambridgeshire villages in the late sixteenth century and early seventeenth century suggests a different pattern. In one of these villages, Chippenham, women usually did receive a life interest in the property, but in the other two they did not. If the children were all minors, the widow controlled the property until the oldest son came of age, and then only if she did not remarry. In the majority of cases adult sons were given control of the property with instructions for the support of their mothers. Spufford suggests that the pattern found in Chippenham must have been very exceptional. On the basis of village censuses in six other counties, dating from 1624 to 1724, which show only 3 percent of widowed people heading households that included a married child, she argues that if widows commonly controlled the farm, a higher proportion should have headed such households. However, she also argues that widows with an interest in land would not long remain unmarried.[51] If so, the low percentage may be deceptive. More direct work with wills needs to be done before we can be sure that Maryland husbands and fathers gave their widows greater control of property and family than did their English counterparts.

Maryland men trusted their widows, but this is not to say that many did not express great anxiety about the future of their children. They asked both wives and overseers to see that the children received "some learning." Robert Sly made his wife sole guardian of his children but admonished her "to take due Care that they be brought up in the true fear of God and instructed in such Literature as may tend to their improvement." Widowers, whose children would be left without any parent, were often the most explicit in prescribing their upbringing. Robert Cole, a middling planter, directed that his children "have such Education in Learning as [to] write and read and Cast accompt I mean my three Sonnes my two daughters to learn to read and sew with their needle and all of them to be keept from Idleness but not to be keept as Comon Servants." John Lawson required his executors to see that his two daughters be reared together, receive learning and sewing instruction, and be "brought up to huswifery."[52] Often present was the fear that orphaned children would be treated as servants and trained only to work in the fields.[53] With stepfathers in mind, many fathers provided that their sons should be independent before the usual age of majority, which for girls was sixteen but for men twenty-one. Sometimes fathers willed that their sons should inherit when they were as young as sixteen, though more often eighteen. The sons could then escape an incompatible stepfather, who could no longer exploit their labor or property. If a son was already close to age sixteen, the father might bind him to his mother until he reached majority or his mother died, whichever came first. If she lived, she could watch out for his welfare, and his labor could contribute to her support. If she died, he and his property would be free from a stepfather's control.[54]

What happened to widows and children if a man died without leaving a will? There was great need for some community institution that could protect children left fatherless or parentless in a society where they usually had no other kin. By the 1660s the probate court and county orphans' courts were supplying this need.[55] If a man left a widow, the probate court—in Maryland a central government agency—usually appointed her or her new husband administrator of the estate with power to pay its creditors under court supervision. Probate procedures provided a large measure of protection. These required an inventory of the movable property and careful accounting of all disbursements, whether or not a man had left a will. William Hollis of Baltimore County, for example, had three stepfathers in seven years, and only the care of the judge of probate prevented the third stepfather from paying the debts of the second with goods that had belonged to William's father. As the judge remarked, William had "an uncareful mother."[56]

Once the property of an intestate had been fully accounted and creditors paid, the county courts appointed a guardian who took charge of the property and gave bond to the children with sureties that he or she would not waste it. If the mother were living, she could be the guardian, or if she had remarried, her new husband would act. Through most of the century bond was waived in these circumstances, but from the 1690s security was required of all guardians, even of mothers. Thereafter the courts might actually take away an orphan's property from a widow or stepfather if she or he could not find sureties—that is, neighbors who judged the parent responsible and hence were willing to risk their own property as security. Children without any parents were assigned new families, who at all times found surety if there were property to manage. If the orphans inherited land, English common law allowed them to choose guardians for themselves at age fourteen—another escape hatch for children in conflict with stepparents. Orphans who had no property, or whose property was insufficient to provide an income that could maintain them, were expected to work for their guardians in return for their maintenance. Every year the county courts were expected to check on the welfare of orphans of intestate parents and remove them or their property from guardians who abused them or misused their estates. From 1681, Maryland law required that a special jury be impaneled once a year to report neighborhood knowledge of mistreatment of orphans and hear complaints.

This form of community surveillance of widows and orphans proved quite effective. In 1696 the assembly declared that orphans of intestates were often better cared for than orphans of testators. From that time forward, orphans' courts were charged with supervision of all orphans and were soon given powers to remove any guardians who were shown false to their trusts, regardless of the arrangements laid down in a will. The assumption was that the deceased parent's main concern was the welfare of the child, and that the orphans' court, as "father to us poor orphans," should implement the parent's intent. In actual fact, the courts never removed children—as opposed to their property—from a household in which the mother was living, except to apprentice them at the mother's request. These powers were mainly exercised over guardians of orphans both of whose parents were dead. The community as well as the husband believed the mother most capable of nurturing his children.

Remarriage was the usual and often the immediate solution for a woman who had lost her husband.[57] The shortage of women made any woman eligible to marry again, and the difficulties of raising a family while running a plantation must have made remarriage necessary for widows who had no son old enough to make tobacco. One indication of the high incidence of remarriage is the fact that there were only sixty women, almost all of them widows, among the 1,735 people who left probate inventories in four southern Maryland counties over the second half of the century.[58] Most other women must have died while married and therefore legally without property to put through probate.

One result of remarriage was the development of complex family structures. Men found themselves responsible for stepchildren as well as their own offspring, and children acquired half-sisters and half-brothers. Sometimes a woman married a second husband who himself had been previously married, and both brought children of former spouses to the new marriage. They then produced children of their own. The possibilities for conflict over the upbringing of children are evident, and crowded living conditions, found even in the households of the wealthy, must have added to family tensions. Luckily, the children of the family very often had the same mother. In Charles County, at least, widows took new husbands three times more often than widowers took new wives.[59] The role of the mother in managing the relationships of half-brothers and half-sisters or stepfathers and stepchildren must have been critical to family harmony.

Early death in this immigrant population thus had broad effects on Maryland society in the seventeenth century. It produced what we might call a pattern of serial polyandry, which enabled more men to marry and to father families than the sex ratios otherwise would have permitted. It produced thousands of orphaned children who had no kin to maintain them or preserve their property, and thus gave rise to an institution almost unknown in England, the orphans' court, which was charged with their protection. And early death, by creating families in which the mother was the unifying element, may have increased her authority within the household.

When the immigrant woman married her first husband, there was usually no property settlement involved, since she was unlikely to have any dowry. But her remarriage was another matter. At the very least, she owned or had a life interest in a third of her former husband's estate. She needed also to think of her children's interests. If she remarried, she would lose control of the property. Consequently, property settlements occasionally appear in the seventeenth-century court records between widows and their future husbands. Sometimes she and her intended signed an agreement whereby he relinquished his rights to the use of her children's portions. Sometimes he deeded to her property which she could dispose of at her pleasure.[60] Whether any of these agreements or gifts would have survived a test in court is unknown. We have not yet found any challenged. Generally speaking, the formal marriage settlements of English law, which bypassed the legal difficulties of the married woman's inability to make a contract with her husband, were not adopted by immigrants, most of whom probably came from levels of English society that did not use these legal formalities.

The wife's dower rights in her husband's estate were a recognition of her role in contributing to his prosperity, whether by the property she had brought to the marriage or by the labor she performed in his household. A woman newly freed from servitude would not bring property, but the benefits of her labor would be great. A man not yet prosperous enough to own a servant might need his wife's help in the fields as well as in the house, especially if he were paying rent or still paying for land. Moreover, food preparation was so time-consuming that even if she worked only at household duties, she saved him time he needed for making tobacco and corn. The corn, for example, had to be pounded in the mortar or ground in a handmill before it could be used to make bread, for there were very few water mills in seventeenth-century Maryland. The wife probably raised vegetables in a kitchen garden; she also milked the cows and made butter and cheese, which might produce a salable surplus. She washed the clothes, and made them if she had the skill. When there were servants to do field work, the wife undoubtedly spent her time entirely in such household tasks. A contract of 1681 expressed such a division of labor. Nicholas Maniere agreed to live on a plantation with his wife and child and a servant. Nicholas and the servant were to work the land; his wife was to "Dresse the Victualls milk the Cowes wash for the servants and Doe allthings necessary for a woman to doe upon the s[ai]d plantation."[61]

We have suggested that wives did field work; the suggestion is supported by occasional direct references in the court records. Mary Castleton, for example, told the judge of probate that "her husband late Deceased in his Life time had Little to sustaine himselfe and Children but what was produced out of ye ground by ye hard Labour of her the said Mary."[62] Household inventories provide indirect evidence. Before about 1680 those of poor men and even middling planters on Maryland's lower Western Shore—the bottom two-thirds of the married decedents—[63] show few signs of household industry, such as appear in equivalent English estates.[64] Sheep and woolcards, flax and hackles, and spinning wheels all were a rarity, and such things as candle molds were nonexistent. Women in these households must have been busy at other work. In households with bound labor the wife doubtless was fully occupied preparing food and washing clothes for family and hands. But the wife in a household too poor to afford bound labor—the bottom fifth of the married decedent group—might well tend tobacco when she could.[65] Eventually, the profits of her labor might enable the family to buy a servant, making greater profits possible. From such beginnings many families climbed the economic ladder in seventeenth-century Maryland.[66]

The proportion of servantless households must have been larger than is suggested by the inventories of the dead, since young men were less likely to die than old men and had had less time to accumulate property. Well over a fifth of the households of married men on the lower Western Shore may have had no bound labor. Not every wife in such households would necessarily work at the hoe—saved from it by upbringing, ill-health, or the presence of small children who needed her care—but many women performed such work. A lease of 1691, for example, specified that the lessee could farm the amount of land which "he his wife and children can tend."[67]

Stagnation of the tobacco economy, beginning about 1680, produced changes that had some effect on women's economic role.[68] As shown by inventories of the lower Western Shore, home industry increased, especially at the upper ranges of the economic spectrum. In these households women were spinning yarn and knitting it into clothing.[69] The increase in such activity was far less in the households of the bottom fifth, where changes of a different kind may have increased the pressures to grow tobacco. Fewer men at this level could now purchase land, and a portion of their crop went for rent.[70]

At this level, more wives than before may have been helping to produce tobacco when they could. And by this time they were often helping as a matter of survival, not as a means of improving the family position.

So far we have considered primarily the experience of immigrant women. What of their daughters? How were their lives affected by the demographic stresses of Chesapeake society?

One of the most important points in which the experience of daughters differed from that of their mothers was the age at which they married. In this woman-short world, the mothers had married as soon as they were eligible, but they had not usually become eligible until they were mature women in their middle twenties. Their daughters were much younger at marriage. A vital register kept in Somerset County shows that some girls married at age twelve and that the mean age at marriage for those born before 1670 was sixteen and a half years.

Were some of these girls actually child brides? It seems unlikely that girls were married before they had become capable of bearing children. Culturally, such a practice would fly in the face of English, indeed Western European, precedent, nobility excepted. Nevertheless, the number of girls who married before age sixteen, the legal age of inheritance for girls, is astonishing. Their English counterparts ordinarily did not marry until their mid- to late twenties or early thirties. In other parts of the Chesapeake, historians have found somewhat higher ages at marriage than appear in Somerset, but everywhere in seventeenth-century Maryland and Virginia most native-born women married before they reached age twenty-one.[71] Were such early marriages a result of the absence of fathers? Evidently not. In Somerset County, the fathers of very young brides—those under sixteen—were usually living.[72] Evidently, guardians were unlikely to allow such marriages, and this fact suggests that they were not entirely approved. But the shortage of women imposed strong pressures to marry as early as possible.

Not only did native girls marry early, but many of them were pregnant before the ceremony. Bridal pregnancy among native-born women was not as common as among immigrants. Nevertheless, in seventeenth-century Somerset County 20 percent of native brides bore children within eight and one half months of marriage. This was a somewhat higher percentage than has been reported from seventeenth-century English parishes.[73]

These facts suggest considerable freedom for girls in selecting a husband. Almost any girl must have had more than one suitor, and evidently many had freedom to spend time with a suitor in a fashion that allowed her to become pregnant. We might suppose that such pregnancies were not incurred until after the couple had become betrothed, and that they were consequently an allowable part of courtship, were it not that girls whose fathers were living were usually not the culprits. In Somerset, at least, only 10 percent of the brides with fathers living were pregnant, in contrast to 30 percent of those who were orphans.[74] Since there was only about one year's difference between the mean ages at which orphan and non-orphan girls married, parental supervision rather than age seems to have been the main factor in the differing bridal pregnancy rates.[75]

Native girls married young and bore children young; hence they had more children than immigrant women. This fact ultimately changed the composition of the Maryland population. Native-born females began to have enough children to enable couples to replace themselves. These children, furthermore, were divided about evenly between males and females. By the mid-1680s, in all probability, the population thus began to grow through reproductive increase, and sexual imbalance began to decline. In 1704 the native-born preponderated in the Maryland assembly for the first time and by then were becoming predominant in the adult population as a whole.[76]

This appearance of a native population was bringing alterations in family life, especially for widows and orphaned minors. They were acquiring kin. St. Mary's and Charles counties wills demonstrate the change.[77] (See Table III.) Before 1680, when nearly all those who died and left families had been immigrants, three-quarters of the men and women who left widows and/or minor children made no mention in their wills of any other kin in Maryland. In the first decade of the eighteenth century, among native-born testators, nearly three-fifths mention other kin, and if we add information from sources other than wills—other probate records, land records, vital registers, and so on—at least 70 percent are found to have had such local connections. This development of local family ties must have been one of the most important events of early Maryland history.[78]

Historians have only recently begun to explore the consequences of the shift from an immigrant to a predominantly native population.[79] We would like to suggest some changes in the position of women that may have resulted from this transition. It is already known that as sexual imbalance disappeared, age at first marriage rose, but it remained lower than it had been for immigrants over the second half of the seventeenth century. At the same time, life expectancy improved, at least for men. The results were longer marriages

TABLE III
Resident Kin of Testate Men and Women Who Left Minor Children, St. Mary's and Charles Counties, Maryland, 1640 to 1710

	Families N	No Kin % Families	Only Wife % Families	Grown Child % Families	Other Kin % Families
A.					
1640–1669	95	23	43	11	23
1670–1679	76	17	50	7	26
1700–1710	71	6	35[a]	25	34[b]
B.					
1700–1710					
Immigrant	41	10	37	37	17
Native	30		33[c]	10	57[d]

Notes: [a] If information found in other records is included, the percentage is 30.
[b] If information found in other records is included, the percentage is 39.
[c] If information found in other records is included, the percentage is 20.
[d] If information found in other records is included, the percentage is 70.
For a discussion of wills as a reliable source for discovery of kin see n. 78. Only 8 testators were natives of Maryland before 1680s; hence no effort has been made to distinguish them from immigrants.

Source: Wills, I–XIV.

and more children who reached maturity.[80] In St. Mary's County after 1700, dying men far more often than earlier left children of age to maintain their widows, and widows may have felt less inclination and had less opportunity to remarry.[81]

We may speculate on the social consequences of such changes. More fathers were still alive when their daughters married, and hence would have been able to exercise control over the selection of their sons-in-law. What in the seventeenth century may have been a period of comparative independence for women, both immigrant and native, may have given way to a return to more traditional European social controls over the creation of new families. If so, we might see the results in a decline in bridal pregnancy and perhaps a decline in bastardy.[82]

We may also find the wife losing ground in the household polity, although her economic importance probably remained unimpaired. Indeed, she must have been far more likely than a seventeenth-century immigrant woman to bring property to her marriage. But several changes may have caused women to play a smaller role than before in household decision-making.[83] Women became proportionately more numerous and may have lost bargaining power.[84] Furthermore, as marriages lasted longer, the proportion of households full of stepchildren and half-brothers and half-sisters united primarily by the mother must have diminished. Finally, when husbands died, more widows would have had children old enough to maintain them and any minor brothers and sisters. There would be less need for women to play a controlling role, as well as less incentive for their husbands to grant it. The provincial marriage of the eighteenth century may have more closely resembled that of England than did the immigrant marriage of the seventeenth century.

If this change occurred, we should find symptoms to measure. There should be fewer gifts from husbands to wives of property put at the wife's disposal. Husbands should less frequently make bequests to wives that provided them with property beyond their dower. A wife might even be restricted to less than her dower, although the law allowed her to choose her dower instead of a bequest.[85] At the same time, children should be commanded to maintain their mothers.

However, St. Mary's County wills do not show these symptoms. (See Table IV.) True, wives occasionally were willed less than their dower, an arrangement that was rare in the wills examined for the period before 1710. But there was no overall decrease in bequests to wives of property beyond their dower, nor was there a tendency to confine the wife's interest to the term of her widowhood or the minority of the oldest son. Children were not exhorted to help their mothers or give them living space. Widows evidently received at least enough property to maintain themselves, and husbands saw no need to ensure the help of children in managing it. Possibly, then, women did not lose ground, or at least not all ground, within the family polity. The demographic disruption of New World settlement may have given women power which they were able to keep even after sex ratios became balanced and traditional family networks appeared. Immigrant mothers may have bequeathed their daughters a legacy of independence which they in turn handed down, despite pressures toward more traditional behavior.

It is time to issue a warning. Whether or not Maryland women in a creole society lost ground, the argument hinges on an interpretation of English behavior that also requires testing. Either position supposes that women in seventeenth-century Maryland obtained power in the household which wives of English farmers did not enjoy. Much of the evidence for Maryland is drawn from the disposition of property in wills. If English wills show a similar pattern, similar inferences might be drawn about English women. We have already discussed evidence from English wills that supports the view

TABLE IV

Bequests of Husbands to Wives with Children, St. Mary's County, Maryland, 1710 to 1776

	N	All Estate	All or Dwelling Plantation for Life	All or Dwelling Plantation for Widowhood	All or Dwelling Plantation for Minority of Child	More than Dower in Other Form	Dower or Less or Unknown	Maintenance or House Room
		%	%	%	%	%	%	%
1710–1714	13	0	46	0	0	23	31	0
1715–1719	25	4	24	4	0	28	36	4
1720–1724	31	10	42	0	0	28	23	3
1725–1729	34	3	29	0	0	24	41	3
1730–1734	31	6	16	13	0	29	35	0
1735–1739	27	0	37	4	4	19	37	0
1740–1744	35	0	40	0	3	23	34	0
1745–1749	39	3	31	8	0	31	28	0
1750–1754	43	2	35	7	0	16	40	0
1755–1759	34	3	41	3	0	41	12	0
1760–1764	48	2	46	10	2	13	27	0
1765–1769	45	4	27	11	2	18	33	4
1770–1774	46	4	26	7	0	37	26	0
1775–1776	19	5	32	26	0	5	32	0
Totals	470	3	33	7	1	24	31	1

Source: Wills, XIV–XLI.

that women in Maryland were favored; but the position of seventeenth-century English women—especially those not of gentle status—has been little explored.[86] A finding of little difference between bequests to women in England and in Maryland would greatly weaken the argument that demographic stress created peculiar conditions especially favorable to Maryland women.

If the demography of Maryland produced the effects here described, such effects should also be evident elsewhere in the Chesapeake. The four characteristics of the seventeenth-century Maryland population—immigrant predominance, early death, late marriage, and sexual imbalance—are to be found everywhere in the region, at least at first. The timing of the disappearance of these peculiarities may have varied from place to place, depending on date of settlement or rapidity of development, but the effect of their existence upon the experience of women should be clear. Should research in other areas of the Chesapeake fail to find women enjoying the status they achieved on the lower Western Shore of Maryland, then our arguments would have to be revised.[87]

Work is also needed that will enable historians to compare conditions in Maryland with those in other colonies. Richard S. Dunn's study of the British West Indies also shows demographic disruption.[88] When the status of wives is studied, it should prove similar to that of Maryland women. In contrast were demographic conditions in New England, where immigrants came in family groups, major immigration had ceased by the mid-seventeenth century, sex ratios balanced early, and mortality was low.[89] Under these conditions, demographic disruption must have been both less severe and less prolonged. If New England women achieved status similar to that suggested for women in the Chesapeake, that fact will have to be explained. The dynamics might prove to have been different;[90] or a dynamic we have not identified, common to both areas, might turn out to have been the primary engine of change. And, if women in England shared the status—which we doubt—conditions in the New World may have had secondary importance. The Maryland data establish persuasive grounds for a hypothesis, but the evidence is not all in.

NOTES

The authors wish to thank Russell R. Menard for sharing his data and insights into family history in the Chesapeake.

1. Russell R. Menard, "Economy and Society in Early Colonial Maryland" (Ph.D. diss., University of Iowa, 1975), 153–212, and "Immigrants and

Their Increase: The Process of Population Growth in Early Colonial Maryland," in Aubrey C. Land, Lois Green Carr, and Edward C. Papenfuse, eds., *Law, Society, and Politics in Early Maryland* (Baltimore, 1977), 88–110, hereafter cited as Menard, "Immigrants and Their Increase"; Lorena S. Walsh and Russell R. Menard, "Death in the Chesapeake: Two Life Tables for Men in Early Colonial Maryland," *Maryland Historical Magazine,* LXIX (1974), 211–227. In a sample of 806 headrights Menard found only two unmarried women who paid their own passage ("Economy and Society," 187).

2. Menard, "Immigrants and Their Increase," Fig. 1; William Hand Browne *et al.*, eds., *Archives of Maryland* (Baltimore, 1883–), XXV, 256, hereafter cited as *Maryland Archives.*

3. Court proceedings for St. Mary's and Calvert counties have not survived.

4. The lists of immigrants are found in John Camden Hotten, ed., *The Original Lists of Persons of Quality: Emigrants; Religious Exiles; Political Rebels; . . . and Others Who Went from Great Britain to the American Plantations, 1600–1700* (London, 1874); William Dodgson Bowman, ed., *Bristol and America: A Record of the First Settlers in the Colonies of North America, 1654–1685* (Baltimore, 1967 [orig. publ. London, 1929]); C. D. P. Nicholson, comp., *Some Early Emigrants to America* (Baltimore, 1965); Michael Ghirelli, ed., *A List of Emigrants to America, 1682–1692* (Baltimore, 1968); and Elizabeth French, ed., *List of Emigrants to America from Liverpool, 1697–1707* (Baltimore, 1962 [orig. publ. Boston, 1913]). Folger Shakespeare Library, MS. V.B. 16 (Washington, D.C.), consists of 66 additional indentures that were originally part of the London records. For studies of these lists see Mildred Campbell, "Social Origins of Some Early Americans," in James Morton Smith, ed., *Seventeenth-Century America: Essays in Colonial History* (Chapel Hill, N.C., 1959), 63–89; David W. Galenson, " 'Middling People' or 'Common Sort'?: The Social Origins of Some Early Americans Reexamined," *William and Mary Quarterly* (forthcoming). See also Menard, "Immigrants and Their Increase," Table 4.1, and "Economy and Society," Table VIII-6; and Lorena S. Walsh, "Servitude and Opportunity in Charles County," in Land, Carr, and Papenfuse, eds., *Law, Society, and Politics in Early Maryland,* 112–114, hereafter cited as Walsh, "Servitude and Opportunity."

5. Campbell, "Social Origins of Some Early Americans," in Smith, ed., *Seventeenth-Century America,* 74–77; Galenson, " 'Middling People' or "Common Sort'?" *WMQ* (forthcoming). When the ages recorded in the London list (Nicholson, comp., *Some Early Emigrants*) and on the Folger Library indentures for servants bound for Maryland and Virginia are combined, 84.5% of the men (N = 354) are found to have been aged 17 to 30, and 54.9% were 18 through 22. Of the women (N = 119), 81.4% were 18 through 25; 10% were older, 8.3% younger, and half (51.2%) immigrated between ages 20 and 22. Russell Menard has generously lent us his abstracts of the London list.

6. This assumption is defended in Walsh, "Servitude and Opportunity," 129.

7. *Ibid.*, 112–114, describes the legislation and the Charles County data base. There is some reason to believe that by 1700, young servants had contracts more often than earlier. Figures from the London list include the Folger Library indentures.

8. Menard, "Immigrants and Their Increase," Table I.

9. Menard, "Economy and Society," 336–356; Lois Green Carr and Rus-

sell R. Menard, "Servants and Freedmen in Early Colonial Maryland," in Thad W. Tate and David A. Ammerman, eds., *Essays on the Chesapeake in the Seventeenth Century* (Chapel Hill, N.C., forthcoming); E. A. Wrigley, "Family Limitation in Pre-Industrial England," *Economic History Review*, 2d Ser., XIX (1966), 82–109; Michael Drake, "An Elementary Exercise in Parish Register Demography," *ibid.*, XIV (1962), 427–445; J. D. Chambers, *Population, Economy, and Society in Pre-Industrial England* (London, 1972).

10. John Hammond, *Leah and Rachel, or the Two Fruitfull Sisters Virginia and Mary-land* . . . , and George Alsop, *A Character of the Province of Maryland* . . . , in Clayton Colman Hall, ed., *Narratives of Early Maryland, 1633–1684*, Original Narratives of Early American History (New York, 1910), 281–308, 340–387; Russell R. Menard, P. M. G. Harris, and Lois Green Carr, "Opportunity and Inequality: The Distribution of Wealth on the Lower Western Shore of Maryland, 1638–1705," *Md. Hist. Mag.*, LXIX (1974), 169–184; Russell R. Menard, "From Servant to Freeholder: Status Mobility and Property Accumulation in Seventeenth-Century Maryland," *WMQ*, 3d Ser., XXX (1973), 37–64; Carr and Menard, "Servants and Freedmen," in Tate and Ammerman, eds., *Essays on the Chesapeake*; Walsh, "Servitude and Opportunity," 111–133.

11. Walsh and Menard, "Death in the Chesapeake," *Md. Hist. Mag.*, LXIX (1974), 211–227; Darrett B. and Anita H. Rutman, "Of Agues and Fevers: Malaria in the Early Chesapeake," *WMQ*, 3d Ser., XXXIII (1976), 31–60.

12. E. A. Wrigley, *Population and History* (New York, 1969), 96–100.

13. Menard, "Economy and Society," Table VII-5.

14. Lorena S. Walsh, "Charles County, Maryland, 1658–1705: A Study in Chesapeake Political and Social Structure" (Ph.D. diss., Michigan State University, 1977), chap. 4.

15. Hammond, *Leah and Rachel*, and Alsop, *Character of the Province*, in Hall, ed., *Narratives of Maryland*, 281–308, 340–387; Mildred Campbell, *The English Yeoman Under Elizabeth and the Early Stuarts*, Yale Historical Publications (New Haven, Conn., 1942), 255–261; Alan Everitt, "Farm Labourers," in Joan Thirsk, ed., *The Agrarian History of England and Wales, 1540–1640* (Cambridge, 1967), 432.

16. Lorena S. Walsh and Russell R. Menard are preparing an article on the history of illegitimacy in Charles and Somerset counties, 1658–1776.

17. Abbot Emerson Smith, *Colonists in Bondage: White Servitude and Convict Labor in America, 1607–1776* (Chapel Hill, N.C., 1947), 271–273. Marriage was in effect a breach of contract.

18. Lois Green Carr, "County Government in Maryland, 1689–1709" (Ph.D. diss., Harvard University, 1968), text, 267–269, 363. The courts pursued bastardy offenses regardless of the social status of the culprits in order to ensure that the children would not become public charges. Free single women were not being overlooked.

19. John Barth, *The Sot-Weed Factor* (New York, 1960), 429.

20. This impression is based on Walsh's close reading of Charles County records, Carr's close reading of Prince George's County records, and less detailed examination by both of all other 17th-century Maryland court records.

21. Walsh, "Charles County, Maryland," chap. 4; Carr, "County Government in Maryland," chap. 4, n. 269. Carr summarizes the evidence from Charles, Prince George's, Baltimore, Talbot, and Somerset counties, 1689–1709, for comparing punishment of fathers and mothers of bastards. Leni-

ency toward fathers varied from county to county and time to time. The length of time served for restitution also varied over place and time, increasing as the century progressed. See Charles County Court and Land Records, MS, L #1, ff. 276–277, Hall of Records, Annapolis, Md. Unless otherwise indicated, all manuscripts cited are at the Hall of Records.

22. Peter Laslett and Karla Osterveen have calculated illegitimacy ratios —the percentage of bastard births among all births registered—in 24 English parishes, 1581–1810. The highest ratio over the period 1630–1710 was 2.4. Laslett and Osterveen, "Long Term Trends in Bastardy in England: A Study of the Illegitimacy Figures in the Parish Registers and in the Reports of the Registrar General, 1561–1960," *Population Studies*, XXVII (1973), 267. In Somerset County, Maryland, 1666–1694, the illegitimacy ratio ranged from 6.3 to 11.8. Russell R. Menard, "The Demography of Somerset County, Maryland: A Preliminary Report" (paper presented to the Stony Brook Conference on Social History, State University of New York at Stony Brook, June 1975), Table XVI. The absence of figures for the number of women in these places of childbearing age but with no living husband prevents construction of illegitimacy rates.

23. Alsop, *Character of the Province*, in Hall, ed., *Narratives of Maryland*, 358.

24. Maryland Headright Sample, 1658–1681 (N = 625); 257.1 men per 100 women; Maryland Inventories, 1658–1679 (N = 584): 320.1 men per 100 women. Menard, "Immigrants and Their Increase," Table I.

25. A comparison of a Virginia Headright Sample, 1648–1666 (N = 4,272) with inventories from York and Lower Norfolk counties, 1637–1675 (N = 168) shows less, rather than more, imbalance in inventories as compared to headrights. This indicates fewer purchases of wives than we have suggested for the period after 1660. However, the inventory sample is small.

26. Only 8% of tenant farmers who left inventories in four Maryland counties of the lower Western Shore owned labor, 1658–1705. St. Mary's City Commission Inventory Project, "Social Stratification in Maryland, 1658–1705" (National Science Foundation Grant GS-32272), hereafter cited as "Social Stratification." This is an analysis of 1,735 inventories recorded from 1658 to 1705 in St. Mary's, Calvert, Charles, and Prince George's counties, which together constitute most of the lower Western Shore of Maryland.

27. Sixty women left inventories. The status of five is unknown. The two who died single died in 1698. Menard, "Immigrants and Their Increase," Table I.

28. Menard, "Demography of Somerset County," Table XVII; Daniel Scott Smith and Michael S. Hindus, "Premarital Pregnancy in America, 1640–1971: An Overview," *Journal of Interdisciplinary History*, V (1975), 541. It was also two to three times the rate found in New England in the late 17th century.

29. In Maryland any proceedings against pregnant brides could have been brought only in the civil courts. No vestries were established until 1693, and their jurisdiction was confined to the admonishment of men and women suspected of fornication unproved by the conception of a child. Churchwardens were to inform the county court of bastardies. Carr, "County Government in Maryland," text, 148–149, 221–223.

30. The data are from Nicholson, comp., *Some Early Emigrants*.

31. Charles County Court and Land Records, MSS, C #1 through B #2.

32. Available ages at arrival are as follows:

Age	under 12	13	14	15	16	17	18	19	20	21	22	23	24	25	26	27	28	29	30
Indentured (1682–1687)			1	1	6	2	9	9	8	29	19	6	5	6	2	3	1	2	3
Unindentured (1666–1705)	8	5	12	4	7	18	16	13	34	9	11	2	1	1					

Terms of service for women without indentures from 1666 on were 5 years if they were aged 22 at arrival; 6 years if 18–21; 7 years if 15–17; and until 22 if under 15. From 1661 to 1665 these terms were shorter by a year, and women under 15 served until age 21. If we assume that (1) indentured women served 4 years; (2) they constituted half the servant women; (3) women under age 12 were not purchased as wives; (4) 20% of women aged 12 or older were purchased; and (5) purchases were spread evenly over the possible years of service, then from 1666, 73.9% were 23 or older at marriage, and 66.0% were 24 or older; 70.8% were 23 or older from 1661 to 1665, and 55.5% were 24 or older. Mean ages at eligibility for marriage, as calculated by dividing person-years by the number of women, were 24.37 from 1666 on and 23.42 from 1661 to 1665. All assumptions except (3) and (5) are discussed above. The third is made on the basis that native girls married as young as age 12.

33. Walsh, "Charles County, Maryland," chap. 2; Menard, "Demography of Somerset County," Tables XI, XII.

34. The impact of later marriages is best demonstrated with age-specific marital fertility statistics. Susan L. Norton reports that women in colonial Ipswich, Massachusetts, bore an average of 7.5 children if they married between ages 15 and 19; 7.1 if they married between 20 and 24; and 4.5 if they married after 24. Norton, "Population Growth in Colonial America: A Study of Ipswich, Massachusetts," *Pop. Studies*, XXV (1971), 444. Cf. Wrigley, "Family Limitation in Pre-Industrial England," *Econ. Hist. Rev.*, 2d Ser., XIX (1966), 82–109.

35. In Charles County the mean interval between first and second and subsequent births was 30.8, and the median was 27.3 months. Walsh, "Charles County, Maryland," chap. 2. Menard has found that in Somerset County, Maryland, the median birth intervals for immigrant women between child 1 and child 2, child 2 and child 3, child 3 and child 4, and child 4 and child 5 were 26, 26, 30, 27 months, respectively ("Demography of Somerset County," Table XX).

36. Walsh, "Charles County, Maryland," chap. 2.

37. Walsh and Menard, "Death in the Chesapeake," *Md. Hist. Mag.*, LXIX (1974), 222.

38. Menard, using all Maryland wills, found a considerably lower number of children per family in a similar period: 1.83 in wills probated 1660–1665; 2.20 in wills probated 1680–1684 ("Economy and Society," 198). Family reconstitution not surprisingly produces slightly higher figures, since daughters are often underrecorded in wills but are recorded as frequently as sons in birth registers. In 17th-century Charles County the mean size of all reconstituted families was 2.75. For marriages contracted in the years 1658–1669 (N = 118), 1670–1679 (N = 79), and 1680–1689 (N = 95), family size was 3.15, 2.58, and 2.86, respectively. In Somerset County, family size for immigrant marriages formed between 1665 and 1695 (N = 41) was 3.9. Walsh, "Charles County, Maryland," chap. 2; Menard, "Demography of Somerset County," Table XXI.

39. For fuller exposition of the process see Menard, "Immigrants and Their Increase."

40. P. E. Razell, "Population Change in Eighteenth-Century England. A Reinterpretation," *Econ. Hist. Rev.*, 2d Ser., XVIII (1965), 315, cites mean age at marriage as 23.76 years for 7,242 women in Yorkshire, 1662–1714, and 24.6 years for 280 women of Wiltshire, Berkshire, Hampshire, and Dorset, 1615–1621. Peter Laslett, *The World We Have Lost: England before the Industrial Age*, 2d ed. (London, 1971), 86, shows a mean age of 23.58 for 1,007 women in the Diocese of Canterbury, 1619–1690. Wrigley, "Family Limitation in Pre-Industrial England," *Econ. Hist. Rev.*, 2d Ser., XIX (1966), 87, shows mean ages at marriage for 259 women in Colyton, Devon, ranging from 26.15 to 30.0 years, 1600–1699.

41. For a brief discussion of Chesapeake and English mortality see Walsh and Menard, "Death in the Chesapeake," *Md. Hist. Mag.*, LXIX (1974), 224–225.

42. George W. Barclay, *Techniques of Population Analysis* (New York, 1958), 136n; Darrett B. and Anita H. Rutman, " 'Now-Wives and Sons-in-Law': Parental Death in a Seventeenth-Century Virginia County," in Tate and Ammerman, eds., *Essays on the Chesapeake;* Rutman and Rutman, "Of Agues and Fevers," *WMQ*, 3d Ser., XXXIII (1976), 31–60. Cf. Peter H. Wood, *Black Majority: Negroes in Colonial South Carolina from 1670 through the Stono Rebellion* (New York, 1974), chap. 3.

43. Walsh and Menard, "Death in the Chesapeake," *Md. Hist. Mag.*, LXIX (1974), 211–227; Menard, "Demography of Somerset County."

44. In Charles County immigrant women who ended childbearing years or died before 1705 bore a mean of 3.5 children (N = 59); the mean for natives was 5.1 (N = 42). Mean completed family size in Somerset County for marriages contracted between 1665 and 1695 was higher, but the immigrant–native differential remains. Immigrant women (N = 17) bore 6.1 children, while native women (N = 16) bore 9.4. Walsh, "Charles County, Maryland," chap. 2; Menard, "Demography of Somerset County," Table XXI.

45. Among 1,735 decedents who left inventories on Maryland's lower Western Shore, 1658–1705, 72% died without children or with children not yet of age. Only 16% could be proved to have a child of age. "Social Stratification."

46. Wills, I, 172.

47. From 1640 to 1710, 17% of the married men named no executor. In such cases, the probate court automatically gave executorship to the wife unless she requested someone else to act.

48. Wills, I, 96, 69.

49. *Ibid.*, 193–194, 167, V, 82. The practice of appointing overseers ceased around the end of the century. From 1690 to 1710, only 13% of testators who made their wives executors appointed overseers.

50. We divided wills according to whether decedents were immigrant, native born, or of unknown origins, and found no differences in patterns of bequests, choice of executors, or tendency to appoint overseers. No change occurred in 17th-century Maryland in these respects as a native-born population began to appear.

51. Margaret Spufford, *Contrasting Communities: English Villagers in the Sixteenth and Seventeenth Centuries* (Cambridge, 1974), 85–90, 111–118, 161–164.

52. Wills, I, 422, 182, 321.

53. For example, *ibid.*, 172, 182.

54. Lorena S. Walsh, " 'Till Death Do Us Part': Marriage and Family in Charles County, Maryland, 1658–1705," in Tate and Ammerman, eds., *Essays on the Chesapeake.*

55. The following discussion of the orphans' court is based on Lois Green Carr, "The Development of the Maryland Orphans' Court, 1654–1715," in Land, Carr, and Papenfuse, eds., *Law, Society, and Politics in Early Maryland*, 41–61.

56. Baltimore County Court Proceedings, D, ff. 385–386.

57. In 17th-century Charles County two-thirds of surviving partners remarried within a year of their spouse's death. Walsh, "Charles County, Maryland," chap. 2.

58. See n. 26.

59. Walsh, " 'Till Death Do Us Part,' " in Tate and Ammerman, eds., *Essays on the Chesapeake.*

60. *Ibid.*

61. *Maryland Archives*, LXX, 87. See also *ibid.*, XLI, 210, 474, 598, for examples of allusions to washing clothes and dairying activities. Water mills were so scarce that in 1669 the Maryland assembly passed an act permitting land to be condemned for the use of anyone willing to build and operate a water mill. *Ibid.*, II, 211–214. In the whole colony only four condemnations were carried out over the next 10 years. *Ibid.*, LI, 25, 57, 86, 381. Probate inventories show that most households had a mortar and pestle or a hand mill.

62. Testamentary Proceedings, X, 184–185. Cf. Charles County Court and Land Records, MS, I #1, ff. 9–10, 259.

63. Among married decedents before 1680 (N = 308), the bottom two-thirds (N = 212) were those worth less than £150. Among all decedents worth less than £150 (N = 451), only 12 (about 3%) had sheep or yarn-making equipment, "Social Stratification."

64. See Everitt, "Farm Labourers," in Thirsk, ed., *Agrarian History of England and Wales*, 422–426, and W. G. Hoskins, *Essays in Leicestershire History* (Liverpool, 1950), 134.

65. Among married decedents, the bottom fifth were approximately those worth less than £30. Before 1680 these were 17% of the married decedents. By the end of the period, from 1700 to 1705, they were 22%. Before 1680, 92% had no bound labor. From 1700 to 1705, 95% had none. Less than 1% of all estates in this wealth group had sheep or yarn-making equipment before 1681. "Social Stratification."

66. On opportunity to raise from the bottom to the middle see Menard, "From Servant to Freeholder," *WMQ*, 3d Ser., XXX (1973), 37–64; Walsh, "Servitude and Opportunity," 111–133, and Menard, Harris, and Carr, "Opportunity and Inequality," *Md. Hist. Mag.*, LXIX (1974), 169–184.

67. Charles County Court and Land Records, MS, R #1, f. 193.

68. For 17th-century economic development see Menard, Harris, and Carr, "Opportunity and Inequality," *Md. Hist. Mag.*, LXIX (1974), 169–184.

69. Among estates worth Q150 or more, signs of diversification in this form appeared in 22% before 1681 and in 67% after 1680. Over the years 1700–1705, the figure was 62%. Only 6% of estates worth less than £40 had such signs of diversification after 1680 or over the period 1700–1705. Knitting

rather than weaving is assumed because looms were very rare. These figures are for all estates. "Social Stratification."

70. After the mid-1670s information about landholdings of decedents becomes decreasingly available, making firm estimates of the increase in tenancy difficult. However, for householders in life cycle 2 (married or widowed decedents who died without children of age) the following table is suggestive. Householding decedents in life cycle 2 worth less than £40 (N = 255) were 21% of all decedents in this category (N = 1,218).

	£0–19				£20–39			
	Decedents	Land Unkn.	With Land	With Land	Decedents	Land Unkn.	With Land	With Land
	N	N	N	%	N	N	N	%
To 1675	10	0	7	70	34	2	29	91
1675 on	98	22	40	53	113	16	64	66

In computing percentages, unknowns have been distributed according to knowns.

A man who died with a child of age was almost always a landowner, but these were a small proportion of all decedents (see n. 45).

Several studies provide indisputable evidence of an increase in tenancy on the lower Western Shore over the period 1660–1706. These compare heads of households with lists of landowners compiled from rent rolls made in 1659 and 1704–1706. Tenancy in St. Mary's and Charles counties in 1660 was about 10%. In St. Mary's, Charles, and Prince George's counties, 1704–1706, 30–35% of householders were tenants. Russell R. Menard, "Population Growth and Land Distribution in St. Mary's County, 1634–1710" (ms report, St. Mary's City Commission, 1971, copy on file at the Hall of Records); Menard, "Economy and Society," 423; Carr, "County Government in Maryland," text, 605.

71. Menard, "Immigrants and Their Increase," Table III; n. 40 above.

72. Menard, "Demography of Somerset County," Table XIII.

73. *Ibid.*, Table XVII; P. E. H. Hair, "Bridal Pregnancy in Rural England in Earlier Centuries," *Pop. Studies,* XX (1966), 237; Chambers, *Population, Economy, and Society in England,* 75; Smith and Hindus, "Premarital Pregnancy in America," *Jour. Interdisciplinary Hist.*, V (1975), 537–570.

74. Menard, "Demography of Somerset County," Table XVIII.

75. Adolescent subfecundity might also partly explain lower bridal pregnancy rates among very young brides.

76. Menard develops this argument in detail in "Immigrants and Their Increase." For the assembly see David W. Jordan, "Political Stability and the Emergence of a Native Elite in Maryland, 1660–1715," in Tate and Ammerman, eds., *Essays on the Chesapeake.* In Charles County, Maryland, by 1705 at least half of all resident landowners were native born. Walsh, "Charles County, Maryland," chaps. 1, 7.

77. The proportion of wills mentioning non-nuclear kin can, of course, prove only a proxy of the actual existence of these kin in Maryland. The reliability of such a measure may vary greatly from area to area and over time, depending on the character of the population and on local inheritance customs. To test the reliability of the will data, we compared them with data from reconstituted families in 17th-century Charles County. These reconstitution data draw on a much broader variety of sources and include many

men who did not leave wills. Because of insufficient information for female lines, we could trace only the male lines. The procedure compared the names of all married men against a file of all known county residents, asking how many kin in the male line might have been present in the county at the time of the married man's death. The proportions for immigrants were in most cases not markedly different from those found in wills. For native men, however, wills were somewhat less reliable indicators of the presence of such kin; when non-nuclear kin mentioned by testate natives were compared with kin found by reconstitution, 29% of the native testators had non-nuclear kin present in the county who were not mentioned in their wills.

78. Not surprisingly, wills of immigrants show no increase in family ties, but these wills mention adult children far more often than earlier. Before 1680, only 11% of immigrant testators in St. Mary's and Charles counties mention adult children in their wills; from 1700 to 1710, 37% left adult children to help the family. Two facts help account for this change. First, survivors of early immigration were dying in old age. Second, proportionately fewer young immigrants with families were dying, not because life expectancy had improved, but because there were proportionately fewer of them than earlier. A long stagnation in the tobacco economy that began about 1680 had diminished opportunities for freed servants to form households and families. Hence, among immigrants the proportion of young fathers at risk to die was smaller than in earlier years.

In the larger population of men who left inventories, 18.2% had adult children before 1681, but in the years 1700–1709, 50% had adult children. "Social Stratification."

79. Examples of some recent studies are Carole Shammas, "English-Born and Creole Elites in Turn-of-the-Century Virginia," in Tate and Ammerman, eds., *Essays on the Chesapeake;* Jordan, "Political Stability and the Emergence of a Native Elite in Maryland," *ibid.;* Lois Green Carr, "The Foundations of Social Order: Local Government in Colonial Maryland," in Bruce C. Daniels, ed., *Town and Country: Essays on the Structure of Local Government in the American Colonies* (Middletown, Conn., forthcoming); Menard, "Economy and Society," 396–440.

80. Allan Kulikoff has found that in Prince George's County the white adult sex ratio dropped significantly before the age of marriage rose. Women born in the 1720s were the first to marry at a mean age above 20, while those born in the 1740s and marrying in the 1760s, after the sex ratio neared equality, married at a mean age of 22. Marriages lasted longer because the rise in the mean age at which men married—from 23 to 27 between 1700 and 1740—was more than offset by gains in life expectancy. Kulikoff, "Tobacco and Slaves: Population, Economy, and Society in Eighteenth-Century Prince George's County, Maryland" (Ph.D. diss., Brandeis University, 1976), chap. 3; Menard, "Immigrants and Their Increase."

81. Inventories and related biographical data have been analyzed by the St. Mary's City Commission under a grant from the National Endowment for the Humanities, "The Making of a Plantation Society in Maryland" (R 010585-74-267). From 1700 through 1776 the percentage of men known to have had children, and who had an adult child at death, ranged from a low of 32.8% in the years 1736–1738 to a high of 61.3% in the years 1707–1709. The figure was over 50% for 13 out of 23 year-groups of three to four years each. For the high in 1707–1709 see comments in n. 78.

82. On the other hand, these rates may show little change. The restraining effect of increased parental control may have been offset by a trend toward increased sexual activity that appears to have become general throughout Western Europe and the United States by the mid-19th century. Smith and Hindus, "Premarital Pregnancy in America," *Jour. Interdisciplinary Hist.*, V (1975), 537–570; Edward Shorter, "Female Emancipation, Birth Control, and Fertility in European History," *American Historical Review*, LXXVIII (1973), 605–640.

83. Page Smith has suggested that such a decline in the wife's household authority had occurred in the American family by—at the latest—the beginning of the 19th century (*Daughters of the Promised Land: Women in American History* [Boston, 1970], chaps. 3, 4).

84. There is little doubt that extreme scarcity in the early years of Chesapeake history enhanced the worth of women in the eyes of men. However, as Smith has observed, "the functioning of the law of supply and demand could not in itself have guaranteed status for colonial women. Without an ideological basis, their privileges could not have been initially established or subsequently maintained" (*ibid.*, 38–39). In a culture where women were seriously undervalued, a shortage of women would not necessarily improve their status.

85. Acts 1699, chap. 41, *Maryland Archives*, XXII, 542.

86. Essays by Cicely Howell and Barbara Todd, printed or made available to the authors since this article was written, point out that customary as opposed to freehold tenures in England usually gave the widow the use of the land for life, but that remarriage often cost the widow this right. The degree to which this was true requires investigation. Howell, "Peasant Inheritance in the Midlands, 1280–1700," in Jack Goody, Joan Thirsk, and E. P. Thompson, eds., *Family and Inheritance: Rural Society in Western Europe, 1200–1800* (Cambridge, 1976), 112–155; Todd, " 'In Her Free Widowhood': Succession to Property and Remarriage in Rural England, 1540–1800" (paper delivered to the Third Berkshire Conference of Women Historians, June 1976).

87. James W. Deen, Jr., "Patterns of Testation: Four Tidewater Counties in Colonial Virginia," *American Journal of Legal History*, XVI (1972), 154–176, finds a life interest in property for the wife the predominant pattern before 1720. However, he includes an interest for widowhood in life interest and does not distinguish a dower interest from more than dower.

88. Richard S. Dunn, *Sugar and Slaves: The Rise of the Planter Class in the English West Indies, 1624–1713* (Chapel Hill, N.C., 1972), 326–334. Dunn finds sex ratios surprisingly balanced, but he also finds very high mortality, short marriages, and many orphans.

89. For a short discussion of this comparison see Menard, "Immigrants and Their Increase."

90. James K. Somerville has used Salem, Massachusetts, wills from 1660 to 1770 to examine women's status and importance within the home ("The Salem [Mass.] Woman in the Home, 1660–1770," *Eighteenth-Century Life*, I [1974], 11–14). See also Alexander Keyssar, "Widowhood in Eighteenth-Century Massachusetts: A Problem in the History of the Family," *Perspectives in American History*, VIII (1974), 83–119, which discusses provisions for 22 widows in 18th-century Woburn, Massachusetts. Both men find provisions for houseroom and care of the widow's property enjoined upon children proportionately far more often than we have found in St. Mary's

County, Maryland, where we found only five instances over 136 years. However, part of this difference may be a function of the differences in age at widowhood in the two regions. Neither Somerville nor Keyssar gives the percentage of widows who received a life interest in property, but their discussions imply a much higher proportion than we have found of women whose interest ended at remarriage or the majority of the oldest son.

2

Vertuous Women Found

New England Ministerial Literature, 1668–1735

■

LAUREL THATCHER ULRICH

People today often have difficulty comprehending or empathizing with the seventeenth-century Puritans' religious involvement. Laurel Ulrich takes seriously the personal meaning and the shaping influence of religion for early New England women. Her comparison of the portraits of the pious woman and the pious man in published Puritan literature yields some surprising results. As is always the case with such sources, more is revealed about norms than about behavior. Nevertheless, her subtle concluding argument about change over time suggests that there are different levels of norms to consider—here spiritual and social—as well as links to be drawn between norms and the range of possible behaviors.

COTTON MATHER CALLED THEM "the hidden ones." They never preached or sat in a deacon's bench. Nor did they vote or attend Harvard. Neither, because they were virtuous women, did they question God or the magistrates. They prayed secretly, read the Bible through at least once a year, and went to hear the minister preach even when it snowed. Hoping for an eternal crown, they never asked to be remembered on earth. And they haven't been. Well-behaved women seldom make history; against Antinomians and witches, these pious matrons have had little chance at all. Most historians, considering the domestic by definition irrelevant, have simply assumed the pervasiveness of similar attitudes in the seventeenth century. Others, noting the apologetic tone of Anne Bradstreet and the banishment of Anne Hutchinson, have been satisfied that New England society, while it valued marriage and allowed women limited participation in economic affairs, discouraged their interest in either poetry or theology. For thirty years no one has bothered to question Edmund Morgan's assumption that a Puritan wife was considered "the weaker vessel in both body and mind" and that "her husband ought not to expect too much from her."[1] John Winthrop's famous letter on the insanity of bookish Mistress Hopkins has been the quintessential source: ". . . if she had attended her household affairs, and such things as belong to women, and not gone out of her way and calling to meddle in such things as are proper for men, whose minds are stronger, etc., she had kept her wits."[2]

Yet there is ample evidence in traditional documents to undermine these conclusions, at least for the late seventeenth and early eighteenth centuries. For the years between 1668 and 1735, Evans' *American Bibliography* lists 55 elegies, memorials, and funeral sermons for females plus 15 other works of practical piety addressed wholly or in part to women.[3] Although historians have looked at such popular works as Cotton Mather's *Ornaments for the Daughters of Zion,* they have ignored the rest.[4] Thus, New England's daughters remain hidden despite the efforts of her publishing ministry. True, a collection of ministerial literature cannot tell us what New England women, even of the more pious variety, were really like. Nor can it describe what "most Puritans" thought of women. It can tell us only what qualities were publicly praised in a specific time by a specific group of men. Yet, in a field which suffers from so little data, there is value in that. A handful of quotations has for too long defined the status of New England's virtuous women. This interesting collection deserves a closer look.

Although 27 of the 70 titles are by Cotton Mather (who wrote more of everything in the period), the remaining 43 are the work of 21 authors. They range from a single sermon by Leonard Hoar, his only published work, to the six poems for women written over a 25-year period by ubiquitous elegist John Danforth. They include four English works republished in America. Only 12 of the titles were printed before 1700, but two others, Samuel Willard's short discourse on marriage from his *Complete Body of Divinity,* posthumously published in 1726, and Hugh Peter's *A Dying Father's Last Legacy,* first reprinted in Boston in 1717, originated earlier. Peter's treatise, written just before his execution, is especially interesting as a link to the first generation of New Englanders.

In spite of personal idiosyncracies and the acknowledged predominance of Mather, this literature is remarkably consistent. Thus, a crude woodcut decorating a broadside published for Madam Susanna Thacher in 1724 is identical to that ornamenting an elegy for Lydia Minot published in 1668. Nor are doctrinal distinctions of any consequence. Benjamin Colman could differ with his brethren over the precise meaning of New England, for example, yet share with them a common attitude toward women.[5] Because these works are so much of a piece, however, subtle shifts in emphasis between authors and across time become significant. A patient examination of this seemingly static and formulaic material reveals nuances in ministerial thought of considerable interest, demonstrating that for women's history, as for so many aspects of social history, the real drama is often in the humdrum.

In ministerial literature, as in public records, women became legitimately visible in only three ways: they married, they gave birth, they died. In the written materials, dying is by far the best documented activity. Although a minister might have had a specific woman in mind as he prepared an idealized portrait of the good wife for a wedding or espousal sermon or as he composed a comforting tract for parishioners approaching childbed, it is only in the funeral literature that he is free to name names and praise individual accomplishments. Not that a funeral sermon is ever very specific. Circumlocution, even a certain coyness in referring to "that excellent person now departed from us," is the rule. Still, it is a rare sermon that does not contain a eulogy, however brief. Some append fuller biographical sketches often containing selections from the writings of the deceased.[6] From these materials a composite portrait emerges.

A virtuous woman sought God early. Hannah Meigs, who died in New London at the age of 22, was typical. She began while still a child to pay attention in church, acquiring the habit of reading and praying at night when the rest of her family was asleep. Becoming preoccupied with her own salvation, she bewailed her sinfulness, at last receiving an assurance of God's mercy. In the sickness which eventually claimed her, she submitted her will to God, from her death bed meekly teaching her brothers and sisters and other "Relatives, Acquaintances, & Companions."[7] Praise of early piety was not confined to sermons for young women. In his eulogy for Mary Rock, who died at the age of 80, Cotton Mather devoted considerable space to her early religiosity and the wise education of her parents.[8] The women eulogized typically found God before marriage, having been, in Danforth's phrase, first "Polish'd and Prepar'd" by pious parents.[9]

A virtuous woman prayed and fasted. Jane Colman was said to have lain awake whole nights mourning for sin, calling on God, praying.[10] Mrs. Increase Mather regularly prayed six times a day. After her death her husband wrote a tribute to her from his study, a spot which had become endeared to him when he discovered in some of her private papers that during his four years absence in England she had "spent many whole Days (some Scores of them) alone with God there" in prayer and fasting for his welfare and that of her children.[11] Thomas Foxcroft characterized a praying mother as "One that *stood in the Breach* to turn away wrath" and concluded that the death of such women was a bad omen for the community.[12] Cotton Mather was fond of saying that good mothers travailed twice for their children, once for their physical birth, again for the spiritual.[13]

A virtuous woman loved to go to church. On the day of her death ailing Sarah Leveret went to hear the sermon even though the weather was bitter. When her friends tried to dissuade her, she answered: "If the Ministers can go abroad to Preach, certainly, it becomes the People to go abroad; and hear them."[14] Sarah was not alone among New England's pious matrons. The ministers who preached the funeral sermons for Anne Mason and Jane Steel both commented on the fact that they came to church even when they were ill.[15] Jabez Fitch said of Mrs. Mary Martin: "The feet of those that brought the glad Tidings of the Gospel, were always beautiful in her Eyes, and it was her great Delight to attend on the Ministry of the Word."[16]

A virtuous woman read. Throughout the eulogies reading is mentioned as often as prayer, and the two activities are occasionally linked as in John Danforth's praise of Hannah Sewall:

> *Observing Ladys* must keep down their Vail,
> 'Till They're as *Full* of Grace, *&* *Free* from Gall,
> As *Void* of Pride, as *High* in Vertue Rare
> As *much* in Reading, and as *much* in Prayer.[17]

After her children were grown, Maria Mather took renewed interest in reading the scriptures, more than doubling the prescribed pace by reading the Bible through twice in less than a year.[18] Her daughter Jerusha was a great reader of history and theology as well as scripture, having been given eyesight so excellent she could read in dim light.[19] Katharin Mather, Cotton's daughter, went beyond her grandmother and her aunt. She mastered music, penmanship, needlework, the usual accomplishments of a gentlewoman, "To which she added this, that she became in her childhood a Mistress of the Hebrew Tongue."[20]

A virtuous woman conversed. Mourning for Elizabeth Hatch, Joseph Metcalf lamented nothing so much as the loss of her pious discourse.[21] For John Danforth, Elizabeth Hutchinson's conversation was "sweeter than Hybla's Drops," while for Cotton Mather, the "fruitfulness" of Mary Rock's "Religious Conferences" made her sick room "A little *Anti-Chamber* of Heaven."[22] James Hillhouse said his mother could converse "on many subjects with the Grandees of the World, and the Masters of Eloquence" yet she was not haughty. "Her incessant and constant Reading, with her good Memory, and clear Judgment, made her expert (even to a degree) in the Bible. Insomuch, that she was capable on many occasions very seasonably and suitably to apply it, and that with great facility and aptness, to the various Subjects of Discourse, that offered themselves."[23] James Fitch said that if he were to "rehearse the many Spiritual, Weighty, and Narrow Questions & Discourses" he had heard from Anne Mason, "it would fill up a large book."[24] Benjamin Wadsworth praised Bridget Usher for promoting "pious and savoury Discourse."[25] Godly matrons were meant to be heard.

A virtuous woman wrote. A quill as well as a distaff was proper to a lady's hand. Despite eight pregnancies in ten years, Katharin Willard was such a good manager and so industrious that she was "hindred not from the Use of her Pen, as well as of her Needle."[26] One form of writing was simply taking notes in church. Mary Terry wrote down the main points of the preacher's sermon, recalling the whole thing later from her notes, a habit which had apparently become less common by Foxcroft's time, for he commented that aged Bridget Usher and her associates had "practiced (even to the last) the good old way of *writing* after the Minister. They were *swift to hear;* and by this laudable (but not too unfashionable) Method, took care to hear *for the time to come,* as the Prophet Speaks."[27]

In preaching a funeral sermon Cotton Mather often included excerpts from the woman's writings. In Elizabeth Cotton's, for example, he drew from writings at several stages of her life, telling his audience that one of these selections was "so expressive and so Instructive, that it may well pass for the Best part of my Sermon, if I now give to you all, and particularly the Daughters of our *Zion,* the Benefit of hearing it Read unto you."[28] In 1711 he edited a selection of the writings of his sister Jerusha and published them with an introduction as *Memorials of Early Piety.* Such a practice was not uncommon. In 1681, Sarah Goodhue's husband published *The Copy of A Valedictory and Monitory Writing,* a letter of "sage counsel" and "pious instructions" which she had written for her family and hidden, having had a premonition of her death in childbirth.[29] Grace Smith's legacy to her children was supposedly "taken from her lips by the Minister of that Town where she died," a strange statement since it included in addition to predictable paragraphs of advice and motherly proverbs, two long passages in verse written in iambic tetrameter with a rather complex internal rhyme scheme.[30] Like the others, she had obviously been sharpening her pen after the spinning was done.

A virtuous woman managed well. Increase Mather said his father's greatest affliction was the death of his wife, "Which Afflication was the more grievous, in that she being a Woman of singular Prudence for the Management of Affairs, had taken off from her Husband all Secular Cares, so that he wholly devoted himself to his Study, and to Sacred Imployments."[31] Women were praised in the funeral sermons not only for being godly but for being practical. Even the saintly Jerusha Oliver was not above dabbling in investments. "When she sent (as now and then she did) her Little *Ventures to Sea,* at the return she would be sure to lay aside the *Tenth* of her gain, for Pious Uses."[32]

Anne Eliot's talents, which included nursing, were so valued that Danforth almost credited her with holding up the world:

Haile! Thou *Sagacious & Advant'rous* Soul!
Haile, Amazon Created to Controll
Weak Nature's Foes, & T'take her part,
The King of Terrours, Thou, (till the command
Irrevocable came to Stay thy Hand,)
Didst oft Repel, by thy Choice Art:
By High Decree
Long didst thou stand
An Atlas, in Heav'n's Hand
To th' World to be.[33]

Mrs. Eliot, like many of her sisters, was no less pious as an "Atlas."

A virtuous woman submitted to the will of God. Increase Mather told the story of a "Person of Quality" whose only son contracted smallpox. She called in the ministers to pray for him. When they prayed that if by God's will the child should die the mother would have the strength to submit, she interrupted, crying: "If He will Take him away; Nay, He shall then *Tear* him away." The child died. Sometime later the mother became pregnant, but when the time for delivery arrived the child would not come and was consequently "Violently *Torn* from her; so she Died."[34] For the godly woman rebellion was not worth the risks. She learned to submit to God, meekly acquiescing to the deaths of husband and children and ultimately to her own as well. Only one minister suggested that a departed sister was less than patient in her final sickness and Samuel Myles cautioned his reader lest he "Uncharitably, and Unchristianly impute that to the *Person,* which was justly chargeable on the *Disease.*"[35] Cotton Mather's women were typically terrified of death until it approached, then they triumphed over the "King of Terrours." Jerusha Oliver sang for joy and sent a message to her sister in Roxbury telling her not to be afraid to die.[36] Rebeckah Burnet, age

17, expired crying, "Holy, Holy, Holy—Lord Jesus, Come unto Me!"[37] In her illness, Abiel Goodwin heard voices and music and was transported by the tolling of funeral bells. In her quieter moments she exhibited a wry sense of humor, agreeing with a visitor that, given her hydropical condition, she was "A going to Heaven by Water" and might soon sing that song with Jesus.[38]

Read directly, the qualities attributed to these women have little meaning. It is easy to conclude from the lavish praise bestowed upon them that they enjoyed an exalted position in the Puritan ethos. It is even more tempting to conclude the opposite, that the limited nature of their intellectual achievement and their continually lauded meekness and submission document a secondary role. It is helpful, then, to compare this portrait of a virtuous woman with a contemporary portrait of a godly man. Richard Mather, according to the eulogy written by his son Increase, found God early, prayed often, read the scriptures, and though he was learned "was exceeding low and little in his own eyes." Though well-educated, he was careful not to display his learning, and he always preached plainly. He loved to listen to sermons and in his last months continued to attend lectures in neighboring congregations until he was too sick to ride. "Yea and usually even to his old Age (as did Mr. Hildersham) he took notes from those whom he heard, professing that he found profit in it." He was patient in affliction, submitting to the will of God in death.[39] The inference is clear. While a godly woman was expected to act appropriately in all the relations in which she found herself, to be a dutiful daughter, an obedient and faithful wife, a wise parent and mistress, a kind friend, and a charitable neighbor, in her relationship with God she was autonomous. The portrait of Richard Mather, the first spiritual autobiography published in America, is duplicated in miniature in dozens of funeral sermons printed in Boston. But it didn't originate there. It is a pattern of godliness basic to the English reformed tradition.[40] This much should be obvious to anyone familiar with Puritan literature, yet it bears repeating in a time when qualities such as "meekness" and "submissiveness" are presumed to have a sexual reference. In a very real sense there is no such thing as *female* piety in early New England: in preaching sermons for women, the ministers universally used the generic male pronouns in enlarging their themes, even when the text had reference to a scriptural Bathsheba or Mary; the same Christ-like bearing was required of both male and female.

Because dying is an individual rather than a social act, it is in the funeral literature that we see most clearly the equality of men and women before God. It is important, then, to try to determine whether this acknowledged spiritual equality impinged on the prescribed social roles described in the general works of practical piety.

In 1709 there appeared in Boston a reprint of a wedding sermon preached at Sherbourn in Dorsetshire by a nonconformist minister named John Sprint. Called *The Bride-Woman's Counsellor,* it virtually ignored the groom. Marital troubles, the author concluded, were mainly the fault of women anyway. "You women will acknowledge that Men can learn to command, and rule fast enough, which as Husbands they ought to do, but tis very rare to find that Women learn so fast to Submit and obey, which as Wives they ought to do."[41] Like Sarah, women should call their husbands "Lord," never presuming to the familiarity of a Christian name lest they in time usurp his authority and place him under the discipline of an Apron-String. Although women might make light of this instruction to obey, he continued, "I know not of any duty belonging to any Men or Women, in the Whole Book of God, that is urged with more vehemency." Authority had been given to the husband as "absolutely and as peremptorily as unto Christ himself."[42]

This is a remarkable document, all the more remarkable because in the whole corpus of materials printed in Boston there is nothing remotely like it in content or in tone. It makes a useful reference point for looking at three other works printed about the same time: Benjamin Wadsworth's *The Well-Ordered Family,* 1712; William Secker's *A Wedding Ring,* an English pamphlet reprinted in Boston in 1690, 1705, 1750, and 1773; and Samuel Willard's exposition of the fifth commandment in *A Complete Body of Divinity,* 1726.

Wadsworth's treatise must be looked at structurally. Like Sprint he reminded wives to "love, honour and obey," but his entire essay was organized around the notion of mutual responsibility, mutual caring. He listed seven duties of husbands and wives. The first six are reciprocal: to cohabit, to love one another, to be faithful to one another, to help one another, to be patient with one another, to honor one another. It is only with the seventh duty that there is any differentiation at all: the husband is to govern gently, the wife to obey cheerfully. It was thus within an ethic of mutual concern and sharing that Wadsworth developed the obedience theme, and he maintained the parallel structure of the essay even in these paragraphs. Both mates were scolded if they should lift up their hands against the other. A woman who struck her husband usurped not just his authority but that of God. A man who twitted his wife affronted not just a Woman but God.[43] Wadsworth thus undercut the subjection of women to their husbands even as he upheld it.

The same tendency is apparent in Secker. *A Wedding Ring* is a frothy bit of writing, a tiny little book which would have fitted a pocket or pouch. Its intention was not so much instruction as celebration, and it appropriated attractive quotations and metaphors at random, regardless of inconsistency. Although there are traditional proverbs enjoining submission, the great weight of the imagery falls on the side of equality. Eve is a "parallel line drawn equal" with Adam. A husband and wife are like two instruments making music, like two streams in one current, like a pair of oars rowing a boat to heaven (with children and servants as passengers), like two milch kine coupled to carry the Ark of God, two cherubims, two tables of stone on which the law is written.[44]

Willard accepted this two-sided view of the marriage relation and in his short disquisition on the family attempted to harmonize it. "Of all the Orders which are unequals," he wrote, "these do come nearest to an Equality, and in several respects they stand upon even ground. These do make a Pair, which infers so far a Parity. They are in the Word of God called *Yoke-Fellows,* and so are to draw together in the Yoke. Nevertheless, God hath also made an imparity between them, in the Order prescribed in His Word, and for that reason there is a Subordination, and they are ranked among unequals." Yet, referring to the duties of the wife "as inferiour," he cautioned that "the word used there is a general word, and signified to be ordered under another, or to keep Order, being a Metaphor from a Band of Souldiers, or an Army." Further he explained that "the Submission here required, is not to be measured by the Notation or import of the Word itself, but by the Quality of the Relation to which it is applied." The husband-wife relation must never be confused with the master-servant or child-parent relation. A husband ought to be able to back his counsels with the word of God "and lay before her a sufficient Conviction of her Duty, to comply with him therein; for he hath no Authority or Compulsion." While in any relation it is the duty of inferiors to obey superiors unless a command is contrary to God, "a wife certainly hath greater liberty of debating the Prudence of the thing." Thus, the emphasis throughout is on discussion, on reasoning, on mediation. Wives as well as husbands have the responsibility to counsel and direct. Each should "chuse the fittest Seasons to Reprove each other, for things which their Love and Duty calls for."[45] The command to obedience, for Willard, was primarily a principle of order.

Sprint's sermon, bristling with assertive females and outraged husbands, is an oddity among the ministerial literature. Harmony, not authority, was the common theme. Thus, the marriage discourses support the implication of the funeral literature that women were expected to be rational as well as righteous, capable of independent judgment as well as deference, and as responsible as their spouses for knowing the word of God and for promoting the salvation of the family. A virtuous woman was espoused to Christ before she was espoused to any man.

That few tracts and sermons on childbirth survive is probably evidence in itself of the reluctance of the ministers to stress "feminine" or "masculine" themes over a common Christianity. The limited writing on parturition is worth examining, however, for here if anywhere authors had an opportunity to expound upon the peculiar failings or virtues of the weaker sex.

A pregnant woman in New England's godly community had two preparations to make for the day of her delivery. On the one hand she had to arrange for a midwife, ready a warm and convenient chamber, prepare childbed linen for herself and clothing for her infant, and plan refreshment for the friends invited to attend her. But she knew, even without a ministerial reminder, that these things could prove "miserable comforters." She might "perchance need no other linen shortly but a winding sheet, and have no other chamber but a grave, no neighbors but worms."[46] Her primary duty, then, was preparing to die. Female mortality is the most pervasive theme of the childbirth literature. The elegists loved to exploit the pathos of death in birth—the ship and cargo sunk together, the fruit and tree both felled, the womb became a grave. In his poem for Mary Brown, for example, Nicholas Noyes dwelt at length on the fruitless pangs of her labor: "A BIRTH of *One*, to Both a Death becomes;/ A Breathless Mother the *Dead Child* Entombs."[47] Thus, it was often in a very particular sense that the ministers spoke of the "fearful sex." In stressing the need for a husband's tenderness, for example, Willard had singled out those bodily infirmities associated with the "breeding, bearing, and nursing" of children.[48]

Yet these grim realities had their joyous side. Cotton Mather was fond of saying that though an equal number of both sexes were born, a larger proportion of females were reborn.[49] He wondered why. Perhaps they had more time to spend in godly activities, "although I must confess, tis often otherwise." No, he concluded, it was probably because in childbirth the curse of Eve had turned into a blessing.[50] Given the spiritual equality of men and women, the only possible explanation for a disparity in religious performance had to be physical. Benjamin Colman resolved the same problem in a similar way in a preface to one of his sermons. Writing later in the period than Mather, he could toy with the idea of a "natural Tenderness of Spirit" given to women through the election of God, yet he too focused upon their bodily experience. Pregnancy and childbirth, by turning female thoughts frequently "towards the Gates of Death, by which We all receive our Life," increased women's susceptibility to the comforts of Christ. Pregnancy was superior to regular human ills in this regard, thought Colman, because it continued for months rather than surprising the victim with an acute attack forgotten as soon as it was over.[51]

Even here the ministers were ready to stress similarities between men and women. Though John Oliver urged husbands to be kind to their pregnant wives because of their increased vulnerability to "hysterical vapours," his argument really rested on an analogy, not a contrast, between the sexes. Husbands should be tolerant of their wives, he insisted, because they "desire or expect the like favour to themselves in their own sickness, wherein all men are lyable to many absurdities, and troublesome humours."[52] Eve in her troubles was no more unstable than Adam.

Thus, the ministers were able to acknowledge the reproductive role of women without giving a sexual content to the psyche and soul. They stressed the *experience* of childbirth, rather than the *nature* of the childbearer. It is significant that the one place where they openly referred to the "curse of Eve" (rather than the more generalized "sin of Adam") was in dealing with the issue of birth. In such a context, Eve's curse had a particular and finite meaning, and it could be overcome. Stressing the redemptive power of childbirth, they transformed a traditional badge of weakness into a symbol of strength. Locating the religious responsiveness of women in their bodily experience rather than in their eternal nature, they upheld the spiritual oneness of the sexes. The childbirth literature, though fragmentary, is consistent with the marriage and funeral sermons.

When New England's ministers sat down to write about women, they were all interested in promoting the same asexual qualities: prayerfulness, industry, charity, modesty, serious reading, and godly writing. From 1660 to 1730 the portrait of the virtuous woman did not change. Her piety was the standard Protestant piety; her virtues were those of her brothers. Although childbearing gave her an added incentive to godliness, she possessed no inherently female spiritual qualities, and her deepest reality was unrelated to her sex. Yet an examination of the ministerial literature is not complete without consideration of an important but subtle shift, not in content but in attitude. This begins around the turn of the century in the work of Cotton Mather and continues, though less strikingly, in the sermons of Foxcroft and Colman. Mather's elegy for Mary Brown of Salem, "Eureka the Vertuous Woman Found," marks the tone:

> Monopolizing HEE's, pretend no more
> Of wit and worth, to hoard up all the store.
> The Females too grow wise & Good & Great.[53]

Everything Mather said about Mary Brown had been said before by other ministers about other women. But his open championship of her sex was new. All of the ministers believed in the inherent equality of men and women, but for some reason first Mather, then others, seemed *compelled* to say so.

If we turn to the earliest of the advice literature, Hugh Peter's *A Dying Father's Last Legacy,* written for his daughter in 1660, this subtle shift becomes immediately apparent. The researcher who combs its tightly-packed pages looking for specific comments on women will come away disappointed. Yet the entire work is a profound comment on his attitude toward the subject. That he would write a long and detailed treatise to Elizabeth without reference to her sex is evidence in itself that he considered her basic responsibilities the same as his. Know Christ, he told her. Read the best books. Study the scriptures, using the annotations of divines. Pray constantly. Keep a journal; write of God's dealings with you and of yours with him. Discuss the workings of salvation with able friends. Seek wisdom. Speak truth. Avoid frothy words. Do your own business; work with your own hands. The one explicit reference to feminine meekness is inextricable from the general Christian context: "Oh that you might be God-like, Christ-like, *Moses*-like. *Michael* contesting with the Dragon, maintained his Meekness; and Paul says, it is the Woman's Ornament." For Peter, virtue had no gender. In putting on the woman's ornament, Elizabeth was clothed in the armor of a dragon-fighter as well. In a short paragraph on marriage, he reminded his daughter that while it was the husband's duty to lead, hers to submit, these duties "need mutual supports." Husbands and wives "need to observe each others Spirits; they need to Pray out, not Quarrel out their first Grablings; They need at first to dwell much in their own duties, before they step into each others." When he told her to stay much at home, he was applying a judgment to his own stormy career and troubled marriage. "For my Spirit it wanted weight, through many tossings, my head that composure others have, credulous, and too careless, but never mischievous nor malicious: I thought my work was to serve others, and so mine own Garden not so well cultivated."[54] Thus, Peter's treatise epitomized the central sermon tradition.

Thirty years later Cotton Mather was promoting the same qualities—but with a difference. Clearly, a contrast between inherent worth and public position was at the heart of his attitude toward women. "There are People, who make no Noise at all in the World, People hardly known to be in the World; Persons of the *Female Sex*, and under all the Covers imaginable. But the world has not many People in it, that are fuller of the Truest Glory."[55] That women made no noise bothered Mather, and he was continually devising metaphorical detours around the Pauline proscriptions. "Yes, those who may not *Speak in the Church*, does our Glorious Lord Employ to *Speak:* to *Speak* to us, and *Speak* by what we *see* in them, such Things as we ought certainly to take much Notice of."[56] He made much of the fact that Abiel Goodwin, a little damsel half his age, had taught him much of salvation, and in her funeral sermon he expressed pleasure that she could finally "without any Disorder" speak in the Church.[57]

But there was a route to worldly honor open to women, one which no epistle denied. "They that might not without *Sin*, lead the Life which old stories ascribe to *Amazons*, have with much Praise done the part of *Scholars* in the World."[58] A long section in *Ornaments for the Daughters of Zion* was devoted to the promotion of female writing. Mather combed the scriptures and the classics for precedents and applauded the efforts of near contemporaries such as Anna Maria Schurman, a Dutch feminist whose tract *The Learned Maid* probably influenced his decision to teach Katharin Hebrew. Schurman's argument, deeply imbedded in traditional piety, would have been congenial to Mather. She excluded from discussion "*Scriptural Theology*, properly so named, as that which without Controversie belongs to all Christians," directing her attention to that wider scholarship commonly denied women. If you say we are weak witted, she wrote, studies will help us. If you say we are not inclined to studies, let us taste their sweetness and you will see. If you say we have no colleges, we can use private teachers. If you say our vocations are narrow, we answer they are merely private; we are not exempt from the universal sentence of Plutarch: "It becomes a perfect Man, to know what is to be Known, and to do what is to be done."[59] She concluded by suggesting that young women be exposed from their infancy to the "encouragement of wise men" and the "examples of illustrious women." In his tracts and in his sermons, Mather enthusiastically provided both.

It is important to understand that we are not dealing with a new concept of women in Mather's work, but a new visibility. Though in 1660 under sentence of death, Peter could hardly have recommended a public role for Elizabeth, there is evidence that he was as ready as

Mather to value female scholarship and writing. In 1651 he had contributed a Prefatory letter to a revolutionary tract by Mary Cary, applauding her clear opening of the scriptures and her rejection of "naked Brests, black Patches" and "long Trains" in favor of a pen. He referred to "Two of this Sexe I have met with, very famous for more than their mother-tongue, and for what we call Learning, yet living." One of these women, "the glory of her sexe in Holland," was apparently Anna Maria Schurman, whom Peter may have met in Utrecht.[60]

As important as Mather's promotion of increased intellectual activity for women was the luster he gave to their more traditional roles. In beginning his funeral sermon for his own mother, he exclaimed: "Oh! The Endearments of our God! Beyond all the Endearments of the Tenderest Mother in the World!" Taking for his text Isaiah 49:15, "Can a Woman forget her Sucking Child, that she should not have Compassion on the Son of her Bowels? Yea, They may forget: yet will not I forget thee," he drew out the parallels between the love of God and the love of a mother. "The Disposition which the Glorious God has to provide for the *Comfort* of His People, has Two Resemblances, in *His Two Testaments;* And in both of them, 'tis Resembled unto the Provision which *Female-Parents* make for their Young-ones." Mothers comfort their children through their good instructions, through their good examples, and through their pious prayers. These, however, are temporary comforts. Mothers feed us, but God does more. Mothers clothe us, but God does more. Mothers guide us, but God does more. Mothers keep us out of harm's way, but God does more. Mothers confer ornaments upon us, but God confers upon us the lasting ornament. Thus God is a better mother than our earthly mothers. At this point, Mather drew back somewhat from his metaphor, assuring his audience that God was also our father. "What is the best of Mothers weigh'd in the Ballance with Such a *Father?* Our *Father* is now the Infinite God." But he went on:

> It has been a little Surprising unto me to find That in some of the Primitive Writers, the *Holy Spirit* is called, *The Mother.* Tertullian uses this Denomination for the *Holy Spirit; the Mother,* who is Invocated with the *Father* and the *Son.*[61]

Instead of recoiling from the heresy, Mather explained the reasonableness of the metaphor. It is through the Holy Ghost that we are born again. The Holy Ghost is spoken of in the scriptures as a comforter. Surely nothing is of greater comfort than a good mother.

Mather did not mean to deify women. In finding female as well as male virtues in the Godhead, he was simply reasserting the spiritual equality of men and women and the essentially asexual nature of godliness. But he was doing something else as well. He was openly and generously bolstering the public image of Boston's women.

If a person believes in the inherent equality of the sexes yet notes an inequity in the way they are regarded in society, he can resolve the discrepancy in three ways. He can try to change women, encouraging them to enlarge those activities which might bring them honor and recognition. He can try to change society, urging recognition and praise for the unsung activities women already excel in. Or he can dismiss the whole problem, deny the importance of status altogether, and turn his attention to the spiritual realm. Mather tried all three. In praising the works of Anna Maria Schurman and in teaching his daughter Hebrew, he put himself on the side of enlarged opportunity. In eulogizing his mother, he gave public recognition to a specifically feminine role. But as a good minister he could not commit himself completely to any worldly activity. His real commitment had to be to the glory of God. Paradoxically, then, one of the attractions of women for Mather seems to have been their very lack of status. In praising them, he was not only encouraging their good works, he was demonstrating his own superiority to earthly standards. Thus he withdrew with one hand what he had given with the other.

Mather's work points to a difficulty in reconciling inherent worth and earthly position. For most of the ministers through most of the period this had been no problem. Either they had seen no discrepancy or they were unconcerned with questions of status. The reasons for Mather's position are not entirely clear, although several explanations suggest themselves. On the one hand, he may have been influenced by European feminist thought; in a letter to his sister-in-law, who was living in England, he mentioned not only Anna Maria Schurman but Marie de Gournay.[62] Yet even with an allowance for the Atlantic, the writings of neither were new. Gournay's essays were published in the 1620's, Schurman's in the 1650's. Nor was Schurman unknown to earlier ministers, as the Hugh Peter friendship shows. More probably, Mather was dealing with changes in his own provincial society. It is a commonplace that by the end of the seventeenth century, New England was becoming more secular as well as more prosperous. The presumed threat of leisure hangs over much of Mather's writing. In his first booklet, he noted that while women often had a great deal to do, "it is as *often* so, that you have little more Worldly Business, than to Spend (I should rather say, to

Save) what others *Get,* and to *Dress* and *Feed* (should I not also say, to *Teach*) the Little Birds, which you are *Dams* unto. And those of you, that are *Women of Quality* are Excused from very much of *this* Trouble too."[63] He picked up the same theme in his tract for midwives, urging mothers to suckle their own infants. "Be not such an Ostrich as to Decline it, merely because you would be One of the Careless Women Living at Ease."[64] Clothing and jewels are pervasive metaphors not only in *Ornaments for the Daughters of Zion* but in *Bethiah,* a similar pamphlet written thirty years later. In both, women are told that if they will resist the temptation to worldly adornment they will be "clothed with the sun."[65] Perhaps changes in the provincial lifestyle gave new impetus to the traditional Puritan distrust of leisure. Such an explanation accounts for Mather's injunctions to piety and his warnings against worldliness, but it does not totally explain his preoccupation with status.

Cotton Mather's writings on women point to a much more fundamental problem, a paradox inherent in the ministerial position from the first. This paper began by noting the obvious—that New England's women could not preach, attend Harvard, or participate in the government of the congregation or commonwealth. It went on to argue that this circumscribed social position was not reflected in the spiritual sphere, that New England's ministers continued to uphold the oneness of men and women before God, that in their understanding of the marriage relationship they moved far toward equality, that in all their writings they stressed the dignity, intelligence, strength, and rationality of women even as they acknowledged the physical limitations imposed by their reproductive role. Cotton Mather may not have been fully conscious of this double view, yet all his writings on women are in one way or another a response to it. Such a position requires a balance (if not an otherworldliness) that is very difficult to maintain. In the work of his younger contemporaries, Benjamin Colman and Thomas Foxcroft, this is even more clearly seen.

Colman's daughter Jane was apparently fond of the sermons of Cotton Mather for she composed a tribute to him on his death. Certainly in her own life she exemplified his teaching, spurning balls, black patches, and vain romances for godly scholarship. She had the run of her father's library, which included, in addition to edifying tomes, the poetry of Sir Richard Blackmore and of Waller. At eleven she began composing rhymes of her own and as a young bride she wrote letters to her father in verse which he sometimes answered in kind. Although intensely religious, she began to measure her own writing against a worldly as well as a heavenly scale, a tendency that must have contributed to her own self-doubts and frequent headaches. In a letter to her father, she expressed the hope that she had inherited his gifts. His answer epitomized the possibilities and the limitations of the ministerial position:

> My poor Gift is in thinking and writing with a little Eloquence, and a Poetical turn of Thought. This, in proportion to the Advantages you have had, under the necessary and useful Restraints of your Sex, you enjoy to the full of what I have done before you. With the Advantages of my liberal Education at School & College, I have no reason to think but that your Genious in Writing would have excell'd mine. But there is no great Progress or Improvement ever made in any thing but by Use and Industry and Time. If you diligently improve your stated and some vacant hours every Day or Week to read your Bible and other useful Books, you will insensibly grow in knowledge & Wisdom, fine tho'ts and good Judgment.[66]

Both the "useful Restraints" and the encouragement of study are familiar themes. If Colman saw no possibility for a university education, neither did he deny her ability to profit by it. Like the other ministers, he made no attempt to extrapolate a different spiritual nature from a contrasting social role. But he fully accepted that role and expected Jane to fulfill it.

In 1735, Jane Colman Turrel died in childbirth. In her father's sermons and in the biography written by her husband, there is little to distinguish her from Katharin Mather or even Jerusha Oliver. But in a poem appended to the sermons, there is a fascinating crack in the portrait. The Reverend John Adams wrote:

> Fair was her Face, but fairer was her Mind,
> Where all the Muses, all the Graces join'd.
> For tender Passions turn'd, and soft to please,
> With all the graceful Negligence of Ease.
> Her Soul was form'd for nicer Arts of Life,
> To show the Friend, but most to grace the Wife.[67]

Negligence, softness, ease! These are concepts alien to the virtuous woman. Jane Colman had been invited into her father's library as an intellectual equal, but to at least one of her male friends she had become only that much more attractive as a drawing-room ornament. It is tempting to conclude that by 1735, even ministers were seducing the Virtuous Woman with worldly standards. But the new prosperity was not entirely to blame. As an instrument of piety, scholarship had its limits. With no other earthly outlet available, dinner-party conversation had to do.

Thomas Foxcroft was either less comfortable with the intellectual role than Mather or Colman or more concerned about its limits. In *Anna the Prophetess* he went to great lengths to deny the implications of his own text, arguing on the one hand that women were worthy of the title of prophet and on the other that they certainly shouldn't be allowed to speak in church. His choice of a text and title were very much in the tradition of Mather, but his handling of it betrayed a discomfort his mentor never acknowledged. When he came to write of motherhood, however, his defense of women blossomed. In his sermon for his own mother, preached in 1721, he described women as the bastions of religion in the home and the community. "At the Gap, which the Death of a wise and good Mother makes, does many times enter a Torrent of Impieties and Vices." Some mothers were simply too good for this world: God might gather them home to prevent them seeing the "Penal Evils" about to befall their children. Foxcroft's praise overlay a more conservative base. He cautioned that the death of a mother might be a punishment for loving her too much as well as for loving her too little. But his own sermon is evidence of where he felt the greater danger lay. "Indeed Children's Love and Regard to their Parents living or dead, commonly needs a Spur, Tho' the Parents too often need a Curb."[68] As a good Puritan, he could not embrace mother love or any other form of human love as an unqualified good, but like Mather he was concerned that Boston's mothers receive the proper respect.

This is a crucial point. In the funeral literature there had been little mention of "motherhood" as opposed to the more generalized concept of "parenthood." Even Colman, who published a baptismal sermon entitled *Some of the Honours that Religion Does Unto the Fruitful Mothers in Israel,* was unable to maintain the sex differentiation much beyond the title. If a distinction between mothers and fathers is ever made in the literature, however, it is over the issue of respect. Wadsworth felt that "persons are often more apt to *despise a Mother,* (the weaker vessel, and frequently most indulgent) than a Father."[69] Despite its text, John Flavell's *A Discourse: Shewing that Christ's Tender Care of His Mother is an Excellent Pattern for all Gracious Children* is about parents rather than about mothers specifically. But the one direct comment on women echoes Wadsworth: "[S]he by reason of her blandishments, and fond indulgence is most subject to the irreverence and contempt of children."[70] Thus Boston's ministers showed a concern for neglect of women well before they identified or elaborated any sex-related virtues. Foxcroft built upon this concern, but with a subtle difference. Although his mother's piety was the traditional piety, it was as a *mother* rather than as a Christian that she was singled out. With a new set of values, a focus upon tenderness and love rather than on godliness and strength, Foxcroft's effusiveness would be indistinguishable from nineteenth-century sentimentality.

Thus, in New England sermons firmly rooted in the reformed tradition of the seventeenth century, we can see developing, as if in embryo, both the "genteel lady" of the eighteenth century and the "tender mother" of the nineteenth. Adams' poem for Jane Turrel shows the short step from Puritan intellectuality to feminine sensibility. Foxcroft's eulogy for his mother demonstrates how praise for a single virtue might obliterate all others. If Puritan piety upheld the oneness of men and women, Puritan polity in large part did not. Nor, we assume, did the increasingly mercantile world of early eighteenth-century Boston. Unwilling or unable to transfer spiritual equality to the earthly sphere, ministers might understandably begin to shift earthly differences to the spiritual sphere, gradually developing sexual definitions of the psyche and soul.

It is important to remember here that the sermon literature deals with a relatively small group of people, that it reveals attitudes not practices. Presumably, few women experienced the conflicts of Jane Turrel. Most housewives in provincial Boston were probably too occupied with the daily round to consider the nature of their position in society. Yet when a minister of the stature of Cotton Mather assumes a defensive tone, telling us that "those *Handmaids of the Lord*, who tho' they ly very much Conceal'd from the World, and may be called *The Hidden Ones*, yet have no little share in the *Beauty* and the *Defence* of the Land," as historians we ought to listen to him.[71] Attitudes are important. Subtle shifts in perception both reflect and affect social practice. Mather's advocacy of women suggests a real tension in early eighteenth century New England between presumed private worth and public position. It demonstrates the need for closer study of the actual functioning of women within congregation and community. But it has ramifications beyond its own time and place. Mather's work shows how discrete and ultimately confining notions of "femininity" might grow out of a genuine concern with equality. Finally, the ministerial literature to which it belongs illustrates the importance of the narrow study, the need to move from static concepts like "patriarchal New England society" to more intricate questions about the interplay of values and practice over time. Zion's daughters have for too long been hidden.

NOTES

1. Edmund S. Morgan, *The Puritan Family: Religion and Domestic Relations in Seventeenth-Century New England* (New York: Harper and Row,

1966), p. 44. Recent works continue to rely on Morgan's study, which was first published in 1944. See, for example, John Demos, *A Little Commonwealth: Family Life in Plymouth* (New York: Oxford Univ. Press, 1970), p. 98. Morgan's description of male dominance within a loving marriage is consistent with descriptions taken from English prescriptive literature in Louis B. Wright, *Middle-Class Culture in Elizabethan England* (Chapel Hill, N.C.: Univ. of North Carolina Press, 1935), chapter VII, and in Charles H. and Katherine George, *The Protestant Mind of the English Reformation, 1570–1640* (Princeton, N.J.: Princeton Univ. Press, 1961), chapter 7.

2. The Winthrop quote appears in Morgan (p. 44) as in many lesser summaries of Puritan attitudes toward women from Thomas Woody, *A History of Women's Education in the United States,* Vol. I (New York: Science Press, 1929), pp. 106–07, to Lyle Koehler, "The Case of the American Jezebels: Anne Hutchinson and Female Agitation During the Years of Antinomian Turmoil, 1636–1640," *William and Mary Quarterly*, 3d Ser., 31 (Jan. 1974), p. 58. Koehler's article exemplifies the common imbalance in favor of deviant women.

3. Charles Evans, *American Bibliography: A Chronological Dictionary of all Books, Pamphlets and Periodical Publications Printed in the USA, 1639–1820* (New York: P. Smith, 1941); Roger Bristol, *Supplement to Charles Evans' American Bibliography* (Charlottesville, Va.: Univ. Press of Virginia, 1970).

4. Mary Sumner Benson, in *Women in Eighteenth-Century America* (New York: Columbia Univ. Press, 1935), quotes extensively from Mather's *Ornaments,* using it as evidence that he believed in the "proper submission of women." Page Smith draws the opposite conclusion from the same document in *Daughters of the Promised Land* (Boston: Little, Brown, 1970), pp. 47ff. Two of the three main sources for Edmund Morgan's description of marital ethics belong to this group of materials: Willard's *Complete Body of Divinity* and Wadsworth's *The Well-Ordered Family,* although he quotes rather selectively from them. William Andrews, "The Printed Funeral Sermons of Cotton Mather," *Early American Literature*, 5 (Fall 1970), pp. 24–44, notes the high percentage of sermons on females and attempts some analysis of the materials but without relating it to the wider corpus of ministerial literature.

5. In his study of prescriptive literature in late seventeenth-century England, Levin L. Schucking noted a similar phenomenon. See *The Puritan Family: A Social Study from the Literary Sources* (London: Routledge and Kegan Paul, 1969), p. xiii. I have made no attempt to define the "Puritanism" of the authors. Although most of them belonged to the congregational majority, Samuel Myles was an Anglican. His eulogy for Elizabeth Riscarrick, though less detailed than many, follows the typical pattern.

6. The funeral sermon with its accompanying biographical "lean-to" was a venerable form by this time. See William Haller, *The Rise of Puritanism* (New York: Harper, 1938), p. 101.

7. John Hart, *The Nature and Blessedness of Trusting in God* (New London, 1728), p. 45.

8. Cotton Mather, *Nepenthes Evangelicum . . . A Sermon Occasion'd by the Death of a Religious Matron, Mrs. Mary Rock* (Boston, 1713), p. 41.

9. John Danforth, "An Elegy upon the much Lamented Decease of Mrs. Elizabeth Foxcroft," appended to Thomas Foxcroft's *Sermon Preach'd at Cambridge after the Funeral of Mrs. Elizabeth Foxcroft* (Boston, 1721), p. 53.

10. Benjamin Colman, *Reliquiae Turellae, et Lachrymae Paternae. Father's*

Tears over his Daughter's Remains . . . to which are added, some Large Memoirs of her Life and Death by her Consort, the Reverend Mr. Ebenezer Turell (Boston, 1735), p. 116.

11. Increase Mather, *A Sermon Concerning Obedience & Resignation To The Will of God in Everything* (Boston, 1714), p. ii, p. 39.

12. Foxcroft, *Sermon Preach'd*, pp. 14–15.

13. This is a common theme throughout Mather's funeral sermons. A typical example is in *Virtue in its Verdure. A Christian Exhibited as a Green Olive Tree . . . with a character of the Virtuous Mrs. Abigail Brown* (Boston, 1725), p. 23.

14. Cotton Mather, *Monica Americana, A Funeral-Sermon Occasioned by Death of Mrs. Sarah Leveret* (Boston, 1705), p. 27.

15. James Fitch, *Peace the End of the Perfect and Upright* (Cambridge, 1672), p. 12; Benjamin Colman, *The Death of God's Saints Precious in His Sight* (Boston, 1723), p. 23.

16. Jabez Fitch, *Discourse on Serious Piety. A Funeral Sermon . . . upon the Death of Mrs. Mary Martyn* (Boston, 1725), p. 18.

17. John Danforth, "Greatness & Goodness Elegized, In a Poem upon the Much Lamented Decease of the Honourable & Vertuous Madam Hannah Sewall" (Boston, 1717), Broadside, p. 1.33ff.

18. Increase Mather, *A Sermon Concerning Obedience*, p. ii.

19. Cotton Mather, *Memorials of Early Piety* (Boston, 1711), pp. 3–4, 13.

20. "An Account of Mrs. Katharin Mather by Another Hand," in Cotton Mather, *Victorina: A Sermon Preach'd on the Decease and at the Desire of Mrs. Katharin Mather* (Boston, 1717), p. 50.

21. [Joseph Metcalf,] "Tears Dropt at the Funeral of . . . Mrs. Elizabeth Hatch" (Boston, 1710), Broadside.

22. John Danforth, "Honour and Vertue Elegized in a Poem Upon an Honourable, Aged, and Gracious Mother in Israel" (Boston, 1713), Broadside; Cotton Mather, *Nepenthes*, pp. 45–46.

23. James Hillhouse, *A Sermon Concerning the Life, Death, and Future State of Saints* (Boston, 1721), pp. 112, 117. Although Hillhouse's sermon was published in Boston after he had settled there, it was originally preached in Ireland.

24. James Fitch, *Peace*, p. 11.

25. Thomas Foxcroft, *The Character of Anna, The Prophetess Consider'd and Apply'd* (Boston, 1723), from the Preface by Benjamin Wadsworth, p. ii.

26. Cotton Mather, *El-Shaddai . . . A brief Essay . . . Produced by the Death of That Virtuous Gentlewoman, Mrs. Katharin Willard* (Boston, 1725), p. 22.

27. Thomas Reynolds, *Practical Religion Exemplify'd In The Lives of Mrs. Mary Terry . . . and Mrs. Clissould* (Boston, 1713), p. 4; and Foxcroft, *Anna*, p. 14.

28. Cotton Mather, *Ecclesiae Monilia. The Peculiar Treasure of the Almighty King Opened . . . Whereof one is more particularly Exhibited in the Character of Mrs. Elizabeth Cotton* (Boston, 1726), p. 25.

29. Sarah Goodhue, *The Copy of a Valedictory and Monitory Writing . . . Directed to her Husband and Children, with other Near Relations and Friends*, reprinted in Thomas Franklin Water, *Ipswich in the Massachusetts Bay Colony* (Ipswich, Mass.: Ipswich Historical Society, 1905), pp. 519–24.

30. Grace Smith, *The Dying Mother's Legacy, or the Good and Heavenly Counsel of that Eminent and Pious Matron* (Boston, 1712).

31. Increase Mather, *The Life and Death of Richard Mather* (Cambridge, 1670), p. 25.

32. Cotton Mather, *Memorials of Early Piety*, p. 45.

33. John Danforth, "A Poem Upon the Triumphant Translation of a Mother in Our Israel," appended to *Kneeling to God* (Boston, 1697), p. 64.

34. Increase Mather, *Sermon Concerning Obedience*, p. 34.

35. Samuel Myles, *Sermon Preach't At the Funeral of Mrs. Elizabeth Riscarrick* (Boston, 1698).

36. Cotton Mather, *Memorials of Early Piety*, p. 49.

37. Cotton Mather, *Light in Darkness, An Essay on the Piety Which by Rememb'ring the Many Days of Darkness, Will Change Them Into a Marvelous Light* (Boston, 1724), p. 20.

38. Cotton Mather, *Juga*, pp. 31–32.

39. Increase Mather, *Richard Mather*, pp. 33, 34.

40. See for example, Cotton Mather, *A Good Man Making A Good End* (Boston, 1698), on the death of a minister; and Thomas Foxcroft, *A Brief Display of Mordecai's Excellent Character* (Boston, 1727), on the death of a public official. For the English tradition (which placed less emphasis on early piety), see Haller, *Rise of Puritanism*, p. 93ff. Robert Middlekauff and David Hall both stress the prototypal quality of Richard Mather's biography. See *The Mathers: Three Generations of Puritan Intellectuals, 1596–1728* (New York: Oxford Univ. Press, 1971), p. 101–02, and *The Faithful Shepherd: A History of the New England Ministry in the Seventeenth Century* (Chapel Hill, N.C.: Univ. of North Carolina Press, 1972), p. 179.

41. John Sprint, *The Bride-Woman's Counsellor, Being A Sermon Preached at a Wedding at Sherbourn, in Dorsetshire* (Boston, 1709), p. 2.

42. Ibid., pp. 16, 11.

43. Benjamin Wadsworth, *The Well-Ordered Family: or, Relative Duties, Being The Substance of Several Sermons About Family Prayer, Duties of Husband & Wives, Duties of Parents & Children, Duties of Masters & Servants* (Boston, 1712), p. 28.

44. William Secker, *A Wedding Ring* (Boston, 1690), unpaged.

45. Samuel Willard, *A Complete Body of Divinity in Two Hundred and Fifty Expository Lectures* (Boston, 1726), pp. 609–12.

46. John Oliver, *A Present for Teeming American Women* (Boston, 1694), p. 3. This was an American edition of a pamphlet first printed in London in 1663. The Evans film is very short and probably includes just the preface.

47. Nicholas Noyes, poem for Mrs. Mary Brown in Cotton Mather, *Eureka the Vertuous Woman Found*, I. 15; see also "Upon the Death of the Virtuous and Religious Mrs. Lydia Minot" (Cambridge, 1668), an anonymous broadside.

48. Willard, *Complete Body of Divinity*, p. 611.

49. See for example, *Tabitha Rediviva, An Essay to Describe and Commend The Good Works of a Virtuous Woman* (Boston, 1713), p. 21.

50. Cotton Mather, *Ornaments for the Daughters of Zion* (Cambridge, 1692), p. 45.

51. Benjamin Colman, *The Duty and Honour of Aged Women* (Boston, 1711), pp. ii–iii.

52. John Oliver, *Teeming Women*, p. 4.

53. Cotton Mather, *Eureka*, p. 1.

54. Hugh Peter, *A Dying Father's Last Legacy* (Boston, 1717), pp. 22, 34, 83. Lyle Koehler quotes merely the phrase "Woman's Ornament" in attempt-

ing to show that Hugh Peter shared a general Puritan belief in the subjection of women. See "The Case of the American Jezebels," p. 59.

55. Cotton Mather, *Bethiah. The Glory Which Adorns the Daughters of God and the Piety, Wherewith Zion Wishes to see her Daughters Glorious* (Boston, 1722), p. 34.

56. Cotton Mather, *Undoubted Certainties, or, Piety Enlivened* (Boston, 1720), p. 26.

57. Cotton Mather, *Juga*, p. 24.

58. Cotton Mather, *Ornaments*, pp. 5–6.

59. Anna Maria Schurman, *The Learned Maid: or, Whether a Maid may be a Scholar? A Logick Exercise* (London, 1659), pp. 1, 37.

60. The entire letter is quoted in Doris Mary Stenton, *The English Woman in History* (London: G. Allen and Unwin, 1957), pp. 136–37.

61. Cotton Mather, *Maternal Consolations of God* (Boston, 1714), pp. 5, 8, 24, 25.

62. *Diary of Cotton Mather, 1709–1724*, Mass. Hist. Soc. Collections, 7th Series, VIII (Boston, 1911), p. 325.

63. Cotton Mather, *Ornaments*, p. 45.

64. Cotton Mather, *Elizabeth*, p. 35. James Axtell, *The School Upon a Hill: Education and Society in Colonial New England* (New Haven and London: Yale Univ. Press, 1974), pp. 75–83, surveys English attitudes toward wet-nurses and speculates on colonial practice.

65. Cotton Mather, *Bethiah*, p. 37. Declension is of course a familiar theme. The sex ratio of church membership is worth further study in this regard. Robert Pope, "New England Versus the New England Mind: The Myth of Declension," *Journal of Social History*, 3 (1969–70), 102, argues that women were becoming less rather than more dominant after 1675. This would undercut the easy assumption made by Andrews, "Funeral Sermons of Cotton Mather," p. 32, that women were getting more attention from ministers because men had abandoned the churches.

66. Colman, *Reliquiae Turellae*, p. 69.

67. Ibid., p. v.

68. Foxcroft, *Sermon*, pp. 14, 20.

69. Wadsworth, *Well-Ordered Family*, p. 92.

70. John Flavell, *A Discourse* (Boston, 1728), p. 5.

71. Cotton Mather, *El-Shaddai*, p. 31.

3

Quaker Marriage Patterns in a Colonial Perspective

ROBERT V. WELLS

The North American colonies were known, in the British empire, for their fecundity. Numerous observers in the seventeenth and eighteenth centuries remarked on the large size of American families. As Robert V. Wells points out, a couple's age at marriage has an important relationship to the size of their completed family: the younger the couple (especially the wife), the longer the potential period of fertility in the marriage. One of the distinct characteristics of colonial marriage was the young age of brides. Child bearing and child rearing thus occupied even more of the adult years of American women's lives than of their British or European counterparts. Wells complements his detailed examination of Quaker families (accomplished by "family reconstitution" techniques) with extensive comparative data to illuminate changing trends in marriage, fertility, and the sex ratio at the end of the eighteenth century.

DESPITE THE OBVIOUS IMPORTANCE of marriage patterns for an understanding of the colonial family, and so of colonial society, the subject has only recently begun to receive close attention from students of the period. In the last few years, the studies of various Massachusetts towns done by John Demos, Philip Greven, and Kenneth Lockridge have led the way in exploring the relationships between marriage and other aspects of colonial society.[1] Because of the focus on New England to date, a study of marriage patterns among colonists from a different region has an obvious interest. Therefore, the first part of this paper will examine some patterns of marriage of a particular group of 276 Quaker families from the middle colonies. The remainder of the essay will consider the possible existence of distinct patterns of marriage in the colonies and will explore the effect that such patterns may have had on family size in seventeenth- and eighteenth-century America.

As defined here, a family consisted of a husband and wife, plus any children born to that particular union. Because of an interest in change over time, the date of birth of the wife was used to divide the 276 Quaker families into three chronological groups. A desire to identify any demographic patterns that might be associated with the American Revolution and a concern to avoid groups with very small numbers were the principal determinants of the division. The first grouping of families included 80 couples in which the wife was born no later than 1730. The second group of families, numbering 65 in all, was defined by wives who were born between 1731 and 1755. A final group, which included the remaining 125 families, was determined by wives born between 1756 and 1785.[2] Although most of the members of these families lived during the eighteenth century, a few unions were formed in the late seventeenth century and children occasionally were born to the couples under study as late as the 1820s. The records of their births, marriages, and deaths are to be found in the registers of the monthly meetings of the Society of Friends of New York City, Flushing, Jericho, and Westbury in New York; Plainfield and Rahway, Salem, and Burlington in New Jersey; and Falls and Philadelphia in Pennsylvania.[3] From these records it has been possible to reconstitute the 276 families.[4] As might be expected, the proportion of families from each geographic area did not remain constant in each of the chronological groups, but this does not seem to have caused the changes over time which will be described later. In fact, it is rather surprising to discover that, in this instance at least, regional variations (including rural-urban differences) in demographic patterns could not be readily identified.

The age at which persons, especially women, first marry is a subject of considerable interest, since a woman seldom is able to bear children for more than the thirty years between ages fifteen and forty-five. The age at which she marries plays, then, an obvious role in determining how many children she can bear and therefore directly affects family size and the growth rate of the population. Women who married at the age of fifteen (and a few of these Quakers did) would have had approximately twice as many years to bear children as women who remained single until thirty. Furthermore, since the ability to bear children tends to decline as age increases, the women who married at a later age could expect to have their childbearing potential reduced still further.

Among the Quakers included in this study the average age at first marriage, as indicated in Table I, was 22.8 for women and 26.5 for men.[5] The median age for first marriages among the women was 20.5 years, while the corresponding figure for the men showed half

TABLE I
First Marriages
(Proportion by age)

	Women			Men		
Married at Age	N	Proportion	Cumulated Proportion	N	Proportion	Cumulated Proportion
15	4	1.5	1.5[b]	—	—	—
16	19	7.1	8.6	—	—	—
17	12	4.5	13.0	—	—	—
18	29	10.8	23.8	2	.9	.9
19	35	13.0	36.8	3	1.4	2.4
20	23	8.6	45.4	8	3.8	6.1
21	28	10.4	55.8	28	13.2	19.3
22	21	7.8	63.6	20	9.4	28.6
23	16	6.0	69.5	26	12.2	40.9
24	14	5.2	74.7	20	9.4	50.2
25	6	2.2	77.0	19	8.9	59.2
26	17	6.3	83.3	16	7.5	66.7
27	9	3.4	86.6	13	6.1	72.8
28	4	1.5	88.1	11	5.2	77.9
29	4	1.5	89.6	8	3.8	81.7
30	1	.4	90.0	6	2.8	84.5
31	5	1.9	91.8	6	2.8	87.3
32	5	1.9	93.7	1	.5	87.8
33	1	.4	94.1	3	1.4	89.2
34	4	1.5	95.5	3	1.4	90.6
35	3	1.1	96.7	3	1.4	92.0
36	2	.7	97.4	4	1.9	93.9
37	0	0.0	97.4	4	1.9	95.8
38	3	1.1	98.5	0	0.0	95.8
39	1	.4	98.9	1	.5	96.2
40 or more	3	1.1	100.0	8	3.8	100.0
Total	269[a]	100.0	100.0	213	100.0	100.0
Average		22.8			26.5	
Median		20.5			24.0	

Notes: [a] The numbers involved in this and following tables will not always equal 276. The persons under consideration change according to differing combinations of restrictions. The restrictions are based on 1.) previous marital status and 2.) the quality of data on the family reconstitution form.
[b] Cumulated proportions were calculated directly, and so, because of rounding differences, may not be exactly equal to the sum of the individual proportions.

of them marrying before age 24.0 and half marrying after that age. These figures indicate that marriage tended to be concentrated in the younger ages, a conclusion which is borne out by the information on the proportions marrying at a given age, also presented in Table I. Of the men who married, 81.7 percent did so before the age of thirty, while only 10.4 percent of the women who married remained single that long. As might be expected, few of either sex married for the first time at an age of forty or more. One of the most striking differences between the marriage patterns of the men and women is in the proportions marrying for the first time under the age of twenty, since over a third of the women married before they were twenty, but only 2.4 percent of the men married before that age. In fact, 93.9 percent of all men waited to marry until they were over twenty years old, but once they had attained the age of twenty-one, more men married at that age than at any other. In the case of the women, more were married at nineteen than at any other age. While women were younger than men on the average when they married for the first time, there were few child brides. The youngest women to marry did so at the age of fifteen, but only 1.5 percent of the brides were that young, and 87.0 percent were eighteen or older before they married.

Custom may have played an important part in determining when a young Quaker might marry, for most of the marriages of both the men and women were concentrated in just a few years. Between the ages of eighteen and twenty-two, 50.6 percent of the women got married, while in a similar five-year span, 53.1 percent of the men were married between the ages of twenty-one and twenty-five. Equally impressive is the fact that fully 75.5 percent of the brides married for the first time between the ages of sixteen and twenty-five; four out of every five men (79.3 percent) marrying for the first time did so between the ages of twenty and twenty-nine. It is difficult to believe that anything but a customary association of marriage with certain ages could produce such concentrations. The fact that marriages were concentrated in much the same way in Andover and Plymouth, Massachusetts, (and elsewhere, as well) lends further support to the conclusion that the age at first marriage was, to some extent, determined by custom in seventeenth- and eighteenth-century America.[6]

When a Quaker man of this study married, his bride was often his age or slightly younger, as the data in Table II indicates. In all, there was a difference of less than one year in the age of the husband and wife 16.1 percent of the time, when the marriage was the first for both partners; there was less than five years' difference in 62.0 percent of the marriages; and 85.1 percent of these couples were

TABLE II
Difference in Age of Husband and Wife
(First marriage for both partners)

	Difference in Years	% of Marriages	Number
Wife older by	5.0– 9.9	1.0	2
	1.0– 4.9	7.2	14
	0.1– 0.9	2.1	4
No difference	0	1.6	3
Husband older by	0.1– 0.9	12.4	24
	1.0– 4.9	38.7	75
	5.0– 9.9	22.2	43
	10.0–14.9	9.8	19
	15.0–19.9	3.6	7
	20.0–24.9	.5	1
	25.0–29.9	1.0	2
Total		100.0	194

separated by less than ten years of age. Interestingly, in 10.3 percent of the marriages the wife was older than the husband, though only 8.2 percent of the wives exceeded their husband's age by a year or more. There seem to have been very few instances of an old man marrying a young girl, for only in 5.1 percent of the marriages was the husband over fifteen years older than his wife, but in no case was the difference in age between husband and wife as much as thirty years.

A similar study of marriages in which at least one of the partners had been previously married produced the same results. The ages of the husband and wife were much the same, as men chose wives who were younger but not far different in age. Only twice in twenty-two known cases involving remarriage was the difference in age between husband and wife twenty years or more, and in neither of these did the difference reach thirty years.

The average age at first marriage of both men and women was examined for each of the three chronological groups described above to see if there was any change in this particular aspect of marriage over time. Table III indicates the changes which occurred.

In the case of the men, the age at first marriage remained fairly stable. Although the men of the middle group married at an average

TABLE III
Changes in the Average Age at First Marriage

	By 1730	Wives Born 1731–1755	1756–1785
Men	26.5	25.8	26.8
Women	22.0	22.8	23.4

age which was lower than for the other two groups, there was less than a third of a year's difference between the first and the last group. The women, on the other hand, experienced a steady rise in their average age at first marriage. The women who were born after 1755 married at an average age of 23.4 years, an increase of 1.4 years over those women born by 1730, who married at 22.0 on the average. These changes in the average age at first marriage suggest a number of significant developments in colonial society that will be discussed later.

Studies which deal primarily with age at marriage emphasize the formation of families and the age at which women begin to bear children. But just as important in determining the size of the family is the duration of marriage, and for obvious reasons. Among the Quakers of this study, marriages lasted until one spouse died, for divorce among the Friends was rare in the eighteenth century.[7]

For these Quakers the average duration of the marriage was surprisingly high. The 271 unions which were formed before the wife was forty-five lasted an average of 30.8 years from the time the wedding took place until the first spouse died. Furthermore, the average duration of marriage increased steadily over time, rising from 28.7 years for the families in which the wife was born by 1730, to averages of 29.6 and 32.8 years among the families in which the wives were born from 1731 to 1755, and from 1756 to 1785 respectively. As a result of this increase, the proportion of couples who remained united until the wife had reached the age of forty-five, and hence had presumably completed her childbearing, rose from 61 percent in the first group of families to 69 percent in the middle group; among the last group of families, the corresponding figure was 73 percent.

In spite of the high average duration of marriage, a sizable proportion of all these unions did end relatively early, as is evident from an examination of Table IV. Although only 1.9 percent of all unions lasted less than a year, almost a fifth (18.8 percent) had been dissolved by the death of one partner before the fifteenth anniversary had been reached, and after twenty-five years 38.4 percent of the

TABLE IV
Duration of Marriage
(Wife less than 45 at marriage)

By Years	Number	% of All Marriages	Cumulative %
Under 1	5	1.9	1.9[a]
1– 4.9	15	5.5	7.4
5– 9.9	11	4.1	11.4
10–14.9	20	7.4	18.8
15–19.9	30	11.1	29.9
20–24.9	23	8.5	38.4
25–29.9	30	11.1	49.5
30–49.9	96	35.4	84.9
50 or more	41	15.1	100.0
Total	271	100.0	100.0

Note: [a] Cumulated proportions were calculated directly, and so, because of rounding differences, may not be exactly equal to the sum of the individual proportions.

unions once formed no longer existed. Just over half (50.5 percent) of all marriages lasted more than thirty years, with 15.1 percent of the couples united for as long as fifty years.[8]

The fact that these Quaker couples had, on the average, a relatively long life together should be enough to cast doubt on the oft held assumption that colonial women frequently died from an excess of childbearing. There is also little evidence to support the notion that only the healthiest and hardiest of women could bear large families in the eighteenth century. A correlation between the age at death of the wife and the total number of children born in families which remained intact until the wife had reached the age of forty-five indicates that there was virtually no relationship between the two factors: having a large number of children seems not to have shortened a woman's life or to indicate that she was unusually healthy and likely to live to a ripe old age.[9] Epidemic or endemic disease was far more likely to cause the death of one of these Quaker women in the eighteenth century than was childbirth.

From the evidence available there can be little doubt that both widows and widowers were common among these Quakers, for the surviving partner often lived a number of years after the union was ended. The length of time that the surviving spouse lived after the marriage was terminated can be determined for each of the 216 families in which the age at death of both husband and wife is known. Of these 216 marriages, 113 were ended by the death of the husband; in two instances death was virtually simultaneous; and 101 were ended by the death of the wife. That the husband died first in the majority of cases helps to substantiate the view that childbearing had nowhere near the effect on the life expectancy of married women as has been thought.[10] The husbands who outlived their wives did so by 16.0 years on the average; wives survived an average of 15.9 years after the death of their husbands.

Historians of colonial America have often assumed that virtually every adult married and that remarriage was common among the colonists. That may be true, but in this instance the proportion of the total number of marriages which were remarriages, the delay between the termination of one marriage and remarriage, and the proportion of adults who lived to age fifty but were never married all suggest that these assumptions need to be reexamined.

As Table V shows, the vast majority of the Quaker marriages studied here involved men and women who had never been married before. In 88.1 percent of the marriages represented both the bride and the groom were being married for the first time. Overall, 88.8 percent of the marriages involved men who were taking their first wife; among the women the proportion marrying for the first time rises to 97.5 percent. In only 1.8 percent of the marriages did the wedding involve both a husband and wife who had been married previously. Obviously remarriage was not too common and there is evidence to suggest that the sample used here is not in this regard unique. Widows accounted for about 10 percent of New Hampshire's adult female population just before the Revolution.[11] Several eighteenth-century Dutch Reformed congregations in New Jersey show much the same pattern as the Quakers. Of these Dutch Reformed marriages, 86.8 percent were between persons never before married. Only 4.6 percent were remarriages for both partners. Of the rest, 5.7

TABLE V
Marital Status at Time of Marriage

		HUSBAND					
		Never Married Before		Widowed		Total	
		Number	%	Number	%	Number	%
WIFE	Never Married Before	243	88.1	26	9.4	269	97.5
	Widow	2	.7	5	1.8	7	2.5
	Total	245	88.8	31	11.2	276	100.0

percent were between spinsters and widowers; 2.9 percent involved widows and single men.[12]

The evidence on the time between the death of a previous spouse and remarriage is sparse, but what little there is supports the view that these eighteenth-century Quakers did not rush into a second or third marriage. Those few who did marry more than once did so after a surprisingly long delay, as can be seen in Table VI. An average wait to remarry of 3.6 years for the men and 6.2 years for the women suggests that prompt remarriage was either not necessary, or perhaps not possible. The delay stands in sharp contrast with the intervals reported for other contemporary communities. Neither the French of Crulai and Bas-Quercy nor the French Canadians waited as long to remarry. In fact, only the women of Crulai delayed remarriage longer than the Quaker men.

In seeking an explanation, one thinks first of the insistence by Quaker meetings upon a delay of at least one year in order to avoid potentially difficult questions of paternity and inheritance.[13] It is worth observing that the shortest time for these Quakers between the death of a spouse and remarriage was ten months for a woman and thirteen months for a man. The French and Canadians remarried much more rapidly as can be seen from the right side of Table VI. In France, almost half the widowers who took another wife did so in less than a year; no Quaker man in this group remarried in that time. Although differences among the women are less striking, it seems nonetheless true that fewer Quaker widows remarried in under

TABLE VI
Remarriage

	Years Between Widowhood and Remarriage		% Remarried Under One Year of Those Who Remarried	
	Men	Women	Men	Women
Quakers	3.6	6.2	0	9
Crulai 1674–1742	2.1	5.5	47	14
Bas-Quercy 1767–1792	1.3	3.5	48	21
Canada 1700–1730	2.1	3.2	—	—

Sources: Gautier and Henry, *Crulai*, 89; Jacques Henripin, *La Population Canadienne au début du XVIIIe Siècle: Nuptialité, Fécondité, Mortalité Infantile* (Paris, 1954), 99; Pierre Valmary, *Familles Paysannes au XVIIIe Siècle en Bas-Quercy: Etude Démographique* (Paris, 1965), 103.

twelve months than did their French counterparts. But no sudden surge in remarriages appeared among the Quaker widows after a year had passed since the death of their spouse. Only 12 percent of all the remarriages of these women occurred in less than twenty months. Presumably if the religious restrictions on widows and widowers were of serious consequence in delaying the formation of a new family, many marriages would have occurred shortly after a year had passed since the death of the previous spouse. That this did not happen indicates that remarriage was delayed mainly for other reasons.

The final aspect of marriage which concerns us here is the proportion of adults who never wed. The amount of celibacy, together with the age at first marriage and the patterns of remarriage, may reflect the extent of need and opportunity to marry in colonial society. At the same time, the proportion of adults who never marry is obviously pertinent to questions related to the growth of population. If fewer women marry, fewer will have children, unless illegitimacy is widespread. Thus, a decline in the number of women marrying can lead to a decline in the birth rate, even though each wife still has the same number of children on the average.

The proportion never marrying is one of the more difficult of the marriage patterns with which to deal. Since the available information is most complete for the families associated with the Plainfield and Rahway meeting, the study of this question has been limited to the evidence drawn from that particular group. The findings are presented in Table VII.

First of all, only 52.0 percent of the daughters and 52.2 percent of the sons born to the Quakers of the Plainfield and Rahway meeting are known to have married.[14] Many who did not marry undoubtedly

TABLE VII
Proportion Marrying
(Plainfield and Rahway only)

			Daughters Born	
	Sons	Daughters	Before 1786	1786 or After
% Born Who Married	52.2	52.0	57.3	45.5
% Single of Those Living to Age 50	12.1	15.9	9.8	23.5
Number Born	291	246	136	110

died before they had an opportunity to marry. But the fact that nearly half the children born never were known to have married has tremendous implications for the rate of growth from one generation to the next.

Since the proportion of adults who never marry is to some extent indicative of the need and opportunity to marry, it is useful to know how many of the celibates were adults who were either unwilling or unable to marry and how many represent children who died young. If a person lives to the age of fifty without marrying, it is generally safe to assume that he will remain single for the rest of his life, since virtually all first marriages involve persons under fifty.[15] Therefore, by studying the deaths of all persons aged fifty or more to see what proportion of them were of single persons, it is possible to estimate the proportion of adults who never married. Among both the sons and daughters of the Plainfield and Rahway Quakers a surprisingly large proportion of those who lived until fifty died unmarried. As indicated in Table VII, 15.9 percent of the women who lived to fifty never married, while 12.1 percent of the men remained single at that age. Since populations rarely have a numerical balance between the sexes at any one age, the fact that the two proportions are not equal is no cause for concern. The fact that men married on the average at a later age than the women may have made the difference in the numbers and the proportions never married greater than if the average ages at marriage of the men and women were equal.

The reader also will notice in Table VII that by the end of the eighteenth century and in the early nineteenth century there was a noticeable increase among the women in the proportion never marrying. Fully 57.3 percent of the daughters of Plainfield and Rahway Quaker families born before 1786 lived to marry, but only 45.5 percent of the daughters born in 1786 or later married. Among the same two groups the proportion who lived to fifty but never married rose from 9.8 percent to 23 percent. Some marriages of women of advanced ages may have been missed by the Quaker registrars after the Hicksite separation split the Friends in 1827, but not enough to explain the shift of this magnitude. Clearly there was a marked rise in the proportion of women who never married among those born after the Revolution.

Many of the marriage patterns of these Quakers were similar to those of other colonists. Furthermore, the available evidence suggests that distinct patterns of marriage existed in seventeenth- and eighteenth-century America that were unlike those found elsewhere at the same time. By the late eighteenth century, however, marriage patterns in the colonies started to move into line with those found in Europe throughout the period under consideration. Recently, J. Hajnal has suggested that a new pattern of marriage emerged in western Europe about the time that colonization was just getting started in the Americas.[16] This new pattern of marriage which Hajnal has called "European" has lasted until today, and its identifying features include late marriage (average age of first marriage for women of at least 23) and a high proportion of people who never married at all (at least 10 percent). Such patterns were quite distinct from the rest of the world at the time, or from those found in western Europe in earlier periods. Marriage patterns which contrasted with the European patterns, and hence were called "non-European" by Hajnal, have a low average age of first marriage (under 21 for women) and a low rate of celibacy (less than 4 percent of the adults never marry).

As the data in Table VIII indicates, women living in America before 1800 may have had "colonial" marriage patterns that were neither European nor non-European. The average age at first marriage for the Quaker women of this study was above that of the non-European pattern of marriage, but below the European pattern. The evidence for Plymouth and Andover in Massachusetts, Bristol in Rhode Island, and French Canada suggests that the Quakers were not unique in this regard. Actually, the earliest group of women listed for Plymouth, Bristol, and Andover had an average age at first marriage which would put them in the non-European category. But none of the colonial women, except for those Quakers born from 1756 to 1785, and the last two groups of Andover wives, had an average age at first marriage which could be classified as European. The information presented in Table VIII is representative of a much larger body of evidence. From New England to the southern colonies, and in the French West Indies as well, the figures show that colonial women had a unique pattern of age at first marriage which does not fit either of Hajnal's categories.[17]

By way of comparison it is worth noting that all of the French and English populations listed in Table VIII met the requirements for the European pattern of marriage with regard to the age at first marriage of the woman. These groups appear typical of the larger populations of which they were a part.[18] A more detailed examination of the table reveals that colonial women were from two to six years younger when they married than any of the contemporary European women included here, with the exception of British noblewomen. As shall be seen later, this earlier age at marriage for the women combined with longer marriages to produce families in the

TABLE VIII
Average Age at First Marriage
(Comparisons)

	Men	Women
America		
Quaker families		
All wives	26.5	22.8
Wives born		
By 1730	26.5	22.0
1756–1785	26.8	23.4
Plymouth, Mass.		
Wives born		
1624–1650	26.1	20.2
1675–1700	24.6	22.3
Bristol, R.I.		
Before 1750	23.9	20.5
After 1750	24.3	21.1
Andover, Mass.		
a. 1630–1790		
First generation	26.8	19.0
Second generation	26.7	22.3
Third generation	27.1	24.5
Fourth generation	25.3	23.2
Canada		
1700–1730	26.9	22.4
Europe		
Crulai		
1674–1742	27.2	24.6
Ile-de-France		
1740–1800	26.2	25.5
Bas-Quercy		
1767–1792	27.1	26.3
British Peers		
1750–1774	29.6	23.9
Colyton		
1720–1769	25.7	26.8
Hajnal		
"European"	—	23.0 or over
"non-European"	—	under 21.0

Sources: Demos, "Plymouth Colony," *WMQ*, 3d Ser., XXII (1965), 275; Demos, "Families in Bristol," *ibid.*, 3d Ser., XXV (1968), 55; Greven, *Four Generations*, 33, 35, 118, 120, 206, 208; Henripin, *La Population Canadienne*, 96; Gautier and Henry, *Crulai*, 84; Ganiage, *Trois Villages*, 56, n. 9; Valmary, *Bas-Quercy*, 101; Hollingsworth, "British Peerage," *Population Studies*, XVIII (1964), 25; E. A. Wrigley, "Family Limitation in Pre-Industrial England," *Econ. Hist. Rev.*, 2d Ser., XIX (1966), 86; Hajnal, "European Marriage Patterns," in Glass and Eversley, eds., *Population in History*, 108.

colonies which were larger than those found in Europe in the period under consideration.

However, the distinct pattern of marriage observed among colonial wives was only temporary. In every case studied here, with the exception of the fourth generation of Andover brides, the average age at which women married for the first time rose steadily with time. The average age at first marriage of the Quaker women of this study increased from 22.0 in the first group to 23.4 in the last, as is shown in Table VIII. A similar shift seems to have occurred among other colonial populations as well. Both in Plymouth and in Bristol the age at marriage for women showed a marked tendency to rise. The Plymouth women who married for the first time at the start of the eighteenth century did so at an average age of 22.3, over two years older than had been the case in the middle of the seventeenth century. The change among the Bristol women was not as great, but it was in the same direction. In Andover, the third generation women were five and a half years older on average than the first generation wives when they married for the first time. Although the fourth generation wives were slightly younger than their immediate predecessors when they married, they were still clearly above the lower limit of the European marriage pattern. Evidence from studies of family genealogies supports the conclusion that the age of marriage among colonial women was rising toward the limits of the European pattern, and in a few instances surpassed it, in the eighteenth century.[19]

In contrast to their wives, colonial men seem to have followed European marriage patterns throughout the seventeenth and eighteenth centuries. As is evident in Table VIII, most colonial men married for the first time at an average age of between twenty-five and twenty-seven, much the same as their contemporaries in England and France. The relative stability of this aspect of marriage among the men is quite surprising in view of the steady increase in the average age at first marriage of the women throughout the colonial period.

The information available on the proportions never marrying is limited, but what there is of it also indicates the existence of distinct colonial patterns of marriage. Two separate studies have concluded that no more than 2 percent of eighteenth-century Yale graduates remained unwed after the age of fifty, a figure which stands in sharp contrast to the minimum of 10 percent never marrying which defines the European marriage pattern; in regard to taking wives, Harvard men of the seventeenth century were much like the later Yale graduates.[20] Likewise, in Andover, Massachusetts, the available figures show a higher proportion ultimately married than in Europe, as only 7.4 percent of the third generation women who lived to the age of twenty-six were known to have been spinsters, while only 3.6 percent of the fourth generation men who lived to twenty-five never married.[21] Only the Quakers studied above remained single in proportions which approached the European standard. As was shown in Table VII, 12.1 percent of the sons who lived to fifty never married, while among the daughters born before 1786 the corresponding figure was 9.8 percent, just below the minimum for the European pattern of marriage described by Hajnal. It is of interest to note, however, that the marital status of every spinster included in this study who died after the age of fifty was carefully recorded in the meeting registers, suggesting that the Friends considered such persons remarkable in the context of colonial society. Indeed, they may have been, for evidence from Canada in 1681 shows only about 5 percent of the women who had reached the age of thirty were still single, while in Mexico in 1793 only 9.6 percent of the women were unmarried once they reached the age of forty.[22] Apparently, the tendency for most women to marry was not limited to the English-speaking colonies.

Only in the case of the Quakers is there readily available information regarding changes in the proportion of women who never married. But this evidence, too, indicates that a shift in marriage patterns occurred from a colonial to a more European pattern of marriage during the eighteenth century. Among women born before 1786, 9.8 percent of those who lived to fifty never married. But by the time the women who were born in 1786 or later were marrying European marriage pattern apparently had become common, at least among these Quakers, for over 20 percent of those who lived to fifty remained unwed. The change in marriage patterns among the Quaker women was consistent for both the age of first marriage and the proportion never marrying.

The extent of remarriage in colonial society can be used to supplement evidence on the proportions never marrying, since both may reflect the need and opportunity for a person to marry. Thus, if the proportion never marrying was, in fact, increasing in the eighteenth century, one should expect to find the number of widows who remarried declining. Such was the case among the Quakers, for the increase in the proportion single was accompanied by a decline in the frequency of remarriage among the women. Of the seven widows listed in Table V who remarried, all were born by 1755. All of the marriages in which the bride was born after 1755 were first marriages for the wife. The decline in remarriage seems to have occurred in other parts of the colonial population, too. The data assembled from genealogies by Carl E. Jones indicates that in the course of the seventeenth and eighteenth centuries the proportion of remarried women among all wives fell from 11 percent from the period 1651–1700 to 5.5 percent a century later.[23] To the extent that the frequency of remarriage reflects the overall prospects for marriage in a society, it seems likely that an American woman living at the end of the eighteenth century had fewer opportunities to wed than if she had lived earlier. This conclusion is consistent with the evidence presented above regarding changes in the age at first marriage and in the proportions never marrying.

Although colonial men also seem to have remarried less often at the end of the eighteenth century than they had earlier, the changes in their patterns were less striking than those of the women. In the case of Quakers studied above, men remarried in roughly the same proportions throughout the period. In Andover, Massachusetts, the percentage of husbands who married only once increased from 67.6 percent in the first generation to 72.1 percent in the third generation, but this change seems relatively small.[24] The proportion of husbands studied by Jones who had married more than once declined by less than a third (from 22 percent to 15 percent) during the eighteenth century, compared to a decrease in remarriage of 50 percent among the women.[25] As in the case of the age at first marriage, this aspect of marriage appears to have been more stable among men than among women.

Any interpretation of the marriage patterns of the Quakers of this study, and of other colonists as well, must explain why there was little apparent change in the marriage patterns of the men, at the same time that among the women the age at first marriage and the proportion never marrying were shifting from distinctive colonial patterns into line with those found in western Europe.

The best explanation which may be offered for this shift involves the opportunity to marry, which was related to the numerical balance between the sexes. Over the course of the eighteenth century certain fundamental demographic changes occurred in the colonies which may explain why the pattern of marriage changed more for women than for men. Migration into a particular colony, whether from Europe or from another colony, tended to be predominantly male. As long as immigrants were an important part of the population, men were likely to be more numerous with the result that at any given age there were far more possible husbands than wives.[26] In order for all the men to marry who wished to do so, it was necessary for them to take wives of a different, and generally younger, age, once most of the eligible women of their own age had married. However, by the end of the eighteenth century immigration was accounting for a smaller proportion of the total population than it had earlier. In some regions it had ceased altogether, or perhaps even reversed. The result was a more equal ratio between men and women by the time of the Revolution.[27] Once men no longer found it necessary to seek younger brides, the age of marriage of the women tended to rise toward that of their prospective husbands. At the same time an increasing proportion of adult women may never have had the opportunity to marry at all. Widows may have found it harder to remarry in such a situation, as most of their possible suitors could find wives who had never been married before. All of these changes in the marriage patterns of the women could occur even though the men experienced no major change in their marriage patterns.

The changes observed above in the marriage patterns of the Quakers of this study were accompanied by precisely this kind of alteration in the ratio between men and women. In the middle colonies and especially Pennsylvania, immigration into the colony continued on an impressive scale to the time of the Revolution, but after 1775 movement into those colonies slowed and was, perhaps, even reversed.[28] It is impossible to know how much the Quakers would have been influenced by the general decline in immigration; but it is clear that after the Revolution a sharp rise in migration to the frontier among Quaker men began. Although precise figures are not available, the records indicate that a surprising number of Quaker families had one or more sons leave the middle colony area for new settlements from Canada to Ohio and Indiana and south to Alabama. An occasional young man who had left the region returned to marry a girl he had probably known from childhood, but many did not. Thus, at the very time that fewer young men were moving into the middle colonies, many of the Quaker youths were leaving the area, thereby reducing the supply of possible husbands. The numerical balance between the sexes was clearly subject to alteration, and that in turn may have had an effect on the marriage patterns of the women. The men married much as they always had, but the women were forced to change as their opportunities to marry declined.

Much the same type of situation seems to have occurred in parts of New England. In Plymouth, for example, a steady increase in the age at first marriage among women (see Table VIII) corresponded in time with a decline in the number of men available for marriage.[29] Andover experienced a similar change, as the average age at first marriage among the women rose from 19.0 in the first generation to

24.5 among their granddaughters. Although the increase began in the decade before large numbers of young men left Andover, it was accompanied by a sharp decrease in the number of women whose husbands came from outside the community.[30] A changing sex ratio seems to have altered marriage patterns in New England as it apparently did among the Quakers.

In view of all this, it is of special interest to find that the status of women and the values placed on marriage seem to have changed considerably in the course of the eighteenth century, and especially at the time of the Revolution. Such changes may well have fostered the alterations in marriage patterns which were resulting from a more balanced sex ratio.

For much of the colonial period the prevailing values clearly encouraged marriage. No colony ever deliberately persecuted persons who were single in order to encourage marriages, although various seventeenth-century statutes make it clear that single persons were considered to require special supervision. For example, New England viewed single men with suspicion if they were not under the shelter and scrutiny of a larger family unit. Their movements were often limited; they were subject to special fines and duties; and they might even be prevented from receiving land grants until after they married.[31] Undoubtedly part of this effort to supervise single persons came from a desire to protect the community from strangers. At the same time, the Puritans encouraged marriage for the simple reason that it provided an acceptable outlet for normal human desires.[32] In Pennsylvania, the Quakers on occasion actually taxed single men on a separate basis. Their purpose seems to have been to include such men within the overall scheme of taxation rather than to encourage marriage. However, at least one foreign observer noted the fact that single persons received special attention in the tax laws.[33] Furthermore, many of Pennsylvania's laws regulating marriage specifically encouraged adults to marry, although none went as far as the suggestions made in 1683 that young men ought to be fined every year they remained unmarried after reaching twenty-one.[34] Nevertheless, to remain single was to reject accepted social patterns.

After the Revolution these values may have changed. At least two scholars have found that the necessity to marry was reduced a little as social and economic values shifted. Men began to accept women as their equals in some matters. A woman's ability to own property improved, for example. As conditions altered the need to find a husband may have been reduced, since adult females could find alternatives other than marrying and raising a family.[35] Those women who married after the Revolution apparently showed an increasing concern with love and happiness in their unions; and they may have expected a greater say in family matters.[36] Of importance here is the fact that the Quakers were among the first people to give formal recognition to the rights of women.[37] Changing values may have made it possible for unmarried men and women to find a satisfying role in post-Revolutionary America. If so, the need to marry no longer would be as great as in the colonial period. Those who wed may have taken longer to consider the implications of such action and the alternatives. Thus, the opinions which emerged at the close of the colonial period regarding the status of women and the importance of marriage were consistent with, and hence may have helped to bring about, changes in the patterns of marriage.

Many of the effects that the colonial marriage patterns had on American society in the seventeenth and eighteenth centuries are of considerable interest. But none is of greater concern than the relationship between the patterns of marriage and the size of colonial families. On average, the size of families in the colonies tended to be larger than those found in contemporary European populations, as the information in Table IX shows. In this table, family size refers to the total number of children born to a particular couple. In the case of completed families, in which the marriage remained intact until the wife had reached the age of forty-five, and hence had normally completed her childbearing, the average number of children born to a couple ranged from a high of 8.7 in Andover, Massachusetts, in the seventeenth century, to a low of 6.2 among the Quakers of this study whose childbearing occurred at the end of the eighteenth century. Apparently, couples who lived together until the wife was at least forty-five could expect an average of between 7 and 9 children, though the number may have fallen slightly by the end of the period under consideration.[38] The figures for the average number of children born per wife, including those families in which childbearing was curtailed by the death of one spouse before the wife was forty-five, naturally are somewhat smaller. Nevertheless, most colonial couples apparently could expect an average of 6 to 7 children in the course of their marriage.[39] As was the case with the marriage patterns, family size in Canada was much the same as in the English colonies.

In contrast, European families appear to have been considerably smaller. The largest average family size listed in Table IX was 5.2 children among the French of the Ile-de-France in the late eighteenth century; the smallest families were those found in Crulai, in France, in the early eighteenth century, where a couple might expect only 4.0

TABLE IX
Family Size
(Comparisons)

Study by	Before 1700	1700–1749	1750–1799
	America		
Completed Families			
Demos—Plymouth	8.6	—	—
Greven—Andover	8.7	7.5	—
Freeman	—	7.2	6.8
Henripin—Canada	—	8.4	—
Wells—Quakers	—	7.5	6.2
Children per Wife			
Wells—Quakers	—	6.7	5.7
Henripin—Canada	—	5.7	—
Crum	7.4	6.8	6.4
Engelmann	6.4	6.6	6.1
Jones	5.8	5.9	6.1
Sage	5.9	6.9	6.0
	Europe		
Children per Wife			
Gautier and Henry—Crulai	—	4.0	—
Ganiage—Ile-de-France	—	—	5.2
Hollingsworth—British Peers	4.6	4.2	4.9
Knodel—Bavaria	—	5.0	5.0

Sources: Demos, *Little Commonwealth*, 192; Greven, *Four Generations*, 202; Freeman, "Fertility and Longevity," *Human Biology*, VII (1935), 403; Henripin, *La Population Canadienne*, 50; Crum, "Decadence of Native American Stock," Am. Stat. Assn., *Pubs.*, XVI (1916-1917), 215–222; George J. Engelmann, "The Increasing Sterility of American Women," *American Medical Association Journal*, XXXVII (1901), 893; Jones, "Genealogical Study," Am. Stat. Assn., *Pubs.*, XVI, (1918–1919), 209; Sage, "Genealogical Records of New England," 10; Gautier and Henry, *Crulai*, 124; Ganiage, *Trois Villages*, 68; Hollingsworth, "British Peerage," *Population Studies*, XVIII (1964), 30; Knodel, "Bavarian Village," *ibid.*, XXIV (1970), 371.

children on average. These figures are in agreement with the standard recently suggested for France in the eighteenth century of between 4 and 5 children per family.[40] A study of families in a Bavarian village indicates an average of 5 children per couple throughout the eighteenth century. In England, the situation was much the same. The average family size of the British peerage was well below the number of children born to colonial couples. A study using a different definition of family size points to the same conclusion regarding the populations of England as a whole, namely, that English families were smaller than American families before 1800. By dividing the total number of persons listed in various censuses by the number of households mentioned in the same documents, Peter Laslett has found that English families averaged about 4.75 persons in the seventeenth and eighteenth centuries.[41] This figure is considerably below corresponding average "family sizes" for various American populations. In Bristol, Rhode Island, the average family size as calculated from a census taken in 1689 was 5.99; Massachusetts families in 1764 and Rhode Island families in 1774 both averaged 5.8 persons; and the first United States census counted 5.7 persons for every family in 1790.[42] Clearly colonial couples had more children on average than did their European counterparts.

In seeking to explain the larger colonial families, one thinks first of the possibility that American women had children more often than did wives on the other side of the Atlantic. But the evidence in Table X indicates that childbearing in America occurred at much the same rate as it did in Europe in the period under study. Wives who

TABLE X
Birth Intervals
(Comparisons)

Study by	Length of Interval Between Births in Months
America	
Demos—Plymouth (Before 1700)	24
Greven—Andover (1705–1724)	26.5
Lockridge—Dedham (1636-1736)	29
Jones (1651–1800)	30
Wells—Quakers (a. 1650–1830)	27.7
Henripin—Canada (1700–1730)	23.3
Europe	
Wrigley—Colyton (1720–1769)	29.1
Ganiage—Ile-de-France (1740–1800)	25.2
Gautier and Henry—Crulai (1674–1742)	27.3
Goubert—Beauvais (1600–1730)	29

Sources: Demos, *Little Commonwealth,* 68–69; Greven, *Four Generations,* 200; Lockridge, "Population of Dedham," *Econ. Hist. Rev.*, 2d Ser., XIX (1966), 332; Jones, "Genealogical Study," Am. Stat. Assn., *Pubs.*, XVI (1918–1919), 213; Henripin, *La Population Canadienne*, 84; Wrigley, "Family Limitation," *Econ. Hist. Rev.*, 2d Ser., XIX (1966), 93; Ganiage, *Trois Villages,* 99; Gautier and Henry, *Crulai,* 147; Pierre Goubert, *Beauvais et le Beauvaisis de 1600 à 1730: Contribution à l'Histoire Sociale de la France du XVII*[e] *Siècle* (Paris, 1960), 35.

lived in the seventeenth and eighteenth centuries could expect to have a child every 24 to 30 months on average, regardless of whether they lived in America or Europe. The French wives of the Ile-de-France and Crulai actually had a shorter interval between births *and smaller families* than did the Quakers studied above. Although the data are not strictly comparable, it is clear that in at least one part of Bavaria families were smaller than those found in America in spite of a birth interval of under 24 months.[43] Apparently, the difference in size between European and American families was not the result of more rapid childbearing in the colonies.

Since childbearing seems to have occurred at similar rates among married women on both sides of the Atlantic in the seventeenth and eighteenth centuries, the only possible explanation for the larger colonial families is that American wives had more time to bear children. By marrying younger and remaining married longer than was common in Europe, wives in the colonies were able to have more children than their English and French contemporaries.[44] Since a higher proportion of women married in the colonies than in Europe, the effect of the larger colonial family size on the birth rate was enhanced. For this reason then, and for others which remain to be explored, the distinct patterns of marriage which seem to have existed in America before 1800 were of considerable importance in determining the character of colonial society.

NOTES

1. See John Demos, "Notes on Life in Plymouth Colony," *William and Mary Quarterly,* 3d Ser., XXII (1965), 264–286; and his article, "Families in Colonial Bristol, Rhode Island: An Exercise in Historical Demography," *ibid.,* 3d Ser., XXV (1968), 40–57. Most of Demos's findings have been included in his recent book, *A Little Commonwealth: Family Life in Plymouth Colony* (New York, 1970). The work by Philip J. Greven, Jr., first published as "Family Structure in Seventeenth-Century Andover, Massachusetts," *WMQ,* 3d Ser., XXIII (1966), 234–256, has been revised and expanded in his *Four Generations: Population, Land, and Family in Colonial Andover, Massachusetts* (Ithaca, N. Y., 1970). See also Kenneth A. Lockridge, "The Population of Dedham, Massachusetts, 1636–1736," *Economic History Review,* 2d Ser., XIX (1966), 318–344.

2. The main study, of which this is a part, was concerned primarily with changes in childbearing patterns. As a result, it was most convenient to divide these families on the basis of the date of birth of the mother. For a fuller explanation of the logic behind these groupings, and a description of the changes observed, see Robert V. Wells, "Family Size and Fertility Control in Eighteenth-Century America: A Study of Quaker Families," *Population Studies,* XXV (1971), 73–82.

3. The records are to be found in *Genealogical Magazine of New Jersey,*

XXVII–XXVIII (1952–1953); William Wade Hinshaw, ed., *Encyclopedia of American Quaker Genealogy*, 6 vols. (Ann Arbor, Mich., 1936–1950); New York Genealogical and Biographical Society, *Record*, VII–XI (1877–1880); Rahway and Plainfield Monthly Meeting Register, manuscript in the Genealogical Society of Pennsylvania, Philadelphia.

4. Families were reconstituted according to the method described in E. A. Wrigley, ed., *An Introduction to English Historical Demography: From the Sixteenth to the Nineteenth Century* (New York, 1966), 96–159.

5. Readers interested in comparing many of the figures which appear below with those current in the United States today should consult Robert V. Wells, "Demographic Change and the Life Cycle of American Families," *Journal of Interdisciplinary History*, II (1971–1972), 273–282.

6. Demos, *Little Commonwealth*, 193; Greven, *Four Generations*, 207, 209. The evidence from Greven's book is of special interest in view of the fact that he argues elsewhere in that work (pp. 125–172) that parents often delayed the marriage of sons until they were mature men by preventing them from acquiring land. The following studies done from genealogical sources support the interpretation advanced here, showing that most marriages occurred at the same few ages in the 18th century: Bettie C. Freeman, "Fertility and Longevity in Married Women Dying After the End of the Reproductive Period," *Human Biology*, VII (1935), 402–403; Carl E. Jones, "A Genealogical Study of Population," American Statistical Association, *Publications*, XVI (1918–1919), 208; and William B. Bailey, "A Statistical Study of Yale Graduates, 1701–1792," *Yale Review*, XVII (1907–1908), 413.

7. George E. Howard, *A History of Matrimonial Institutions . . .* , II (Chicago, 1904), last section.

8. See Etienne Gautier and Louis Henry, *La Population de Crulai, Paroisse Normande: Etude Historique* (Paris, 1958), 84, 125, 191. In Crulai at the end of the 17th century, a life expectancy of 30 years combined with later marriages to produce much shorter unions on average.

9. The correlation coefficient was .042 (not significant at .05). For similar conclusions, see Freeman, "Fertility and Longevity," *Human Biology*, VII (1935), 404–416; and Robert Higgs and H. Louis Stettler, III, "Colonial New England Demography: A Sampling Approach," *WMQ*, 3d Ser., XXVII (1970), 286.

10. A similar situation seems to have existed in at least one part of France where the husband died first 54% of the time in three villages of the Ile-de-France. Jean Ganiage, *Trois Villages de l'Ile-de-France au XVIII*[e] *Siècle: Etude Démographique* (Paris, 1963), 61.

11. U. S. Department of Commerce, Bureau of the Census, *A Century of Population Growth: From the First Census of the United States to the Twelfth* (Washington, D.C., 1909), 149–151.

12. Based on my study of 981 marriages, with information on marital status for the Hackensack and Schraalenburg Dutch Reformed Church in W. A. Whitehead *et al.*, eds., *New Jersey Archives*, XXII: *Marriage Records, 1665–1800* (Paterson, N. J., 1900), 467–548. Similar findings for the South are given in Roland M. Harper, "A Statistical Study of a Typical Southern Genealogy," *Journal of Heredity*, XXV (1934); see below, pp. 425–426, for a further discussion of remarriage.

13. Albert C. Applegarth, *Quakers in Pennsylvania*, Johns Hopkins University Studies in Historical and Political Science, X (Baltimore, 1892), 33–34.

14. For similar figures for 18th-century England, see T. H. Hollingsworth, "The Demography of the British Peerage," supplement to *Population Studies*, XVIII (1964), 22.

15. Out of 482 first marriages in Table I, only 4 involved persons of 50 or more, 2 men and 2 women.

16. J. Hajnal, "European Marriage Patterns in Perspective," in D. V. Glass and D. E. C. Eversley, eds., *Population in History: Essays in Historical Demography* (Chicago, 1965), 101–143.

17. See Bailey, "Yale Graduates," *Yale Rev.*, XVII (1907–1908), 415; Frederick S. Crum, "The Decadence of the Native American Stock: A Statistical Study of Genealogical Records," Am. Stat. Assn., *Pubs.*, XIV (1916–1917), 214–222; Freeman, "Fertility and Longevity," *Human Biology*, VII (1935), 402–403; Harper, "A Typical Southern Genealogy," *Jour. Heredity*, XXV (1934), 366; Higgs and Stettler, "Colonial New England Demography," *WMQ*, 3d Ser., XXVII (1970), 285; Jones, "Genealogical Study," Am. Stat. Assn., *Pubs.*, XVI (1918–1919), 208; Lockridge, "Population of Dedham," *Econ. Hist. Rev.*, 2d Ser., XIX (1966), 330; David Sage, "A Statistical Study of the Genealogical Records of New England" (M.A. thesis, Clark University, 1917), 13; Jacques Houdaille, "Trois Paroisses de Saint-Domingue au XVIIIe Siècle," *Population*, XVIII (1963), 99.

18. Similar data on other European populations may be found in Raymond Deniel and Louis Henry, "La Population d'un Village du Nord de la France," *Population*, XX (1965), 572; P. Deprez, "The Demographic Development of Flanders in the Eighteenth Century," in Glass and Eversley, eds., *Population in History*, 615; Pierre Girard, "Aperçus de la Démographie de Sotteville-les-Rouen vers la Fin du XVIIIe Siècle," *Population*, XIV (1959), 489; Louis Henry, *Anciennes Familles Genévoises. Etude Démographique: XVIe–XXe Siècle* (Paris, 1956), 55; Jacques Houdaille, "La Population de Boulay (Moselle) avant 1850," *Population*, XXII (1967), 1063, 1078; Houdaille, "Un Village du Morvan: Saint-Agnan," *ibid.*, XVI (1961), 302; John Knodel, "Two and a Half Centuries of Demographic History in a Bavarian Village," *Population Studies*, XXIV (1970), 361; Peter Laslett, *The World We Have Lost* (New York, 1965), 83; Claude Levy and Louis Henry, "Ducs et Pairs sous l'Ancien Régime, Characteristiques Démographiques d'une Caste," *Population*, XV (1960), 813; Michel Terrisse, "Un Faubourg du Havre: Ingouville," *ibid.*, 286.

19. See Crum, "Decadence of Native American Stock," Am. Stat. Assn., *Pubs.*, XVI (1916–1917), 215–222; Freeman, "Fertility and Longevity," *Human Biology*, VII (1935), 402–403; Jones, "Genealogical Study," Am. Stat. Assn., *Pubs.*, XVI (1918–1919), 208; Sage, "Genealogical Records of New England," 13.

20. Bailey, "Yale Graduates," *Yale Rev.*, XVII (1907–1908), 410–412; G. Stanley Hall and Theodate L. Smith, "Marriage and Fecundity of College Men and Women," *Pedagogical Seminary*, X (1903), 283, 298.

21. Greven, *Four Generations*, 121, 207.

22. Henripin, *La Population Canadienne*, 20; S. F. Cook, "The Population in Mexico in 1793," *Human Biology*, XIV (1942), 508.

23. Jones, "Genealogical Study," Am. Stat. Assn., *Pubs.*, XVI (1918–1919), 204, 209.

24. Greven, *Four Generations*, 29, 111.

25. Jones, "Genealogical Study," Am. Stat. Assn., *Pubs.*, XVI (1918–1919), 204, 209. In view of the fact that the absolute decline among the men

of 7% was greater than the 5.5% decrease observed among the women, it is necessary to treat this particular evidence with caution. Fortunately, the ambiguity of this item of information does not destroy the main thrust of the argument.

26. The evidence on the impact of migration on the sex ratio and marriage patterns in the colonies has been ably presented in Herbert Moller, "Sex Composition and Correlated Culture Patterns of Colonial America," *WMQ*, 3d Ser., II (1945), 113–153.

27. *Ibid.*, 113–129.

28. *Ibid.*, 120–124; J. Potter, "The Growth of Population in America," in Glass and Eversley, eds., *Population in History*, 542–660, 666–667.

29. Demos, "Plymouth Colony," *WMQ*, 3d Ser., XXII (1965), 276.

30. Greven, *Four Generations*, 120–122, 211.

31. Alice Morse Earle, *Customs and Fashions in Old New England* (New York, 1893), 36–37; J. Hammond Trumbull and Charles J. Hoadly, eds., *The Public Records of the Colony of Connecticut*, I (Hartford, 1850), 8.

32. Edmund S. Morgan, "The Puritans and Sex," *New England Quarterly*, XV (1942), 591–594.

33. J. P. Brissot de Warville, *New Travels in the United States of America, 1788*, ed. Durand Echeverria, trans. Mara Soceanu Vamos and Durand Echeverria (Cambridge, Mass., 1964), 272; James T. Mitchell and Henry Flanders, comps., *The Statutes at Large of Pennsylvania from 1682 to 1801* (Harrisburg, Pa., 1896–1911), V, 8.

34. Mitchell and Flanders, comps., *Pennsylvania Statutes*, II, 161; Applegarth, *Quakers in Pennsylvania*, 32.

35. Thomas P. Monahan, *The Pattern of Age at Marriage in the United States* (Philadelphia, 1951), 51, 78–79; Mary Sumner Benson, *Women in Eighteenth-Century America: A Study of Opinion and Social Usage* (New York, 1935), 76, 119, 168–169, 240–242, 248, 263–267, 274–313. See also Richard B. Morris, *Studies in the History of American Law, with Special Reference to the Seventeenth and Eighteenth Centuries* (New York, 1930), Chap. 3, "Women's Rights in Early American Law."

36. See Herman R. Lantz *et al.*, "Pre-Industrial Patterns in the Colonial Family in America: A Content Analysis of Colonial Magazines," *American Sociological Review*, XXXIII (1968), 413–426.

37. See Jerry William Frost, "The Quaker Family in Colonial America: A Social History of the Society of Friends" (Ph.D. diss., University of Wisconsin, 1968), 386–387, 405–407, for evidence that in practice Quaker women found their rights ignored by the men.

38. For a study of a population which clearly did experience such a decline, apparently because of deliberate family limitation, see Wells, "Family Size and Fertility Control," *Population Studies*, XXV (1971), 73–82.

39. These figures are borne out by Bailey, "Yale Graduates," *Yale Rev.*, XVII (1907–1908), 420; Wendell H. Bash, "Factors Influencing Family and Community Organization in a New England Town, 1730–1940" (Ph.D. diss., Harvard University, 1941), 205; Harper, "A Typical Southern Genealogy," *Jour. Heredity*, XXV (1934), 369; Alfred J. Lotka, "The Size of American Families in the Eighteenth Century," Am. Stat. Assn., *Journal*, XXII (1927), 154–170. Only Kenneth Lockridge has found evidence of a much smaller colonial family (average size of about 4), but see also pp. 329–330 for his comments on poor birth records which may explain the small family size. "Population of Dedham," *Econ. Hist. Rev.*, 2d Ser., XIX (1966), 343, n. 1.

40. Louis Henry, "The Population of France in the Eighteenth Century," in Glass and Eversley, eds., *Population in History*, 456.

41. Peter Laslett, "Size and Structure of the Household in England Over Three Centuries," *Population Studies*, XXIII (1969), 199–223.

42. Demos, "Families in Bristol," *WMQ*, 3d Ser., XXV (1968), 52; Census Bureau, *Century of Population Growth*, 96, 158–163.

43. Knodel, "Bavarian Village," *Population Studies*, XXIV (1970), 371, 374.

44. For a similar conclusion, see Deniel and Henry, "Village du Nord de la France," *Population*, XX (1965), 593–594. The principal evidence for longer colonial marriages comes from the Quakers studied above, pp. 421–422. However, other findings which support this conclusion are Demos, *Little Commonwealth*, 192–193; Greven, *Four Generations*, 192, 195; and Massachusetts Historical Society, *Collections*, 1st Ser., VI (Boston, 1800), 288.

4

Eighteenth-Century Family and Social Life Revealed in Massachusetts Divorce Records

■

NANCY F. COTT

Although studies in family history and women's history have developed along separate lines, there has been cross-fertilization between the two fields, especially concerning the transition from traditional to modern society. Questions and methods arising from both fields coincide in Nancy F. Cott's essay. Drawing on the rich materials contained in divorce records, Cott explores attitudes and practices involved in several sets of social and familial relationships. Her findings regarding privacy, ties between members of one sex and between the sexes, the different marital roles of husbands and wives, romantic love, and sex expose complex patterns in women's and men's transition to modern behaviors.

AN INTERDISCIPLINARY FIELD, beset by subjective judgments of value and freighted with half-defined social implications, the history of family life is one in which revisions have rapidly succeeded assertions and contradictory evidence constantly undermines what seems established. If painstaking researchers in parish registers and local censuses have found that American colonists and their English forebears lived in nuclear families, still insufficient grasp of the life cycles of nuclear families and their relationships to wider kin connections makes this at best a partial revelation. If theorists have proposed that premodern family life edged imperceptibly into community life, while families in modern industrial society have strict psychological boundaries, some evidence of earlier and later social networks rebukes them. If historians have suggested that before the modern period adults did not distinguish childhood as a special stage of life nor parents view small children as individuated characters, personal documents can be found to subvert their claims.[1] The mistaken assumption that there was a prevailing type of "the" family at any one time, rather than several types of families in different classes, regions, etc., has caused distortion and confusion; but amid the welter of debate it seems clear that the size, functions, values, and attitudes, if not the structure of premodern families, contrast with those of modern families. For the case of the United States, historians have usually drawn the contrast between preindustrial and industrial (which in practice has meant seventeenth- and nineteenth-century) families. They have relied chiefly on census and church records to reconstitute families and establish basic demographic information, searched both religious and secular prescriptive literature to discover norms of family life, and combed diaries and letters for evidence of individual family habits.

Court records (especially those of domestic relations cases) have some of the advantages of census and church records, because they deal with an "ordinary" population, and some of the advantages of prescriptive and personal documents, because they reveal values, attitudes, and individual practices, but they have not been as commonly used. It happens that the records of divorce in eighteenth-century Massachusetts—229 petitions for divorce or separation between 1692 and 1786—have been well preserved.[2] They include dramatic new evidence on debated issues about family and social life, privacy and community, and relations among family members. This is material that can contribute to the resolution of persistent questions. Since the eighteenth century is the most mysterious of times in the history of American families (historians' energies so far having been concentrated on the seventeeth and the nineteenth centuries), these documents are especially important. Elsewhere I have examined the patterns of frequency of these petitions and the causes for which divorce or separation was granted, analyzed men's and women's success in obtaining divorce, and drawn conclusions about women's legal and familial status and the operation of the double standard in the Revolutionary period.[3] But the asset of the divorce records most appealing to the social historian is the wealth of detail about intimate aspects of life conveyed in petitions and depositions. Since they are concentrated in the mid- to late eighteenth century—only 27 of the cases occurred before 1735, but 158 between 1755 and 1786—the divorce suits can illuminate what seems to be a period of critical change in familial roles.[4]

The obvious caveat is whether inferences drawn from divorce materials can apply to the general population. Divorce was clearly atypical in this period in Massachusetts, but it would be a mistake to assume therefore that the practices and expectations of domestic life divulged in the records were unrepresentative. Divorce was more accessible and more frequent in Massachusetts than in contemporary England or several of the other American colonies; petitioners there ranged from black slaves to wealthy heiresses, and came from tiny remote towns as well as urban places.[5] The causes that gave rise to divorce petitions should show the boundaries of normal marital expectations, just as actions construed as criminal indicate societal limits. And while the defendants' behavior threatened accepted norms, the petitioners and the deponents—who supplied almost all of the information in the records—preserved them. There seems every reason to accept the portrayal of domestic life and social surroundings in the divorce records as valid, while maintaining caution about possible distortions introduced by the defendants' behavior.

Eighteenth-century Massachusetts residents lived in nuclear families. That is, a household typically contained a mother and father and their children, while it might also house unrelated young persons acting as servants or apprentices, and for some years a widowed parent of one of the spouses. The extended-family household of several generations or several married siblings was uncommon, although in almost all Massachusetts towns in 1764, when a colony-wide census was taken, "families" outnumbered "houses," meaning that some families shared dwellings (likely occupying separate "ends" of the house).[6] From the predominance of nuclear family *structure* we cannot ascertain all we would like to, however, for census or family reconstitution data do not tell how individuals lived; whether, for instance, goings-on within the family were open or closed to outside view, whether people focused their emotions on family life, whether the community maintained family norms or vice-versa. Since Philippe Ariès' extraordinary book, *Centuries of Childhood,* led the way, historians have contrasted the premodern with the modern family in terms of the "promiscuity" or "sociability" of the former and the "intimacy" or "isolation" of the latter.[7] Their impression is that the boundaries of the premodern family were permeable—people lived "in the street," in the community—so that the family served to establish lineage and to organize production but not to contain or define social life.

When men and women of eighteenth-century Massachusetts complained to the court of marital travesties such as desertion, adultery, or neglect, they inadvertently brought these issues to light. Families there experienced none of the isolation or withdrawal from community overseership which presumably characterize the modern family. On the contrary, the divorce records reveal the interconnectedness of family and community, particularly in the form of community members' guardianship over family affairs. Divorce petitioners successfully relied on the proximity and curiosity of neighbors, lodgers, and kin, and on their motives to preserve community norms, in order to obtain material to substantiate their cases. Mary Angel, for example, out walking in Boston with Abigail Galloway one day, saw through an open window her neighbor Adam Air "in the Act of Copulation" with a woman named Pamela Brichford. Nor did she stop there:

> on Seeing this We went into the House, & stood behind them as they lay on the Floor, and after observing them some time, the said Abigail Galloway spoke, & asked him if he was not Ashamed to act so when he had a Wife at home, he got up & answered, one Woman was as good to him as another he then put up his nakedness before our faces, & went away, and she on his getting off her, jumped up & ran away into another part of the House.[8]

John Andrews used similar directness upon hearing suspicious noises from the house of Caleb Morey, a married man, in Brunswick. He took a light, "went into the House or Camp, & to the bedside, tuck [sic] hold of a persons hand" and ascertained that Caleb was in bed with Mary Knowles.[9] At social gatherings and at inns surveillance was even more immediate. After John Backus and Chloe Gleason disappeared from the company at Roswell Downing's in Sheffield, one night in 1784, others went searching for them and found them in bed. Since the observers threatened that "they must get up or be puled [sic] out of bed," the couple arose and dressed and John, who was married, "agreed to treat said Company for his misconduct."[10] Occasionally an individual protested against this kind of interference. When a neighboring widow discovered Ebenezer Simpson, a Boston blacksmith, in bed with a strange woman, and "told him it was a Shame for him who had a Wife & children to behave in such a manner," he summarily responded "with cursing . . . that It was none of . . . [her] business."[11]

Whether avid observers were attempting to uphold community standards by surveillance, when it came to adultery—or simply satisfying their own curiosity—may be a fine distinction. When Mary Cole witnessed Hannah Wales invite a strange man to lie down with her in Boston in 1785, Mary left the room, but later admitted that "Curiosity led me to Look thro' a hole in the door, when I plainly saw said man Lying upon Mrs. Wales, his breeches were down . . . ," and the couple was caught in the act.[12] Mary Knight, living with her husband Russell in William Parham's household in Lancaster, was constantly subject to the Parhams' and their neighbors' observation because they doubted her fidelity. One night William and a neighbor, hearing noises in Mary's chamber, rushed up through a cellar trap door to confront her in bed with a strange man. Mary later accused William of sending the man to assault her and "frame" her in the act of adultery. When the justice of the peace asked William whether he had burst into Mary's room "to find out the Man and to secure him or not"—for he allowed the man to escape—William replied, "I went into the Room to Satisfy myself whether the sd Russells Wife was such a lewd Person as I suspected—and not to apprehend the Man."[13]

Not only did neighbors know each others' business with predictable small-town alacrity.[14] The very circumstances of household life facilitated the intervention of neighbors, and even more readily, of lodgers, into a couple's affairs. The construction and population of houses were respectively so thin, and so thick, that privacy was hard to come by. Mary Angel, who caught Adam Air in the act, also testified that she "live[d] the next door, where only a thin Partition divided us have often heard him beat . . . [his wife] & heard her scream in Consequence of the beating." In Katherine and Elijah Cobb's house in Taunton in 1766, only a single wall separated Ruth Cushman's chamber from the Cobbs', and she "had frequent opportunity of hearing their conversation."[15] The presence and transience of servants, hired laborers, nurses, relatives, and other lodgers in households assured numerous omnipresent eyes and ears.[16] The practice for several persons to share sleeping quarters particularly undermined privacy in bed. The James and McCarthy families, for example, lived under the same roof in Boston in 1754–1755. It was accepted as "no matter" that William Stone, a transient, slept in the same room with Daniel McCarthy's wife Mary, since there were two beds; but Ann James incriminated Mary by divulging that Mary and William slept in one bed while Ann and Mary's two sisters slept in the other.[17] When William Chambers was at sea, his wife Susanna frequently had thirteen-year-old Mary Salmon sleep with her, a redundant gesture for the four nights that Sergeant George Hatton occupied the same bed. Mary reported that "on the third night Mrs. Chambers lay in the middle, at which time it appeared to me I being awake, that Sergt Hatton had carnal knowledge of Mrs. Sus[a] Chambers. . . . Mrs. Chambers gave me three Coppers, & charged me to tell nobody what I saw."[18] Captain Peter Staples regularly lodged about two feet away from the bed of Thomas and Abigail Hammet in their house in Berwick in 1761, and often climbed into bed with Abigail after Thomas arose in the morning. Two women lodgers, who saw this through a crack in the partition dividing their room from the Hammets', reported it.[19] Cracks and knotholes in walls and floors readily supplied eyepieces and listening posts.[20]

Any evaluation of the qualities of family life in eighteenth-century New England must take into account the permeability of the boundaries of the household, lodgers' and neighbors' presence and transience, and the physical construction of households,[21] and add to these the apparently inquisitive temperament of New England folk. The predisposition to be one's brother's and sister's keeper found support in both religious and social values. Household residents and neighbors—in a word, the local community—kept continuous check on family and marital norms. Nathaniel Haskell, for example, justified his intervention in his kinsman's adulterous affair in 1760 by saying, "I ought not to Suffer Sin in My Fellow Creature or Neighbour."[22] In the Puritan view, breaches of the marital covenant were sins against God, and thus utterly reprehensible; the Puritan's religious duty directed him to attempt to remedy marital irregularities where he saw them. In the mid-eighteenth century, however, it seems that social expectations or community norms regarding marriage and personal life motivated observers more than intense piety did. When Hannah and Ebenezer Medberry of Rehoboth, a widow and widower married to each other for a short time, began to trade recriminations, an old neighbor "being infirm in body not being able to go abroad sent for both of them over to . . . [his] house to Examien [sic] them."[23] The informal institution of the social network surrounding a couple attempted to maintain social order by preserving domestic harmony, as formal institutions such as church and civil government had more regularly done in earlier years.[24]

Members of the local community functioned as overseers, guardians, and conciliators: in their minds the rights of husbands and wives were clearly defined and ready to be imposed on any nonconforming couple for their own and the common benefit. Sometimes a dozen or more persons involved themselves in sorting out a couple's allegations against one another and advising them what to do. In the Medberry case "the s^{d} Neighbours" more than once descended on their house *en masse* "haveing [sic] come in in order to see if the Difficulty could not be made up between s^{d} Medbury [sic] and his wife."[25] When a young wife of Rehoboth left her husband to return to her parents' house, and the couple thereafter accused each other of wrongs, numerous community members (especially gentlemen) took the responsibility to lecture them on the realities of married life and to urge them "in the Strongest terms possible to come to a Reconciliation and be at Peace." One upstanding gentleman pressed the young wife whether she had understood the marriage covenant when she married, and she unsatisfactorily replied "She Did not think much about it."[26]

All of this goes to point out that privacy within the family and household as we know it—the privacy that relies on insulated walls, anonymity in a mass society, *and* the usual belief that what goes on in a family group is and should remain "their own business"—simply did not prevail in eighteenth-century Massachusetts towns. I do not claim that solitude was never sought or valued, or that individuals failed to distinguish activities that were appropriately hidden from public view. Job Keith of Sutton testified, for example, regarding Nehemiah Adams' adultery with Ziporah Rawson, "I have seen him behave wantonly in the bed towards her, and do that which a husband would not do before folks."[27] Adulterers wished to escape detection—but circumstances foiled their attempts.[28] Mary Angel's interruption of Adam Air in the act of adultery, John Andrews' investigation of the sleeping arrangements of Caleb Morey and his housekeeper, Widow Hoar's reprimand to Ebenezer Simpson, William Parham's desire to satisfy his mind about Mary Knight's "lewdness," and the local squires' attempts to reconcile Amos and Phebe Bliss—all of these bespoke assumptions about the rights (even the duties) of community members to step in and straighten individual detours from the accepted path of family and personal life. Living conditions, including small and thinly partitioned houses and the ubiquity of lodgers and neighbors, made it all the more unlikely for the household to be a scene of personal privacy and familial intimacy.

While demonstrating the interconnections between nuclear families and networks of other persons, the divorce records also provide a means to assess relative proportions of kin and non-kin, household co-residents and neighbors, within those social networks. Both the petitioner and the defendant could call witnesses; I assume that they called upon the persons best acquainted with themselves and the circumstances of their marriages. To identify these witnesses (or deponents, as they were called) should be to draw the outlines of the couples' closest social relationships. Categorizing 770 deponents from 102 cases as exactly as possible within the limits of the records produced striking results. (See Table I.) Only 2% of the deponents were kin living in the same household as the petitioner, and only 9% were other nonresident kin of the couple; 11% of the deponents

TABLE 1
Relation of Deponents to Petitioners and Spouses

Deponents Who Were:	N	%	
Kin (nonresident)	70	9	
Kin (co-resident)	16	2	total kin: 11%
Non-kin co-resident	83	11	total co-resident: 13%
Neighbors	377	49	
Officials	83	11	
Non-identifiable above	141	18	possible neighbors: 78%
Total	770	100	

were residents in the household, but not kin; while at least half of the deponents were neighbors. The remaining quarter of the deponents were either persons called upon to testify in an official capacity (e.g., doctors, midwives, justices of the peace, marriage witnesses), or persons not surely identifiable in any of the other categories. Most of the persons in these groups were likely neighbors as well.

Neighbors thus greatly outnumbered kin among the deponents and, by inference, in the divorcing couples' social networks. This is an unexpected result, because of the persistent assumption that kinfolk composed the social environment of nuclear families.[29] The definite identification of "kin" among the deponents does, however, present a problem. Those who described themselves as family members, were referred to as such by others, or had the same unmistakable name as petitioner or defendant, were almost always mothers, fathers, siblings, offspring, or the same relations by marriage (i.e., "in-laws")—only occasionally aunts, uncles, cousins, nieces or nephews. While deponents usually found it pertinent to mention their relationship to the petitioner, some neighbors or others—particularly if they were more distant relations—may not have revealed their kinship in the written record. I cannot ascertain the extent of this possible error without reconstituting the families of the divorcing couples; but even with allowance for some error of this sort, the prevalence of neighbors over kin is impressive.[30]

If, perhaps, married persons purposely declined to call on family members to testify in divorce suits, then the equation of the deponents with the couples' social networks is mistaken. Feelings of shame or remorse could have been involved. Perhaps family members were there, but were unwilling to testify. To account for the small number of kin among deponents without implying that kin networks were absent, one could hypothesize that extended-family members avoided intervening in cases involving conjugal-family conflict in order not to exacerbate it.[31] Since at least 11% of the deponents were kin, however, there apparently was no general bar to family members' testimony. Furthermore, it is as logical (or more logical) to assume that family members were especially eager to defend or support their innocent, wronged, or unfairly accused relatives. In some of the most conflict-ridden cases, kin of both spouses testified on opposing sides.[32] The motives to rely on family members in particular as deponents may have balanced, or overbalanced, reasons to pass them by.

Measured by the identity of deponents, married couples' social relationships involved nonresidents of their households more than residents (as would be expected, simply because of available numbers), and non-related persons more than family members. Not only did community residents' interest and presence cross the boundaries of the conjugal family, in other words, but chiefly non-kin composed that community. Identifying the sex of deponents, in addition, may shed some light on the question of whether friendships, interests, and "social world" were divided by gender in this society. In the study of American women's history it has become almost commonplace to note that sex-role prescriptions were less elaborate and rigid when men and women worked together in the context of family production than in the nineteenth century when men's and women's places of work became separate.[33] This implies that same-sex affiliations—particularly women's affiliations within their own "sphere"—were less intense and less exclusive in the preindustrial period than in their later formulation.

Carroll Smith-Rosenberg has recently described in impressive detail the "female world" in which well-to-do women of the nineteenth century circulated, giving, expecting, and receiving emotional sustenance within their own gender-group and indicating by the same token the emotional poverty of cross-sex relationships, including marriage.[34] If same-sex affiliation was at all as important in eighteenth-century Massachusetts, I would expect to find divorce petitioners and defendants relying primarily on members of their own sex to substantiate their cases; but that result did not materialize. Female deponents were in the minority, which meant that husbands as petitioners or defendants relied more heavily on deponents of their own sex, while wives did not. As petitioners, wives in fact called upon a smaller proportion of female deponents than husbands did. (See Table 2.) Perhaps the presence, not the absence, of same-sex affiliations could cause this result: wives might have found relatively more male deponents to testify about their husbands' wrongdoing because their husbands' usual confidants and companions

TABLE 2. Gender Composition of Deponents
(Total deponents: 762; 521 m, 421 f—31% f)

Petitioner	Deponents					
	For Petitioner		For Accused		Neutral	
Wife	179 m 71 f	28.4% f	37 m 23 f	38.3% f	97 m 21 f	17.8% f
Husband	115 m 69 f	37.5% f	51 m 34 f	40% f	42 m 23 f	35% f

were male, and husbands might have found relatively more female deponents to testify about their wives' wrongdoing because their wives had female confidants and companions.

The sex of deponents supporting *accused* spouses may be a less ambiguous measure. The accused, often guilty, presumably had more difficulty than the petitioner in finding supportive witnesses, and needed to call on intimate friends. The proportion of females defending accused wives, nonetheless, was only minutely higher than the proportion of females defending accused husbands. Furthermore, wives as petitioners called on a much smaller proportion of females than husbands did for neutral deponents (those who filled in information without confirming one side of the story or the other). This, together with wives' greater reliance upon male supporting witnesses, suggests that they wanted to corroborate their cases with male testimony, perhaps because they felt a general disadvantage as women in civil actions.

These statistics equivocate about the separation of sexual spheres when they speak at all, and the actions and statements of divorce petitioners and witnesses add little more. Only two instances of especially defensive or collusive friendship between persons of the same sex occurred, both between women.[35] There are equally few but tantalizing evidences of intimate confidences exchanged between men and women.[36] Fragments such as these cannot be conclusive, but they tend to diminish rather than stress the importance of gender-group segregation. Men's and women's evident freedom in conversation suggests openness rather than restrictions in social interaction between the sexes, but it is difficult to interpret whether this indicates anything more than simple lack of prudishness.

Even if non-kin relations in the community outnumbered the extended-family relationships of the divorcing couples, the latter also deserve particular investigation. Examining how and why parents intervened, whenever they did so, in their children's married lives, should clarify issues of intergenerational intimacy and control. The economic links between generations in a traditional agricultural community are presumably very strong; but recent study of mid- to late eighteenth-century Massachusetts suggests that it was no longer a traditional agricultural society and that patterns of intergenerational control and stability were being eroded.[37] In the divorce records parents most frequently played the role of financial resource or resort for their married children. Seven wives who were deserted or severely abused by their husbands went back to their fathers' households for support; three went to their widowed mothers'; two went to their brothers'; and two wives who abandoned their husbands did not hesitate to return to their fathers' houses—one of them even carried on her adulteries there. Only one deserted *husband* cited his parents' help, in supporting and caring for his five children.[38] Parents also typically supported their children's side of the story in divorce controversies, usually when they were the innocent or aggrieved, but even in a few cases when they appeared to be in the wrong. Mary Knight's father accepted her account that William Parham had "framed" her, for instance; he accused Russell Knight of scheming together with William in order to manufacture cause to divorce Mary, claimed that his daughter was an honest woman, and warned Russell that he would "smart" for his contrivance.[39] Sometimes parental support or intervention appeared to heighten a married couple's animosities toward one another. Amos Bliss of Rehoboth attributed many of his difficulties with his young wife Phebe to her family, who, living nearby, he said, "had ocationed [sic] a great Deal of Trouble; as well as Loss, to his Interest." Although he charged Phebe with adultery and desertion—and, on the contrary, the essential problem appeared to be Phebe's feeling after eight months of marriage that she had chosen the wrong mate—Amos persisted in blaming Phebe's family for the failure of his expectations. Phebe's sister described Amos' habit of cursing her family, "O Dam ye, Dam the whole Company, Dam the Whole Billing of ye: you [Phebe] shall renounce the Whole Dam Club. . . ." Phebe's father reported Amos' declaration (in 1781) that he was at war with them, "as much at variance with that Family as Ever Great Britain and America was or is." Nonetheless, Phebe's father evidently was trying to reconcile the young couple, as were several Bliss relatives; but Phebe's family gave her refuge when she deserted Amos.[40]

Married couples felt their parents' presence, in great or small ways, in less than a score of the divorce cases. By this measure, parents only infrequently expressed responsibility for adult married children; and when they did, it was primarily to provide emergency financial help, notably to daughters who were not self-supporting. Mortality must partially account for parents' slight concern. Many divorce petitioners were no longer young, and probably had no parents to turn to. Even allowing for mortality, however, I would estimate that parents played a role in only a fifth of the cases in which they likely could have.[41]

As the parents of the divorce petitioners displayed minimal and chiefly financial responsibility for their children, the same kind of relationship recurred in the next generation, between the petitioners and their minor children. Likely as it was that any first marriage of that era would have produced a child within two years, just over one-third of the divorce cases mentioned children—even when I discount the marriages of short duration, those involving sexual incapacity, and the poorly recorded suits.[42] Probably a much higher proportion of the petitioners had children but did not allude to them, because they considered the matter nonessential. References to offspring in the petitions, when present at all, suggested that parents did not consider their children's well-being of overriding importance. Most often a petitioner mentioned offspring in order to show the former viability of the marriage and his or her own dutiful performance in it. The number of children was not always declared, and the sex, never. Also, deserted spouses cited their children as economic responsibilities. Wives, usually those saddled with tasks of support beyond their competence, made up almost three-fourths of the petitioners who referred to children. Only two petitioners explicitly requested to keep their children.[43] In all of the other cases the question of child custody was either neglected, or, I assume, resolved in favor of the innocent (and often burdened) spouse.

Several historians have suggested that parents in premodern times viewed their children with little of the sentiment or affection, and reared them with little of the emotional intimacy, that we have become accustomed to since the Romantic idolization of childhood in the early nineteenth century. Ariès' book proposed that the very concept of childhood as a separate stage (which it had to be before becoming a *precious* stage) of life only gradually evolved between the fourteenth and the eighteenth centuries in Europe. More recently Lloyd DeMause has hypothesized that the experience of childhood was a terror—a nightmare—before parents began to introduce a more humanitarian and enlightened approach toward the middle of the eighteenth century. Edward Shorter sees a revolution in maternal sentiment as a central event in the transformation from the premodern to the modern family.[44] While there have been some opposing examples of tender treatment of children in the New England colonies—Edmund Morgan, for example, stresses the solicitude of Puritan parents[45]—the developing consensus seems to be that parents' attitudes in the early period were matter-of-fact, if not cavalier, and that children's early development could depend as much on other caretakers, such as siblings, neighbors, masters, as on their parents.

The evidence about children in the divorce records supports that consensus. Petitioners and their spouses pictured their children in economic terms. Virtually the only manifestation of parental concern was remarried widows' or widowers' desire to assure provision for the offspring of their first marriages.[46] Some parents saw children purely as burdens: in 1710, for instance, Abigail Emery of Newbury accused her husband of Onan's "abominable" sin, which he practiced, she claimed, because "he feared the charge of children." Russell Knight stopped sleeping with his wife Mary because of her ill treatment, and told her that he would not risk producing "a Parcel of young Children more to make him a Slave as long as he lived when she [Mary] would not do anything to help him."[47] Other comments indicated only neglect or abuse of children. When asked how she could elope with her lover and leave her children behind, Tabitha Lufkin said she never thought about them. Susanna Chambers, hearing her small daughter reveal to a neighbor her presence in the bedroom, where she was with a lover, "unhook'd the door, & called her daughter little Bitch & said she would sacrifice her if she did not get away. Upon which the Child went up Stairs crying." Hannah Wales apparently did not care what her four-year-old daughter saw or said; the child told a maidservant she saw a man "lay on the bed with her mamma, and she saw her thighs, and the man told her to lay up higher."[48] (These parents' heedlessness of protecting their children's sexual "innocence" recalls Ariès' claim that in premodern families children were assumed not to sense sexual significance nor, on the other hand, to have any "innocence" to preserve.)[49] Mary Higerty, wife of a mariner of Salem, neither hid her promiscuity from her fourteen-year-old son nor ended it even when he threatened to tell his father. Stephen Temple of Upton "violated the chastity" of his daughter in 1772—that is, raped her, when she was sick in bed, and could not have been more than fourteen years old, and "was afraid of him and thought I must obey him."[50] Chiefly the words of cruel or adulterous spouses, these examples may be much more vicious than general attitudes toward children. Nonetheless, together with the minimal concern for children in the divorce records, and the tendency of even the righteous petitioners to view children as economic quantities, they suggest that an unsentimental, instrumental approach to children prevailed within families. Stephen Temple's wife Sarah even forgave him his incest, on his apology and promise to behave better at that time, and did not divorce him until eleven years later when he fathered an Upton girl's illegitimate child.

The primarily economic bond between parents and children reflected the same characteristic in the marital relationship. Petitioners' and deponents' statements repeatedly made it clear that marriage was seen as a relationship in which the husband agreed to provide food, clothing, and shelter for his wife, and she agreed to return frugal management and obedient service. To "act like a man" meant to support one's wife. Yet just as parents might disregard their duties to their children, so spouses travestied the requirements of marriage. Of the 128 petitions brought by wives, 65% included the charge of desertion and/or non-support, alone or in combination with charges of adultery, bigamy, or cruelty. Thirty-seven % of the 101 husbands' petitions included the charge of desertion. Husbands frequently accused their wives of squandering provisions, or mismanaging the household—deserted husbands lamented the lack of their wives' services, or alleged that they had stolen goods—and wives had even more serious economic complaints.[51] John Chapin, a Springfield farmer, claimed greater hardship than other deserted men; his 1786 petition said that for six years he had supported and cared for his five small children, with his parents' help, but finally had to break up his household and place the children elsewhere.[52] Wives whose husbands deserted or failed to support them almost always had tales of woe. Martha Dickinson, for example, was an orphan in 1762 when she married a tailor of Hadley named William Jones. Within two years he fell heavily in debt, and then absconded, leaving her caring for one child and pregnant with another. Creditors took all of William's estate and her own, including wearing apparel. For almost ten years, up to the time when she heard that William had remarried in another place and she sued for divorce, she lived by the sufferance of friends and relations.[53]

Wives who endured nonsupport also found that the marriage contract hindered their own efforts to earn. Common law gave the use and profit of a woman's real estate, and the ownership of her personal property and earnings, to her husband.[54] Without their husbands' consent married women could not contract or sue to collect debts, so they virtually could not engage in business while still legally bound to untrustworthy husbands. Henrietta East Caine, who had run a fashionable millinery shop on Boston's Marlborough

Street in her earlier years, lamented that after her marriage, her husband's desertion, and her discovery that he was a bigamist, "her Friends will not supply her with Goods to carry on her business as before," so long as her marriage contract lasted.[55] Wives with large marriage portions might find themselves destitute because of their husbands' inept or reckless or malevolent management; Mary Hunt of Boston was one whose husband not only beat her, but also spent her fortune of fifteen hundred pounds, in twelve years of marriage, leaving her and three children to fend for themselves.[56] The divorce records contain numerous instances such as these, in which wives' adherence to the norm of economic dependence resulted in their own economic powerlessness. These economic defaults of marriage took place with little effective counteraction. With two exceptions (both male), petitioners did not obtain divorce on the grounds of simple desertion or non-support in eighteenth-century Massachusetts. And, as women's repeated petitions regarding nonpayment of alimony demonstrated, the law offered no foolproof compulsion to make a man support his wife.[57]

Despite women's economic subjection in marriage (or, perhaps, because of it), they clung to married status longer than men did, even when aware of their spouses' wrongs. Almost two-thirds of the divorce suits provided enough information to allow reckoning the length of time between one spouse's first offense (e.g., the first occasion of adultery, the beginning of cruelty, the point of desertion) and the other's petition for divorce. Aggrieved wives waited a longer time before suing for divorce than aggrieved husbands did, whether all offenses are considered together or each type figured separately. (See Table 3.)[58] On the average, wives waited almost five years, while husbands petitioned after only two and a half years. In cases involving adultery both spouses acted faster than in other instances, but wives still waited longer to sue than husbands did, suggesting that a double standard of sexual morality was operating. Women consistently manifested greater tolerance—or, one could say, greater resignation—in marriage than men did. Despite its disadvantages, women hesitated to abandon married status for its alternative. Of course other considerations besides pure tolerance or resignation must have figured in an individual's decision to wait or to sue for divorce. Awareness of divorce procedure, estimation of how likely a divorce was to be obtained, or appraisal of what benefit or shame a divorce would produce, could counterbalance the desire to be rid of an unworthy partner, and more effectively did so, it seems, for wives than for husbands. Some cases are truly remarkable. Abigail Daniels of Grafton finally petitioned in 1781 to divorce her husband of thirty

TABLE 3. Years Elapsed Before Petitioning for Divorce[a]

Petitioner	Grounds[b]				Yrs. Married at Pet. Date
	All	Adultery	Desertion	Cruelty	
Median					
Wife	4 (N:81)	2 (N:53)	4 (N:44)	4 (N:44)	10 (N:73)
Husband	1 (N:64)	1 (N:61)	1 (N:18)	n.a.	11 (N:62)
Mean					
Wife	4.9 (N as above)	3	4.9	4.5	11.65
Husband	2.5	2	2.9	n.a.	10.69

[a] The figures represent *minimum* number of years since petitioner's *awareness* of the offense.

[b] While the number of years elapsed in cases involving adultery, cruelty, and desertion are figured separately, these causes in fact overlapped in individual cases. If a petitioner's spouse had deserted ten years earlier, for example, and committed adultery eight years before, each of these has been counted separately in the desertion and adultery median and mean.

years, when for as long as eight years he had been cohabiting at home with her sister, as well as frequenting taverns and failing to support Abigail and their children.[59] Several wives who sued on the grounds of cruelty said they had endured five or ten years of physical abuse, and women often waited as long, or longer, to petition after being deserted.[60] There were some exceptional cases of extremely tolerant or resigned husbands, such as John Bragg of Andover, who allowed nine years of flagrant promiscuity on his wife's part to elapse before he petitioned for divorce.[61]

Were characteristics besides the economic ones identifiable in marriage in this period—romantic love expectations, perhaps? In recent attempts to test the theoretical alignment of romantic love choice with the modern conjugal family, historians and sociologists have asserted not only that romantic love themes appeared in the elite literature of the last quarter of the eighteenth century, but also that certain demographic indicators, such as rates of prebridal pregnancy and the marriage order of siblings, point by mid-century to autonomous, love-directed choices of marriage partners. Such developments imply that traditional, parent-dominated, chiefly economic determinants of marriage were breaking down.[62] My finding that parents of divorcing couples involved themselves minimally with their children's marital problems allows—although it does not demand—the interpretation that emotional life had in these cases become concentrated on the conjugal pair, rather than being diffused in a wider kin network; that regardless of the ubiquity of neighbors and lodgers, a husband's and wife's most important relations were reciprocal, with one another. The rising frequency of divorce petitions as the century progressed also suggests that people were becoming more willing to take drastic steps if disappointed in their expectations of marital happiness. This supports the interpretation that greater emotional investment in marriage was the developing pattern.[63]

The actual language and content of petitions, however, display little in the way of romantic love ideals—partially because petitioners, for pragmatic reasons, detailed more palpable grievances than the loss of conjugal love—and also, I suspect, because romantic love was not a *primary* value in their definition of marriage. The petitions later in the century can be distinguished from the earlier ones in this regard. They more frequently manifested awareness of and hope for romantic love. Petitioners *never* named loss of conjugal affection among their grievances in 58 petitions between 1736 and 1765, although they mentioned conduct unbecoming a wife or husband, neglect of family, and wasting of provisions, as general faults to support specific accusations. More than a tenth of 121 suits between 1766 and 1786, in contrast, contained complaints such as "her affections were thereby alienated from him," "all conjugal affection has fled," "he lost all affection for her," her actions "opposed nuptial happiness," he "ceased to cherish her," she had "almost broken his heart."[64] While the earlier petitioners as well as the later differentiated between cruel and kind treatment, that is not the same as calling attention to the presence or absence of conjugal affection.

A comparison of two suits may illustrate some shifts of emphasis in the marital relationship. Both are cases in which a husband charged his wife with adultery. Stephen Lufkin, a mariner and fisherman of Gloucester, had a solid case in 1760 against his wife Tabitha, whose affair and planned elopement with William Haskell was well known in the neighborhood. Tabitha, claiming she was innocent, at first opposed the divorce action, but then changed her mind; while still alleging that her husband could not prove his accusations, she said she wished to be divorced from him. Her reasons are worth detailing: first, Stephen had been an unkind husband, always checking up on her, finding fault, and getting angry, and only giving her to eat the food he liked, whether or not it agreed with her stomach; second, he had refused to pay for a jug of cider she had bought in his absence, although she had drunk only water for seven or eight months; third, he had argued with her about cloth that she bought for his coat, and had shut her out of the house until she, on her knees, begged him to be reconciled; fourth, he falsely accused her of wasting his goods, for they had had little when they married (six years before) and now had several hundred pounds despite the fact that he was only a fisherman; fifth, Stephen had faults too, including a penchant for stealing rum; sixth, he had stripped her bare, not even allowing her an apron and coat in which to appear at court. Tabitha said that she desired a divorce because Stephen was "so Encenced [sic] against me that we never shall live well together again."[65] Although Tabitha's conclusion revealed that she had a norm of marital harmony in mind, in order to make her grievances plausible and shift the blame she raised only objections which were economic in origin, and dealt with the basics of food, clothing, and shelter. Neither partner seemed particularly interested in their emotional relationship; Stephen stated the simple objections that Tabitha had behaved in ways unbecoming a wife, had committed adultery, and had wasted his property.

In Amos Bliss' suit against his wife Phebe in 1781 the emphasis had changed. Amos could not prove his charge that Phebe committed adultery with Nathan Turner, and Phebe's countercharges about Amos' physical abuse, which she said had forced her out of the house, were also questionable. What was evident was a failure of romantic expectations on both sides of this young marriage. Amos only wanted Phebe to stop provoking and "twitting" him, to be his "friend" and "be in Subjection to him" and he would live with her gladly; he said he loved Phebe but not her recent actions, and would be more satisfied to have her live with him happily than to have "both the Endias [sic]." Phebe said, on the other hand, that she had loved Amos when he courted her, but had been young and foolish; since marriage his behavior had become so insufferable that she hated him, and would rather beg her bread, or die, than live with him. She told several people that she could never live with Amos again, and that she thought him a fool. Both of them had some economic grievances—Amos accused Phebe of carting away his goods to benefit her father's family; and Phebe, according to one informant, resented the failure of her mother's promise that if she married Amos she would "Live Like a Lady and Never need fetch the water to wash . . . [her] hand"—but clearly the real source of bitterness was the rupture of a romantic and emotional bond, which neither family nor community efforts at conciliation could heal.[66] The Bliss case epitomized as no other did a conception of marriage founded in romantic attraction and conjugal loyalty. It may have heralded the direction in which marriage ideals were to develop, however, since the language of contemporaneous petitions began to suggest the same thing.

These divorce records divulge remarkable information about sexual behavior—more often extramarital than marital—because over two-thirds of the petitioners charged adultery, and usually had to substantiate their allegations with witnesses' descriptions of sexual relations. Even though it was illicit, the sexual activity described must have manifested some typical habits and expectations. Deponents' testimonies thus provide an unusual opportunity to remedy our ignorance, or test ill-founded assumptions, about sexual practices in a pre-Kinsey era. Shorter, for example, trusts that "marital sex for most people in traditional Europe was simple up-and-down, man on top, woman on bottom, little foreplay, rapid ejaculation, masculine unconcern with female orgasm."[67] The divorce records portray a somewhat different case. When the position of sexual intercourse was indicated it was virtually always the "missionary," e.g., "I observed him to get upon her & they hugg'd each other"; "I saw s[d] Miller Laying on M[rs] Crosley, her petticoats being up & his Briches unbuttoned & down, & Lascivious Shaking"; "[Hannah was] lying on a bed on her back with her Cloath [sic] turned up and her thighs bare and a man (not her husband) lying on her"; "she luying [sic] on the Ground & he upon her."[68] There were only slight variations, the most unusual being Tabitha Lufkin's "taking said Haskell round the Wast [sic] throwing her Legs over him told him that was the way to lay."[69]

Women were not expected to make sexual advances as Tabitha Lufkin did, these records suggest, but if women made advances they were presumed to be irresistible. William Haskell attempted to explain the beginning of his affair with Tabitha in such terms: she met him at the mill and followed him in, then "She Said to him what are you Scared at me, Do not Let a woman Scare you She Said or to this Effects [sic], upon this He made some motion to her, and She was so Forwards in y[e] Affair that He had no power to withstand her Temptations." William tried to justify the continuance of the affair to his relatives by saying "if She had not ben [sic] more forward than He it would never come to this." In the Knight case, Joshua Green reported Mary Knight's saying to him, when they were in a room alone, that he was a likely young man whom she would like to sleep with but she supposed he would scorn such a "dried up Woman" as she. (Married for fourteen years, she was probably about thirty-five.) Joshua "just then though of the Peakhole [sic] & concluded that they [the omnipresent observers] would think that I was going to lodge with the s[d] Russells wife & upon that thought I went directly out of the Room."[70] Only men were explicit sexual aggressors, however. Caleb Morey acted upon his belief that "a Man had a right to be concerned with as many Women as he pleased whenever he could have a chance." Bostonian Adam Air defiantly maintained that "one Woman was as good to him as another." Sutton trader Steven Holman acknowledged "that He Had Rogred other Woman [sic] [besides his wife] and ment [sic] to Roger Every Likely Woman He Could and as many as would Let Him," and that "he had deceaved [sic] Many Woman [sic] in Order to get his will of them."[71]

These fragments suggest that the norm of male rather than female "forwardness" (sexual initiative) prevailed along with the assumption that women as well as men needed and enjoyed sex. This formulation may have encouraged mutual sexual pleasure but also, given men's predominance, allowed men to exploit women sexually and blame their sexual aggression on women. Another justification that William Haskell used for his behavior with Tabitha Lufkin was that "to his Certain Knowledge She would Never do without a man"; she had told William that "if She Did not Comply with him She Should with Some other Man For She Did not Love her Husband Lufkin." For his own part, William had to confess "she was the best for that game that ever he meet [sic] with."[72] Men articulated concern for women's sexual pleasure a few times. Mary Knight's supposed lover was overheard to apologize to her, "I have not made out so well as I intended to for I have fired my Charge too soon"; to which Mary charitably replied, "that is no strange thing . . . for my Husband has done so often when he has been gone a few Nights." John Donnell discovered Caleb Morey and Mary Knowles in bed because he overheard "a Mans Voice say does it feel good." Mary Stokell, a witness to Abel Sawyer's adultery with Mary Lancaster, reported that "while he was upon her he Asked her if it felt good; after s[d] Sawyer Was gone s[d] Lancaster Said he was a Glorious hand."[73] It appears that if sexual position was typically "man on top," and women were not expected to initiate sexual advances, some did; both men and women were assumed to desire and take pleasure in sex.

All of this evidence tends to confirm the view that the mid- to late eighteenth century was a period of important transition in family life, and it may help demonstrate how modern patterns emerged gradually out of the matrix of the traditional by multiple overlapping steps, not by sudden transformation. In the extent of community control and surveillance over individuals, in the lack of privacy and intimacy in families, in parents' instrumental and economic approach to minor children, in wives' economic subjection to and resigned tolerance of husbands, in the predominantly non-emotional definition of marriage, and in the frank admission of men's and women's sexuality, the patterns of family and personal life revealed here are those of a traditional society. Yet the apparent severing of parents' control over adult married children's lives, the inchoate influence of romantic love in marriage, and the improvement in women's status suggested by their more frequent petitions for divorce and their greater success in obtaining it, point to modern conceptions of family life and relations between the sexes. It remains to be seen how other sources will elucidate this shift, explain its causes, and refine—even complicate—the contrast between traditional and modern so that it becomes a less schematic one.

NOTES

1. A current critical review of historical literature on the family is Christopher Lasch, "The Family and History," *New York Review of Books,* XXII:18 (November 13, 1975). Two good examples of "revisionist" writing in the field are Lutz Berkner, "The Stem Family and the Developmental Cycle of the Peasant Household: An 18th-Century Austrian Example," *Amer. Historical Review,* LXXVII (April, 1972), and Tamara K. Hareven, "The Family as Process," *Journal of Social History,* VII (1974).

2. The most informative records are the original petitions and depositions preserved for most of the cases between 1739 and 1786 in volumes 793 through 796 of the Suffolk Court Files [hereafter cited as SF followed by case number] in the Suffolk County Courthouse, Boston. A single bound manuscript volume labeled "Divorces 1760–1786," [hereafter cited as Div. followed by page number], in the same location, summarizes most of the divorce petitions and decrees for those years. Documents of some earlier cases appear in Mass. Archives, volume 9 [hereafter cited as M.A. 9]; and the existence of still more cases is disclosed in the executive records of the Council of Massachusetts [hereafter cited as C.R. followed by volume and page number or date]. Jurisdiction over divorce between 1692 and 1786 was held by the Governor and Council.

3. See my "Divorce and the Changing Status of Women in Eighteenth-Century Massachusetts," *William and Mary Quarterly,* (Oct. 1976). Over half of the divorce petitions occurred after 1765, and over a third between 1775 and 1786. More women (128) than men (101) filed suit. Husbands had better success overall in obtaining divorce, but wives' rate of success improved during the century so that by the Revolutionary years it almost equalled husbands'. The Governor and Council granted annulments for bigamous marriages or impotence; separate bed and board for cruelty; and divorces for desertion (in two cases only) or for adultery itself or in combination with desertion, remarriage, or cruelty. Wives, with a few notable exceptions, were *not* able to obtain divorce for their husbands' adultery before 1773, but after that year did so regularly.

4. For indications of change in sexual and marital patterns in the mid- to late eighteenth century, see Daniel Scott Smith, "Parental Power and Marriage Patterns—An Analysis of Historical Trends in Hingham, Massachusetts," *Journal of Marriage and the Family,* 35 (Aug. 1973); Daniel Scott

Smith and Michael Hindus, "Premarital Pregnancy in America," *Journal of Interdisciplinary History*, 5 (1975); Robert V. Wells, "Quaker Marriage Patterns in a Colonial Perspective," *William and Mary Quarterly*, 3d ser., 29 (1972); Edward Shorter, *The Making of the Modern Family* (N.Y., 1975); and Lonna Myers Malmsheimer, "New England Funeral Sermons and Changing Attitudes toward Women, 1672–1792," unpubl. Ph.D. diss., Univ. of Minn., 1973.

5. I discuss the accessibility of divorce, and the geographical and occupational distribution of petitioners more fully in "Divorce and the Changing Status . . ." Briefly, three-quarters of the petitioners or their husbands had middle-range occupations such as farmer, mariner, craftsman; three-quarters of the petitioners lived in all sizes of Massachusetts towns and the other quarter in Boston; almost three-quarters of the female petitioners and 95% of the male petitioners could sign their names.

6. See J. H. Benton, Jr., comp., *Early Census-Making in Massachusetts* (Boston, 1905), which contains a facsimile reprint of the 1764–65 census; and Philip J. Greven, Jr., "The Average Size of Families and Households in the Province of Massachusetts in 1764 and in the United States in 1790," in Peter Laslett and Richard Wall, eds., *Household and Family in Past Time* (Cambridge, 1972), chapter 20.

7. Philippe Ariès, *Centuries of Childhood: A Social History of Family Life*, trans. Robert Baldick (N.Y., 1962). Shorter's new book *The Making of the Modern Family* stresses this contrast.

8. Martha Air v. Adam Air (1773), SF 129779, depositions of Mary Angel and Abigail Galloway, pp. 86–87. See also Edward Holman v. Rebeccah Holman (1763), Div., pp. 18–20; William Chambers v. Susanna Chambers (1769), SF 129753, p. 136.

9. Mary Morey v. Caleb Morey (1783), SF 129844, p. 95. Neighbor John Andrews, who wanted to know if Caleb slept with his housekeeper, as rumored, purposely spied on him: after saying good night he retraced his steps to Caleb's house, "looked through a large Crack in the Wall & saw by the light of a Candle which was there" Caleb in bed and his housekeeper in the same room with him. Deposition of John Andrews, p. 96.

10. Sarah Backus v. John Backus (1784), SF 129846, depositions of John Huggins and Moses Westover, pp. 104–5. John Backus fared no better in his neighbors' eyes for his general treatment of his wife. Elijah Austin and Gad Austin, p. 102, attested that John neglected his trade, left his wife without provisions, and frequented taverns; one said that he "and others with whom he conversed" all felt that Sarah was unfortunate to be connected with John. Cf. the denouement of the affair between William Cornell and Elizabeth Cook at an inn in Tiverton, in 1785: three men found them in bed, "took hold of the [bed]clothes that cover^{d} them and hawled [sic] them off on the floor and there they ware [sic] with Nothing on them but their Shirts." Patience Cornell v. William Cornell (1785), SF 129845, deposition of Jeremiah Dwelly, p. 98. N.B. in both the Cornell and Backus cases married *men's* behavior was restricted by their companions. For an example of a married woman and her lover being uncovered in an inn, see Jacob Miller v. Hannah Miller (1785), SF 129847. See also, as further instances of surveilance, Joshua Gay v. Sarah Gay (1777), SF 129784; Phineas Chamberlain v. Sybil Chamberlain (1783), SF 129826, p. 27; Samuel Hemenway v. Hannah Hemenway (1781), SF 129804, p. 78; Francis Burnham v. Sarah Burnham (1752), M.A. 9, p. 368.

11. Rebecca Simpson v. Ebenezer Simpson (1785), SF 129854, deposi-

tion of Mary Hoar, p. 141. Cf. the retorts of Moses Elwell to Elisha Cranson and Barzillai Banister, depositions in Hannah Elwell v. Moses Elwell (1785), SF 129850, p. 123.

12. John Wales v. Hannah Wales (1785), p. 132. Cf. the acknowledgement by a spinster who lodged with James and Hannah Thompson in Boston, that her "Curiosity excited [her]" to spy through a partly open door to see Mrs. Thompson and a man in bed; she "did not stay so long as . . . [her] Curiosity would otherwise have prompted" because she was afraid of being seen. James Thompson v. Hannah Thompson (1778), SF 129786, p. 128. Cf. also Phineas Chamberlain v. Sybil Chamberlain, SF 129826, depositions of Betty Chamberlain and Abigail Willis, pp. 27, 29; Rebecca Carr v. Andrew Carr (1786), SF 129855, deposition of William Sadler, p. 368.

13. Russell Knight v. Mary Knight (1766), SF 129745, depositions of Ephraim Fairbanks, Joshua Green, Ebenezer Dexter, Jonathan Knight, Timothy Knight, Reuben Leppenwell, William Parham, Sarah Phelps, and John and Zerviah Woods, pp. 71–75.

14. Viz. comments such as "[we have] lived near too [sic] and hard by to s^{d} Lydia the s^{d} term of ten years and are well knowing to her and the circumstances of her children . . . ," or "as I have liv'd in the same neighborhood I have seen & known a good deal." Lydia Kellogg v. Ephraim Kellogg, M.A. 9, depositions of Noah Baker and Zebulon Ballard, p. 408; Mary Lobb v. George Lobb (1781), SF 129800, deposition of John Ballard, p. 6—see also deposition of Margaret Clarke, p. 6. Cf. numerous depositions in Ann Leonard v. Henry Leonard (1743), M.A. 9, pp. 278–281; Jacob Brown v. Ruth Brown (1758), M.A. 9, pp. 424–425; and Ephraim Fairbanks' testimony in Russell Knight v. Mary Knight, SF 129745, p. 71, that Mary had led Russell a bitter life for the two years he had been their neighbor in Boston, "as was generally Reported by those that lived in the House with them and nearest to them."

15. SF 129779, p. 86; Katherine Cobb v. Elijah Cobb (1767), SF 129748, p. 99—see also the testimony of three other former lodgers, pp. 99–101. William Parham claimed that his suspicions of Mary Knight arose because he overheard her in incriminating conversation with a man in her room; SF 129745, p. 74.

16. E.g., a nurse and a hired laborer testified in Mary Fairservice v. John Fairservice (1767), SF 129749, p. 109; four hired men and two other former lodgers, in James Richardson v. Hannah Richardson (1772), SF 129769, pp. 42, 46–48; six lodgers, including nurses, craftsmen, and kin, in Persis Adams v. Daniel Adams (1781), SF 129805, pp. 83–85, 88, 91; five fellow-lodgers or householders in Benjamin Ingersoll v. Lydia Ingersoll (1765), SF 129741, pp. 60–62. The woman who nursed Mary Higerty at her lying-in in 1781 gave the interesting testimony that she saw Mary lying on a bed with Robert Bates about three or four weeks after she gave birth, when "she was as well as any body." This is the only bit of evidence regarding post-partum sexual behavior. SF 129828, p. 38.

17. Daniel McCarthy v. Mary McCarthy (1757), SF 129734, p. 33.

18. SF 129753, p. 136. Sexual adventures on shipboard were also very likely to be observed, because of crowded conditions. See Andrew Shenk v. Sarah Shenk (1771), SF 129766, pp. 33–35—this case was dismissed because it appeared that the witnesses had been bribed; John Crosley v. Jane Crosley (1771), SF 129763, p. 27; William Sturgis v. Sarah Sturgis (1778), SF 129785, pp. 111, 113, 115, 118, 120, 122.

19. Thomas Hammet v. Abigail Hammet (1766), SF 129747, depositions

of Sarah and Mary Guptail, pp. 90–91. Cf. lodgers' alertness to illicit sexual encounters in Domenicus Record v. Martha Record (1785), SF 129851, depositions of Caleb Young and Mary Dailey, pp. 129, 127; Thomas Crippen v. Rosanna Crippen (1781), deposition of Biah Black, p. 139; Sarah Sawyer v. Abel Sawyer (1783), SF 129827, deposition of Mary Stokell, p. 36; James Thompson v. Hannah Thompson, SF 129786, deposition of Rebeccan George, p. 128.

20. E.g., a servant in the household of James and Mary Dougherty in Shirley in 1768 saw from his upper chamber, on a bright moonlit night, Mary Dougherty commit adultery with Thomas Little, "there being only some Boards thrown Downloose for a floor, there being Considerable Distances between s^{d} Boards," SF 129750 (1768), deposition of "Jacko," p. 120; a singlewoman lodger saw Jane Crosley commit adultery with Leonard Miller by looking "through a large Crack In the door, the door being Locked," John Crosley v. Jane Crosley, SF 129763 (1771), deposition of Sarah Powell, p. 27. Cf. methods of observation in Stephen Lufkin v. Tabitha Lufkin (1760), SF 129735, deposition of Judith Ball, p. 42; and Benjamin Ingersoll v. Lydia Ingersoll (1765), SF 129741, deposition of Lydia Emerson, p. 61.

21. Cf. John Demos' discussion of the relevance of the physical construction of households to privacy and to family life in seventeenth-century Plymouth in *A Little Commonwealth* (N.Y., 1970), pp. 24–51.

22. Stephen Lufkin v. Tabitha Lufkin, SF 129735, p. 45.

23. Hannah v. Ebenezer Medberry (1767), SF 129746, deposition of Leavitt Cushing, p. 81.

24. On seventeenth-century aims by church and civil government to maintain family order, see Edmund S. Morgan, *The Puritan Family* (rev. ed., N.Y., 1966), esp. chap. 6.

25. SF 129746, depositions of Abigail Turner (quotation), Abiel Carpenter, Dr. Joseph Bridgham, John Bowen, Jr., Leavitt Cushing, Mathew Cushing, Jr., Silence Cushing, Silvanus Martin, pp. 80–84.

26. Amos Bliss v. Phebe Bliss (1781), SF 129799, depositions of Thomas Allyn (quotations), Betty Bliss, Joseph Allen 3d., Daniel Bliss, Sarah Bowen, Amos Lane, Silvanus Martin, Shubael Peck, Benjamin Pidge, Huldah Tower, pp. 41–44, 48–49, 52–54.

27. Hannah Adams v. Nehemiah Adams (1784), SF 129832, p. 56. Cf. Sarah Lufkin's testimony regarding an instance in which she suspected that William Haskell and Tabitha Lufkin had sexual relations in the orchard, *although* it was daytime, SF 129735, p. 46.

David H. Flaherty, in *Privacy in Colonial New England* (Charlottesville, Va., 1972), affirms that the New England colonists valued, sought, and obtained privacy, but it seems to me that his own intentions and contemporary point of view, rather than his impressive research findings, dictated his conclusions.

28. It should be noted that divorce records have an inherent tendency to emphasize absence of privacy—since petitions for divorce could be substantiated with only those adulteries that did *not* escape notice, those cruelties that *were* observed—and thus are not the most neutral source to use to examine this issue. Nevertheless, taken as a whole the testimonies in these divorce records strongly suggest that privacy-denying conditions were typical and only the discoveries in these cases (i.e., the wrongs observed) were atypical.

29. For a demonstration of significant extended-family linkages in colonial Andover, Massachusetts, see Philip J. Greven, Jr., *Four Generations* (Ithaca, N.Y., 1970).

30. Another objection might be that neighbors at risk to become deponents were likely more numerous than relatives. Most couples, however, called upon few enough deponents that family members alone could conceivably have supplied them. In 102 cases the average number of deponents was between 7 and 8; excluding the dozen exceptional cases with an average of about 27 deponents each, the average number of deponents per case was under five (4.8).

The dozen cases that had exceptionally high numbers of deponents, and thus seemed to exhibit wider and more complex family/community networks, involved couples of relatively high wealth and status levels. Couples of low occupational strata did not call upon such large networks—only those in the middling to upper range, and all property owners, with one exception: they included five yeomen, two traders, two Captains, one doctor, one "Esquire," and one cooper. The deponents in these dozen cases were composed of 12.1% non-resident kin, 2.4% resident kin, 12.5% non-kin coresidents, 54% neighbors, 3% officials, 15.5% unidentifiable.

31. In at least two cases a parent of the petitioner or defendant was mentioned but did not become a deponent. Deponent Joshua Green mentioned Mary Knight's father and brother, neither of whom testified; SF 129745, p. 71. Katherine Cobb's mother did not testify but deponents Joseph Cobb and John Harvey referred to her in Cobb v. Cobb, SF 129748, pp. 98, 101; since both men referred to incidents two or more years earlier, however, Katherine's mother may no longer have been alive at the time of the divorce suit.

32. E.g., Amos Bliss v. Phebe Bliss, SF 129799; Andrew Gage v. Elizabeth Gage (1783), SF 129829; Stephen Lufkin v. Tabitha Lufkin, SF 129735.

33. This contrast does not account for the assignment of work tasks by gender in the earlier period, or for the hierarchical view of women as mentally and morally inferior to men, but it has the virtue of placing women's "separate sphere" of the nineteenth century in historical perspective.

34. Carroll Smith-Rosenberg, "The Female World of Love and Ritual," *Signs: A Journal of Women in Culture and Society*, I (1975).

35. In Mary Knight's case, between her and Abigail Kendall; see SF 129745, deposition of William Parham, p. 74. And in the Hammet case, between Abigail Hammet and lodger Sarah Guptail; see SF 129747, deposition of Hannah Warren, p. 92.

36. E.g., William Haskell told the full details of his affair with Tabitha Lufkin to two women—both of whom disapproved—as well as to several men; SF 129735, depositions of Sarah Jacques and Hannah Sargent, pp. 46, 48. Abigail Bradstreet discussed her marital problems in company with her husband and four other men at her mother's house, including her objection that "*her husband would do it for her* (meaning, as . . . [the deponent] understood her, that he would have carnal knowledge of her body) *which, as She was with child, put her to great pain, & almost killed her* the next day"; SF 129762 (1771), deposition of Jonathan Knight, p. 19. Abigail, who was well-to-do, apparently expected a cessation of sexual intercourse during pregnancy; whereas Isabella Dawes, the wife of a Boston peruke-master, just advised her lover "that he must use her gently as she was with Child." Edward Dawes v. Isabella Dawes (1779), deponent's name blurred, p. 136.

37. See, e.g., Greven, *Four Generations;* Kenneth A. Lockridge, "Land, Population, and the Evolution of New England Society, 1630–1790," *Past and Present,* 39 (1968); Smith, "Parental Power"; Smith/Hindus, "Premarital Pregnancy"; Richard D. Brown, "The Emergence of Urban Society in Rural Massachusetts, 1760–1820," *Journal of American History,* 61 (1974).

38. To fathers': Sarah Rogers, M.A. 9, p. 148; Thankfull Winehall, C.R. V, p. 238; Hannah Marshall, M.A. 9, pp. 206–07; Priscilla Howard, SF 129771; Phebe Bliss, SF 129799; Sarah Sturgis, SF 129785; Rachel King, SF 129780.

To mothers': Mary Fairservice, SF 129756; Abigail Bradstreet, SF 129762; Sarah Hill, SF 129812.

To brothers': Eleanor Gray, M.A. 9, pp. 296–311; Elizabeth G. Bemis, SF 129797.

Deserted to fathers': Hannah Anthony, M.A. 9, 237–243; Margaret Chapin, SF 129856. Margaret Chapin's husband John, in the last-mentioned case, used his parents' help.

39. SF 129745, deposition of Joshua Green, p. 71. Cf. the actions of Mary Finney's father and brother, who got Gill Belcher drunk and dragged him before the justice of the peace to marry Mary (who was pregnant) in 1738, without publication of banns. Gill subverted their achievement by obtaining an annulment; Gill Belcher v. Mary Finney alias Belcher, SF 129726. On the other hand, in the affair between William Haskell and Tabitha Lufkin, which was adulterous on both sides, relatives opposed the wrong. Tabitha's mother attempted to bribe her into virtue, promising that if Tabitha would "Give no Further Occasion for such Storeys [sic] to be Told about her I would Give her a Good Russet Gown"; SF 129735, deposition of Judith Ball, p. 42.

40. SF 129799: quotations are from depositions of Silvanus Martin, p. 49; Releaf Munro, p. 50; and Rosbotham Munro, p. 51. See also depositions of David Turner, Jr., p. 55, and Eleazar Bliss, p. 43. See also Abigail Bradstreet v. Joseph Bradstreet, SF 129762; and William Sturgis v. Sarah Sturgis, SF 129783—a case in which the wife, accused by her husband of adultery, charged that his father (her father-in-law) had raped her. Charlotte McDaniel Ford blamed her husband's father for his divorce suit against her, SF 129764 (1771); and Puella Kelley found that her husband's father was more interested than her husband in contesting her charge of adultery and suit for divorce, SF 129824 (1782).

41. That is, mention of parents' involvement, however slight, occurred in 19 out of 229 cases. Documentation in about 50 of the 229 cases was too minimal to have revealed such information. And probably half of the remaining 180 petitioners were too old to expect their parents to be alive: the median number of years married of *all* petitioners was over ten (see Table 2), whereas the median number of years married for the petitioners whose parents were known to be involved was *five* years. Therefore, halving the remaining cases to account for mortality, I estimate that the proportion of cases showing parental involvement—of those that reasonably *could* have—is 19 out of 90 cases = 21%.

42. I have no way to estimate how many couples had no surviving children or none living at home. Of 229 cases, fifty were poorly recorded, seven involve marriages of less than two years' duration; four possibly involved sexual incapacity. Among the remaining 168, 61 showed evidence of children, 56 of these through the petitioner's remarks, the remaining 5 through deponents' testimony.

43. Of the 56 petitioners who mentioned their children, 41 were wives. The two who requested custody (there was only one child in each case) were Lucy Purnam, in her suit against Scipio Purnam, SF 129751 (1766), and John Crosley, in his suit against his wife Jane, SF 129763.

44. Ariès, *Centuries of Childhood;* Lloyd de Mause, "The Evolution of Childhood," in de Mause, ed., *The History of Childhood* (N.Y., 1974); Shorter, *Making of the Modern Family.* See also David Hunt, *Parents and Children in History: The Psychology of Family Life in Early Modern France* (N.Y., 1970), and John Demos, *A Little Commonwealth.*

45. *The Puritan Family,* esp. chaps. 3 and 7.

46. E.g., as in Hannah Medberry v. Ebenezer Medberry, SF 129746, or Persis Adams v. Daniel Adams, SF 129805.

47. Abigail Emery v. John Emery (1710), M.A. 9, pp. 162–173; SF 129745, deposition of Jonathan Knight, p. 72.

48. SF 129735, deposition of Sarah Lufkin, p. 46; SF 129753, deposition of Tabitha Steuart, p. 137; John Wales v. Hannah Wales (1785), SF 129852, deposition of Mary Cole, p. 132.

49. Cf. Ariès, *Centuries of Childhood,* pp. 100–106. But when thirteen-year-old Mary Salmon's mother found out that Sgt. Hatton had been sleeping in the same bed with Mrs. Susanna Chambers and Mary, she took "the child" away. SF 129753, deposition of Mary Hay, p. 135.

50. Jeremiah Higerty v. Mary Higerty (1784), SF 129828, deposition of Jeremiah Higerty, Jr., p. 39; Sarah Temple v. Stephen Temple (1783), SF 129821, deposition of Susanna Temple Wood, p. 150. The *Memoirs of Mrs. Abigail Bailey . . . written by herself . . . ,* edited by Ethan Smith (Boston, 1815), recount a tale of incest contemporary with the Temple case and quite similar to it.

51. For husbands' complaints, see for example Francis Burnham v. Sarah Burnham, M.A. 9, pp. 365–369; Benjamin Green v. Jemima Green (1751), SF 129731; Edward Holman v. Rebeccah Holman, Div., pp. 18–20; James Torry v. Mary Torry (1763), Div., pp. 21–23; Squire Baker v. Dorcas Baker (1783), SF 129811; David Harwood v. Mary Harwood (1783), SF 129820.

52. SF 129856, p. 144.

53. Martha Jones v. William Jones (1774), SF 129781. Cf. Sarah Kingsley v. Enoch Kingsley (1771), SF 129773.

54. Common law as effected in Massachusetts included some protections for married women. A husband could not convert or dispose of his wife's real property without her consent. A wife had a virtually absolute right of dower—not contravened by divorce, if she were the innocent party —in one-third of her husband's personal property and the lifetime use and profit of one-third of his real property. Prenuptial contracts, by which a canny and well-advised wife with some property could protect her own interests, were upheld in eighteenth-century Massachusetts. See Richard B. Morris, *Studies in the History of Early American Law* (N.Y., 1930), pp. 135–138, 162–163, 170. Nothing in the law, however, could keep a husband from using abuse or threats to try to force his wife to give up her common-law prerogatives. Such attempts caused two divorce suits: Elizabeth Keith v. Mark Keith (1764), SF 129738 and M.A. 9, pp. 441–42; Abigail Bradstreet v. Joseph Bradstreet, SF 129762. Abigail Bradstreet hired John Adams as her lawyer: see L. Kinvin Wroth and Hiller B. Zobel, eds., *The Legal Papers of John Adams* (Cambridge, 1965), I, pp. 280–285.

55. Henrietta M. East (alias) Caine v. Hugh Caine (1759), SF 129736. See

Carl Bridenbaugh, *Cities in the Wilderness* (N.Y., 1966), p. 342, regarding East's millinery shop at the "Sign of the Fan." Cf. wives' complaints in Sarah Bloget v. John Bloget (1736), M.A. 9, p. 211; Mary Hunt v. Richard Hunt (1760), Div., pp. 8–9; Sarah Backus v. John Backus, SF 129846, p. 100. A husband could more directly stymie his wife's efforts, as John Lovell did: a Boston merchant who degenerated into an idle tyrant in the 1770s, he not only failed to support his wife for five years but also prevented her, by his threats and violence, from taking in sewing or placing their daughter with another family. Ann Lovell v. John Lovell (1773), SF 129778.

56. Div., pp. 8–9. See also Kezia Downing v. Nathaniel Downing (1765), SF 129742; Mary Arthur v. George Arthur (1754), SF 129733b. Cases of economic conflict in second marriages seemed to put husband and wife on somewhat more equal footing, because the wife more likely had property and children to protect. The Medberry (SF 129746), Cobb (SF 129748), and Adams (SF 129805) cases had this character, but in none of them did the wife succeed in obtaining the divorce or separation that she was seeking.

57. On desertion pleas, and alimony, see "Divorce and the Changing Status of Women . . ."

58. The pertinent figure is the number of years the aggrieved spouse waited after having *knowledge* of the offense. In many adultery cases, especially cases of wives' adultery while the husband was away, the innocent spouse did not know about the offense until some time after it occurred. I have made every attempt in this calculation to use the correct figure for the number of years since the innocent spouse's *awareness* of the offense.

59. Abigail Daniels v. John Daniels (1781), SF 129803, esp. depositions of Benjamin Rockwood and John Thurston, p. 76.

60. E.g., Katherine Cobb said she endured eight years of abuse; Ann Lovell, five years; Mary Arthur, nine years; Ann Gardner (SF 129813), twelve years. Sarah Rogers had been deserted ten years; Deborah Briseo (M.A. 9, p. 353), for seventeen years; Agnes Caldwell (M.A. 9, pp. 429–430), for six years. N.B. The presumption of the law was that seven years' absence of one spouse enabled the other to remarry. See "An Act against Adultery and Polygamy" of 1694, *Acts and Resolves . . . of the Province of Massachusetts Bay* (Boston, 1869), I, pp. 171–72.

61. John Bragg v. Anna Bragg (1770), SF 129752.

62. See Herman R. Lantz, et. al., "Pre-Industrial Patterns in the Colonial Family in America: A Content Analysis of Colonial Magazines," *American Sociological Review*, 33 (1968); Frank F. Furstenberg, Jr., "Industrialization and the American Family: A Look Backward," *ibid.*, 31 (1966); Smith, "Parental Power," Smith/Hindus, "Premarital Pregnancy," and Shorter, *Making of the Modern Family*, esp. chaps. 2, 3, 4. Lantz's group distinguishes five themes of romantic love: idealization of the loved one, "the one and only," love at first sight, love wins out over all, and glorification of personal emotions (p. 419).

63. See "Divorce and the Changing Status of Women . . ."

64. Quotations are from petitions in Thomas Hammet v. Abigail Hammet, SF 128747; John Bragg v. Anna Bragg, SF 129752; Rebecca Dunnell v. Jacob Dunnell (1780), SF 129795; Thomas Crippen v. Rosanna Crippen, SF 129817; Abel Fitch v. Ann Fitch (1783), SF 129825; David Harwood v. Mary Harwood, SF 129819. See also language in Mary Fairservice v. John Fairservice, SF 129749; John Barry v. Sarah Barry (1770), SF 129757; Sarah Gould v. William Gould (1773), SF 129772—William Gould's reply to Sarah's petition;

Mary Lobb v. George Lobb, SF 129800; John B. Barrere v. Elizabeth Barrere (1778), Div. pp. 156–158; David Hoit v. Mary Hoit (1782), SF 129806; Samuel Crafts v. Margaret Crafts (1783), SF 129823; Hannah Dudley v. Daniel Dudley (1784), SF 129831; Domenicus Record v. Martha Record, SF 129851; John Wales v. Hannah Wales, SF 129852. Only 58 suits between 1736 and 1765, and 121 between 1766 and 1786, were considered, because the others were too poorly recorded to have yielded this kind of information. Fourteen of the latter group included "romantic" language.

65. SF 129735, Tabitha's reply to the court, February 11, 1761, p. 41.

66. SF 129799, depositions of Eleazar Bliss, David Turner, Shubael Peck, Silvanus Martin, David Turner, Joseph Allen, and Sarah Bowen, pp. 41, 43–44, 49, 52, 54. Amos' suit was dismissed, because the adultery was not proved.

67. Edward Shorter, "Capitalism, Culture, and Sexuality: Some Competing Models," *Social Science Quarterly*, 53 (1972), p. 339.

68. SF 129753, deposition of Mary Salmon, p. 136; SF 129763, deposition of Sarah Powell, p. 27; SF 129769, deposition of Tilly Wilder, Jr., p. 49; SF 129851, deposition of Benjamin Teague, p. 128. See also SF 129784, deposition of Joel Richards, p. 101; SF 129852, depositions of Mary Cole and Abigail Edes, p. 132; SF 129766, deposition of Benjamin Palmer, p. 34; SF 129826, depositions of Jonathan Adams and Abigail Willis, pp. 27, 28.

69. SF 129735, deposition of Hannah Sargent, p. 48. Persis Joy observed Hannah Richardson on a bed with an unmarried man "in lude [sic] & Scandalous postures with the said Hannah Closed in . . . [his] arms and their Legs & Thighs crossing each others," SF 129769, p. 45; William Sadler caught his master in the act of adultery with a woman against the back fence, "the woman . . . bending her body backward with her belly towards him & hugging him round his waist . . . ," SF 129855, p. 143.

70. SF 129735, depositions of Thomas Jaques and Sarah Jaques, pp. 45–46; SF 129745, p. 71. Cf. depositions of James Pearson and Bimsley Stevens, SF 129752, p. 132. Martha Record was direct: after committing adultery with a young hired man, she said to him, "Don't you intend to Roger me again? To which he replied, no, I vow I have rogered you twice today, and I think that is enough." SF 129851, deposition of Benjamin Teague, p. 128.

71. SF 129844, deposition of John Andrews, p. 95; SF 129779, deposition of Mary Angel, p. 86; SF 129815, depositions of Marven Moore and Benjamin Hovey, p. 129.

72. SF 129735, depositions of Thomas Jaques, Samuel Proctor, and Francis Haskell, pp. 45, 47, 44. Elizabeth Gage of Beverly bore two children while her husband was gone during the Revolutionary war, but did not hide the fact that they were other men's children, "& often said her husband was gone & other people sometimes behaved as bad as she had." Andrew Gage v. Elizabeth Gage (1783), SF 129829, deposition of Miriam Crafts, p. 44.

73. SF 129745, deposition of William Parham, p. 74; SF 129844, deposition of John Donnell, p. 95; SF 129827, deposition of Mary Stokell, p. 36.

5

Eighteenth-Century American Women in Peace and War

The Case of the Loyalists

■

MARY BETH NORTON

In histories of the American Revolution women have not been wholly neglected, but a very partial view of their experience has been given. The spotlight has shone on the handful of women who served as daring spies or go-betweens, the patriotic ones who sewed shirts and knit socks for the army, the wives of famous generals and statesmen. Mary Beth Norton here investigates the common circumstances of women during the Revolutionary era, by making innovative use of long-known historical documents: the claims for reimbursement of confiscated property filed with the British government after the war by loyalists (i.e., those who opposed the war for independence and remained loyal to Britain). Norton scrutinizes wives' familiarity with their husbands' property and livelihoods, compares their independent economic activity to their household ties, and uses the language of women's self-perceptions to understand better their positions. Her findings question the historiography that emphasizes women's exercise of initiative and economic independence in the eighteenth century.

IN RECENT YEARS historians have come to recognize the central role of the family in the shaping of American society. Especially in the eighteenth century, when "household" and "family" were synonymous terms, and when household manufactures constituted a major contribution to the economy, the person who ran the household—the wife and mother—occupied a position of crucial significance. Yet those who have studied eighteenth-century women have usually chosen to focus on a few outstanding, perhaps unrepresentative individuals, such as Eliza Lucas Pinckney, Abigail Smith Adams, and Mercy Otis Warren. They have also emphasized the activities of women outside the home and have concentrated on the prescriptive literature of the day. Little has been done to examine in depth the lives actually led by the majority of colonial women or to assess the impact of the Revolution upon them.[1]

Such a study can illuminate a number of important topics. Demographic scholars are beginning to discover the dimensions of eighteenth-century households, but a knowledge of size alone means little without a delineation of roles filled by husband and wife within those households.[2] Historians of nineteenth-century American women have analyzed the ideology which has been termed the "cult of true womanhood" or the "cult of domesticity," but the relationship of these ideas to the lives of women in the preceding century remains largely unexplored.[3] And although some historians of the Revolution now view the war as a socially disruptive phenomenon, they have not yet applied that insight specifically to the study of the family.[4]

Fortunately, at least one set of documents contains material relevant to an investigation of all these aspects of late eighteenth-century American family life: the 281 volumes of the loyalist claims, housed at the Public Record Office in London. Although these manuscripts have been used extensively for political and economic studies of loyalism, they have only once before been utilized for an examination of colonial society.[5] What makes the loyalist claims uniquely useful is the fact that they contain information not only about the personal wartime experiences of thousands of Americans but also about the modes of life the war disrupted.

Among the 3,225 loyalists who presented claims to the British government after the war were 468 American refugee women. The analysis that follows is based upon an examination of the documents —formal memorials, loss schedules, and private letters—submitted by these women to the loyalist claims commission, and on the commission's nearly verbatim records of the women's personal appearances before them.[6] These women cannot be said to compose a statistically reliable sample of American womanhood. It is entirely possible that loyalist families differed demographically and economically, as well as politically, from their revolutionary neighbors, and it is highly probable that the refugee claimants did not accurately represent even the loyalist population, much less that of the colonies as a whole.[7] Nonetheless, the 468 claimants included white women of all descriptions, from every colony and all social and economic levels: they were educated and illiterate; married, widowed, single, and deserted; rural and urban; wealthy, middling, and poverty-stricken. Accordingly, used with care, the loyalist claims can tell us much about the varieties of female experience in America in the third quarter of the eighteenth century.[8]

One aspect of prewar family life that is systematically revealed in the claims documents is the economic relationship of husband and wife within the household. All claimants, male and female alike, had to supply the commission with detailed estimates of property losses. Given the circumstances of the war, documentary evidence such as deeds, bills of sale, and wills was rarely available in complete form, and the commission therefore relied extensively upon the sworn testimony of the claimants and their witnesses in assessing losses. The claimants had nothing to gain by withholding information, because the amount of compensation they received depended in large part on their ability to describe their losses. Consequently, it may be assumed that what the loyalists told the commission, both orally and in writing, represented the full extent of their knowledge of their families' income and property.[9] The women's claims thus make it possible to determine the nature of their participation in the financial affairs of their households.

Strikingly, although male loyalists consistently supplied detailed assessments of the worth of their holdings, many women were unable to place precise valuations on the property for which they claimed compensation. Time after time similar phrases appear in the records of oral testimony before the commission: "She cant say what the Houses cost or what they woud have sold for" (the widow of a Norfolk merchant); "Says she is much a Stranger to the state of Her Husband's Concerns" (the widow of a storekeeper from Ninety-Six, South Carolina); "It was meadow Land, she cannot speak of the Value" (a New Jersey farmer's widow); "Her husband was a Trader and had many Debts owing to him She does not know how much they amounted to" (a widow from Ninety-Six); "She can't speak to the Value of the Stock in Trade" (a Rhode Island merchant's widow); "It was a good Tract but does not know how to value it" (the widow of a Crown Point farmer).[10]

Even when women submitted detailed loss schedules in writing, they frequently revealed at their oral examinations that they had relied on male relatives or friends, or even on vaguely recalled statements made by their dead husbands, in arriving at the apparently knowledgeable estimates they had initially given to the commission. For example, a New Jersey woman, questioned about her husband's annual income, referred the commissioners to her father and other male witnesses, admitting that she did not know the amount he had earned. Similarly, the widow of a Charleston saddler told the commissioners that "she does not know the Amount of Her husband's Property, but she remembers to have heard him say in the year 1777 that he was worth £2,000 sterling clear of all Debts." Such statements abound in the claims records: "She is unable to speak to the value of the Plantn herself, but refers to Mr. Cassills"; "Says she cannot speak to the Value—the Valuatn was made by Capt McDonald and Major Munro"; "Says her Son in Law Capt Douglas is better acquainted with the particulars of her property than herself and she refers to him for an Account thereof."[11]

Although many female claimants thus lacked specific knowledge of their families' finances, there were substantial variations within the general pattern. The very wealthiest women—like Isabella Logan of Virginia (who could say only that she and her husband had lived in "a new Elegant, large double Brick House with two wings all finish'd in the best taste with Articles from London") and Mrs. Egerton Leigh of South Carolina (who gave it as her opinion that her husband had "a considerable real Estate as well as personal property . . . worth more than £10,000 . . . tho' she cannot herself speak to it with accuracy")—also tended to be the ones most incapable of describing their husbands' business affairs.[12] Yet some wealthy, well-educated women were conversant with nearly every detail of the family finances. For the most part, this latter group was composed of women who had brought the property they described to their husbands at marriage or who had been widowed before the war and had served as executrixes of the estates in question for some time. A case in point is that of Sarah Gould Troutbeck, daughter, executrix, and primary heir of John Gould, a prosperous Boston merchant. Her husband John, an Anglican clergyman, died in 1778, and so she carried the full burden of presenting the family's claim to the commission. Although she deprecatingly described herself to the board as "a poor weak Woman unused to business," she supplied the commissioners with detailed evidence of her losses and unrelentingly pursued her debtors. "Your not hearing from me for so long a time may induce you to think I have relinquishd my claim to the intrest due on your note," she informed one man in 1788. "If you realy entertain any such thoughts I must beg leave to undeceive you." In addition, she did what few loyalists of either sex had the courage to attempt—return to the United States to try to recover her property. When she arrived in 1785, she found her estates "in the greatest confusion" but nevertheless managed within several months to repossess one house and to collect some debts. In the end she apparently won restoration of most of her holdings.[13]

Yet not all the female loyalists who had inherited property in their own right were as familiar with it as was Sarah Troutbeck. Another Massachusetts woman admitted to the commissioners that she did not know the value of the 550 acres left her by a relative, or even how much of the land was cultivated. "Her Brother managed everything for her and gave her what Money she wanted," she explained. In the same vein, a New Yorker was aware that her father had left her some property in his will, but "she does not know what property." A Charleston resident who had owned a house jointly with her brother commented that "it was a good House," but the commission noted, "she does not know the Value of it." And twice-widowed Jane Gibbes, claiming for the farms owned by her back-country South Carolina husbands, told the commission that she had relied on neighbors to assess the worth of the property, for "she can't speak positively to the value of her Lands herself."[14]

But if Jane Gibbes could not precisely evaluate the farms she had lived on, she still knew a good deal about them. She described the total acreage, the amount of land under cultivation, the crops planted, and the livestock that had been lost. In this she was representative of most rural female loyalists with claims that were not complicated by the existence of mortgages or outstanding debts. Although they did not always know the exact value of the land for which they requested reimbursement, they could supply the commission with many important details about the family property: the number of cattle, horses, sheep, and hogs; the types of tools used; the acreage planted, and with what crops; the amounts of grain and other foodstuffs stored for the winter; and the value of such unusual possessions as beehives or a "Covering Horse." It was when they were asked about property on which they had not lived, about debts owed by their husbands, or about details of wills or mortgages that they most often admitted ignorance.[15]

A good example is Mary McAlpin, who had settled with her husband on a farm near Saratoga, New York, in 1767. She did not know what her husband had paid for some unimproved lands, or the acreage of another farm he had purchased, but she was well acquainted with the property on which they had lived. The farm, she told the commissioners, "had been wholly cleared and Improved and was in the most perfect State of Cultivation." There were two "Log Houses plaistered and floored," one for them and one for their hired laborers, and sufficient materials on hand to build "a large and Commodious Brick House." Her husband had planted wheat, rye, peas, oats, barley, corn, turnips, potatoes, and melons; and "the Meadows had been laid down or sown with Clover and Timothy Grass, the two kind of Grass Seeds most Valued in that Country." The McAlpins had had a kitchen garden that produced "in great abundance every Vegitable usually cultivated in that part of America." Moreover, the farm was "well Provided" with such utensils as "a Team waggon, Carts sledges Carwls [*sic*] Wheels for Waggons,

Wheels for Carts, Wheelbarrows, drags for Timber Ploughs, Harrows Hay Sythes Brush Sythes Grubbling Harrows, and all sorts of Carpenters Tools Shoemakers Tools Shovels, Spades, Axes Iron Crow Barrs etc."

After offering all these details, however, Mrs. McAlpin proved unable to assess the value of the property accurately. She gave the commission a total claim of £6,000, clearly an estimate, and when asked to break down a particular item on her schedule into its component parts she could not do so, saying that "She valued the Whole in the Lump in that Sum." Moreover, she proved ignorant of the terms of her husband's will, confusedly telling the commissioners that he had "left his real personal Estate to his Son—This she supposes was his Lands" (the board's secretary noted carefully, "This is her own Expression"), when in fact she had been left a life interest in the real estate plus half the personal estate.[16] In short, Mary McAlpin typifies the rural female claimant, though her husband's property was substantially larger than average. She knew what he had owned, but she did not know exactly how much it was worth. She was well acquainted with the day-to-day operations of the farm but understood very little about the general family finances. And she knew nothing at all about legal or business terminology.

The pattern for urban dwellers was more varied. In the first place, included in their number were most of the wealthy women mentioned earlier, both those who knew little or nothing about their husbands' estates and those who, like Sarah Troutbeck, were conversant with the family holdings. Secondly, a higher percentage of urban women engaged directly in business. Among the 468 female claimants there were forty-three who declared either that they had earned money on their own or that they had assisted their husbands in some way. Only three of these forty-three can be described as rural: a tavernkeeper's wife from Ticonderoga, a small shopkeeper from Niagara, and the housekeeper for the family of Col. Guy Johnson. All the other working women came from cities such as Boston, Philadelphia, Charleston, and New York, or from smaller but substantial towns like Williamsburg, Wilmington, N.C., and Baltimore. The urban women's occupations were as varied as the urban centers in which they resided. There were ten who took lodgers, eighteen shopkeepers and merchants of various sorts, five tavernkeepers, four milliners, two mantua makers, a seamstress, a midwife, an owner of a coffeehouse, a schoolteacher, a printer, one who did not specify an occupation, and two prostitutes who described themselves as owners of a small shop and declared that their house had been "always open" to British officers needing "aid and attention."[17]

As might be expected, the women who had managed businesses or assisted their husbands (one wrote that she was "truly his Partner" in a "steady Course of painfull Industry") were best informed about the value of their property. Those who had been grocers or milliners could usually list in detail the stock they had lost; the midwife had witnesses to support her claim to a high annual income from her profession; the boardinghouse keepers knew what they had spent for furniture and supplies; and the printer could readily value her shop's equipment.[18] But even these working women could not give a full report on all aspects of their husbands' holdings: the widow of a Boston storekeeper, for example, could accurately list their stock in trade but admitted ignorance of the value of the property her husband had inherited from his father, and although the widow of another Boston merchant had carried on the business after her husband was wounded at Bunker Hill, she was not familiar with the overall value of their property.[19]

It is therefore not surprising that women claimants on the average received a smaller return on their claims than did their male counterparts. Since the commissioners reimbursed only for fully proven losses, the amounts awarded are a crude indicator of the relative ability of individual refugees to describe their losses and to muster written and oral evidence on their own behalf. If women had known as much as their husbands about the family estates, there would have been little or no difference between the average amounts granted to each sex. But of the claims heard in England for which complete information is available, 660 loyalist men received an average return of 39.5 percent, while for 71 women the figure was 34.1 percent. And this calculation does not take into account the large number of women's claims, including some submitted by businesswomen, which were entirely disallowed for lack of proof.[20]

In the absence of data for other time periods and populations, it is difficult to assess the significance of the figures that show that slightly less than 10 percent (9.2 percent, to be exact) of the loyalist refugee women worked outside the home. Historians have tended to stress the widespread participation of colonial women in economic enterprise, usually as a means of distinguishing them from their reputedly more confined nineteenth-century counterparts.[21] The claims documents demonstrate that some women engaged in business, either alone or with their husbands, but 9.2 percent may be either a large or a small proportion of the total female population, depending on how one looks at it. The figures themselves must remain somewhat ambiguous, at least until additional data are obtained.[22] What is not at all ambiguous, however, is the distinctive pattern of the female claimants' knowledge.

For regardless of whether they came from rural or urban areas, and regardless of their background or degree of participation in business, the loyalist women testified almost exclusively on the basis of their knowledge of those parts of the family property with which their own lives brought them into regular contact. What they uniformly lacked were those pieces of information about business matters that could have been supplied only by their husbands. Evidently, late eighteenth-century American men, at least those who became loyalists, did not systematically discuss matters of family finances with their wives. From that fact it may be inferred that the men—and their wives as well, perhaps—accepted the dictum that woman's place was in the home. After all, that was where more than 90 percent of the loyalist women stayed, and their ignorance of the broader aspects of their families' economic circumstances indicates that their interest in such affairs was either minimal or else deliberately thwarted by their husbands.[23]

It would therefore appear that the 9 percent figure for working women is evidence not of a climate favorable to feminine enterprise but rather of the opposite: women were expected to remain largely within the home unless forced by necessity, such as the illness or death of their husbands, to do otherwise. The fact that fewer than one-half (seventeen, to be precise) of the working women enumerated earlier had healthy, living husbands at the time they engaged in business leads toward the same conclusion. The implication is that in mid-eighteenth-century America woman's sphere was rigidly defined at all levels of society, not merely in the wealthy households in which this phenomenon has been recognized.[24]

This tentative conclusion is supported by evidence drawn from another aspect of the claims, for a concomitant of the contention that colonial women often engaged in business endeavors has been the assertion that colonial men, as the theoretical and legal heads of household, frequently assumed a large share of domestic responsibilities.[25] Yet if men had been deeply involved in running their households—in keeping accounts and making purchases, even if not in doing day-to-day chores—they should have described household furnishings in much the same detail as their wives used. But just as female claimants were unable to delineate their husbands' business dealings accurately, so men separated from their wives—regardless of their social status—failed to submit specific lists of lost household items like furniture, dishes, or kitchen utensils. One such refugee observed to the commission in 1788, "As Household Furniture consists of a Variety of Articles, at this distance of time I cannot sufficiently recollect them so as to fix a Value on them to the Satisfaction of my mind."[26] It is impossible to imagine a loyalist woman making a comparable statement. For her, what to a man was simply "a Variety of Articles" resolved itself into such familiar and cherished objects as "1 Compleat set blue and white Tea and Table China," "a Large new Goose feather Bed, bolster Pillows and Bedstead," "a Small painted Book Case and Desk," "1 Japan Tea Board," "2 smoothing Irons," and "1 old brass Coffee Pott." Moreover, although men usually noted losses of clothing in a general way, by listing a single undifferentiated sum, women frequently claimed for specific articles of jewelry and apparel. For example, Mary Swords of Saratoga disclosed that she had lost to rebel plunderers a "Long Scarlet Cloak" and a "Velvet Muff and Tippett," in addition to "One pair of Ear Rings French paste set in Gold," "One small pair of Ear Rings Garnets," and "one Gold Broatch with a small diamond Top."[27]

The significance of such lists lies not only in the fact that they indicate what kinds of property the claimants knew well enough to describe accurately and in detail, but also in the insight they provide into the possessions which claimants thought were sufficiently important to mention individually. For example, a rural New York woman left no doubt about her pride in "a fine large new stove"; a resident of Manhattan carefully noted that one of her lost beds was covered in "Red Damask"; and a Rhode Islander called attention to the closets in her "large new dwelling house."[28] The differentiated contents of men's and women's claims thus take on more importance, since the contrasting lists not only suggest the extent of the claimants' knowledge but also reveal their assessments of the relative importance of their possessions. To men, furniture, dishes, and clothing could easily be lumped together under general headings; to women, such possessions had to be carefully enumerated and described.

In the end, all of the evidence that can be drawn from the loyalist claims points to the conclusion that the lives of the vast majority of women in the Revolutionary era revolved around their immediate households to a notable degree. The economic function of those households in relation to the family property largely determined the extent of their knowledge of that property. In rural areas, where women's household chores included caring for the stock and perhaps occasionally working in the fields, women were conversant with a greater proportion of the family estates than were urban women, whose knowledge was for the most part confined to the furnishings of the houses in which they lived, unless they had been widowed before the war or had worked outside the home. The wealth of the family was thus a less significant determinant of the woman's role than was the nature of the household. To be sure, at the extreme ends of the economic scale, wealth and education, or the lack of them, affected a woman's comprehension of her family's property, but what the women displayed were relative degrees of ignorance. If the loyalist claimants are at all representative, very few married colonial women were familiar with the broader aspects of their families' financial affairs. Regardless of where they lived, they were largely insulated from the agricultural and business worlds in which their husbands engaged daily. As a result, the Revolutionary War, which deprived female loyalists of the households in which they had lived and worked, and which at the same time forced them to confront directly the wider worlds of which they had had little previous knowledge, was for them an undeniably traumatic experience.

At the outbreak of the war, loyalist women expected that "their Sex and the Humanity of a civilized People" would protect them from "disrespectfull Indignities." Most of them soon learned otherwise. Rebel men may have paid lip service to the ideal that women and children should be treated as noncombatants, but in practice they consigned female loyalists to much the same fate as their male relatives. Left behind by their fleeing husbands (either because of the anticipated difficulties of a journey to the British lines or in the hope that the family property might thereby be preserved), loyalist wives, with their children, frequently found themselves "stripped of every Thing" by American troops who, as one woman put it, "not contented with possessing themselves of her property were disposed to visit severity upon her person and Those of her friends."[29] Female loyalists were often verbally abused, imprisoned, and threatened with bodily harm even when they had not taken an active role in opposing the rebel cause.[30]

When they had assisted the British—and many aided prisoners or gathered intelligence—their fate was far worse. For example, the New Yorker Lorenda Holmes, who carried letters through the lines in 1776, was stripped by an angry band of committeemen and dragged "to the Drawing Room Window . . . exposing her to many Thousands of People Naked." On this occasion Mrs. Holmes admitted that she "received no wounds or bruises from them only shame and horror of the Mind," but a few months later, after she had shown some refugees the way to the British camp, an American officer came to her house and held her "right foot upon the Coals until he had burnt it in a most shocking manner," telling her "he would learn her to carry off Loyalists to the British Army."[31]

As can readily be imagined, the women did not come through such experiences emotionally unscathed. One Massachusetts mother reported that her twelve-year-old daughter suffered from "nervous Fits" as a result of "the usage she met with from the Mobs"; and another New England woman, the wife of a merchant who was an early target of the local committee because he resisted the nonimportation movement, described to a female friend her reaction to a threatening letter they had received: "I have never injoyed one hours real Sattisfaction since the receipt of that Dreadfull Letter my mind is in continual agitation and the very rustling of the Trees alarms me." Some time later the same woman was unfortunate enough to be abused by a rebel militiaman. After that incident, she reported, "I did not recover from my fright for several days. The sound of drum or the sight of a gun put me into such a tremor that I could not command myself."[32] It was only natural for these women to look forward with longing to the day when they could escape to Canada or, better still, to England, "a land of peace, liberty and plenty." It seemed to them that their troubles would end when they finally left America. But, as one wrote later with the benefit of hindsight, their "severest trials were just begun."[33]

Male and female refugees alike confronted difficult problems in England and Canada—finding housing, obtaining financial support, settling into a new environment. For women, especially widows with families, the difficulties were compounded. The Bostonian Hannah Winslow found the right words: it was a "cruell" truth, she told her sister-in-law, that "when a woman with a family, and Particularly a large one, looses her Husband and Protector People are afraid to keep up the Acquaintance least they may ask favrs."[34] Many of the men quickly reestablished their American friendship networks through the coffeehouses and refugee organizations; the women were deprived not only of the companionship such associations provided but also of the information about pensions and claims that was transmitted along the male networks. As a result, a higher proportion of female than male loyalists made errors in their applications of government assistance, by directing the memorials to the wrong officials and failing to meet deadlines, often because they learned too late about compensation programs. Their standard excuses—that they "had nobody to advise with" and that they "did not know how to do it"—were greeted with skepticism by the claims commission, but they were undoubtedly true.[35]

On the whole, female loyalists appear to have fared worse in England than their male counterparts, and for two major reasons. In the first place, the commissioners usually gave women annual pensions that were from £10 to £20 lower than those received by men, apparently because they believed that the women had fewer expenses, but also because in most cases the women could not claim the extra merit of having actively served the royal cause.[36] Second, fewer women than men found work to supplement the sums they received from the government. To the wealthier female refugees work seemed so automatically foreclosed as an option that only a small number thought it necessary to explain to the commission why they could not contribute to their own support. Mary Serjeant, the widow of a Massachusetts clergyman, even regarded her former affluence as a sufficient reason in itself for her failure to seek employment. In 1782 she told the commissioners, "Educated as a Gentlewoman myself and brought up to no business I submit it to your [torn], Gentlemen, how very scanty must be the Subsistence which my Own Industry [can] procure us." Those who did try to earn additional income (many of whom had also worked outside the home in America) usually took in needlework or hired out as servants or housekeepers, but even they had trouble making ends meet. One orphaned young woman reported, "I can support myself with my needle: but not my two Sisters and infant Brother"; and another, who had learned the trade of mantua making, commented, "I now got Work for my selef [*sic*]—but being oblidged to give long credit and haveing no Money of my one [*sic*] to go on with, I lived Cheifly upon tea which with night working brought me almost into the last stadge of a Consumtion so that when I rec'd my Money for work it went almost [all] to dockters."[37]

Many of the loyalist women displayed a good deal of resilience. Some managed to support themselves, among them the Wells sisters of Charleston, who in 1789 opened a London boardinghouse for young ladies whose parents wished them to have a "suitable" introduction to society. Others survived what might seem an overwhelming series of setbacks—for example, Susannah Marshall of Maryland, who, after running taverns in Baltimore and Head of Elk and trying but failing to join Lord Dunmore off Norfolk in 1776, finally left the United States by sea the following year, only to have her chartered ship captured first by the Americans and then by the British. In the process she lost all the goods she had managed to salvage from her earlier moves, and when she arrived in England she not only learned of her husband's death but was unsuccessful in her application for a subsistence pension. Refusing to give up, she went to work as a nurse to support her children, and although she described herself to the commission in 1785 as "very Old and feeble," she lived long enough to be granted a permanent annual allowance of £20 in 1789.[38]

Susannah Marshall, though, had years of experience as a tavernkeeper behind her and was thus more capable of coping with her myriad difficulties than were women whose prewar experience had been restricted to their households. Such women recognized that they were "less able than many who never knew happier days to bear hardships and struggle with adversity." These women, especially those who had been, as one of them put it, *"born to better expectations"* in America, spoke despairingly of encounters with "difficultys of which she had no experience in her former life," of "Adversities which not many years before she scarcely thought it possible, that in any situation, she should ever experience."[39]

For women like these, exile in England or Canada was one long nightmare. Their relief requests have a desperate, supplicating tone that is largely absent from those submitted by men. One bewailed the impending birth of her third child, asking, "What can I do in my Condishtion deprived of helth with out Friends or mony with a helpless family to suffer with me?" Another begged the commission's secretary for assistance "with all humility" because "the merciless man I lodge with, threatens to sell the two or three trifling articles I have and put a Padlock on the Room unless I pay him the Rent amounting to near a Pound." By contrast, when a man prepared a memorial for the exceptionally distressed Mrs. Sarah Baker, he coolly told the commissioners that they should assist her because her children "as Soldiers or Sailors in his Majesty's Service may in future compensate the present Expence of saving them."[40]

The straits to which some of the female refugees were driven were dramatically illustrated in early 1783 when a South Carolina woman appeared before the commission "in Rags," explaining that she had been "obliged to pawn her Goods." It was but the first incident of many. Time and again women revealed that they had sold or pawned their clothes—which were usually their most valuable possessions—to buy food for themselves and their children. One was literally "reduced to the last shift" when she testified before the commission; another, the New Yorker Alicia Young, pawned so much that "the want of our apparel made our situation very deplorable" until friends helped her to redeem some of her possessions. Strikingly, no man ever told the commission stories like these. Either male refugees were able to find alternatives to pawning their clothes, or, if they did not, they were too ashamed to admit it.[41]

Such hardships took a terrible mental as well as physical toll. Evidence of extreme mental stress permeates the female loyalists' petitions and letters, while it is largely absent from the memorials of male exiles. The women speak constantly of their "Fear, Fatigue and Anxiety of Mind," their "lowness of Spirit," their "inexpressable" distress, their "accumulated anguish." They repeatedly describe themselves as "desolate and distressed," as "disconsolate, Distressed and helpless . . . with a broken Spirit Ruined health and Constitution," as "Oppressed in body and distressed in mind."[42] "I am overwhelm'd with misfortunes," wrote one. Poverty "distracts and terrifies me," said another; and a third begged "that she may not be left a Prey to Poverty, and her constant companons [*sic*], Calamity and Sorrow." "My pen is unable to describe the horrors of My Mind—or the deploreable Situation of Myself and Infant family," Alicia Young told a member of the commission. "Judge then Dr Sir what is to become of me, or what we are to exist upon—I have no kind of resource. . . . oh Sir the horrors of my Situation is almost too much for me to bear." Most revealing of all was the wife of a Connecticut refugee: "Nature it self languishes," Mary Taylor wrote, "the hours that I should rest, I awake in such an aggitation of mind, as though I had to suffer for sins, that I neaver committed, I allmost shudder when I approache the Doone [doom?]—as every thing appears to be conspired against me, the Baker, and Bucher, seams to be weary of serving me oh porvity what is its Crime, may some have Compassion on those who feeals its power—for I can doo nothing —but baith my infant with my tears—while seeing my Husbands sinking under the waight of his misfortuens, unable to afford me any release."[43]

Even taking into account the likelihood that it was more socially acceptable for women to reveal their emotions, the divergence between men's and women's memorials is too marked to be explained by that factor alone. It is necessary to probe more deeply and to examine men's and women's varying uses of language in order to delineate the full dimensions of the difference.[44] As C. Wright Mills pointed out in an influential article some years ago, actions or motives and the vocabularies utilized to describe them cannot be wholly separated, and commonly used adjectives can therefore reveal the limitations placed on one's actions by one's social role. Mills asserted that "the 'Real Attitude or Motive' is not something different in kind from the verbalization or the 'opinion,' " and that "the long acting out of a role, with its appropriate motives, will often induce a man [or, one is compelled to add, a woman] to become what at first he merely sought to appear." Furthermore, Mills noted, people perceive situations in terms of specific, "delimited" vocabularies, and thus adjectives can themselves promote or deter certain actions. When adjectives are "typical and relatively unquestioned accompaniments of typal situations, " he concluded, "such words often function as directives and incentives by virtue of their being the judgements of others as anticipated by the actor."[45]

In this theoretical context the specific words used by female loyalists may be analyzed as a means of understanding the ways in which they perceived themselves and their circumstances. Their very phraseology—and the manner in which it differs from that of their male counterparts—can provide insights into the matrix of attitudes that helped to shape the way they thought and acted. If Mills is correct, the question whether the women were deliberately telling the commission what they thought it wanted to hear becomes irrelevant: it is enough to say that they were acting in accordance with a prescribed role, and that that role helped to determine how they acted.[46]

With these observations in mind, the fact that the women refugees displayed an intense awareness of their own femininity assumes a crucial significance. The phrases permeate the pages of the petitions from rich and poor alike: "Though a Woman"; "perhaps no Woman in America in equal Circumstances"; "being done by a Woman"; "being a poor lame and infirm Woman." In short, in the female loyalists' minds their actions and abilities were to a certain extent defined by their sex. Femininity was the constant point of reference in measuring their achievements and making their self-assessments. Moreover, the fact of their womanhood was used in a deprecating sense. In their own eyes, they gained merit by not acting like women. Her services were "allmost Matchless, (being done by a Woman)," wrote one; "tho' a Woman, she was the first that went out of the Gates to welcome the Royal Army," declared another. Femininity also provided a ready and plausible excuse for failures of action or of knowledge. A South Carolinian said she had not signed the address to the king in Charleston in 1780 because "it was not posable for a woman to come near the office." A Pennsylvanian apologized for any errors in her loss estimate with the comment, "as far as a Woman can know, she believes the contents to be true." A Nova Scotian said she had not submitted a claim by the deadline because of "being a lone Woman in her Husband's Absence and not having any person to Advise with." A Vermonter made the ultimate argument: "had she been a man, Instead, of a poor helpless woman —should not have faild of being in the British Servace."[47]

The pervasive implication is one of perceived inferiority, and this implication is enhanced by the word women used most often to describe themselves: "helpless." "Being a Poor helpless Widow"; "she is left a helpless Widow"; "a helpless woman advanced in life"; "being a helpless woman": such phrases appear again and again in the claims memorials.[48] Male loyalists might term themselves "very unhappy," "wretched," "extremely distressed," or "exceedingly embarrassed," but *never* were they "helpless." For them, the most characteristic self-description was "unfortunate," a word that carried entirely different, even contrary, connotations.[49] Male loyalists can be said to have seen their circumstances as not of their own making, as even being reversible with luck. The condition of women, however, was inherent in themselves; nothing they could do could change their circumstances. By definition, indeed, they were incapable of helping themselves.

It should be stressed here that, although women commonly described themselves as "helpless," their use of that word did not necessarily mean that they were in fact helpless. It indicates rather that they perceived themselves thus, and that that perception in turn perhaps affected the way they acted (for example, in seeking charitable support instead of looking for work). Similarly, the fact that men failed to utilize the adjective "helpless" to refer to themselves does not mean that they were not helpless, for some of them surely were; it merely shows that—however incorrectly—they did think that they could change their circumstances. These two words, with all their connotations, encapsulate much of the divergence between male and female self-perceptions in late eighteenth-century America, even if they do not necessarily indicate much about the realities of male-female relationships in the colonies.[50]

There was, of course, more to the difference in sex roles than the sex-related ways in which colonial Americans looked at themselves. The claims documents also suggest that women and men placed varying emphases on familial ties. For women, such relationships seemed to take on a special order of magnitude. Specifically, men never said, as several women did, that after their spouses' deaths they were so "inconsolable" that they were unable to function. One woman declared that after her husband's execution by the rebels she was "bereft of her reason for near three months," and another described herself as "rendred almost totally incapable of Even writing my own Name or any assistance in any Shape that Could have the least Tendency to getting my Bread."[51] Furthermore, although loyalist men expressed concern over the plight of the children they could not support adequately, women were much more emotionally involved in the fate of their offspring. "Your goodness will easily conceive, what I must feel for My *Children*," Alicia Young told a claims commissioner; "for myself—I care not—Misfortunes and distress have long since made me totally indifferent to everything in the World but *Them*—they have no provision—no provider—no protector—but God—and me." Women noted that their "Sorrows" were increased by the knowledge that their children were "Partners in this Scene of Indigence." Margaret Draper, widow of a Boston printer, explained that although she had been ill and suffering from a "disorderd Mind," "what adds to my affliction is, my fears for my Daughter, who may soon be left a Stranger and friendless." In the same vein, a New Jersey woman commented that she had "the inexpressible mortification of seeing my Children in want of many necessaries and conveniences. . . . and what still more distresses me, is to think that I am obliged by partaking of it, to lessen even the small portion they have."[52]

The women's emphasis on their families is entirely compatible with the earlier observation concerning the importance of their households in their lives. If their menfolk were preoccupied with the monetary consequences of adhering to the crown, the women were more aware of the human tragedy brought about by the war. They saw their plight and that of their children in much more personal terms than did their husbands. Likewise, they personalized the fact of their exile in a way that male loyalists did not, by almost invariably commenting that they were "left friendless in a strange Country." Refugee men, though they might call themselves "strangers," rarely noted a lack of friends, perhaps because of the coffeehouse networks. To women, by contrast, the fact that they were not surrounded by friends and neighbors seemed calamitous. "I am without Friends or Money," declared one; I am "a friendless, forlorn Woman . . . a Stranger to this Country, and surrounded by evils," said another. She is "far from her native Country, and numerous Friends and Relations where she formerly lived, much respected," wrote a third of her own condition.[53]

When the female refugees talked of settling elsewhere or of returning to the United States, they spoke chiefly of the friends and relatives they would find at their intended destinations. Indeed, it appears from the claims that at least six women went into exile solely because their friends and relatives did. A loyalist woman who remained in the United States after the war explained that she did so because she chose "to reside near my relations [rather] than to carry my family to a strange Country where in case of my death they would be at the mercy of strangers." And Mary Serjeant's description of her situation in America as it would have been had her husband not been a loyalist carried the implication that she wished she too had stayed at home: "His poor Children and disconsolate Widow would now have had a House of their own and some Land adjoining to it And instead of being almost destitute in a Land of Strangers would have remained among some Relatives."[54]

In sum, evidence drawn from the loyalist claims strongly suggests that late-eighteenth-century women had fully internalized the roles laid out for them in the polite literature of the day. Their experience was largely confined to their households, either because they chose that course or because they were forced into it. They perceived themselves as "helpless"—even if at times their actions showed that they were not—and they strongly valued ties with family and friends. When the Revolution tore them from the familiar patterns of their lives in America, they felt abandoned and adrift, far more so than did their male relatives, for whom the human contacts cherished by the women seemed to mean less or at least were more easily replaced by those friendships that persisted into exile.

The picture of the late-eighteenth-century woman that emerges from the loyalist claims, therefore, is of one who was almost wholly domestic, in the sense that that word would be used in the nineteenth-century United States. But at the same time the colonial woman's image of herself lacked the positive attributes with which her nineteenth-century counterpart could presumably console herself. The eighteenth-century American woman was primarily a wife and a mother, but America had not yet developed an ideology that would proclaim the social value of motherhood. That was to come with republicanism—and loyalist women, by a final irony, were excluded by their political allegiance from that republican assurance.[55]

NOTES

Ms. Norton wishes to thank Carol Berkin, Carl Kaestle, Pauline Maier, Robert Wells, and Peter Wood for their comments on an earlier version of this article. A portion of it was read at the Second Berkshire Conference on the History of Women, held at Radcliffe College, Oct. 1974.

1. See, for example, such works as Mary Sumner Benson, *Women in Eighteenth-Century America: A Study of Opinion and Social Usage* (New York, 1935); Elisabeth Anthony Dexter, *Colonial Women of Affairs,* 2d ed. (New York, 1931); and Joan Hoff Wilson, "Dancing Dogs of the Colonial Period: Women Scientists," *Early American Literature,* VII (1973), 225–235. Notable exceptions are Julia Cherry Spruill, *Women's Life and Work in the Southern Colonies* (Chapel Hill, N.C., 1938), and Eugenie Andruss Leonard, *The Dear-Bought Heritage* (Philadelphia, 1965). On the importance of the early American family see David Rothman, "A Note on the Study of the Colonial Family," *William and Mary Quarterly,* 3d Ser., XXIII (1966), 627–634.

2. Two recent works that deal with family size, among other topics, are Robert V. Wells, "Household Size and Composition in the British Colonies in America, 1675–1775," *Journal of Interdisciplinary History,* IV (1974), 543–570, and Daniel Scott Smith, "Population, Family and Society in Hingham, Massachusetts, 1635–1880" (Ph.D. diss., University of California, Berkeley,

1973). Internal household relationships in 17th-century New England have been analyzed by Edmund S. Morgan, *The Puritan Family: Religion & Domestic Relations in Seventeenth-Century New England* (Boston, 1944), and John Demos, *A Little Commonwealth: Family Life in Plymouth Colony* (New York, 1970).

3. Barbara Welter, "The Cult of True Womanhood, 1820–1860," *American Quarterly*, XVII (1966), 151–174, was the first to outline the dimensions of this ideology. For writings dealing with some of the implications of the "cult of domesticity" see Carroll Smith-Rosenberg, "The Hysterical Woman: Sex Roles and Role Conflict in 19th-Century America," *Social Research*, XXXIX (1972), 652–678; Ann Douglas Wood, "Mrs. Sigourney and the Sensibility of the Inner Space," *New England Quarterly*, XLV (1972), 163–181; Kathryn Kish Sklar, *Catharine Beecher: A Study in American Domesticity* (New Haven, Conn., 1973); and Nancy Falik Cott, "In the Bonds of Womanhood: Perspectives on Female Experience and Consciousness in New England, 1780–1830" (Ph.D. diss., Brandeis University, 1974), esp. chap. 6. An explicit assertion that women were better off in 18th-century America than they were later is found in Dexter, *Colonial Women of Affairs*, vii, 189–192, and in Page Smith, *Daughters of the Promised Land* (Boston, 1970), 37–76. But two European historians have appropriately warned that it may be dangerous to assume the existence of a "golden, preindustrial age" for women, noting that the "goldenness is seen almost exclusively in terms of women's work and its presumed relationship to family power, not in terms of other vital aspects of their lives, including the physical burdens of work and child bearing." Patricia Branca and Peter N. Stearns, "On the History of Modern Women, a Research Note," *AHA Newsletter*, XII (Sept. 1974), 6.

4. For example, John Shy, "The American Revolution: The Military Conflict Considered as a Revolutionary War," in Stephen G. Kurtz and James H. Hutson, eds., *Essays on the American Revolution* (Chapel Hill, N.C., 1973), 121–156; John Shy, "The Loyalist Problem in the Lower Hudson Valley: The British Perspective," in Robert A. East and Jacob Judd, eds., *The Loyalist Americans: A Focus on Greater New York* (Tarrytown, N.Y., 1975), 3–13; and Ronald Hoffman, *A Spirit of Dissension: Economics, Politics, and the Revolution in Maryland* (Baltimore, 1973), esp. chaps. 6, 8.

5. Catherine S. Crary, "The Humble Immigrant and the American Dream: Some Case Histories, 1746–1776," *Mississippi Valley Historical Review*, XLVI (1959), 46–66.

6. For a detailed examination of the claims process see Mary Beth Norton, *The British-Americans: The Loyalist Exiles in England, 1774–1789* (Boston, 1972), 185–222. More than 468 women appear in the claims documents; excluded from the sample selected for this article are all female children, all English women who never lived in America (but who were eligible for compensation as heirs of loyalists), and all American women who did not personally pursue a claim (that is, whose husbands took the entire responsibility for presenting the family's claims). In addition to those requesting reimbursement for property losses, the sample includes a number of women —mostly the very poor, who had lost only a small amount of property, if any —who applied solely for the subsistence pensions which were also awarded by the claims commissioners. On the allowance system see *ibid.*, 52–61, 111–121, and 225–229.

7. On the statistical biases of the loyalist claims see Eugene Fingerhut, "Uses and Abuses of the American Loyalists' Claims: A Critique of Quantitative Analyses," *WMQ*, 3d Ser., XXV (1968), 245–258.

8. This approach to women in the Revolutionary era differs from the traditional focus on their public contributions to the war effort. See, for example, Elizabeth F. Ellet, *The Women of the American Revolution* (New York, 1848–1850); Walter Hart Blumenthal, *Women Camp Followers of the American Revolution* (Philadelphia, 1952); Elizabeth Cometti, "Women in the American Revolution," *NEQ*, XX (1947), 329–346; and Linda Grant DePauw, *Four Traditions: Women of New York during the American Revolution* (Albany, 1974).

9. Only if they intended to commit fraud could loyalists gain by withholding information from the commission; two refugees, for example, requested compensation for property they had already sold during the war. But the commissioners found deliberately fraudulent only 10 of the claims submitted to them, and although they disallowed others for "gross prevarication," none of the claims falling into either category were submitted by women. See Norton, *British-Americans*, 217–219, on the incidence of fraud, and 203–205, 216–217, on the importance of accurate testimony.

10. Joyce Dawson, testimony, May 5, 1787, A.O. 12/56, 330, Public Record Office; Isabella McLaurin, testimony, Nov. 27, 1784, A.O. 12/47, 233; Margaret Hutchinson, testimony, Aug. 10, 1786, A.O. 12/16, 34; Margaret Reynolds, testimony, Dec. 9, 1783, A.O. 12/46, 168; case of Mrs. Bowers, Feb. 24, 1783, A.O. 12/99, 48; Elizabeth Campbell, testimony, n.d., A.O. 12/26, 267. For other similar statements see A.O. 12/10, 254, A.O. 12/48, 233, A.O. 12/50, 390–391, and A.O. 13/68, pt. 1, 183.

11. Frances Dongan, testimony, Dec. 6, 1784, A.O. 12/13, 267–272; case of Charlotte Pollock, June 27, 1783, A.O. 12/99, 336; Mary Ann Balfour, testimony, Mar. 13, 1786, A.O. 12/48, 242; Janet Murchison, testimony, July 26, 1786, A.O. 12/34, 405; Mary Kearsley, testimony, Apr. 28, 1785, A.O. 12/38, 282. Cf. Mrs. Kearsley's testimony with her written memorial, A.O. 13/102, 324–329. And see, for other examples, A.O. 12/4, 220, A.O. 12/14, 265, A.O. 12/47, 239, A.O. 13/63, 342, and A.O. 13/94, 318–326.

12. Isabella Logan, loss schedule, Feb. 17, 1784, A.O. 13/32, 129; case of Lady Leigh, July 1, 1783, A.O. 12/99, 313. See also the claim of Mary Auchmuty, A.O. 12/24, 114–117, 264–266, and A.O. 13/63, 133–140.

13. Sarah Troutbeck to commissioners, June 5, 1787, A.O. 13/49, pt. 2, 565; Troutbeck to Samuel Peters, May 22, 1788, Peters Papers, III, fol. 83 (microfilm), New-York Historical Society, New York City; Troutbeck to commissioners, Jan. 3, 1785, A.O. 13/137, 609. Her total claim covers fols. 539–590 in A.O. 13/49, pt. 2, and fols. 726–740 in A.O. 13/74. On the recovery of her property see A.O. 12/81, 47. For other examples of well-to-do women with a good knowledge of the family property see A.O. 13/134, 571–574, and A.O. 12/54, 61–71 (Mary Rothery), A.O. 13/64, 81–99, and A.O. 13/97, 344–348 (Henrietta Colden), and A.O. 12/13, 311–314 (Mary Poynton). Mary Winslow knew her own property in detail but was not so familiar with her husband's (A.O. 13/79, 757–758).

14. Case of Mrs. Dumaresq, Mar. 31, 1783, A.O. 12/99, 134; case of Margaret Smithies, Nov. 13, 1783, A.O. 12/100, 66; case of Barbara Mergath, May 8, 1783, A.O. 12/99, 234; Jane Gibbes, testimony, Dec. 15, 1783, A.O. 12/46, 245–247.

15. Jane Gibbes, testimony, Dec. 16, 1783; A.O. 12/46, 247–249; Widow Boyce, loss schedule, Oct 16, 1783, A.O. 13/90, 181; Elizabeth Hogal, loss schedule, n.d., A.O. 12/27, 37. Typical examples of claims submitted by rural women may be found in A.O. 13/56, 91–93, A.O. 13/138, 475, A.O. 12/4, 72–74, A.O. 12/20, 270–271, A.O. 12/26, 14–16, and A.O. 12/29, 79. Cf. claims

from rural men in A.O. 13/79, 73–77, 211–216. For a claim involving property owned elsewhere see that of Elinor Maybee, A.O. 12/28, 343–346, and A.O. 12/64, 1; for one involving both a mortgage and a misread will see that of Margaret Hutchinson, A.O. 12/16, 33–37, and A.O. 12/63, 61.

16. Mary McAlpin, loss schedule, n.d., A.O. 13/131, 10–11, and testimony, Nov. 14, 1785, A.O. 12/21, 51–65.

17. The list totals more than 40 because some women listed two enterprises. The women divided as follows: 10 each from New York City and Charleston, 7 each from Boston and Philadelphia, 2 from Baltimore, and 1 each from Savannah, Williamsburg, Wilmington, N.C., and St. Augustine. Twenty-eight were long-time widows or single, or were married but operated businesses independently of their husbands; 8 assisted their husbands; and 7 took over businesses after the death or incapacitation of their husbands.

18. The quotation is from Rachel Wetmore, claims memorial, Mar. 25, 1786, A.O. 13/16, 271. For a milliner's claim see Margaret Hutchinson's, A.O. 13/96, 601–602; for a grocer and boardinghouse keeper's see Sarah Simpson's, A.O. 12/25, 25–28. The midwife, Janet Cumming, claimed to have made £400 sterling annually, and her witnesses confirmed that estimate (A.O. 12/50, 347–348). See also Margaret Draper's original and revised loss estimates, A.O. 13/44, 342–344, 387, and Mary Airey's schedule, A.O. 12/24, 79.

19. Hannah Pollard, claims memorial and testimony, A.O. 13/49, pt. 1, 158–159, 166; testimony re: claim of Mary Campbell, Oct 24, 1786, A.O. 12/50, 103–105. The detailed schedule presented by the tavernkeeper Rachel Brain had been prepared by her husband before his death; see A.O. 12/26, 308–310.

20. For a general discussion of claims receipts see Norton, *British-Americans,* 216–220. Property claims submitted by 10 of the businesswomen were disallowed, and at least another 10 of them apparently did not pursue a claim for lost property. (Because of the destruction and disappearance of some of the claims records it is impossible to be more precise.)

21. This emphasis appears to have resulted from the influence of Dexter's *Colonial Women of Affairs.* Although she was careful to explain that she had searched only for examples of women who worked outside the home, and although she did not attempt to estimate the percentage of such women in the female population as a whole, historians who draw upon her book invariably stress the wide-ranging economic interests of colonial women. See, for example, Gerda Lerner, *The Woman in American History* (Reading, Mass., 1971), 15–19, and Carol Ruth Berkin, *Within the Conjuror's Circle: Women in Colonial America* (Morristown, N.J., 1974), 8–10.

22. If anything, the loyalist claimants tended to be more urban than other loyalists and the rest of the American population, and therefore would presumably overrepresent working women. See the analysis in Norton, *British-Americans,* 37–39, and Fingerhut, "Uses and Abuses of Loyalists' Claims," *WMQ,* 3d Ser., XXV (1968), 245–258. Further, the method of choosing the sample—including only those women who themselves submitted claims and pension applications—would also tend to bias the result in favor of working women, since they would be the most likely to act on their own.

23. The failure of 18th-century men to discuss finances with their wives is also revealed in such letters as that of Jane Robbins to her daughter Hannah Gilman, Sept. 1799, Gilman Papers, Massachusetts Historical Society,

Boston. Mrs. Robbins declared that, although her husband had made his will some years before, "I never saw it till after his death." Further, she informed her daughter, on his deathbed he told her, "I should have many debts to pay that I knew nothing about."

24. Berkin, *Conjuror's Circle,* 12–14, and Nancy F. Cott, ed., *Root of Bitterness: Documents of the Social History of American Women* (New York, 1972), 8–10, link sex role differentiation specifically to the upper classes that were emerging in the process which has been called "Europeanization" or "Anglicization."

25. See, for example, Spruill, *Women's Life and Work,* 78–79.

26. David Ingersoll to commissioners, July 30, 1788, A.O. 13/74, 288. For rare cases of men who did list household furnishings see A.O. 13/98, 431–432, and A.O. 13/73, 140–155.

27. Martha Leslie, loss schedule, Mar. 25, 1784, A.O. 13/91, 2–3; Frances Dongan, inventory, [Nov. 1, 1783], A.O. 13/109, 45; Catherine Bowles, loss schedule, May 10, 1783, A.O. 13/90, 175–176; Mary Swords, "Things Plundered from me by the Rebels," n.d., A.O. 13/67, 311.

28. Mary Gibbins, loss schedule, n.d., A.O. 13/80, 167; "Estimate of Losses sustained at New York by Hannah Foy in the year 1775" [1782], A.O. 13/54, 431; Elizabeth Bowers, loss schedule, n.d., A.O. 13/68, pt. 1, 64.

29. Sarah Stuart, memorial to Lords of Treasury, Jan. 22, 1786, A.O. 13/135, 702; Elizabeth Phillips, affidavit, Oct. 9, 1788, A.O. 13/67, 303; Phebe Stevens, claims memorial, Mar. 23, 1784, A.O. 13/83, 580. For accounts of rebel looting see, for example, A.O. 12/56, 326–327, A.O. 13/73, 485, A.O. 13/91, 190, A.O. 13/93, 556, A.O. 13/102, 1278, A.O. 13/109, 43, A.O. 13/121, 478, and A.O. 13/126, 589.

30. See, for example, A.O. 12/21, 53–54, A.O. 13/110, 351, A.O. 13/112, 55, A.O. 13/123, 240–241; A.O. 13/128, 7, and A.O. 13/135, 698. Two women said they suffered miscarriages as a result of scuffles with Revolutionary troops (A.O. 13/81, 59, and A.O. 13/64, 76–77), and a third was raped by a rebel soldier. The latter incident is discussed in Thomas Goldthwait to his daughter Catherine, Aug. 20, 1779, J. M. Robbins Papers, Mass. Hist. Soc.

31. Lorenda Holmes, claims memorial, n.d., A.O. 13/65, 529–530. Similar though less graphic tales were recounted by other women whose assistance to the British was also discovered by the Revolutionaries. See A.O. 12/49, 56–58, A.O. 12/102, 80. A.O. 13/45, 530, A.O. 13/67, 192, A.O. 13/68, 125, A.O. 13/96, 263, and A.O. 13/102, 1107.

32. Mary Serjeant, loss schedule, Feb. 19, 1783, A.O. 13/49, pt. 1, 285; Christian Barnes to Elizabeth Smith, July 13–28, 1770, Christian Barnes Letterbook, Library of Congress; Barnes to Elizabeth Smith Inman, Apr. [2]9, [1775], in Nina Moore Tiffany, ed., *Letters of James Murray, Loyalist* (Boston, 1901), 187–188.

33. Louisa Susannah Wells Aikman, *The Journal of a Voyage from Charlestown, S.C., to London undertaken during the American Revolution . . .* (New York, 1906), 52; Catherine Goldthwait to Elizabeth [Inman], Mar. 27, 1780, Robbins Papers, Mass. Hist. Soc. For a discussion of the loyalists' initial optimism and subsequent disillusionment see Mary Beth Norton, "The Loyalists' Image of England: Ideal and Reality," *Albion,* III (1971), 62–71.

34. Hannah Winslow to [a sister-in-law], June 27, 1779, Winslow Papers, Mass. Hist. Soc. See also Rebecca Dolbeare to John Dolbeare, Aug. 30, 1780, Dolbeare Papers, Mass. Hist. Soc.; Polly Dibblee to William Jarvis,

Nov. 1787, A.O. 13/41, 248. For a general discussion of the exiles' financial problems see Norton, *British-Americans*, 49–61. For another similar observation by a single woman see Louisa Oliver to Andrew Spooner, Mar. 1, 1788, Hutchinson-Oliver Papers, Mass. Hist. Soc.

35. The quotation is from the case of Mary Hind, Feb. 1783, A.O. 12/99, 35. For examples of other women who claimed ignorance of proper forms and application procedures see A.O. 12/46, 165, A.O. 12/99, 238, A.O. 13/24, 284, A.O. 13/26, 63, 199, 282, 360, A.O. 13/113, 88, A.O. 13/131, 65, and A.O. 13/137, 150. Of course, a few men also made similar claims; see, for example, A.O. 12/43, 322–325, 328–331, and A.O. 12/46, 63. On the male networks see Norton, *British Americans*, 63–79, 162–164, 186–196, 206–216. The memorials submitted by women were not only more prone to error but also more informal, less likely to be written in the third person, less likely to contain the sorts of ritualistic phrases and arguments used by the men, and consequently more likely to be personally revealing.

36. Norton, *British-Americans*, 52–61, 111–121, discusses the bases of pension decisions. It was standard practice for the commission to lower a family's allotment immediately after the death of the husband, regardless of the fact that the widow usually had to meet medical and funeral expenses at exactly that time. The pension records (A.O. 12/99–105, and T. 50/11ff, Public Record Office) show that women's pensions were normally smaller than men's. In addition, T. 50/11 reveals a clear case of discrimination: in 1789 the Charleston midwife Janet Cumming (see note 18 above) was, under the commission's rules, entitled to an annual pension of £200 for loss of profession (she was the only woman to qualify for one in her own right); instead, she was granted only a £50 widow's allowance.

37. Mary Serjeant to John Wilmot and Daniel P. Coke, Dec. 1, 1782, A.O. 13/49, pt. 1, 283; Ann Asby to commissioners, Apr. 14, 1788, A.O. 13/43, 147; Susanna Sandys, memorial, n.d., A.O. 13/84, 613. (Sandys was English, though the daughter of a refugee, and is quoted here because of the detailed nature of her comments.) For a statement similar to Mrs. Serjeant's see Margaret Smythies to Lords of Treasury, Jan. 23, 1782, A.O. 13/67, 230. For two women who did explain why they could not work see A.O. 13/75, 627, and A.O. 13/53, 193. Information about nearly all the loyalist women who worked in England may be located in the following documents: A.O. 12/30, 230, A.O. 12/99, 50, 244, 264, A.O. 12/101, 137, A.O. 12/102, 87, 136, 164, 165, 175, 187, A.O. 13/43, 661, A.O. 13/44, 427, A.O. 13/71, 156, and A.O. 13/131, 359.

38. On the Wells sisters' enterprise see Steuart Papers, 5041, fol. 123, National Library of Scotland, Edinburgh; Ann Elmsley to James Parker [1789?], Parker Papers, Pt. IV, no. 15, Liverpool Record Office, England; and Aikman, *Journal of a Voyage*, 71. Susannah Marshall's story may be traced in A.O. 13/62, 4, 7, A.O. 12/6, 257–263, and A.O. 12/99, 244.

39. Harriet, Mary, Sarah, and Elizabeth Dawson and Ann Dawson Murray to commissioners, n.d., A.O. 13/113, 195; Mary Muirson to Lords of Treasury, May 28, 1784, A.O. 13/56, 342; Isabella Logan, claims memorial, Feb. 17, 1784, A.O. 13/32, 126; Patience Johnston, claims memorial, Dec. 21, 1785, A.O. 13/26, 196. For similar statements see A.O. 13/40, 93, A.O. 13/75, 354, 603, A.O. 13/132, 257, and A.O. 13/134, 504.

40. Mary Lowry to [Samuel Remnant], n.d., A.O. 13/31, 202; Mary Curtain to Charles Monro, July 7, 1789, A.O. 13/137, 98; Samuel Peters to Daniel P. Coke, Nov. 20, 1784, A.O. 13/43, 352. Cf. the statements in the text with

those of men; for example, Samuel Porter to Lords of Treasury, Feb. 23, 1776, T. 1/520, 27; Thomas Banks to Lords of Treasury, Feb. 9, 1779, T. 1/552, 3; John Saunders to Lords of Treasury, Mar. 31, 1785, F.O. 4/1, 248, Public Record Office.

41. Case of Margaret Reynolds, Mar. 26, 1783, A.O. 12/99, 116; Charlotte Mayne to—[Aug. 1783], H.O. 42/3, Public Record Office; Alicia Young to Robert Mackenzie, June 3, 1789, A.O. 13/67, 641. Mrs. Young gave the commissioners a detailed list of the items she had pawned (A.O. 13/67, 646). For other similar accounts of women pawning or selling their goods see A.O. 12/99, 13, 56, 60. A.O. 12/101, 196, 364, A.O. 13/43, 350, A.O. 13/64, 76, and A.O. 13/135, 81, 426.

42. "Mrs Derbage's Narrative," Mar. 1789, A.O. 13/34, 298; Penelope Nicoll, deposition, July 6, 1787, A.O. 13/68, 267; Mary Broadhead to commissioners, Nov. 12, 1788, A.O. 13/125, 626; Margaret Draper to John Robinson, June 27, 1777, A.O. 13/44, 345; Rose Brailsford to Lords of Treasury, Dec. 29, 1779, A.O. 13/125, 580; Joyce Dawson to Lord Dunmore, July 24, 1781, A.O. 13/28, 220; Charlotte Pollock to Lords of Treasury, n.d., A.O. 13/133, 442.

43. Lucy Necks to Lady North, Aug. 14, 1781, A.O. 13/32, 155; Elizabeth Barkesdale to commissioners, Nov. 24, 1786, A.O. 13/125, 402; Lydia Doty to Lords of Treasury, May 8, 1782, A.O. 13/113, 328; Alicia Young to Robert Mackenzie, June 6, 1789, A.O. 13/67, 643; Mary Taylor to commissioners, Apr. 12, 1783, A.O. 13/42, 590. In sharp contrast to such statements, Andrew Allen, a male refugee, wrote in Feb. 1783, "Notwithstanding what has happened I have the Satisfaction to feel my Spirits unbroken and my Mind prepared to look forwards without Despondency." Allen to James Hamilton, Feb. 3, 1783, Dreer Collection, Historical Society of Pennsylvania, Philadelphia.

44. Recent articles by linguists raise provocative questions about sex differences in speech. Most of them are concerned with 20th-century oral expression, however, and it is difficult to determine how accurately they apply to 18th-century documents. Among the most interesting are Nancy Faires Conklin, "Toward a Feminist Analysis of Linguistic Behavior," *University of Michigan Papers in Women's Studies*, I (1974), 51–73; Mary Ritchie Key, "Linguistic Behavior of Male and Female," *Linguistics: An International Review*, LXXXVIII (1972), 15–31; Cheris Kramer, "Women's Speech: Separate but Unequal?," *The Quarterly Journal of Speech*, LX (1974), 14–24; and Robin Lakoff, "Language and Woman's Place," *Language in Society*, II (1974), 45–79.

45. C. Wright Mills, "Situated Actions and Vocabularies of Motive," *American Sociological Review*, V (1940), 904–913, esp. 906–909.

46. The only woman claimant who appears to have manipulatively assumed a "feminine" role was Sarah Troutbeck. It is also difficult to determine, first, what it was that the commission "wanted" to hear from female loyalists and, second, how the women would know what the commission wanted, given their isolation from the male information networks. It could perhaps be argued that every 18th-century woman "knew" what every 18th-century man expected of her, but the fact is that the women claimants had a great deal to gain by displaying a very "unfeminine" knowledge of their husband's estates and by demonstrating their competence to the commission. See, for example, A.O. 12/101, 186, A.O. 12/40, 40–44, and A.O. 12/66, 6.

47. The long quotations: Margaret Hutchinson, claims memorial, Feb.

23, 1784, A.O. 13/96, 601; Eleanor Lestor, claims memorial, n.d., A.O. 12/48, 359; Elizabeth Thompson to John Forster, Dec. 21, 1785, A.O. 13/136, 8; Mary Kearsley, testimony, Apr. 28, 1785, A.O. 12/38, 282; Mary Williams, affidavit, Dec. 21, 1785, A.O. 13/26, 535; Catherine Chilsom, claims memorial, Mar. 11, 1786, A.O. 13/24, 90. The shorter phrases: A.O. 13/16, 271, A.O. 13/24, 357, A.O. 13/26, 357.

48. A.O. 13/118, 488, A.O. 13/67, 234, A.O. 13/73, 586, A.O. 13/81, 59. Men also described women in the same terms; for examples see A.O. 13/28, 215, and A.O. 12/101, 235. The widows of Revolutionary soldiers also called themselves "helpless"; see, for example, Papers of the Continental Congress, V, 16 (M-41), Roll 50, V, 37, 122 (M-42), Roll 55, National Archives.

49. T. 1/612, 157, A.O. 13/53, 62, A.O. 13/137, 574, A.O. 12/8, 124. For a few "unfortunate" men see A.O. 12/46, 104, A.O. 12/51, 208, A.O. 12/13, 188, and A.O. 12/42, 132.

50. The women who were most definitely not helpless (for example, Susannah Marshall, Janet Cumming, and Sarah Troutbeck) did not use that word to describe themselves. Consequently, it appears that the term was not simply a formulaic one utilized by all women indiscriminately, but rather that it represented a real self-perception of those who did use it. At least one 18th-century woman recognized the sex-typed usage of the word "helpless." In her book of essays, Judith Sargent Murray noted that she hoped that "the term, *helpless widow*, might be rendered as unfrequent and inapplicable as that of *helpless widower*." See Judith Sargent Murray, *The Gleaner*, III (Boston, 1789), 223.

51. Isabella Logan, claims memorial, Feb. 17, 1784, A.O. 13/32, 126; Jane Hilding, claims memorial, July 30, 1788, A.O. 13/46, 315; Joyce Dawson to Lord Dunmore, July 24, 1781, A.O. 13/28, 220. Also of interest is Jane Constable to Lords of Treasury, n.d., A.O. 13/73, 374.

52. Alicia Young to Robert Mackenzie, June 6, 1789, A.O. 13/67, 643; Jane Roberts, claims memorial, Mar. 17, 1784, A.O. 13/71, 245; Margaret Draper to Lord ______, Oct. 15, 1782, A.O. 13/44, 349; Elizabeth Skinner to commissioners, Aug. 28, 1786, A.O. 13/112, 61. Mrs. Draper lived to see her daughter well married (Margaret Draper to the Misses Byles, June 21, 1784, Byles Papers, I, 134, Mass. Hist. Soc.). Cf. men's attitudes toward their children and other dependents in A.O. 13/75, 556, A.O. 12/105, 115, A.O. 13/131, 399, and A.O. 13/137, 2.

53. Elizabeth Putnam to Thomas Dundas, Nov. 7, 1789, A.O. 13/75, 309; Elizabeth Dumaresq to Lord Shelburne, Sept. 14, 1872, A.O. 13/44, 429; Elizabeth Barkesdale to commissioners, Nov. 24, 1786, A.O. 13/125, 402, Rachel Wetmore, claims memorial, Mar. 25, 1786, A.O. 13/16, 272. Other comments on neighbors and relatives may be found in A.O. 12/3, 231, A.O. 12/56, 339, A.O. 13/25, 275, A.O. 13/32, 595, A.O. 13/44, 345, A.O. 13/75, 544, 641, and A.O. 13/107, 271. Mr. and Mrs. James Parker had an interesting exchange of letters on the subject of whether she would join him in England, in which her ties to her American friends figured strongly. "Tho I would not hesitate one moment to go with you my Dearest friend to any place on earth, yet I cannot think of parting forever with my Dear and valuable friends on this side the atlantick, without many a heart felt sigh," she wrote on July 24, 1783. His response (Mar. 5, 1784) recognized her concern: "I realy sympathize with you on this trying scene of leaving of your Country and all our friends." Parker Papers, Pt. VIII, nos. 26, 31, Liverpool Record Office.

54. Elizabeth Macnair to John Hamilton, Dec. 27, 1789, A.O. 13/131,

400; Mary Serjeant to John Wilmot and Daniel P. Coke, Dec. 1, 1782, A.O. 13/49, pt. 1, 283. See also A.O. 13/34, 471, and A.O. 13/70B, 145, on resettlement. For women who followed friends and relatives into exile see A.O. 13/116, 468, A.O. 13/114, 662, A.O. 12/102, 24, and A.O. 13/37, 3.

55. On the development of republican ideology pertaining to women see Linda K. Kerber, "Daughters of Columbia: Educating Women for the Republic, 1787–1805," in Stanley Elkins and Eric McKitrick, eds., *The Hofstadter Aegis* (New York, 1974), 36–59.

6

Passionlessness

An Interpretation of Victorian Sexual Ideology, 1790–1850

■

NANCY F. COTT

In our own post-Freudian era most people frankly acknowledge the formative power of sexuality and sexual drives in both men and women, and distinguish current attitudes by means of an implicit contrast to more restrictive Victorian ideas. There are as forceful stereotypes of the "Victorian" as of the "Puritan" in circulation today (and the two are often conflated, although they represent two very different eras and personalities). A hallmark of Victorian sexual ideology, in most people's minds, is its insistence that women properly lacked sexual passion. Nancy F. Cott appraises the origins and meaning of that idea, examining it from the two perspectives of cultural prescription and women's consciousness.

IN 1903 HAVELOCK ELLIS announced that the notion of women's sexual "anaesthesia," as he called it, was a nineteenth-century creation. He had researched literary and medical sources from ancient Greece to early modern Europe and discovered, to his own amazement, that women had generally been thought to desire and enjoy sexual relations more than men.[1] Ellis and his contemporaries initially sought the source of the idea that women lacked sexual passion in the generations immediately preceding their own. The late nineteenth century was an era of contention over female sexuality, physiology, health, dress, and exercise, and one in which medical opinion had become an authoritative sector of public opinion. Since investigators have found rich documentation on these controversies, particularly in medical sources, they have been little induced to look beyond them. Until quite recently, historians tended not only to follow Ellis's chronological bias but, like him, to associate the idea that women lacked sexual passion with social repression and dysfunction. Now that attitude has been challenged by the possibility that nineteenth-century sexual ideology held some definite advantages for women, and by the claim that ideology reflected or influenced behavior far less than had been thought.[2]

A full appraisal of the idea that women lacked sexual passion requires an investigation of its origins. My purpose is to offer a hypothesis, if not a proven case, regarding the initiation and reception of that central tenet of Victorian sexual ideology which I call "passionlessness." I use the term to convey the view that women lacked sexual aggressiveness, that their sexual appetites contributed a very minor part (if any at all) to their motivations, that lustfulness was simply uncharacteristic. The concept of passionlessness represented a cluster of ideas about the comparative weight of woman's carnal nature and her moral nature; it indicated more about drives and temperament than about actions and is to be understood more metaphorically than literally.

Obviously, a single conception of women's sexuality never wholly prevails. Western civilization up to the eighteenth century, as Ellis discovered, accentuated women's concupiscence: a fifteenth-century witch-hunters' guide warned, for instance, that "carnal lust . . . in women is insatiable."[3] But the Christian belief system that called unsanctified earthly women the devil's agents allowed, on the other hand, that women who embodied God's grace were more spiritual, hence less susceptible to carnal passion, than men. Nineteenth-century views of female sexuality were also double edged: notions of women's inherent licentiousness persisted, to be wielded against women manifesting any form of deviance under the reign of passionlessness. Acknowledging that notions of women's sexuality are never monolithic, I would nonetheless emphasize that there was a traditionally dominant Anglo-American definition of women as *especially* sexual which was reversed and transformed between the seventeenth and the nineteenth centuries into the view that women (although still primarily identified by their female gender) were *less* carnal and lustful than men.

The following pages focus on early appearances of the idea of female passionlessness, discuss its social context, and analyze if and why it was acceptable, especially to women. The documents in this test case are limited to New England; to apply the interpretive paradigm to literate, Protestant, middle-class women elsewhere would require further testing. I have looked to women's public and private writings in order to put the women involved in the forefront and prevent viewing them as passive recipients of changing ideas. My other sources are largely didactic and popular works, especially religious ones, which influenced women. Most of what is known about sexual ideology before the twentieth century comes from "prescriptive" sources—those manuals, essays, and books that tried to establish norms of behavior. Although religious views, expressed in sermons and tracts, were the most direct and commanding "prescriptions" from the seventeenth through the early nineteenth centuries, they have not been so finely combed for evidence of sexual norms as has been medical advice, a comparable source of "prescriptions" for the later nineteenth century.[4] Religious opinion is particularly relevant to this inquiry because of the churches' hold on the female population. Women became a majority in the Protestant churches of America in the mid-seventeenth century and continued to increase their numerical predominance until, by the mid-nineteenth century, "Christian" values and virtues and "female" values and virtues were almost identical.[5] In my view, the ideology of passionlessness was tied to the rise of evangelical religion between the 1790s and the 1830s. Physicians' adoption of passionlessness was a second wave, so to speak, beginning at mid-century. By the time that physicians took up the question of passionlessness and attempted to reduce the concept to "scientific" and somatic quantities the idea had been diffused through the spiritual realm and had already engendered its own opposition.[6]

Early American prescriptive and legal documents suggest that the New England colonists expected women's sexual appetites to be comparable with men's, if not greater.[7] Calvinists assumed that men and women in their "fallen" state were equally licentious, that sexual drives were natural and God-given in both sexes, and had their proper outlet in marriage. If anything, the daughters of Eve were considered more prone to excess of passion because their rational control was seen as weaker. And yet it was objectionable for women to exercise the sexual initiative; regardless of women's sexual drives, the religious and social context required female subordination. Puritan theology weakened but did not destroy the double standard of sexual morality. In colonial law, for example, fornication was punished equally in either sex, but adultery was defined by the participation of a married woman. A married man did not commit adultery but fornication—unless he took up with another man's wife. In Massachusetts until the Revolutionary period, a wife's adultery was always cause for her husband to divorce her, but wives had little success in freeing themselves from unfaithful husbands. Men also won suits to recover "damages" from their wives' lovers.[8] As Keith Thomas has put it, such suits reflected the underlying tenet of the double standard: "the view that men have property in women and that the value of this property is immeasurably diminished if the woman at any time has sexual relations with anyone other than her husband."[9] There was vast potential for sexual exploitation in a society in which women's sexual nature was considered primary and their social autonomy was slight.[10] The physical and biological consequences of sexual adventure also burdened women more heavily than men in an era lacking effective means to prevent conception or infection.

In the second century of colonial settlement one finds many more numerous prescriptions for the role of women. The reasons for this increase are diverse: new class concern for standards of distinction and taste, the spread of literacy, the growth of printing and journalism, and "enlightened" interest in reformulating social systems and personal relations in "natural," "rational," rather than scriptural, terms. Britain led in discussions of female character and place, setting sex-role conventions for the literate audience.[11] Since British social ideals became more influential in the mid-eighteenth century with the decline in Puritanism, the diffusion of Protestant energies, and the growth of an affluent urban class in the colonies, British "prescriptions" must be taken into consideration. At least three phases of British opinion contributed to the development of the idea of passionlessness. In the beginning of the century when spokesmen for the new professional and commercial middle class began explicitly to oppose aristocratic pretension, vanity, and libertinism, reforming writers such as Daniel Defoe, Jeremy Collier, Richard Steele, and Samuel Richardson portrayed sexual promiscuity as one of those aristocratic excesses that threatened middle-class virtue and domestic security. Their kind of propriety led to an ideal of sexual self-control, verbal prudery, and opposition to the double standard of sexual morality (for the sake of purity for men rather than justice for women). Due to their influence, in part, "the eighteenth century witnessed a redefinition of virtue in primarily sexual terms," Ian Watt has pointed out. By elevating sexual control highest among human virtues the middle-class moralists made female chastity the archetype for human morality.[12]

Out of the upper class came a different prescriptive genre, the etiquette manual. The ones most available to middle-class women in America, such as George Savile's *A Lady's New Year's Gift* or John Gregory's *A Father's Legacy to His Daughters,* consistently held that woman was made for man's pleasure and service; woman was strong only insofar as she could use her own weakness to manipulate the opposite sex (within the bounds of social propriety).[13] These authors advised a great deal of restraint and affectation (not to mention deception) in women's behavior. At the same time, modesty and demureness took center stage among the female virtues enshrined. According to Keith Thomas, the idea of passionlessness emerged in this context as an extension of the ideal of chastity needed to protect men's property rights in women; it was a reification in "nature" of the double standard.[14] Yet it must be objected that in the nineteenth century women who believed in passionlessness usually rejected the double standard of sexual morality. Modesty was the quintessential female virtue in works such as Gregory's, but, amid the manipulative and affected tactics advised, it connoted only demure behavior —a good act—not, necessarily, passionlessness. Indeed, the underlying theme that women had to appeal to men turned modesty into a sexual ploy, emphasizing women's sex objectification.[15] John Gregory did hint that sexual desire was weaker in women, with their "superior delicacy," than in men. He was sure that nature had assigned to wives rather than husbands the "reserve" which would prevent "satiety and disgust" in marital relations.[16] But not until a third phase at the close of the century did emphasis move implacably from modesty to passionlessness, under the Evangelical aegis.

The British Evangelicals were conservative reformers horrified at the French Revolution and its "godlessness"; they worked to regenerate Protestantism in order to secure social and political order. Like earlier middle-class moralists, the Evangelicals opposed aristocratic blasphemies and profligacy, cherished family life, and advocated chastity and prudence in both sexes. Because they observed women's greater piety, and hoped that women would influence men and the next generation, they focused much of their proselytizing zeal on women. In contrast to earlier eighteenth-century didacts, they harped on the theme that women were made for God's purposes, not man's. Thomas Gisborne, for example, clearly considered women moral beings responsible for themselves and to society. His call for self-conscious moral integrity on women's part directly opposed Gregory's insinuations about the shaping of women's behavior to men's tastes; he objected that such behavior was "not discretion, but art. It is dissimulation, it is deliberate imposition."[17] Evangelical works of the 1790s argued that aristocratic models of vanity, artifice, and irreligion had undermined and corrupted women's valuable potential. They claimed that female piety and sincerity would bring "effectual reformation . . . in every department of society," because "all virtues, all vices, and all characters are intimately connected with the manners, principles, and dispositions of our women."[18] The Evangelicals transformed the truism of etiquette books, that individual women influenced individual men's manners, into the proposition that the collective influence of women was an agency of moral reform.

More to the point, the Evangelicals linked moral agency to female character with a supporting link to passionlessness. Their insistence on sincerity or "simplicity," accompanying their emphasis on women's moral potential, caused them to imply that women were virtuous by nature. Continuing to stress the female virtue of modesty, Evangelicals could not (in contrast to Gregory) allow that modesty was a behavior assumed to suit society's conventions and men's preferences. If women were to act modest and sexually passive, and also act without affectation, then, logically, they must be passionless. Gisborne said women had "quicker feelings of native delicacy, and a stronger sense of shame" than men. The anonymous author of *Female Tuition* claimed the female sex was "naturally attached to purity."[19]

Hannah More's work perfected the transformation of woman's image from sexual to moral being. Her *Strictures on the Modern System of Female Education* called for the rescue of religion and morality and located her constituency among her own sex. She detailed further than any predecessor the power that women could command, first making clear that this was power derived from their moral and spiritual endowment, not from their winning or endearing (sexual) ways. "It is humbling to reflect," More began her *Strictures*, "that in those countries in which fondness for the mere persons of women is carried to the highest excess, *they are slaves;* and that their moral and intellectual degradation increases in direct proportion to the adoration which is paid to mere external charms."[20] More offered a resounding alternative to the idea that women were made for men's pleasure—but at the price of a new level of self-control. Since she believed that human nature was corrupt, her educational program consisted of repression as much as enhancement.[21] Her outlook revealed to women a source of power (in moral influence) and an independence of men (through reliance on God) in a female world view that inspired and compelled women throughout the nineteenth century.[22] In her refusal to see women as childish and affectedly weak beings, designed only "to gratify the appetite of man, or to be the upper servant," she agreed with her contemporary, Mary Wollstonecraft. Despite the spectrum of difference between More and Wollstonecraft in politics and personal behavior, they both abhorred "libertine notions of beauty" and "weak elegancy of mind" in women, wished to emphasize women's moral and intellectual powers rather than their "mere animal" capacities, and expected reformed women to reform the world.[23] Their two critiques rose from shared indignation that women were degraded by their sexual characterization.

The new focus on moral rather than sexual determinants of female character in didactic works at the end of the eighteenth century required a reversal in Protestant views of women. In Puritan ideology, earthly women were the inheritors of Eve's legacy of moral danger. By the mid-eighteenth century, however, New England ministers had discarded similes to Eve, probably in deference to their predominantly female congregations, and portrayed women as more sensitive to the call of religion than men.[24] Nineteenth-century Protestantism relied on women for its prime exemplars and symbols. Between 1790 and 1820 particularly, as an evangelical united front spread across the United States and Britain, the clergy intensified their emphasis on women as crucial advocates of religion.[25] Evangelical Protestants constantly reiterated the theme that Christianity had raised women from slaves in status to moral and intellectual beings.[26] The tacit condition for that elevation was the suppression of female sexuality. Christian women were "exalted above human nature, raised to that of angels"; proper understanding of the gospel enabled women to dismiss the earthly pride or sensuality that subjected them to men's whims.[27] The clergy thus renewed and generalized the idea that women under God's grace were more pure than men, and they expected not merely the souls but the bodies of women to corroborate that claim.

The pastors had a double purpose in training their eyes on the moral rather than the sexual aspect of woman's being. It enabled them to welcome women as worthy allies and agents of Protestantism, which seemed more and more essential as men's religious commitment dissipated. Second, a world view in which woman's sexual nature was shadowed behind her moral and spiritual endowment eclipsed her primitive and original power over men, the power of her sexuality.[28] The evangelical view, by concentrating on women's spiritual nature, simultaneously elevated women as moral and intellectual beings and disarmed them of their sexual power. Passionlessness was on the other side of the coin which paid, so to speak, for women's admission to moral equality.

The correlation between passionlessness and a distinctly improved view of women's character and social purpose begins to suggest the appeal of the concept to women. By replacing sexual with moral motives and determinants, the ideology of passionlessness favored women's power and self-respect. It reversed the tradition of Christian mistrust based on women's sexual treacherousness. It elevated women above the weakness of animal nature, stressing instead that they were "formed for exalted purity, felicity, and glory."[29] It postulated that woman's influence was not ensnaring but disinterested. It routed women out of the cul-de-sac of education for attractiveness, thus allowing more intellectual breadth.[30] To women who wanted means of self-preservation and self-control, this view of female nature may well have appealed, as Hannah More's views appealed. It remains to be seen in what social circumstances such views came to the fore.

There was extraordinary turbulence in sexual patterns and definitions in the late eighteenth century. The traditional system under which parents exercised authority over their children's marriage choices was breaking down.[31] This change might seem to imply greater freedom for youth of both sexes in choosing their spouses. Since men conventionally exercised the sexual/marital initiative, however, the demise of parental control probably meant a relative decline in the leverage available to marriageable women, who no longer had their parents operating openly on their behalf and could not assume that role themselves. Eliza Southgate, an articulate and well-to-do eighteen-year-old of Maine, remarked in 1800 that women sensed their "inequality of privilege" most grievously "in the liberty of choosing a partner in marriage; true, we have the liberty of refusing those we don't like, but not of selecting those we do."[32] Owing primarily to the changing sex ratio, the average age at which women first married rose from a low of about twenty years in the early colonies to about twenty-three by the Revolutionary period, while men's age at first marriage fell slightly. The proportion of women who never married rose appreciably in the same period, and the remarriage rate of widows dropped. One might interpret these statistics favorably to mean that "those who wed may have taken longer to consider the implications of such actions and the alternatives," or even that it was now "possible for unmarried men and women to find a satisfying role."[33] But since marriage was the principal means women had of supporting themselves, one could argue that the number of desperate and exploitable women multiplied. While marriage was the likeliest source for economic security for a woman, marital subjection remained the living symbol of women's general subjection to men. In Abigail Adams's famous request to her husband John in 1776 to "remember the ladies," her central complaint was not women's political disenfranchisement but husbands' legal exercise of "unlimited power" over their wives. Turning Revolutionary rhetoric to marital relations, Abigail reminded John that "all men would be tyrants if they could," and urged that a new law code "put it out of the power of the vicious and lawless to use us with cruelty and indignity with impunity."[34] Her objections evoke the double spectres, of sharper victimization or greater equity, borne before women's eyes during these Revolutionary years. Did women's marital status trouble her because it had become, of late, more abject, or because some hints of improvement in women's marital power precipitated her demand for further change?

During the same decades, the prebridal pregnancy rate rose dramatically. At peak years between 1760 and 1800, one-third to one-half of all recorded legitimate first births were the result of premarital sexual intercourse in several New England towns where the same measure was one-tenth or one-twentieth in the seventeenth century.[35] Again, numerous and contradictory interpretations can be drawn from these figures. The increase in prebridal pregnancy could be ascribed to a general increase in premarital sexual activity, which in itself could possibly represent greater individual and sexual freedom for both sexes, or just as possibly indicate greater vulnerability and exploitation of women. Or, premarital sexual activity could have remained constant but have led more frequently to marriage and legitimation.[36] The continued reign of a double standard of sexual morality made it unlikely that sexual "freedom" came without cost to women. A content analysis of nine New England magazines between 1777 and 1794 has shown that characters in both fiction and nonfiction regularly advocated punishment or ostracism for the male partner in illicit sex and sympathy for the female as the victim of force or misguided ignorance. In actual portrayals of illicit sexual encounters, however, the males involved escaped scot-free and the women almost always suffered punishment or ostracism.[37] On this injustice the young wife of a lawyer in Haverhill, Massachusetts, reflected in 1802: "Man boasts superior strength of mind, I would have him prove it, by avoiding or conquering temptation; but man disgraces his godlike reason, and yields to a thousand follies, to give them no harsher name—and passes through the world in high repute, such conduct would blast the reputation of poor weak woman. . . . 'tis an unrighteous custom, which gives such license to our lords of the creation." She was not alone in protesting men's combination of sexual license with their claim to righteous social power. On the eve of her marriage, Sarah Connell of Concord, New Hampshire, lamented a local instance of seduction and betrayal, empathizing with the many unprotected girls who had "fallen victim to the baseness of those who call themselves lords of the Creation."[38]

The sexual exploitation possible in contemporary disruption of marital and sexual patterns was probably more obvious to women because of heightened expectations on their part. The clergy, adopting a more positive image of women in their sermons, no longer presented marriage as a hierarchical relationship but stressed that women were complementary, and piously influential, marriage partners. The rhetoric of the American Revolution glorified women's role further by connecting it with the success of the national experiment. In an abrupt reversal in 1773, Massachusetts women were victorious if they petitioned their governor and council for divorce on account of their husbands' adulteries; and women's overall success in obtaining divorce was almost equal to men's in the decade after 1776.[39] If not the most isolated farmers' wives, then literate women, living in populated areas sharing in the commerce of goods and ideas, were particularly likely to anticipate better treatment.[40]

A vision of sexual equity arising from awareness of sexual injustice brought feminist writers into the open during the same years. Judith Sargent Murray of Gloucester, Massachusetts, began criticizing female education in the 1770s, anticipating the themes of More and Wollstonecraft. Under the pseudonym "Constantia" she argued that men's presumed superiority in rationality was due to their superior education and continued advantages, not to any inherent preeminence. She demanded that women have opportunity to cultivate other means than sexual attraction. Pointing out that the typical upbringing of girls trivialized their minds and made them rely on physical beauty, she urged women to develop aspirations, a "reverence of self," moral and intellectual integrity, and the capacity for self-fulfillment.[41] Constantia put her hopes in the female academies springing up. Another pseudonymous feminist, an "aged matron" of Connecticut who published *The Female Advocate* in 1801, wished to disabuse the world of the idea that woman was inferior to man or made for men's uses. God and Nature, she claimed, had given the two sexes "equality of talents, of genius, of morals, as well as intellectual worth," and only male arrogance had invaded that equality. Men had deprived women of education and experience while they themselves "engross[ed] all the emoluments, offices, honors and merits, of church and state." In her eyes the sexual double standard epitomized male usurpation of power, because it allowed a man to flaunt the arts of seduction without losing public esteem while it condemned a woman forever if she once succumbed to a deceiver. *The Female Advocate*'s images of women's powerlessness and vulnerability contrasted with its portrayal of men's aggrandizement of power and seductive wiles. Yet its author was optimistic that "well informed mind[s]" would be "the mean of enabling us [women] to possess some command over ourselves."[42]

Polite ladies' magazines, which first appeared in the 1780s with the growth of a literate female audience, unintentionally paraded the contemporary controversy over sexual definitions. They celebrated female intellectual accomplishments and aimed not to cater to homemakers' tastes but to "improve and amuse" ladies' minds. In this "polite" entertainment, the subjects of fornication, prostitution, adultery, seduction, and betrayal were legion.[43] By and large, the stories and essays in these magazines broadcast the view that women's modus operandi was sexual, and consisted in manipulating men. But they also gave the impression that women met victimization and downfall more often than they gained influence and happiness through the solicitation of men's passions. The sexual definition of women could undermine their control of encounters with men, as Patty Rogers, a young woman of Exeter, New Hampshire, discovered for herself and confided to her diary.[44] Some writers in ladies' magazines were restless or indignant with the sexual characterization of women. A "Fragment on Prostitutes" argued that so-called women of pleasure were really women of grief and suffering, who had been betrayed by their seducers and abandoned by unsympathetic kin. The author railed against the injustice of prostitutes being punished by laws made by men, their seducers.[45] Another author, opposing "what is called Amiable Weakness in women," asserted that women deserved the chance to cultivate their knowledge, intelligence, and self-discipline, because they were moral beings and not merely decorative objects or household drudges. A serious "Scheme for Increasing the Power of the Ladies" called on women to end the double standard by refusing to tolerate fashionable "rakes"; like Hannah More, the writer emphasized that it was up to women to reverse their complaisance with and degradation under the existing code. Sarah Connell concluded her account of her acquaintance's seduction with similar sentiment: "Did every virtuous female show her detestation of the libertine by wholly renouncing his society, there would be a much smaller number of them."[46]

Only a handful of New England women at this time questioned the political inequities of their situation, but sexual and marital subjection—unequal sexual prerogatives—seem to have rankled a much larger population. As *The Female Advocate* pointed out, women had to conform to male tastes and wait to be chosen but resist seduction or suffer ostracism for capitulating; men, meanwhile, were free to take the first step, practice flattery, and escape the consequences of illicit sexual relations. In sexual encounters women had more than an even chance to lose, whether by censure under the double standard, unwanted pregnancy and health problems, or ill-fated marriage. In this perspective, women might hail passionlessness as a way to assert control in the sexual arena—even if that "control" consisted in denial. Some scholars have claimed that women adhered to the ideology of passionlessness to bolster their position in a disadvantageous marriage market, that is, to play "hard to get" with conviction.[47] More essentially, passionlessness served women's larger interests by downplaying altogether their sexual characterization, which was the cause of their exclusion from significant "human" (i.e., male) pursuits.[48] The positive contribution of passionlessness was to replace that sexual/carnal characterization of women with a spiritual/moral one, allowing women to develop their human faculties and their self-esteem. The belief that women lacked carnal motivation was the cornerstone of the argument for women's moral superiority, used to enhance women's status and widen their opportunities in the nineteenth century. Furthermore, acceptance of the idea of passionlessness created sexual solidarity among women; it allowed women to consider their love relationships with one another of higher character than heterosexual relationships because they excluded (male) carnal passion. "I do not believe that men can ever feel so pure an enthusiasm for women as we can feel for one another," Catherine Sedgwick recorded in her diary of 1834, upon meeting Fanny Kemble, "—ours is nearest to the love of angels."[49] "Love is spiritual, only passion is sexual," Mary Grew wrote at the end of the century to vindicate her intense and enduring friendship with Margaret Burleigh. That sense of the angelic or spiritual aspect of female love ennobled the experience of sisterhood which was central to the lives of nineteenth-century women and to the early woman's rights movement.[50] Women considered passionlessness an important shared trait which distinguished them favorably from men.[51]

It must not be assumed that women who internalized the concept of passionlessness necessarily shunned marriage. The pervasive ideology of romantic love, and also the evangelical conflation of the qualities of earthly and spiritual love, bridged the gap and refuted the ostensible contradiction between passionlessness and marriage. On a practical level, belief in female passionlessness could aid a woman to limit sexual intercourse within marriage and thus limit family size. Daniel Scott Smith has postulated a direct relation between women's exertion of that sort of power within the family, which he calls "domestic feminism," and the decline of the birthrate during the nineteenth century.[52] The conviction and the demand that it was woman's right to control reproduction, advocated by health reformers in the 1850s and promulgated in the movement for "voluntary motherhood" in subsequent decades, depended on the ideology of female passionlessness. Linda Gordon has shown the feminist basis of the argument for voluntary motherhood in the claim that women had the right to refuse their husbands' sexual demands, despite the legal and customary requirements of submission to marital "duty."[53]

The degree to which a woman might incorporate the idea of passionlessness is revealed in an 1845 letter of Harriet Beecher Stowe to her husband. Responding to his revelations about "licentiousness" on the part of certain clergymen, she wrote: "What terrible temptations lie in the way of your sex—till now I never realized it—for tho I did love you with an almost insane love before I married you I never knew yet or felt the pulsation which showed me that I could be tempted in that way—there never was a moment when I felt anything by which you could have drawn me astray—for I loved you as I now love God. . . ."[54] Angelina Grimké's passionless attitude was a feminist affirmation of woman's dignity in revulsion from male sexual domination. To the man who would become her husband she revealed her judgment "that men in general, the vast majority, believe most seriously that women were made to gratify their animal appetites, *expressly* to minister to their pleasure—yea Christian men too." She continued: "My soul abhors such a base letting down of the high dignity of my nature as a woman. How I have feared the possibility of ever being married to one who regarded *this* as the *end*—the great design of marriage. In truth I may say that I never was reconciled to the compound [relat]ions of marriage until I read Combe on the Constitution of man this winter."[55]

Yet a belief so at odds with the traditional appreciation of female sexuality, and one which seems to mid-twentieth-century sensibilities so patently counterproductive, so symbolic of the repression and subordination of women, cannot be interpreted simply. Historians' frequent assumption that men devised the ideology of female passionlessness to serve their own interests—"to help gentlemen cope with the problem of controlling their own sexuality"—is partial (in both senses of the word) but not illogical.[56] An ideal of male continence, of virtuous and willed repression of existing carnal desires (as distinct from passionlessness, which implied absence of carnal motivation), figures in nineteenth-century directions for men's respectability and achievement in the bustling new world of industrial capitalism.[57] In one aspect, female passionlessness was a keystone in men's construction of their own self-control. But Howard Gadlin has underlined the paradox of the ideology, as well as reason for its diffusion and rootedness, in his remark that "the nineteenth-century double standard was the vehicle for a desexualization desired by both men and women for opposing purposes. Men wanted to desexualize relationships to maintain their domination; women wanted to desexualize relationships to limit male domination."[58]

Both women's participation in the creation of Victorian sexual standards and the place of passionlessness in the vanguard of feminist thought deserve more recognition. The serviceability of passionlessness to women in gaining social and familial power should be acknowledged as a primary reason that the ideology was quickly and widely accepted. Yet feminists were the first to question and oppose the ideology once it was entrenched. When prudery became confused with passionlessness, it undermined women physically and psychologically by restricting their knowledge of their own sexual functioning. From the first, women health reformers and moral reformers rejected this injurious implication while fostering the positive meanings of passionlessness.[59] Feminist opposition arose when the medical establishment adopted passionlessness and moved the grounds for judging the concept from the spiritual to the somatic. When female passionlessness came to be insisted upon literally, more than one woman reacted as Rebecca Harding Davis did: "In these rough and tumble days, we'd better give [women] their places as flesh and blood, with exactly the same wants and passions as men." Mary Gove Nichols claimed: "A healthy and loving woman is impelled to material union as surely, often as strongly, as man. . . . The apathy of the sexual instinct is caused by the enslaved and unhealthy condition in which she lives."[60] Several woman's rights activists of the later part of the century, including Isabella Beecher Hooker, Alice Stockham, and Elizabeth Cady Stanton, discussed among themselves their belief in the existence and legitimacy of female sexual drives, even while the movement of which they were part banked on women's superior morality and maternal instinct as chief supports.[61] Consistent with the general conflicts and contradictions in sexual ideology after 1860, feminists perceived oppression in prudery while clinging to the promises that passionlessness held out.

The ideology of passionlessness, conceived as self-preservation and social advancement for women, created its own contradictions: on the one hand, by exaggerating sexual propriety so far as to immobilize women and, on the other, by allowing claims of women's moral influence to obfuscate the need for other sources of power. The assertion of moral integrity within passionlessness had allowed women to retrieve their identity from a trough of sexual vulnerability and dependence. The concept could not assure women full autonomy —but what transformation in sexual ideology alone could have done so?

NOTES

I am grateful to the friends who have kindly read and criticized one or another version of this essay over the past several years. I would especially like to thank Sacvan Bercovitch, Mari Jo Buhle, Laurie Crumpacker, John Demos, David B. Davis, Ellen DuBois, David H. Fischer, Linda Gordon, James R. Green, Jean Humez, Janet W. James, Carol Karlsen, Ann Margolis, Michael McGiffert, Mary Beth Norton, and Kathryn Kish Sklar. In addition, the anonymous readers for *signs* were exceptionally helpful in bringing the essay to its final form.

1. Havelock Ellis, *Studies in the Psychology of Sex,* 2d ed., rev. (1903; Philadelphia: F. A. Davis Co., 1913), 3:193–94.

2. On the former challenge, see Carroll Smith-Rosenberg, "Beauty, the Beast, and the Militant Woman," *American Quarterly* 23 (1971): 562–84, and "The Female World of Love and Ritual," *Signs* 1 (1975): 1–29; Linda Gordon, "Voluntary Motherhood: The Beginnings of Feminist Birth Control Ideology in the U.S.," in *Clio's Consciousness Raised,* ed. Mary Hartman and Lois Banner (New York: Harper Torchbook, 1974), and *Woman's Body, Woman's Right* (New York: Grossman Publishers, 1976); John S. Haller, Jr., and Robin M. Haller, *The Physician and Sexuality in Victorian America* (Urbana: University of Illinois Press, 1974), esp. p. xii; Daniel Scott Smith, "Family Limitation, Sexual Control and Domestic Feminism in Victorian America," in Hartman and Banner; and Randall Collins, "A Conflict Theory of Sexual Stratification," *Social Problems* 19 (Summer 1971): 7, 13–19. The latter point has been raised most recently by Carl N. Degler, "What Ought to Be and What Was: Women's Sexuality in the Nineteenth Century," *American Historical Review* 79 (December 1974): 1467–90. Historians' focus on the later part of the nineteenth century in discussions of sexual ideology is evident in Haller and Haller's and Degler's works as well as in Peter T. Cominos, "Innocent Femina Sensualis in Unconscious Conflict," in *Suffer and Be Still,* ed. Martha Vicinus (Bloomington: University of Indiana Press, 1972), and "Late Victorian Sexual Respectability and the Social System," *International Review of Social History* 8 (1963): 18–48, 216–50; Nathan G. Hale, Jr., *Freud and the Americans* (New York: Oxford University Press, 1971); and Charles E. Rosenberg and Carroll Smith-Rosenberg, "The Female Animal: Medical and Biological Views of Woman in Nineteenth-Century America," *Journal of American History* 60 (September 1973): 332–56. Daniel Scott Smith, "The Dating of the American Sexual Revolution: Evidence and Interpretation," in *The American Family in Social-Historical Perspective,* ed. Michael Gordon (New York: St. Martin's Press, 1974), pp. 328–32, and Michael Gordon, "From an Unfortunate Necessity to a Cult of Mutual Orgasm: Sex in Marital Education Literature, 1830–1940," in *Studies in the Sociology of Sex,* ed. James Henslin (New York: Appleton-Century-Crofts, Inc., 1971), note conflict and change in sexual opinion in the last third of the century.

3. Quoted from *Malleus Maleficarum* in Deirdre English and Barbara English, *Witches, Midwives and Nurses: A History of Women Healers* (Oyster Bay, N.Y.: Glassmountain Pamphlets, 1972), p. 10. I remain indebted to Eleanor McLaughlin for conversations, at Wellesley in 1974, about medieval views of women and passionlessness.

4. Historians have noted that doctors took over the advisory role of

ministers in the late nineteenth century (see Haller and Haller, pp. x–xi; Gordon, *Woman's Body*, p. 170; Barbara Sicherman, "The Uses of Diagnosis: Doctors, Patients, and Neurasthenia," *Journal of the History of Medicine and Allied Sciences* 32 [January 1977]: 53–54). The new function of doctors as spiritual counselors highlights the shift of moral authority from religion to science during the course of the century.

5. See Barbara Welter, "The Feminization of American Religion," in Hartman and Banner; and Nancy F. Cott, *The Bonds of Womanhood: 'Woman's Sphere' in New England, 1780–1835* (New Haven, Conn.: Yale University Press, 1977), chap. 4.

6. Degler, pp. 1469–79, cites numerous conflicts within medical opinion. Physicians were never of one mind, and the British physician William Acton, who announced in the 1850s that "the majority of women . . . are not very much troubled with sexual feeling of any kind," represented one end of the range of opinion (see Gordon, "From an Unfortunate Necessity," pp. 57–58).

7. See Edmund Morgan, "The Puritans and Sex," *New England Quarterly* 15 (1942): 592–93, and *The Puritan Family*, rev. ed. (New York: Harper Torchbooks, 1966), pp. 37–42; and Otho T. Beall, Jr., "Aristotle's Masterpiece in America: A Landmark in the Folklore of Medicine," *William and Mary Quarterly*, 3d ser. 20 (1963): 216–20.

8. George E. Howard, *A History of Matrimonial Institutions* (1904: New York: Humanities Press, 1964), 2:169–70, 173, 331, 348, 351, 354; John P. Demos, *A Little Commonwealth* (New York: Oxford University Press, 1970), pp. 96–97; Nancy F. Cott, "Eighteenth-Century Family and Social Life Revealed in Massachusetts Divorce Records," *Journal of Social History* 10 (Fall 1976): 34–35, and "Divorce and the Changing Status of Women in Eighteenth-Century Massachusetts," *William and Mary Quarterly*, 3d ser. 33 (October 1976): 586–614.

9. Keith Thomas, "The Double Standard," *Journal of the History of Ideas* 20 (1959): 210.

10. See Morgan, "Puritans and Sex," pp. 594–600, for examples.

11. On the sex-role distinctions employed in British and American writings, see Mary S. Benson, *Women in Eighteenth-Century America* (New York: Columbia University Press, 1935), pp. 37–39. Frank L. Mott notes, in his *History of American Magazines*, 1741–1850 (Cambridge, Mass.: Belknap Press, 1957), pp. 64–65, that titles such as "Advice to the Fair" and "Counsel upon Female Virtues" became "sickeningly frequent" in the last quarter of the eighteenth century.

12. Ian Watt, "The New Woman: Samuel Richardson's Pamela," in *The Family: Its Structure and Functions*, ed. Rose L. Coser (New York: St. Martin's Press, 1964), pp. 281–82. On the rise of middle-class morality, see also Watt, pp. 286–88; Thomas, p. 204; Gordon Rattray Taylor, *The Angel-Makers: A Study in the Psychological Origins of Historical Change, 1750–1850* (London: William Heinemann, 1958), pp. 12–24; Christopher Hill, "Clarissa Harlowe and Her Times," *Essays in Criticism* 5 (1955): 320. Samuel Richardson's *Pamela* (1742) first portrayed a heroine whose delicacy verged on passionlessness. On the American attention paid to these British moralists and novelists, see Lawrence A. Cremin, *American Education: The Colonial Experience* (New York: Harper Torchbooks, 1970), pp. 366–67, 371; Benson, p. 46; and Robert Palfrey Utter and Gwendolyn B. Needham, *Pamela's Daughters* (New York: Macmillan Publishing Co., 1936).

13. [George Savile, Marquis of Halifax], *The Lady's New Year's Gift, or,*

Advice to a Daughter (London: Randal Taylor, 1688); Dr. [John] Gregory, *A Father's Legacy to His Daughters* (London: J. Sharpe, 1822). James Fordyce, *Sermons to Young Women,* new ed. (Philadelphia: Thomas Dobson, 1787), should be grouped with these although it was not an etiquette book in the traditional sense. Savile's book, which went through fifteen British editions, circulated in the colonies during the first two-thirds of the eighteenth century. Fordyce's work was first published in England in 1765 and was reprinted in America by 1787; it was then frequently excerpted in magazines and reprinted in entirety. Gregory's appeared in England in 1774, was published in Philadelphia the following year, and had sixteen more editions in the United States before 1794 plus selections in compilations and serials. Editions continued to appear into the nineteenth century. See Julia C. Spruill, *Woman's Life and Work in the Southern Colonies* (1935; New York: W. W. Norton & Co., 1969), pp. 215–25, and Benson, pp. 60–61, on the circulation of these books. Direct evidence of Gregory's readership in America appears in the manuscript diaries of Ruth Henshaw of Leicester, Mass., July 1, 1792, and Sally Ripley of Greenfield, Mass., December 1, 1799, both in the collection of the American Antiquarian Society, Worcester, Mass. American essayists frequently echoed the themes of the British didactic works (see, e.g., *Gentleman's and Lady's Town and Country Magazine* [Boston] 1 [May 1784]: 28; and Noah Webster's *American Magazine* [1788], quoted in Mott, p. 64).

14. Thomas, p. 214.

15. The eighteenth-century prescriptive work which made the connection between modesty and sexual ploy most obvious was Rousseau's *Emile* (1762), book 5, on the character of the ideal woman.

16. Gregory, pp. 11, 36, 72, 83.

17. Thomas Gisborne, *An Enquiry into the Duties of the Female Sex* (London: reprint ed. Philadelphia: J. Humphreys, 1798), pp. 2–3, 187, 193. On the British Evangelicals, see Charles I. Foster, *An Errand of Mercy: The Evangelical United Front, 1790–1837* (Chapel Hill: University of North Carolina Press, 1960); and M. G. Jones, *Hannah More* (Cambridge: Cambridge University Press, 1952).

18. Quotations from *Female Tuition, or, An Address to Mothers, on the Education of Daughters* (London: J. Murray, 1784), preface, and p. 34; see also pp. 2–3, 42–47; and Gisborne, chaps. 2, 4, 7, 9; *The Female Aegis* (London: J. Ginger, 1798) an anonymous plagiarism of Gisborne's book; Thomas Branagan, *The Excellency of the Female Character Vindicated* (1807; Harrisburg, Pa.: Francis Wyeth, 1828), chap. 2; Hannah More, *Strictures on the Modern System of Female Education,* 9th ed. (1799; London: T. Cadell & W. Davies, 1801), 1:70–72, 75–79, 111–12, 256–57.

19. Gisborne, p. 183; *Female Tuition,* p. 243. On "simplicity" see, e.g., Gisborne, pp. 104–11, 187, 193; *Female Tuition,* p. 112–75.

20. More, 1:3 (quotation) and passim. Her *Strictures* followed upon her two other successful critiques of aristocratic manners, *Thoughts on the Importance of the Manners of the Great* (1788) and *An Estimate of the Religion of the Fashionable World* (1790) (see Jones, n. 17 above, on her life and work.)

21. *Strictures,* see esp. pp. 17–18, 29, 32–33, 137–38, 154–55.

22. During the first several decades of the nineteenth century all sorts of literate women—farm-bred daughters, society girls, schoolteachers, and matrons, from rural towns to commercial seaports—read and quoted Hannah More. For examples see *The Writings of Nancy Maria Hyde* (Norwich,

Conn.: Russell Hubbard, 1816), diary entry for June 14, 1812; manuscript journal of Margaret Searle, August 22, 1812, Curson Family Papers, Houghton Library, Harvard University; manuscript book of extracts of Lucinda Read, 1815–16, Massachusetts Historical Society, Boston; manuscript journal of Mehitable May Dawes, June 12, 1815, May-Goddard Papers, Schlesinger Library, Radcliffe College. Jones, p. 193, states that More's novel *Coelebs in Search of a Wife* (which personified her ideals for female character) sold out thirty editions in the United States between 1808 and 1834. The British visitor Harriet Martineau was mightily impressed, in the 1830s, with the impact More had on American women: her comments and others are cited by Keith Melder, "Ladies Bountiful," *New York History* 48 (July 1967): 233–34, 254n. Jill K. Conway assembles other evidence of More's wide-ranging influence on American women in "Evangelical Protestantism and Its Influence on Women in North America, 1790–1860" (paper read at the American Historical Association Convention, New Orleans, December 1972).

23. Mary Wollstonecraft, *A Vindication of the Rights of Women* (1792), ed. Charles W. Hagelman, Jr. (New York: W. W. Norton & Co., 1967), pp. 34–35, 49–72, 77, 84, 91–92, 191–92, 206–10.

24. Lonna Myers Malmsheimer, "New England Funeral Sermons and Changing Attitudes toward Women, 1692–1792" (Ph.D. diss., University of Minnesota, 1973), esp. pp. 178–79.

25. See Cott, *Bonds of Womanhood*, pp. 128–35, 146–48; Foster, pp. 92–100, 115–32.

26. See Cott, p. 130.

27. *The Female Friend, or, the Duties of Christian Virgins* (Baltimore: H. S. Keatinge, 1809), pp. 40–42; Samuel Worcester, *Female Love to Christ* (Salem, Mass.: Pool & Palfrey, 1809), pp. 12–13.

28. See Karen Horney, "The Dread of Woman," *International Journal of Psychoanalysis* 13 (1932): 348–60; and H. R. Hays, *The Dangerous Sex: The Myth of Feminine Evil* (New York: Putnam Books, 1966).

29. Worcester, pp. 12–13.

30. Cf. Emma Willard's protest, in her *Plan for Improving Female Education* (1819; reprint ed., Middlebury, Vt.: Middlebury College, 1918), pp. 14–15, that current female education was far too attuned to pleasing the opposite sex.

31. Daniel Scott Smith, "Parental Power and Marriage Patterns—an Analysis of Historical Trends in Hingham, Massachusetts," *Journal of Marriage and the Family* 35 (1973): 326.

32. Eliza Southgate to Moses Porter, 1800, reprinted in *A Girl's Life Eighty Years Ago*, ed. Clarence Cook (New York: Scribner's, 1887).

33. Robert V. Wells, "Quaker Marriage Patterns in a Colonial Perspective," *William and Mary Quarterly*, 3d ser. 29 (1972): 437–39 (quotations); and Daniel Scott Smith, personal communication. Wells's figures for the proportion of women never marrying, and for remarriage of widows, are based on a New Jersey population; those on age at marriage reflect both the New England and the middle colonies population.

34. Abigail Adams to John Adams, March 31, 1776, reprinted in *The Feminist Papers*, ed. Alice Rossi (New York: Bantam Books, 1974), pp. 10–11.

35. Daniel Scott Smith and Michael S. Hindus, "Premarital Pregnancy in America: An Overview and Interpretation," *Journal of Interdisciplinary History* 6 (1975): 537–71; cf. David H. Flaherty, "Law and the Enforcement of Morals in Early America," *Perspectives in American History* 5 (1971): 246–47.

36. If premarital sexual activity remained constant while bridal pregnancy increased then illegitimate births would have decreased. This is unlikely. Although the figures for illegitimacy in early America are not known, as Smith and Hindus point out, illegitimacy and bridal pregnancy usually rise and fall together. Another factor affecting the rise and fall of bridal pregnancy is nutrition, but Smith and Hindus tend to discount its relevance in this case.

37. Herman R. Lantz et al., "Preindustrial Patterns in the Colonial Family in America: A Content Analysis of Colonial Magazines," *American Sociological Review* 33 (1968): 422–23.

38. Manuscript diary of Mary Orne Tucker, May 7, 1802, James Duncan Phillips Library, Essex Institute, Salem, Mass.; Sarah Connell to Susan Kittredge, March 13, 1810, in *Diary of Sarah Connell Ayer* (Portland, Me.: n. p., 1910), pp. 372–73.

39. Malmsheimer, pp. 138–79; Gordon S. Wood, *The Creation of the American Republic* (New York: W. W. Norton & Co., 1969), pp. 65–70, 123–24; Cott, "Divorce and the Changing Status of Women."

40. Kenneth R. Lockridge, *Literacy in Colonial New England* (New York: W. W. Norton & Co., 1974), pp. 38–42, 57–58, estimates that half of New England women were literate in the 1780s (see also Cott, "Divorce and the Changing Status of Women," pp. 595–96; and Richard D. Brown, "The Emergence of Urban Society in Rural Massachusetts, 1760–1830," *Journal of American History* 61 [June 1974: 29–51]).

41. Constantia, "On the Equality of the Sexes," *Massachusetts Magazine* 2 (March 1790): 32–35, reprinted in Aileen S. Kraditor, ed., *Up from the Pedestal* (Chicago: Quadrangle Books, 1968), pp. 31–33; "Desultory Thoughts upon the Utility of Encouraging a Degree of Self-complacency, Especially in Female Bosoms," *Gentleman's and Lady's Town and Country Magazine* 1 (October 1784): 251–53.

42. *The Female Advocate*, Written by a Lady (New Haven, Conn.: Thomas Green & Son, 1801), pp. 6, 13–17, 22, 27–28.

43. My discussion is based on *Gentleman's and Lady's Town and Country Magazine*, Boston, 1784; *Gentlemen's and Ladies' Town and Country Magazine*, Boston, 1789–90; *Lady's Magazine and Repository of Entertaining Knowledge*, Philadelphia, 1792–93; *Lady* [sic] *and Gentleman's Pocket Magazine of Literary and Polite Amusement*, New York, 1796; *Ladies' Museum*, Philadelphia, 1800–1801; *Lady's Magazine and Musical Repository*, New York, 1801; *Ladies' Monitor*, New York, 1801–2; *Ladies' Miscellany, or the Weekly Visitor*, New York, 1802–5; *Ladies' Visitor*, Boston, 1806–7; *Ladies' Weekly Miscellany*, New York, 1805–8.

44. Manuscript diary of Polly [Patty] Rogers, August 4, September 14, September 21, 1785, in the collection of the American Antiquarian Society.

45. *Weekly Visitor*, vol. 2 (January 21, 1804).

46. *Lady and Gentleman's Pocket Magazine* (October 1796), pp. 174–79; *Lady's Magazine* (June 1792); *Diary of Sarah Connell Ayer*, p. 373.

47. See D. S. Smith (n. 2 above), pp. 129–31; Collins (n. 2 above), pp. 7, 13–19; Watt (n. 12 above).

48. Cf. Harriot Hunt's defensive line of argument in her application for admission to the Harvard Medical School in 1850: "In opening your doors to woman, it is mind that will enter the lecture room, it is intelligence that will ask for food; sex will never be felt where science leads for the atmosphere of thought will be around every lecture" (quoted in Mary Roth Walsh, *Doctors*

Wanted: No Women Need Apply [New Haven, Conn.: Yale University Press, 1977], p. 31).

49. Manuscript diary of Catherine Maria Sedgwick, May 16, 1834, Massachusetts Historical Society, Boston.

50. Mary Grew to Isabel Howland, April 27, 1892, quoted in Carroll Smith-Rosenberg, "The Female World of Love and Ritual," p. 27, an essay which describes in rich detail female friendships during the nineteenth century. See also Cott, *Bonds of Womanhood,* chap. 5.

51. At the end of her life Sarah Grimké opined to Elizabeth Smith Miller that "the sexual passion in man is ten times stronger than in woman," and that woman was innately man's superior (quoted in Ronald G. Walters, "The Erotic South: Civilization and Sexuality in American Abolitionism," *American Quarterly* 25 [May 1973]: 196).

52. See Smith (n. 2 above).

53. Gordon, *Woman's Body*, p. 103.

54. Quoted in Edmund Wilson, *Patriotic Gore* (New York: Oxford University Press, 1966), p. 22. I am indebted to Kathryn Kish Sklar for bringing this letter to my attention.

55. Angelina Grimké to Theodore Dwight Weld, March 4, 1838, in *Letters of Theodore Dwight Weld, Angelina Grimké Weld, and Sarah Grimké,* ed. Gilbert Barnes and D. L. Dumond (New York: D. Appleton-Century, 1934), 2:587. "Combe" is the Scottish phrenologist George Combe.

56. Cominos (n. 2 above), p. 162 and passim.

57. See Charles E. Rosenberg, "Sexuality, Class and Role in Nineteenth-Century America," *American Quarterly* 25 (1973): 131–53; and Stephen Nissenbaum, "Sex, Reform, and Social Change, 1830–1840" (paper delivered at the annual meeting of the Organization of American Historians, Washington, D.C., April 6, 1972).

58. Howard Gadlin, "Private Lives and Public Order: A Critical View of the History of Intimate Relations in the U.S.," *Massachusetts Review* 17 (Summer 1976): 318.

59. See Catharine E. Beecher, *Letters to the People on Health and Happiness* (New York: Harper & Bros., 1855); Smith-Rosenberg, "Beauty, the Beast," p. 571; Walsh, pp. 40–41.

60. Rebecca Harding Davis, "Paul Blecker," *Atlantic Monthly* (June/July 1863), quoted in introduction by Tillie Olsen to Davis's *Life in the Iron Mills* (New York: Feminist Press, 1972), p. 168n; Mary Gove Nichols (with T. L. Nichols), *Marriage; Its History, Character and Results . . .* (New York: T. L. Nichols, 1854), quoted in Nancy F. Cott, ed., *Root of Bitterness,* (New York: E. P. Dutton & Co., 1972), p. 286. Cf. Elizabeth Cady Stanton's response to Walt Whitman's poem "There Is a Woman Waiting for Me" in her diary of 1883: "Whitman seems to understand everything in nature but woman. . . . He speaks as if the female must be forced to the creative act, apparently ignorant of the great natural fact that a healthy woman has as much passion as a man, that she needs nothing stronger than the law of attraction to draw her to the male" (quoted in *Feminist Papers,* p. 393).

61. Gordon, *Woman's Body*, pp. 98–100, 183.

7

The Lady and the Mill Girl

Changes in the Status of Women in the Age of Jackson, 1800–1840

■

GERDA LERNER

Historians have for decades been interested in finding the reasons why the first outright organizing of women's rights sentiment occurred in the 1830s and 1840s. Beginning from that familiar starting point and drawing on Elisabeth Anthony Dexter's interpretation of the contraction in women's economic and political activities from the colonial period to the early nineteenth century, Gerda Lerner in 1969 heralded new directions. Her pathbreaking essay introduced vital characteristics of the new women's history, by using social history to explicate political questions, focusing on the transition from rural-artisanal to industrial society, combining recognition of sex-role demands with investigation of class divisions, and regarding women's status as a relative attribute. The essay as presented here includes revisions made by Lerner in 1979.

THE PERIOD 1800–1840 is one in which decisive changes occurred in the status of American women. It has remained surprisingly unexplored. With the exception of a recent, unpublished dissertation by Keith Melder and the distinctive work of Elisabeth Dexter, there is a dearth of descriptive material and an almost total absence of interpretation.[1] Yet the period offers essential clues to an understanding of later institutional developments, particularly the shape and nature of the woman's rights movement. This analysis will consider the economic, political, and social status of women and examine the changes in each area. It will also attempt an interpretation of the ideological shifts which occurred in American society concerning the "proper" role for women.

Periodization always offers difficulties. It seemed useful here, for purposes of comparison, to group women's status before 1800 roughly under the "colonial" heading and ignore the transitional and possibly atypical shifts which occurred during the American

Revolution and the early period of nationhood. Also, regional differences were largely ignored. The South was left out of consideration entirely because its industrial development occurred later.

The status of colonial women has been well studied and described and can briefly be summarized for comparison with the later period. Throughout the colonial period there was a marked shortage of women, which varied with the regions and always was greatest in the frontier areas.[2] This (from the point of view of women) favorable sex ratio enhanced their status and position. The Puritan world view regarded idleness as sin; life in an underdeveloped country made it absolutely necessary that each member of the community perform an economic function. Thus work for women, married or single, was not only approved, it was regarded as a civic duty. Puritan town councils expected single girls, widows, and unattached women to be self-supporting and for a long time provided needy spinsters with parcels of land. There was no social sanction against married women working; on the contrary, wives were expected to help their husbands in their trade and won social approval for doing extra work in or out of the home. Needy children, girls as well as boys, were indentured or apprenticed and were expected to work for their keep.

The vast majority of women worked within their homes, where their labor produced most articles needed for the family. The entire colonial production of cloth and clothing and in part that of shoes was in the hands of women. In addition to these occupations, women were found in many different kinds of employment. They were butchers, silversmiths, gunsmiths, upholsterers. They ran mills, plantations, tan yards, shipyards, and every kind of shop, tavern and boarding house. They were gate keepers, jail keepers, sextons, journalists, printers, "doctoresses," apothecaries, midwives, nurses, and teachers. Women acquired their skills the same way as did the men, through apprenticeship training, frequently within their own families.[3]

Absence of a dowry, ease of marriage and remarriage, and a more lenient attitude of the law with regard to women's property rights were manifestations of the improved position of wives in the colonies. Under British common law, marriage destroyed a woman's contractual capacity; she could not sign a contract even with the consent of her husband. But colonial authorities were more lenient toward the wife's property rights by protecting her dower rights in her husband's property, granting her personal clothing, and upholding pre-nuptial contracts between husband and wife. In the absence of the husband, colonial courts granted women "femme sole" rights, which enabled them to conduct their husband's business, sign contracts, and sue. The relative social freedom of women and the esteem in which they were held was commented upon by most early foreign travelers in America.[4]

But economic, legal, and social status tells only part of the story. Colonial society as a whole was hierarchical, and rank and standing in society depended on the position of the men. Women did not play a determining role in the ranking pattern; they took their position in society through the men of their own family or the men they married. In other words, they participated in the hierarchy only as daughters and wives, not as individuals. Similarly, their occupations were, by and large, merely auxiliary, designed to contribute to family income, enhance their husbands' business or continue it in case of widowhood. The self-supporting spinsters were certainly the exception. The underlying assumption of colonial society was that women ought to occupy an inferior and subordinate position. The settlers had brought this assumption with them from Europe; it was reflected in their legal concepts, their willingness to exclude women from political life, their discriminatory educational practices. What is remarkable is the extent to which this felt inferiority of women was constantly challenged and modified under the impact of environment, frontier conditions, and a favorable sex ratio.

By 1840 all of American society had changed. The Revolution had substituted an egalitarian ideology for the hierarchical concepts of colonial life. Privilege based on ability rather than inherited status, upward mobility for all groups of society, and unlimited opportunities for individual self-fulfillment had become ideological goals, if not always realities. For men, that is; women were, by tacit consensus, excluded from the new democracy. Indeed their actual situation had in many respects deteriorated. While, as wives, they had benefitted from increasing wealth, urbanization, and industrialization, their role as economic producers and as political members of society differed sharply from that of men. Women's work outside of the home no longer met with social approval; on the contrary, with two notable exceptions, it was condemned. Many business and professional occupations formerly open to women were now closed, many others restricted as to training and advancement. The entry of large numbers of women into low status, low pay, and low skill industrial work had fixed such work by definition as "woman's work." Women's political status, while legally unchanged, had deteriorated relative to the advances made by men. At the same time the genteel lady of fashion had become a model of American femininity, and the definition of "woman's proper sphere" seemed narrower and more confined than ever.

Within the scope of this essay only a few of these changes can be more fully explained. The professionalization of medicine and its impact on women may serve as a typical example of what occurred in all the professions.

In colonial America there were no medical schools, no medical journals, few hospitals, and few laws pertaining to the practice of the healing arts. Clergymen and governors, barbers, quacks, apprentices, and women practiced medicine. Most practitioners acquired their credentials by reading Paracelsus and Galen and serving an apprenticeship with an established practitioner. Among the semi-trained "physics," surgeons, and healers the occasional "doctoress" was fully accepted and frequently well rewarded. County records of all the colonies contain references to the work of the female physicians. There was even a female Army surgeon, a Mrs. Allyn, who served during King Philip's war. Plantation records mention by name several slave women who were granted special privileges because of their useful service as midwives and "doctoresses."[5]

The period of the professionalization of American medicine dates from 1765, when Dr. William Shippen began his lectures on midwifery in Philadelphia. The founding of medical faculties in several colleges, the standardization of training requirements, and the proliferation of medical societies intensified during the last quarter of the 18th century. The American Revolution dramatized the need for trained medical personnel, afforded first-hand battlefield experience to a number of surgeons and brought increasing numbers of semi-trained practitioners in contact with the handful of European-trained surgeons working in the military hospitals. This was an experience from which women were excluded. The resulting interest in improved medical training, the gradual appearance of graduates of medical colleges, and the efforts of medical societies led to licensing legislation. In 1801 Maryland required all medical practitioners to be licensed; in 1806 New York enacted a similar law, followed by all but three states.[6] This trend was reversed in the 1830s and 40s when most states repealed their licensure requirements. This was due to pressure from eclectic, homeopathic practitioners, the public's dissatisfaction with the "heroic medicine" then practiced by licensed physicians, and to the distrust of state regulation, which was widespread during the Age of Jackson. Licensure as prime proof of qualification for the practice of medicine was reinstituted in the 1870s.

In the middle of the 19th century it was not so much a license of an M.D. which marked the professional physician as it was graduation from an approved medical college, admission to hospital practice and to a network of referrals through other physicians. In 1800 there were four medical schools, in 1850, forty-two. Almost all of them excluded women from admission. Not surprisingly, women turned to eclectic schools for training. Harriot Hunt, a Boston physician, was trained by apprenticeship with a husband and wife team of homeopathic physicians. After more than twenty years of practice she attempted to enter Harvard Medical School and was repeatedly rebuffed. Elizabeth Blackwell received her M.D. from Geneva (New York) Medical College, an eclectic school. Sarah Adamson found all regular medical schools closed against her and earned an M.D. in 1851 from Central College at Syracuse, an eclectic institution. Clemence Lozier graduated from the same school two years later and went on to found the New York Medical College and Hospital for women in 1862, a homeopathic institution which was later absorbed into the Flower-Fifth Avenue Hospital.

Another way in which professionalization worked to the detriment of women can be seen in the cases of Drs. Elizabeth and Emily Blackwell, Marie Zakrzewska, and Ann Preston, who despite their M.D.s and excellent training were denied access to hospitals, were refused recognition by county medical societies, and were denied customary referrals by male colleagues. Their experiences were similar to those of most of the pioneer women physicians. Such discrimination caused the formation of alternate institutions for the training of women physicians and for hospitals in which they might treat their patients.[7] The point here is not so much that any one aspect of the process of professionalization excluded women but that the process, which took place over the span of almost a century, proceeded in such a way as to institutionalize an exclusion of women, which had earlier been accomplished irregularly, inconsistently, and mostly by means of social pressure. The end result was an *absolute* lowering of status for all women in the medical profession and a *relative* loss. As the professional status of all physicians advanced, the status differential between male and female practitioners was more obviously disadvantageous and underscored women's marginality. Their vital exclusion from the most prestigious and lucrative branches of the profession and their concentration in specializations relating to women and children made such disadvantaging more obvious by the end of the 19th century.

This process of pre-emption of knowledge, of institutionalization of the profession, and of legitimation of its claims by law and public acceptance is standard for the professionalization of the sciences, as George Daniels has pointed out.[8] It inevitably results in the elimination of fringe elements from the profession. It is interesting to note that women had been pushed out of the medical profession in 16th-century Europe by a similar process.[9] Once the public had come to accept licensing and college training as guarantees of up-to-date practice the outsider, no matter how well qualified by years of experience, stood no chance in the competition. Women were the casualties of medical professionalization.

In the field of midwifery the results were similar, but the process was more complicated. Women had held a virtual monopoly in the profession in colonial America. In 1646 a man was prosecuted in Maine for practicing as a midwife.[10] There are many records of well-trained midwives with diplomas from European institutions working in the colonies. In most of the colonies midwives were licensed, registered, and required to pass an examination before a board. When Dr. Shippen announced his pioneering lectures on midwifery, he did it to "combat the widespread popular prejudice against the man-midwife" and because he considered most midwives ignorant and improperly trained.[11]

Yet he invited "those women who love virtue enough, to own their Ignorance, and apply for instruction" to attend his lectures, offering as an inducement the assurance that female pupils would be taught privately. It is not known if any midwives availed themselves of the opportunity.[12]

Technological advances, as well as scientific, worked against the interests of female midwives. In 16th-century Europe the invention and use of obstetrical forceps had for three generations been the well-kept secret of the Chamberlen family and had greatly enhanced their medical practice. Hugh Chamberlen was forced by circumstances to sell the secret to the Medical College in Amsterdam, which in turn transmitted the precious knowledge to licensed physicians only. By the time the use of the instrument became widespread it had become associated with male physicians and male midwives. Similarly in America, introduction of the obstetrical forceps was associated with the practice of male midwives and served to their advantage. By the end of the 18th century a number of male physicians advertised their practice of midwifery. Shortly thereafter female midwives also resorted to advertising, probably in an effort to meet the competition. By the early 19th century male physicians had virtually monopolized the practice of midwifery on the Eastern seaboard. True to the generally delayed economic development in the Western frontier regions, female midwives continued to work on the frontier until a much later period. It is interesting to note that the concepts of "propriety" shifted with the prevalent practice. In 17th-century Maine the attempt of a man to act as a midwife was considered outrageous and illegal; in mid-19th-century America the suggestion that women should train as midwives and physicians was considered equally outrageous and improper.[13]

Professionalization similar to that in medicine, with the elimination of women from the upgraded profession, occurred in the field of law. Before 1750, when law suits were commonly brought to the courts by the plaintiffs themselves or by deputies without specialized legal training, women as well as men could and did act as "attorneys-in-fact." When the law became a paid profession and trained lawyers took over litigation, women disappeared from the court scene for over a century.[14]

A similar process of shrinking opportunities for women developed in business and in the retail trades. There were fewer female storekeepers and business women in the 1830s than there had been in colonial days. There was also a noticeable shift in the kind of merchandise handled by them. Where previously women could be found running almost every kind of retail shop, after 1830 they were mostly found in businesses which served women only.[15]

The only fields in which professionalization did not result in the elimination of women from the upgraded profession were nursing and teaching. Both were characterized by a severe shortage of labor. Nursing lies outside the field of this inquiry since it did not become an organized profession until after the Civil War. Before then it was regarded peculiarly as a woman's occupation, although some of the hospitals and the Army during wars employed male nurses. These bore the stigma of low skill, low status, and low pay. Generally, nursing was regarded as simply an extension of the unpaid services performed by the housewife—a characteristic attitude that haunts the profession to this day.

Education seems, at first glance, to offer an entirely opposite pattern from that of the other professions. In colonial days women had taught "Dame schools" and grade schools during summer sessions. Gradually, as educational opportunities for girls expanded, they advanced just a step ahead of their students. Professionalization of teaching occurred between 1820 and 1860, a period marked by a sharp increase in the number of women teachers. The spread of female seminaries, academies, and normal schools provided new opportunities for the training and employment of female teachers.

This trend, which runs counter to that found in the other professions, can be accounted for by the fact that women filled a desperate need created by the challenge of the common schools, the ever-increasing size of the student body, and the westward growth of the nation. America was committed to educating its children in public schools, but it was insistent on doing so as cheaply as possible. Women were available in great numbers, and they were willing to work cheaply. The result was another ideological adaptation: in the very period when the gospel of the home as woman's only proper sphere was preached most loudly, it was discovered that women were the natural teachers of youth, could do the job better than men, and were to be preferred for such employment. This was always provided, of course, that they would work at the proper wage differential—30 to 50 per cent of the wages paid male teachers was considered appropriate. The result was that in 1888 in the country as a whole, 63 per cent of all teachers were women, while the figure for the cities only was 90.04 per cent.[16]

It appeared in the teaching field, as it would in industry, that role expectations were adaptable provided the inferior status group filled a social need. The inconsistent and peculiar patterns of employment of black labor in the present-day market bear out the validity of this generalization.

There was another field in which the labor of women was appreciated and which they were urged to enter—industry. From Alexander Hamilton to Matthew Carey and Tench Coxe, advocates of industrialization sang the praises of the working girl and advanced arguments in favor of her employment. The social benefits of female labor particularly stressed were those bestowed upon her family, who now no longer had to support her. Working girls were "thus happily preserved from idleness and its attendant vices and crimes," and the whole community benefitted from their increased purchasing power.[17]

American industrialization, which occurred in an underdeveloped economy with a shortage of labor, depended on the labor of women and children. Men were occupied with agricultural work and were not available or were unwilling to enter the factories. This accounts for the special features of the early development of the New England textile industry: the relatively high wages, the respectability of the job and relatively high status of the mill girls, the patriarchal character of the model factory towns, and the temporary mobility of women workers from farm to factory and back again to farm. All this was characteristic only of a limited area and of a period of about two decades. By the late 1830s the romance had worn off: immigration had supplied a strongly competitive, permanent work force willing to work for subsistence wages; early efforts at trade union organization had been shattered, and mechanization had turned semi-skilled factory labor into unskilled labor. The process led to the replacement of the New England-born farm girls by immigrants in the mills and was accompanied by a loss of status and respectability for female workers.

The lack of organized social services during periods of depression drove ever greater numbers of women into the labor market. At first, inside the factories distinctions between men's and women's jobs were blurred. Men and women were assigned to machinery on the basis of local need. But as more women entered industry the limited number of occupations open to them tended to increase competition among them, thus lowering pay standards. Generally, women regarded their work as temporary and hesitated to invest in apprenticeship training, because they expected to marry and raise families. Thus they remained untrained, casual labor and were soon, by custom, relegated to the lowest paid, least skilled jobs. Long hours, overwork, and poor working conditions would characterize women's work in industry for almost a century.[18]

Another result of industrialization was in increasing differences in life styles between women of different classes. When female occupations, such as carding, spinning, and weaving, were transferred from home to factory, the poorer women followed their traditional work and became industrial workers. The women of the middle and upper classes could use their newly gained time for leisure pursuits: they became ladies. And a small but significant group among them chose to prepare themselves for professional careers by advanced education. This group would prove to be the most vocal and troublesome of the near future.

As class distinctions sharpened, social attitudes toward women became polarized. The image of "the lady" was elevated to the accepted ideal of femininity toward which all women would strive. In this formulation of values lower-class women were simply ignored. The actual lady was, of course, nothing new on the American scene; she had been present ever since colonial days. What was new in the 1830s was the cult of the lady, her elevation to a status symbol. The advancing prosperity of the early 19th century made it possible for middle-class women to aspire to the status formerly reserved for upper-class women. The "cult of true womanhood" of the 1830s became a vehicle for such aspirations. Mass circulation newspapers and magazines made it possible to teach every woman how to elevate the status of her family by setting "proper" standards of behavior, dress, and literary tastes. *Godey's Lady's Book* and innumerable gift books and tracts of the period all preach the same gospel of "true womanhood"—piety, purity, domesticity.[19] Those unable to reach the goal of becoming ladies were to be satisfied with the lesser goal—acceptance of their "proper place" in the home.

It is no accident that the slogan "woman's place is in the home" took on a certain aggressiveness and shrillness precisely at the time when increasing numbers of poorer women *left* their homes to become factory workers. Working women were not a fit subject for the concern of publishers and mass media writers. Idleness, once a disgrace in the eyes of society, had become a status symbol. Thorstein Veblen, one of the earliest and sharpest commentators on the subject, observed that it had become almost the sole social function of the lady "to put in evidence her economic unit's ability to pay." She was "a means of conspicuously unproductive expenditure," devoted to displaying her husband's wealth.[20] Just as the cult of white womanhood in the South served to preserve a labor and social system based on race distinctions, so did the cult of the lady in an egalitarian society serve as a means of preserving class distinctions. Where class distinctions were not so great, as on the frontier, the position of women was closer to what it had been in colonial days; their economic contribution was more highly valued, their opportunities were less restricted, and their positive participation in community life was taken for granted.

In the urbanized and industrialized Northeast the life experience of middle-class women was different in almost every respect from that of the lower-class women. But there was one thing the society lady and the mill girl had in common—they were equally disfranchised and isolated from the vital centers of power. Yet the political status of women had not actually deteriorated. With very few exceptions women had neither voted nor stood for office during the colonial period. Yet the spread of the franchise to ever wider groups of white males during the Jacksonian age, the removal of property restrictions, the increasing numbers of immigrants who acquired access to the franchise, made the gap between these new enfranchised voters and the disfranchised women more obvious. Quite naturally, educated and propertied women felt this deprivation more keenly. Their own career expectations had been encouraged by widening educational opportunities; their consciousness of their own abilities and of their potential for power had been enhanced by their activities in the reform movements of the 1830s; the general spirit of upward mobility and venturesome entrepreneurship that pervaded the Jacksonian era was infectious. But in the late 1840s a sense of acute frustration enveloped these educated and highly spirited women. Their rising expectations had met with frustration, their hopes had been shattered; they were bitterly conscious of a relative lowering of status and a loss of position. This sense of frustration led them to action; it was one of the main factors in the rise of the woman's rights movement.[21]

The women who at the first woman's rights convention at Seneca Falls, New York, in 1848 declared boldly and with considerable exaggeration that "the history of mankind is a history of repeated injuries and usurpations on the part of man toward woman, having in direct object the establishment of an absolute tyranny over her," did not speak for the truly exploited and abused working woman.[22] As a matter of fact, they were largely ignorant of her condition and, with the notable exception of Susan B. Anthony, indifferent to her fate. But they judged from the realities of their own life experience. Like most revolutionaries, they were not the most downtrodden but rather the most status-deprived group. Their frustrations and traditional isolation from political power funneled their discontent into fairly utopian declarations and immature organizational means. They would learn better in the long, hard decades of practical struggle. Yet it is their initial emphasis on the legal and political "disabilities" of women which has provided the framework for most of the historical work on women.* For almost a hundred years sympathetic historians have told the story of women in America by deriving from the position of middle-class women a generalization concerning all American women. To avoid distortion, any valid generalization concerning American women after the 1830s should reflect a recognition of class stratification.

For lower-class women the changes brought by industrialization were actually advantageous, offering income and advancement opportunities, however limited, and a chance for participation in the ranks of organized labor.† They, by and large, tended to join men in their struggle for economic advancement and became increasingly concerned with economic gains and protective labor legislation. Middle- and upper-class women, on the other hand, reacted to actual and fancied status deprivation by increasing militancy and the formation of organizations for woman's rights, by which they meant especially legal and property rights.

The four decades preceding the Seneca Falls Convention were decisive in the history of American women. They brought an actual deterioration in the economic opportunities open to women, a relative deterioration in their political status, and a rising level of expectation and subsequent frustration in a privileged elite group of educated women. It was in these decades that the values and beliefs that clustered around the assertion "Woman's place is in the home" changed from being descriptive of an existing reality to becoming an ideology. "The cult of true womanhood" extolled woman's predominance in the domestic sphere, while it tried to justify women's ex-

* To the date of the first printing of this article (1969).

† In 1979, I would not agree with this optimistic generalization.

clusion from the public domain, from equal education and from participation in the political process by claims to tradition, universality, and a history dating back to antiquity, or at least to the *Mayflower*. In a century of modernization and industrialization women alone were to remain unchanging, embodying in their behavior and attitudes the longing of men and women caught in rapid social change for a mythical archaic past of agrarian family self-sufficiency. In preindustrial America the home was indeed the workplace for both men and women, although the self-sufficiency of the America yeoman, whose economic well-being depended on a network of international trade and mercantilism, was even then more apparent than real. In the 19th and 20th centuries the home was turned into the realm of woman, while the workplace became the public domain of men. The ideology of "woman's sphere" sought to upgrade women's domestic function by elaborating the role of mother, turning the domestic drudge into a "homemaker" and charging her with elevating her family's status by her exercise of consumer functions and by her display of her own and her family's social graces. These prescribed roles never *were* a reality. In the 1950s Betty Friedan would describe this ideology and rename it "the feminine mystique," but it was no other than the myth of "woman's proper sphere" created in the 1840s and updated by consumerism and the misunderstood dicta of Freudian psychology.[23]

The decades 1800–1840 also provide the clues to an understanding of the institutional shape of the later women's organizations. These would be led by middle-class women whose self-image, life experience, and ideology had largely been fashioned and influenced by these early, transitional years. The concerns of middle-class women—property rights, the franchise, and moral uplift—would dominate the woman's rights movement. But side by side with it, and at times co-operating with it, would grow a number of organizations serving the needs of working women.

American women were the largest disfranchised group in the nation's history, and they retained this position longer than any other group. Although they found ways of making their influence felt continuously, not only as individuals but as organized groups, power eluded them. The mill girl and the lady, both born in the age of Jackson, would not gain access to power until they learned to cooperate, each for her own separate interests. It would take almost six decades before they would find common ground. The issue around which they finally would unite and push their movement to victory was the "impractical and utopian" demand raised at Seneca Falls—the means to power in American society—female suffrage.

NOTES

This article first appeared in *American Studies,* Vol. 10, No. 1, Spring 1969. Research for this article was facilitated by a research grant provided by Long Island University, Brooklyn, N.Y., which is gratefully acknowledged.

The generalizations in this article are based on extensive research in primary sources, including letters and manuscripts of the following women: Elizabeth Cady Stanton, Susan B. Anthony, Abby Kelley, Lucretia Mott, Lucy Stone, Sarah and Angelina Grimké, Maria Weston Chapman, Lydia Maria Child, and Betsey Cowles. Among the organizational records consulted were those of the Boston Female Anti-Slavery Society, the Philadelphia Female Anti-Slavery Society, Anti-Slavery Conventions of American Women, all the Woman's Rights Conventions prior to 1870, and the records of various female charitable organizations.

1. Keith E. Melder, "The Beginnings of the Women's Rights Movement in the United States: 1800–1840" (Dissertation, Yale, 1963); Elisabeth A. Dexter, *Colonial Women of Affairs: Women in Business and Professions in America before 1776* (Boston, 1931) and *Career Women of America: 1776–1840* (Francestown, N.H., 1950).

2. Herbert Moller, "Sex Composition and Corresponding Culture Patterns of Colonial America," *William and Mary Quarterly*, Ser. 3, II (April 1945), 113–53.

3. The summary of the status of colonial women is based on the following sources: Mary Benson, *Women in 18th Century America: A Study of Opinion and Social Usage* (New York, 1935); Arthur Calhoun, *A Social History of the American Family* (3 vols.; Cleveland, 1918); Dexter, *Colonial Women;* Dexter, *Career Women;* Edmund S. Morgan, *Virginians at Home: Family Life in the 18th Century* (Williamsburg, 1952); Julia C. Spruill, *Women's Life and Work in the Southern Colonies* (Chapel Hill, 1938).

4. E. M. Boatwright, "The Political and Legal Status of Women in Georgia: 1783–1860," *Georgia Historical Quarterly*, XXV (April 1941); Richard B. Morris, *Studies in the History of American Law* (New York, 1930), chap. 3. A summary of travelers' comments on American woman may be found in: Jane Mesick, *The English Traveler in America: 1785–1835* (New York, 1922), pp. 83–99.

5. For facts on colonial medicine the following sources were consulted: Wyndham B. Blanton, *Medicine in Virginia* (3 vols.; Richmond, 1930); N. S. Davis, M.D., *History of Medical Education and Institutions in the United States . . .* (Chicago, 1851); Dexter, *Career Women;* K. C. Hurd-Mead, M.D., *A History of Women in Medicine: from the Earliest Times to the Beginning of the 19th Century* (Haddam, Conn., 1938); Geo. W. Norris, *The Early History of Medicine in Philadelphia* (Philadelphia, 1886); Joseph M. Toner, *Contributions to the annals of Medical Progress in the United States before and during the War of Independence* (Washington, D.C., 1874). The citation regarding Mrs. Allyn is from Hurd-Mead, *Women in Medicine*, p. 487.

6. Fielding H. Garrison, M.D., *An Introduction to the History of Medicine* (Philadelphia, 1929). For licensing legislation: Davis, 88–103; see also: Martin Kaufman, "American Medical Diploma Mills," *The Bulletin of the Tulane University Medical Faculty*, Vol. 26, No. 1 (Feb. 1967), 53–57.

7. Among the alternate institutions founded are: New England Female

Medical College (1848); Female (later Women's) Medical College of Philadelphia (1850); Women's Medical College and New York Infirmary for Women (1865); Woman's Hospital of Philadelphia (1861); New England Hospital for Women and Children (1862).

For information on the training of pioneer women physicians see: James R. Chadwick, M.D., *The Study and Practice of Medicine by Women* (New York, 1879).

For instances of discrimination see: Harriot K. Hunt, M.D., *Glances and Glimpses or Fifty Years Social including Twenty Years Professional Life* (Boston, 1856); Elizabeth Blackwell, *Pioneer Work in Opening the Medical Profession to Women* (New York, 1865); "Preamble and Resolution of the Philadelphia County Medical Society Upon the Status of Women Physicians with *A Reply by a Woman*" (Philadelphia, 1867), pamphlet.

See also biographies of women physicians in Edward and Janet James (eds.), *Notable American Women, 1607–1950: A Biographical Dictionary* (3 vols.; Cambridge, Mass., 1972).

For a recent work offering a somewhat different interpretation see Mary Roth Walsh, *Doctors Wanted: No Women Need Apply: Sexual Barriers in the Medical Profession, 1835–1975* (New Haven, 1977).

8. George Daniels, "The Professionalization of American Science: The Emergent Period, 1820–1860," paper delivered at the joint session of the History of Science Society and the Society of the History of Technology, San Francisco, December 28, 1965.

9. Hurd-Mead, *Women in Medicine*, p. 391.

10. *Ibid.*, p. 486.

11. Betsy E. Corner, *William Shippen Jr.: Pioneer in American Medical Education* (Philadelphia, 1951), p. 103.

12. *Ibid.*

13. Benjamin Lee Gordon, *Medieval and Renaissance Medicine* (New York, 1959), pp. 689–91. Blanton, *Medicine*, II, 23–24; Hurd-Mead, *Women in Medicine*, pp. 487–88; Annie Nathan Meyer, *Woman's Work in America* (New York, 1891); Harriot K. Hunt, M.D., *Glances* . . . pp. 127–40; Eleanor Flexner, *Century of Struggle: The Woman's Rights Movement in the United States* (Cambridge, Mass., 1959), pp. 115–19.

14. Sophie H. Drinker, "Women Attorneys of Colonial Times," *Maryland Historical Society Bulletin*, vol. LVI, No. 4 (Dec. 1961).

15. Dexter, *Colonial Women*, pp. 34–35, 162–65.

16. Harriet W. Marr, *The Old New England Academies* (New York, 1959), chap. 8; Thomas Woody, *A History of Women's Education in the United States* (2 vols.; New York, 1929), pp. 100–109, 458–60, 492–93.

17. Matthew Carey, *Essays on Political Economy* . . . (Philadelphia, 1822), p. 459.

18. The statements on women industrial workers are based on the following sources: Edith Abbott, *Women in Industry* (New York, 1910), pp. 66–80, and "Harriet Martineau and the Employment of Women in 1836," *Journal of Political Economy*, XIV (Dec. 1906), 614–26; Matthew Carey, *Miscellaneous Essays* (Philadelphia, 1830), pp. 153–203; Helen L. Sumner, *History of Women in Industry in the United States*, in *Report on Condition of Woman and Child Wage-Earners in the United States* (19 vols., Washington, D.C., 1910), IX; also: Elizabeth F. Baker, *Technology and Woman's Work* (New York, 1964), chaps. 1–5.

19. Emily Putnam, *The Lady: Studies of Certain Significant Phases of Her*

History (New York, 1910), pp. 319–20; Barbara Welter, "The Cult of True Womanhood: 1820–1860," *American Quarterly,* Vol. XVIII, No. 2, Part I (Summer 1966), 151–74.

20. Veblen generalized from his observations of the society of the Gilded Age and fell into the usual error of simply ignoring the lower-class women, whom he dismissed as "drudges . . . fairly content with their lot," but his analysis of women's role in "conspicuous consumption" and of the function of women's fashions is unsurpassed. For references see: Thorstein Veblen, *The Theory of the Leisure Class* (New York, 1962, first printing, 1899), pp. 70–71, 231–32, and "The Economic Theory of Woman's Dress," *Essays in Our Changing Order* (New York, 1934), pp. 65–77.

21. Like most groups fighting status oppression women formulated a compensatory ideology of female superiority. Norton Mezvinsky has postulated that this was clearly expressed only in 1874; in fact this formulation appeared in the earliest speeches of Elizabeth Cady Stanton and in the speeches and resolutions of the Seneca Falls conventions and other pre-Civil War woman's rights conventions. Rather than a main motivating force, the idea was a tactical formulation, designed to take advantage of the popularly held male belief in woman's "moral" superiority and to convince reformers that they needed the votes of women. Those middle-class feminists who believed in woman's "moral" superiority exploited the concept in order to win their major goal—female equality. For references see: Norton Mezvinsky, "An Idea of Female Superiority," *Midcontinent American Studies Journal,* Vol. II, No. 1 (Spring 1961), 17–26; Stanton *et al., HWS,* I, 72, 479, 522, 529, and *passim;* Alan P. Grimes, *The Puritan Ethic and Woman Suffrage* (New York, 1967), chaps. 2 and 3.

22. Stanton *et al., HWS,* I, 70.

23. Betty Friedan, *The Feminine Mystique* (New York, 1963).

8

Beauty, the Beast, and the Militant Woman

A Case Study in Sex Roles and Social Stress in Jacksonian America

■

CARROLL SMITH-ROSENBERG

The Seneca Falls Declaration of Sentiments of 1848, in which women asserted a long list of economic, educational, legal, and political grievances, has traditionally been considered the initial appearance of organized feminism in America. One of the first historians to recognize the complex role evangelical religion played in shaping the activities of women in the early nineteenth century, Carroll Smith-Rosenberg focuses on evangelically-motivated moral reform societies and finds in their attack on the double standard of sexual morality an incipient rebellion on women's part more than a decade ahead of Seneca Falls. Her essay of 1971 is already regarded as a classic in the field for its innovative and fruitful application of concepts of social psychology, its broadening of the definition of feminism by inclusion of protests respecting sexual norms, its illumination of the importance of women's associative activity, and its comparison of the evangelical stream of women's activism with mainstream feminism.

ON A SPRING EVENING in May 1834, a small group of women met at the revivalistic Third Presbyterian Church in New York City to found the New York Female Moral Reform Society. The Society's goals were ambitious indeed; it hoped to convert New York's prostitutes to evangelical Protestantism and close forever the city's numerous brothels. This bold attack on prostitution was only one part of the Society's program. These self-assertive women hoped as well to confront that larger and more fundamental abuse, the double standard, and the male sexual license it condoned. Too many men, the Society defiantly asserted in its statement of goals, were aggressive destroyers of female innocence and happiness. No man was above suspicion. Women's only safety lay in a militant effort to reform American sexual mores—and, as we shall see, to reform sexual mores meant in practice to control man's sexual values and autonomy. The rhetoric of the Society's spokesmen consistently betrayed an unmistakable and deeply felt resentment toward a male-dominated society.[1]

Few if any members of the Society were reformed prostitutes or the victims of rape or seduction. Most came from middle-class native American backgrounds and lived quietly respectable lives as pious wives and mothers. What needs explaining is the emotional logic which underlay the Society's militant and controversial program of sexual reform. I would like to suggest that both its reform program and the anti-male sentiments it served to express reflect a neglected area of stress in mid-19th century America—that is, the nature of the role to be assumed by the middle-class American woman.

American society from the 1830s to the 1860s was marked by advances in political democracy, by a rapid increase in economic, social and geographic mobility, and by uncompromising and morally relentless reform movements. Though many aspects of Jacksonianism have been subjected to historical investigation, the possibly stressful effects of such structural change upon family and sex roles have not. The following pages constitute an attempt to glean some understanding of women and women's role in antebellum America through an analysis of a self-consciously female voluntary association dedicated to the eradication of sexual immorality.

Women in Jacksonian America had few rights and little power. Their role in society was passive and sharply limited. Women were, in general, denied formal education above the minimum required by a literate early industrial society. The female brain and nervous system, male physicians and educators agreed, were inadequate to sustained intellectual effort. They were denied the vote in a society which placed a high value upon political participation; political activity might corrupt their pure feminine nature. All professional roles (with the exception of primary school education) were closed to women. Even so traditional a female role as midwife was undermined as male physicians began to establish professional control over obstetrics. Most economic alternatives to marriage (except such burdensome and menial tasks as those of seamstress or domestic) were closed to women. Their property rights were still restricted and females were generally considered to be the legal wards either of the state or of their nearest male relative. In the event of divorce, the mother lost custody of her children—even when the husband was conceded to be the erring party.[2] Women's universe was bounded by their homes and the career of father or husband; within the home it was woman's duty to be submissive and patient.

Yet this was a period when change was considered a self-evident good, and when nothing was believed impossible to a determined free will, be it the conquest of a continent, the reform of society or the eternal salvation of all mankind. The contrast between these generally accepted ideals and expectations and the real possibilities available to American women could not have been more sharply drawn. It is not implausible to assume that at least a minority of American women would find ways to manifest a discontent with their comparatively passive and constricted social role.

Only a few women in antebellum America were able, however, to openly criticize their socially defined sexual identity. A handful, like Fanny Wright, devoted themselves to overtly subversive criticism of the social order.[3] A scarcely more numerous group became pioneers in women's education. Others such as Elizabeth Cady Stanton, Lucretia Mott and Susan B. Anthony founded the women's rights movement. But most respectable women—even those with a sense of ill-defined grievance—were unable to explicitly defy traditional sex-role prescriptions.

I would like to suggest that many such women channeled frustration, anger and a compensatory sense of superior righteousness into the reform movements of the first half of the 19th century; and in the controversial moral reform crusade such motivations seem particularly apparent. While unassailable within the absolute categories of a pervasive evangelical world-view, the Female Moral Reform Society's crusade against illicit sexuality permitted an expression of anti-male sentiments. And the Society's "final solution"—the right to control the mores of men—provided a logical emotional redress for those feelings of passivity which we have suggested. It should not be surprising that between 1830 and 1860 a significant number of militant women joined a crusade to establish their right to define —and limit—man's sexual behavior.

Yet adultery and prostitution were unaccustomed objects of reform even in the enthusiastic and millennial America of the 1830s. The mere discussion of these taboo subjects shocked most Americans; to undertake such a crusade implied no ordinary degree of commitment. The founders of the Female Moral Reform Society, however, were able to find both legitimization for the expression of grievance normally unspoken and an impulse to activism in the moral categories of evangelical piety. Both pious activism and sex-role anxieties shaped the early years of the Female Moral Reform Society. This conjunction of motives was hardly accidental.

The lady founders of the Moral Reform Society and their new organization represented an extreme wing of that movement within American Protestantism known as the Second Great Awakening. These women were intensely pious Christians, convinced that an era of millennial perfection awaited human effort. In this fervent generation, such deeply felt millennial possibilities made social action a moral imperative. Like many of the abolitionists, Jacksonian crusaders against sexual transgression were dedicated activists, compelled to attack sin wherever it existed and in whatever form it assumed—even the unmentionable sin of illicit sexuality.

New Yorkers' first awareness of the moral reform crusade came in the spring of 1832 when the New York Magdalen Society (an organization which sought to reform prostitutes) issued its first annual report. Written by John McDowall, their missionary and agent, the report stated unhesitatingly that 10,000 prostitutes lived and worked in New York City. Not only sailors and other transients, but men from the city's most respected families, were regular brothel patrons. Lewdness and impurity tainted all sectors of New York society. True Christians, the report concluded, must wage a thoroughgoing crusade against violators of the Seventh Commandment.[4]

The report shocked and irritated respectable New Yorkers—not only by its tone of righteous indignation and implied criticism of the city's old and established families. The report, it seemed clear to many New Yorkers, was obscene, its author a mere seeker after notoriety.[5] Hostility quickly spread from McDowall to the Society itself; its members were verbally abused and threatened with ostracism. The society disbanded.

A few of the women, however, would not retreat. Working quietly, they began to found church-affiliated female moral reform societies. Within a year, they had created a number of such groups, connected for the most part with the city's more evangelical congregations. These pious women hoped to reform prostitutes, but more immediately to warn other God-fearing Christians of the pervasiveness of sexual sin and the need to oppose it. Prostitution was after all only one of many offenses against the Seventh Commandment; adultery, lewd thoughts and language, and bawdy literature were equally sinful in the eyes of God. These women at the same time continued unofficially to support their former missionary, John McDowall, using his newly established moral reform newspaper to advance their cause not only in the city, but throughout New York State.[6]

After more than a year of such discreet crusading, the women active in the moral reform cause felt sufficiently numerous and confident to organize a second city-wide moral reform society, and renew their efforts to reform the city's prostitutes. On the evening of May 12, 1834, they met at the Third Presbyterian Church to found the New York Female Moral Reform Society.[7]

Nearly four years of opposition and controversy had hardened the women's ardor into a militant determination. They proposed through their organization to extirpate sexual license and the double standard from American society. A forthright list of resolves announced their organization:

> Resolved, That immediate and vigorous efforts should be made to create a public sentiment in respect to this sin; and also in respect to the duty of parents, church members and ministers on the subject, which shall be in stricter accordance with . . . the word of God.
>
> . . . .
>
> Resolved, That the licentious man is no less guilty than his victim, and ought, therefore, to be excluded from all virtuous female society.
>
> Resolved, That it is the imperious duty of ladies everywhere, and of every religious denomination, to co-operate in the great work of moral reform.

A sense of urgency and spiritual absolutism marked this organizational meeting, and indeed all of the Society's official statements for years to come. "It is the duty of the virtuous to use every consistent moral means to save our country from utter destruction," the women warned. "The sin of licentiousness has made fearful havoc . . . drowning souls in perdition and exposing us to the vengeance of a holy God." Americans hopeful of witnessing the promised millennium could delay no longer.[8]

The motivating zeal which allowed the rejection of age-old proprieties and defied the criticism of pulpit and press was no casual and fashionable enthusiasm. Only an extraordinary set of legitimating values could have justified such commitment. And this was indeed the case. The women moral reformers acted in the conscious conviction that God imperiously commanded their work. As they explained soon after organizing their society: "As Christians we must view it in the light of God's word—we must enter into His feelings on the subject—engage in its overthrow just in the manner he would have us. . . . We must look away from all worldly opinions or influences, for they are perverted and wrong; and individually act only as in the presence of God."[9] Though the Society's pious activism had deep roots in the evangelicalism of the Second Great Awakening, the immediate impetus for the founding of the Moral Reform Society came from the revivals Charles G. Finney conducted in New York City between the summer of 1829 and the spring of 1834.[10]

Charles Finney, reformer, revivalist and perfectionist theologian from western New York State, remains a pivotal figure in the history of American Protestantism. The four years Finney spent in New York had a profound influence on the city's churches and reform movements, and upon the consciences generally of the thousands of New Yorkers who crowded his revival meetings and flocked to his churches. Finney insisted that his disciples end any compromise with sin or human injustice. Souls were lost and sin prevailed, Finney urged, because men chose to sin—because they chose not to work in God's vineyard converting souls and reforming sinners.[11] Inspired by Finney's sermons, thousands of New Yorkers turned to missionary work; they distributed Bibles and tracts to the irreligious, established Sunday schools and sent ministers to the frontier.[12] A smaller, more zealous number espoused abolition as well, determined, like Garrison, never to be silent and to be heard. An even smaller number of the most zealous and determined turned—as we have seen—to moral reform.[13]

The program adopted by the Female Moral Reform Society in the spring of 1834 embraced two quite different, though to the Society's founders quite consistent, modes of attack. One was absolutist and millennial, an attempt to convert all of America to perfect moral purity. Concretely the New York women hoped to create a militant nationwide women's organization to fight the double standard and indeed any form of licentiousness—beginning of course in their own homes and neighborhoods. Only an organization of women, they contended, could be trusted with so sensitive and yet monumental a task. At the same time, the Society sponsored a parallel and somewhat more pragmatic attempt to convert and reform New York City's prostitutes. Though strikingly dissimilar in method and geographic scope, both efforts were unified by an uncompromising millennial zeal and by a strident hostility to the licentious and predatory male.

The Society began its renewed drive against prostitution in the fall of 1834 when the executive committee appointed John McDowall their missionary to New York's prostitutes and hired two young men to assist him.[14] The Society's three missionaries visited the female wards of the almshouse, the city hospital and jails, leading prayer meetings, distributing Bibles and tracts. A greater proportion of their time, however, was spent in a more controversial manner, systematically visiting—or, to be more accurate, descending upon—brothels, praying with and exhorting both the inmates and their patrons. The missionaries were especially fond of arriving early Sunday morning—catching women and customers as they awoke on the traditionally sacred day. The missionaries would announce their arrival by a vigorous reading of Bible passages, followed by prayer and hymns. At other times they would station themselves across the street from known brothels to observe and note the identity of customers. They soon found their simple presence had an important deterring effect, many men, with doggedly innocent expressions, pausing momentarily and then hastily walking past. Closed coaches, they also reported, were observed to circle suspiciously for upwards of an hour until, the missionary remaining, they drove away.[15]

The Female Moral Reform Society did not depend completely on paid missionaries for the success of such pious harassment. The Society's executive committee, accompanied by like-thinking male volunteers, regularly visited the city's hapless brothels. (The executive committee minutes for January 1835, for example, contain a lengthy discussion of the properly discreet makeup of groups for such "active visiting.")[16] The members went primarily to pray and to exert moral influence. They were not unaware, however, of the financially disruptive effect that frequent visits of large groups of praying Christians would have.[17] The executive committee also aided the concerned parents (usually rural) of runaway daughters who, they feared, might have drifted to the city and been forced into prostitution. Members visited brothels asking for information about such girls; one pious volunteer even pretended to be delivering laundry in order to gain admittance to a brothel suspected of hiding such a runaway.[18]

In conjunction with their visiting, the Moral Reform Society opened a House of Reception, a would-be refuge for prostitutes seeking to reform. The Society's managers and missionaries felt that if the prostitute could be convinced of her sin, and then offered both a place of retreat and an economic alternative to prostitution, reform would surely follow. Thus they envisioned their home as a "house of industry" where the errant ones would be taught new trades and prepared for useful jobs—while being instructed in morality and religion. When the managers felt their repentant charges prepared to return to society, they attempted to find them jobs with Christian families—and, so far as possible, away from the city's temptations.[19]

Despite their efforts, however, few prostitutes reformed; fewer still appeared, to their benefactresses, to have experienced the saving grace of conversion. Indeed, the number of inmates at the Society's

House of Reception was always small. In March 1835, for instance, the executive committee reported only fourteen women at the House. A year later, total admissions had reached but thirty—only four of whom were considered saved.[20] The final debacle came that summer when the regular manager of the House left the city because of poor health. In his absence, the executive committee reported unhappily, the inmates seized control, and discipline and morality deteriorated precipitously. The managers reassembled in the fall to find their home in chaos. Bitterly discouraged, they dismissed the few remaining unruly inmates and closed the building.[21]

The moral rehabilitation of New York's streetwalkers was but one aspect of the Society's attack upon immorality. The founders of the Female Moral Reform Society saw as their principal objective the creation of a woman's crusade to combat sexual license generally and the double standard particularly. American women would no longer willingly tolerate that traditional—and role-defining—masculine ethos which allotted respect to the hearty drinker and the sexual athlete. This age-old code of masculinity was as obviously related to man's social preeminence as it was contrary to society's explicitly avowed norms of purity and domesticity. The subterranean mores of the American male must be confronted, exposed and rooted out.

The principal weapon of the Society in this crusade was its weekly, *The Advocate of Moral Reform*. In the fall of 1834, when the Society hired John McDowall as its agent, it voted as well to purchase his journal and transform it into a national women's paper with an exclusively female staff. Within three years, the *Advocate* grew into one of the nation's most widely read evangelical papers, boasting 16,500 subscribers. By the late 1830s the Society's managers pointed to this publication as their most important activity.[22]

Two themes dominated virtually every issue of the *Advocate* from its founding in January 1835, until the early 1850s. The first was an angry and emphatic insistence upon the lascivious and predatory nature of the American male. Men were the initiators in virtually every case of adultery or fornication—and the source, therefore, of that widespread immorality which endangered America's spiritual life and delayed the promised millennium. A second major theme in the *Advocate*'s editorials and letters was a call for the creation of a national union of women. Through their collective action such a united group of women might ultimately control the behavior of adult males and of the members' own children, particularly their sons.

The founders and supporters of the Female Moral Reform Society entertained several primary assumptions concerning the nature of human sexuality. Perhaps most central was the conviction that women felt little sexual desire; they were in almost every instance induced to violate the Seventh Commandment by lascivious men who craftily manipulated not their sensuality, but rather the female's trusting and affectionate nature. A woman acted out of romantic love, not carnal desire; she was innocent and defenseless, gentle and passive.[23] "The worst crime alleged against [the fallen woman] in the outset," the *Advocate*'s editors explained, "is . . . 'She is without discretion.' She is open-hearted, sincere, and affectionate. . . . She trusts the vows of the faithless. She commits her all into the hands of the deceiver."[24]

The male lecher, on the other hand, was a creature controlled by base sexual drives which he neither could nor would control. He was, the *Advocate*'s editors bitterly complained, powerful and decisive; unwilling (possibly unable) to curb his own willfulness, he callously used it to coerce the more passive and submissive female. This was an age of rhetorical expansiveness, and the *Advocate*'s editors and correspondents felt little constraint in their delineation of the dominant and aggressive male. "Reckless," "bold," "mad," "drenched in sin" were terms used commonly to describe erring males; they "robbed," "ruined" and "rioted." But one term above all others seemed most fit to describe the lecher—"The Destroyer."[25]

A deep sense of anger and frustration characterized the *Advocate*'s discussion of such all-conquering males, a theme reiterated again and again in the letters sent to the paper by rural sympathizers. Women saw themselves with few defenses against the determined male; his will was far stronger than that of woman.[26] Such letters often expressed a bitterness which seems directed not only against the specific seducer, but toward all American men. One representative rural subscriber complained, for example: "Honorable men; they would not plunder; . . . an imputation on their honour might cost a man his life's blood. And yet they are so passingly mean, so utterly contemptible, as basely and treacherously to contrive . . . the destruction of happiness, peace, morality, and all that is endearing in social life; they plunge into degradation, misery, and ruin, those whom they profess to love. O let them not be trusted. Their 'tender mercies are cruel.' "[27]

The double standard seemed thus particularly unjust; it came to symbolize and embody for the Society and its rural sympathizers the callous indifference—indeed at times almost sadistic pleasure—a male-dominated society took in the misfortune of a passive and defenseless woman. The respectable harshly denied her their friendship; even parents might reject her. Often only the brothel offered food and shelter. But what of her seducer? Conventional wisdom found it easy to condone his greater sin: men will be men and right-thinking women must not inquire into such questionable matters.[28]

But it was just such matters, the Society contended, to which women must address themselves. They must enforce God's commandments despite hostility and censure. "Public opinion must be operated upon," the executive committee decided in the winter of 1835, "by endeavoring to bring the virtuous to treat the guilty of both sexes alike, and exercise toward them the same feeling." "Why should a female be trodden under foot," the executive committee's minutes questioned plaintively, "and spurned from society and driven from a parent's roof, if she but fall into sin—while common consent allows the male to habituate himself to this vice, and treats him as not guilty. Has God made a distinction in regard to the two sexes in this respect?"[29] The guilty woman too should be condemned, the Moral Reform Society's quarterly meeting resolved in 1838: "But let not the most guilty of the two—the deliberate destroyer of female innocence—be afforded even an 'apron of fig leaves' to conceal the blackness of his crimes."[30]

Women must unite in a holy crusade against such sinners. The Society called upon pious women throughout the country to shun all social contact with men suspected of improper behavior—even if that behavior consisted only of reading improper books or singing indelicate songs. Church-going women of every village and town must organize local campaigns to outlaw such men from society and hold them up to public judgment.[31] "Admit him not to your house," the executive committee urged, "hold no converse with him, warn others of him, permit not your friends to have fellowship with him, mark him as an evildoer, stamp him as a villain and exclaim, 'Behold the Seducer.' " The power of ostracism could become an effective weapon in the defense of morality.[32]

A key tactic in this campaign of public exposure was the Society's willingness to publish the names of men suspected of sexual immorality. The *Advocate*'s editors announced in their first issue that they intended to pursue this policy, first begun by John McDowall in his *Journal*.[33] "We think it proper," they stated defiantly, "even to expose names, for the same reason that the names of thieves and robbers are published, that the public may know them and govern themselves accordingly. We mean to let the licentious know, that if they are not ashamed of their debasing vice, we will not be ashamed to expose them. . . . It is a justice which we owe each other."[34] Their readers responded enthusiastically to this invitation. Letters from rural subscribers poured into the *Advocate,* recounting specific instances of seduction in their towns and warning readers to avoid the men described. The editors dutifully set them in type and printed them.[35]

Within New York City itself the executive committee of the Society actively investigated charges of seduction and immorality. A particular target of their watchfulness was the city's employment agencies—or information offices as they were then called; these were frequently fronts for the white-slave trade. The *Advocate* printed the names and addresses of suspicious agencies, warning women seeking employment to avoid them at all costs.[36] Prostitutes whom the Society's missionaries visited in brothels, in prison or in the city hospital were urged to report the names of men who had first seduced them and also of their later customers; they could then be published in the *Advocate.*[37] The executive committee undertook as well a lobbying campaign in Albany to secure the passage of a statute making seduction a crime for the male participant.[38] While awaiting the passage of this measure, the executive committee encouraged and aided victims of seduction (or where appropriate their parents or employers) to sue their seducers on the grounds of loss of services.[39]

Ostracism, exposure and statutory enactment offered immediate, if unfortunately partial, solutions to the problem of male licentiousness. But for the seduced and ruined victim such vengeance came too late. The tactic of preference, women moral reformers agreed, was to educate children, especially young male children, to a literal adherence to the Seventh Commandment. This was a mother's task. American mothers, the *Advocate's* editors repeated endlessly, must educate their sons to reject the double standard. No child was too young, no efforts too diligent in this crucial aspect of socialization.[40] The true foundations of such a successful effort lay in an early and highly pietistic religious education and in the inculcation of a related imperative—the son's absolute and unquestioned obedience to his mother's will. "Obedience, entire and unquestioned, must be secured, or all is lost." The mother must devote herself whole-heartedly to this task for self-will in a child was an ever-recurring evil.[41] "Let us watch over them continually . . . Let us . . . teach them when they go out and when they come in—when they lie down, and when they rise up. . . ."[42] A son must learn to confide in his mother instinctively; no thought should be hidden from her.

Explicit education in the Seventh Commandment itself should

begin quite early for bitter experience had shown that no child was too young for such sensual temptation.[43] As her son grew older, his mother was urged to instill in him a love for the quiet of domesticity, a repugnance for the unnatural excitements of the theater and tavern. He should be taught to prefer home and the companionship of pious women to the temptations of bachelor life.[44] The final step in a young man's moral education would come one evening shortly before he was to leave home for the first time. That night, the *Advocate* advised its readers, the mother must spend a long earnest time at his bedside (ordinarily in the dark to hide her natural blushes) discussing the importance of maintaining his sexual purity and the temptations he would inevitably face in attempting to remain true to his mother's religious principles.[45]

Mothers, not fathers, were urged to supervise the sexual education of sons. Mothers, the Society argued, spent most time with their children; fathers were usually occupied with business concerns and found little time for their children. Sons were naturally close to their mothers and devoted maternal supervision would cement these natural ties. A mother devoted to the moral reform cause could be trusted to teach her son to reject the traditional ethos of masculinity and accept the higher—more feminine—code of Christianity. A son thus educated would be inevitably a recruit in the women's crusade against sexual license.[46]

The Society's general program of exposure and ostracism, lobbying and education depended for effectiveness upon the creation of a national association of militant and pious women. In the fall of 1834, but a few months after they had organized their Society, its New York officers began to create such a woman's organization. At first they worked through the *Advocate* and the small network of sympathizers John McDowall's efforts had created. By the spring of 1835, however, they were able to hire a minister to travel through western New York State "in behalf of Moral Reform causes."[47] The following year the committee sent two female missionaries, the editor of the Society's newspaper and a paid female agent, on a thousand-mile tour of the New England states. Visiting women's groups and churches in Brattleboro, Deerfield, Northampton, Pittsfield, the Stockbridges and many other towns, the ladies rallied their sisters to the moral reform cause and helped organize some forty-one new auxiliaries. Each succeeding summer saw similar trips by paid agents and managers of the Society throughout New York State and New England.[48] By 1839, the New York Female Moral Reform Society boasted some 445 female auxiliaries, principally in greater New England.[49] So successful were these efforts that within a few years the bulk of the Society's membership and financial support came from its auxiliaries. In February 1838, the executive committee voted to invite representatives of these auxiliaries to attend the Society's annual meeting. The following year the New York Society voted at its annual convention to reorganize as a national society—the American Female Moral Reform Society; the New York group would be simply one of its many constituent societies.[50]

This rural support was an indispensable part of the moral reform movement. The local auxiliaries held regular meetings in churches, persuaded hesitant ministers to preach on the Seventh Commandment, urged Sunday school teachers to confront this embarrassing but vital question. They raised money for the executive committee's ambitious projects, convinced at least some men to form male moral reform societies, and did their utmost to ostracize suspected lechers. When the American Female Moral Reform Society decided to mount a campaign to induce the New York State legislature to pass a law making seduction a criminal offense, the Society's hundreds of rural auxiliaries wrote regularly to their legislators, circulated petitions and joined their New York City sisters in Albany to lobby for the bill (which was finally passed in 1848).[51]

In addition to such financial and practical aid, members of the moral reform society's rural branches contributed another crucial, if less tangible, element to the reform movement. This was their commitment to the creation of a feeling of sisterhood among all morally dedicated women. Letters from individuals to the *Advocate* and reports from auxiliaries make clear, sometimes even in the most explicit terms, that many American women experienced a depressing sense of isolation. In part, this feeling merely reflected a physical reality for women living in rural communities. But since city- and town-dwelling women voiced similar complaints, I would like to suggest that this consciousness of isolation also reflected a sense of status inferiority. Confined by their non-maleness, antebellum American women lived within the concentric structure of a family organized around the needs and status of husbands or fathers. And such social isolation within the family—or perhaps more accurately a lack of autonomy both embodied in and symbolized by such isolation—not only dramatized, but partially constituted, a differentiation in status.[52] The fact that social values and attitudes were established by men and oriented to male experiences only exacerbated women's feelings of inferiority and irrelevance. Again and again the Society's members were to express their desire for a feminine-sororial community which might help break down this isolation, lighten the monotony and harshness of life, and establish a counter-system of female values and priorities.

The New York Female Moral Reform Society quite consciously sought to inspire in its members a sense of solidarity in a cause peculiar to their sex, and demanding total commitment, to give them a sense of worthiness and autonomy outside woman's traditionally confining role. Its members, their officers forcefully declared, formed a united phalanx twenty thousand strong, "A UNION OF SENTIMENT AND EFFORT AMONG . . . VIRTUOUS FEMALES FROM MAINE TO ALABAMA."[53] The officers of the New York Society were particularly conscious of the emotional importance of female solidarity within their movement—and the significant role that they as leaders played in the lives of their rural supporters. "Thousands are looking to us," the executive committee recorded in their minutes with mingled pride and responsibility, "with the expectation that the principles we have adopted, and the example we have set before the world will continue to be held up & they reasonably expect to witness our *united onward* movements till the conflict shall end in Victory."[54]

For many of the Society's scattered members, the moral reform cause was their only contact with the world outside farm or village —the *Advocate* perhaps the only newspaper received by the family.[55] A sense of solidarity and of emotional affiliation permeated the correspondence between rural members and the executive committee. Letters and even official reports inevitably began with the salutation, "Sisters," "Dear Sisters" or "Beloved Sisters." Almost every letter and report expressed the deep affection Society members felt for their like-thinking sisters in the cause of moral reform—even if their contact came only through letters and the *Advocate*. "I now pray and will not cease to pray," a woman in Syracuse, New York, wrote, "that your hearts may be encouraged and your hands strengthened."[56] Letters to the Society's executive committee often promised unfailing loyalty and friendship; members and leaders pledged themselves ever ready to aid either local societies or an individual sister in need.[57] Many letters from geographically isolated women reported that the Society made it possible for them for the first time to communicate with like-minded women. A few, in agitated terms, wrote about painful experiences with the double standard which only their correspondence with the *Advocate* allowed them to express and share.[58]

Most significantly, the letters expressed a new consciousness of power. The moral reform society was based on the assertion of female moral superiority and the right and ability of women to reshape male behavior.[59] No longer did women have to remain passive and isolated within the structuring presence of husband or father. The moral reform movement was, perhaps for the first time, a movement within which women could forge a sense of their own identity.

And its founders had no intention of relinquishing their newfound feeling of solidarity and autonomy. A few years after the Society was founded, for example, a group of male evangelicals established a Seventh Commandment Society. They promptly wrote to the Female Moral Reform Society suggesting helpfully that since men had organized, the ladies could now disband; moral reform was clearly an area of questionable propriety. The New York executive committee responded quickly, firmly—and negatively. Women throughout America, they wrote, had placed their trust in a female moral reform society and in female officers. Women, they informed the men, believed in both their own right and ability to combat the problem; it was decidedly a woman's, not a man's issue.[60] "The paper is now in the right hands," one rural subscriber wrote: "This is the appropriate work for *women*. . . . Go on Ladies, go on, in the strength of the Lord."[61]

In some ways, indeed, the New York Female Moral Reform Society could be considered a militant woman's organization. Although it was not overtly part of the woman's rights movement, it did concern itself with a number of feminist issues, especially those relating to woman's economic role. Society, the *Advocate*'s editors argued, had unjustly confined women to domestic tasks. There were many jobs in society that women could and should be trained to fill. They could perform any light indoor work as well as men. In such positions—as clerks and artisans—they would receive decent wages and consequent self-respect.[62] And this economic emphasis was no arbitrary or inappropriate one, the Society contended. Thousands of women simply had to work; widows, orphaned young women, wives and mothers whose husbands could not work because of illness or intemperance had to support themselves and their children. Unfortunately, they had now to exercise these responsibilities on the pathetically inadequate salaries they received as domestics, washerwomen or seamstresses—crowded, underpaid and physically unpleasant occupations.[63] By the end of the 1840s, the Society had adopted the cause of the working woman and made it one of their principal concerns—in the 1850s even urging women to join unions and, when mechanization came to the garment industry, helping underpaid seamstresses rent sewing machines at low rates.[64]

The Society sought consciously, moreover, to demonstrate woman's ability to perform successfully in fields traditionally reserved for men. Quite early in their history they adopted the policy of hiring only women employees. From the first, of course, only women had been officers and managers of the Society. And after a few years, these officers began to hire women in preference to men as agents and to urge other charitable societies and government agencies to do likewise. (They did this although the only salaried charitable positions held by women in this period tended to be those of teachers in girls' schools or supervisors of women's wings in hospitals and homes for juvenile delinquents.) In February 1835, for instance, the executive committee hired a woman agent to solicit subscriptions to the *Advocate*. That summer they hired another woman to travel through New England and New York State organizing auxiliaries and giving speeches to women on moral reform. In October of 1836, the executive officers appointed two women as editors of their journal—undoubtedly among the first of their sex in this country to hold such positions.[65] In 1841, the executive committee decided to replace their male financial agent with a woman bookkeeper. By 1843 women even set type and did the folding for the Society's journal. All these jobs, the ladies proudly, indeed aggressively stressed, were appropriate tasks for women.[66]

The broad feminist implications of such statements and actions must have been apparent to the officers of the New York Society. And indeed the Society's executive committee maintained discreet but active ties with the broader woman's rights movement of the 1830s, 40s and 50s; at one point at least, they flirted with official endorsement of a bold woman's rights position. Evidence of this flirtation can be seen in the minutes of the executive committee and occasionally came to light in articles and editorials appearing in the *Advocate*. As early as the mid-1830s, for instance, the executive committee began to correspond with a number of women who were then or were later to become active in the woman's rights movement. Lucretia Mott, abolitionist and pioneer feminist, was a founder and secretary of the Philadelphia Female Moral Reform Society; as such she was in frequent communication with the New York executive committee.[67] Emma Willard, a militant advocate of women's education and founder of the Troy Female Seminary, was another of the executive committee's regular correspondents. Significantly, when Elizabeth Blackwell, the first woman doctor in either the United States or Great Britain, received her medical degree, Emma Willard wrote to the New York executive committee asking its members to use their influence to find her a job.[68] The Society did more than that. The *Advocate* featured a story dramatizing Dr. Blackwell's struggles. The door was now open for other women, the editors urged; medicine was a peculiarly appropriate profession for sensitive and sympathetic womankind. The Society offered to help interested women in securing admission to medical school.[69]

One of the most controversial aspects of the early woman's rights movement was its criticism of the subservient role of women within the American family, and of the American man's imperious and domineering behavior toward women. Much of the Society's rhetorical onslaught upon the male's lack of sexual accountability served as a screen for a more general—and less socially acceptable—resentment of masculine social preeminence. Occasionally, however, the *Advocate* expressed such resentment overtly. An editorial in 1838, for example, revealed a deeply felt antagonism toward the power asserted by husbands over their wives and children. "A portion of the inhabitants of this favored land," the Society admonished, "are groaning under a despotism, which seems to be modeled precisely after that of the Autocrat of Russia. . . . We allude to the tyranny exercised in the HOME department, where lordly man, 'clothed with a little brief authority,' rules his trembling subjects with a rod of iron, conscious of entire impunity, and exalting in his fancied superiority." The Society's editorialist continued, perhaps even more bitterly: "Instead of regarding his wife as a help-mate for him, an equal sharer in his joys and sorrows, he looks upon her as a useful article of furniture, which is valuable only for the benefit derived from it, but which may be thrown aside at pleasure."[70] Such behavior, the editorial carefully emphasized, was not only commonplace, experienced by many of the Society's own members—even the wives of "Christians" and of ministers—but was accepted and even justified by society; was it not sanctioned by the Bible?

At about the same time, indeed, the editors of the *Advocate* went so far as to print an attack upon "masculine" translations and interpretations of the Bible, and especially of Paul's epistles. This appeared in a lengthy article written by Sarah Grimké, a "notorious" feminist and abolitionist.[71] The executive committee clearly sought to associate their organization more closely with the nascent woman's rights movement. Calling upon American women to read and interpret the Bible for themselves, Sarah Grimké asserted that God had created woman the absolute equal of man. But throughout history, man, being stronger, had usurped woman's natural rights. He had subjected wives and daughters to his physical control and had evolved religious and scientific rationalizations to justify this domination. "Men have endeavored to entice, or to drive women from almost every sphere of moral action." Miss Grimké charged: " 'Go home and spin' is the . . . advice of the domestic tyrant. . . . The first duty, I believe, which devolves on our sex now is to think for themselves. . . . Until we take our stand side by side with our brother; until we read all the precepts of the Bible as addressed to woman as well as to man, and lose . . . the consciousness of sex, we shall never fulfil the end of our existence." "Those who do undertake to labor," Miss Grimké wrote from her own and her sister's bitter experiences, "are the scorn and ridicule of their own and the other sex." "We are so little accustomed *to think for ourselves,*" she continued,

> that we submit to the dictum of prejudice, and of usurped authority, almost without an effort to redeem ourselves from the unhallowed shackles which have so long bound us; almost without a desire to rise from that degradation and bondage to which we have been consigned by man, and by which the faculties of our minds, and the powers of our spiritual nature, have been prevented from expanding to their full growth, and are sometimes wholly crushed.

Each woman must re-evaluate her role in society; no longer could she depend on husband or father to assume her responsibilities as a free individual. No longer, Sarah Grimké argued, could she be satisfied with simply caring for her family or setting a handsome table.[72] The officers of the Society, in an editorial comment following this article, admitted that she had written a radical critique of woman's traditional role. But they urged their members, "It is of immense importance to our sex to possess clear and *correct* ideas of our rights and duties."[73]

Sarah Grimké's overt criticism of woman's traditional role, containing as it did an attack upon the Protestant ministry and orthodox interpretations of the Bible, went far beyond the consensus of the *Advocate's* rural subscribers. The following issue contained several letters sharply critical of her and of the managers, for printing her editorial.[74] And indeed the *Advocate* never again published the work of an overt feminist. Their membership, the officers concluded, would not tolerate explicit attacks upon traditional family structure and orthodox Christianity. Anti-male resentment and anger had to be expressed covertly. It was perhaps too threatening or—realistically—too dangerous for respectable matrons in relatively close-knit semi-rural communities in New York, New England, Ohio or Wisconsin so openly to question the traditional relations of the sexes and demand a new and ominously forceful role for women.

The compromise the membership and the officers of the Society seemed to find most comfortable was one that kept the American woman within the home—but which greatly expanded her powers as pious wife and mother. In rejecting Sarah Grimké's feminist manifesto, the Society's members implicitly agreed to accept the role traditionally assigned woman: the self-sacrificing, supportive, determinedly chaste wife and mother who limited her "sphere" to domesticity and religion. But in these areas her power should be paramount. The mother, not the father, should have final control of the home and family—especially of the religious and moral education of her children. If the world of economics and public affairs was his, the home must be hers.[75]

And even outside the home, woman's peculiar moral endowment and responsibilities justified her in playing an increasingly expansive role, one which might well ultimately impair aspects of man's traditional autonomy. When man transgressed God's commandments, through licentiousness, religious apathy, the defense of slavery, or the sin of intemperance—woman had both the right and duty of leaving the confines of the home and working to purify the male world.

The membership of the New York Female Moral Reform Society chose not to openly espouse the woman's rights movement. Yet many interesting emotional parallels remain to link the moral reform crusade and the suffrage movement of Elizabeth Cady Stanton, the Grimké sisters and Susan B. Anthony. In its own way, indeed, the war for purification of sexual mores was far more fundamental in its implications for woman's traditional role than the demand for woman's education—or even the vote.

Many of the needs and attitudes, moreover, expressed by suffragette leaders at the Seneca Falls Convention and in their efforts in the generation following are found decades earlier in the letters of rural women in the *Advocate of Moral Reform.* Both groups found woman's traditionally passive role intolerable. Both wished to assert female worth and values in a heretofore entirely male world. Both welcomed the creation of a sense of feminine loyalty and sisterhood that could give emotional strength and comfort to women isolated within their homes—whether in a remote farmstead or a Gramercy Park mansion. And it can hardly be assumed that the demand for votes for women was appreciably more radical than a moral absolutism which encouraged women to invade bordellos, befriend harlots and publicly discuss rape, seduction and prostitution.

It is important as well to re-emphasize a more general historical perspective. When the pious women founders of the Moral Reform Society gathered at the Third Free Presbyterian Church, it was fourteen years before the Seneca Falls Convention—which has traditionally been accepted as the beginning of the woman's rights movement in the United States. There simply was no woman's movement in the 1830s. The future leaders were either still adolescents or just becoming dissatisfied with aspects of their role. Women advocates of moral reform were among the very first American women to challenge their completely passive, home-oriented image. They were among the first to travel throughout the country without male chaperones. They published, financed, even set type for their own paper and defied a bitter and long-standing male opposition to their cause. They began, in short, to create a broader, less constricted sense of female identity. Naturally enough, they were dependent upon the activist impulse and legitimating imperatives of evangelical religion. This was indeed a complex symbiosis, the energies of pietism and the grievances of role discontent creating the new and activist female consciousness which characterized the history of the American Female Moral Reform Society in antebellum America. Their experience, moreover, was probably shared, though less overtly, by the thousands of women who devoted time and money to the great number of reform causes which multiplied in Jacksonian America. Women in the abolition and the temperance movements (and to a less extent in more narrowly evangelical and religious causes) also developed a sense of their ability to judge for themselves and of their right to publicly criticize the values of the larger society. The lives and self-image of all these women had changed—if only so little—because of their new reforming interests.

NOTES

1. "Minutes of the Meeting of the Ladies' Society for the Observance of the Seventh Commandment held in Chatham Street Chapel, May 12, 1834," and "Constitution of the New York Female Moral Reform Society," both in ledger book entitled "Constitution and Minutes of the New York Female Moral Reform Society, May, 1834 to July 1839," deposited in the archives of the American Female Guardian Society (hereinafter referred to as A.F.G.S.), Woodycrest Avenue, Bronx, New York. (The Society possesses the executive committee minutes from May 1835–June 1847, and from Jan. 7, 1852–Feb. 18, 1852.) For a more detailed institutional history of the Society see Carroll Smith-Rosenberg, *Religion and the Rise of the American City* (Ithaca, N.Y.: Cornell Univ. Press, 1971), chaps. 4 and 7. The New York Female Moral Reform Society changed its name to American Female Guardian Society in 1849. The Society continues today, helping children from broken homes. Its present name is Woodycrest Youth Service.

2. For a well-balanced though brief discussion of American women's role in antebellum America see Eleanor Flexner, *A Century of Struggle* (Cambridge: Harvard Univ. Press, 1959), chaps. 1–4.

3. There are two modern biographies of Fanny Wright, both rather thin:

W. R. Waterman, *Frances Wright* (New York: Columbia Univ. Press., 1924); Alice J. Perkins, *Frances Wright, Free Enquirer* (New York: Harper & Bros., 1939). Fanny Wright was one of the first women in America to speak about women's rights before large audiences of both men and women. Yet she attracted very few women into the woman's rights movement, probably because her economic and political views and her emphatic rejection of Christianity seemed too radical to most American women.

4. John R. McDowall, *Magdalen Report*, rpr. *McDowall's Journal*, 2 (May 1834), 33–38. For the history of the New York Magdalen Society see *First Annual Report of the Executive Committee of the New York Magdalen Society, Instituted January 1, 1830*. See as well, Rosenberg, *Religion*, chap. 4.

5. Flora L. Northrup, *The Record of a Century* (New York: American Female Guardian Soc., 1934), pp. 13–14; cf. *McDowall's Defence*, 1, No. 1 (July 1836), 3; *The Trial of the Reverend John Robert McDowall by the Third Presbytery of New York in February, March, and April, 1836* (New York, 1836). [Thomas Hastings Sr.], *Missionary Labors through a Series of Years among Fallen Women by the New York Magdalen Society* (New York: N.Y. Magdalen Soc., 1870), p. 15.

6. Northrup, *Record of a Century*, pp. 14–15; only two volumes of *McDowall's Journal* were published, covering the period Jan. 1833 to Dec. 1834. Between the demise of the New York Magdalen Society and the organization of the New York Female Moral Reform Society (hereinafter, N.Y.F.M.R.S.), McDowall was connected, as agent, with a third society, the New York Female Benevolent Society, which he had helped found in February of 1833. For a more detailed account see Carroll S. Rosenberg, "Evangelicalism and the New City," Ph.D. Diss. Columbia University, 1968, chap. 5.

7. *McDowall's Journal*, 2 (Jan. 1834), 6–7.

8. "Minutes of the Meeting of the Ladies' Society for the Observance of the Seventh Commandment . . . May 12, 1834," and "Preamble," "Constitution of the New York Female Moral Reform Society."

9. *Advocate of Moral Reform* (hereinafter, *Advocate*) 1 (Jan.–Feb. 1835), 6. The *Advocate* was the Society's official journal.

10. Close ties connected the N.Y.F.M.R.S. with the Finney wing of American Protestantism. Finney's wife was the Society's first president. The Society's second president, Mrs. William Green, was the wife of one of Finney's closest supporters. The Society's clerical support in New York City came from Finney's disciples. Their chief financial advisers and initial sponsors were Arthur and Lewis Tappan, New York merchants who were also Charles Finney's chief financial supporters. For a list of early "male advisers" to the N.Y.F.M.R.S. see Joshua Leavitt, *Memoir and Select Remains of the Late Reverend John R. McDowall* (New York: Joshua Leavitt, Lord, 1838), pp. 248, also pp. 99, 151, 192. See as well L. Nelson Nichols and Allen Knight Chalmers, *History of the Broadway Tabernacle of New York City* (New Haven: Tuttle, Morehouse & Taylor, 1940), pp. 49–67, and William G. McLoughlin Jr., *Modern Revivalism* (New York: Ronald Press, 1959), pp. 50–53.

11. For an excellent modern analysis of Finney's theology and his place in American Protestantism see McLoughlin, *Modern Revivalism*. McLoughlin has as well edited Finney's series of New York Revivals which were first published in 1835. Charles Grandison Finney, *Lectures on Revivals of Religion*, ed. William G. McLoughlin (Cambridge: Harvard Univ. Press, 1960). McLoughlin's introduction is excellent.

12. Rosenberg, *Religion*, chaps. 2 and 3.

13. These reforms were by no means mutually exclusive. Indeed there was a logical and emotional interrelation between evangelical Protestantism and its missionary aspects and such formally secular reforms as peace, abolition and temperance. The interrelation is demonstrated in the lives of such reformers as the Tappan brothers, the Grimké sisters, Theodore Dwight Weld, Charles Finney and in the overlapping membership of the many religious and "secular" reform societies of the Jacksonian period. On the other hand, the overlap was not absolute, some reformers rejecting evangelical Protestantism, others pietism, or another of the period's reforms.

14. *Advocate,* 1 (Jan.–Feb. 1835), 4; Northrup, *Record,* p. 19.

15. *Advocate,* 1 (Mar. 1835), 11–12; 1 (Nov. 1835), 86; N.Y.F.M.R.S., "Executive Committee Minutes, June 6, 1835 and April 30, 1836." These pious visitors received their most polite receptions at the more expensive houses, while the girls and customers of lower-class, slum brothels met them almost uniformly with curses and threats.

16. N.Y.F.M.R.S., "Executive Committee Minutes, Jan. 24, 1835."

17. *Advocate,* 1 (Jan.–Feb. 1835), 7.

18. For a description of one such incident see *Advocate,* 4 (Jan. 15, 1838), 15.

19. *Advocate,* 1 (Sept. 1, 1835), 72; Northrup, *Record,* p. 19.

20. *Advocate,* 1 (Mar. 1835), 11; N.Y.F.M.R.S., "Executive Committee Minutes, Apr. 5, 1836, May 30, 1835."

21. N.Y.F.M.R.S., "Executive Committee Minutes, Oct. 4, 1836."

22. N.Y.F.M.R.S., "Executive Committee Minutes, June 6 and June 25, 1835, June (n.d.), 1836"; N.Y.F.M.R.S., *The Guardian or Fourth Annual Report of the New York Female Moral Reform Society presented May 9, 1838,* pp. 4–6.

23. "Budding," "lovely," "fresh," "joyous," "unsuspecting lamb," were frequent terms used to describe innocent women before their seduction. The *Advocate* contained innumerable letters and editorials on this theme. See, for example, *Advocate,* 4 (Jan. 1, 1838), 1; *Advocate,* 10 (Mar. 1, 1844), 34; *Advocate and Guardian* (the Society changed the name of its journal in 1847), 16 (Jan. 1, 1850), 3.

24. Letter in *Advocate,* 1 (Apr. 1835), 19.

25. "Murderer of Virtue" was another favorite and pithy phrase. For a sample of such references see: *Advocate,* 4 (Feb. 1, 1838), 17, *Advocate,* 10 (Jan. 1, 1844), 19–20; *Advocate,* 10 (Jan. 15, 1844), 29; *Advocate,* 10 (Mar. 1, 1844), 33.

26. *Advocate,* 1 (Jan.–Feb. 1835), 3; *Advocate,* 1 (Apr. 1835), 19; *Advocate and Guardian,* 16 (Jan. 1, 1850), 3.

27. Letter in *McDowall's Journal,* 2 (Apr. 1834), 26–27.

28. Many subscribers wrote to the *Advocate* complaining of the injustice of the double standard. See, for example: *Advocate,* 1 (Apr. 1835), 22; *Advocate,* 1 (Dec. 1835), 91; *Advocate and Guardian,* 16 (Jan. 1, 1850), 5.

29. *Advocate,* 1 (Jan.–Feb. 1835), 6–7.

30. Resolution passed at the Quarterly Meeting of the N.Y.F.M.R.S., Jan. 1838, printed in *Advocate,* 4 (Jan. 15, 1838), 14.

31. This was one of the more important functions of the auxiliaries, and their members uniformly pledged themselves to ostracize all offending males. For an example of such pledges see *Advocate,* 4 (Jan. 15, 1838), 16.

32. *Advocate and Guardian,* 16 (Jan. 1, 1850), 3.

33. McDowall urged his rural subscribers to report any instances of seduction. He dutifully printed all the details, referring to the accused man

by initials, but otherwise giving the names of towns, counties and dates. Male response was on occasion bitter.

34. *Advocate,* 1 (Jan.–Feb. 1835), 2.

35. Throughout the 1830s virtually every issue of the *Advocate* contained such letters. The *Advocate* continued to publish them throughout the 1840s.

36. For detailed discussions of particular employment agencies and the decision to print their names see: N.Y.F.M.R.S., "Executive Committee Minutes, Feb. 12, 1845, July 8, 1846."

37. N.Y.F.M.R.S., "Executive Committee Minutes, Mar. 1, 1838, Mar. 15, 1838"; *Advocate,* 4 (Jan. 15, 1838), 15.

38. The Society appears to have begun its lobbying crusade in 1838. N.Y.F.M.R.S., "Executive Committee Minutes, Oct. 14, 1838, Jan. 4, 1842, Feb. 18, 1842, Apr. 25, 1844, Jan. 8, 1845"; American Female Moral Reform Society (the Society adopted this name in 1839), *Tenth Annual Report for . . . 1844,* pp. 9–11; American Female Moral Reform Soc., *Fourteenth Annual Report for . . . 1848.*

39. The N.Y.F.M.R.S.'s Executive Committee Minutes for the years 1837, 1838, 1843 and 1844 especially are filled with instances of the committee instituting suits against seducers for damages in the case of loss of services.

40. *Advocate,* 1 (Jan.–Feb. 1835), 6–7; 4 (Jan. 1, 1838), 1.

41. *Advocate,* 10 (Feb. 1, 1844), 17–18; *Advocate and Guardian,* 16 (Jan. 1, 1850), 3–4.

42. *Advocate,* 10 (Jan. 1, 1844), 7–8.

43. *Advocate,* 2 (Jan. 1836), 3; *Advocate,* 4 (Jan. 15, 1838), 13.

44. *Advocate,* 4 (Jan. 1, 1838), 1–2; *Advocate,* 10 (Feb. 15, 1844), 26; *Advocate and Guardian,* 16 (Jan. 15, 1850), 15.

45. *Advocate,* 1 (Jan.–Feb. 1835), 5–6.

46. An editorial in the *Advocate* typified the Society's emphasis on the importance of child rearing and religious education as an exclusively maternal role. "To a mother.—You have a child on your knee. . . . It is an immortal being; destined to live forever! . . . And who is to make it happy or miserable? You—the mother! You who gave it birth, the mother of its body, . . . its destiny is placed in your hands" (*Advocate,* 10 [Jan. 1, 1844], 8).

47. N.Y.F.M.R.S., "Executive Committee Minutes, June 25, 1835."

48. N.Y.F.M.R.S., "Executive Committee Minutes, Oct. 4, 1836, and May 22, 1837, and Sept. 11, 1839." Indeed, as early as 1833 a substantial portion of John McDowall's support seemed to come from rural areas. See, for example, *McDowall's Journal,* 1 (Aug. 1833), 59–62.

49. N.Y.F.M.R.S., "Executive Committee Minutes, Oct. 4, 1838"; Northrup, *Record,* p. 22.

50. N.Y.F.M.R.S., "Executive Committee Minutes, May 10, 1839"; N.Y.F.M.R.S., "Quarterly Meeting, July, 1839." Power within the new national organization was divided so that the president and the board of managers were members of the N.Y.F.M.R.S. while the vice presidents were chosen from the rural auxiliaries. The annual meeting was held in New York City, the quarterly meetings in one of the towns of Greater New England.

51. Virtually every issue of the *Advocate* is filled with letters and reports from the auxiliaries discussing their many activities.

52. The view that many women held of their role is perhaps captured in the remarks of an editorialist in the *Advocate* in 1850. Motherhood was unquestionably the most correct and important role for women. But it was a very hard role. "In their [mothers'] daily rounds of duty they may move in

a retired sphere—secluded from public observation, oppressed with many cares and toils, and sometimes tempted to view their position as being adverse to the highest usefulness. The youthful group around them tax their energies to the utmost limit—the wants of each and all . . . must be watched with sleepless vigilance; improvement is perhaps less marked and rapid than is ardently desired. . . . Patience is tried, faith called into exercise; and all the graces of the Spirit demanded, to maintain equanimity and exhibit a right example. And *such* with all its weight of care and responsibility is the post at which God in his providence has placed the mothers of our land." The ultimate reward of motherhood which the writer held out to her readers, significantly, was that they would be the ones to shape the character of their children. *Advocate and Guardian*, 16 (Jan. 15, 1850), 13.

53. N.Y.F.M.R.S., *Guardian*, p. 8.

54. N.Y.F.M.R.S., "Executive Committee Minutes, Oct. 24, 1836."

55. See two letters, for example, to the *Advocate* from rural subscribers. Although written fifteen years apart and from quite different geographic areas (the first from Hartford, Conn., the second from Jefferson, Ill.), the sentiments expressed are remarkably similar. Letter in *Advocate*, 1 (Apr. 1835), 19; *Advocate and Guardian*, 16 (Jan. 15, 1850), 14.

56. Letter in *Advocate*, 4 (Jan. 1, 1838), 6.

57. Letters and reports from rural supporters expressing such sentiments dotted every issue of the *Advocate* from its founding until the mid-1850s.

58. The editors of the *Advocate* not infrequently received (and printed) letters from rural subscribers reporting painfully how some young woman in their family had suffered social censure and ostracism because of the machinations of some lecher—who emerged from the affair with his respectability unblemished. This letter to the *Advocate* was the first time they could express the anguish and anger they felt. For one particularly pertinent example see an anonymous letter to the *Advocate*, 1 (Mar. 1835), 15–16.

59. N.Y.F.M.R.S., "Executive Committee Minutes, Oct. 4, 1836"; *Advocate*, 1 (Apr. 1835), 19–20; *Advocate*, 3 (Jan. 15, 1837), 194; *Advocate*, 4 (Jan. 1, 1838), 5, 7–8; *Advocate*, 4 (Apr. 1838), 6–7. An integral part of this expression of power was the women's insistence that they had the right to investigate male sexual practices and norms. No longer would they permit men to tell them that particular questions were improper for women's consideration. See for example, N.Y.F.M.R.S., "Circular to the Women of the United States," rpr. in *Advocate*, 1 (Jan.–Feb. 1835), 6–7, 4.

60. N.Y.F.M.R.S., "Executive Committee Minutes, June 28, 1837."

61. Letter in *Advocate*, 1 (Apr. 1835), 19.

62. *Advocate and Guardian*, 16 (Jan. 15, 1850), 9.

63. *Advocate*, 1 (May 1835), 38; N.Y.F.M.R.S., *Guardian*, pp. 5–6. The Society initially became concerned with the problems of the city's poor and working women as a result of efforts to attack some of the economic causes of prostitution. The Society feared that the low wages paid seamstresses, domestics or washerwomen (New York's three traditional female occupations) might force otherwise moral women to turn to prostitution. The Society was, for example, among the earliest critics of the low wages and bad working conditions of New York's garment industry.

64. Significantly, the Society's editors and officers placed the responsibility for the low wages paid seamstresses and other female workers on ruthless and exploitative men. Much the same tone of anti-male hostility is evident in their economic exposés as in their sexual exposés.

65. N.Y.F.M.R.S., "Executive Committee Minutes, Feb. 20, 1835, Oct. 4 and Oct. 5, 1836"; N.Y.F.M.R.S., *Fifth Annual Report,* p. 5.

66. A.F.G.S., *Eleventh Annual Report,* pp. 5, 6. For details of replacing male employees with women and the bitterness of the male reactions, see N.Y.F.M.R.S., "Executive Committee Minutes," *passim,* for early 1843. Nevertheless, even these aggressively feminist women did not feel that women could with propriety chair public meetings, even those of their own Society. In 1838, for instance, when the ladies discovered that men expected to attend their annual meeting, they felt that they had to ask men to chair the meeting and read the women's reports. Their decision was made just after the Grimké sisters had created a storm of controversy by speaking at large mixed gatherings of men and women. Northrup, *Record,* pp. 21–25. For the experiences of the Grimké sisters with this same problem, see Gerda Lerner's excellent biography, *The Grimké Sisters from South Carolina* (Boston: Houghton Mifflin, 1967), chaps. 11–14.

67. N.Y.F.M.R.S., "Executive Committee Minutes, Aug. 3, 1837."

68. N.Y.F.M.R.S., "Executive Committee Minutes, June 2, 1847, Mar. 28, 1849." The *Advocate* regularly reviewed her books, and indeed made a point of reviewing books by women authors.

69. *Advocate and Guardian,* 16 (Jan. 15, 1850), 10.

70. *Advocate,* 4 (Feb. 15, 1838), 28.

71. See Lerner, *The Grimké Sisters.*

72. *Advocate,* 4 (Jan. 1, 1838), 3–5.

73. *Ibid.,* p. 5.

74. See, for example, *Advocate,* 4 (Apr. 1, 1838), 55; 4 (July 16, 1838), 108.

75. For examples of the glorification of the maternal role see *Advocate,* 10 (Mar. 15, 1844), 47 and *Advocate and Guardian,* 16 (Jan. 15, 1850), 13–14.

9

Family Limitation, Sexual Control, and Domestic Feminism in Victorian America

■

DANIEL SCOTT SMITH

Social historians often try to elucidate political trends by linking them to deep-lying social change. Here, Daniel Scott Smith uses his knowledge of the demographic and fertility patterns of American families over several centuries as the basis for a venturesome reinterpretation of the meaning of women's rights in American history. Smith's deductive jump from statistics to interpretation sparked controversy when the article first appeared, and his argument has since generated responses on both the supporting and the deflating sides. His invention of the term "domestic feminism" has generally been adopted, and expanded upon, in the literature of women's history. A 1979 postscript by Smith appears at the end of the essay.

THE HISTORY OF WOMEN IS inextricably connected with the social evolution of the family. The revitalization of the American feminist movement and the surge of interest in social history among professional historians during the past decade have combined to make the study of women in the family a crucial concern. The central insight of the new feminism—the critical relationship of family structure and roles to the possibilities for full participation by women in the larger society—provides an immediate impetus to the historical study of that relationship. To isolate a central historical question conceptually, however, is far easier than to examine it empirically. Women in the family do not generate written documents describing their ordinary life experiences. It is easier, for example, to describe historical attitudes toward women's proper role than to determine what the roles actually were at any given time. Only painstaking research into local history, a systematic study of personal documents describing ordinary behavior, and tracing life histories of women through manuscript lists can bridge this major gap in the historiography of American women.[1] At this point, then, a different approach seems necessary and useful.

An examination of three rather well-established quantitative indicators showing the relationship of the entire population of American women to the family suggests the hypothesis that over the course of the nineteenth century the average woman experienced a great increase in power and autonomy *within* the family. The important contribution women made to the radical decline in nineteenth-century marital fertility provides the central evidence for this hypothesis. Empirical data on the details of family limitation and the control of sexuality in the nineteenth century unfortunately are limited. However, an analysis of nineteenth century sexual ideology supports the theory that women acquired an increasing power over sex and reproduction within marriage. The hypothesis that women's power increased within the nineteenth-century family also accords well with such important themes as the narrow social base of the women's movement in America before the late nineteenth century, the flourishing of women's groups opposed to female suffrage, and the centrality of the attack on aspects of male culture in such movements as temperance. A long-term perspective is essential for understanding the history of women in the family. I shall suggest how the situation of women varied in three periods: the pre-industrial (seventeenth and eighteenth century); industrial (nineteenth century); and the post-industrial (recent) phases of American society.

From the colonial period to the present, *an overwhelming majority*—from 89 to 96 percent—*of American women surviving past the age of forty-five have married* (Table 1). The proportion who never married was highest for those born in the last four decades of the nineteenth century. Small percentage changes represent, of course, thousands of women. While marriage was overwhelmingly the typical experience for American women, before the present century roughly a third of all females did not survive long enough to be eligible for marriage.[2] In addition, the numerically tiny minority who remained single had a far larger historical importance than their percentage would suggest. For example, 30.1 percent of 45–49-year-old native-white female college graduates in 1940 were unmarried.[3] Before the marked increase in life-expectancy in the late nineteenth and early twentieth century, the average American woman married in her early-to-mid-

TABLE 1
Percentage of American Women Who Never Married

	Census or Survey, and Birth Cohort	Age at Enumeration	Percentage Never Married
1910	1835–39	70–74	7.3
	1840–44	65–69	7.1
	1845–49	60–64	8.0
	1850–54	55–59	7.7
	1855–59	50–54	8.9
	1860–64	45–49	10.0
1940	1865–69	70–74	11.1
	1870–74	65–69	10.9
	1875–79	60–64	10.4
	1880–84	55–59	8.7
	1885–89	50–54	8.8
	1890–94	45–49	8.6
1950	1895–99	50–54	7.7
	1900–04	45–49	8.0
1960	1905–09	50–54	7.6
	1910–14	45–49	6.5
1965	1915–19	45–49	4.8
1969	1921–25	45–49	4.5
	1926–30	40–44	5.0

Source: Calculated from Irene B. Taeuber, "Growth of the Population of the United States in the Twentieth Century," Table 11, p. 40 in *Demographic and Social Aspects of Population Growth*, eds., Charles F. Westoff and Robert Parke, Jr., vol. 1, U.S. Commission on Population Growth and the American Future (Washington: Government Printing Office, 1972).

twenties, survived with her husband for some three decades, and, if widowed, spent an additional decade or so in widowhood.[4]

The implications of these figures for historians of women are obvious but must still be emphasized. Labor historians now realize that most workers historically did not belong to unions, black historians have been conscious that most Negroes were not in civil-rights organizations, and urban historians have discovered that groups other than politicians and elites dwell in cities. The search for the history of "anonymous Americans" has generally focused on population elements that in one sense or another have been defined as "social problems." For these groups there exists at least some information imbedded in contemporary myths and prejudices. It will be more difficult to write the history of the average or modal American woman, a person substantively akin to William Graham Sumner's

Forgotten Man. She was, in 1880, for example, a 38-year-old white wife of a farmer living eight miles west-by-south of Cincinnati and the mother eventually of five or six children.[5] Intensive study of local records may reveal a surprising degree of social participation in church and voluntary associations and perhaps performance in other roles as well. Yet the primary statuses of the modal woman were those of wife and mother.

While nearly all American women have married, *married American women did not work outside the home until the twentieth century*, with the major increase coming in the last three decades (Table 2). Only one white married woman in forty was classified in the labor force in 1890 and only one in seven in 1940; today two-fifths of all married women are working according to official definition.[6] The increase in labor-force participation for single women in the twentieth century has been less dramatic. More generally, many indicators (an increase in single-person households for the young and widowed, the disappearance of boarders and lodgers from family units, the decline in the age at marriage, an increase in premarital intercourse, and the legalization of abortion and no-fault divorce) point to an emerging post-industrial family pattern in the post-World-

TABLE 2

Female Participation in the Labor Force (in Percentage)

		White Only		Native-White, Age 35–44	
Year	Total	Single	Married	Single	Married
1830[a]	(7)	—	—	—	—
1890[a]	12.1	35.2	2.5	39.3	2.3
1940[a]	26.9	47.9	14.6	73.6	17.9
1960[a]	34.1	45.5	29.6	76.5	29.9

	All Women			Age 35–44		
	Single	Married, Husband Present	Widowed, Divorced, Separated	Single	Married, Husband Present	Widowed, Divorced, Separated
1950[b]	50.5	23.8	37.8	83.6	28.5	65.4
1960[b]	44.1	30.5	40.0	79.7	36.2	67.4
1972[b]	54.9	41.5	40.1	71.5	48.6	71.7

[a] Stanley Lebergott, *Manpower in Economic Growth* (New York: McGraw Hill, 1964), Table A-10, p. 519.

[b] Bureau of Labor Statistics, summarized in *The New York Times*, January 31, 1973, pp. 20.

War-II period. This major shift in the family has important implications for the periodization of women's history.

The final statistical trend presents an interesting historical problem. During the nineteenth century, some ninety percent of women got married, over ninety-five percent of the married were not employed outside the home, yet *women progressively bore fewer and fewer children*. The average number born to a white woman surviving to menopause fell from 7.04 in 1800 to 6.14 in 1840, to 4.24 in 1880, and finally to 3.56 in 1900 (Table 3). The same decline is also apparent in U.S. census data on completed fertility.[7] Between 1800 and 1900 the total fertility rate decreased by half. By the late nineteenth century, France was the only European country whose fertility rate was lower than America's.[8] Despite the demographic effects of a later marriage age and of more women remaining permanently single, from one-half to three-fourths of the nineteenth-century decline in fertility may be attributed to the reduction of fertility within marriage.[9]

The decline in marital fertility is of critical importance in structuring the possibilities open to the average woman. A fifteen-to-twenty-year cycle of conception-birth-nursing-weaning-conception (broken not infrequently by spontaneous abortions) at the height of active adulthood obviously limits chances for social and economic participation as well as for individual development. Child-rearing must be added to this onerous cycle. The great transition in fertility is a central event in the history of woman. A dominant theme in the

TABLE 3

Total Fertility Rates (TFR) for Whites, 1800–1968

Year	TFR	Year	TFR	Year	TFR
1800	7.04	1860	5.21	1920	3.17
1810	6.92	1870	4.55	1930	2.45
1820	6.73	1880	4.24	1940	2.19
1830	6.55	1890	3.87	1950	3.00
1840	6.14	1900	3.56	1960	3.52
1850	5.42	1910	3.42	1968	2.36

Sources: For 1800–1960, Ansley J. Coale and Melvin Zelnik, *New Estimates of Fertility and Population in the United States* (Princeton: Princeton University Press, 1963), Table 2, p. 36; 1968 calculated from Irene B. Taueber, "Growth of the Population of the United States in the Twentieth Century," in *Demographic and Social Aspects of Population Growth*, eds. Charles F. Westoff and Robert Parke, Jr., U.S. Commission on Population Growth and the American Future, vol. 1 (Washington, D.C.: Government Printing Office, 1972), Table 7, p. 33.

history is that women have not shaped their own lives. Things are done to women, not by them. Thus it is important to examine the extent to which nineteenth-century women did gain control over their reproductive lives.

Many forces, to be mentioned later, were clearly at work in curbing fertility, but the power of the wife to persuade or coerce her husband into practicing birth control deserves examination. While women did employ contraceptive methods in the nineteenth century (principally douching and the sponge), the major practices involved the control of male sexuality—*coitus interruptus* (withdrawal) and abstinence.[10] Following Kraditor's excellent definition of the essence of feminism as the demand for autonomy, sexual control of the husband by the wife can easily be subsumed under the label of "domestic feminism."[11]

Before marshalling empirical data showing the strengthening of the position of women within the nineteenth-century American family, it is first necessary to consider certain misconceptions about women's place in the industrial and pre-industrial periods. Many of the recent interpretations of the history of American women have been devoted to an autopsy of the "failure" of women's suffrage. According to Kraditor, late nineteenth- and early-twentieth-century American women became conservative and were co-opted into the general progressive movement.[12] In Degler's view, women lacked an ideology that could properly guide them to full status as human beings.[13] For O'Neill, the "failure" lay in the refusal of the movement to assault the ideology and reality of the conjugal family structure that sustained women's inferior position.[14] This "what-went-wrong" approach implicitly assumes the constancy of woman's role within the family, and, more damagingly, interprets the behavior and responses of women as deviations from a preconceived standard rather than as responses to their actual situations. The turn toward conservatism in the leadership of active American women, for example, is seen as a tactical mistake rather than as the result of interaction between the leaders and their female constituency.

The extremely low percentage of married women in the nineteenth-century labor force suggests that the domestic-sphere versus social-participation dichotomy is not appropriate for the interpretation of women's history during the industrial period. If the average woman in the last century failed to perceive her situation through the modern feminist insight, this did not mean she was not increasing her autonomy, exercising more power, or even achieving happiness within the domestic sphere. Rather than examining Victorian culture and especially the Victorian family at its heart through a twentieth-century perspective, it is more useful and revealing to contrast nineteenth-century values and institutions with their pre-industrial antecedents.

Misconceptions about women in the pre-industrial family fit integrally into the pessimistic view of the Victorian era derived from the modern feminist perspective. Having portrayed the nineteenth century as something of a nadir for women, by implication, all other eras must be favorable by comparison. In order to show that women are not inevitably entrapped by the family, it has seemed important to emphasize that somewhere or sometime the status and role of women were quite different. While cross-cultural evidence supports this argument adequately, more compelling are conclusions drawn from as little as two centuries ago in American or Western culture. Historians, however, have been properly cautious about more than hinting at a Golden Age for the pre-industrial American woman. There is, to be sure, a sharp difference between the pre-industrial and industrial family and the corresponding position of women in each. A conjugal family system, in the sense of the centrality of the married pair, in contrast to the dominance of the family line, did emerge in the United States during the early nineteenth century.[15]

The effects of this shift for women are complex. The conventional belief in the more favorable position of the average woman in pre-industrial society rests on three arguments: the intimacy and complementary nature of sex roles in an undifferentiated economy; Ariès' thesis that the boundary between the pre-industrial family and society was very permeable; and finally, in the American case, the favorable implications for women of the relative female and labor scarcity on the frontier. The first argument may be compared to George Fitzhugh's defense of slavery, but extreme subordination and superordination do not require a highly differentiated economy and society. The very absence of complexity in the pre-industrial family doubtless contributed to the subordination of women. While the identity of the place of work and residence in an agricultural economy inevitably meant some sharing of productive tasks by husband and wife, the husband's presence, given the prevailing ideological and cultural values, deterred the wife from gaining a sense of autonomy. Just as the gender stereotypes of masculine and feminine were not as rigidly defined as in the Victorian period, the prestige attached to the status of wife and mother was less than in the nineteenth century. Social prestige depended on the position of the woman's family in the hierarchical structure of pre-industrial society. Daughters and wives shared in the deference paid to important families. When this system collapsed in the nineteenth century, women of high-status families experienced considerable deprivation compared to their high-ranking colonial counterparts. Women born to more modest circumstances, however, derived enhanced status from the shift away from deference and ascription.

Although Ariès has little to say about women, his thesis that the line between the Western pre-industrial family and community was not sharply delineated is of considerable importance here.[16] There does exist scattered evidence of women's nonfamilial activity, e.g., voting, operating businesses, etc., in the pre-industrial period. The incidence of women's nonfamilial activity over time, its relationship to family and conventional sex roles, and finally, its importance in the social structure as a whole have not been explored. The existing social history of colonial women has successfully demonstrated that wider participation was not unknown.[17] The details of such nonfamilial participation have been much more fully researched for the colonial period than for the nineteenth century. Spinsters almost certainly were more marginal and deviant in pre-industrial American society than during the nineteenth century. Only widows who controlled property may have been in a more favorable position. While changes in colonial American law permitted a married woman to exercise certain rights, these innovations related mainly to acting as a stand-in for a husband.[18] By negating the impact of male absence because of travel and death, these modifications in colonial law made the family a more efficient economic unit; historians should not confuse a response to high mortality and slow transportation with normative support for women's being outside the family. In fact, nonfamilial participation by pre-industrial women must generally be viewed as a substitution for the activities of absent husbands. In effect, a woman's activity outside the pre-industrial family was a *familial* responsibility.

Systematic evidence comparing the position of women in the pre-industrial and industrial phases of American society is scarce; what exists points to the comparatively unfavorable place of women in the earlier stage. In most populations, for example, women live considerably longer than men. Yet this was not the case in four (Andover, Hingham, Plymouth and Salem) of the five seventeenth-century New England communities studied to date. Only in seventeenth-century Ipswich did the typical pattern of longer survival for adult females exist.[19] In Hingham, furthermore, an inverse relationship between family wealth and mortality is apparent only for eighteenth-century married women, not for their husbands or children.[20] Literacy is a good index of the potential to perform complex tasks. The scattered published data on the frequency of signatures on documents suggest that there may have been some narrowing of the historic differential between male and female literacy during the eighteenth century. The gap, however, was not fully closed until the nineteenth century.[21] The sex differential in literacy is, of course, also a class differential. Compared to those of pre-industrial men, the burdens of life were harsh for women, particularly those of low status. Finally, the resemblance in that era of the sexual act itself to the Hobbesian state of nature is revealing. Marital sex, succinctly summarized by Shorter as "simple up-and-down, man on top, woman on bottom, little foreplay, rapid ejaculation, masculine unconcern with feminine orgasm,"[22] perhaps mirrored the broader social relationship between men and women.

It may be argued that America was not Europe and that the relative strength of the woman's movement in nineteenth-century America can be attributed to a decline from a more favorable situation during the colonial period. The existence of protest, however, is not an index of oppression, but rather a measure of the ambiguities and weaknesses of the system of control. It is ironic that the Turnerian frontier theory, implicitly biased by its emphasis on male experience, survives most strongly in the field of women's history.[23] As Domar has shown, however, labor scarcity and free land are intimately related to the institutions of slavery and serfdom.[24] The economic factor associated with the exceptional freedom of white American males was a precondition of the equally exceptional degree of suppression of blacks. For a group to gain from favorable economic conditions, it must be able to benefit from the operation of the market. While this was true for single women in the nineteenth century (but not in the pre-industrial period), it decidedly was not true for married women. Wives were not free to strike a better bargain with a new mate. What appears to be crucial in determining the turn toward freedom or suppression of the vulnerable group are the ideology and values of the dominant group.[25] Neither the position of the labor force nor of women can be mechanistically reduced to simple economic factors.[26]

The empirical basis for the importance of the frontier in the history of women is not impressive. On the nineteenth-century frontier at least, the high male-to-female sex ratio was a transitory phenomenon.[27] For the entire American population, the high rate of natural increase during the colonial period quickly narrowed the differential in the sex ratio created by immigration.[28] The truth left in the frontier argument is also ironic. Women's suffrage undeniably came earlier in the West. That development, as Grimes has argued, reflected the potential usefulness of women as voters along the conservative wife-mother line rather than a recognition of Western women as citizens per se.[29] Farber's interesting analysis of the East-Midwest variation in marriage prohibition statutes points to a relative emphasis on the conjugal family in the newer areas of the country. Midwestern states tend to prohibit marriages of cousins while certain affinal marriages are illegal in the East and South.[30] In summary, then, the frontier and the general newness of social institutions in America benefitted women chiefly as part of the elevation of conjugality in family structure.

The majority of women in nineteenth-century families had good reason to perceive themselves as better off than their pre-industrial forebearers. This shift involved not merely the level of material comfort but, more importantly, the quality of social and familial relationships. Since being a wife and mother was now evaluated more positively, women recognized an improvement within their "sphere" and thus channelled their efforts within and not beyond the family unit. It is not surprising that contemporary and later critics of the Victorian family referred to it as patriarchal, since that was the older form being superseded. If a descriptive label with a Latin root is wanted, however, "matriarchal" would be more suitable for the nineteenth-century family. Men had inordinate power within the Victorian family, but it was as husbands—not as fathers. The conservative conception of woman's role focused, after all, on the submissive wife rather than the submissive daughter.[31] Nineteenth-century women, once married, did not retain crucial ties to their family of birth; marriage joined individuals and not their families.[32]

While the interpretation being advanced here stresses the significance of the new autonomy of women within the family as an explanation of the decline of fertility during the nineteenth century, this is not to deny the importance of economic, instrumental, or "male" considerations. The shift from agriculture, the separation of production from the family, the urbanization of the population, and the loss of child labor through compulsory education doubtless also contributed. Indeed, the wife's demand for a smaller family may have been so successful precisely because it was not contrary to the rational calculations of her husband. Since the fertility decline was nationwide and affected urban and rural areas simultaneously, attitudes and values as well as structural factors are obviously of relevance.[33] The romantic cult of childhood, for example, may have induced a change from quantitative to qualitative fertility goals on the part of parents.

The social correlates of lower fertility found in modern populations are relevant to this discussion of the history of American fertility. A common finding of cross-national studies, for example, is a strong negative relationship between fertility and female participation in the labor force.[34] The American historical record, however, does not provide much support for this theory. During the 1830–1890 period, there was probably only a slight increase in the labor-force participation of married women and yet marital fertility continuously declined.[35] During both the post-World-War-II baby boom and the fertility decline since 1957, labor-force activity of married women increased.[36] For lower fertility, what is important is the meaning women assign to themselves and their work, either in or out of the home.[37] Since work is compatible with a traditional orientation for women,[38] the converse may also be true. Finally, the strong relationship between lower fertility and the educational attainment of a woman may involve more than a response to the higher financial return of nonfamilial activity for the better educated.[39] Education may be a proxy variable for the degree to which a woman defines her life in terms of self rather than others.

Some quantitative support for the hypothesis that the wife significantly controlled family planning in the nineteenth century derives from a comparison of sex ratios of last children in small and large families, and an analysis of the sex composition of very small families in Hingham, Massachusetts. Most studies indicate that men and women equally prefer boys to girls.[40] Given a residue of patriarchal bias in nineteenth-century values, it is not an unlikely assumption that women would be more satisfied than men with girl children. A suggestive psychological study supports this notion. In a sample of Swedish women expecting their first child, those preferring a boy were found to have less of a sense of personal autonomy. Of the eleven of the eighty-one women in the sample who considered themselves dominant in their marriages, only two wanted sons. The "no-preference" women were better adjusted psychologically and scored higher on intelligence tests.[41] In short, the less autonomous and adjusted the woman, the more likely she is to want her first child to be a boy.

In Hingham marriages formed between 1821 and 1860, the last child was more likely to be a girl in small families and a boy in the larger families (see Table 4). The difference between the sex ratios of the final child in families with one to four children as compared to those with five and more is statistically significant only at the 0.1 level. Given the complexity of the argument here, this is not impressive. Small families, however, tended to contain only girls. Sixty percent of only children were girls (21 of 35); 27 percent and 17 percent of two-child families were both girls (14) and boys (9) re-

TABLE 4

Sex ratio of last versus other children of stated parity and the probability of having another child according to sex of the last child: Hingham women in complete families marrying before age twenty-five between 1821 and 1860.

	Sex Ratio		Parity Progression Ratios		
Parity	Last	Not Last	Male Last	Female Last	Difference
1	57(22)	124(242)	.944	.885	+.059
2	113(32)	82(211)	.848	.855	−.037
3	69(49)	83(165)	.789	.756	+.033
4	83(42)	114(124)	.776	.716	+.060
5	107(31)	114(94)	.758	.746	+.012
6	237(22)	74(66)	.596	.826	−.230
7	150(20)	77(46)	.625	.764	−.139
8&+	124(47)	105(86)	.628	.667	−.039

Note: Sample sizes in parentheses. Chi-Square (1–4) vs. (5 and more) 2.882, significant at 0.1 level.

Source: Daniel Scott Smith, "Population, Family and Society in Hingham, Massachusetts, 1635–1880," (unpublished Ph.D. dissertation, University of California, Berkeley, 1973), p. 360.

spectively; and 14 percent and 6 percent of three-child families were all girls (9) and all boys (4) respectively. The independent probability of these differences is less than one in ten, one in four, and one in twenty respectively. With a slight biological tendency toward males in births to young women, these figures suggest that differing sex-preferences of husbands and wives may explain the pattern. On the other hand, twentieth-century sex-ratio samples show either no difference or a bias toward males in the sex ratio of the last-born child.[42] In the absence of very marked differences in the preference of husbands and wives and with less than perfect contraceptive methods available to nineteenth-century couples, no extreme relationship should appear. This quantitative pattern does suggest that the Victorian family had a domestic-feminist rather than a patriarchal orientation.

Recognition of the desirability and even the existence of female control of marital sexual intercourse may be found in nineteenth-century marital advice literature. In these manuals, "marital excess," i.e., too-frequent coitus, was a pervasive theme. Although conservative writers, such as William Alcott, proclaimed that "the submissive wife should do everything for your husband which your strength and a due regard to your health would admit,"[43] women rejected submission. In fact, Dio Lewis claimed that marital excess was the topic best received by his female audience during his lecture tours of the 1850s. The Moral Education Society, according to Lewis, asserted the right "of a wife to be her own person, and her sacred right to deny her husband if need be; and to decide how often and when she should become a mother."[44] The theme of the wife's right to control her body and her fertility was not uncommon. "It is a woman's right, not her privilege, to control the surrender of her person;" she should have pleasure or not allow access unless she wanted a child.[45]

It should be emphasized that both the husband and the wife had good (albeit different) reasons for limiting the size of their family. In most marriages, perhaps, these decisions were made jointly by the couple. Nor is it necessarily true that the wife imposed abstinence on her husband. While *coitus interruptus* is the male contraceptive par excellence, the wife could assist "with voluntary [though unspecified] effort."[46] Withdrawal was, according to one physician, "so universal it may be called a national vice, so common that it is unblushingly acknowledged by its perpetrators, *for the commission of which the husband is even eulogized by his wife and applauded by her friends* [italics added]."[47] In the marriage manuals, withdrawal was the most denounced means of marital contraception and, it may be inferred, the most common method in actual practice.

There are serious questions about the applicability of this literary evidence to actual behavior. Even among the urban middle classes (presumably the consumers of these manuals and tracts) reality and ideology probably diverged considerably. Historical variation in sexual ideology doubtless is much greater than change in actual sexual behavior.[48] The anti-sexual themes of the nineteenth century should not, however, be ignored. One may view this ideology as the product of underlying social circumstances—the conscious tip, so to speak, of the submerged iceberg of sexual conflict. While the influence of this literature is difficult to assess, its functions can be examined. It can be argued that anti-sexual themes had little to do with family limitation. Nor was contraception universally condemned by respectable opinion. The *Nation* in June 1869 called family limitation "not the noblest motive of action, of course; but there is something finely human about it."[49] Male sexual self-control was necessary, it has been suggested, to produce ordered, disciplined personalities who could focus relentlessly on success in the marketplace.[50] The conventional interpretation of these anti-sexual themes, of course, is that Victorian morality was but another means for suppressing women. The trouble with these arguments is that men more than women should be expected to favor, support, and extend the operation of this morality.

To understand the function of this ideology we must examine the market system involving the exchange of services between women and men. In historical, pre-industrial, hierarchical society, male control and suppression of female sexuality focused especially on the paternal control of daughters. This system of control existed for the establishment of marriage alliances and for the protection of one's females from the intrusions of social inferiors. Sexual restrictiveness need not, however, imply direct male domination. In a system of equality between males in which females are denied access to other resources, a sexually restrictive ideology is predictable. Nineteenth-century mate-choice was more or less an autonomous process uncontrolled by elders. American women, as Tocqueville and others noted, had considerable freedom before marriage. Lacking economic resources, however, they could bargain with their only available good—sex. The price of sex, as of other commodities, varies inversely with the supply. Since husbands were limited by the autonomy of single women in finding sexual gratification elsewhere, sexual restrictiveness also served the interests of married women. Furthermore, in a democratic society, men could not easily violate the prerogatives of their male equals by seducing their wives. Thus Victorian morality functioned in the interest of both single and married women.[51] By having an effective monopoly on the supply of sexual gratification, married women could increase the "price" since their husbands still generally expressed a traditional uncontrolled demand for sex. Instead of being "possessed," women could now bargain. Respectable sexual ideology argued, it is true, that men should substitute work for sex. This would reduce the price that wives could exact. At the same time, according to the prevailing sexual ideology, marital sex was the least dangerous kind. In contrast to masturbation or prostitution, marital intercourse was evaluated positively. But, contrary to these ideological trends, prostitution appears to have increased during the nineteenth century. Whether or not prostitution was a substitute for marital sex or merely a reflection of the relative increase in the proportion of unattached males created by late marriage and high geographical mobility is uncertain. This brief economic analysis of the supply and demand of sex at least suggests the possibility that Victorian morality had distinctly feminist overtones.

In principle, Victorian sexual ideology did advance the interest of individual women. Whether or not this represented a genuine feminist ideology depends to some extent on the behavior of women as a group. The evidence seems to be fairly clear on this point. If women as individuals had wished to maximize their advantage, they could have furthered the devaluation of non-marital sex for men by drawing more firmly the line between "good" and "bad" women, between the lady and the whore. While mothers may have done this on an individual basis, for example, by threatening their daughters with the dishonor of being a fallen woman, collectively they tended to sympathize with the prostitute or fallen woman and condemn the male exploiter or seducer.[52] The activity of the New York Female Moral Reform Society is an instructive case in point.[53]

Historians have had some difficulty in interpreting the anti-sexual theme in nineteenth-century women's history. Although Rosenberg recognizes the implicit radicalness of the assault on the double standard and the demand for a reformation in male sexual behavior, she tends to apologize for the failure of sexual reformers to link up with the "real" feminism represented by Sarah Grimké's feminist manifesto.[54] More serious is the distortion of the central question of the periodization of women's history. Cott's labeling of the first half of the nineteenth century as a question of "the cult of domesticity vs. social change," Kraditor's similar choice of "the family vs. autonomy," and Lerner's dichotomy of "the lady and the mill girl" all perpetuate the half-truth that the family served only as a source of social stability and change for women occurred only outside of the family.[55] I am arguing here, however, that the domestic roles of women and the perceptions that developed out of these roles were not an alternative to social change but presented a significant and positive development for nineteenth-century women.

Linking the decline of marital fertility to women's increasing autonomy within the family—the concept of "domestic feminism"—conflicts with several other theories held by scholars. To stress the failure of the woman's movement to support family limitation, as the Bankses do in their analyses for England, ignores the possibility of a parallel domestic feminist movement. It may be more to the point that anti-feminists blamed the revolt against maternity and marital sexual intercourse on the public feminists.[56] The Bankses suggest that individual feminists may have fought a battle to gain control over their own reproduction.[57] The nineteenth-century neo-Malthusians and the woman's movement had different purposes; the former attempted to control the fertility of "others," i.e., the working classes, while the latter sought reforms in its own interest. Since mechanical means of contraception were associated with non-marital sex of a kind exploitative of women, the opposition of women to these devices was an expression of the deeper hostility to the double standard.

A more serious objection to identifying the increasing power and autonomy of women within the family as feminism is, of course, the existence of the parallel tradition of "real" or "public" feminism. This tradition—linking Wollstonecraft, Seneca Falls, Stanton, Anthony, and Gilman—at least partially recognized the centrality of the role and position of women in the family to the general subjugation of women in society. In contrast, the goals of domestic feminism, at least in its initial stage, were situated entirely within marriage. Clearly some explanation is needed of why both strands of feminism existed. A possible answer relates to the evolution of the family in the process of modernization. With the democratization of American society, prestige ascribed by birth declined. Women born into families of high social status could not obtain deference if they remained single; even if a woman married a man of equally high status, his position would not assure her prestige; his status depended on his achievement. The satisfactory and valued performance in the roles of wife and mother could not compensate for the loss of status associated with the family line in pre-industrial society. Thus public feminism would be most attractive to women of high social origin.[58] This conception of the woman as an atomistic person and citizen naturally drew on the Enlightenment attack on traditional social ties. The modeling of the Seneca Falls manifesto on the Declaration of Independence is suggestive in this regard.[59]

The liberal origins of public feminism were both its strength and its weakness. Because it emphasized a clear standard of justice and stressed the importance of human individuality, it was consistent with the most fundamental values in American political history. But it was also limiting as a political ideology in that it cast its rhetoric against nearly obsolete social forms that had little relevance in the experience of the average American woman, i.e., patriarchalism and arbitrary male authority. Paradoxically, public feminism was simultaneously behind and ahead of the times. Resting on eighteenth-century notions, it clashed with the romantic and sentimental mood of the nineteenth century. The social basis of the appeal of public feminism—the opportunity for married women to assume both family and social roles—would not be created for the average woman until the post-industrial period.

Domestic feminism, on the other hand, was a nineteenth-century creation, born out of the emerging conjugal family and the social stresses accompanying modern economic growth. Instead of postulating woman as an atom in competitive society, domestic feminism viewed woman as a person in the context of relationships with others. By defining the family as a community, this ideology allowed women to engage in something of a critique of male, materialistic, market society and simultaneously proceed to seize power within the family. Women asserted themselves within the family much as their husbands were attempting to assert themselves outside the home. Critics such as de Tocqueville concluded that the Victorian conjugal family was really a manifestation of selfishness and a retreat from the older conception of community as place. As one utopian-communitarian put it, the basic social question of the day was "whether the existence of the marital family is compatible with that of the universal family which the term 'Community' signifies."[60]

Community—"that mythical state of social wholeness in which each member has his place and in which life is regulated by cooperation rather than by competition and conflict,"[61]—is not fixed historically in one social institution. Rather, as Kirk Jeffrey has argued, the nineteenth-century home was conceived of as a utopian community—at once a retreat, refuge and critique of the city.[62] Jeffrey, however, does not fully realize the implications of his insight. He admits that the literature of the utopian home demanded that husbands consult their wives, avoid sexual assault on them, and even consciously structure their own behavior on the model of their spouses. Yet he still concludes that "there seems little doubt that they (women) suffered a notable decline in autonomy and morale during the three-quarters of a century following the founding of the American republic."[63] He suggests that women who engaged in writing, social activities, political reform, drug use, and sickliness were "dropping out" of domesticity. On the contrary, these responses reflect both the time and autonomy newly available to women. The romantic ideal of woman as wife and mother in contrast to the Enlightenment model of woman as person and citizen did not have entirely negative consequences—particularly for the vast majority of American women who did not benefit from the position of their family in society.

The perspective suggested above helps to explain why the history of the suffrage movement involved a shift from the woman-as-atomistic-person notion toward the ideology of woman as wife-and-mother. Drawing on the perceptions gained from their rise within the family, women finally entered politics in large numbers at the turn of the twentieth century. Given the importance of family limitation and sexual control in domestic feminism, it is not surprising that women were involved in and strongly supported the temperance and social purity movements—reform attempts implicitly attacking male culture. Since these anti-male responses and attitudes were based on the familial and social experience of women, it seems beside the point to infer psychological abnormality from this emphasis.[64]

In an important sense, the traditions of domestic and public feminism merged in the fight for suffrage in the early twentieth century. In a study of "elite" women surveyed in 1913, Jensen found that mothers of completed fertility actually exhibited more support for suffrage than childless married women.[65] Women in careers involving more social interaction, for example, medicine, law, administration, tended to favor suffrage more strongly than women in more privatistic occupations, for example, teaching, writing, art.[66] In short, the dichotomy between women trapped or suppressed within marriage and women seeking to gain freedom through social participation does not accurately represent the history of American women in the nineteenth century.

It has been argued that historians must take seriously the changing roles and behavior of women within the Victorian conjugal family. That women eventually attained a larger arena of activity was not so much an alternative to the woman-as-wife-and-mother as an extension of the progress made within the family itself. Future research doubtless will qualify, if not completely obviate, the arguments presented in this essay. Although power relationships within contemporary marriages are poorly understood by social scientists, this critical area very much needs a historical dimension.[67] The history of women must take into account major changes in the structure of society and the family. During the pre-industrial period, women (mainly widows) exercised power as replacements for men. In the industrializing phase of the last century, married women gained power and a sense of autonomy within the family. In the post-industrial era, the potentiality for full social participation of women clearly exists. The construction of these historical stages inevitably involves over-simplification. Drawing these sharp contrasts, however, permits the historian to escape from the present-day definition of the situation. Once it is clear just what the long-run course of change actually was, more subtlety and attention to the mechanism of change will be possible in the analysis of women's history.

POSTSCRIPT (1979)

There was an important omission from the essay, an unstated premise whose centrality I did not fully grasp at the time. The rise of domestic feminism—the extension of autonomy of women within the family and the gradual enlargement of the social territory assigned to the domestic sphere—was essentially the only opening in the system. The distinction between public and private and the corresponding allocation of men to the former and women to the latter is a central (if not *the* central) theme in the history of gender.[68] The hostility to female participation in the public sphere was one reason for the trial of Anne Hutchinson in 1637; it precipitated the woman's issue within abolitionist ranks in the 1830s. At this late date in American history it helps to explain the delay and possible defeat of the ratification of the Equal Rights Amendment.

By assuming rather than analyzing this central definition, much of the attention of the essay was misplaced. While my contrast of "domestic" and "public" feminism may have some validity in terms of the intellectual origins of ideas, it is historically inaccurate. In her study of feminist abolitionists Hersh has shown that these types of feminism are not dichotomous but continuous.[69] Nearly all feminist abolitionists favored female autonomy within the family and the Victorian ideology of sex and the family. They were, in effect, also domestic feminists. Because of the persistent importance of the public/private distinction, most domestic feminists, on the other hand, could not be public feminists.

Suffrage for women, advocated by a tiny minority, was radical for two reasons. The ideological climate of liberalism made it radical. Given the assumption that injustice had only political origins and therefore was to be cured by a political remedy, the vote was the most advanced position possible. The vote for women, just as the Reconstruction Fifteenth Amendment for freedmen, was at the boundary of nineteenth-century reform. Land redistribution in the South or a public role for women lay outside. As DuBois has argued, the demand for female suffrage was radical because it represented an explicit assault on the all-important distinction between public and private.[70]

NOTES

I wish to thank Carl Degler, A. William Hoglund, Peter Stearns, and especially Ellen DuBois for their comments and suggestions on an earlier version of this analysis; none of the above should be held responsible for its flaws and errors.

1. The attempt to examine systematically the lives of ordinary women is well under way; for example, see Theodore Hershberg, "A Method for the Computerized Study of Family and Household Structure Using the Manuscript Schedules of the U.S. Census of Population." *Family in Historical Perspective Newsletter* 3 (Spring 1973): 6–20.

2. For a suggestive illustration of the impact of changing mortality on the average female, see Peter R. Uhlenberg, "A Study of Cohort Life Cycles: Cohorts of Native-Born Massachusetts Women, 1830–1920," *Population Studies* 23 (November 1969): 407–420.

3. Wilson H. Grabill, Clyde V. Kiser, and Pascal K. Whelpton, *The Fertility of American Women* (New York: John Wiley & Sons, Inc., 1958), Table 67, p. 145.

4. Robert V. Wells, "Demographic Change and the Life Cycle of American Families," *Journal of Interdisciplinary History* 2 (Autumn 1971): Table 2, p. 282.

5. This modal woman was constructed from the median age of household heads (less four years) from U.S. Bureau of the Census, *Historical Statistics of the United States, Colonial Times to 1957* (Washington, D.C.: Government Printing Office, 1960), Series A-263, p. 16; from the center of population gravity, from *U.S. Statistical Abstract* (87th ed., 1966), Table 11; from the mean number (5.6) of children born to rural-farm women in the north-central region born between 1835 and 1844 and married only once, U.S. Bureau of the Census, Sixteenth Census, *Population: Differential Fertility 1940 and 1910, Women by Number of Children ever Born* (Washington: Government Printing Office, 1945), Table 81, p. 237; and from the fact that 51.3 percent of the workforce in 1880 was employed in agriculture, Stanley Lebergott, *Manpower in Economic Growth* (New York: McGraw Hill, 1964), Table A-1, p. 510.

6. Some working women may have been counted as housewives by the census takers. Lebergott, *Manpower*, pp. 70–73, however, makes a cogent case for accepting the census figures.

7. Grabill *et al.*, *Fertility*. Table 9, p. 22.

8. Ansley J. Coale and Melvin Zelnik, *New Estimates of Fertility and Population in the United States* (Princeton: Princeton University Press, 1963), p. 41.

9. Yasukichi Yasuba, *Birth Rates of the White Population in the United States, 1800–1860* (Baltimore: Johns Hopkins Press, 1961), Table IV-9, p. 119, attributes 64.3 percent of the Connecticut fertility decline between 1774 and 1890 and 74.3 percent of the New Hampshire decline between 1774 and 1890 to change in marital fertility. Longer birth intervals and an earlier age at the termination of childbearing contributed nearly equally to the decrease in marital fertility. See Daniel Scott Smith, "Change in American Family Structure before the Demographic Transition: The Case of Hingham, Massachusetts," (unpublished paper presented to the American Society for Ethnohistory, October 1972), p. 3.

10. For a summary of the importance of withdrawal in the history of European contraception, see D. V. Glass, *Population: Policies and Movements in Europe* (New York: Augustus M. Kelley, Booksellers, 1967), p. 46–50.

11. For this definition, see Aileen S. Kraditor, *Up from the Pedestal* (Chicago: Quadrangle Books, 1968), p. 5.

12. Aileen S. Kraditor, *The Ideas of the Woman Suffrage Movement* (New York: Anchor Books, 1971).

13. Carl N. Degler, "Revolution without Ideology: The Changing Place of Women in America," *Daedalus* 93 (Spring 1964): 653–670.

14. William L. O'Neill, *Everyone was Brave* (Chicago: Quadrangle Books, 1969).

15. My use of the term conjugal is intended to be much broader than the strict application to household composition. On the relatively unchanging conjugal (or nuclear) structure of the household see Peter Laslett, ed., *Household and Family in Past Time* (Cambridge: Cambridge University Press, 1972). For an empirical demonstration of the types of changes involved see

my article, "Parental Power and Marriage Patterns: An Analysis of Historical Trends in Hingham, Massachusetts," in the special historical issue of *Journal of Marriage and the Family* 35 (August 1973).

16. Phillipe Ariès, *Centuries of Childhood: A Social History of Family Life*, trans. Robert Baldick (New York: Vintage Books, 1962).

17. Julia Cherry Spruill, *Women's Life and Work in the Southern Colonies* (Chapel Hill: University of North Carolina Press, 1938) and Elisabeth Anthony Dexter, *Colonial Women of Affairs* (Boston: Houghton Mifflin Company, 1924).

18. Richard B. Morris, *Studies in the History of American Law*, 2nd ed. (Philadelphia: Joseph M. Mitchell Co., 1959), pp. 126–200.

19. Maris Vinovskis, "Mortality Rates and Trends in Massachusetts before 1860," *Journal of Economic History* 12 (March 1972): 198–199. In the eighteenth century women began to live longer than men with the exception again of Ipswich.

20. Daniel Scott Smith, "Population, Family and Society in Hingham, Massachusetts, 1635–1880," (unpublished Ph.D. dissertation, University of California, Berkeley, 1973), pp. 225–227.

21. Scattered American data are available in Lawrence A. Cremin, *American Education: The Colonial Experience, 1607–1783* (New York: Harper Torchbooks, 1970), pp. 526, 533, 540. Also see Carlo M. Cipolla, *Literacy and Development in the West* (Baltimore: Penguin Books, 1969), Table 1, p. 14. Professor Kenneth Lockridge of the University of Michigan, who is undertaking a major study of literacy in early America has written me, however, that women using a mark may have been able to read.

22. Edward Shorter, "Capitalism, Culture and Sexuality: Some Competing Models," *Social Science Quarterly* 53 (September 1972): 339.

23. David M. Potter, "American Women and the American Character," in *History and American Society: Essays of David M. Potter*, ed. Don E. Fehrenbacher (New York: Oxford University Press, 1973), pp. 227–303.

24. Evsey D. Domar, "The Causes of Slavery or Serfdom: A Hypothesis," *Journal of Economic History* 30 (March 1970): 18–32.

25. See Edmund S. Morgan, "Slavery and Freedom: An American Paradox," *Journal of Economic History* 59 (June 1972): 3–29.

26. Stanley Engerman, "Some Considerations Relating to Property Rights in Man," *Journal of Economic History* 33 (March 1973): 56–65.

27. Jack E. Eblen, "An Analysis of Nineteenth Century Frontier Populations," *Demography* 2 (1965): 399–413.

28. See Herbert Moller, "Sex Composition and Correlated Culture Patterns of Colonial America," *William and Mary Quarterly* 2 (April 1945): 113–153 for data on sex ratios.

29. Alan P. Grimes, *The Puritan Ethic and Woman Suffrage* (New York: Oxford University Press, 1967).

30. Bernard Farber, *Comparative Kinship Systems* (New York: John Wiley & Sons, Inc., 1968), pp. 23–46.

31. Walter E. Houghton, *The Victorian Frame of Mind* (New Haven: Yale University Press, 1957), pp. 348–353.

32. See Smith, "Parental Power and Marriage Patterns . . ." *Journal of Marriage and the Family* (August 1973).

33. Grabill *et al.*, *Fertility*, pp. 16–19. For insights based on differentials in census child-woman ratios see Yasuba, *Birth Rates*, as well as Colin Forster and G. S. L. Tucker, *Economic Opportunity and White American Fertility Ra-*

tios, 1800–1860 (New Haven: Yale University Press, 1972). For a brief statement of the structural argument see Richard Easterlin, "Does Fertility Adjust to the Environment?" *American Economic Review* 61 (1971): 394–407.

34. John D. Kasarda, "Economic Structure and Fertility: A Comparative Analysis," *Demography* 8 (August 1971): 307–317.

35. Lebergott, *Manpower*, p. 63.

36. Kingsley Davis, "The American Family in Relation to Demographic Change," in *Demographic and Social Aspects of Population Growth*, eds. Charles F. Westoff and Robert Parke, Jr. (Washington, D.C.: Government Printing Office, 1972), p. 245.

37. One study involving seven Latin American cities has suggestively concluded that the "wife's motivation for employment, her education, and her preferred role seem to exert greater influence on her fertility than her actual role of employee or homemaker," Paula H. Hass, "Maternal Role Incompatability and Fertility in Urban Latin America," *Journal of Social Issues* 28 (1972): 111–127.

38. Virginia Yans McLaughlin, "Patterns of Work and Family Organization: Buffalo's Italians," *Journal of Interdisciplinary History* 2 (Autumn 1971): 299–314.

39. For the relationship between fertility and individual characteristics see the special issue of the *Journal of Political Economy* 81, pt. 2 (March/April 1973) on "new economic approaches to fertility."

40. See the summary by Gerald E. Markle and Charles B. Nam, "Sex Determination: Its Impact on Fertility," *Social Biology* 18 (March 1971): 73–82.

41. N. Uddenberg, P. E. Almgren and A. Nilsson, "Preference for Sex of Child among Pregnant Women," *Journal of Biosocial Science* 3 (July 1971): 267–280.

42. In a study of early twentieth century *Who's Who*, cited by Markle and Nam, the sex ratio of the last child was 117.4 in 5,466 families. No differences appear in Harriet L. Fancher, "The Relationship between the Occupational Status of Individuals and the Sex Ratio of their Offspring." *Human Biology*, 28 (September 1966): 316–322.

43. William A. Alcott, *The Young Man's Wife, or Duties of Women in the Marriage Role* (Boston: George W. Light, 1837), p. 176.

44. Dio Lewis, *Chastity, or Our Secret Sins* (New York: Canfield Publishing Company, 1888), p. 18.

45. Henry C. Wright, *Marriage and Parentage* (Boston: Bela Marsh, 1853), pp. 242–255.

46. Anon, *Satan in Society* (Cincinnati: C. V. Vent, 1875), p. 153.

47. Ibid., p. 152.

48. For a discussion of the gradualness of change in sexual behavior see Daniel Scott Smith, "The Dating of the American Sexual Revolution: Evidence and Interpretation," in *The American Family in Social-Historical Perspective*, ed., Michael Gordon (New York: St. Martin's Press, 1973), pp. 321–335.

49. Quoted by George Humphrey Napheys, *The Physical Life of Women* (Philadelphia: H. C. Watts Co., 1882), p. 119.

50. Peter C. Cominos, "Late Victorian Sexual Respectability and the Social System," *International Review of Social History* 8 (1963): 18–48, 216–250.

51. Although the basic argument here was formulated independently.

Randall Collins, "A Conflict Theory of Sexual Stratification," *Social Problems* 19 (Summer 1971): 3–21; and David G. Berger and Morton C. Wenger, "The Ideology of Virginity," (paper read at the 1972 meeting of the National Council on Family Relations) were very helpful in developing this theme.

52. On attitudes toward prostitution, see Margaret Wyman, "The Rise of the Fallen Woman," *American Quarterly* 3 (Summer 1951): 167–177; and Robert E. Riegel, "Changing American Attitudes Toward Prostitution," *Journal of the History of Ideas* 29 (July-September 1968): 437–452.

53. Carroll Smith-Rosenberg, "Beauty, the Beast and the Militant Woman: a Case Study in Sex Roles in Jacksonian America," *American Quarterly* 23 (October 1971): 562–584.

54. Ibid.

55. Nancy F. Cott, *Root of Bitterness* (New York: E. P. Dutton & Co., Inc., 1972): 11–14; Kraditor, *Up from the Pedestal*, p. 21; Gerda Lerner, "The Lady and the Mill Girl: Changes in the Status of Women in the Age of Jackson," *Midcontinent American Studies Journal* 10 (Spring 1969): 5–14.

56. J. A. and Olive Banks, *Feminism and Family Planning in Victorian England* (Liverpool: Liverpool University Press, 1964); esp. pp. 53–57.

57. Ibid., p. 125.

58. In his book, *Daughters of the Promised Land* (Boston: Little, Brown, 1970), Page Smith argues that many prominent feminists had strong fathers. It might be that the true relationship, if any in fact exists, is between public feminism and high status fathers.

59. Robert A. Nisbet, *The Sociological Tradition* (New York: Basic Books, 1966), ch. 3, esp. pp. 47–51.

60. Quoted by John L. Thomas, "Romantic Reform in America, 1815–1865," *American Quarterly* 17 (Winter 1965): p. 677.

61. Charles Abrams, *The Language of Cities* (New York: Viking Press, 1971), p. 60.

62. Kirk Jeffrey effectively develops this theme in "The Family as Utopian Retreat from the City: The Nineteenth Century Contribution" in *The Family, Communes and Utopian Societies*, ed. Sallie Teselle (New York: Harper Torchbooks, 1972), pp. 21–41.

63. Ibid., p. 30.

64. For a psychological emphasis see James R. McGovern, "Anna Howard Shaw: New Approaches to Feminism," *Journal of Social History* 3 (Winter 1969–70): 135–153.

65. Richard Jensen, "Family, Career, and Reform: Women Leaders of the Progressive Era," in *The American Family in Social-Historical Perspective*, Table 7, p. 277.

66. Ibid., Table 2, p. 273.

67. An analysis of recent literature of this important topic is presented by Constantina Safilios-Rothschild, "The Study of Family Power Structure: A Review 1960–1969," *Journal of Marriage and the Family* 32 (November 1970): 539–552.

68. Michelle Zimbalist Rosaldo, "Woman, Culture, and Society: A Theoretical Overview," in Rosaldo and Louise Lamphere, eds., *Woman, Culture, and Society* (Stanford: Stanford University Press, 1974), 17–42. The boundaries and definition of the public/private distinction vary among societies. My stress here is on the lack of variance concerning its definition in American history, at least before the twentieth century.

69. Blanche Glassman Hersh, *The Slavery of Sex: Feminists-Abolitionists in America* (Champaign, University of Illinois Press, 1978).

70. Ellen DuBois, "The Radicalism of the Woman Suffrage Movement: Notes Toward the Reconstruction of Nineteenth-Century Feminism," *Feminist Studies* 3 (1975): 63–71.

10

Women and Their Families on the Overland Trail to California and Oregon, 1842–1867

■

JOHNNY FARAGHER and CHRISTINE STANSELL

The pioneer is a stock figure in American history, and a male stereotype in many Americans' minds. What of the pioneer who was a woman? In their searching analysis of the conditions of life for women and their families traveling to the West coast in the mid-nineteenth century, John Faragher and Christine Stansell draw upon rich stores of surviving diaries and letters to delve behind the stereotypes. Rather than assuming that all members of a family traveling West shared the same outlook, the authors distinguish the women's from the men's experience. They are interested in whether Eastern conventions regarding women's roles carried over to a new, undefined situation. Their questions about family roles, work tasks, cultural expectations, and bonding among women evoke a portrait that is at once surprising and realistic.

I am not a wheatfield
nor the virgin forest

I never chose this place
yet I am of it now

—Adrienne Rich
"From an Old House in America"

From 1841 until 1867, the year in which the transcontinental railroad was completed, nearly 350,000 North Americans emigrated to the Pacific coast along the western wagon road known variously as the Oregon, the California, or simply the Overland Trail. This migration was essentially a family phenomenon. Although single men constituted the majority of the party which pioneered large-scale emigration on the Overland Trail in 1841, significant numbers of women and children were already present in the wagon trains of the next season. Families made up the preponderant proportion of the migrations throughout the 1840s. In 1849, during the overwhelmingly male Gold Rush, the number dropped precipitously, but after 1851 families once again assumed dominance in the overland migration.[1] The contention that "the family was the one substantial social institution" on the frontier is too sweeping, yet it is undeniable that the white family largely mediated the incorporation of the western territories into the American nation.[2]

The emigrating families were a heterogeneous lot. Some came from farms in the midwest and upper South, many from small midwestern towns, and others from northeastern and midwestern cities. Clerks and shopkeepers as well as farmers outfitted their wagons in Independence, St. Louis, or Westport Landing on the Missouri. Since costs for supplies, travel, and settlement were not negligible,[3] few of the very poor were present, nor were the exceptionally prosperous. The dreams of fortune which lured the wagon trains into new lands were those of modest men whose hopes were pinned to small farms or larger dry-goods stores, more fertile soil or more customers, better market prospects and a steadily expanding economy.

For every member of the family, the trip West was exhausting, toilsome, and often grueling. Each year in late spring, westbound emigrants gathered for the journey at spots along the Missouri River and moved out in parties of ten to several hundred wagons. Aggregates of nuclear families, loosely attached by kinship or friendship, traveled together or joined an even larger caravan.[4] Coast-bound families traveled by ox-drawn wagons at the frustratingly slow pace of fifteen to twenty miles per day. They worked their way up the Platte River valley through what is now Kansas and Nebraska, crossing the Rockies at South Pass in southwestern Wyoming by midsummer. The Platte route was relatively easy going, but from present-day Idaho, where the roads to California and Oregon diverged, to their final destinations, the pioneers faced disastrous conditions: scorching deserts, boggy salt flats, and rugged mountains. By this time, families had been on the road some three months and were only at the midpoint of the journey; the environment, along with the wear of the road, made the last months difficult almost beyond endurance. Finally, in late fall or early winter the pioneers straggled into their promised lands, after six months and over two thousand miles of hardship.[5]

As this journey progressed, bare necessity became the determinant of most of each day's activities. The primary task of surviving and getting to the coast gradually suspended accustomed patterns of dividing work between women and men. All able-bodied adults worked all day in one way or another to keep the family moving. Women's work was no less indispensable than men's; indeed, as the summer wore on, the boundaries dividing the work of the sexes were threatened, blurred, and transgressed.

The vicissitudes of the trail opened new possibilities for expanded work roles for women, and in the cooperative work of the family there existed a basis for a vigorous struggle for female-male equality. But most women did not see the experience in this way. They viewed it as a male enterprise from its very inception. Women experienced the breakdown of the sexual division of labor as a dissolution of their own autonomous "sphere." Bereft of the footing which this independent base gave them, they lacked a cultural rationale for the work they did, and remained estranged from the possibilities of the enlarged scope and power of family life on the trail. Instead, women fought *against* the forces of necessity to hold together the few fragments of female subculture left to them. We have been bequeathed a remarkable record of this struggle in the diaries, journals, and memoirs of emigrating women. In this study, we will examine a particular habit of living, or culture, in conflict with the new material circumstances of the Trail, and the efforts of women to maintain a place, a sphere of their own.

The overland family was not a homogeneous unit, its members imbued with identical aspirations and desires. On the contrary, the period of westward movement was also one of multiplying schisms within those families whose location and social status placed them in the mainstream of national culture.[6] Child-rearing tracts, housekeeping manuals, and etiquette books by the hundreds prescribed and rationalized to these Americans a radical separation of the work responsibilities and social duties of mothers and fathers; popular thought assigned unique personality traits, spiritual capacities, and forms of experience to the respective categories of man, woman, and child.[7] In many families, the tensions inherent in this separatist ideology, often repressed in the everyday routines of the East, erupted under the strain of the overland crossing. The difficulties of the emigrants, while inextricably linked to the duress of the journey itself, also revealed family dynamics which had been submerged in the less eventful life "back home."

A full blown ideology of "woman's place" was absent in pre-industrial America. On farms, in artisan shops, and in town marketplaces, women and children made essential contributions to family income and subsistence; it was the family which functioned as the basic unit of production in the colony and the young nation. As commercial exchanges displaced the local markets where women had sold surplus dairy products and textiles, and the workplace drifted away from the household, women and children lost their breadwinning prerogatives.[8]

In Jacksonian America, a doctrine of "sexual spheres" arose to facilitate and justify the segregation of women into the home and men into productive work.[9] While the latter attended to politics, economics, and wage-earning, popular thought assigned women the refurbished and newly professionalized tasks of child-rearing and housekeeping.[10] A host of corollaries followed on the heels of these shifts. Men were physically strong, women naturally delicate; men were skilled in practical matters, women in moral and emotional concerns; men were prone to corruption, women to virtue; men belonged in the world, women in the home. For women, the system of sexual spheres represented a decline in social status and isolation from political and economic power. Yet it also provided them with a psychological power base of undeniable importance. The "cult of true womanhood" was more than simply a retreat. Catharine Beecher, one of the chief theorists of "woman's influence," proudly quoted Tocqueville's observation that "in no country has such constant care been taken, as in America, to trace two clearly distinct lines of action for the two sexes, and to make them keep pace with the other, but in two pathways which are always different."[11] Neither Beecher nor her sisters were simply dupes of a masculine imperialism. The supervision of child-rearing, household economy, and the moral and religious life of the family granted women a certain degree of real autonomy and control over their lives as well as those of their husbands and children.

Indeed, recent scholarship has indicated that a distinctly female subculture emerged from "woman's sphere." By "subculture" we simply mean a "habit of living"—as we have used "culture" above—of a minority group which is self-consciously distinct from the dominant activities, expectations, and values of a society. Historians have seen female church groups, reform associations, and philanthropic activity as expressions of this subculture in actual behavior, while a large and rich body of writing by and for women articulated the subcultural impulses on the ideational level. Both behavior and thought point to child-rearing, religious activity, education, home life, associationism, and female communality as components of women's subculture. Female friendships, strikingly intimate and deep in this period, formed the actual bonds.[12] Within their tight and atomized family households, women carved out a life of their own.

At its very inception, the western emigration sent tremors through the foundations of this carefully compartmentalized family structure. The rationale behind pulling up stakes was nearly always economic advancement;[13] since breadwinning was a masculine concern, the husband and father introduced the idea of going West and made the final decision. Family participation in the intervening time ran the gamut from enthusiastic support to stolid resistance. Many women cooperated with their ambitious spouses: "The motive that induced us to part with pleasant associations and the dear friends of our childhood days, was to obtain from the government of the United States a grant of land that 'Uncle Sam' had promised to give to the head of each family who settled in this new country."[14] Others, however, only acquiesced. "Poor Ma said only this morning, 'Oh, I wish we never had started,' " Lucy Cooke wrote her first day on the trail, "and she looks so sorrowful and dejected. I think if Pa had not passengers to take through she would urge him to return; not that he should be so inclined."[15] Huddled with her children in a cold, damp wagon, trying to calm them despite the ominous chanting of visiting Indians, another woman wondered "what had possessed my husband, anyway, that he should have thought of bringing us away out through this God forsaken country."[16] Similar alienation from the "pioneer spirit" haunted Lavinia Porter's leave-taking:

> I never recall that sad parting from my dear sister on the plains of Kansas without the tears flowing fast and free. . . . We were the eldest of a large family, and the bond of affection and love that existed between us was strong indeed . . . as she with the other friends turned to leave me for the ferry which was to take them back to home and civilization, I stood alone on that wild prairie. Looking westward I saw my husband driving slowly over the plain; turning my face once more to the east, my dear sister's footsteps were fast widening the distance between us. For the time I knew not which way to go, nor whom to follow. But in a few moments I rallied my forces . . . and soon overtook the slowly moving oxen who were bearing my husband and child over the green prairie . . . the unbidden tears would flow in spite of my brave resolve to be the courageous and valiant frontierswoman.[17]

Her dazed vacillation soon gave way to a private conviction that the family had made a dire mistake: "I would make a brave effort to be cheerful and patient until the camp work was done. Then starting out ahead of the team and my men folks, when I thought I had gone beyond hearing distance, I would throw myself down on the unfriendly desert and give way like a child to sobs and tears, wishing myself back home with my friends and chiding myself for consenting to take this wild goose chase."[18] Men viewed drudgery, calamity, and privation as trials along the road to prosperity, unfortunate but inevitable corollaries of the rational decision they had made. But to those women who were unable to appropriate the vision of the upwardly mobile pilgrimage, hardship and loss only testified to the inherent folly of the emigration, "this wild goose chase."

If women were reluctant to accompany their men, however, they were often equally unwilling to let them go alone. In the late 1840s, the conflict between wives and their gold-crazed husbands reveals the determination with which women enforced the cohesion of the nuclear family. In the name of family unity, some obdurate wives simply chose to blockbust the sexually segregated Gold Rush: "My husband grew enthusiastic and wanted to start immediately," one woman recalled, "but I would not be left behind. I thought where he could go I could and where I went I could take my two little toddling babies."[19] Her family departed intact. Other women used their moral authority to smash the enterprise in its planning stages. "We were married to live together," a wife acidly reminded her spouse when he informed her of his intention to join the Rush: "I am willing to go with you to any part of *God's Foot Stool* where you think you can do best, and under these circumstances you have no right to go where I cannot, and if you do you need never return for I shall look upon you as dead."[20] Roundly chastised, the man postponed his journey until the next season, when his family could leave with him. When included in the plans, women seldom wrote of their husbands' decisions to emigrate in their diaries or memoirs. A breadwinner who tried to leave alone, however, threatened the family unity upon which his authority was based; only then did a wife challenge his dominance in worldly affairs.[21]

There was an economic reason for the preponderance of families on the Trail. Women and children, but especially women, formed an essential supplementary work force in the settlements. The ideal wife in the West resembled a hired hand more than a nurturant Christian housekeeper.[22] Narcissa Whitman wrote frankly to aspiring settlers of the functional necessity of women on the new farms: "Let every young man bring a wife, for he will want one after he gets here, if he never did before."[23] In a letter from California, another seasoned woman warned a friend in Missouri that in the West women became "hewers of wood and drawers of water everywhere."[24] Mrs. Whitman's fellow missionary Elkanah Walker was unabashedly practical in beseeching his wife to join him: "I am tired of keeping an old bachelor's hall. I want someone to get me a good supper and let me take my ease and when I am very tired in the morning I want someone to get up and get breakfast and let me lay in bed and take my rest."[25] It would be both simplistic and harsh to argue that men brought their families West or married because of the labor power of women and children; there is no doubt, however, that the new Westerners appreciated the advantages of familial labor. Women were not superfluous; they were workers. The migration of women helped to solve the problem of labor scarcity, not only in the early years of the American settlement on the coast, but throughout the history of the continental frontier.[26]

In the first days of the overland trip, new work requirements were not yet pressing and the division of labor among family members still replicated familiar patterns. Esther Hanna reported in one of her first diary entries that "our men have gone to build a bridge across the stream, which is impassable," while she baked her first bread on the prairie.[27] Elizabeth Smith similarly described her party's day: "rainy . . . Men making rafts. Women cooking and washing. Children crying."[28] When travel was suspended, "the men were generally busy mending wagons, harnesses, yokes, shoeing the animals etc., and the women washed clothes, boiled a big mess of beans, to warm over for several meals, or perhaps mended clothes."[29] At first, even in emergencies, women and men hardly considered integrating their work. "None but those who have cooked for a family of eight, crossing the plains, have any idea of what it takes," a disgruntled woman recalled: "My sister-in-law was sick, my niece was much younger than I, and consequently I had the management of all the cooking and planning on my young shoulders."[30] To ask a man to help was a possibility she was unable even to consider.[31]

The relegation of women to purely domestic duties, however, soon broke down under the vicissitudes of the Trail. Within the first few weeks, the unladylike task of gathering buffalo dung for fuel (little firewood was available *en route*) became women's work.[32] As one traveler astutely noted, "force of surroundings was a great leveler";[33] miles of grass, dust, glare, and mud erased some of the most rudimentary distinctions between female and male responsibilities. By summer, women often helped drive the wagons and the livestock.[34] At one Platte crossing, "the men drawed the wagons over by hand and the women all crossed in safety"; but at the next, calamity struck when the bridge collapsed, "and then commenced the hurry and bustle of repairing; all were at work, even the women and children."[35] Such crises, which compounded daily as the wagons moved past the Platte up the long stretches of desert and coastal mountains, generated equity in work; at times of Indian threats, for example, both women and men made bullets and stood guard.[36] When mountain fever struck the Pengra family as they crossed the Rockies, Charlotte relieved her incapacitated husband of the driving while he took care of the youngest child.[37] Only such severe afflictions forced men to take on traditionally female chores. While women did men's work, there is little evidence that men reciprocated.

Following a few days in the life of an overland woman discloses the magnitude of her work. During the hours her party traveled, Charlotte Pengra walked beside the wagons, driving the cattle and gathering buffalo chips. At night she cooked, baked bread for the next noon meal, and washed clothes. Three successive summer days illustrate how trying these small chores could be. Her train pulled out early on a Monday morning, only to be halted by rain and a flash flood; Mrs. Pengra washed and dried her family's wet clothes in the afternoon while doing her daily baking. On Tuesday the wagons pushed hard to make up for lost time, forcing her to trot all day to keep up. In camp that night there was no time to rest. Before going to bed, she wrote, "Kept busy in preparing tea and doing other things preparatory for the morrow. I baked a cracker pudding, warm biscuits and made tea, and after supper stewed two pans of dried apples, and made two loaves of bread, got my work done up, beds made, and child asleep, and have written in my journal. Pretty tired of course." The same routine devoured the next day and evening: "I have done a washing. Stewed apples, made pies and baked a rice pudding, and mended our wagon cover. Rather tired." And the next: "baked biscuits, stewed berries, fried meat, boiled and mashed potatoes, and made tea for supper, afterward baked bread. Thus you see I have not much rest."[38] Children also burdened women's work and leisure. During one quiet time, Helen Stewart retreated in mild defiance from her small charges to a tent in order to salvage some private time: "It exceeding hot . . . some of the men is out hunting and some of them sleeping. The children is grumbling and crying and laughing and howling and playing all around."[39] Although children are notably absent in women's journals, they do appear, frightened and imploring, during an Indian scare or a storm, or intrude into a rare and precious moment of relaxation, "grumbling and crying."[40]

Because the rhythm of their chores was out of phase with that of the men, the division of labor could be especially taxing to women.

Men's days were toilsome but broken up at regular intervals with periods of rest. Men hitched the teams, drove or walked until noon, relaxed at dinner, traveled until the evening camp, unhitched the oxen, ate supper, and in the evening sat at the campfire, mended equipment, or stood guard. They also provided most of the labor in emergencies, pulling the wagons through mires, across treacherous river crossings, up long grades, and down precipitous slopes. In the pandemonium of a steep descent,

> you would see the women and children in advance seeking the best way, some of them slipping down, or holding on to the rocks, now taking an "otter slide," and then a run til some natural obstacle presented itself to stop their accelerated progress and those who get down safely without a hurt or a bruise, are fortunate indeed. Looking back to the train, you would see some of the men holding on to the wagons, others slipping under the oxen's feet, some throwing articles out of the way that had fallen out, and all have enough to do to keep them busily occupied.[41]

Women were responsible for staying out of the way and getting themselves and the children to safety, men for getting the wagons down. Women's work, far less demanding of brute strength and endurance, was nevertheless distributed without significant respite over all waking hours: mealtimes offered no leisure to the cooks. "The plain fact of the matter is," a young woman complained,

> we *have no time for sociability*. From the time we get up in the morning, until we are on the road, it is hurry scurry to get breakfast and put away the things that necessarily had to be pulled out last night—while under way there is no room in the wagon for a visitor, nooning is barely long enough to eat a cold bite—and at night all the cooking utensils and provisions are to be gotten about the camp fire, and cooking enough to last until the next night.[42]

After supper, the men gathered together, "lolling and smoking their pipes and guessing, or maybe betting, how many miles we had covered during the day,"[43] while the women baked, washed, and put the children to bed before they finally sat down. Charlotte Pengra found "as I was told before I started that there is no rest in such a journey."[44]

Unaccustomed tasks beset the travelers, who were equipped with only the familiar expectation that work was divided along gender lines. The solutions which sexual "spheres" offered were usually irrelevant to the new problems facing families. Women, for example, could not afford to be delicate: their new duties demanded far greater stamina and hardiness than their traditional domestic tasks. With no tradition to deal with the new exigencies of fuel-gathering, cattle-driving, and cooking, families found that "the division of labor in a party . . . was a prolific cause of quarrel."[45] Within the Vincent party, "assignments to duty were not accomplished without grumbling and objection . . . there were occasional angry debates while the various burdens were being adjusted," while in "the camps of others who sometimes jogged along the trail in our company . . . we saw not a little fighting . . . and these bloody fisticuffs were invariably the outcome of disputes over division of labor."[46] At home, these assignments were familiar and accepted, not subject to questioning. New work opened the division of labor to debate and conflict.

By midjourney, most women worked at male tasks. The men still retained dominance within their "sphere," despite the fact that it was no longer exclusively masculine. Like most women, Lavinia Porter was responsible for gathering buffalo chips for fuel. One afternoon, spying a grove of cottonwoods half a mile away, she asked her husband to branch off the trail so that the party could fell trees for firewood, thus easing her work. "But men on the plains I had found were not so accommodating, nor so ready to wait upon women as they were in more civilized communities." Her husband refused and Porter fought back: "I was feeling somewhat under the weather and unusually tired, and crawling into the wagon told them if they wanted fuel for the evening meal they could get it themselves and cook the meal also, and laying my head down on a pillow, I cried myself to sleep."[47] Later that evening her husband awakened her with a belated dinner he had prepared himself, but despite his conciliatory spirit their relations were strained for weeks: "James and I had gradually grown silent and taciturn and had unwittingly partaken of the gloom and somberness of the dreary landscape."[48] No longer a housewife or a domestic ornament, but a laborer in a male arena, Porter was still subordinate to her husband in practical matters.

Lydia Waters recorded another clash between new work and old consciousness: "I had learned to drive an ox team on the Platte and my driving was admired by an officer and his wife who were going with the mail to Salt Lake City." Pleased with the compliment, she later overheard them "laughing at the thought of a woman driving oxen."[49] By no means did censure come only from men. The officer's wife as well as the officer derided Lydia Waters, while her own mother indirectly reprimanded teenaged Mary Ellen Todd. "All along our journey, I had tried to crack that big whip," Mary Ellen remembered years later:

> Now while out at the wagon we kept trying until I was fairly successful. How my heart bounded a few days later when I chanced to hear father say to mother, "Do you know that Mary Ellen is beginning to crack the whip." Then how it fell again when mother replied, "I am afraid it isn't a very lady-like thing for a girl to do." After this, while I felt a secret joy in being able to have a power that set things going, there was also a sense of shame over this new accomplishment.[50]

To understand Mrs. Todd's primness, so incongruous in the rugged setting of the Trail, we must see it in the context of a broader struggle on the part of women to preserve the home in transit. Against the leveling forces of the Plains, women tried to maintain the standards of cleanliness and order that had prevailed in their homes back East:

> Our caravan had a good many women and children and although we were probably longer on the journey owing to their presence —they exerted a good influence, as the men did not take such risks with Indians . . . were more alert about the care of teams and seldom had accidents; more attention was paid to cleanliness and sanitation and, lastly, but not of less importance, meals were more regular and better cooked thus preventing much sickness and there was less waste of food.[51]

Sarah Royce remembered that family wagons "were easily distinguished by the greater number of conveniences, and household articles they carried."[52] In the evenings, or when the trains stopped for a day, women had a chance to create with these few props a flimsy facsimile of the home.

Even in camp women had little leisure time, but within the "hurry scurry" of work they managed to re-create the routine of the home. Indeed, a female subculture, central to the communities women had left behind, reemerged in these settings. At night, women often clustered together, chatting, working, or commiserating, instead of joining the men: "High teas were not popular, but tatting, knitting, crochetting, exchanging recipes for cooking beans or dried apples or swopping food for the sake of variety kept us in practice of feminine occupations and diversions."[53] Besides using the domestic concerns of the Trail to reconstruct a female sphere, women also consciously invoked fantasy: "Mrs. Fox and her daughter are with us and everything is so still and quiet we can almost imagine ourselves at home again. We took out our Daguerreotypes and tried to live over again some of the happy days of 'Auld Lang Syne.' "[54] Sisterly contact kept "feminine occupations" from withering away from disuse: "In the evening the young ladies came over to our house and we had a concert with both guitars. Indeed it seemed almost like a pleasant evening at home. We could none of us realize that we were almost at the summit of the Rocky Mountains."[55] The hostess added with somewhat strained sanguinity that her young daughter seemed "just as happy sitting on the ground playing her guitar as she was at home, although she does not love it as much as her piano."[56] Although a guitar was no substitute for the more refined instrument, it at least kept the girl "in practice with feminine occupations and diversions": unlike Mary Ellen Todd, no big whip would tempt her to unwomanly pleasure in the power to "set things going."

But books, furniture, knick-knacks, china, the daguerreotypes that Mrs Fox shared, or the guitars of young musicians—the "various articles of ornament and convenience"—were among the first things discarded on the epic trash heap which trailed over the mountains. On long uphill grades and over sandy deserts, the wagons had to be lightened; any materials not essential to survival were fair game for disposal. Such commodities of woman's sphere, although functionally useless, provided women with a psychological lifeline to their abandoned homes and communities, as well as to elements of their identities which the westward journey threatened to mutilate or entirely extinguish.[57] Losing homely treasures and memorabilia was yet another defeat within an accelerating process of dispossession.

The male-directed venture likewise encroached upon the Sabbath, another female preserve. Through the influence of women's magazines, by mid-century Sunday had become a veritable ladies' day; women zealously exercised their religious influence and moral skill on the day of their families' retirement from the world. Although parties on the Trail often suspended travel on Sundays, the time only provided the opportunity to unload and dry the precious cargo of the wagons—seeds, food, and clothing—which otherwise would rot from dampness. For women whose creed forbade any worldly activity on the Sabbath, the work was not only irksome and tedious but profane.

> This is Sabath it is a beautiful day but indeed we do not use it as such for we have not traveled far when we stop in a most lovely place oh it is such a beautiful spot and take everything out of our wagon to air them and it is well we done it as the flower was damp and there was some of the other ones flower was rotten

> . . . and we baked and boiled and washed oh dear me I did not think we would have abused the sabeth in such a manner. I do not see how we can expect to get along but we did not intend to do so before we started.[58]

Denied a voice in the male sphere that surrounded them, women were also unable to partake of the limited yet meaningful power of women with homes. On almost every Sunday, Helen Stewart lamented the disruption of a familiar and sustaining order of life, symbolized by the household goods strewn about the ground to dry: "We took everything out the wagons and the side of the hill is covered with flower biscut meat rice oat meal clothes and such a quantity of articles of all discertions to many to mention and childre[n] included in the number. And hobos that is neather men nor yet boys being in and out hang about."[59]

The disintegration of the physical base of domesticity was symptomatic of an even more serious disruption in the female subculture. Because the wagon trains so often broke into smaller units, many women were stranded in parties without other women. Since there were usually two or more men in the same family party, some male friendships and bonds remained intact for the duration of the journey. But by midway in the trip, female companionship, so valued by nineteenth-century women, was unavailable to the solitary wife in a party of hired men, husband, and children that had broken away from a larger train. Emergencies and quarrels, usually between men, broke up the parties. Dr. Powers, a particularly ill-tempered man, decided after many disagreements with others in his train to make the crossing alone with his family. His wife shared neither his misanthropy nor his grim independence. On the day they separated from the others, she wrote in her journal: "The women came over to bid me goodbye, for we were to go alone, all alone. They said there was no color in my face. I felt as if there was none." She perceived the separation as a banishment, almost a death sentence: "There is something peculiar in such a parting on the Plains, one there realizes what a goodbye is. Miss Turner and Mrs. Hendricks were the last to leave, and they bade me adieu the tears running down their sunburnt cheeks. I felt as though my last friends were leaving me, for what—as I thought then—was a Maniac."[60] Charlotte Pengra likewise left Missouri with her family in a large train. Several weeks out, mechanical problems detained some of the wagons, including those of the other three women. During the month they were separated, Pengra became increasingly dispirited and anxious: "The roads have been good today—I feel lonely and almost disheartened. . . . Can hear the wolves howl very distinctly. Rather ominis, perhaps you think. . . . Feel very tird and lonely—our folks not having come—I fear some of them ar sick." Having waited as long as possible for the others, the advance group made a major river crossing. "Then I felt that indeed I had left all my friends," Pengra wrote, "save my husband and his brother, to journey over the dreaded Plains, without one female acquaintance even for a companion—of course I wept and grieved about it but to no purpose."[61]

Others echoed her mourning. "The whipporwills are chirping," Helen Stewart wrote, "they bring me in mind of our old farm in pensillvania the home of my childhood where I have spent the happiest days I will ever see again. . . . I feel rather lonesome today oh solitude solitude how I love it if I had about a dozen of my companions to enjoy it with me."[62] Uprootedness took its toll in debilitation and numbness. After a hard week, men "lolled around in the tents and on their blankets seeming to realize that the 'Sabbath was made for man,' "[63] resting on the palpable achievements of miles covered and rivers crossed. In contrast, the women "could not fully appreciate physical rest, and were rendered more uneasy by the continual passing of emigrant trains all day long. . . . To me, much of the day was spent in meditating over the past and in forebodings for the future."[64]

The ultimate expression of this alienation was the pressure to turn back, to retrace steps to the old life. Occasionally anxiety or bewilderment erupted into open revolt against going on.

> This morning our company moved on, except one family. The woman got mad and wouldn't budge or let the children go. He had the cattle hitched on for three hours and coaxed her to go, but she wouldn't stir. I told my husband the circumstances and he and Adam Polk and Mr. Kimball went and each one took a young one and crammed them in the wagon, and the husband drove off and left her sitting. . . . She cut across and overtook her husband. Meantime he sent his boy back to camp after a horse he had left, and when she came up her husband said, "Did you meet John?" "Yes," was the reply, "and I picked up a stone and knocked out his brains." Her husband went back to ascertain the truth and while he was gone she set fire to one of the wagons. . . . He saw the flames and came running and put it out, and then mustered spunk enough to give her a good flogging.[65]

Short of violent resistance, it was always possible that circumstances would force a family to reconsider and turn back. During a cholera scare in 1852, "women cried, begging their men to take them back."[66] When the men reluctantly relented, the writer observed that "they did the hooking up of their oxen in a spiritless sort of way," while "some of the girls and women were laughing."[67] There was little lost and much regained for women in a decision to abandon the migration.

Both sexes worked, and both sexes suffered. Yet women lacked a sense of inclusion and a cultural rationale to give meaning to the suffering and the work; no augmented sense of self or role emerged from augmented privation. Both women and men also complained, but women expanded their caviling to a generalized critique of the whole enterprise. Margaret Chambers felt "as if we had left all civilization behind us"[68] after crossing the Missouri, and Harriet Ward's cry from South Pass—"Oh, shall we ever live like civilized beings again?"[69]—reverberated through the thoughts of many of her sisters. Civilization was far more to these women than law, books, and municipal government; it was pianos, church societies, daguerreotypes, mirrors—in short, their homes. At their most hopeful, the exiles perceived the Trail as a hellish but necessary transition to a land where they could renew their domestic mission: "Each advanced step of the slow, plodding cattle carried us farther and farther from civilization into a desolate, barbarous country. . . . But our new home lay beyond all this and was a shining beacon that beckoned us on, inspiring our hearts with hope and courage."[70] At worst, temporary exigencies became in the minds of the dispossessed the omens of an irrevocable exile: "We have been travelling with 25-18-14-129-64-3 wagons—now all alone—how dreary it seems. Can it be that I have left my quiet little home and taken this dreary land of solitude in exchange?"[71]

Only a minority of the women who emigrated over the Overland Trail were from the northeastern middle classes where the cult of true womanhood reached its fullest bloom. Yet their responses to the labor demands of the Trail indicate that "womanliness" had penetrated the values, expectations, and personalities of midwestern farm women as well as New England "ladies." "Woman's sphere" provided them with companionship, a sense of self-worth, and most important, independence from men in a patriarchal world. The Trail, in breaking down sexual segregation, offered women the opportunities of socially essential work. Yet this work was performed in a male arena, and many women saw themselves as draftees rather than partners.

Historians have generally associated "positive work roles"[72] for women with the absence of narrowly defined notions of "woman's place." In the best summary of literature on colonial women, for example, the authors of *Woman in American Society* write: "In general, neither men nor women seemed concerned with defining what women were or what their unique contribution to society should be. . . . Abstract theories about the proper role of women did not stand in the way of meeting familial and social needs."[73] Conversely, the ascendancy of "true womanhood" and the doctrine of sexual spheres coincided with the declining importance of the labor of middle- and upper-class women in a rapidly expanding market economy. On the Overland Trail, cultural roles and self-definitions conflicted with the immediate necessities of the socioeconomic situation. Women themselves fought to preserve a circumscribed role when material circumstances rendered it dysfunctional. Like their colonial great-grandmothers on premarket subsistence farms, they labored at socially indispensable tasks. Yet they refused to appropriate their new work to their own ends and advantage. In their deepest sense of themselves they remained estranged from their function as "able bodies."

It could be argued that the time span of the trip was not long enough to alter cultural values. Yet there is evidence that the tensions of the Trail haunted the small and isolated market farms at the journey's end.[74] Women in the western settlements continued to try to reinstate a culture of domesticity, although their work as virtual hired hands rendered obsolete the material base of separate arenas for women and men.

The notion of subculture employed in this and other studies of nineteenth-century women is hazy and ill-defined. We need to develop more rigorous conceptions of society, culture, and subculture, and to clarify the paradoxes of women's position, both isolated and integrated, in the dominant social and cultural movements of their time. Nonetheless, the journals of overland women are irrefutable testimony to the importance of a separate female province. Such theorists as Catharine Beecher were acutely aware of the advantages in keeping life divvied up, in maintaining "two pathways which are always different" for women and men.[75] The women who traveled on the Overland Trail experienced firsthand the tribulations of integration which Beecher and her colleagues could predict in theory.

NOTES

We wish to thank Howard Lamar for his continuing support and Peter H. Wood, Ann Douglas, and Michele Hoffnung for their help and criticism. C. Stansell wants to acknowledge the importance of the experiences she shared with Joan Neuman Fleming and Katherine Fleming in this interpretation of women's history in the West. A National Endowment for the Humanities

Youth Grant AY-7451-72-482 supported J. Faragher's portion of the research for this article.

1. The 1841 Bidwell-Bartelson party of about fifty people included only five women three of them wives—and ten children. Contemporary figures for the forties' migrations indicate that men made up roughly 50 percent of the parties, women and children the other 50 percent. These proportions prevailed until the Gold Rush. In contrast, the composition of the 1849 emigration was men-92 percent, women-6 percent, and children-2 percent; in 1850, men-97 percent, women and children-3 percent. In 1852 the proportions shifted toward the pre-1849 norm: men-70 percent, women-13 percent, children-20 percent. These percentages are rough estimates, and indicate no more than trends.

For overall figures see Merrill Mattes, *The Great Platte River Road* (Lincoln, Nebraska: Nebraska State Historical Society, 1969), p. 23. For the early forties on the Oregon Trail, see David Lavender, *Westward Vision: The Story of the Oregon Trail* (New York: McGraw-Hill, 1963), pp. 349–50, 365. For the California branch: George R. Stewart, *The California Trail: An Epic With Many Heroes* (New York: McGraw-Hill, 1962), pp. 8, 54–55, 85, 147, 187, 195, 232, 303, 310. For the Gold Rush: Georgia Willis Read, "Women and Children on the Oregon-California Trail in the Gold-Rush Years," *Missouri Historical Review* 34 (1944–1945): 6.

2. Arthur W. Calhoun, *A Social History of the American Family from Colonial Times to the Present* 3 vols. (New York: Barnes & Noble, 1945) 2:11. Calhoun's statement has stood up well to demographic tests; after analysis of nineteenth-century census data, Jack Eblen concludes that "the deeply entrenched ideal and institution of the family provided the mechanism by which people were bound together during the process of cultural transplantation and adaptation" ("An Analysis of Nineteenth Century Frontier Populations," *Demography* 2, no. 4 [1965]: 341).

3. A simple enumeration of the special equipment necessary for the trip indicates the expense. Each family needed a light wagon, harnesses, and a team, usually oxen; the team alone could easily cost two hundred dollars. Arms and ammunition were purchased specially for the trip; such weapons as shotguns and rifles cost around twenty-five dollars. Since there was practically no chance for resupply along the route, a family had to stock for the entire six-month trip, a considerable investment that only the economically stable could afford. For discussion and details see Mattes, *Great Platte River Road,* pp. 37–50; Stewart, *The California Trail,* pp. 106–26.

4. Neighbors and friends often moved as a "party," later joining a larger train. Brothers, cousins, and their families, or parents and one or two married children and their families, might set out together. Conjugal and parental ties usually survived under stress, while other relations disintegrated or exploded. Interestingly, the most enduring extrafamilial bonds may have been between nuclear families and the single men who traveled with them. The latter saved money by attaching themselves to family parties rather than outfitting a wagon alone. Some paid for their passage, while others worked as drivers or cattle drovers. For examples of various groupings, see Phoebe Goodell Judson, *A Pioneer's Search for an Ideal Home* (Bellingham, Washington: United Printing, Binding and Stationery Co., 1925), pp. 15–17; Mary E. Ackley, *Crossing the Plains and Early Days in California* (San Francisco: the author, 1928), p. 17; Sarah J. Cummins, *Autobiography and Reminiscences* (Walla Walla, Oregon: The Walla Walla Bulletin, 1920), p. 22; Mrs. J. T.

Gowdy, *Crossing the Plains: Personal Recollections of the Journey to Oregon in 1852* (Dayton, Oregon: n.p., 1906), p. 1; Nancy A. Hunt, "By Ox Team to California," *Overland Monthly* 67 (April 1916): 10; Mrs. M. A. Looney, *A Trip Across the Plains in the Year of 1852 with Ox Teams* (McMinnville, Oregon: n.p., 1915), p. 8; and Mrs. Lee Whipple-Halsam, *Early Days in California: Scenes and Events of the '60s as I Remember Them* (Jamestown, California: n.p., 1923), p. 8.

5. For a recent revision of work on the Overland Trail see Mattes, *The Great Platte River Road.*

6. Most of the research on the Victorian family has been based on middle- and upper-class northeastern and midwestern families. We do not yet know to what extent the ideology of domesticity affected poor, proletarianized, or southern families.

Although our suggestions about the geographic and class composition of the migrations are generally accepted ones, they remain hypothetical in the absence of demographic research. An overwhelming majority of the women who kept the journals upon which much of our research is based *did* come from the northeastern and midwestern middle class. Nevertheless, until we know much more about the inarticulate families from backwoods Missouri, we cannot pretend to describe the "normative" experience of the overland family. Our interpretation is limited to families whose structure and consciousness were rooted in American bourgeois culture.

7. The ten volumes of Sarah Hale's *Ladies' Magazine* (1828–1837) are rich primary sources for antebellum ideals of sex roles and the family. For secondary works see the introductory pieces in Nancy Cott, ed., *Root of Bitterness* (Boston: E. P. Dutton, 1972), and Kathryn Kish Sklar, *Catharine Beecher* (New Haven: Yale University Press, 1973). A relatively inaccessible essay remains one of the most illuminating treatments of the period: Nancy Osterud, "Sarah Josepha Hale: A Study of the History of Women in Nineteenth Century America" (unpublished honors thesis, Harvard College, 1971).

8. See Cott, *Root of Bitterness,* pp. 11–14; Alice Clark, *Working Life of Women in the Seventeenth Century* (London: G. Routledge & Sons, 1919); Elisabeth Dexter, *Colonial Women of Affairs: Women in Business and Professions in America Before 1776* (Boston: Houghton Mifflin Co., 1924); Alice M. Earle, *Home Life in Colonial Days* (New York: Macmillan Co., 1899); and Nancy Osterud, "The New England Family, 1790–1840" (unpublished manuscript, Old Sturbridge Village Education Department; Sturbridge, Mass., n.d.).

9. We do not use "productive" as a value judgment but as a historically specific concept: labor which produces surplus value within the capitalist mode of production. Within the work process itself, both men's *and* women's labor was "useful," but only men's, in the accepted sex division, resulted in the creation of commodities. For a provocative discussion of this problem see Ian Gough, "Marx's Theory of Productive and Unproductive Labor," *New Left Review* 76 (November-December 1972): 47–72, and Lise Vogel, "The Earthly Family," *Radical America* 7 (July-October 1973): 9–50.

10. See Sklar, *Catharine Beecher,* and Ann D. Gordon, Mari Jo Buhle, and Nancy E. Schrom, "Women in American Society," *Radical America* (1972): 25–33.

11. Quoted in Catharine Beecher, *A Treatise on Domestic Economy* (New York: Harper Brothers, 1858), p. 28.

12. The most comprehensive account to date of domesticity, culture, and sexual spheres is Sklar, *Catharine Beecher;* see especially pp. 151–67 and

204–16. For the cultural importance of reform to women, see Carroll Smith-Rosenberg, "Beauty, the Beast, and the Militant Woman: A Case Study in Sex Roles in Jacksonian America," *American Quarterly* 23 (Fall 1971): 562–84 and Gail Parker, *The Oven Birds: American Women on Womanhood 1820–1920* (New York: Doubleday and Co., 1972), pp. 1–56. Nancy Cott's argument in *Root of Bitterness*, pp. 3–4, is a concise summary of the subculture argument. See Ann Douglas Wood, "The 'Scribbling Women' and Fanny Fern: Why Women Wrote," *American Quarterly* 23 (Spring 1971): 1–24, and "Mrs. Sigourney and the Sensibility of the Inner Space," *New England Quarterly* 45 (June 1972): 163–81 for women's cultural impulses in literature.

13. The Great Pacific migration began in the wake of the depression of 1837–40. The Pacific Northwest and California seemed to offer unfailing markets at Hudson's Bay forts, Russian settlements, even the massive Orient. The Pacific itself was to be the great transportation network that backwoods farmers needed so desperately. The 1841 migration was the result of the work of the Western Emigration Society, specifically organized to overcome the economic problems of the depressed Midwest. In short, the coast was rich in fertile, free land and unlimited chances for economic success. See Lavender, *Westward Vision*, pp. 327–28. The major exception to this generalization is the Mormon emigration.

14. Judson, *A Pioneer's Search*, p. 9.

15. Lucy Rutledge Cooke, *Crossing the Plains in 1852 . . . as told in Letters Written During the Journey* (Modesto, California: the author, 1923), p. 5. See also James Robertson, *A Few Months in America* (London: n.p., 1855), p. 150; Nancy A. Hunt, "By Ox-Team," p. 9; and Elias Johnson Draper, *An Autobiography* (Fresno, California: the author, 1904), p. 9.

16. Margaret M. Hecox, *California Caravan: the 1846 Overland Trail Memoir of Margaret M. Hecox* (San Jose, California: Harlan-Young Press, 1966), p. 31.

17. Lavinia Honeyman Porter, *By Ox Team to California: A Narrative of Crossing the Plains in 1860* (Oakland, California: author, 1910), p. 7; see also Margaret White Chambers, *Reminiscences* (n.p.: n.p. 1903), pp. 5–7.

18. Porter, *By Ox Team*, p. 41.

19. Luzena Stanley Wilson, *Luzena Stanley Wilson, '49er* (Oakland, California: The Eucalyptus Press, 1937), p. 1.

20. Mary Jane Hayden, *Pioneer Days* (San Jose, California: Murgotten's Press, 1915), pp. 7–8.

21. Our sample of women's diaries and memoirs is by definition biased toward those women who successfully challenged their husbands. A more comprehensive view requires reading another set of journals—those of men who left their families behind. This work, as a part of a general history of the family, women, and men on the Overland Trail, is now in progress: John Faragher, "Women, Men and Their Families on the Overland Trail" (Ph.D. thesis, Yale University, in progress [1978]).

22. For a particularly striking record of marriage proposals, see *Mollie: The Journal of Mollie Dorsey Sanford in Nebraska and Colorado Territories, 1857–66* (Lincoln, Nebraska: University of Nebraska Press, 1959), pp. 20, 58, 59, 74, 91.

23. Quoted in Nancy Ross, *Westward the Women* (New York: Alfred A. Knopf, 1944), p. 110.

24. Mrs. John Wilson, quoted in Read, "Women and Children on the Oregon-California Trail in the Gold-Rush Years," p. 7.

25. Ross, *Westward the Women*, p. 111.

26. See Mari Sandoz's biography of her father, *Old Jules* (Lincoln, Nebraska: University of Nebraska Press, 1955) for a dramatic illustration of a male homesteader's functional view of wives and children.

The conventional view that the American west was predominantly male dies hard. Jack Eblen, in "Nineteenth Century Frontier Populations," conclusively demonstrates that the sex ratio in the West was little different from that in the East: women were nearly always present in numbers equal to men. See Christine Stansell, "Women on the Plains," *Women's Studies* (forthcoming).

27. Esther Allen, *Canvas Caravans: Based on the Journal of Esther Belle McMillan Hanna* (Portland, Oregon: Binfords & Mort, 1946), p. 18.

28. Mrs. Elizabeth Dixon Smith Geer, "Diary," in Oregon Pioneer Association, *Transactions of the Thirty-fifth Annual Reunion* (1907), p. 169.

29. Catherine Margaret Haun, quoted in Read, "Women and Children on the Oregon-California Trail in the Gold-Rush Years," p. 9.

30. Chambers, *Reminiscences*, p. 8.

31. See Adrietta Applegate Hixon, *On to Oregon! A True Story of a Young Girl's Journey Into the West* (Wesler, Idaho: Signal-American Printers, 1947), p. 17, for one of the few instances in the diaries when men took on women's work.

32. See Charles Howard Crawford, *Scenes of Earlier Days: In Crossing the Plains to Oregon, and Experiences of Western Life* (Chicago: Quadrangle, 1962), p. 9, for an account of women's resistance to assuming this particular responsibility.

33. Cummins, *Autobiography and Reminiscences*, p. 28.

34. See Gowdy, *Crossing the Plains*, p. 2; John Barnett, *Long Trip in a Prairie Schooner* (Whittier, California: Western Stationery Co., 1928), p. 105; and Lydia Milner Waters, "A Trip Across the Plains in 1855," *Quarterly of the Society of California Pioneers* 6 (June 1929): 66.

35. Charlotte Emily Pengra, "Diary of Mrs. Byron J. Pengra," (unpublished typescript in Lane Country Historical Society, Eugene, Oregon, n.d.), p. 8.

36. Mary Burrell, "Mary Burrell's Book" (manuscript diary, Beinecke Library, Yale University), no pagination; Cummins, *Autobiography*, p. 27; E. Allene Dunham, *Across the Plains in a Covered Wagon* (Milton, Iowa: n.p., n.d.), p. 10.

37. Pengra, "Diary," p. 5.

38. Ibid., pp. 6, 8–9, 12.

39. Helen Marnie Stewart, "Diary" (unpublished typescript at Lane County Historical Society, Eugene, Oregon, 1961), p. 13.

40. The place of children in the structure of the overland family is an intriguing question that we are reserving for more research and reflection. On the basis of their infrequent appearance in the journals, it seems that in this area, too, nineteenth-century patterns were modified. Many historians have pointed to the antebellum period as the time when "the child" emerged from obscurity to a special social status. In the overland sources, however, children over the age of five are rarely discussed except as younger and more vulnerable members of the working group, requiring little extra or special attention.

41. Elizabeth Wood, "Journal of a Trip to Oregon, 1851," *Oregon Historical Society Quarterly* 17 (1926): 4.

42. Helen M. Carpenter, "A Trip Across the Plains in an Ox Wagon, 1857" (manuscript diary, Huntington Library, San Marino, California), pp. 27–28.

43. Hixon, *On to Oregon!* p. 17.

44. Pengra, "Diary," p. 5.

45. Emery T. Bray, ed., *Bray Family Genealogy and History* (n.p.: n.p., 1927), p. 10.

46. Ibid.

47. Porter, *By Ox Team to California*, p. 43.

48. Ibid., p. 118.

49. Waters, "A Trip Across the Plains in 1855," p. 77.

50. Hixon, *On to Oregon!* p. 45.

51. Catherine Haun in Read, "Women and Children During the Gold-Rush Years," p. 9. See also Hixon, *On to Oregon!* p. 15 and *passim;* and William Smedley, "Across the Plains in Sixty-two," *The Trail* 19 (March 1927): 11.

52. Sarah Royce, *A Frontier Lady: Recollections of the Gold Rush and Early California* (New Haven: Yale University Press, 1932), pp. 8–9.

53. Haun in Read, "Women and Children During the Gold-Rush Years," p. 9.

54. Harriet Sherril Ward, *Prairie Schooner Lady: The Journal of Harriet Sherril Ward* (Los Angeles: Westernlore Press, 1959), p. 60.

55. Ibid., p. 95. See also Celinda E. Hines, "Diary of Celinda E. Hines," in Oregon Pioneer Association, *Transactions of the Forty-sixth Annual Reunion* (1918), pp. 82–83 and *passim.*

56. Ward, *Prairie Schooner Lady*, p. 69.

57. See Narcissa Whitman, "Diary," (manuscript, Beinecke Library, Yale University), p. 18, or in any one of its many published versions—e.g., *Oregon Historical Quarterly* 35 (1936). Also Esther and Joseph Lyman, "Letters About the Lost Wagon Train of 1853" (unpublished typescript in Lane County Historical Society, Eugene, Oregon), p. 6; and Georgia Read and Ruth Gaines, eds., *Gold Rush: the Journals, Drawings, and Other Papers of J. Goldsborough Bruff . . . April 2, 1849–July 20, 1851* (New York: n.p., 1949), p. 45 and *passim.*

58. Stewart, "Diary," entry for June 6, 1853. See also Whitman, "Diary," p. 21; Pengra, "Diary," p. 3; and Royce, *Frontier Lady*, p. 11.

59. Stewart, "Diary," entry for June 12, 1853.

60. Mrs. Mary Rockwood Power, "The Overland Route: Leaves from the Journal of a California Emigrant," *Amateur Book Collector* 1 (November 1950): 6.

61. Pengra, "Diary," entries for May 2, 3, 8, and 10, and entries for June 5, 24, and July 7, 1853. See also, Royce, *Frontier Lady*, p. 9; and Mrs. Mary A. Frink, *Journal of the Adventures of a Party of California Gold Seekers* (Oakland, California: n.p. 1897), p. 67.

62. Stewart, "Diary," entry for May 1, 1853.

63. Judson, *A Pioneer's Search*, p. 23.

64. Ibid.

65. Geer, "Diary," pp. 165–66.

66. Hixon, *On to Oregon!* p. 18.

67. Ibid.

68. Chambers, *Reminiscences*, p. 7.

69. Ward, *Prairie Schooner Lady*, p. 128. See also Allen, *Canvas Caravans*, p. 28.

70. Judson, *A Pioneer's Search*, p. 18.

71. Maria Parsons Belshaw, "Diary of a Bride Written on the Trail in 1853," *Oregon Historical Society Quarterly* 33 (March-December 1932): 334.

72. Cott, *Root of Bitterness*, p. 5.

73. Gordon, Buhle, and Schrom, *Woman in American Society, p. 22.*

74. Stansell, "Women on the Plains."

75. Catharine Beecher, *Domestic Economy*, p. 28.

11

The Life Cycles and Household Structure of American Ethnic Groups

Irish, Germans, and Native-born Whites in Buffalo, New York, 1855

■

LAURENCE A. GLASCO

One of the hallmarks of the new social history is the analysis of manuscript censuses from the nineteenth and early twentieth centuries for aggregate data about occupational distribution and mobility, geographic mobility, and household patterns. Laurence Glasco's use of one manuscript state census schedule is unusual because of his thoroughgoing comparative approach. Rather than looking at changing trends over time, he compares the life-cycle, occupational, and residential experiences of the two sexes in three nationality groupings. His disclosure of differentiation by age and sex as well as ethnic group makes possible a much more complex social profile of ordinary Americans. His statistical findings, bare of interpretation, suggest a host of questions which call for further investigation. For women's history, perhaps the most interesting questions concern the patterns of acculturation set up by the very high proportion of adolescent immigrant girls living as domestic servants in the homes of American-born employers.

DESPITE INCREASED INTEREST in the ethnic dimension of American history, we still know relatively little about the social and economic characteristics of the immigrants themselves, especially their family patterns. And most of what we do know centers primarily around those who were both adult and male.[1] An understanding of ethnic groups—or of any population for that matter—should be based on all the component age and sex groupings: women as well as men; children and adolescents as well as adults.

Life-cycle analysis offers a useful method for doing this. The systematic age-related analysis of a population enables us to observe and compare the social characteristics of all its members as they pass through the age stations of childhood, adolescence, adulthood, and old age.[2]

The technique has other advantages as well. A division of the life cycle into separate stages can deepen our understanding of the two major themes of ethnic study: work and acculturation. If we relate stages of the life cycle to economic behavior and household organization, we can delineate patterns of "economic" and household cycles. Most of what we know in this area is based on the experiences of adult males. It is their occupation and income which is investigated in studies of ethnic stratification; it is they who are pictured as agents of change or acculturation, and the women as bastions of conservatism. In the present case, we have used life-cycle analysis to examine these issues, and have compared the age-related household and work experiences of men and women for each of three ethnic groups—Irish, Germans, and native-born whites—in a mid-nineteenth-century American city. The procedure helps to clarify how age and sex were related to the processes of ethnic stratification and acculturation.

Few studies have employed the method of life-cycle analysis because the sources are difficult to locate and utilize. The present study, using Buffalo, New York as an example, takes the city's three major ethnic groups at one point in time, 1855, and describes their changing life situations in relation to age. It was possible to do this because the New York State manuscript census of 1855 provides not only the usual information on each person's age, sex, race, birthplace, and occupation, but also his or her marital condition and relationship to the head of the household. This material, transcribed and machine encoded for the city's entire population, enabled us to compare ethnic differences in the timed sequence by which both men and women passed through the various stages of childhood, adolescence, marriage, childbearing, and retirement, as well as corresponding household statuses of husband, wife, child, boarder, servant, and relative. Finally, it enabled us to trace and describe the age-related patterns of work and property ownership.

Such a description of the life cycle at one point in time cannot tell us whether any particular age cohort had previously followed, or in the future would follow, such patterns. That is, young children would not necessarily follow the example of their older brothers in regard to the timing or the sequence in which they left home, married, and established their own households. In fact, given the rapidly modernizing society of mid-nineteenth-century America, there is every chance that they would not. The complete answer to that question can be found only in cohort analysis, tracing the life cycles of specific age groups back in time and forward into the future. The form of analysis employed here, however, does tell us the age and age-related life patterns prevailing in a given period and provides a baseline from which to measure future deviations.

By the mid-nineteenth century, nationality virtually defined Buffalo's population and social structure. Like many northern cities at that time, Buffalo had a large, rapidly growing immigrant population jostling alongside a native-born, in-migrant population drawn mainly from New England and the eastern part of New York State. Between 1845 and 1855 the city's population more than doubled, to over 70,000 residents, about one-fourth of whom were native-born, one-fifth Irish and forty percent German, the latter coming mainly from Bavaria and other southern principalities.

These residents had been attracted by the city's booming economy, based on the commerce of the Erie Canal and a rapidly growing manufacturing sector, especially of iron. Occupations tended to divide along ethnic lines, with Irish men holding many of the unskilled jobs along the docks, German men dominating the construction crafts, and native-born men controlling the finances, professions, and trade of the city.[3]

Ethnic differences of occupation and income were reflected in the life experiences of all members of society. As we will see, they extended through the entire life span, and included both the household and work cycles. Finally, as revealed by an examination of the household and work cycles, first of the men and then of the women, ethnic differences were as pronounced among young women as they were among adult men.

NATIVE-BORN MEN

The life cycle of native-born men reveals a rather prolonged childhood and adolescence. They did not begin to leave home until late adolescence, around age 19, and it was not until age 29 that virtually all had left the shelter of their parents' home. Many who left home, particularly if they were new to the city, became boarders. The practice of boarding, which has been associated generally with immigrants, involved one-third of all native-born men between the ages of 19 and 29, and over half of those present less than one year in the city. Most of these boarders—about four-fifths—were single, and less than one-half had a permanent occupation listed by the census.

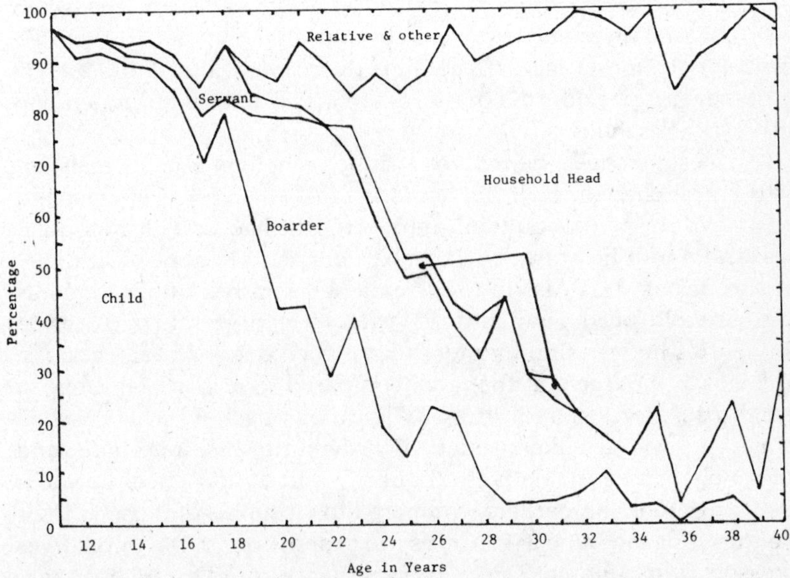

Figure 1. NATIVE-BORN MALES: HOUSEHOLD STATUS BY AGE.

The longer they remained in the city, the less likely they were to board out. After residing in the city for five years, only about one-third of those in their early or late twenties and a fifth of those in their early thirties boarded out; among eight-year residents this was true of only 8% to 13% (Figure 1).

The typical native-born boarder lived with a family, almost always a native-born family, along with perhaps one or two other boarders who were also native-born. He was, in short, only semi-independent since in this situation his comings and goings were subject to supervision by the family with which he lived. The large, impersonal boarding house which characterized seaport towns housed less than half of the city's boarders. For the majority of young boarders, this practice was structured to provide a moderate amount of adult supervision, in a family setting, and to insulate the young men from intimate, unsupervised contact with the wider world.[4]

Native-born men who had been in the city a few years seldom became boarders. Instead, they got married as soon as they left home and quickly established their own household. For this reason there was great variation in the average age at which native-born men got married. Marriage began as early as age 20 for about 10% of native-born men and did not include half of any age group until age 26.[5]

Thereafter, the process speeded up and by age 28 three-fourths of that age group were married. Those who married early tended to delay the establishment of a separate household. Less than half the married men under age 24 had their own household. From age 25 on, however, three-fourths or more of married native-born men had their own household.

Once established, the native-born household was quite resistant to structural change. Half of the households consisted of husband and wife (with or without children); a fourth had one or more relatives; and a fifth had one or more boarders and roomers.[6] With only two exceptions, this distribution remained relatively unchanged as the household head grew older. When the household head was in his twenties he was slightly more likely to take in boarders: about a third took in boarders at that age, compared to a fourth of those in their thirties, forties, and fifties. When the household head reached old age, he was less likely to take boarders into his household, and more likely to take in relatives; about a fourth of household heads in their sixties took in boarders, compared to only 14% of those in their seventies. For the same age groups the proportion taking in relatives increased from 19% to 32%. Over the large middle range of age, however—the thirties, forties, fifties, and sixties—the native-born household was remarkably stable in form, with consistently close to half being nuclear, a fifth being extended, and a fourth being augmented.[7]

Although the native-born household head did not significantly alter the composition of his household with advancing age, he did change his status within that household by purchasing his own home. Almost a fourth of native-born family heads in their twenties owned real property. This proportion increased with age, and included two-fifths of those in their thirties, half of those in their forties and fifties, and three-fifths of those over sixty years of age.

Aiding him in the acquisition of his home was a clear occupational advantage. Native-born men dominated the white-collar, professional, and entrepreneurial positions in the city, and made up at least their share of the painters and mechanics. Moreover, they enjoyed these advantages over the entire course of their working years. There were not substantial age-related differences in their occupational chances. In their twenties, thirties, or forties, native-born men were likely to be clerks; when older, in their fifties and sixties, they tended to be entrepreneurs. Regardless of age, almost all native-born men were able to avoid the low-paying, unskilled position of day laborer. Moreover, the work career of native-born men extended over forty years. They began work fairly early, about age 16; by age 19 one-fourth were employed and by age 24 over half. As they aged, an increasing proportion of native-born men retired from the work force. Retirement began in their early sixties, when the percentage of men listed with an occupation decreased from 58% of those in their late fifties to 48% of those in their early sixties. For men in their late sixties the figure dropped to 40% and decreased still further among those in their seventies.

As they retired from the labor force, an increasing proportion ceased to head their own household. About one-third of native-born men over the age of sixty were living outside their own household, compared to about a tenth of those in their forties and fifties. Of those who did not maintain their own household, only a fifth went to live among possible strangers as a roomer or boarder. The great majority went to live with relatives. In over half of the cases, they lived with one of their children, while about 15% lived with an in-law.

This, then, briefly summarizes the age-related life experiences of native-born white men in a mid-nineteenth-century American city. Their household cycle was typically characterized by a prolonged childhood and adolescence, followed by a brief, relatively sheltered boarding experience, designed especially for those who were single, young, and new to the city. They generally married in their mid to late twenties and began a family. During middle age their household consisted of a wife, two or three children and, for about half, either a relative or boarder, plus a servant. Increasing age brought its economic satisfactions. An examination of the economic cycle shows that they dominated the white-collar, professional, and entrepreneurial occupations, as well as certain of the skilled trades—especially metal working—and avoided the unskilled, day-laboring positions. This preferential occupational standing was enjoyed throughout the native-born man's occupational career. It paid off over the years. By the time they were in their sixties, about two-thirds continued to head their own household, and almost all of those who did so owned their own home. Most of the rest went to live with one of their children, such that only a few were left to live alone or to board out among strangers. All in all, the patterns suggest a fairly stable life experience.

IRISH MEN

To a remarkable degree the household cycle of Irish men resembled that of the native-born.[8] Like their native-born counterparts, Irish men began leaving home relatively late in adolescence, around age

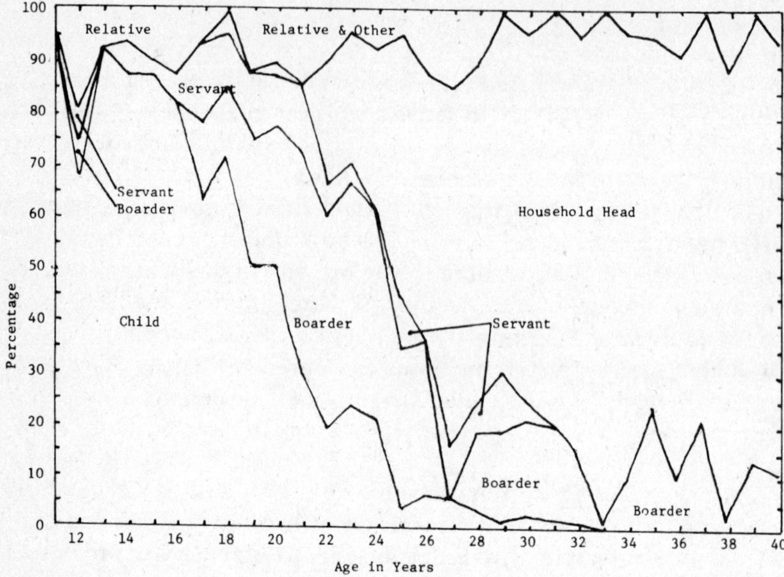

Figure 2. IRISH MALES: HOUSEHOLD STATUS BY AGE.

19, although they completed the leaving process somewhat earlier, around age 25. As with the native-born, this amounted to just under a third of Irish men aged 19 to 29 and 40% of those aged 20 to 24 became boarders (Figure 2). Nearly all of these boarders were single and most were new to the city as well. Of Irish men aged 20 to 24 years, 70% of those present for less than one year were boarders, compared to a third among those present five years, and just over a tenth of those present eight years. Among those in their late twenties the corresponding decline was from 58% to between 7% and 12%. Again, as with the native-born, most Irish boarders lived with families of their own ethnic background, with perhaps one other boarder.

Irish men passed from a dependent to an independent status somewhat more quickly than native-born men. First, the process of leaving home was more accelerated, being virtually completed by age 25, compared to age 29 for the native-born. Second, the Irish boarding experience was somewhat shorter. Impressions to the contrary of boarding being primarily an immigrant phenomenon, boarding for Irish males was virtually over by the age of 27, whereas there were still a moderate number of native-born boarders in their early thirties.

The Irish marriage experience was similar too, but somewhat more compressed than that of native-born men. It began two years later (age 22) and was completed at about the same age—28 or 29. Irish married men achieved independence somewhat earlier, however, in that there was not a notable delay between marriage and the establishment of a separate household. Whereas only half the native-born men through age 23 headed their own household, two-thirds or more of Irish married men from age 22 (when they began marrying in substantial numbers) headed their own households.

In contrast to the native-born household, the Irish household was more likely to be nuclear in composition. Only 15% took in relatives and 13% took in roomers and boarders, compared to 25% and 20% respectively, for the native-born. The practice of taking in boarders did not vary with the age of the household head, and in this regard, too, the Irish pattern resembled the native-born.

The similarities between native-born and Irish break down in regard to the presence of relatives, however. The likelihood of an Irish household including relatives was clearly articulated to the life cycle. The proportion of Irish households containing extended kin declined from about 20% of those in their twenties to only about 10% of those in their forties; thereafter the trend reversed, such that older household heads were more likely to have relatives—about 15% of those in their sixties and 30% of those in their seventies. The causes of this inverted, or U-shaped, pattern are not clear. Possibly it is related to particular Irish migration patterns, in which young unmarried brothers and sisters came to America and set up a sibling household when young, which was followed by marriage in middle age and the establishment of independent households. This possibility, however, has not been tested.

The difference in the experience of Irish and native-born was also reflected in property ownership. Native-born household heads, as they grew older, were increasingly successful in buying their own home. This was not true for Irish men. Those owning real estate increased from 16% of those in their twenties to 26% of those in their thirties. The trend then stabilized, and ownership actually decreased among those over sixty years of age.

The reason for such a relatively low proportion of Irish home owners was their unfavorable occupational structure. Irish men dominated no specific occupation, but were overrepresented among teamsters, sailors, ship carpenters, and especially among unskilled day laborers. As a result, two-thirds of Irish family heads either were unskilled or—especially older men—had no occupation listed. Examination of this aspect of the economic cycle, furthermore, reveals that this maldistribution of occupational skills did not significantly vary with age; at no point in their working lives did a majority of Irish men have a chance for stable, well-paying work. The impact of this occupational pattern can be gauged by the fact that semi-skilled and skilled Irish workers were as successful as their native-born counterparts in acquiring property. This was not true for unskilled Irish laborers, suggesting the operation of cultural values as well in the matter of property acquisition.

To maintain even this position, many Irish men had to work past what was a normal retirement age for native-born men. Irish boys began working at about age 17, one year later than native-born boys. One fourth were employed by the age 19, and the proportion rose to one half by the time they reached age 22. They worked substantially longer, however. By the early seventies, when only 14% of native-born men had a listed occupation, this was the case of one third of Irish men.

In old age, the household status of Irish men came once again to resemble that of native-born men. Most were able to maintain their position as household heads. Indeed, the proportion who did so (three-fourths) exceeded that for native-born household heads (two-thirds). Of those who did not remain household heads, only about a fifth boarded out, and an insignificant number went to live with collateral kin. Almost half went to live with a child, and a third went to live with an in-law. In this way, their pattern resembled that of the native-born.

This, then, summarizes the age-related life experiences of Irish men. The greatest differences emerged in their economic cycle, specifically in the type of jobs held and the amount of property acquired over a lifetime. In certain respects there were striking, unexpected parallels in regard to their household cycles. They left home at about the same age, became boarders at about the same age and in about the same proportions, and in a similarly structured situation that provided adult supervision in a family setting and reduced contact with peers outside the ethnic group. Their households differed somewhat in composition, since fewer Irish families took in boarders or relatives. Yet the differences seem more one of degree than of kind.

There were similarities in the aging process as well. About the same proportion of Irish and native-born men headed their own households in old age, although a greater proportion of native-born men owned the dwelling in which they lived. Finally, the experience of those who left their households was similar: few of either group had to live among possible strangers in a boarding situation; a ma-

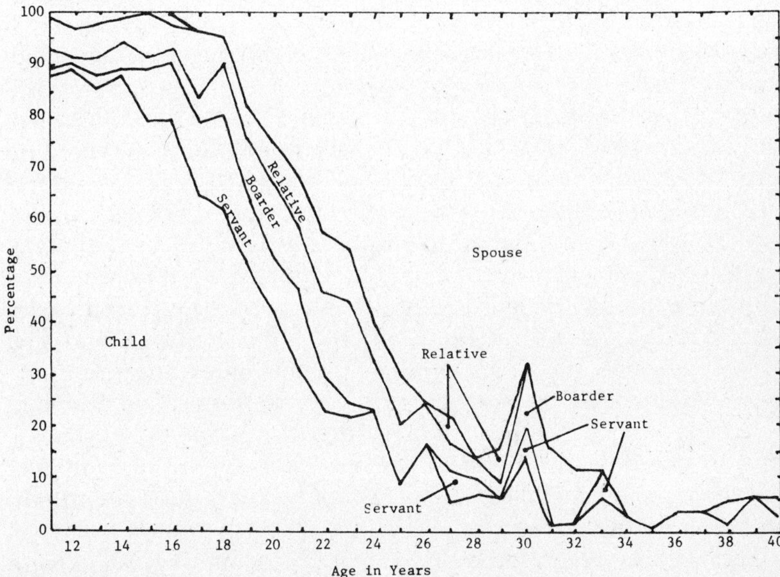

Figure 3. GERMAN MALES: HOUSEHOLD STATUS BY AGE.

jority of both went to live with their children or, less frequently, with their in-laws.

GERMAN MEN

At first glance, the life cycle of German men differed from that of native-born and Irish men. German men began leaving home at a substantially earlier age—16 years, compared to 19 years for the other two groups. Moreover, they practiced apprenticeship as an additional intermediate step between childhood and boarding or marriage. This practice was brought over from Germany and continued in Buffalo because of German domination of the city's crafts. It was most pronounced among young men between the ages of 18 and 22, when about one-fourth of German young men lived with a master craftsman (Figure 3).

Except for apprenticeship, the household cycle of German men broadly resembled that of the other two groups. About one-third of German young men between the ages of 21 and 24, and as many as 10% up to age 31 were boarders. The corresponding figures for those in their late teens and twenties were substantially lower (by about half) and were insignificant for most other age groups.

The marriage pattern for German men was compressed like that for Irish men, although it began and concluded about a year earlier, at ages 21 and 27, respectively.[9] Also like the Irish, German men experienced no delay in establishing their own household once they married.

Of the three ethnic groups, Germans had the most intensely nuclear household pattern. There existed few German boarding houses; boarders lived primarily with a German family. Once established, the German household was only moderately subject to modification as the household head grew older. Only 8% of German families took in a roomer or boarder, and the figure varied very slightly over the life cycle of the household head. The percentage of family heads taking in relatives fell slowly, but steadily, from 11% of those in their twenties to 5% of those in their fifties; thereafter, the trend reversed, as 11% among those in their sixties headed extended households and 20% of those in their seventies. German households taking in boarders and roomers declined very slightly, but noticeably, among older members, from 12% of those in their twenties to 6% of those in their seventies.

German men experienced a fairly stable economic cycle and were substantially more successful than their Irish counterparts in buying a home. During their early adult years—the twenties and thirties—their patterns of home ownership were similar to those of natives, with about one-fourth and two-fifths of the family heads in those age categories owning their own homes. Thereafter, the German percentage stabilized while that of the native-born advanced, such that by the time they were sixty years or older, less than half of German family heads owned their own homes, compared to almost three-fifths of native-born family heads. If one allows for length of residence in the city (German family heads had been present eight years on the average, compared to thirteen years for the native-born), the differences disappear entirely. Finally, although home ownership among the Germans did not advance with old age as did that for the native-born, neither did it decline, as was the case for the Irish.

Part of the German success in acquiring a home, of course, can be attributed to their occupational patterns. Although they lacked any significant number of white-collar, professional, or entrepreneurial occupations, and over half of their family heads were unskilled or without occupation, they had a firm grip on the city's crafts and dominated many of the lucrative building trades. As a result, over a third of their family heads were skilled workers, compared to only a fifth of the native-born and a sixth of the Irish. There were proportionately more young skilled workers than older ones. Moreover, German men stayed longer in the labor force than either of the other two groups. At age 16, when native-born men were just entering the labor force and a year before Irish young men began to work, one-fourth of German boys were already employed. By age 20, almost half were listed with an occupation, a level not reached by the native-born and Irish until age 22. They also retired from the labor force at a later age than either of the other two groups. Whereas half of the native-born and Irish men retired in their early sixties, less than 40% of German men had retired before their late sixties.

Despite the undoubted significance of work, occupational patterns accounted for only part of the German success in acquiring property. Cultural preferences undoubtedly operated as well, for if one allows for differences in age and length of residence in the city, German family heads not only equaled, but often exceeded, their native-born and Irish counterparts in the proportion owning real property. It was particularly among unskilled workers that German family heads bested their ethnic competitors.

As with the Irish and native-born men, advanced age brought relatively few unsettling changes in their life patterns. About one German man in three past the age of sixty was not the head of his own household. The great majority (three-fifths) of those who were not household heads lived with a child or grandchild; somewhat over one-tenth lived with an in-law, and somewhat fewer than one in ten lived with a nephew or niece. Only 12% lived as a boarder or roomer.

The notable aspect of this comparison of age-related life experiences of native-born, Irish, and German men is that alongside the not unexpected socioeconomic differences—occupation and property ownership—there existed such remarkable similarities in the timing and form of their respective family cycles. As we will now see, it was the women who demonstrated the most striking and pervasive ethnic differences in their family and economic cycles.

NATIVE-BORN WOMEN

Native-born women began leaving home at age 16—several years before their brothers. Few left, however, to take a job; at no age did more than 5% of native-born women have an occupation listed in the census other than that of domestic servant. Few became servants. Only 12% to 17% of native-born women aged 16 to 19 were classified as domestic servants. By age 24, virtually none were domestics.

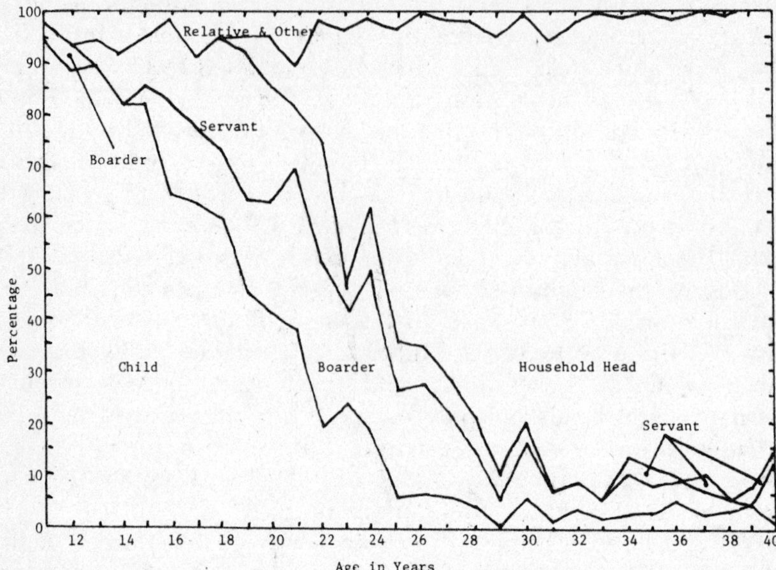

Figure 4. NATIVE-BORN FEMALES: HOUSEHOLD STATUS BY AGE.

Boarding was an equally rare experience, occurring primarily between the ages of 22 and 23 and even then involving less than one-fifth of the native-born women. Thus, except for a very brief period in their late teens, these women never lived in a household other than that of their parents (Figure 4).

Beginning at age 19 native-born women began to marry. By age 21 over half were listed as wives and by age 25 over three-fourths.[10] Most established their own household shortly after marrying. Three-fifths had done so between the ages of 19 and 22, and by age 27 virtually all had married. Native-born women delayed bearing children until a household was established. This conclusion is based on the following evidence: first, some 69% of native-born married women aged 20 to 24, and 89% of those aged 25 to 29 had their own households; second, there were 69 children aged 0-4 years per 100 married native-born women aged 20-24, and 91 children per 100 women aged 25-29 years. If the assumption is that most of these women had only one child under five years of age, this would mean that most of those without their own household had no children.

Even after they began to bear children, native-born women restricted their family size. They had a very low fertility ratio, only 585 children aged 0–4 years per 100 married women of childbearing years, 15–44.[11] They achieved this low rate by having most of their children before age 35. The fertility rate was 188 for native-born women in their late teens, 685 for women in their early twenties. It peaked at 910 for those in their late twenties and then declined rapidly, to 600 and 452 among women in their early and late thirties and to only 286 among those in their early forties. All this suggests a conscious pattern of limited childbearing.

Had native-born women not restricted their childbearing years, their households would have become rather large, and would have remained so, until the women reached middle age. As noted above, children of native-born parents did not leave home until late adolescence—the boys around age 19 and the girls around age 16 or 17. Thus, a native-born woman who began raising children in her mid-twenties could not expect them even to begin leaving until she was in her forties. During such a sixteen-year fertile period, if she gave birth every other year (the rate to be expected for a population not practicing birth control, but engaged in breast feeding), she would have had seven or eight children before the oldest daughters began leaving home. An examination of age-specific family size, however, shows that native-born families peaked in size while the family head was in his late thirties, with two to three children—2.56 on the average. Such a low figure reveals the extent to which most native-born women limited their family size.

As they aged, the death of the husband and/or financial pressures meant that fewer women were able to maintain their previous status as wife in an independent household. The first major decline in the proportion listed as "spouse" of their own household occurred among those in their early fifties. Prior to that, over two-thirds of any particular age group were so listed; after age sixty only about a fifth. What happened to the others? Of the women over sixty years of age who were not living with their husbands in their own households, only a few (16%) became household heads in their own right, half went to live with one of their children, and slightly less than a fifth went to live with in-laws. As with the men, a negligible percentage lived as boarders or with collateral kin.

IRISH WOMEN

While the life cycles of Irish and native-born men converged at several points, the pattern for Irish and native-born women was one of sharp and persistent differences. The divergence began in early adolescence. At age 17, when native-born women were just beginning

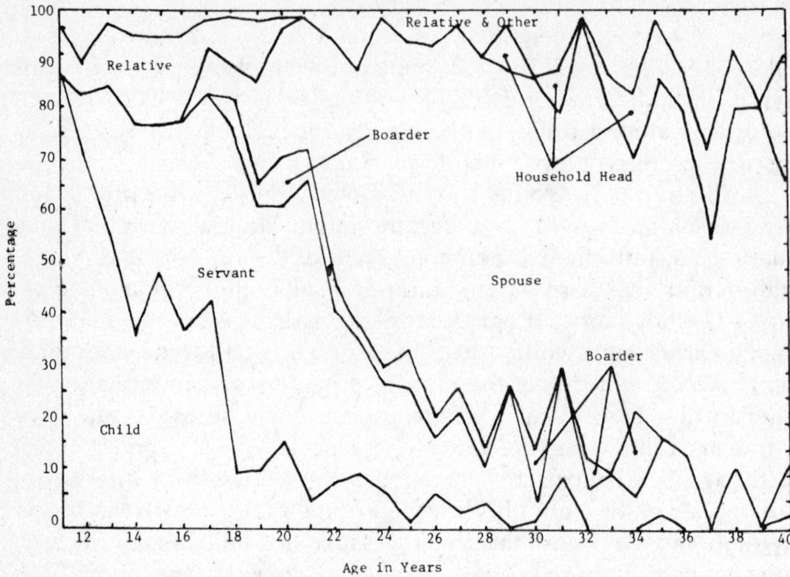

Figure 5. IRISH FEMALES: HOUSEHOLD STATUS BY AGE.

to leave home, over half of the Irish girls had already left theirs to take on domestic work, starting as early as 11 years of age; and by age 21 virtually all of them were living apart from their parents. This was not true of native-born women until age 25. Whereas only a few native-born women ever lived outside the household of either their parents or of their husbands, live-in domestic service claimed the energies of more than one-fourth of Irish girls between the ages of 13 and 25, and from half to two-thirds of those aged 18 to 21 years (Figure 5).

Domestic service was closely related to at least two demographic factors—age and length of residence in the city. Undoubtedly, Irish parents did not want their daughters to work as live-in domestics. These girls typically lived and worked among native-born families who themselves had adolescent sons living at home. Those who were new to the city, however, were unable to keep even their very young daughters out of domestic service. One-fourth of Irish girls aged 10 to 14 who were present in the city for one year or less worked as live-in domestics, compared to less than 15% of those present more than three years. The corresponding drop among those aged 15 to 19 was equally dramatic, from 75% to 32%. Among older girls, however, those in their early twenties, the decline was only from 52% to

39%; among those in their late twenties the decline was from about 30% to about 15%. Domestic service was the female counterpart of boarding out for the men and was much more widely practiced. Regardless of how long they had been in the city, however, domestic service was not a permanent feature of Irish women's lives. Beginning at age 21 Irish girls rapidly left such work and by age 26 virtually none were so employed.

Irish girls left domestic service in their late teens in order to get married. One fourth were married by age 19, half by age 21, and three-fourths by age 25. Despite domestic service (or perhaps financially because of it), Irish women caught up with their native-born counterparts in terms of age at marriage. As with the native-born women, about half of those who married early set up their own household. By age 22 over four-fifths of married Irish women had their own, independent household.

By contrast to the severely restricted overall fertility rate of native women, Irish women had a fertility rate high enough to suggest virtually unregulated childbearing. The Irish figure was 1000, for married women 15–44, almost double that of native-born women. Inspection of the age-specific fertility rates for Irish women in comparison to their native-born counterparts reinforces this impression. Thus, among married Irish women aged 15 to 19 the fertility rate was 313, or about two-thirds higher than that for native-born women of the same age. Among Irish women in their twenties and early thirties the fertility rate was much higher, 1,130 among those aged 25 to 29, and 1,290 among those aged 30 to 34 years. The latter figure was over twice as high as that for native-born women of the same age. Not until their late thirties did the Irish rate decline. It fell to 927 among the 35 to 39 age group and to 446 among the 40 to 44 age group. By the late thirties, however, simple biological restraints would have been operating, as many women drew toward the end of their fertile period.

Despite higher fertility rates and longer periods of childbearing, Irish families were not substantially larger than native-born families. Irish families had an average of 2.37 children, not significantly higher than the figure of 2.06 for native-born families. Moreover, native-born families peaked in the average number of children living at home with 2.56; Irish families peaked (at age 50) with 3.43. The maximum average differences between the two, then, were just one child. The only plausible explanation of this small divergence in family size in light of such major differences in fertility is related to the household cycle, by which native-born families kept their children home until late adolescence, whereas Irish families sent their children, particularly their young girls, out for a prolonged period of domestic service. Domestic service, then, served as an important regulator of Irish family size.

In describing the transition to old age for men, whether native-born or Irish, we focused on the age group over sixty because that was the period of major shifts in household status. The same was true for native-born women. For Irish women, however, shifts in household status began much earlier—in the age group 41 to 60. Beginning in their forties, the Irish woman's household began to break up. Only half of Irish women in their forties and fifties were wives living in their own households compared to three-fifths of native-born women. Similarly, one-fourth of all Irish women in that age bracket headed their own household, compared to less than 15% of native-born women. The reasons for this unusually high number of female-headed households among the Irish is not clear. It is possible that Irish men had a higher death rate than Irish women, but in the 41 to 60 age group there were 604 men compared to 565 women, suggesting that mortality alone is not a sufficient cause. Whatever the cause—death, separation, or divorce—it is clear that many middle-aged Irish women did not remarry.

Among older women, those over sixty years of age, Irish women continued to head a disproportionate number of households. About a fourth of those not living with a husband headed their own household (compared to 16% among the native-born). Half had gone to live with children, another 15% had gone to live with other in-laws, and an insignificant proportion boarded.

The life cycle of Irish women, therefore, diverged substantially from that of native-born women. The differences emerged in early adolescence, as most Irish girls went to live and work as servants in native-born households. This prolonged period of domestic service, however, was not a permanent part of their lives. Between the ages of 20 and 24, most Irish girls left that service in order to get married. At that point their age-related life experiences diverged again from the native-born pattern. Irish mothers had a much higher rate of childbearing, lasting over a longer period of time. While native-born mothers kept their daughters home until the time for them to marry, this was not possible for most Irish mothers. Perhaps out of both economic necessity and considerations of space in the house, their daughters spent most of their adolescence living with, and working for, those native-born families. During much of the middle and later years, Irish women were more likely than native-born women to head their own households, a type of independence which they probably did not relish. An insignificant number of Irish women

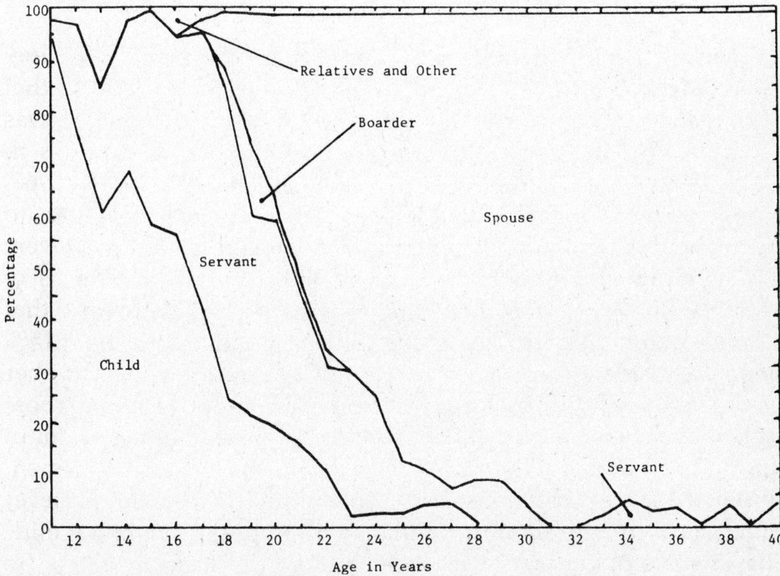

Figure 6. GERMAN FEMALES: HOUSEHOLD STATUS BY AGE.

were listed in the census with an occupation, reflecting the fact that Buffalo was not a city with an industry which could provide outside sources of income for working women. We may assume, however, that these women heading households did work; it probably only consisted of such poorly remunerative work as taking in other people's laundry.

GERMAN WOMEN

Like Irish girls, German girls left home at a very early age. The transition began at the age of 11 years, but was more gradual. Not until age 23, two years after almost all Irish girls had left home, was it completed (Figure 6).

As with the Irish, nearly all German girls at some point during their adolescence served as live-in domestics, almost invariably for native-born families. For the Germans, however, the length of service was shorter. Only between the ages of 17 and 18 did as many as two-thirds work in such a capacity, a figure which characterized Irish women in the age group from 18 to 21. Finally, German girls married and helped to establish a household earlier than either Irish or native-born girls. They began at age 17 (two or three years before the Irish), and by age 25 over 80% were listed as wives of household heads, compared to only 60% of Irish women and 70% of native-born women. After marriage, never more than 5% were listed with an occupation.

As with the Irish, once German women married, they experienced little or no delay in setting up a household. Nor was there any delay in beginning a family. German women aged 15 to 44 had the same overall fertility rate as Irish women, but a review of age-specific fertility shows that among the young and the old, German women had a higher rate than the Irish, and among the middle childbearing years, a rate only slightly under that of the Irish. As with the Irish, the suggestion is that their childbearing was regulated primarily by biological consideration.

Despite their high, prolonged fertility, the German family averaged just over two children (2.13), somewhat more than native-born families (2.06), and less than Irish families (2.37). The explanation is not related to age differences between the groups, for the average number of children present in German families peaked among family heads 45 years old at just over three children (3.08), again not substantially higher than the peak for native-born families at 2.56 and below the Irish figure of 3.43. As with the Irish, family size was regulated by sending children out of the household. German girls went into domestic service among the native-born; German boys became apprentices for German master craftsmen. Among the Germans, then, both domestic service and apprenticeship served as important regulators of effective family size.

As they aged, German women were more fortunate than either native-born or Irish women in remaining spouses in their own households. Among those over sixty years of age, over a third had that status, compared to a fifth or less among the native-born and Irish. Of those whose position changed, about a fifth became household heads in their own right, half went to live with their children and 14% went to live with in-laws. Thus, as with the other ethnic groups, boarding or living with collateral kin was seldom resorted to by the elderly.

CONCLUSION

Irish, Germans, and native-born whites, then, had distinctive life cycles. This was true for both the men and the women, but the men's patterns differed primarily in their economic cycles, while the women's patterns differed in terms of both the economic and the household cycles.

Among the men the household cycle was more notable for similarities than for differences among the ethnic groups. The most impressive differences among the men involved not the timing, but the content, of their life cycles. Thus, throughout their working lives, native-born men dominated the white-collar and entrepreneurial occupations, virtually to the exclusion of immigrant men; the ranks of the unskilled were composed largely of immigrant men, and most of the crafts, especially in the construction industry, were dominated by Germans. Occupational differences among them were largely independent of age.

Age-related patterns, and ethnic differences in those patterns, were also pronounced for the men in terms of property ownership. A substantial proportion of each group owned their own homes, but the differences were nonetheless substantial—one-fourth of the Irish, two-fifths of the Germans, and over two-fifths of the native-born. Moreover, the differences became even greater as the household head aged, reflecting presumably age-related differences in the earning potential among the types of occupations.

It was among the women that there existed the most consistent ethnic differences in life cycles. The years of "adolescence" for immigrant girls were strikingly different, not only from their native-born counterparts, but also from their brothers. For an extended period of time they lived and worked with native-born families. Their brothers, however, were never exposed to an intimate living situation with persons of another ethnic group. They remained home until late adolescence, boarded among families of the same nationality, married a girl also of the same nationality, and established a household usually in an ethnically homogeneous neighborhood. Their only chance for contact with the native-born occurred in the work situation, but, given the degree of occupational specialization along ethnic lines, this was probably neither extensive nor significant.

This early departure of girls from their parents' household was functional, both in terms of their later marriage prospects being increased from the earnings and especially as a regulator of the household size. In this way, although Irish and German fertility rates were almost double that for the native-born, and although the childbearing period for them extended ten years longer, immigrant families were not substantially larger than those of the native-born population.

The implications of these age-related sex differences are enormous, especially for the question of acculturation. The contact of immigrant girls with native-born families occurred at an impressionable age, when patterns of behavior, dress, language, and cultural values were still being learned. For foreign-language groups like the Germans, in particular, the girls probably learned English before their brothers. For the second generation it would be they who taught and translated such behavior to their children, years before the schools did their work. For working-class populations of immigrant background, the institution of domestic service was probably as important a force for acculturation as the more widely known institutions of work and schooling. These are only some of the perspectives that a comparative life-cycle analysis can offer for all of a community's members, young and old, male and female.

NOTES

1. Earlier historical studies of immigration give scant treatment to family composition or to age-related aspects of immigrant adjustment. A partial exception would be Oscar Handlin, *Boston's Immigrants: A Study in Acculturation* (Cambridge, Mass., 1941, 1959), which describes a wide range of social characteristics of Boston's Irish immigrants. The focus of much subsequent history, particularly the "new" urban history, has been on occupation and geographic mobility. Only lately has attention shifted to studies of the family and household. See Tamara K. Hareven, "The History of the Family as an Interdisciplinary Field," *Journal of Interdisciplinary History*, 2 (1970); *Journal of Marriage and the Family*, 35 (1973); Michael Gordon, ed., *The American Family in Social-Historical Perspective* (New York, 1973); Peter Laslett and Richard Wall, eds., *The Household and Family in Past Time* (Cambridge, England, 1972).

2. Paul C. Glick and Robert Parke, Jr., "New Approaches in Studying the Life Cycle of the Family," *Demography*, 2 (1965), 187–202, summarizes much of the sociological literature on the life cycle applied to the family. Tamara K. Hareven, "The Family as Process: The Historical Study of the Family Cycle," *Journal of Social History* (March 1974), 322–329, urges historians to adapt, in a creative fashion, this analytical tool for their own purposes. There are no studies comparing the life cycles of ethnic groups in nineteenth-century America, but see Robert V. Wells, "Demographic Change and the Life Cycle of American Families," *Journal of Interdisciplinary History*, 2 (1971), 273–282; Howard P. Chudacoff, "The Non-Private Newlyweds: Familial Extension in the First Stage of the Family Cycle, Providence, Rhode Island, 1864–1865 and 1879–1880," paper submitted to the MSSB Conference on Family History, Williams College, July 1974. Because of lack of space, not all the tables were included in this paper. For tables see Laurence A. Glasco, "Ethnicity and Social Structure: Irish, Germans and Native-Born of Buffalo, N.Y., 1850–1860," Ph.D. dissertation, State University of New York at Buffalo, 1973; esp. ch. 3, "Household and Family Structure."

3. Laurence A. Glasco, "Ethnicity and Occupation in the Mid-19th Century: Irish, Germans and Native-born Whites in Buffalo, N.Y.," paper delivered at the Conference on Immigrants in Industrial America, Eleutherian Mills Historical Library and the Balch Institute, November 1973; Theodore Hershberg et al., "Occupation and Ethnicity in Five Nineteenth-Century Cities: A Collaborative Inquiry," *Historical Methods Newsletter*, 7 (1974), 174–216.

4. Michael Anderson found that in mid-nineteenth-century Preston, England about half of the lodgers were single and between the ages of 15 and 24. Only one-fifth lived in a household containing more than five lodgers. Anderson, *Family Structure in Nineteenth Century Lancashire* (Cambridge, England, 1971), 47. Compare with John Modell and Tamara K. Hareven, "Urbanization and the Malleable Household: An Examination of Boarding and Lodging in American Families," *Journal of Marriage and the Family*, 35 (1973) 478–479.

5. The same as in 1890 for all white males in the United States. See Paul C. Glick and Robert Parke, Jr., "New Approaches in Studying the Life Cycle of the Family," *Demography*, 2 (1965), 189.

6. These figures for relatives and lodgers are almost identical to those for Preston, England. Anderson, *Family Structure in Nineteenth Century Lancashire*, 46.

7. The distribution of households with relatives and boarders—one fourth and one-fifth, respectively—does not quite agree with the distribution of extended and augmented household—one-fifth and one-fourth, respectively—because the classification "augmented" includes households which contained both relatives and boarders.

8. Unfortunately, the printed U.S. census does not provide information of the family and household characteristics of immigrants. For information on the Irish, see K. H. Connell, *The Population of Ireland, 1750–1845* (Oxford, England, 1950).

9. John Knodel, "Law, Marriage and Illegitimacy in Nineteenth-Century Germany," *Population Studies*, 20 (1966–1967), 279–294, deals with the effects on marriage age and illegitimacy of marriage restriction by various German states.

10. From the late eighteenth century onward, this has been the median age at marriage for American women. Wells, "Demographic Change and the Life Cycle of American Families," 280 ff. Cf. Tamara K. Hareven and Maris A. Vinovskis, "Marital Fertility, Ethnicity and Occupation in Urban Families: An Analysis of South Boston and the South End in 1880," paper presented at the MSSB Conference on Family History, Williams College, July 1974.

11. A rate only moderately below that for other cities of its size in the mid-nineteenth century. Warren S. Thompson and P. K. Whelpton, *Population Trends in the U.S.* (New York, 1933), 263, 279.

12

Life in the Big House

EUGENE D. GENOVESE

In his award-winning study Roll, Jordan, Roll: The World the Slaves Made, *Eugene D. Genovese argues that the antebellum South constituted a peculiar system of class rule, in which masters justified their domination as a benevolent paternalism which required duties and responsibilities of them as well as of the slaves. In the following selection, Genovese employs that perspective to analyze one of the most mystifying and ambiguous of ties, the one between "Mammy"—head servant, nurse, and substitute mother—and her owners. To gain a sense of both sides of the master-slave relationship, Genovese relies on the letters and autobiographies of plantation owners and mistresses and on the oral histories of ex-slaves. His juxtaposition of the situations of whites and blacks in the Big House permits some contemplation of the bonds between women of divergent race, class, and status.*

THE BLACK AND WHITE WOMEN of the Big House needed each other. They lived as part of a single family, although by no means always a happy, peaceful, or loving one. If black Mammies and nurses usually delivered the white babies, white mistresses sometimes delivered the black and more often helped look after both mother and infant. If Mammies and nurses raised the white children, mistresses helped raise the black, so that the children, white and black, were constantly underfoot and a joy and a trial to all. Mistresses with drunken, dissolute, spendthrift, or brutal husbands poured out their troubles to their maids, who poured out their own troubles to their mistresses and to each other. If a woman, white or black, woke up at night terrified by a dream of impending death, she would run to her maid or her mistress for comfort.[1] . . .

Mistress and servants found themselves bound together in mutual dependency in spite of themselves. The house servants required the protection and support of their white folks, much as the field hands did, and in addition, they needed to maintain their special advantages. The whites required that the house servants, like the field hands, work to provide for them, but in addition, they required their love and emotional support far beyond anything the servants needed in return. In the reciprocal dependency of slavery, especially in the Big House, the slaves needed masters and mistresses they could depend on; they did not need masters and mistresses to love them. But the whites needed their servants' love and trust. The slaves had the upper hand, and many of them learned how to use it.

The black and white women of the Big House reached the peak of intimacy in their involvement in each other's love lives. The young white ladies occupied much of their time in exchanging love letters with beaux and arranging rendezvous, the safe execution of which—not to mention half the fun—required secrecy and cunning in a society that demanded female chastity and feared sexual scandal. Loyal and discreet allies among the house servants became the *sine qua non* of romance. As Annie Laurie Broidrick of Mississippi insisted, "Many a romantic tale was confided by mistress and maid to each other during the hours the hair was being brushed and the soft wrapper donned."[2]

The servants often had access to information not easily obtained by their mistresses. If the beau lived on a nearby plantation, the servants of the two households probably knew each other or could arrange to know each other. The young lady's servants then became privy to the beau's private life and could report on his character, morals, and other love interests. They could learn much about his true feelings for their mistress. When he lived a bit farther away, this access to private information might even be enhanced, for an excuse could be found to send a servant to his home, and she would be likely to receive an invitation to spend the night among his house servants. Sometimes, the servants decided against a gentleman whose attentions their mistress fancied and were not bashful about saying so. The servants appropriated to themselves some of the duties and rights of Big Sister, not to say Mother.[3]

The presumption cut both ways. Young Missus normally expected to have something to say about whom her favorite servants cavorted with and did not hesitate to intervene in their marital affairs. Yet, the black women seem to have protected their independence better than the white. In any case, the bonds between mistress and servant grew stronger with each shared secret. And so did the boldness and pretensions of the servants, who readily felt the strength that shared secrets carry with them. . . .

The intimacy of shared secret lives brought the black and white women of the Big House together in a relationship of mutual dependence, but it thereby threatened the mistress-servant relation itself.

At its best, the women's feelings for each other would deepen, but the inevitable resentments easily generated moments of hatred and fierce violence.

When the house servants could, they risked pressing their masters and mistresses into a reversal of roles. They throve on the manifest dependency of their superiors. When the mistress of the Dabney plantation died and her daughters had to step in, the servants made their bid for supremacy. Susan Dabney Smedes recalled: "These were days of trial and perplexity for the young mistresses. The old house-servants, though having at heart an affection for them, considered or pretended to consider them too young to know what they wanted." Mrs. Smedes paraphrased the servants' attitude: "Besides, had they not known these young ladies ever since they were born? And did they not call them mammy or aunt in consideration of superior age? The young white ladies had no easy time establishing their authority and might have failed if Mammy had not rallied to them and helped put the others in their place."[4] . . .

[Mammy] remains the most elusive and important black presence in the Big House. To understand her is to move toward understanding the tragedy of plantation paternalism.

First, the white legend. Lewis H. Blair, attacking racial segregation in 1889, wrote:

> Most of us above thirty years of age had our mammy, and generally she was the first to receive us from the doctor's hands, and was the first to proclaim, with heart bursting with pride, the arrival of a fine baby. Up to the age of ten we saw as much of the mammy as of the mother, perhaps more, and we loved her quite as well. The mammy first taught us to lisp and to walk, played with us and told us wonderful stories, taught us who made us and who redeemed us, dried our tears and soothed our bursting hearts, and saved us many a well-deserved whipping. . . .[5]

A few years later, Annie Laurie Broidrick of Mississippi provided her own sketch:

> Consequential, important, and next in authority to the owners were the old "black mammies," who raised and superintended the care of the children. As they grew old they were exempt from hard work, and ruled white and black with impartial severity. Our old "mammy Harriet" raised two or three generations of children. We had the greatest love for her, but it was tempered with fear, for she never overlooked a fault and was ready to tell "old miss" how "de chillun was carrying on." She never allowed us to go into the kitchen. That was considered extremely low taste; and she would say with an emphatic shake of her old,

> turbaned head, "Nobody but niggers go in thar. Sit in de parlor wid'er book in y'or hand like little white ladies." Once mammy was in disgrace, when she slapped my mother, after her marriage. My father said he used some pretty strong language to the old lady, and she never repeated the offense.

But if Mammy punished, Mammy forgave and consoled. She would wipe away the white child's tears while defending her mistress's action: "But, honey, why does yer make y'r ma so mad, acting like sich po'r white trash?" The report concluded:

> Numbers of little "darkies" were always around and the children often begged the privilege of having them in the house to show off an accomplishment, such as a dance, or a tune on the jewsharp or banjo. I have seen dusky feet flying over the velvet carpet in the large drawing-room, and heard the hearty applause given by master and mistress. . . . Then mammy would come in, "hustle" them all out, grumbling that she "would like to know what white folks meant having all these niggers bout starting things."[6]

Without contradicting Mrs. Broidrick's implicit reading, a skeptic might at least wonder if Mammy was not as shamed by the spectacle being made of the black children as she was concerned with the maintenance of class and racial mores in the Big House. . . .

Who were these Mammies? What did they actually do?[7] Primarily, the Mammy raised the white children and ran the Big House either as the mistress's executive officer or her *de facto* superior. Her power extended over black and white so long as she exercised restraint, and she was not to be crossed. She carried herself like a surrogate mistress—neatly attired, barking orders, conscious of her dignity, full of self-respect. She played the diplomat and settled the interminable disputes that arose among the house servants; when diplomacy failed, she resorted to her whip and restored order. She served as confidante to the children, the mistress, and even the master. She expected to be consulted on the love affairs and marriages of the white children and might even be consulted on the business affairs of the plantation. She presided over the dignity of the whole plantation and taught the courtesies to the white children as well as to those black children destined to work in the Big House. On the small and medium-sized plantations she had to carry much of the house work herself, and her relationship to the field slaves drew closer. In general, she gave the whites the perfect slave—a loyal, faithful, contented, efficient, conscientious member of the family who always knew her place; and she gave the slaves a white-approved standard of black behavior. She also had to be a tough, worldly-wise, enormously resourceful woman; that is, she had to develop all the strength of character not usually attributed to an Aunt Jane.

Mammy supposedly paid more attention to the white children than to her own. Even W. E. B. Du Bois, who was rarely taken in by appearances and legends, thought so. He described the Mammy as "one of the most pitiful of the world's Christs. . . . She was an embodied Sorrow, an anomaly crucified on the cross of her own neglected children for the sake of the children of masters who bought and sold her as they bought and sold cattle."[8] The Mammy typically took her responsibilities to the white family as a matter of high personal honor and in so doing undoubtedly could not give her own children as much love and attention as they deserved. House nannies, white and black, free and slave, have often fallen into this trap, as Olmsted, for one, observed.[9] But willful neglect of or indifference to their own children cannot be deduced from their behavior. In particular, the idea that the Mammies actually loved the white children more than their own rests on nothing more than wishful white perceptions. That they loved the white children they themselves raised—hardly astonishing for warm, sensitive, generous women—in no way proves that they loved their own children the less. Rather, their position in the Big House, including their close attention to the white children sometimes at the expense of their own, constituted the firmest protection they could have acquired for themselves and their immediate families. Mammies did not often have to worry about being sold or about having their husbands or children sold. The sacrifices they made for the whites earned them genuine affection in return, which provided a guarantee of protection, safety, and privilege for their own children. The relationship between the Mammies and their white folks exhibited that reciprocity so characteristic of paternalism. "Of course," a planter in Virginia told a northern reporter in 1865, "if a servant has the charge of one of my little ones, and I see the child grown fond of her, and that she loves the child, I cannot but feel kindly towards her." Of course, Mom Genia Woodbury, who had been a slave in South Carolina, acknowledged that when white folks treat you kindly, you develop kind feelings toward their children.[10]

The devotion of the white children, who regularly sought her as their protector, confidante, and substitute mother, established a considerable barrier against the abuse of Mammy or her family. . . .

The immunity that Mammy secured for herself did not fully cover husband and children, but it went far enough to shield them from the worst. Mammy distraught, hurt, or angry was not to be borne. More than one overseer learned to his cost to walk gingerly around her and hers. Ma Eppes of Alabama said that an overseer had whipped the plantation Mammy when the mistress was away.

> When Miss Sarah comed back and found it out she was the maddest white lady I ever seed. She sent for the overseer and she say, "Allen, what you mean by whipping Mammy? You know I don't allow you to touch my house servants. . . . I'd rather see them marks on my old shoulders than to see 'em on Mammy's. They wouldn't hurt me no worse." Then she say, "Allen, take your family and git offen my place. Don't you let sundown catch you here." So he left. He wasn't nothing but white trash nohow.[11]

Another overseer made the incredible mistake of asking his employer for permission to punish Mammy. The reply: "What! What! Why I would as soon think of punishing my own mother! Why man you'd have four of the biggest men in Mississippi down on you if you even dare suggest such a thing, and she knows it! All you can do is to knuckle down to Mammy."[12]

Violence against Mammies and old nurses did sometimes occur. Francis Henderson, who fled a plantation near Washington, D.C., and settled in Canada, said that his master's son treated all the slaves cruelly: "I have known him to kick my aunt, an old woman who had raised and nursed him. . . ." And Ellen Cragin of Mississippi said that her mother fell asleep at a loom one day to be wakened by blows from her master's young son. She grabbed a stick and beat him badly, crying out, "I'm going to kill you. These black titties sucked you, and then you come here to beat me."[13]

The Mammies, strictly speaking, inhabited only the large plantation households. A much larger group, the nurses, took on many of their attributes. Even where a powerful Mammy presided, one or more nurses would be on hand, and plantations and good-sized farms usually had a black nurse for the white children, as well as a midwife, when the two were not the same person. Frequently, one black woman nursed and raised black and white children alike. White opinion of the nurses' qualities as midwives and medical practitioners varied, but the sources reveal much more praise than censure.[14] Beyond their medical services, to these nurses fell most of the duties associated with the more formally designated and prestigious Mammies. It was they who imparted the speech of the quarters to the children of the Big House, who introduced them to black folklore, who taught them to love black music, and who helped bend their Christianity in the folkish direction the black preachers were taking it.

The uses to which Mammy put her power and influence included protection of her own family. If her loyalty to her white folks took priority over her loyalty to the blacks in the quarters—and it did not always—she cannot be convicted of slighting her own flesh and blood. At the end of the war some Mammies did choose to stay with their white folks in preference to following a husband or children. But the departing children were usually full-grown and ready to make their own lives, and there is no evidence that the Mammy left her husband in cases other than those in which the marriage had deteriorated anyway. Normally, the husband held a position of importance in his own right—butler, coachman, blacksmith—and the couple would have been foolish to leave white people with whom they had developed kind and warm relationships for the vicissitudes of life in an uncertain world. The decision to stay demonstrated genuine affection and loyalty to the whites; it did not demonstrate servility or disloyalty to their own color, much less to their own family.

The same testimony from the Big House that created the legend of the faithful Mammy as contented slave *par excellence* also provided some warnings. Mrs. Chesnut wrote in 1865: "My ideas of those last days in Columbia are confused. The Martins left the Friday before I did, and their Mammy refused to go with them. That daunted me."[15] Elizabeth Allston Pringle, of a great low-country slaveholding family, told of her mother's attempt to return to the plantation during the war and of Mammy's message to desist or take another road:

> I never understood that message from Maum Milly, whether it was genuine anxiety on her part, or whether it was to keep mamma from coming and asserting her rights, by intimidating her. Maum Milly had always been greatly considered and trusted. She held herself and her family as vastly superior to the ordinary run of negroes, the aristocracy of the race.[16]

And Eliza Frances Andrews told how "dear old mammy—Sophia by name—while so superior, and as genuine a 'lady' as I ever knew," fell under suspicion of being a Yankee spy.[17] . . .

And in her own way Mammy defended black dignity. . . . She was not, as is so easily assumed, some "white man's nigger," some pathetic appendage to the powerful whites of the Big House. Her strength of character, iron will, and impressive self-discipline belie any glib generalizations. More than any other slave, she had absorbed the paternalist ethos and accepted her place in a system of reciprocal obligations defined from above. In so doing, she developed pride, resourcefulness, and a high sense of responsibility to white and black people alike, as conditioned by the prevalent system of values and notions of duty. She did not reject her people in order to identify with stronger whites, but she did place herself in a relationship to her own people that reinforced the paternalist social order. Thus, she carried herself with courage, compassion, dignity, and self-respect and might have provided a black model for these qualities among people who needed one, had not the constricting circumstances of her own development cut her off, in essential respects, from playing that role. Her tragedy lay, not in her abandonment of her own people, but in her inability to offer her individual power and beauty to black people on terms they could accept without themselves sliding further into a system of paternalistic dependency.

NOTES

1. For some specific illustrations see Rawick, ed., *Indiana Narr.*, VI (2), 138; Cornish Diary, Dec. 8, 1846; K. M. Jones, ed., *Ladies of Richmond*, pp. 95–96; Chesnut, *Diary from Dixie*, July 9, 1861 (p. 79).
2. Broidrick, "Recollection of Thirty Years Ago," ms. p. 5.
3. See Bateman Diary, 1856, esp. p. 25; Bayne Autobiographical Sketch, ms. p. 4; Rawick, ed., *Mo. Narr.*, XI, 244–245; Thomas Diary, Sept. 16, 1866; Chesnut, *Diary from Dixie*, pp. 295, 321.
4. Smedes, *Southern Planter*, p. 151.
5. Blair, *Southern Prophecy*, p. 144.
6. Broidrick, "Recollection of Thirty Years Ago," ms. pp. 6–7.
7. For a useful review of Mammy's position and role see Jessie W. Parkhurst, "The Role of the Black Mammy in the Plantation Household," *JNH*, XXIII (July, 1938), 349–369. Parkhurst, however, draws different conclusions than the ones presented here.
8. Du Bois, *Gift of Black Folk*, pp. 188–189.
9. Olmstead, *Seaboard*, p. 556.
10. Dennett, *South as It Is*, p. 14; Rawick, ed. *S.C. Narr.*, III (4), 218.
11. Botkin, ed., *Lay My Burden Down*, p. 173.
12. Quoted in Parkhurst, "Role of the Black Mammy in the Plantation Household," p. 355.
13. Drew, *Refugee*, p. 156; Botkin, ed., *Lay My Burden Down*, p. 174.
14. *DBR*, V (Jan., 1858), 321; Kemble, *Journal*, pp. 28–29; Walker Diary, Feb. 17, 1856; Mrs. E. C. Hamilton to William Hamilton, May 31, 1860, in the Lester Collection. For critical views see C. C. Jones, *Religious Instruction*, p. 137; Pringle, *Chicora Wood*, p. 82.
15. Chesnut, *Diary from Dixie*, Feb. 16, 1865 (p. 478).
16. Pringle, *Chicora Wood*, p. 251.
17. E. F. Andrews, *War-Time Journal of a Georgia Girl*, pp. 293–294 n.; also p. 355.

13

Marital and Sexual Norms Among Slave Women

HERBERT G. GUTMAN

Trends within the field of women's history have in several important respects repeated trends in the development of black history. In both fields initial emphasis on the oppression and powerlessness of the subjected group was succeeded by recognition of cultural strengths and individual accomplishments achieved in counterpoint to the pressures of domination. Less than a decade ago, the common wisdom was that slavery had destroyed cultural and family life among blacks, leaving only the pairing of mother and child. Herbert Gutman's research on slave cultural life, represented here in a selection on attitudes and norms with regard to sexuality, constitutes a major intellectual breakthrough. His recurrent likening of slaves to other preindustrial social groups and his interest in values and rituals reflect the influence of cultural anthropology on his work.

THE FULLEST RECORD of northern observation of slave sexual behavior is found among the witnesses, mostly whites familiar with the South Carolina Sea Island blacks, before the American Freedmen's Inquiry Commission in 1863, a record that emphasized the absence of slave sexual norms and confused prenuptial intercourse with "licentiousness."[1] The Commission entirely ignored, perhaps even consciously suppressed, this testimony in its published reports. A few witnesses, like General Rufus Saxton's aide-de-camp E. W. Hooper, said the slaves "appreciate [chastity] . . . thoroughly." But most agreed with Saxton, the Sea Island military commander, that "the [slave] system . . . destroyed that feeling," that masters "never inculcated it," and that women were "paid . . . a premium to breed as fast as possible." Saxton said women bore children at a "very young age," "often [at] fourteen." Henry Judd believed prenuptial intercourse "universal." "Before marriage," said James Redpath, who spent the early war years with Kansas slaves, there was "no such thing" as chastity. Richard Hinton, who had been with the Missouri slaves, "never heard of one" fifteen- or sixteen-year-old slave girl who had not "copulated with somebody." The most important testimony came from two former slaves; both described widespread prenuptial intercourse. Then about forty years old, Harry McMillan had been born in Georgia but grown up a Beaufort, South Carolina, slave. Asked if "colored women have a great deal of sexual passion" and "all go out with men," McMillan replied, "Yes, sir, there is a great idea of that. I do not think you will find four out of a hundred that do not; they begin at fifteen or sixteen." The well-known Robert Smalls was even more explicit:

QUESTION: Have not colored women a good deal of sexual passion?
ANSWER: Yes, sir.
QUESTION: Are they not carried away by their passions to have intercourse with men?
ANSWER: Yes, sir, but very few lawful married women are carried away if their husbands take care of them.
QUESTION: How is it with young women?
ANSWER: They are very wild and run around a good deal.

Asked "what proportion" had "sexual intercourse before marriage," Smalls answered, "The majority do, but they do not consider this intercourse an evil thing. . . ."[2]

That many slaves distinguished between prenuptial intercourse and "licentiousness" and believed prenuptial intercourse and pregnancy compatible with settled marriage escaped the notice of all but a few observers. A visit to the Sea Islands in 1863 convinced the Yankee journalist Charles Nordhoff that "indiscriminate intercourse" did not exist among slave women "to any great extent." Young women, however, were "not eminently chaste." Angered by a British journalist who condemned black plantation women for not being "vestal virgins," Mary Chesnut confided in her Civil War diary that Virginia and South Carolina slave women "have a chance here that women have nowhere else. They can redeem themselves —the 'impropers' can. They can marry decently, and nothing is remembered against these colored ladies." A Yazoo, Mississippi, owner explained to Frederick Olmsted: "They don't very often get married for good . . . without trying each other out, as they say, for two or three weeks, to see how they are going to like each other." (Eighty years later, an ex-slave called such behavior "a make-out.") Harriet Beecher Stowe learned from a southern white correspondent that after a South Carolina woman's husband was sold to Florida she had to take a new spouse and agreed to what appears to have been a trial marriage, explaining later that "we lib along two year—he watchin my ways and I watchin his ways."[3]

Despite their cultural-bound moralism, observers like Chesnut, the Yazoo owner, and Nordhoff were describing aspects of the sexual and social behavior disclosed by the Good Hope slaves, who demonstrated that prenuptial intercourse and settled marriage were compatible. Their behavior, which distinguished their norms from the prevalent Victorian ones, closely resembled practices found in many other premodern cultures. In 1833, for example, the British physician Peter Gaskell said that "sexual intercourse was almost universal prior to marriage in the [English] agricultural districts," but that "it existed only between parties where a tacit understanding had all the weight of obligation—and that was that marriage be the result." "The moral, customary, and legal rules of most human communities," Bronislaw Malinowski observed a century later, ". . . dissociate the two sides of procreation, that is sex and parenthood." In these cultures, marriage did not mean the "licensing of sexual intercourse but rather the licensing of parenthood." Prenuptial intercourse often served as "a method of arranging marriage by trial and error."[4] . . .

The acceptance of a slave norm that placed great emphasis upon a settled union and the belief that prenuptial pregnancy should be followed by marriage did not mean, of course, that all slaves behaved accordingly. "Sometimes," one old ex-slave recalled, "they would slip there and sleep with the woman and wouldn't marry them at all." Another ex-slave said, "Some of them had children for them what wasn't married to you. No, they would do nothing; they were glad of it. They would be glad to have them little bastards; brag about it." Competing values existed among the slaves, as among their owners and other peoples. In describing his 1828 marriage, the former North Carolina slave Lunsford Lane made it plain that he wanted no part of bridal pregnancy: "When we had been married nine months and one day, we were blessed with a son." Charles Nordhoff met an unhappily married Sea Islander in 1863 who had lived secretly with a younger woman for more than a year. She was about to bear his child, and he was "extremely anxious to marry her before the child is born." The man's slave wife consented to the separation. A plantation white noted in his 1854 diary: "The girl Martha, the wife of Willis, is delivered of a Daughter this morning—she has been married only two months. Her mother says 'she makes quick work of it' and seems distressed. I comfort her, by telling her such things often happen with the first born, but never afterwards." The young woman's mother worried more about her daughter's behavior than did the young woman's owner. . . .[5]

Despite the fact that some slaves everywhere rejected the dominant norm, marriage followed most prenuptial slave pregnancies. "If you fooled up a girl with a arm full of you," said an elderly male ex-slave, "you had to take care of her." Men who refused to marry such women may even have repudiated common norms and thereby won such women communal favor or special concern, an attitude that very much troubled Yankee missionaries and teachers among the wartime Sea Islanders. "It was held no shame for a girl to bear a child under any circumstances," said the journalist Nordhoff, and it dismayed Austa French to find that unmarried mothers were not ostracized. "There is no great gulf between them and the poor, as there is with the voluntary fallen," complained French. Such beliefs so upset one Island Yankee superintendent that he distributed a "very simple" outfit of clothing to the mothers of newborn children but only if they were married. Older women approached the teacher Elizabeth Botume "many times" to ask support for young unmarried mothers, behavior which conformed to their belief system. They once sought help for "poor sick Cumber," an unmarried woman who had suffered much in childbirth and was "bad off." They gave "united testimony," said Botume, aware that "we would have nothing to do with one like her." Botume sent a bundle of clothing, explaining that "their readiness to help the poor erring girl made me ashamed." Time and again, Botume heard the "touching appeals of these poor, ignorant, tender-hearted women for their down-fallen sisters." She finally rejected the plea of the old nurse Aunt Judy, hoping to make "this case an example."[6] . . .

Fidelity was expected from slave men and women after marriage. "If a woman loses her husband," Robert Smalls told the American Freedmen's Inquiry Commission in 1863, "she mourns for him and will not marry for a year and a half unless she is driven to it by want and must have somebody to help her." Aggressive slave husbands guarded their wives. Henry Gladney said his South Carolina father ("Bill de Giant") "didn't 'low other slave men to look at my mammy." A North Carolina Supreme Court Justice observed in 1853 that "as a general rule" slaves "respect the exclusive rights of fellow-slaves who are married." Violence, even murder, sometimes followed suspected or actual infidelity. . . .

Fidelity was also expected of married men. A Sea Islander caused a stir by taking a new wife, and when the couple came forward to marry in a missionary church, his mother rose and protested, "I take Becca (the second wife) in dis han' and carry her to punishment, an' Sarah in dis han' an' carry her to Christ." Decades later, Zora Hurston described conjuration beliefs and practices among Florida blacks meant to restrain men from engaging in extramarital intercourse. A practice by one woman supposedly prevented her husband from having an erection while with other women. "Tings we lub," a South Carolina slave woman said, "we don't like anybody else hab 'em. . . . What I hide behind de curtain now, I can't hide behind de curtain when I stand before God—de whole world know it den." Mary Chesnut summed up these beliefs. "Negro women are married," said Chesnut, "and after marriage behave as well as other people." "Bad men," she went on, "are hated here as elsewhere."[7] . . .

Group pressures often enforced dominant slave marital norms. For at least a quarter century prior to the Civil War, the Beaufort Baptist Church, most if not all of its members South Carolina slaves, punished people guilty of adultery and fornication. To commit adultery meant suspension from the church for three months. An affirmative vote by church members resulted in readmission. Second offenders were put out for six months. The role played by a black clergyman in a Camden, South Carolina, plantation church strongly impressed Mary Chesnut. After spending an afternoon in his church in October 1861, she wrote scornfully of his sermon: "Those who stole before, steal on, in spite of sobs and shouts on Sunday. Those who drink, drink when they can get it." But "for any open, detected sin they are turned out of church." The slave preacher "requires them to keep the Commandments. If they are not married—and show they ought to be—out of church they go. If the married mothers are not true to their vows, and it is made plain to him by their conduct, he has them up before the church." She believed the slaves were "devoted to their church membership"; the church was "a keen police court." The slave Harry McMillan put it differently to the American Freedmen's Inquiry Commission in 1863 when asked if some slave women had children prior to marriage. "Yes, sir," he replied, "but they are thought low of among their companions unless they get a husband before the child is born and if they cannot the shame grows until they do get a husband." Also emphasizing communal sanctions was the former Darien, Georgia, slave Priscilla McCullough. She described adaptations of West African practices. "I heard many times," she recollected, "bout how in Africa when a girl dohn act jis lak day should, dey drum uh out uh town. . . . In Africa dey gits punished. Sometimes wen dey bad, dey put um on duh banjo. Dat was in dis country. . . . When dey play dat night, dey sing bout dat girl and dey tell all bout uh. Das puttin on duh banjo. Den ebrybody know an dat girl she bettuh change."[8]

It is even possible that slave church initiation served as a social device to redefine the changing social and sexual status of maturing women. That was suggested by Robert Smalls and the Yankee schoolteacher Laura M. Towne to the American Freedmen's Inquiry

Commission. Smalls explained that church *initiation*—not mere membership—transformed the sexual behavior of young unmarried black women, publicly bridging the difficult transition from prenuptial sexual freedom to marital fidelity:

> QUESTION: What proportion of the colored girls join the Church?
> ANSWER: Most all girls join the Church. Generally between fifteen and sixteen years of age. They go through a certain probation and are admitted as members. No matter how bad a girl may have been as soon as she joins the Church she is made respectable.
> QUESTION: Does joining the Church make a difference in her behavior?
> ANSWER: Yes, sir, the change is very great—as great as between sun shine and a hail storm. She stops all this promiscuous intercourse with men. The rules of the Church are very strict about it.

The *process* by which they achieved full church membership (what Smalls called "a certain probation") impressed upon young and unmarried women a changed communal expectation as to their sexual behavior. Without connecting it directly to that function, Towne detailed a syncretic Afro-Christian church initiation among coastal South Carolina plantation blacks that apparently applied only to "a young girl" (or "young woman"):

> Their church government is most exact and rigid. Those who know about the examination of candidates for membership in Christian Churches say that among them there is nothing like such a strict examination before admission as obtains here. They have *secret religious societies* and *all their religious ways are peculiar*. When a young girl or young woman begins to have *the desire for a change of heart* she ties an old white handkerchief round her head and wears the poorest and dirtiest clothes she can procure. She must not be seen to [illegible] nor to look up and sometimes she goes into the fields and stays which is called *"being in the bush,"* or "seeking for pray." Then, after being in this state *three months* and attending prayer meetings three times a week, besides Sunday evenings for all that. There the candidate is examined by the *elder* who generally belongs to the society. After he has examined [her] and is satisfied that she is thoroughly in earnest she is admitted as a member of the society, when after undergoing another probation, she is admitted as a candidate for baptism. Then the elders of the church examine the candidate on doctrinal points, subjecting her to a searching inquiry on theological questions. If the result is satisfactory, the candidate is admitted to full membership. [Italics added.]

"Then," the teacher concluded, such women "dress in white and deck themselves with the gayest clothes they can get." Towne and Smalls indicated one way in which the slaves managed the difficult transition to adulthood and from prenuptial sexual freedom to postmarital fidelity.[9]

Church rules also imposed a submissive role upon married slave women. . . . After Frances Butler Leigh (Fanny Kemble's daughter) returned to the Georgia Sea Islands to manage her dead father's postwar plantation properties, she noticed that "the negroes had their own ideas of morality, and they held to them very strictly; they did not consider it wrong for a girl to have a child before she married, but afterwards were very strict upon anything like infidelity on her part." Moreover, "the good old law of female submission to the husband's will on all points held good." Once she saw a black woman who had been dropped from the church and was "sitting on the church steps, rocking herself backwards and forwards in great distress." On asking why, Leigh learned "she refused to obey her husband in a small matter." Leigh intervened in her behalf. Church readmission followed but only after the offending woman made "a public apology before the whole congregation."[10] . . .

Prenuptial intercourse and bridal pregnancy usually followed by settled marriage are not peculiar to slave populations but are also to be found in diverse "premodern" populations; the decline of these phenomena is often associated with the early stages of "modernization."[11] That decline, however, did not occur among Afro-American slaves and their immediate descendants, a fact made clear in the 1880 and 1900 manuscript federal census schedules and in later studies by scholars like Woofter and Johnson. Much remains to be studied before these continuities are understood. The sexual, courting, and mating practices of African slaves and their *early* (eighteenth-century) Afro-American descendants, for example, have been little studied, so it is hard to describe how enslavement affected such early practices. Nevertheless, much indirect evidence suggests a close relationship between the relatively early age of slave women at the birth of a first child, prenuptial intercourse, slave attachments to a family of origin and to enlarged slave kin networks, and the economic needs of slaveowners.

Enslavement required more than that human chattel produce commodities: it also required—especially after the abolition of the overseas slave trade—that the slave labor force reproduce itself. Few realized this better than the slaveowners themselves. . . . Scant evidence shows that owners discouraged prenuptial intercourse among their slaves; in fact, only a single such instance has been found. The aged former planter John Witherspoon DuBose recollected that when his family and their slaves left their Darlington, South Carolina, plantation in 1850 for Marengo County, Alabama, some additional slaves joined them. They were "presents to my mother from her father" and included "half a dozen buxom wenches" and "under the wagon cover . . . a bastard pickaninny of each wench." DuBose's grandfather "had passed a sentence of banishment upon Mittie & Amelia & the others for producing pickaninnies outside of the plantation rule." (DuBose also said that during the trek to Alabama each woman "capture[d] a sturdy buck and all had firmly pledged their hearts and hands in marriage as soon as the new home should be reached." He found their courting practices "very amusing and spectacular." DuBose apparently did not remember that marriage following the birth of a child had been a common slave practice.) DuBose's recollection is very unusual. Chancellor Harper, for example, tolerated what DuBose's grandfather forbade. To Harper it was "just" that free society proclaimed "the unmarried woman who becomes a mother . . . an outcast from society," "cut off from the hope of useful and profitable employment and driven by necessity to further vice." But the unmarried slave mother was "not a less useful member of society than before." "She has not impaired her means of support, not materially lowered her character, or lowered her station in society; she has done no great injury to herself, or any other human being. Her offspring is not a burden but an acquisition to her owner." Harper did not advocate "fornication," but his attitude helps to explain why prenuptial intercourse—so common among diverse "premodern" populations—survived much longer among the slaves and their immediate descendants than among the descendants of eighteenth-century New England Puritans and indentured southern white servants.

Reproducing the slave labor force required only the simple *biological* dyad "mother and child." The *social* dyads "husband and wife" and "father and child" were not essential. Neither was the completed nuclear family. But many owners, who did little to discourage prenuptial intercourse among their slaves, nevertheless encouraged the formation of completed slave families. Some did so for moral reasons, and others did so for economic reasons that had much more to do with the production of commercial crops and the performance of other unskilled and skilled tasks than with the reproduction of the labor force. Slave women mostly counted in the calculations of their owners as mothers, and slave men counted mostly as laborers. Although the reproduction of the labor force did not require the existence of completed slave families, maintenance of labor discipline did. Only those slaves who lived in affective familial groupings (and especially the greatly prized slave husband and father) could respond to indirect and direct incentives that exploited their familial bonds. Monetary rewards based on family labor (such as the slave garden plot) and incentive payments for "extra" work balanced the threat of the sale of relatives and especially of grown children. A husband and father might work harder to get extra rations for his children, to earn cash to purchase a luxury item for his wife, or to prevent his children from being sold.

Ideologues among the slaveowners mixed Christian obligation and economic reality in emphasizing the utility of "family government" among the slaves. The Baptist cleric Holland McTyeire urged owners to encourage slave marriages and to divide slaves "into families." It paid to "gratify the *home feeling* of the servant."

> Local as well as family associations, thus cast about him, are strong yet pleasing cords binding him to his master. His welfare is so involved in the order of things that he would not for any consideration have it disturbed. He is made happier and safer; put beyond discontent, or temptations to rebellion and abduction; for he gains nothing in comparison with what he loses. His comforts cannot be removed with him, and he will stay with them.

A cotton plantation overseer near Natchez made the same point differently. Those runaway men who outwitted the dogs, he told Frederick Olmsted, "almost always kept in the neighborhood, because they did not like to go where they could not sometimes get back and see their families. . . . [T]hey would come round their quarters to see their families and to get food, and as soon as he knew it, he would find their tracks and put the dogs on again. . . ."[12]

Pressures within the slave system encouraged early childbirth among slave women, but patterns of sexual behavior among slaves, particularly women, disclose that slaves made difficult choices, often beyond the master's influence. "Old Buford," said an elderly Tennessee ex-slave, "his darkies had chillun by him, and mammy wouldn't do it; and I've seen him take a paddle with holes in it and beat her." "Some of them," another Tennessee woman remembered, "thought it was an honor to have the marsa, but I didn't want no white foolin' with me." The worst whipping John Finnelly recollected from his slave childhood "was give to Clarinda; she hit massa with de hoe 'cause he try to 'fere with her and she try stop him." In an 1865 Georgia divorce trial, the ex-slave Louisa supported her old owner's complaint that the white woman's husband had slept with slave women. She had resisted his advances: once she slept with the white children; another time, she "nailed up the windows of her house." When he got into her room once, she "blew up the light to keep him off her, and he would blow it out." The white persisted and even offered her "two dollars to feel her titties." Occasional reports in southern medical journals and elsewhere described how slave women made yet other choices involving abortive and contraceptive practices. Among Good Hope women who had a first child by one man and later settled into an enduring relationship with a second man, sometimes several years passed before the birth of a second child. It is hard to believe that during that time they practiced sexual abstinence. Nancy, for example, had a first child by Tony in 1829. A second child, the first of seven fathered by Burge over a seventeen-year period, was born to her in 1836. Lettice's first child was born in 1848 by a man whose name is unknown, and she gave birth to the first of two children by Major six years later. The recollections by elderly ex-slaves suggest yet other choices made by slave adults. A few—nearly all women and nearly always interviewed by blacks—said their parents withheld sexual information from them as young teen-agers. Some learned about menstruation after the fact. ("When it first come on," remembered an elderly woman, "I ran to the branch trying to make it stop. . . . But it didn't bother me. I was trying to stop it for I didn't know whether I was going to get a killing for it or not. I didn't know what it was.") Others said they were "most grown befo' we knowed a thing 'bout man and woman." Some children learned from their mothers that babies were born in "hollow logs" (or that "Aunt Sarah brought the babies"). Adult reproductive functions became known to some only upon marriage. A few described a modified trundle bed that hid parental lovemaking from them, and the South Carolina ex-slave Jacob Stroyer detailed efforts to maintain privacy and even to keep grown siblings apart. Cabins "were built so as to contain two families," and Stroyer remembered how the slaves coped with overcrowding:

> Some had partitions, while others had none. When there were not partitions each family would fit up his own part as he could, sometimes they got old boards and nailed them up, stuffing the cracks with old rags; when they could not get boards they hung up old clothes. When the family increased, the children all slept together, both boys and girls, until either got married, then a part of another cabin was assigned to the one that was married, but the rest would have to remain with their mother and father as they did when children unless they could get with some of

> their relatives or friends who had small families. . . . [T]he young men slept in the apartment known as the kitchen and the young women slept in the room with their mother and father.

Such decisions reveal the presence of sociosexual standards that affected the choices made by slaves.[13]

NOTES

1. For other contemporary observations about slave sexual behavior see *Facts Concerning the Freedmen, Their Capacities, and Their Destinies. Collected and Published by the Emancipation League* (Boston, 1863), 3–12; "Interview with J. R. Roudanez," in James MacKaye, *The Mastership and Its Fruits* (1864), 4–6. See also Charles Lyell, *A Second Visit to the United States of North America* I (1849), 271–73. Lyell's wife came to know an Alabama woman who had raised "a colored girl" to be "modest and well behaved." The young slave woman became the mother of "a mulatto child." "The mistress," Lyell reported, "reproached her very severely for her misconduct, and the girl at first took the rebuke much to heart; but having gone home one day to visit her mother, a native African, she returned, saying that her parent had assured her she had done nothing wrong, and had no reason to be ashamed." Lyell felt this to be evidence of "the loose code of morality which the Africans have inherited from their parents."

2. Testimony before the American Freedmen's Inquiry Commission, 1863, file 2 (pp. 4–5), file 3 (pp. 4–7, 42–43, 63–64, 70, 85, 100–105, 125–26, 160, 223–24), file 8 (p. 28). Letters Received, Office of the Adjutant General, 1861–1870, Main Series, Reels 200 and 201, National Archives.

3. Charles Nordhoff, "Freedmen of South Carolina," in Frank Moore, ed., *Papers of the Day #1* (1863), 21–24; Mary B. Chesnut, *A Diary from Dixie* (1949), 121–23; F. L. Olmsted, *Journey in the Back Country* (1863), 113–14, 153–55; Harriet Beecher Stowe, *Key to Uncle Tom's Cabin* (1854), 298–301; *American Slave, South Carolina Narratives*, III, iv, 208–9.

4. Peter Gaskell, *Manufacturing Population of England* (1833), quoted Margaret Hewitt, *Wives and Mothers in Victorian England* (1958), 54; Bronislaw Malinowski, "Parenthood—the Basis of Social Structure," in V. F. Calverton and Samuel D. Schmalhausen, eds., *New Generation* (1930), 129–43; *id., Sex and Repression in Savage Society* (1927), 195.

5. *Unwritten History . . . (Fisk)*, 1–6, 67–69, 77–79, 123–27, 153–54; *American Slave, Texas Narratives*, IV, i, 62–65, *South Carolina Narratives*, II, ii, 200–203; 1854 diary notation quoted in Bobby Frank Jones, "A Cultural Middle Passage: Slave Marriage and Family in the Antebellum South," unpublished Ph.D. dissertation, University of North Carolina, 1965, 169; Lunsford Lane, *Narrative of Lunsford Lane* (1842), 11; Nordhoff, "Freedmen of the South," in Frank Moore, ed., *Papers of the Day #1*, 23–24.

6. Botume, *First Days Amongst the Contrabands* (1893), 125–27, 162–167; Nordhoff, "Freedmen of the South," 21–24; Austa French, *Slavery in South Carolina* (1863), 180–87, 190–91.

7. *Alvany (a free woman of color) v. Powell*, 1 Jones Esq. 35, December 1853, printed in Catterall, *Judicial Cases Concerning Slavery*, II, 179–80; *State*

v. Tackett, 1 Hawks 210–22, December 1820; *State v. Samuel, a slave,* 2 Devereux and Battle's Law, 177–185, December 1836; *State v. John, a slave,* 8 Tredell 330–39, June 1848; *Alfred, a slave v. The State of Mississippi,* 37 Miss. 296–99, October 1859; *Samuel Adams v. William Adams,* 36 Ga. 236–37, June 1867; *Timmons v. Lacy,* 30 Texas 126, April 1867; *American Slave, South Carolina Narratives,* II, i, 13–16, ii, 129–33; testimony of Robert Smalls, A. D. Smith, and E. G. Dudley, American Freedmen's Inquiry Commission, 1863, file 3, Office of the Adjutant General, Letters Received, Main Series, 1861–1870, Reel 200, National Archives; *Letters from Port Royal* (1906), ed. E. W. Pearson, 86–87; Zora Hurston, "Hoodoo in America," *Journal of American Folklore,* 44 (October–December 1931), 391, 400–401; Stowe, *Key to Uncle Tom's Cabin* (1854), 298–301; Chesnut, *Diary from Dixie,* 122. See also *Smith, a slave, v. The State,* 9 Ala. 990–98, June 1846; *William v. The State,* 33 Ga. Supp. 85–94, March 1864; Johnson, *Ante-bellum North Carolina: A Social History,* 538–39; Johnston, *Race Relations in Virginia,* 305–6.

8. Chesnut, *Diary from Dixie,* 148–49; testimony of Henry Judd and Harry McMillan, American Freedmen's Inquiry Commission, 1863, file 3, Letters Received, Office of the Adjutant General, Main Series, Reel 200, National Archives; *Drums and Shadows* (1940), 154.

9. Testimony of Robert Smalls and Laura M. Towne, American Freedmen's Inquiry Commission, 1863, file 3, Letters Received, Office of the Adjutant General, Main Series, Reel 200, National Archives.

In a little-read essay, E. Franklin Frazier asserted that after emancipation southern blacks "rationalized between the 'natural' impulse to seek sexual satisfaction outside of marriage and the teachings of the Church" with "the quasi-theological doctrine that 'two clean sheets cannot soil each other.' " Premarital and extra-marital sexual intercourse, accordingly, were not "sinful" when involving two Christians. I have found no evidence suggesting such beliefs. See EFF, "Sex Life of the African and American Negro," printed in Albert Ellis and Albert Abarbanel, eds., *Encyclopedia of Sexual Behavior* (1961), and reprinted in Robert Staples, ed., *The Black Family: Essays and Studies* (1971), 109–18. Similarly, no evidence sustains Eugene Genovese's confused contention that the "slaves did not separate marriage or sex itself from love" but instead "held the theory that good Christians did not sin by sleeping together out of wedlock, for they were pure and therefore could not defile each other" (Genovese, *Roll, Jordan, Roll,* 472).

10. Botume, *First Days Amongst the Contrabands,* 125–27, 162–67; Frances Butler Leigh, *Ten Years on a Georgia Plantation Since the War* (1883), 164, 227–28, 246–48.

11. See, for example, P. E. H. Hair, "Bridal Pregnancies in Rural England in Earlier Centuries," *Population Studies* XX (November 1966), 233–43; D. S. Smith and Michael S. Hindus, "Premarital Pregnancy in America, 1640–1971: An Overview and Interpretation," *Journal of Interdisciplinary History,* V (Spring 1975), 537–570; John Knodel, "Two and a Half Centuries of Demographic History in a Bavarian Village," *Population Studies,* XXIV (November 1970), 353–70; P. E. H. Hair, "Bridal Pregnancy in Earlier Rural England Further Examined," *Population Studies,* XXIV (March 1970), 59–70.

12. Frederic Bancroft, *Slave Trading in the Old South* (1931), 74–75, 79–86; *Proslavery Argument* (1852), 40–44, 368; *American Cotton Planter,* I. n.s., 295, II, 331, III, 76; Olmsted, *Seaboard States* (1857), 280; J. C. Reed, *The Brother's War* (1905), 48–49, 156, 334, 432; J. S. Bassett, *Plantation Overseer* (1925), 21–22, 260–61; Phillips, *American Negro Slavery* (1918), 85–86; Phil-

lips, ed., *Plantation Documents* (1909), I, 179; W. K. Scarborough, *The Overseer: Plantation Management in the Old South* (1966), 68–70, 91–92, 97; W. D. Postell, *The Health of Slaves on Southern Plantations* (1951), 111, 119; Thomas W. Knox, *Camp-Fire and Cotton-Field: Southern Adventures in Time of War* (1865), 355–359; *Southern Cultivator,* V (1847), 142–43, VI (1848), 120, XVI (1858), 273–74, 319; J. W. DuBose, "Recollections . . ." *Alabama History Quarterly,* I (Spring 1930), 65–66; *DeBow's Review,* XVIII (1855), 715 XX (1856), 656, XXII (1857), 44, XXVIII (1860), 52–53.

13. *Odom v. Odom,* 36 Ga. 286–320, June 1867; *American Slave, South Carolina Narratives,* II, ii, 11–26, 166–70, 200–203, III, iii, 17–19; *Texas Narratives,* IV, ii, 35–40, V, iv, 190–94; *Arkansas Narratives,* IX, ix, 9–13; *Unwritten History (Fisk),* 1–6, 55–58, 67–69, 77–79, 103–8, 141–51; *Negro in Virginia (WPA),* 89; Jacob Stroyer, *Sketches of My Life in the South* (1879), 8–12, 31–33.

14

The Female World of Love and Ritual

Relations Between Women in Nineteenth-Century America

■

CARROLL SMITH-ROSENBERG

The increased freedom in sexual attitudes and sexual experimentation in the 1960s led some scholars to inject a healthy dose of relativism into their views of sexual practices of the past. Rather than assuming that Victorian sexual ideology was simply repressive and dysfunctional, researchers began to look for the functions it served. Among those investigating sexuality and sex roles in American history, Carroll Smith-Rosenberg has been one of the most innovative, recognizing, as she does in the following essay, that the uniqueness of Victorian sexual ideology pertained not only to heterosexual relations but to relations between members of one sex. In its adaptation of anthropological, sociological, and psychological theory, and in its focus on women's consciousness, the essay is an outstanding example of the new women's history. It represents a major advance in the field because it moves from abstract assertion to a rich and evocative depiction of a female subculture.

THE FEMALE FRIENDSHIP of the nineteenth century, the long-lived, intimate, loving friendship between two women, is an excellent example of the type of historical phenomena which most historians know something about, which few have thought much about, and which virtually no one has written about.[1] It is one aspect of the female experience which consciously or unconsciously we have chosen to ignore. Yet an abundance of manuscript evidence suggests that eighteenth- and nineteenth-century women routinely formed emotional ties with other women. Such deeply felt, same-sex friendships were casually accepted in American society. Indeed, from at least the late eighteenth through the mid-nineteenth century, a female world of varied and yet highly structured relationships appears to have been an essential aspect of American society. These relationships ranged from the supportive love of sisters, through the enthusiasms of adolescent girls, to sensual avowals of love by mature women. It was a world in which men made but a shadowy appearance.[2]

Defining and analyzing same-sex relationships involves the historian in deeply problematical questions of method and interpretation. This is especially true since historians, influenced by Freud's libidinal theory, have discussed these relationships almost exclusively within the context of individual psychosexual developments or, to be more explicit, psychopathology.[3] Seeing same-sex relationships in terms of a dichotomy between normal and abnormal, they have sought the origins of such apparent deviance in childhood or adolescent trauma and detected the symptoms of "latent" homosexuality in the lives of both those who later became "overtly" homosexual and those who did not. Yet theories concerning the nature and origins of same-sex relationships are frequently contradictory or based on questionable or arbitrary data. In recent years such hypotheses have been subjected to criticism both from within and without the psychological professions. Historians who seek to work within a psychological framework, therefore, are faced with two hard questions: Do sound psychodynamic theories concerning the nature and origins of same-sex relationships exist? If so, does the historical datum exist which would permit the use of such dynamic models?

I would like to suggest an alternative approach to female friendships—one which would view them within a cultural and social setting rather than from an exclusively individual psychosexual perspective. Only by thus altering our approach will we be in the position to evaluate the appropriateness of particular dynamic interpretations. Intimate friendships between men and men and women and women existed in a larger world of social relations and social values. To interpret such friendships more fully they must be related to the structure of the American family and to the nature of sex-role divisions and of male-female relations both within the family and in society generally. The female friendship must not be seen in isolation; it must be analyzed as one aspect of women's overall relations with one another. The ties between mothers and daughters, sisters, female cousins and friends, at all stages of the female life cycle constitute the most suggestive framework for the historian to begin an analysis of intimacy and affection between women. Such an analysis would not only emphasize general cultural patterns rather than the internal dynamics of a particular family or childhood; it would shift the focus of the study from a concern with deviance to that of defining configurations of legitimate behavioral norms and options.[4]

This analysis will be based upon the correspondence and diaries of women and men in thirty-five families between the 1760s and the 1880s. These families, though limited in number, represented a broad range of the American middle class, from hard-pressed pioneer families and orphaned girls to daughters of the intellectual and social elite. It includes families from most geographic regions, rural and urban, and a spectrum of Protestant denominations ranging from Mormon to orthodox Quaker. Although scarcely a comprehensive sample of America's increasingly heterogeneous population, it does, I believe, reflect accurately the literate middle class to which the historian working with letters and diaries is necessarily bound. It has involved an analysis of many thousands of letters written to women friends, kin, husbands, brothers, and children at every period of life from adolescence to old age. Some collections encompass virtually entire life spans; one contains over 100,000 letters as well as diaries and account books. It is my contention that an analysis of women's private letters and diaries which were never intended to be published permits the historian to explore a very private world of emotional realities central both to women's lives and to the middle-class family in nineteenth-century America.[5]

The question of female friendships is peculiarly elusive; we know so little or perhaps have forgotten so much. An intriguing and almost alien form of human relationship, they flourished in a different social structure and amidst different sexual norms. Before attempting to reconstruct their social setting, therefore, it might be best first to describe two not atypical friendships. These two friendships, intense, loving, and openly avowed, began during the women's adolescence and, despite subsequent marriages and geographic separation, continued throughout their lives. For nearly half a century these women played a central emotional role in each other's lives, writing time and again of their love and of the pain of separation. Paradoxically to twentieth-century minds, their love appears to have been both sensual and platonic.

Sarah Butler Wister first met Jeannie Field Musgrove while vacationing with her family at Stockbridge, Massachusetts, in the summer of 1849.[6] Jeannie was then sixteen, Sarah fourteen. During two subsequent years spent together in boarding school, they formed a deep and intimate friendship. Sarah began to keep a bouquet of flowers before Jeannie's portrait and wrote complaining of the intensity and anguish of her affection.[7] Both young women assumed nom de plumes, Jeannie a female name, Sarah a male one; they would use these secret names into old age.[8] They frequently commented on the nature of their affection: "If the day should come," Sarah wrote Jeannie in the spring of 1861, "when you failed me either through your fault or my own, I would forswear all human friendship, thenceforth." A few months later Jeannie commented: "Gratitude is a word I should never use toward you. It is perhaps a misfortune of such intimacy and love that it makes one regard all kindness as a matter of course, as one has always found it, as natural as the embrace in meeting."[9]

Sarah's marriage altered neither the frequency of their correspondence nor their desire to be together. In 1864, when twenty-nine, married, and a mother, Sarah wrote to Jeannie: "I shall be entirely alone [this coming week]. I can give you no idea how desperately I shall want you. . . ." After one such visit Jeannie, then a spinster in New York, echoed Sarah's longing: "Dear darling Sarah! How I love you & how happy I have been! You are the joy of my life. . . . I cannot tell you how much happiness you gave me, nor how constantly it is all in my thoughts. . . . My darling how I long for the time when I shall see you. . . ." After another visit Jeannie wrote: "I want you to tell me in your next letter, to assure me, that I am your dearest. . . . I do not doubt you, & I am not jealous but I long to hear you say it once more & it seems already a long time since your voice fell on my ear. So just fill a quarter page with caresses & expressions of endearment. Your silly Angelina." Jeannie ended one letter: "Goodbye dearest, dearest lover—ever your own Angelina." And another, "I will go to bed . . . [though] I could write all night—A thousand kisses—I love you with my whole soul—your Angelina."

When Jeannie finally married in 1870 at the age of thirty-seven, Sarah underwent a period of extreme anxiety. Two days before Jeannie's marriage Sarah, then in London, wrote desperately: "Dearest darling—How incessantly have I thought of you these eight days—all today—the entire uncertainty, the distance, the long silence—are all new features in my separation from you, grevious to be borne. . . . Oh Jeannie. I have thought & thought & yearned over you these two days. Are you married I wonder? My dearest love to you wherever and *who*ever you are."[10] Like many other women in this collection of thirty-five families, marriage brought Sarah and Jeannie physical separation; it did not cause emotional distance. Although at first they may have wondered how marriage would affect their relationship, their affection remained unabated throughout their lives, underscored by their loneliness and their desire to be together.[11]

During the same years that Jeannie and Sarah wrote of their love and need for each other, two slightly younger women began a similar odyssey of love, dependence and—ultimately—physical, though not emotional, separation. Molly and Helena met in 1868 while both attended the Cooper Institute School of Design for Women in New

York City. For several years these young women studied and explored the city together, visited each other's families, and formed part of a social network of other artistic young women. Gradually, over the years, their initial friendship deepened into a close intimate bond which continued throughout their lives. The tone in the letters which Molly wrote to Helena changed over these years from "My dear Helena," and signed "your attached friend," to "My dearest Helena," "My Dearest," "My Beloved," and signed "Thine always" or "thine Molly."[12]

The letters they wrote to each other during these first five years permit us to reconstruct something of their relationship together. As Molly wrote in one early letter:

> I have not said to you in so many or so few words that I was happy with you during those few so incredibly short weeks but surely you do not need words to tell you what you must know. Those two or three days so dark without, so bright with firelight and contentment within I shall always remember as proof that, for a time, at least—I fancy for quite a long time—we might be sufficient for each other. We know that we can amuse each other for many idle hours together and now we know that we can also work together. And that means much, don't you think so?

She ended: "I shall return in a few days. Imagine yourself kissed many times by one who loved you so dearly."

The intensity and even physical nature of Molly's love was echoed in many of the letters she wrote during the next few years, as, for instance in this short thank-you note for a small present: "Imagine yourself kissed a dozen times my darling. Perhaps it is well for you that we are far apart. You might find my thanks so expressed rather overpowering. I have that delightful feeling that it doesn't matter much what I say or how I say it, since we shall meet so soon and forget in that moment that we were ever separated. . . . I shall see you soon and be content."[13]

At the end of the fifth year, however, several crises occurred. The relationship, at least in its intense form, ended, though Molly and Helena continued an intimate and complex relationship for the next half-century. The exact nature of these crises is not completely clear, but it seems to have involved Molly's decision not to live with Helena, as they had originally planned, but to remain at home because of parental insistence. Molly was now in her late twenties. Helena responded with anger and Molly became frantic at the thought that Helena would break off their relationship. Though she wrote distraught letters and made despairing attempts to see Helena, the relationship never regained its former ardor—possibly because Molly had a male suitor.[14] Within six months Helena had decided to marry a man who was, coincidentally, Molly's friend and publisher. Two years later Molly herself finally married. The letters toward the end of this period discuss the transition both women made to having male lovers—Molly spending much time reassuring Helena, who seemed depressed about the end of their relationship and with her forthcoming marriage.[15]

It is clearly difficult from a distance of 100 years and from a post-Freudian cultural perspective to decipher the complexities of Molly and Helena's relationship. Certainly Molly and Helena were lovers—emotionally if not physically. The emotional intensity and pathos of their love becomes apparent in several letters Molly wrote Helena during their crisis: "I wanted so to put my arms round my girl of all the girls in the world and tell her . . . I love her as wives do love their husbands, as *friends* who have taken each other for life—and believe in her as I believe in my God. . . . If I didn't love you do you suppose I'd care about anything or have ridiculous notions and panics and behave like an old fool who ought to know better. I'm going to hang on to your skirts. . . . You can't get away from [my] love." Or as she wrote after Helena's decision to marry: "You know dear Helena, I really was in love with you. It was a passion such as I had never known until I saw you. I don't think it was the noblest way to love you." The theme of intense female love was one Molly again expressed in a letter she wrote to the man Helena was to marry: "Do you know sir, that until you came along I believe that she loved me almost as girls love their lovers. *I know I loved her so*. Don't you wonder that I can stand the sight of you." This was in a letter congratulating them on their forthcoming marriage.[16]

The essential question is not whether these women had genital contact and can therefore be defined as heterosexual or homosexual. The twentieth-century tendency to view human love and sexuality within a dichotomized universe of deviance and normality, genitality and platonic love, is alien to the emotions and attitudes of the nineteenth century and fundamentally distorts the nature of these women's emotional interaction. These letters are significant because they force us to place such female love in a particular historical context. There is every indication that these four women, their husbands and families—all eminently respectable and socially conservative—considered such love both socially acceptable and fully compatible with heterosexual marriage. Emotionally and cognitively, their heterosocial and their homosocial worlds were complementary.

One could argue, on the other hand, that these letters were but an example of the romantic rhetoric with which the nineteenth century surrounded the concept of friendship. Yet they possess an emotional intensity and a sensual and physical explicitness that is difficult to dismiss. Jeannie longed to hold Sarah in her arms; Molly mourned her physical isolation from Helena. Molly's love and devotion to Helena, the emotions that bound Jeannie and Sarah together, while perhaps a phenomenon of nineteenth-century society were not the less real for their Victorian origins. A survey of the correspondence and diaries of eighteenth- and nineteenth-century women indicates that Molly, Jeannie, and Sarah represented one very real behavioral and emotional option socially available to nineteenth-century women.

This is not to argue that individual needs, personalities, and family dynamics did not have a significant role in determining the nature of particular relationships. But the scholar must ask if it is historically possible and, if possible, important, to study the intensely individual aspects of psychosexual dynamics. Is it not the historian's first task to explore the social structure and the world view which made intense and sometimes sensual female love both a possible and an acceptable emotional option? From such a social perspective a new and quite different series of questions suggests itself. What emotional function did such female love serve? What was its place within the hetero- and homosocial worlds which women jointly inhabited? Did a spectrum of love-object choices exist in the nineteenth century across which some individuals, at least, were capable of moving? Without attempting to answer these questions it will be difficult to understand either nineteenth-century sexuality or the nineteenth-century family.

Several factors in American society between the mid-eighteenth and the mid-nineteenth centuries may well have permitted women to form a variety of close emotional relationships with other women. American society was characterized in large part by rigid gender-role differentiation within the family and within society as a whole, leading to the emotional segregation of women and men. The roles of daughter and mother shaded imperceptibly and ineluctably into each other, while the biological realities of frequent pregnancies, childbirth, nursing, and menopause bound women together in physical and emotional intimacy. It was within just such a social framework, I would argue, that a specifically female world did indeed develop, a world built around a generic and unself-conscious pattern of single-sex or homosocial networks. These supportive networks were institutionalized in social conventions or rituals which accompanied virtually every important event in a woman's life, from birth to death. Such female relationships were frequently supported and paralleled by severe social restrictions on intimacy between young men and women. Within such a world of emotional richness and complexity devotion to and love of other women became a plausible and socially accepted form of human interaction.

An abundance of printed and manuscript sources exists to support such a hypothesis. Etiquette books, advice books on child rearing, religious sermons, guides to young men and young women, medical texts, and school curricula all suggest that late eighteenth- and most nineteenth-century Americans assumed the existence of a world composed of distinctly male and female spheres, spheres determined by the immutable laws of God and nature.[17] The unpublished letters and diaries of Americans during this same period concur, detailing the existence of sexually segregated worlds inhabited by human beings with different values, expectations, and personalities. Contacts between men and women frequently partook of a formality and stiffness quite alien to twentieth-century America and which today we tend to define as "Victorian." Women, however, did not form an isolated and oppressed subcategory in male society. Their letters and diaries indicate that women's sphere had an essential integrity and dignity that grew out of women's shared experiences and mutual affection and that, despite the profound changes which affected American social structure and institutions between the 1760s and the 1870s, retained a constancy and predictability. The ways in which women thought of and interacted with each other remained unchanged. Continuity, not discontinuity, characterized this female world. Molly Hallock's and Jeannie Fields's words, emotions, and experiences have direct parallels in the 1760s and the 1790s.[18] There are indications in contemporary sociological and psychological literature that female closeness and support networks have continued into the twentieth century—not only among ethnic and working-class groups but even among the middle class.[19]

Most eighteenth- and nineteenth-century women lived within a world bounded by home, church, and the institution of visiting—that endless trooping of women to each others' homes for social purposes. It was a world inhabited by children and by other women.[20] Women helped each other with domestic chores and in times of sickness, sorrow, or trouble. Entire days, even weeks, might be spent almost exclusively with other women.[21] Urban and town women could devote virtually every day to visits, teas, or shopping trips with other women. Rural women developed a pattern of more extended visits that lasted weeks and sometimes months, at times even dislodging husbands from their beds and bedrooms so that dear friends might spend every hour of every day together.[22] When husbands traveled, wives routinely moved in with other women, invited women friends to teas and suppers, sat together sharing and comparing the letters they had received from other close women friends. Secrets were exchanged and cherished, and the husband's return at times viewed with some ambivalence.[23]

Summer vacations were frequently organized to permit old friends to meet at water spas or share a country home. In 1848, for example, a young matron wrote cheerfully to her husband about the delightful time she was having with five close women friends whom she had invited to spend the summer with her; he remained at home alone to face the heat of Philadelphia and a cholera epidemic.[24] Some ninety years earlier, two young Quaker girls commented upon the vacation their aunt had taken alone with another woman; their remarks were openly envious and tell us something of the emotional quality of these friendships: "I hear Aunt is gone with the Friend and wont be back for two weeks, fine times indeed I think the old friends had, taking their pleasure about the country . . . and have the advantage of that fine woman's conversation and instruction, while we poor young girls must spend all spring at home. . . . What a disappointment that we are not together. . . ."[25]

Friends did not form isolated dyads but were normally part of highly integrated networks. Knowing each other, perhaps related to each other, they played a central role in holding communities and kin systems together. Especially when families became geographically mobile women's long visits to each other and their frequent letters filled with discussions of marriages and births, illness and deaths, descriptions of growing children, and reminiscences of times and people past provided an important sense of continuity in a rapidly changing society.[26] Central to this female world was an inner core of kin. The ties between sisters, first cousins, aunts, and nieces provided the underlying structure upon which groups of friends and their network of female relatives clustered. Although most of the women within this sample would appear to be living within isolated nuclear families, the emotional ties between nonresidential kin were deep and binding and provided one of the fundamental existential realities of women's lives.[27] Twenty years after Parke Lewis Butler moved with her husband to Louisiana, she sent her two daughters back to Virginia to attend school, live with their grandmother and aunt, and be integrated back into Virginia society.[28] The constant letters between Maria Inskeep and Fanny Hampton, sisters separated in their early twenties when Maria moved with her husband from

New Jersey to Louisiana, held their families together, making it possible for their daughters to feel a part of their cousins' network of friends and interests.[29] The Ripley daughters, growing up in western Massachusetts in the early 1800s, spent months each year with their mother's sister and her family in distant Boston; these female cousins and their network of friends exchanged gossip-filled letters and gradually formed deeply loving and dependent ties.[30]

Women frequently spent their days within the social confines of such extended families. Sisters-in-law visited each other and, in some families, seemed to spend more time with each other than with their husbands. First cousins cared for each others' babies—for weeks or even months in times of sickness or childbirth. Sisters helped each other with housework, shopped and sewed for each other. Geographic separation was borne with difficulty. A sister's absence for even a week or two could cause loneliness and depression and would be bridged by frequent letters. Sibling rivalry was hardly unknown, but with separation or illness the theme of deep affection and dependency reemerged.[31]

Sisterly bonds continued across a lifetime. In her old age a rural Quaker matron, Martha Jefferis, wrote to her daughter Anne concerning her own half-sister, Phoebe: "In sister Phoebe I have a real friend—she studies my comfort and waits on me like a child. . . . She is exceedingly kind and this to all other homes (set aside yours) I would prefer—it is next to being with a daughter." Phoebe's own letters confirmed Martha's evaluation of her feelings. "Thou knowest my dear sister," Phoebe wrote, "there is no one . . . that exactly feels [for] thee as I do, for I think without boasting I can truly say that my desire is for thee."[32]

Such women, whether friends or relatives, assumed an emotional centrality in each others' lives. In their diaries and letters they wrote of the joy and contentment they felt in each others' company, their sense of isolation and despair when apart. The regularity of their correspondence underlines the sincerity of their words. Women named their daughters after one another and sought to integrate dear friends into their lives after marriage.[33] As one young bride wrote to an old friend shortly after her marriage: "I want to see you and talk with you and feel that we are united by the same bonds of sympathy and congeniality as ever."[34] After years of friendship one aging woman wrote of another: "Time cannot destroy the fascination of her manner . . . her voice is music to the ear. . . ."[35] Women made elaborate presents for each other, ranging from the Quakers' frugal pies and breads to painted velvet bags and phantom bouquets.[36] When a friend died, their grief was deeply felt. Martha Jefferis was unable to write to her daughter for three weeks because of the sorrow she felt at the death of a dear friend. Such distress was not unusual. A generation earlier a young Massachusetts farm woman filled pages of her diary with her grief at the death of her "dearest friend" and transcribed the letters of condolence other women sent her. She marked the anniversary of Rachel's death each year in her diary, contrasting her faithfulness with that of Rachel's husband who had soon remarried.[37]

These female friendships served a number of emotional functions. Within this secure and empathetic world women could share sorrows, anxieties, and joys, confident that other women had experienced similar emotions. One mid-nineteenth-century rural matron in a letter to her daughter discussed this particular aspect of women's friendships: "To have such a friend as thyself to look to and sympathize with her—and enter into all her little needs and in whose bosom she could with freedom pour forth her joys and sorrows—such a friend would very much relieve the tedium of many a wearisome hour. . . ." A generation later Molly more informally underscored the importance of this same function in a letter to Helena: "Suppose I come down . . . [and] spend Sunday with you quietly," she wrote Helena ". . . that means talking all the time until you are relieved of all your latest troubles, and I of mine. . . ."[38] These were frequently troubles that apparently no man could understand. When Anne Jefferis Sheppard was first married, she and her older sister Edith (who then lived with Anne) wrote in detail to their mother of the severe depression and anxiety which they experienced. Moses Sheppard, Anne's husband, added cheerful postscripts to the sisters' letters—which he had clearly not read—remarking on Anne's and Edith's contentment. Theirs was an emotional world to which he had little access.[39]

This was, as well, a female world in which hostility and criticism of other women were discouraged, and thus a milieu in which women could develop a sense of inner security and self-esteem. As one young woman wrote to her mother's longtime friend: "I cannot sufficiently thank you for the kind unvaried affection & indulgence you have ever shown and expressed both by words and actions for me. . . . Happy would it be did all the world view me as you do, through the medium of kindness and forbearance."[40] They valued each other. Women, who had little status or power in the larger world of male concerns, possessed status and power in the lives and worlds of other women.[41]

An intimate mother-daughter relationship lay at the heart of this female world. The diaries and letters of both mothers and daughters attest to their closeness and mutual emotional dependency. Daughters routinely discussed their mother's health and activities with their own friends, expressed anxiety in cases of their mother's ill health and concern for her cares.[42] Expressions of hostility which we would today consider routine on the part of both mothers and daughters seem to have been uncommon indeed. On the contrary, this sample of families indicates that the normal relationship between mother and daughter was one of sympathy and understanding.[43] Only sickness or great geographic distance was allowed to cause extended separation. When marriage did result in such separation, both viewed the distance between them with distress.[44] Something of this sympathy and love between mothers and daughters is evident in a letter Sarah Alden Ripley, at age sixty-nine, wrote her youngest and recently married daughter: "You do not know how much I miss you, not only when I struggle in and out of my mortal envelop and pump my nightly potation and no longer pour into your sympathizing ear my senile gossip, but all the day I muse away, since the sound of your voice no longer rouses me to sympathy with your joys or sorrows. . . . You cannot know how much I miss your affectionate demonstrations."[45] A dozen aging mothers in this sample of over thirty families echoed her sentiments.

Central to these mother-daughter relations is what might be described as an apprenticeship system. In those families where the daughter followed the mother into a life of traditional domesticity, mothers and other older women carefully trained daughters in the arts of housewifery and motherhood. Such training undoubtedly occurred throughout a girl's childhood but became more systematized, almost ritualistic, in the years following the end of her formal education and before her marriage. At this time a girl either returned home from boarding school or no longer divided her time between home and school. Rather, she devoted her energies on two tasks: mastering new domestic skills and participating in the visiting and social activities necessary to finding a husband. Under the careful supervision of their mothers and of older female relatives, such late-adolescent girls temporarily took over the household management from their mothers, tended their young nieces and nephews, and helped in childbirth, nursing, and weaning. Such experiences tied the generations together in shared skills and emotional interaction.[46]

Daughters were born into a female world. Their mother's life expectations and sympathetic network of friends and relations were among the first realities in the life of the developing child. As long as the mother's domestic role remained relatively stable and few viable alternatives competed with it, daughters tended to accept their mother's world and to turn automatically to other women for support and intimacy. It was within this closed and intimate female world that the young girl grew toward womanhood.

One could speculate at length concerning the absence of that mother-daughter hostility today considered almost inevitable to an adolescent's struggle for autonomy and self-identity. It is possible that taboos against female aggression and hostility were sufficiently strong to repress even that between mothers and their adolescent daughters. Yet these letters seem so alive and the interest of daughters in their mothers' affairs so vital and genuine that it is difficult to interpret their closeness exclusively in terms of repression and denial. The functional bonds that held mothers and daughters together in a world that permitted few alternatives to domesticity might well have created a source of mutuality and trust absent in societies where greater options were available for daughters than for mothers. Furthermore, the extended female network—a daughter's close ties with her own older sisters, cousins, and aunts—may well have permitted a diffusion and a relaxation of mother-daughter identification and so have aided a daughter in her struggle for identity and autonomy. None of these explanations are mutually exclusive; all may well have interacted to produce the degree of empathy evident in those letters and diaries.

At some point in adolescence, the young girl began to move outside the matrix of her mother's support group to develop a network of her own. Among the middle class, at least, this transition toward what was at the same time both a limited autonomy and a repetition of her mother's life seemed to have most frequently coincided with a girl's going to school. Indeed education appears to have played a crucial role in the lives of most of the families in this study. Attending school for a few months, for a year, or longer, was common even among daughters of relatively poor families, while middle-class girls routinely spent at least a year in boarding school.[47] These school years ordinarily marked a girl's first separation from home. They served to wean the daughter from her home, to train her in the essential social graces, and, ultimately, to help introduce her into the marriage market. It was not infrequently a trying emotional experience for both mother and daughter.[48]

In this process of leaving one home and adjusting to another, the mother's friends and relatives played a key transitional role. Such older women routinely accepted the role of foster mother; they supervised the young girl's deportment, monitored her health and introduced her to their own network of female friends and kin.[49] Not infrequently women, friends from their own school years, arranged to send their daughters to the same school so that the girls might form bonds paralleling those their mothers had made. For years Molly and Helena wrote of their daughters' meeting and worried over each others' children. When Molly finally brought her daughter east to school, their first act on reaching New York was to meet Helena and her daughters. Elizabeth Bordley Gibson virtually adopted the daughters of her school chum, Eleanor Custis Lewis. The Lewis daughters soon began to write Elizabeth Gibson letters with the salutation "Dearest Mama." Eleuthera DuPont, attending boarding school in Philadelphia at roughly the same time as the Lewis girls, developed a parallel relationship with her mother's friend, Elizabeth McKie Smith. Eleuthera went to the same school and became a close friend of the Smith girls and eventually married their first cousin. During this period she routinely called Mrs. Smith "Mother." Indeed Eleuthera so internalized the sense of having two mothers that she casually wrote her sisters of her "Mamma's" visits at her "mother's" house—that is at Mrs. Smith's.[50]

Even more important to this process of maturation than their mother's friends were the female friends young women made at school. Young girls helped each other overcome homesickness and endure the crises of adolescence. They gossiped about beaux, incorporated each other into their own kinship systems, and attended and gave teas and balls together. Older girls in boarding school "adopted" younger ones, who called them "Mother."[51] Dear friends might indeed continue this pattern of adoption and mothering throughout their lives; one woman might routinely assume the nurturing role of pseudomother, the other the dependency role of daughter. The pseudomother performed for the other woman all the services which we normally associate with mothers; she went to absurd lengths to purchase items her "daughter" could have obtained from other sources, gave advice and functioned as an idealized figure in her "daughter's" imagination. Helena played such a role for Molly, as did Sarah for Jeannie. Elizabeth Bordley Gibson bought almost all Eleanor Parke Custis Lewis's necessities—from shoes and corset covers to bedding and harp strings—and sent them from Philadephia to Virginia, a procedure that sometimes took months. Eleanor frequently asked Elizabeth to take back her purchases, have them redone, and argue with shopkeepers about prices. These were favors automatically asked and complied with. Anne Jefferis Sheppard made the analogy very explicitly in a letter to her own mother written shortly after Anne's marriage, when she was feeling depressed about their separation: "Mary Paulen is truly kind, almost acts the part of a mother and trys to aid and *comfort me*, and also to *lighten my new cares*."[52]

A comparison of the references to men and women in these young women's letters is striking. Boys were obviously indispensable to the elaborate courtship ritual girls engaged in. In these teenage letters and diaries, however, boys appear distant and warded off —an effect produced both by the girls' sense of bonding and by a highly developed and deprecatory whimsy. Girls joked among themselves about the conceit, poor looks or affectations of suitors. Rarely, especially in the eighteenth and early nineteenth centuries, were favorable remarks exchanged. Indeed, while hostility and criticism of other women were so rare as to seem almost tabooed, young women permitted themselves to express a great deal of hostility toward peer-group men.[53] When unacceptable suitors appeared, girls might even band together to harass them. When one such unfortunate came to court Sophie DuPont she hid in her room, first sending her sister Eleuthera to entertain him and then dispatching a number of urgent notes to her neighboring sister-in-law, cousins, and a visiting friend who all came to Sophie's support. A wild female romp ensued, ending only when Sophie banged into a door, lacerated her nose, and retired, with her female cohorts, to bed. Her brother and the presumably disconcerted suitor were left alone. These were not the antics of teenagers but of women in their early and mid-twenties.[54]

Even if young men were acceptable suitors, girls referred to them formally and obliquely: "The last week I received the unexpected intelligence of the arrival of a friend in Boston," Sarah Ripley wrote in her diary of the young man to whom she had been engaged for years and whom she would shortly marry. Harriet Manigault assiduously kept a lively and gossipy diary during the three years preceding her marriage, yet did not once comment upon her own engagement nor indeed make any personal references to her fiancé—who was never identified as such but always referred to as Mr. Wilcox.[55] The point is not that these young women were hostile to young men. Far from it; they sought marriage and domesticity. Yet in these letters and diaries men appear as an other or out group, segregated into different schools, supported by their own male network of friends and kin, socialized to different behavior, and coached to a proper formality in courtship behavior. As a consequence, relations between young women and men frequently lacked the spontaneity and emotional intimacy that characterized the young girls' ties to each other.

Indeed, in sharp contrast to their distant relations with boys, young women's relations with each other were close, often frolicsome, and surprisingly long lasting and devoted. They wrote secret missives to each other, spent long solitary days with each other, curled up together in bed at night to whisper fantasies and secrets.[56] In 1862 one young woman in her early twenties described one such scene to an absent friend: "I have sat up to midnight listening to the confidences of Constance Kinney, whose heart was opened by that most charming of all situations, a seat on a bedside late at night, when all the household are asleep & only oneself & one's confidante survive in wakefulness. So she has told me all her loves and tried to get some confidences in return but being five or six years older than she, I know better. . . ."[57] Elizabeth Bordley and Nelly Parke Custis, teenagers in Philadelphia in the 1790s, routinely secreted themselves until late each night in Nelly's attic, where they each wrote a novel about the other.[58] Quite a few young women kept diaries, and it was a sign of special friendship to show their diaries to each other. The emotional quality of such exchanges emerges from the comments of one young girl who grew up along the Ohio frontier:

> Sisters CW and RT keep diaries & allow me the inestimable pleasure of reading them and in turn they see mine—but O shame covers my face when I think of it; theirs is so much better than mine, that every time. Then I think well now I *will* burn mine but upon second thought it would deprive me the pleasure of reading theirs, for I esteem it a very great privilege indeed, as well as very improving, as we lay our hearts open to each other, it heightens our love & helps to cherish & keep alive that sweet soothing friendship and endears us to each other by that soft attraction.[59]

Girls routinely slept together, kissed and hugged each other. Indeed, while waltzing with young men scandalized the otherwise flighty and highly fashionable Harriet Manigault, she considered waltzing with other young women not only acceptable but pleasant.[60]

Marriage followed adolescence. With increasing frequency in the nineteenth century, marriage involved a girl's traumatic removal from her mother and her mother's network. It involved, as well, adjustment to a husband, who, because he was male came to marriage with both a different world view and vastly different experiences. Not surprisingly, marriage was an event surrounded with supportive, almost ritualistic, practices. (Weddings are one of the last female rituals remaining in twentieth-century America.) Young women routinely spent the months preceding their marriage almost exclusively with other women—at neighborhood sewing bees and quilting parties or in a round of visits to geographically distant friends and relatives. Ostensibly they went to receive assistance in the practical preparations for their new home—sewing and quilting a trousseau and linen—but of equal importance, they appear to have gained emotional support and reassurance. Sarah Ripley spent over a month with friends and relatives in Boston and Hingham before her wedding; Nelly Custis Lewis exchanged visits with her aunts and first cousins throughout Virginia.[61] Anne Jefferis, who married with some hesitation, spent virtually half a year in endless visiting with cousins, aunts, and friends. Despite their reassurance and support, however, she would not marry Moses Sheppard until her sister Edith and her cousin Rebecca moved into the groom's home, met his friends, and explored his personality.[62] The wedding did not take place until Edith wrote to Anne: "I can say in truth I am entirely willing thou shouldst follow him even away in the Jersey sands believing if thou are not happy in thy future home it will not be any fault on his part. . . ."[63]

Sisters, cousins, and friends frequently accompanied newlyweds on their wedding night and wedding trip, which often involved additional family visiting. Such extensive visits presumably served to wean the daughter from her family of origin. As such they often contained a note of ambivalence. Nelly Custis, for example, reported homesickness and loneliness on her wedding trip. "I left my Beloved and revered Grandmamma with sincere regret," she wrote Elizabeth Bordley. "It was sometime before I could feel reconciled to traveling without her." Perhaps they also functioned to reassure the young woman herself, and her friends and kin, that though marriage might alter it would not destroy old bonds of intimacy and familiarity.[64]

Married life, too, was structured about a host of female rituals. Childbirth, especially the birth of the first child, became virtually a *rite de passage*, with a lengthy seclusion of the woman before and after delivery, severe restrictions on her activities, and finally a dramatic reemergence.[65] This seclusion was supervised by mothers, sisters, and loving friends. Nursing and weaning involved the advice and assistance of female friends and relatives. So did miscarriage.[66] Death, like birth, was structured around elaborate unisexed rituals. When Nelly Parke Custis Lewis rushed to nurse her daughter who was critically ill while away at school, Nelly received support, not from her husband, who remained on their plantation, but from her old school friend, Elizabeth Bordley. Elizabeth aided Nelly in caring for her dying daughter, cared for Nelly's other children, played a major role in the elaborate funeral arrangements (which the father did not attend), and frequently visited the girl's grave at the mother's request. For years Elizabeth continued to be the confidante of Nelly's anguished recollections of her lost daughter. These memories, Nelly's letters make clear, were for Elizabeth alone, "Mr. L knows nothing of this," was a frequent comment.[67] Virtually every collection of letters and diaries in my sample contained evidence of women turning to each other for comfort when facing the frequent and unavoidable deaths of the eighteenth and nineteenth centuries.[68] While mourning for her father's death, Sophie DuPont received elaborate letters and visits of condolence—all from women. No man wrote or visited Sophie to offer sympathy at her father's death.[69] Among rural Pennsylvania Quakers, death and mourning rituals assumed an even more extreme same-sex form, with men or women largely barred from the deathbeds of the other sex. Women relatives and friends slept with the dying woman, nursed her, and prepared her body for burial.[70]

Eighteenth- and nineteenth-century women thus lived in emotional proximity to each other. Friendships and intimacies followed the biological ebb and flow of women's lives. Marriage and pregnancy, childbirth and weaning, sickness and death involved physical and psychic trauma which comfort and sympathy made easier to bear. Intense bonds of love and intimacy bound together those women who, offering each other aid and sympathy, shared such stressful moments.

These bonds were often physical as well as emotional. An undeniably romantic and even sensual note frequently marked female relationships. This theme, significant throughout the stages of a woman's life, surfaced first during adolescence. As one teenager from a struggling pioneer family in the Ohio Valley wrote in her diary in 1808: "I laid with my dear R[ebecca] and a glorious good talk we had until about 4 [A.M.]—O how hard I do *love* her. . . ."[71] Only a few years later Bostonian Eunice Callender carved her initials and Sarah Ripley's into a favorite tree, along with a pledge of eternal love, and then waited breathlessly for Sarah to discover and respond to her declaration of affection. The response appears to have been affirmative.[72] A half-century later urbane and sophisticated Katherine Wharton commented upon meeting an old school chum: "She was a great pet of mine at school & I thought as I watched her light figure how often I had held her in my arms—how dear she had once been to me." Katie maintained a long intimate friendship with another girl. When a young man began to court this friend seriously, Katie commented in her diary that she had never realized "how deeply I loved Eng and how fully." She wrote over and over again in that entry: "Indeed I love her!" and only with great reluctance left the city that summer since it meant also leaving Eng with Eng's new suitor.[73]

Peggy Emlen, a Quaker adolescent in Philadelphia in the 1760s, expressed similar feelings about her first cousin, Sally Logan. The girls sent love poems to each other (not unlike the ones Elizabeth Bordley wrote to Nellie Custis a generation later), took long solitary walks together, and even haunted the empty house of the other when one was out of town. Indeed Sally's absences from Philadelphia caused Peggy acute unhappiness. So strong were Peggy's feelings that her brothers began to tease her about her affection for Sally and threatened to steal Sally's letters, much to both girls' alarm. In one letter that Peggy wrote the absent Sally she elaborately described the depth and nature of her feelings: "I have not words to express my impatience to see My Dear Cousin, what would I not give just now for an hours sweet conversation with her, it seems as if I had a thousand things to say to thee, yet when I see thee, everything will be forgot thro' joy. . . . I have a very great friendship for several Girls yet it dont give me so much uneasiness at being absent from them as from thee. . . . [Let us] go and spend a day down at our place together and there unmolested enjoy each others company."[74]

Sarah Alden Ripley, a young, highly educated woman, formed a similar intense relationship, in this instance with a woman somewhat older than herself. The immediate bond of friendship rested on their atypically intense scholarly interests, but it soon involved strong emotions, at least on Sarah's part. "Friendship," she wrote Mary Emerson, "is fast twining about her willing captive the silken hands of dependence, a dependence so sweet who would renounce it for the apathy of self-sufficiency?" Subsequent letters became far more emotional, almost conspiratorial. Mary visited Sarah secretly in her room, or the two women crept away from family and friends to meet in a nearby woods. Sarah became jealous of Mary's other young woman friends. Mary's trips away from Boston also thrust Sarah into periods of anguished depression. Interestingly, the letters detailing their love were not destroyed but were preserved and even reprinted in a eulogistic biography of Sarah Alden Ripley.[75]

Tender letters between adolescent women, confessions of loneliness and emotional dependency, were not peculiar to Sarah Alden, Peggy Emlen, or Katie Wharton. They are found throughout the letters of the thirty-five families studied. They have, of course, their parallel today in the musings of many female adolescents. Yet these eighteenth- and nineteenth-century friendships lasted with undiminished, indeed often increased, intensity throughout the women's lives. Sarah Alden Ripley's first child was named after Mary Emerson. Nelly Custis Lewis's love for and dependence on Elizabeth Bordley Gibson only increased after her marriage. Eunice Callender remained enamored of her cousin Sarah Ripley for years and rejected as impossible the suggestion by another woman that their love might some day fade away.[76] Sophie DuPont and her childhood friend, Clementina Smith, exchanged letters filled with love and dependency for forty years while another dear friend, Mary Black Couper, wrote of dreaming that she, Sophie, and her husband were all united in one marriage. Mary's letters to Sophie are filled with avowals of love and indications of ambivalence toward her own husband. Eliza Schlatter, another of Sophie's intimate friends, wrote to her at a time of crisis: "I wish I could be with you present in the body as well as the mind & heart—I would turn your *good husband out of bed*—and snuggle into you and we would have a long talk like old times in Pine St.—I want to tell you so many things that are not *writable*. . . ."[77]

Such mutual dependency and deep affection is a central existential reality coloring the world of supportive networks and rituals. In the case of Katie, Sophie, or Eunice—as with Molly, Jeannie, and Sarah—their need for closeness and support merged with more intense demands for a love which was at the same time both emotional and sensual. Perhaps the most explicit statement concerning women's lifelong friendships appeared in the letter abolitionist and reformer Mary Grew wrote about the same time, referring to her own love for her dear friend and lifelong companion, Margaret Burleigh. Grew wrote, in response to a letter of condolence from another woman on Burleigh's death: "Your words respecting my beloved friend touch me deeply. Evidently . . . you comprehend and appreciate, as few persons do . . . the nature of the relation which existed, which exists, between her and myself. Her only surviving niece . . . also does. To me it seems to have been a closer union than that of most marriages. We know there have been other such between two men and also between two women. And why should there not be. Love is spiritual, only passion is sexual."[78]

How then can we ultimately interpret these long-lived intimate female relationships and integrate them into our understanding of Victorian sexuality? Their ambivalent and romantic rhetoric presents us with an ultimate puzzle: the relationship along the spectrum of human emotions between love, sensuality, and sexuality.

One is tempted, as I have remarked, to compare Molly, Peggy, or Sophie's relationships with the friendships adolescent girls in the twentieth century routinely form—close friendships of great emotional intensity. Helene Deutsch and Clara Thompson have both described these friendships as emotionally necessary to a girl's psychosexual development. But, they warn, such friendships might shade into adolescent and postadolescent homosexuality.[79]

It is possible to speculate that in the twentieth century a number of cultural taboos evolved to cut short the homosocial ties of girlhood and to impel the emerging women of thirteen or fourteen toward heterosexual relationships. In contrast, nineteenth-century American society did not taboo close female relationships but rather recognized them as a socially viable form of human contact—and, as such, acceptable throughout a woman's life. Indeed it was not these homosocial ties that were inhibited but rather heterosexual leanings. While closeness, freedom of emotional expression, and uninhibited physical contact characterized women's relationships with each other, the opposite was frequently true of male-female relationships. One could thus argue that within such a world of female support, intimacy, and ritual it was only to be expected that adult women would turn trustingly and lovingly to each other. It was a behavior they had observed and learned since childhood. A different type of emotional landscape existed in the nineteenth century, one in which Molly and Helena's love became a natural development.

Of perhaps equal significance are the implications we can garner from this framework for the understanding of heterosexual marriages in the nineteenth century. If men and women grew up as they did in relatively homogeneous and segregated sexual groups, then marriage represented a major problem in adjustment. From this perspective we could interpret much of the emotional stiffness and distance that we associate with Victorian marriage as a structural consequence of contemporary sex-role differentiation and gender-role socialization. With marriage, both women and men had to adjust to life with a person who was, in essence, a member of an alien group.

I have thus far substituted a cultural or psychosocial for a psychosexual interpretation of women's emotional bonding. But there are psychosexual implications in this model which I think it only fair to make more explicit. Despite Sigmund Freud's insistence on the bisexuality of us all or the recent American Psychiatric Association decision on homosexuality, many psychiatrists today tend explicitly or implicitly to view homosexuality as a totally alien or pathological behavior—as totally unlike heterosexuality. I suspect that in essence they may have adopted an explanatory model similar to the one used in discussing schizophrenia. As a psychiatrist can speak of schizophrenia and of a borderline schizophrenic personality as both ultimately and fundamentally different from a normal or neurotic personality, so they also think of both homosexuality and latent homosexuality as states totally different from heterosexuality. With this rapidly dichotomous model of assumption, "latent homosexuality" becomes the indication of a disease in progress—seeds of a pathology which belie the reality of an individual's heterosexuality.

Yet at the same time we are well aware that cultural values can effect choices in the gender of a person's sexual partner. We, for instance, do not necessarily consider homosexual-object choice among men in prison, on shipboard or in boarding schools a necessary indication of pathology. I would urge that we expand this relativistic model and hypothesize that a number of cultures might well tolerate or even encourage diversity in sexual and nonsexual relations. Based on my research into this nineteenth-century world of female intimacy, I would further suggest that rather than seeing a gulf between the normal and the abnormal we view sexual and emotional impulses as part of a continuum or spectrum of affect gradations strongly effected by cultural norms and arrangements, a continuum influenced in part by observed and thus learned behavior. At one end of the continuum lies committed heterosexuality, at the other uncompromising homosexuality; between, a wide latitude of emotions and sexual feelings. Certain cultures and environments permit individuals a great deal of freedom in moving across this spectrum. I would like to suggest that the nineteenth century was such a cultural environment. That is, the supposedly repressive and destructive Victorian sexual ethos, may have been more flexible and responsive to the needs of particular individuals than those of mid-twentieth century.

NOTES

Research for this paper was supported in part by a grant from the Grant Foundation, New York, and by National Institutes of Health trainee grant 5 FO3 HD48800-03. I would like to thank several scholars for their assistance and criticism in preparing this paper: Erving Goffman, Roy Schafer, Charles E. Rosenberg, Cynthia Secor, Anthony Wallace. Judy Breault, who has just completed a biography of an important and introspective nineteenth-century feminist, Emily Howland, served as a research assistant for this paper and her knowledge of nineteenth-century family structure and religious history proved invaluable.

1. The most notable exception to this rule is now eleven years old: William R. Taylor and Christopher Lasch, "Two 'Kindred Spirits': Sorority and Family in New England, 1839–1846," *New England Quarterly* 36 (1963): 25–41. Taylor has made a valuable contribution to the history of women and the history of the family with his concept of "sororial" relations. I do not, however, accept the Taylor-Lasch thesis that female friendships developed in the mid-nineteenth century because of geographic mobility and the breakup of the colonial family. I have found these friendships as frequently in the eighteenth century as in the nineteenth and would hypothesize that the geographic mobility of the mid-nineteenth century eroded them as it did so many other traditional social institutions. Helen Vendler (*Review of Notable American Women, 1607–1950*, ed. Edward James and Janet James, *New York Times*) [November 5, 1972]: sec. 7) points out the significance of these friendships.

2. I do not wish to deny the importance of women's relations with particular men. Obviously, women were close to brothers, husbands, fathers, and sons. However, there is evidence that despite such closeness relationships between men and women differed in both emotional texture and frequency from those between women. Women's relations with each other, although they played a central role in the American family and American society, have been so seldom examined either by general social historians or by historians of the family that I wish in this article simply to examine their nature and analyze their implications for our understanding of social relations and social structure. I have discussed some aspects of male-female relationships in two articles: "Puberty to Menopause: The Cycle of Femininity in Nineteenth-Century America," *Feminist Studies* 1 (1973): 58–72, and, with Charles Rosenberg, "The Female Animal: Medical and Biological Views of Women in 19th Century America," *Journal of American History* 59 (1973): 331–56.

3. See Freud's classic paper on homosexuality, "Three Essays on the Theory of Sexuality," in *The Standard Edition of the Complete Psychological Works of Sigmund Freud*, trans. James Strachey (London: Hogarth Press, 1953), 7:135–72. The essays originally appeared in 1905. Prof. Roy Shafer, Department of Psychiatry, Yale University, has pointed out that Freud's view of sexual behavior was strongly influenced by nineteenth-century evolutionary thought. Within Freud's schema, genital heterosexuality marked the height of human development (Schafer, "Problems in Freud's Psychology of Women," *Journal of the American Psychoanalytic Association* 22 [1974]: 459–85).

4. For a novel and most important exposition of one theory of behavioral norms and options and its application to the study of human sexuality, see Charles Rosenberg, "Sexuality, Class and Role," *American Quarterly* 25 (1973): 131–53.

5. See, e.g., the letters of Peggy Emlen to Sally Logan, 1768–72, Wells Morris Collection, Box 1, Historical Society of Pennsylvania; and the Eleanor Parke Custis Lewis Letters, Historical Society of Pennsylvania, Philadelphia.

6. Sarah Butler Wister was the daughter of Fanny Kemble and Pierce Butler. In 1859 she married a Philadelphia physician, Owen Wister. The novelist Owen Wister is her son. Jeannie Field Musgrove was the half-orphaned daughter of constitutional lawyer and New York Republican politician David Dudley Field. Their correspondence (1855–98) is in the Sarah Butler Wister Papers, Wister Family Papers, Historical Society of Pennsylvania.

7. Sarah Butler, Butler Place, S.C., to Jeannie Field. New York, September 14, 1855.

8. See, e.g., Sarah Butler Wister, Germantown, Pa., to Jeannie Field, New York, September 25, 1862, October 21, 1863; or Jeannie Field, New York, to Sarah Butler Wister, Germantown, July 3, 1861, January 23 and July 12, 1863.

9. Sarah Butler Wister, Germantown, to Jeannie Field, New York, June 5, 1861, February 29, 1864; Jeannie Field to Sarah Butler Wister November 22, 1861, January 4 and June 14, 1863.

10. Sarah Butler Wister, London, to Jeannie Field Musgrove, New York, June 18 and August 3, 1870.

11. See, e.g., two of Sarah's letters to Jeannie: December 21, 1873, July 16, 1878.

12. This is the 1868–1920 correspondence between Mary Hallock Foote

and Helena, a New York friend (the Mary Hallock Foote Papers are in the Manuscript Division, Stanford University). Wallace E. Stegner has written a fictionalized biography of Mary Hallock Foote (*Angle of Repose* [Garden City, N.Y.: Doubleday & Co., 1971]). See, as well, her autobiography: Mary Hallock Foote, *A Victorian Gentlewoman in the Far West: The Reminiscences of Mary Hallock Foote*, ed. Rodman W. Paul (San Marino, Calif.: Huntington Library, 1972). In many ways these letters are typical of those women wrote to other women. Women frequently began letters to each other with salutations such as "Dearest," "My Most Beloved," "You Darling Girl," and signed them "tenderly" or "to my dear dear sweet friend, good-bye." Without the least self-consciousness, one woman in her frequent letters to a female friend referred to her husband as "my other love." She was by no means unique. See, e.g., Annie to Charlene Van Vleck Anderson, Appleton, Wis., June 10, 1871, Anderson Family Papers, Manuscript Division, Stanford University; Maggie to Emily Howland, Philadelphia, July 12, 1851. Howland Family Papers, Phoebe King Collection, Friends Historical Library, Swarthmore College; Mary Jane Burleigh to Emily Howland, Sherwood, N.Y., March 27, 1872, Howland Family Papers, Sophia Smith Collection, Smith College; Mary Black Couper to Sophia Madeleine DuPont, Wilmington, Del.: n.d. [1834] (two letters), Samuel Francis DuPont Papers, Eleutherian Mills Foundation, Wilmington, Del.; Phoebe Middleton, Concordiville, Pa., to Martha Jefferis, Chester County, Pa., February 22, 1848; and see in general the correspondence (1838–49) between Rebecca Biddle of Philadelphia and Martha Jefferis, Chester County, Pa., Jefferis Family Correspondence, Chester County Historical Society, West Chester, Pa.; Phoebe Bradford Diary, June 7 and July 13, 1832, Historical Society of Pennsylvania; Sarah Alden Ripley, to Abba Allyn, Boston, n.d. [1818–20], and Sarah Alden Ripley to Sophia Bradford, November 30, 1854, in the Sarah Alden Ripley Correspondence, Schlesinger Library, Radcliffe College; Fanny Canby Ferris to Anne Biddle, Philadelphia, October 11 and November 19, 1811, December 26, 1813, Fanny Canby to Mary Canby, May 27, 1801, Mary R. Garrigues to Mary Canby, five letters n.d., [1802–8], Anne Biddle to Mary Canby, two letters n.d., May 16, July 13, and November 24, 1806, June 14, 1807, June 5, 1808, Anne Sterling Biddle Family Papers, Friends Historical Society, Swarthmore College; Harriet Manigault Wilcox Diary, August 7, 1814, Historical Society of Pennsylvania. See as well the correspondence between Harriet Manigault Wilcox's mother, Mrs. Gabriel Manigault, Philadelphia, and Mrs. Henry Middleton, Charleston, S.C., between 1810 and 1830, Cadwalader Collection, J. Francis Fisher Section, Historical Society of Pennsylvania. The basis and nature of such friendships can be seen in the comments of Sarah Alden Ripley to her sister-in-law and long-time friend, Sophia Bradford: "Hearing that you are not well reminds me of what it would be to lose your loving society. We have kept step together through a long piece of road in the weary journey of life. We have loved the same beings and wept together over their graves" (Mrs. O. J. Wister and Miss Agnes Irwin, eds., *Worthy Women of Our First Century* [Philadelphia: J. B. Lippincott & Co., 1877] p. 195).

13. Mary Hallock [Foote] to Helena, n.d. [1869–70], n.d. [1871–72], Folder 1, Mary Hallock Foote Letters, Manuscript Division, Stanford University.

14. Mary Hallock [Foote] to Helena, September 15 and 23, 1873, n.d. [October 1873], October 12, 1873.

15. Mary Hallock [Foote] to Helena, n.d. [January 1874], n.d. [Spring 1874].

16. Mary Hallock [Foote] to Helena, September 23, 1873; Mary Hallock [Foote] to Richard, December 13, 1873. Molly's and Helena's relationship continued for the rest of their lives. Molly's letters are filled with tender and intimate references, as when she wrote, twenty years later and from 2,000 miles away: "It isn't because you are good that I love you—but for the essence of you which is like perfume" (n.d. [1890s?]).

17. I am in the midst of a larger study of adult gender-roles and gender-role socialization in America, 1785–1895. For a discussion of social attitudes toward appropriate male and female roles, see Barbara Welter, "The Cult of True Womanhood: 1820–1860," *American Quarterly* 18 (Summer 1966): 151–74; Anne Firor Scott, *The Southern Lady: From Pedestal to Politics, 1830–1930* (Chicago: University of Chicago Press, 1970), chaps. 1–2; Smith-Rosenberg and Rosenberg.

18. See, e.g., the letters of Peggy Emlen to Sally Logan, 1768–72, Wells Morris Collection, Box 1, Historical Society of Pennsylvania; and the Eleanor Parke Custis Lewis Letters, Historical Society of Pennsylvania.

19. See esp. Elizabeth Bott, *Family and Social Network* (London: Tavistock Publications, 1957); Michael Young and Peter Willmott, *Family and Kinship in East London*, rev. ed. (Baltimore: Penguin Books, 1964).

20. This pattern seemed to cross class barriers. A letter that an Irish domestic wrote in the 1830s contains seventeen separate references to women and but only seven to men, most of whom were relatives and two of whom were infant brothers living with her mother and mentioned in relation to her mother (Ann McGrann, Philadelphia, to Sophie M. DuPont, Philadelphia, July 3, 1834, Sophie Madeleine DuPont Letters, Eleutherian Mills Foundation).

21. Harriett Manigault Diary, June 28, 1814, and passim; Jeannie Field, New York, to Sarah Butler Wister, Germantown, April 19, 1863; Phoebe Bradford Diary, January 30, February 19, March 4, August 11, and October 14, 1832, Historical Society of Pennsylvania; Sophie M. DuPont, Brandywine, to Henry DuPont, Germantown, July 9, 1827, Eleutherian Mills Foundation.

22. Martha Jefferis to Anne Jefferis Sheppard, July 9, 1843; Anne Jefferis Sheppard to Martha Jefferis, June 28, 1846; Anne Sterling Biddle Papers, passim, Biddle Family Papers, Friends Historical Society, Swarthmore College; Eleanor Parke Custis Lewis, Virginia, to Elizabeth Bordley Gibson, Philadelphia, November 24 and December 4, 1820, November 6, 1821.

23. Phoebe Bradford Diary, January 13, November 16–19, 1832, April 26 and May 7, 1833; Abigail Brackett Lyman to Mrs. Catling, Litchfield, Conn., May 3, 1801, collection in private hands; Martha Jefferis to Anne Jefferis Sheppard, August 28, 1845.

24. Lisa Mitchell Diary, 1860s, passim, Manuscript Division, Tulane University; Eleanor Parke Custis Lewis to Elizabeth Bordley [Gibson] February 5, 1822; Jeannie McCall, Cedar Park, to Peter McCall, Philadelphia, June 30, 1849, McCall Section, Cadwalader Collection, Historical Society of Pennsylvania.

25. Peggy Emlen to Sally Logan, May 3, 1769.

26. For a prime example of this type of letter, see Eleanor Parke Custis Lewis to Elizabeth Bordley Gibson, passim, or Fanny Canby to Mary Canby,

Philadelphia, May 27, 1801; or Sophie M. DuPont, Brandywine, to Henry DuPont, Germantown, February 4, 1832.

27. Place of residence is not the only variable significant in characterizing family structure. Strong emotional ties and frequent visiting and correspondence can unite families that do not live under one roof. Demographic studies based on household structure alone fail to reflect such emotional and even economic ties between families.

28. Eleanor Parke Custis Lewis to Elizabeth Bordley Gibson, April 20 and September 25, 1848.

29. Maria Inskeep to Fanny Hampton Correspondence, 1823–60, Inskeep Collection, Tulane University Library.

30. Eunice Callender, Boston, to Sarah Ripley [Stearns], September 24 and October 29, 1803, February 16, 1805, April 29 and October 9, 1806, May 26, 1810.

31. Sophie DuPont filled her letters to her younger brother Henry (with whom she had been assigned to correspond while he was at boarding school) with accounts of family visiting (see, e.g., December 13, 1827, January 10 and March 9, 1828, February 4 and March 10, 1832; also Sophie M. DuPont to Victorine DuPont Bauday, September 26 and December 4, 1827, February 22, 1828; Sophie M. DuPont, Brandywine, to Clementina B. Smith, Philadelphia, January 15, 1830; Eleuthera DuPont, Brandywine, to Victorine DuPont Bauday, Philadelphia, April 17, 1821, October 20, 1826; Evelina DuPont [Biderman] to Victorine DuPont Bauday, October 18, 1816). Other examples, from the Historical Society of Pennsylvania, are Harriet Manigault [Wilcox] Diary, August 17, September 8, October 19 and 22, December 22, 1814; Jane Zook, Westtown School, Chester County, Pa., to Mary Zook, November 13, December 7 and 11, 1870, February 26, 1871; Eleanor Parke Custis [Lewis] to Elizabeth Bordley [Gibson], March 30, 1796, February 7 and March 20, 1798; Jeannie McCall to Peter McCall, Philadelphia, November 12, 1847; Mary B. Ashew Diary, July 11 and 13, August 17, Summer and October 1858, and, from a private collection, Edith Jefferis to Anne Jefferis Sheppard, November 1841, April 5, 1842; Abigail Brackett Lyman, Northampton, Mass., to Mrs. Catling, Litchfield, Conn., May 13, 1801; Abigail Brackett Lyman, Northampton, to Mary Lord, August 11, 1800. Mary Hallock Foote vacationed with her sister, her sister's children, her aunt, and a female cousin in the summer of 1874; cousins frequently visited the Hallock farm in Milton, N.Y. In later years Molly and her sister Bessie set up a joint household in Boise, Idaho (Mary Hallock Foote to Helena, July [1874?] and passim). Jeannie Field, after initially disliking her sister-in-law, Laura, became very close to her, calling her "my little sister" and at times spending virtually every day with her (Jeannie Field [Musgrove] New York, to Sarah Butler Wister, Germantown, March 1, 8, and 15, and May 9, 1863).

32. Martha Jefferis to Anne Jefferis Sheppard, January 12, 1845; Phoebe Middleton to Martha Jefferis, February 22, 1848. A number of other women remained close to sisters and sisters-in-law across a long lifetime (Phoebe Bradford Diary, June 7, 1832, and Sarah Alden Ripley to Sophia Bradford, cited in Wister and Irwin, p. 195).

33. Rebecca Biddle to Martha Jefferis, 1838–49, passim; Martha Jefferis to Anne Jefferis Sheppard, July 6, 1846; Anne Jefferis Sheppard to Rachael Jefferis, January 16, 1865; Sarah Foulke Farquhar [Emlen] Diary, September 22, 1813, Friends Historical Library, Swarthmore College; Mary Garrigues to Mary Canby [Biddle], 1802–8, passim; Anne Biddle to Mary Canby [Biddle], May 16, July 13, and November 24, 1806, June 14, 1807, June 5, 1808.

34. Sarah Alden Ripley to Abba Allyn, n.d., Schlesinger Library.

35. Phoebe Bradford Diary, July 13, 1832.

36. Mary Hallock [Foote] to Helena, December 23 [1868 or 1869]: Phoebe Bradford Diary, December 8, 1832; Martha Jefferis and Anne Jefferis Sheppard letters, passim.

37. Martha Jefferis to Anne Jefferis Sheppard, August 3, 1849; Sarah Ripley [Stearns] Diary, November 12, 1808, January 8, 1811. An interesting note of hostility or rivalry is present in Sarah Ripley's diary entry. Sarah evidently deeply resented the husband's rapid remarriage.

38. Martha Jefferis to Edith Jefferis, March 15, 1841; Mary Hallock Foote to Helena, n.d. [1874–75?]; see also Jeannie Field, New York, to Sarah Butler Wister, Germantown, May 5, 1863, Emily Howland Diary, December 1879, Howland Family Papers.

39. Anne Jefferis Sheppard to Martha Jefferis, September 29, 1841.

40. Frances Parke Lewis to Elizabeth Bordley Gibson, April 29, 1821.

41. Mary Jane Burleigh, Mount Pleasant, S.C., to Emily Howland, Sherwood N.Y., March 27, 1872, Howland Family Papers; Emily Howland Diary, September 16, 1879, January 21 and 23, 1880; Mary Black Couper, New Castle, Del., to Sophie M. DuPont, Brandywine, April 7, 1834.

42. Harriet Manigault Diary, August 15, 21, and 23, 1814 Historical Society of Pennsylvania; Polly [Simmons] to Sophie Madeleine DuPont, February 1822; Sophie Madeleine DuPont to Victorine Bauday, December 4, 1827; Sophie Madeleine DuPont to Clementina Beach Smith, July 24, 1828, August 19, 1829; Clementina Beach Smith to Sophie Madeleine DuPont, April 29, 1831; Mary Black Couper to Sophie Madeleine DuPont, December 24, 1828, July 21, 1834. This pattern appears to have crossed class lines. When a former Sunday school student of Sophie DuPont's (and the daughter of a worker in her father's factory) wrote to Sophie she discussed her mother's health and activities quite naturally (Ann McGrann to Sophie Madeleine DuPont, August 25, 1832; see also Elizabeth Bordley to Martha, n.d. [1797], Eleanor Parke Custis [Lewis] to Elizabeth Bordley [Gibson], May 13, 1796, July 1, 1798; Peggy Emlen to Sally Logan, January 8, 1786. All but the Emlen/Logan letters are in the Eleanor Parke Custis Lewis Correspondence, Historical Society of Pennsylvania).

43. Mrs. S. S. Dalton, "Autobiography," (Circle Valley, Utah, 1876), pp. 21–22. Bancroft Library, University of California, Berkeley; Sarah Foulke Emlen Diary, April 1809; Louisa G. Van Vleck, Appleton, Wis., to Charlena Van Vleck Anderson. Göttingen, n.d. [1875], Harriet Manigault Diary, August 16, 1814, July 14, 1815; Sarah Alden Ripley to Sophy Fisher [early 1860s], quoted in Wister and Irwin (n. 12 above), p. 212. The Jefferis family papers are filled with empathetic letters between Martha and her daughters, Anne and Edith. See, e.g., Martha Jefferis to Edith Jefferis, December 26, 1836, March 11, 1837, March 15, 1841; Anne Jefferis Sheppard to Martha Jefferis, March 17, 1841, January 17, 1847; Martha Jefferis to Anne Jefferis Sheppard, April 17, 1848, April 30, 1849. A representative letter is this of March 9, 1837 from Edith to Martha: "My heart can fully respond to the language of my own precious Mother, that absence has not diminished our affection for each other, but has, if possible, strengthened the bonds that have united us together & I have had to remark how we had been permitted to mingle in sweet fellowship and have been strengthened to bear one another's burdens. . . ."

44. Abigail Brackett Lyman, Boston, to Mrs. Abigail Brackett (daughter to mother), n.d. [1797], June 3, 1800; Sarah Alden Ripley wrote weekly to her

daughter, Sophy Ripley Fisher, after the latter's marriage (Sarah Alden Ripley Correspondence, passim); Phoebe Bradford Diary, February 25, 1833, passim, 1832–33; Louisa G. Van Vleck to Charlena Van Vleck Anderson, December 15, 1873, July 4, August 15 and 29, September 19, and November 9, 1875. Eleanor Parke Custis Lewis's long correspondence with Elizabeth Bordley Gibson contains evidence of her anxiety at leaving her foster mother's home at various times during her adolescence and at her marriage, and her own longing for her daughters, both of whom had married and moved to Louisiana (Eleanor Parke Custis [Lewis] to Elizabeth Bordley [Gibson], October 13, 1795, November 4, 1799, passim, 1820s and 1830s). Anne Jefferis Sheppard experienced a great deal of anxiety on moving two days' journey from her mother at the time of her marriage. This loneliness and sense of isolation persisted through her marriage until, finally a widow, she returned to live with her mother (Anne Jefferis Sheppard to Martha Jefferis, April 1841, October 16, 1842, April 2, May 22, and October 12, 1844, September 3, 1845, January 17, 1847, May 16, June 3, and October 31, 1849; Anne Jefferis Sheppard to Susanna Lightfoot, March 23, 1845, and to Joshua Jefferis, May 14, 1854). Daughters evidently frequently slept with their mothers—into adulthood (Harriet Manigault [Wilcox] Diary, February 19, 1815; Eleanor Parke Custis Lewis to Elizabeth Bordley Gibson, October 10, 1832). Daughters also frequently asked mothers to live with them and professed delight when they did so. See, e.g., Sarah Alden Ripley's comments to George Simmons, October 6, 1844, in Wister and Irwin, p. 185: "It is no longer 'Mother and Charles came out one day and returned the next,' for mother is one of us: she has entered the penetratice, been initiated into the mystery of the household gods, . . . Her divertissement is to mend the stockings . . . whiten sheets and napkins, . . . and take a stroll at evening with me to talk of our children, to compare our experiences, what we have learned and what we have suffered, and, last of all, to complete with pears and melons the cheerful circle about the solar lamp. . . ." We did find a few exceptions to this mother-daughter felicity (M. B. Ashew Diary, November 19, 1857, April 10 and May 17, 1858). Sarah Foulke Emlen was at first very hostile to her stepmother (Sarah Foulke Emlen Diary, August 9, 1807), but they later developed a warm supportive relationship.

45. Sarah Alden Ripley to Sophy Thayer, n.d. [1861].

46. Mary Hallock Foote to Helena [winter 1873] (no. 52); Jossie, Stevens Point, Wis., to Charlena Van Vleck [Anderson], Appleton, Wis., October 24, 1870; Pollie Chandler, Green Bay, Wis., to Charlena Van Vleck [Anderson], Appleton, n.d. [1870]; Eleuthera DuPont to Sophie DuPont, September 5, 1829; Sophie DuPont to Eleuthera DuPont, December 1827; Sophie DuPont to Victorine Bauday, December 4, 1827; Mary Gilpin to Sophie DuPont, September 26, 1827; Sarah Ripley Stearns Diary, April 2, 1809; Jeannie McCall to Peter McCall, October 27 [late 1840s]. Eleanor Parke Custis Lewis's correspondence with Elizabeth Bordley Gibson describes such an apprenticeship system over two generations—that of her childhood and that of her daughters. Indeed Eleanor Lewis's own apprenticeship was quite formal. She was deliberately separated from her foster mother in order to spend a winter of domesticity with her married sisters and her remarried mother. It was clearly felt that her foster mother's (Martha Washington) home at the nation's capital was not an appropriate place to develop domestic talents (October 13, 1795, March 30, May 13, and [summer] 1796, March 18 and April 27, 1797, October 1827).

47. Education was not limited to the daughters of the well-to-do. Sarah Foulke Emlen, the daughter of an Ohio Valley frontier farmer, for instance, attended day school for several years during the early 1800s. Sarah Ripley Stearns, the daughter of a shopkeeper in Greenfield, Mass., attended a boarding school for but three months, yet the experience seemed very important to her. Mrs. S. S. Dalton, a Mormon woman from Utah, attended a series of poor country schools and greatly valued her opportunity, though she also expressed a great deal of guilt for the sacrifices her mother made to make her education possible (Sarah Foulke Emlen Journal, Sarah Ripley Stearns Diary, Mrs. S. S. Dalton, "Autobiography").

48. Maria Revere to her mother [Mrs. Paul Revere], June 13, 1801, Paul Revere Papers, Massachusetts Historical Society. In a letter to Elizabeth Bordley Gibson, March 28, 1847, Eleanor Parke Custis Lewis from Virginia discussed the anxiety her daughter felt when her granddaughters left home to go to boarding school. Eleuthera DuPont was very homesick when away at school in Philadelphia in the early 1820s (Eleuthera DuPont, Philadelphia, to Victorine Bauday, Wilmington, Del., April 7, 1821; Eleuthera DuPont to Sophie Madeleine DuPont, Wilmington Del., February and April 3, 1821).

49. Elizabeth Bordley Gibson, a Philadelphia matron, played such a role for the daughters and nieces of her lifelong friend, Eleanor Parke Custis Lewis, a Virginia planter's wife (Eleanor Parke Custis Lewis to Elizabeth Bordley Gibson, January 29, 1833, March 19, 1826, and *passim* through the collection). The wife of Thomas Gurney Smith played a similar role for Sophie and Eleuthera DuPont (see, e.g., Eleuthera DuPont to Sophie Madeleine DuPont, May 22, 1825; Rest Cope to Philema P. Swayne [niece] West Town School, Chester County, Pa., April 8, 1829, Friends Historical Library, Swarthmore College). For a view of such a social pattern over three generations, see the letters and diaries of three generations of Manigault women in Philadelphia: Mrs. Gabrielle Manigault, her daughter, Harriet Manigault Wilcox, and granddaughter, Charlotte Wilcox McCall. Unfortunately the papers of the three women are not in one family collection (Mrs. Henry Middleton, Charleston, S.C., to Mrs. Gabrielle Manigault, n.d. [mid 1800s]; Harriet Manigault Diary, vol. 1; December 1, 1813, June 28, 1814; Charlotte Wilcox McCall Diary, vol. 1, 1842, *passim*. All in Historical Society of Philadelphia).

50. Frances Parke Lewis, Woodlawn, Va., to Elizabeth Bordley Gibson, Philadelphia, April 11, 1821, Lewis Correspondence; Eleuthera DuPont, Philadelphia, to Victorine DuPont Bauday, Brandywine, December 8, 1821, January 31, 1822; Eleuthera DuPont, Brandywine, to Margaretta Lammont [DuPont], Philadelphia, May 1823.

51. Sarah Ripley Stearns Diary, March 9 and 25, 1810; Peggy Emlen to Sally Logan, March and July 4, 1769; Harriet Manigault [Wilcox] Diary, vol. 1, December 1, 1813, June 28 and September 18, 1814, August 10, 1815; Charlotte Wilcox McCall Diary, 1842, passim; Fanny Canby to Mary Canby, May 27, 1801, March 17, 1804; Deborah Cope, West Town School, to Rest Cope, Philadelphia, July 9, 1828, Chester County Historical Society, West Chester, Pa.; Anne Zook, West Town School, to Mary Zook, Philadelphia, January 30, 1866, Chester County Historical Society, West Chester, Pa.; Mary Gilpin to Sophie Madeleine DuPont, February 25, 1829; Eleanor Parke Custis [Lewis] to Elizabeth Bordley [Gibson], April 27, July 2, and September 8, 1797, June 30, 1799, December 29, 1820; Frances Parke Lewis to Elizabeth Bordley Gibson, December 20, 1820.

52. Anne Jefferis Sheppard to Martha Jefferis, March 17, 1841.

53. Peggy Emlen to Sally Logan, March 1769, Mount Vernon, Va.; Eleanor Parke Custis [Lewis] to Elizabeth Bordley [Gibson], Philadelphia, April 27, 1797, June 30, 1799; Jeannie Field, New York, to Sarah Butler Wister, Germantown, July 3, 1861, January 16, 1863, Harriet Manigault Diary, August 3 and 11–13, 1814; Eunice Callender, Boston, to Sarah Ripley [Stearns], Greenfield, May 4, 1809. I found one exception to this inhibition of female hostility. This was the diary of Charlotte Wilcox McCall, Philadelphia (see, e.g., her March 23, 1842 entry).

54. Sophie M. DuPont and Eleuthera DuPont, Brandywine, to Victorine DuPont Bauday, Philadelphia, January 25, 1832.

55. Sarah Ripley [Stearns] Diary and Harriet Manigault Diary, *passim*.

56. Sophie Madeleine DuPont to Eleuthera DuPont, December 1827; Clementina Beach Smith to Sophie Madeleine DuPont, December 26, 1828; Sarah Faulke Emlen Diary, July 21, 1808, March 30, 1809; Annie Hethroe, Ellington, Wis., to Charlena Van Vleck [Anderson], Appleton, Wis., April 23, 1865; Frances Parke Lewis, Woodlawn, Va., to Elizabeth Bordley [Gibson], Philadelphia, December 20, 1820; Fanny Ferris to Debby Ferris, West Town School, Chester County, Pa., May 29, 1826. An excellent example of the warmth of women's comments about each other and the reserved nature of their references to men are seen in two entries in Sarah Ripley Stearns' diary. On January 8, 1811 she commented about a young woman friend: "The amiable Mrs. White of Princeton . . . one of the loveliest most interesting creatures I ever knew, young fair and blooming . . . beloved by everyone . . . formed to please & to charm. . . ." She referred to the man she ultimately married always as "my friend" or "a friend" (February 2 or April 23, 1810).

57. Jeannie Field, New York, to Sarah Butler Wister, Germantown, April 6, 1862.

58. Elizabeth Bordley Gibson, introductory statement to the Eleanor Parke Custis Lewis Letters [1850s], Historical Society of Pennsylvania.

59. Sarah Foulke [Emlen] Diary, March 30, 1809.

60. Harriet Manigault Diary, May 26, 1815.

61. Sarah Ripley [Stearns] Diary, May 17 and October 2, 1812; Eleanor Parke Custis Lewis to Elizabeth Bordley Gibson, April 23, 1826; Rebecca Ralston, Philadelphia, to Victorine DuPont [Bauday], Brandywine, September 27, 1813.

62. Anne Jefferis to Martha Jefferis, November 22 and 27, 1840, January 13 and March 17, 1841; Edith Jefferis, Greenwich, N.J., to Anne Jefferis, Philadelphia, January 31, February 6 and February 1841.

63. Edith Jefferis to Anne Jefferis, January 31, 1841.

64. Eleanor Parke Custis Lewis to Elizabeth Bordley, November 4, 1799. Eleanor and her daughter Parke experienced similar sorrow and anxiety when Parke married and moved to Cincinnati (Eleanor Parke Custis Lewis to Elizabeth Bordley Gibson, April 23, 1826). Helena DeKay visited Mary Hallock the month before her marriage; Mary Hallock was an attendant at the wedding; Helena again visited Molly about three weeks after her marriage; and then Molly went with Helena and spent a week with Helena and Richard in their new apartment (Mary Hallock [Foote] to Helena DeKay Gilder [Spring 1874] (no. 61), May 10, 1874 [May 1874], June 14, 1874 [Summer 1874]. See also Anne Biddle, Philadelphia, to Clement Biddle (brother), Wilmington, March 12 and May 27, 1827; Eunice Callender, Boston, to Sarah

Ripley [Stearns], Greenfield, Mass., August 3, 1807, January 26, 1808; Victorine DuPont Bauday, Philadelphia, to Evelina DuPont [Biderman], Brandywine, November 25 and 26, December 1, 1813; Peggy Emlen to Sally Logan, n.d. [1769–70?]; Jeannie Field, New York, to Sarah Butler Wister, Germantown, July 3, 1861).

65. Mary Hallock to Helena DeKay Gilder [1876] (no. 81); n.d. (no. 83), March 3, 1884; Mary Ashew Diary, vol. 2, September–January, 1860; Louisa Van Vleck to Charlena Van Vleck Anderson, n.d. [1875]; Sophie DuPont to Henry DuPont, July 24, 1827; Benjamin Ferris to William Canby, February 13, 1805; Benjamin Ferris to Mary Canby Biddle, December 20, 1825; Anne Jefferis Sheppard to Martha Jefferis, September 15, 1884; Martha Jefferis to Anne Jefferis Sheppard, July 4, 1843, May 5, 1844, May 3, 1847, July 17, 1849; Jeannie McCall to Peter McCall, November 26, 1847, n.d. [late 1840s]. A graphic description of the ritual surrounding a first birth is found in Abigail Lyman's letter to her husband Erastus Lyman, October 18, 1810.

66. Fanny Ferris to Anne Biddle, November 19, 1811; Eleanor Parke Custis Lewis to Elizabeth Bordley Gibson, November 4, 1799, April 27, 1827; Martha Jefferis to Anne Jefferis Sheppard, January 31, 1843, April 4, 1844; Martha Jefferis to Phoebe Sharpless Middleton, June 4, 1846; Anne Jefferis Sheppard to Martha Jefferis, August 20, 1843, February 12, 1844; Maria Inskeep, New Orleans, to Mrs. Fanny G. Hampton, Bridgeton, N.J., September 22, 1848; Benjamin Ferris to Mary Canby, February 14, 1805; Fanny Ferris to Mary Canby [Biddle], December 2, 1816.

67. Eleanor Parke Custis Lewis to Elizabeth Bordley Gibson, October–November 1820, passim.

68. Emily Howland to Hannah, September 30, 1866; Emily Howland Diary, February 8, 11, and 27, 1880; Phoebe Brandford Diary, April 12 and 13, and August 4, 1833; Eunice Callender, Boston, to Sarah Ripley [Stearns], Greenwich, Mass., September 11, 1802, August 26, 1810; Mrs. H. Middleton, Charleston, to Mrs. Gabrielle Manigault, Philadelphia, n.d. [mid 1800s]; Mrs. H. C. Paul to Mrs. Jeannie McCall, Philadelphia, n.d. [1840s]; Sarah Butler Wister, Germantown, to Jeannie Field [Musgrove], New York, April 22, 1864; Jeannie Field [Musgrove] to Sarah Butler Wister, August 25, 1861, July 6, 1862; S. B. Raudolph to Elizabeth Bordley [Gibson], n.d. [1790s]. For an example of similar letters between men, see Henry Wright to Peter McCall, December 10, 1852; Charles McCall to Peter McCall, January 4, 1860, March 22, 1864; R. Mercer to Peter McCall, November 29, 1872.

69. Mary Black [Couper] to Sophie Madeleine DuPont, February 1827, [November 1, 1834], November 12, 1834, two letters [late November 1834]; Eliza Schlatter to Sophie Madeleine DuPont, November 2, 1834.

70. For a few of the references to death rituals in the Jefferis papers see: Martha Jefferis to Anne Jefferis Sheppard, September 28, 1843, August 21 and September 25, 1844, January 11, 1846, summer 1848, passim; Anne Jefferis Sheppard to Martha Jefferis, August 20, 1843; Anne Jefferis Sheppard to Rachel Jefferis, March 17, 1863, February 9, 1868. For other Quaker families, see Rachel Biddle to Anne Biddle, July 23, 1854; Sarah Foulke Farquhar [Emlen] Diary, April 30, 1811, February 14, 1812; Fanny Ferris to Mary Canby, August 31, 1810. This is not to argue that men and women did not mourn together. Yet in many families women aided and comforted women and men, men. The same-sex death ritual was one emotional option available to nineteenth-century Americans.

71. Sarah Foulke [Emlen] Diary, December 29, 1808.

72. Eunice Callender, Boston, to Sarah Ripley [Stearns] Greenfield, Mass., May 24, 1803.

73. Katherine Johnstone Brinley [Wharton] Journal, April 26, May 30, and May 29, 1856, Historical Society of Pennsylvania.

74. A series of roughly fourteen letters written by Peggy Emlen to Sally Logan (1768–71) has been preserved in the Wells Morris Collection, Box 1, Historical Society of Pennsylvania (see esp. May 3 and July 4, 1769, January 8, 1768).

75. The Sarah Alden Ripley Collection, the Arthur M. Schlesinger, Sr., Library, Radcliffe College, contains a number of Sarah Alden Ripley's letters to Mary Emerson. Most of these are undated, but they extend over a number of years and contain letters written both before and after Sarah's marriage. The eulogistic biographical sketch appeared in Wister and Irwin (n. 12 above). It should be noted that Sarah Butler Wister was one of the editors who sensitively selected Sarah's letters.

76. See Sarah Alden Ripley to Mary Emerson, November 19, 1823. Sarah Alden Ripley routinely, and one must assume ritualistically, read Mary Emerson's letters to her infant daughter, Mary. Eleanor Parke Custis Lewis reported doing the same with Elizabeth Bordley Gibson's letters, passim. Eunice Callender, Boston, to Sarah Ripley [Stearns], October 19, 1808.

77. Mary Black Couper to Sophie M. DuPont, March 5, 1832. The Clementina Smith–Sophie DuPont correspondence of 1,678 letters is in the Sophie DuPont Correspondence. The quotation is from Eliza Schlatter, Mount Holly, N.J., to Sophie DuPont, Brandywine, August 24, 1834. I am indebted to Anthony Wallace for informing me about this collection.

78. Mary Grew, Providence, R.I., to Isabel Howland, Sherwood, N.Y., April 27, 1892, Howland Correspondence, Sophia Smith Collection, Smith College.

79. Helena Deutsch, *Psychology of Women* (New York: Grune & Stratton, 1944), vol. 1, chaps. 1–3; Clara Thompson, *On Women*, ed. Maurice Green (New York: New American Library, 1971).

15

"Where Are the Organized Women Workers?"

ALICE KESSLER-HARRIS

Low wages and sex-typing of occupations have been chronic conditions in the history of women's gainful employment. Both are linked to prevalent beliefs about women's primary role in the family. Alice Kessler-Harris connects the question of labor organization among women to this constellation of working women's circumstances, concentrating on the period at the beginning of this century. Her essay is a good example of the benefits of analyzing by sex within given social groupings. She not only discusses how employers and women workers were at odds, but also distinguishes the interests of female workers and unionists from those of male workers and unionists.

"THE ORGANIZATION OF WOMEN," wrote Fannia Cohn, an officer of the International Ladies Garment Workers Union to William Green, newly elected president of the American Federation of Labor, "is not merely a moral question, but also an economic one. Men will never be certain with their conditions unless the conditions of the millions of women are improved."[1] Her letter touched a home truth and yet in 1925, the year in which Cohn's letter was written, the A. F. of L., after nearly forty years of organizing, remained profoundly ambivalent about the fate of more than eight million wage-earning women.

During these four decades of industrial growth, the women who worked in the industrial labor force had not passively waited to be organized. Yet their best efforts had been tinged with failure. Figures for union members are notoriously unreliable, and estimates fluctuate widely. But something like 3.3 percent of the women who were engaged in industrial occupations in 1900 were organized into trade unions. As low as that figure was, it was to decline even further. Around 1902 and 1903 trade union membership among women began to decrease, reaching a low of 1.5 percent in 1910. Then, a surge of organization among garment workers lifted it upwards. A reasonable estimate might put 6.6 percent of wage-earning women into trade unions by 1920. In a decade that saw little change in the relative proportion of female and male workers, the proportion of women who were trade union members quadrupled, increasing at more than twice the rate for trade union members in general. Even so, the relative numbers of wage-earning women who were trade union members remained tiny. One in every five men in the industrial workforce belonged to a union, compared to one in every fifteen women. Although more than 20 percent of the labor force was female, less than 8 percent of organized workers were women. And five years later, when Fannia Cohn was urging William Green to pay attention to female workers, these startling gains had already been eroded.[2]

Figures like these have led historians of the working class to join turn-of-the-century labor organizers in lamenting the difficulty of unionizing female workers. Typically, historians argue that the traditional place of women in families, as well as their position in the workforce, inhibited trade unionism. Statistical overviews suggest that these arguments have much to be said for them. At the turn of the century, most wage-earning women were young temporary workers who looked to marriage as a way to escape the shop or factory. Eighty-five percent of these women were unmarried and nearly half were under twenty-five years old. Most women worked at traditionally hard-to-organize unskilled jobs: a third were domestic servants and almost one quarter worked in the garment and textile industries. The remainder were scattered in a variety of industrial and service jobs, including the tobacco and boot and shoe industries, department stores, and laundries. Wage-earning women often came from groups without a union tradition: about one half of all working women were immigrants or their daughters who shared rural backgrounds. In the cities, that figure sometimes climbed to 90 percent.[3]

For all these reasons, women in the labor force unionized with difficulty. Yet the dramatic fluctuations in the proportions of organized working women testify to their potential for organization. And the large numbers of unions in which the proportion of women enrolled exceeded their numbers in the industry urge us to seek further explanations for the small proportions of women who actually became union members.[4]

No apparent change either in the type of women who worked or in the structure of jobs explains the post-1902 decline in the proportion of unionized women. On the contrary, several trends would suggest the potential for a rise in their numbers. The decline began just at the point when union membership was increasing dramatically after the devastating depression of 1893–1897. The proportion of first-generation immigrant women who were working dropped after the turn of the century only to be matched by an increase in the proportion of their Americanized daughters who worked. Married women entered the labor force in larger numbers suggesting at once a more permanent commitment to jobs and greater need for the security unions could provide. Large declines in the proportion of domestic workers reduced the numbers of women in these isolated, low-paying, and traditionally hard-to-organize jobs. At the same time, increases in office and clerical workers, department store clerks, and factory operatives, offered fertile areas for promoting unionization among women. Strenuous organizing campaigns by and among women in all these areas achieved few results.

Although cultural background, traditional roles, and social expectations hindered some unionizing efforts, they were clearly not insurmountable barriers. Given a chance, women were devoted and successful union members, convinced that unionism would serve them as it seemed to be serving their brothers. In the words of a seventeen-year-old textile worker, "We all work hard for a mean living. Our boys belong to the miners' union so their wages are better than ours. So I figured that girls must have a union. Women must act like men, ain't?"[5] In the garment workers union where women were the majority of members, they often served as shop "chairladies" and reached positions of minor importance in the union structure. Faige Shapiro recalled how her union activity began at the insistence of a business agent but quickly became an absorbing interest. In these unions, women arrested on picket lines thought highly enough of the union to try to save it bail money by offering to spend the night in jail before they returned to the line in the morning.[6]

In mixed unions, women often led men in militant actions. Iowa cigar makers reported in 1899 that some striking men had resumed work, while the women were standing pat.[7] Boot and shoe workers in Massachusetts were reported in 1905 to be tough bargainers. "It is harder to induce women to compromise," said their president, "they are more likely to hold out to the bitter end . . . to obtain exactly what they want."[8] The great uprising of 1909 in which 20,000 women walked out of New York's garment shops occurred over the objections of the male leadership, striking terror into the hearts of Jewish men afraid "of the security of their jobs."[9] Polish "spool girls" protesting a rate cut in the textile mills of Chicopee, Massachusetts, refused their union's suggestion that they arbitrate and won a resounding victory. Swedish women enrolled in a Chicago Custom Clothing Makers local, lost a battle against their bosses' attempts to subdivide and speed up the sewing process when the United Garment Workers union, largely male, agreed to the bosses' conditions. The bosses promptly locked out the women forcing many to come to terms and others to seek new jobs.[10] At the turn of the century, female garment workers in San Francisco and tobacco strippers, overall and sheepskin workers, and telephone operators in Boston ran highly successful sex-segregated unions.[11]

If traditional explanations for women's failure to organize extensively in this period are not satisfying, they nevertheless offer clues to understanding the unionization process among women. They reveal the superficiality of the question frequently asked by male organizers and historians alike: "Why don't women organize?" And they encourage us to adopt economist Theresa Wolfson's more sensitive formulation: "Where are the organized women workers?"[12] For when we stop asking why women have not organized themselves, we are led to ask how women were, and are, kept out of unions.

The key to this question lies, I think, in looking at the function that wage earning women have historically played in the capitalist mode of production. Most women entered the labor force out of economic necessity. They were encouraged by expanding technology and the continuing division of labor which in the last half of the nineteenth century reduced the need for skilled workers and increased the demand for cheap labor. Like immigrant men, and blacks today, women formed a large reservoir of unskilled workers. But they offered employers additional advantages. They were often at the mercy of whatever jobs happened to be available in the towns where their husbands or fathers worked, and they willingly took jobs that offered no access to upward mobility. Their extraordinarily low pay and exploitative working conditions enabled employers to speed up the process of capital accumulation. Their labor was critical to industrial expansion, yet they were expected to have few job-related aspirations and to look forward instead to eventual marriage. Under these circumstances, employers had a special incentive to resist unionization among women. As John Andrews, writing in the 1911 Report on the Condition of Women and Child Wage Earners, put it: ". . . the moment she organizes a union and seeks by organization to secure better wages she diminishes or destroys what is to the employer her chief value."[13]

If the rising numbers of working women are any gauge, women for the most part nicely filled the expectations of employers. Traditional social roles and the submissive behavior expected of women with primary attachments to home and family precisely complemented the needs of their bosses. To those women whose old world or American family norms encouraged more aggressive and worldly behavior—Russian Jews, for example—unionization came easier. Yet, for the most part, women fought on two fronts: against the weight of tradition and expectation, and against employers. If that were not enough, there was yet a third battlefront.

Unionists, if they thought about it at all, were well aware of women's special economic role. Samuel Gompers, head of the American Federation of Labor, editorialized in 1911 that some companies had "taken on women not so much to give them work as to make dividends fatter."[14] In a competitive labor market unionists tended to be suspicious of women who worked for wages and to regard them as potentially threatening to men's jobs. "Every woman employed," wrote an editor in the A. F. of L. journal, *American Federationist*, "displaces a man and adds one more to the idle contingent that are fixing wages at the lowest limit."[15]

Since employers clearly had important economic incentives for hiring women, male trade unionists felt they had either to eliminate that incentive, or to offer noneconomic reasons for restricting women's labor-force participation. In the early 1900s they tried to do both. In order to reduce the economic threat, organized labor repeatedly affirmed a commitment to unionize women wage earners and to extract equal pay for them. Yet trade unionists simultaneously argued that women's contributions to the home and their duties as mothers were so valuable that women ought not to be in the labor force at all. Their use of the home-and-motherhood argument had two negative effects: it sustained the self-image on which the particular exploitation of women rested, and it provided employers with a weapon to turn against the working class as a whole.

Buttressed by the grim realities of exploitative working conditions and the difficulties of caring for children while working ten or more hours a day, and supported by well-intentioned social reformers, the argument to eliminate women from the work force, in the end, held sway. It was, of course, impossible to achieve, so the A. F. of L. continued to organize women and to demand equal pay for equal work. But genuine ambivalence tempered its efforts. The end result was to divide the working class firmly along gender lines and to confirm women's position as a permanently threatening underclass of workers who finally resorted to the protection of middle-class reformers and legislators to ameliorate intolerable working conditions. The pattern offers us some lessons about what happens to the work force when one part of it attacks another.

The published sources of the A. F. of L. reveal some of the attitudes underlying A. F. of L. actions, and I have focused attention on these because I want to illustrate not only how open and prevalent the argument was, but because the A. F. of L.'s affiliated unions together constituted the largest body of collective working-class opinion. We have amassed enough evidence by now to know that the A. F. of L. was a conservative force whose relatively privileged members sacrificed the larger issues of working-class solidarity for a piece of the capitalist pie. In the creation of what labor economist Selig Perlman called "a joint partnership of organized labor and organized capital," the Federation cooperated extensively with corporation-dominated government agencies, sought to exclude immigrants, and supported an imperialist foreign policy.[16] Its mechanisms for dealing with the huge numbers of women entering the labor force are still unclear. Yet they are an integral part of the puzzle surrounding the interaction of ideological and economic forces in regulating labor market participation.

In the period from 1897 to 1920, the A. F. of L. underwent dramatic expansion. It consolidated and confirmed its leadership over a number of independent unions, including the dying Knights of Labor. Membership increased from about 265,000 members in 1897 to more than four million by 1920, and included four-fifths of all organized workers. In the same period, the proportion of women working in the industrial labor force climbed rapidly. Rapid and heady expansion offered a golden opportunity for organizers. That they didn't take advantage of it is one of the most important facts in the history of labor organizing in America.

Union leaders were sure that women did not belong in the work force. Anxious about losing jobs to these low-paid workers, they tried instead to drive women out of the labor force. "It is the so-called competition of the unorganized defenseless woman worker, the girl and the wife, that often tends to reduce the wages of the father and husband," proclaimed Samuel Gompers.[17] And the *American Federationist* was filled with tales of men displaced by women and children. "One house in St. Louis now pays $4 per week to women where men got $16," snapped the journal in 1896. "A local typewriter company has placed 200 women to take the place of unorganized men," announced an organizer in 1903.[18]

The Federation's fears had some basis. In the late nineteenth and early twentieth century, new technology and techniques of efficiency pioneered by Frederick Taylor eroded the control and the jobs of skilled workmen, replacing them with managerial experts and the unskilled and semiskilled. Skilled members of the A. F. of L. who might appropriately have directed their anger at the way technology was being manipulated, lashed out instead at women who dared to work. Gompers offers a good example. In an article published in 1904, he declared, "The ingenuity of man to produce the world's wealth easier than ever before, is utilized as a means to pauperize the worker, to supplant the man by the woman and the woman by the child. . . ."[19] Some of the least appropriate bitterness was expressed by Thomas O'Donnell, secretary of the National Spinners Union whose constituency, once largely female, had been replaced by men after the Civil War. The advent of simple electric-powered machinery caused him to complain that "the manufacturers have been trying for years to discourage us by dispensing with the spinning mule and substituting female and child labor for that of the old time skilled spinners. . . ."[20]

Real anxieties about competition from women stimulated and supported rationalizations about woman's role as wife and mother. Working men had argued even before the Civil War that women belonged at home, and both the harsh conditions of labor and the demands of rearing a family supported their contention. But the women who worked for wages in the early 1900s were overwhelmingly single, and often supported widowed mothers and younger siblings with their meagre pay. An argument that could have been used to improve conditions for all workers was directed at eliminating women from the work force entirely. By the early 1900s it had become an irrepressible chorus. "The great principle for which we fight," said the A. F. of L.'s treasurer in 1905, "is opposed to taking . . . the women from their homes to put them in the factory and the sweatshop."[21] "We stand for the principle," said another A. F. of L. member, "that it is wrong to permit any of the female sex of our country to be forced to work, as we believe that the man should be provided with a fair wage in order to keep his female relatives from going to work. The man is the provider and should receive enough for his labor to give his family a respectable living."[22] And yet a third proclaimed, "Respect for women is apt to decrease when they are compelled to work in the factory or the store. . . . More respect for women brings less degeneration and more marriages . . . if women labor in factories and similar institutions they bring forth weak children who are not educated to become strong and good citizens."[23] No language was too forceful or too dramatic. "The demand for female labor," wrote an official of the Boston Central Labor Union in 1897, is "an insidious assault upon the home . . . it is the knife of the assassin, aimed at the family circle."[24] The *American Federationist* romanticized the role of women's jobs at home, extolling the virtues of refined and moral mothers, of good cooking and even of beautiful needlework and embroidery.[25]

These sentiments did not entirely prevent the A. F. of L. from attempting to unionize women. Gompers editorialized on the subject in 1904: "We . . . shall bend every energy for our fellow workmen to organize and unite in trade unions; to federate their effort without regard to . . . sex."[26] Yet the limited commitment implied by the wish that women would get out of the work force altogether was tinged with the conviction and perhaps the hope that women would in the end, fail. The Federation's first female organizer, Mary Kenny, had been appointed as early as 1892. But the Federation had supported her only half-heartedly and allowed her position to expire when she gave up the job to marry. It was 1908 before the organization appointed another woman, Annie Fitzgerald, as full-time organizer. While Gompers and others conceded the "full and free opportunity for women to work whenever and wherever necessity requires," Gompers did not address himself to the problem of how to determine which women were admissible by these standards, and his actions revealed that he thought their numbers relatively few.[27] The A. F. of L. repeatedly called for an end to discriminatory pay for women and men: "Equal compensation for equal service performed."[28] The demand was a double-edged sword. While it presumably protected all workers from cheap labor, in the context of the early 1900s labor market it often functioned to deprive women of jobs. The Boston Typographical Union, noted one observer, saw "its only safety in maintaining the principle of equal pay for men and women. . . ."[29] Officials must have been aware that equal compensation for women often meant that employers would as soon replace them with men. It was no anomaly, then, to find an A. F. of L. organizer say of his daughters in 1919 that though he had "two girls at work [he] . . . wouldn't think of having them belong to a labor organization."[30]

When the A. F. of L. did organize women, its major incentive was often the need to protect the earning power of men. Women were admitted to unions after men recognized them as competitors better controlled from within than allowed to compete from without. "It has been the policy of my associates and myself," wrote Gompers in 1906, "to throw open wide the doors of our organization and invite the working girls and working women to membership for their and our common protection."[31] *American Federationist* articles that began with pleas that women stay out of the work force concluded with equally impassioned pleas to organize those who were already in it. Alice Woodbridge, writing in 1894, concluded an argument that women who worked for wages were neglecting their duties to their "fellow creatures" with the following statement: "It is to the interest of both sexes that women should organize . . . until we are well organized there is little hope of success among organizations of men."[32] The A. F. of L. officially acknowledged competition as a primary motivation for organizing women in 1923. "Unorganized they constitute a menace to standards established through collective action. Not only for their protection, but for the protection of men . . . there should be organization of all women. . . ."[33]

These were not of course the only circumstances of which men suspended their hostility toward women's unions. Occasionally in small towns female and male unions in different industries supported each other against the hostile attacks of employers. Minersville, Pennsylvania miners, for example, physically ousted railroad detectives who tried to break up a meeting of female textile workers.[34] The women in this case were the daughters, sisters and sweethearts of miners. Far from competing with men for jobs, women were helping to support the same families as the miners. Similarly, women and men in newly established industries could cooperate more effectively in unionizing together. The garment industry saw parallel but equally effective organization among its various branches. Though female organizers complained bitterly of the way they were treated, male leadership depended on the numerical majority of female workers to bargain successfully with employers and did not deny women admission. Yet, even here, union leadership successfully eliminated "home work" without offering to the grossly underpaid and often needy female workers who did it a way of recouping their financial losses.

Occasional exceptions notwithstanding, the general consequence of union attitudes toward women was to isolate them from the male work force. Repeatedly women who organized themselves into unions applied for entry to the appropriate parent body only to be turned down or simply ignored. Pauline Newman, who had organized and collected dues from a group of candy makers in Philadelphia, in 1910 offered to continue to work with them if the International Bakery and Confectionery Workers union would issue a charter. The International stalled and put them off until the employers began to discharge the leaders and the group disintegrated.[35] Waitresses in Norfolk, Virginia, suffered a similar fate. Mildred Rankin, who requested a charter for a group of fifteen, was assured by the local A. F. of L. organizer that she was wasting her time. "The girls were all getting too much money to be interested," was his comment on denying the request.[36] New York's International Typographical Union refused to issue female copyholders a charter on the grounds that they were insufficiently skilled. When the group applied to the parent A. F. of L. for recognition, they were refused on the grounds that they were within the ITU's jurisdiction. The Women's Trade Union League got little satisfaction when it raised this issue with the A. F. of L.'s executive council the following year. Though the Federation had agreed to issue charters to black workers excluded from all-white unions, it refused to accord the same privilege to women. The parent body agreed only to "take up the subject with the trade unions and to endeavor to reach an understanding" as far as women were concerned.[37]

A strong union could simply cut women out of the kinds of jobs held by unionized men. This form of segmenting the labor market ran parallel to, and sometimes contradicted the interests of employers who would have preferred cheap labor. A Binghamton, New York printing establishment, for example, could not hire women linotype operators because "the men's union would not allow it."[38] The technique was as useful for excluding racial minorities as it was for restricting women.[39] Like appeals to racist beliefs, arguments based on the natural weakness of women worked well as a rationale, as the following examples will indicate. Mary Dreier, then President of the New York Chapter of the Women's Trade Union League, recalled a union of tobacco workers whose leaders refused to admit women because "they could only do poor sort of work . . . , because women had no colour discrimination."[40] A Boston metal polishers union refused to admit women. "We don't want them," an official told a Women's Bureau interviewer. "Women can only do one kind of work while men can polish anything from iron to gold and frame the smallest part to the largest," and besides, he added, "metal polishing is bad for the health."[41]

Women were often excluded from unions in less direct but equally effective ways. The International Retail Clerks Union charged an initiation fee of $3, and dues of 50¢ a month. Hilda Svenson, a local organizer in 1914, complained that she had been unable to negotiate a compromise with the International. "We want to be affiliated with them," she commented, "but on account of the dues and initiation fee we feel it is too high at the present time for the salaries that the girls in New York are getting."[42] Sometimes union pay scales were set so high that the employer would not pay the appropriate wage to women. Joining the union could mean that a female printer would lose her job, so women simply refused to join.

Though the A.F. of L. supported its few female organizers only half-heartedly, male organizers complained of the difficulty of organizing women. Social propriety hindered them from talking to women in private or about moral or sanitary issues. Women felt keenly the absence of aid. When the Pennsylvania State Federation of Labor offered to finance the Philadelphia Women's Trade Union League's program for organizing women, its secretary pleaded with Rose Schneiderman to take the job. "We have never had a wise head to advise, or an experienced worker," she wrote.[43]

But even membership in a union led by men guaranteed little to women. Such well known tactics as locating meetings in saloons, scheduling them at late hours, and ridiculing women who dared to speak deprived women of full participation. And unions often deliberately sabotaged their female members. Fifteen hundred female street railway conductors and ticket agents, dues-paying members of New York City's Amalgamated Street Workers Union, complained in 1919 that their brother union members had supported a reformers' bill to deprive them of their jobs. When the women discovered they had been betrayed they resigned from the union and formed their own organization sending women throughout the state to Albany "to show them that they . . . were able to take care of their own health and morals." To no avail. Eight hundred of the 1500 women lost their jobs and the remaining 700 continued to work only at reduced hours.[44] Supporting union men was not likely to benefit women either. Mary Anderson, newly appointed head of the Women's Bureau, got a frantic telegram from a WTUL organizer in Joliet, Illinois, early in 1919. The women in a Joliet steel plant who, in return for the promise of protection, had supported unionized men in a recent strike, were fighting desperately for jobs that the union now insisted they give up. The company wanted to retain the women, but union men argued the work was too heavy for them.[45]

As the idea of home-and-motherhood was used to exclude women from unions, so it enabled unionized workers to join legislatures and middle-class reformers in restricting women's hours and regulating their working condition through protective labor legislation. The issue for the Federation's skilled and elite corps of male workers was clearly competition. Their wives did not work for wages, and most could afford to keep their daughters outside the marketplace. In an effort to preserve limited opportunity, they attacked fellow workers who were women, attempting to deny them access to certain kinds of jobs. Abused by employers who valued women primarily for their "cheap labor," women were isolated by male workers who were afraid their wages and their jobs would fall victim to the competition. Arguments used by male workers may have undercut their own positions, confirming the existence of a permanent underclass of workers and locking men psychologically and economically into positions of sole economic responsibility for their families. Appeals to morality and to the duties of motherhood obscured the economic issues involved, encouraging women and men alike to see women as impermanent workers whose major commitment would be to families and not to wage earning. Women would, therefore, require the special protection of the state for their presumably limited wage-earning lives.

The argument reached back at least as far as the 1880s and it was firmly rooted in the idea that the well-being of the state depended on the health of future mothers. But the line between the interests of the state and those of working men was finely drawn, and occasionally a protagonist demonstrated confusion about the issue. A few examples will illustrate the point. The cigar maker, Adolph Strasser, testifying before a Congressional Committee in 1882, concluded a diatribe against the number of women entering the trade with a plea to restrict them. "Why?" asked his questioner. "Because," replied Strasser, "I claim that it is the duty of the government to protect the weak and the females are considered among the weak in society."[46] Nearly forty years later, a Women's Bureau investigator reported that the Secretary of the Amalgamated Clothing Workers Union, fearful that women were taking jobs from men, had argued that women were "going into industry so fast that home life is very much in danger, not to mention the propagation of the race."[47] As the idea spread, it took on new forms, leading a Boston streetcar union secretary to acknowledge that "he would not care to see [women] employed as conductors. . . . It coarsened [them] to handle rough crowds on cars."[48] But in more sophisticated form, the argument for protective legislation appeared as a patriotic appeal to enlightened national self-interest. "Women may be adults," argued one A.F. of L. columnist in 1900, "and why should we class them as children? Because it is to the interest of all of us that female labor should be limited so as not to injure the motherhood and family life of a nation."[49] Sometimes pleas were more dramatic. In a piece entitled, "The Kingdom of God and Modern Industry," Ira Howerth, a sociologist writing for the *American Federationist*, asserted:

> The highest courts in some of our states declare that a law limiting the hours of labor for these women is unconstitutional. It may be so, but if it is so, so much the worse for the state. The state or nation that permits its women to stunt their bodies and dwarf their minds by over-exertion in insanitary [sic] stores and

> mills and factories is thereby signing its own death warrant. For the degeneracy of women is the degeneracy of the race. A people can never be any better than its mothers.[50]

Gompers, as well as other Federation officials, at first opposed the idea of legislation. But in the period following World War I, their attitudes changed, perhaps as a result of what seemed like an enormous increase in the number of women in the industrial labor force. The A.F. of L. encouraged the Department of Labor to set up a Women's Bureau to defend the interests of wage earning women.[51] The Bureau, on investigation, found that many union officials viewed unionization and protective legislation as alternate means to the same goal: better working conditions. Sara Conboy, United Textile Workers' official and a WTUL activist, told a Women's Bureau interviewer that she believed in "legislation to limit long hours of work for women where and when the union [was] not strong enough to limit hours."[52] Some unionized workers thought legislation surer and faster or remarked that it was more dependable than possibly untrustworthy union leaders. A. J. Muste, then secretary of the Amalgamated Textile Workers Union of America, preferred unionization, but was said to have believed that legislation did not hinder organization and might be essential in industries with many women and minors.[53] But some women union leaders were not so sanguine. Fannia Cohn of the International Garment Workers Union only reluctantly acquiesced to the need for protective legislation. "I did not think the problem of working women could be solved in any other way than the problem of working men and that is through trade union organization," she wrote in 1927, "but considering that very few women are as yet organized into trade unions, it would be folly to agitate against protective legislation."[54] Cohn laid the problems of female workers on the absence of organization.

In any event, exclusion from unions merely confirmed the discomfort many women felt about participating in meetings. Italian and Southern families disliked their daughters going out in the evenings. Married and self-supporting women and widows had household duties at which they spent after-work hours. Women who attended meetings often participated reluctantly. They found the long discussions dull and were often intimidated by the preponderance of men. Men, for their part, resented the indifference of the women and further excluded them from leadership roles, thereby discouraging more women from attending. Even fines failed to spark attendance. Some women preferred to pay them rather than to go to the meetings.[55]

Self-images that derived from a paternalistic society joined ethnic ties in hindering unionization. Wage-earning women, anxious to marry, were sometimes reluctant to join unions for what they felt would be a temporary period. Occasionally, another role conflict was expressed: "No nice girl would belong to one," said one young woman.[56] An ILG organizer commented that most women who did not want to join a union claimed that "the boss is good to us and we have nothing to complain about and we don't want to join the union."[57] A woman who resisted unionization told an organizer that she knew "that $6 a week is not enough pay but the Lord helps me out. He always provides . . . I won't ever join a union. The Lord doesn't want me to."[58] A recent convert to unionism apologized for her former reticence. She had always scabbed because church people disapproved of unions. Moreover she and her sister had only with difficulty, she told an organizer, overcome their fear of the Italian men who were organizing their factory.[59]

Exceptions to this pattern occurred most often among women whose ethnic backgrounds encouraged both wage labor and a high level of social consciousness, as in the American Jewish community for example. Young Jewish women constituted the bulk of the membership of the International Ladies Garment Workers Union in the period from 1910 to 1920. Their rapid organization and faithful tenure is responsible for at least one quarter of the increased number of unionized women in the second decade of the twentieth century. And yet, they were unskilled and semi-skilled workers, employed in small, scattered shops, and theoretically among the least organizable workers. These women, unionized at their own initiative, formed the backbone of the ILGWU, which had originally been directed toward organizing the skilled, male, cutters in the trade.

As it became clear to many laboring women that unionists would offer them little help, many women turned to such middle-class allies as the Women's Trade Union League. Established in 1905, the WTUL, an organization founded by female unionists and upper-middle-class reformers, offered needed financial and moral support for militant activity. Its paternalistic and benevolent style was not unfamiliar to women and those who came from immigrant families seemed particularly impressed with its Americanizing aspects. Young immigrant girls spoke with awe of the "fine ladies" of the WTUL and did not object to the folk-dancing classes that were part of the Chicago League's program.[60] But help from these nonwage-earning women came at a price. Working women who became involved in the WTUL moved quickly from working class militance to the search for individual social mobility through vocational training, legislation, and the social refinements that provided access to better paying and rapidly increasing clerical and secretarial jobs. Rose Schneiderman illustrates this syndrome well. Beginning as a fiery organizer of the hat-and-cap makers, she moved through the WTUL to become Secretary of the New York State Department of Labor. Like the WTUL, which had begun by organizing women into trade unions, she began in the 1920s to devote herself to attaining protective legislation, even borrowing some of the arguments used by men who did not wish women to compete with them.

By this time many working women were themselves moving in the direction of legislative solutions to exploitative working conditions. It seemed to be the most accessible solution to the problems of exploitation. Female workers interviewed by the Women's Bureau at first felt that both women and men should be included in any legislation. Later, they asked that office workers be exempted.[61] Other women acquiesced reluctantly. "I have always been afraid," wrote a supervisor in a Virginia silk mill, "that if laws were made discriminating for women, it would work a hardship upon them." By 1923 she had changed her mind: ". . . it would in time raise the entire standard rather than make it hard for women."[62] As women came to accept the necessity for legislation, they, like men, saw it as an alternative to unionization and rationalized its function in terms of their female "roles." A Women's Bureau agent noted of the reactions to a 48-hour law passed in Massachusetts that "the girls felt that legislation establishing a 48-hour week was more 'dignified' and permanent than one obtained through the union as it was not so likely to be taken away."[63] By the mid-1920s only business and professional women remained staunchly opposed to protective legislation.

Within this framework of trade-union ambivalence and the real need of wage-earning women for some form of protection employers who were particularly anxious that women not unionize pressed their advantage. Using crude techniques, rationalized by the home-and-motherhood argument, they contributed more than their share toward keeping women out of unions. In the small businesses in which women most often worked, employers used a variety of techniques to discourage organization, some of them familiar to men. Department store employees whose union membership became known were commonly fired. Many stores had spy systems so that employees could not trust their coworkers. Blacklists were common. A representative of the year-old retail clerks union testifying before a Congressional Committee in 1914 was afraid even to reveal the number of members in her union. Owners of New York's garment shops, fighting a losing battle by 1910, nevertheless frequently discharged employees who were thought to be active organizers or union members.[64]

Other tactics were no more subtle. Employers often played on ethnic and racial tensions in order to prevent women from unionizing. Rose Schneiderman, who formed the Hat and Cap Makers Union in 1903, fought against bosses who urged immigrant workers to stick to the "American shop"—a euphemism for an antiunion shop. Jewish owners sometimes hired only Italian workers who were thought to be less prone to unionization than Jews.[65] Others hired "landsmen" from the same old country community, hoping that fraternal instincts might keep them from striking. Blacks were played off against whites. Waitresses picketing Knab's restaurant in Chicago were met with counterpickets paid by the employers. A representative of the waitresses union reported indignantly that the employer "placed colored pickets on the street, colored women who wore signs like this 'Gee, I ain't mad at nobody and nobody ain't mad at Knab.' " When the nonunion pickets attracted a crowd, police moved in and arrested the union members. The women were further discouraged by trials engineered by employers who had previously given "every policeman a turkey free."[66]

Police routinely broke up picket lines and outdoor union meetings. Women who were accused of obstructing traffic or were incited into slapping provocateurs were arrested. More importantly, women who might have been interested in unionization were intimidated by police who surrounded open air meetings or by department store detectives who mingled obtrusively with potential recruits. Department store owners diverted workers from street meetings by locking all but one set of doors or sending trucks, horns honking full blast, to parade up and down the street in which a meeting was scheduled.[67]

Small employers formed mutual assistance associations to help them resist their employees' attempts to unionize. The Chicago Restaurant Keepers Association, for example, denied membership to any "person, firm or corporation . . . having signed agreements with any labor organization."[68] Garment manufacturers in both New York and Chicago created protective associations to combat what they called "the spreading evil of unionism."[69] In small towns, the power of town officials was called into play. Ann Washington Craton, organizing textile workers in Minersville, Pennsylvania, was warned by the town burgess: "You are to let our girls alone . . . Mr. Demsky will shut the factory down rather than have a union. . . . The town council brought this factory here to provide work for worthy widows and poor girls. We don't intend to have any trouble about it."[70]

Employers justified continued refusal to promote women or to offer them access to good jobs on the grounds that women's major contribution was to home and family. When they were challenged with the argument that bad working conditions were detrimental to that end, they responded slowly with paternalistic amelioration of the worst conditions and finally by acquiescing to protective labor legislation. Often concessions to workers were an effort to undercut mounting union strength, as for example when department store owners voluntarily closed their shops one evening a week. Some employers introduced welfare work in their factories, providing social workers, or other women, to help smooth relationships between them and their female employees. Mutual benefit associations, sometimes resembling company unions, were a more familiar tactic. Though they were presumably cooperative and designed to incorporate input from workers, membership in them was compulsory and dues of ten to twenty-five cents per month were deducted from wages. In return employees got sickness and health benefits of varying amounts but only after several months of continuous employment. A 1925 investigation of one widely publicized cooperative association operated by Filene's department store in Boston revealed that in all its twelve years, only store executives had ever served on its board of directors.[71]

Manufacturers seemed to prefer legislation regulating the hours and conditions of women's work to seeing their workers join unions. One, for example, told the Women's Bureau of the Department of Labor that a uniform 48-hour week for women would equalize competition and would, in any event, only confirm existing conditions in some shops. Some went even further hoping for federal legislation that would provide uniform standards nationwide.[72]

When occasionally employers found it in their interests to encourage unionism they did so in return for certain very specific advantages. One of these was the union label. In the garment industry the label on overalls in certain parts of the country assured higher sales. To acquire the right to use it, some employers rushed into contracts with the United Garment Workers and quite deliberately urged their workers into the union.[73] New York garment manufacturers negotiated a preferential union shop, higher wages, and shorter hours with the ILGWU in return for which the union agreed to discipline its members and to protect employers against strikes. The garment manufacturers' protective association urged employers to "make every effort to increase the membership in the union so that its officers may have complete control of the workers and be enabled to discipline them when necessary."[74] Southern textile mill owners, otherwise violently opposed to unions, were similarly interested in the disciplinary functions of unionism. They would, an observer reported, modify their opposition "if the purposes of the union were to improve the educational, moral and social conditions of the workers."[75]

In general, however, employers made valiant attempts to keep women out of unions. The paternalism, benevolence, and welfare they offered in compensation were supported by other sectors of their society, including the trade unions. Middle-class reformers and government investigators had long viewed the harsh conditions under which women worked as detrimental to the preservation of home and family, and government regulation or voluntary employer programs seemed to many an adequate alternative. Unions played into this competitive structure adopting the home-and-motherhood argument to restrict women's labor-force participation. In the process they encouraged women to see their interests apart from those of male workers.

Limited labor-force opportunities, protective labor legislation and virtual exclusion from labor unions institutionalized women's isolation from the mainstream of labor. Not accidentally, these tendencies confirmed traditional women's roles, already nurtured by many ethnic groups and sustained by prevailing American norms. Together they translated into special behavior on the part of female workers that isolated them still further from male workers and added up to special treatment as members of the labor force.

In acquiescing, women perhaps bowed to the inevitable, seeking for themselves the goals of employers who preferred not to see them in unions, of male workers who hoped thereby both to limit competition and to share in the advantages gained, and of middle-class reformers who felt they were helping to preserve home and motherhood. Echoing labor union arguments of twenty years earlier, Women's Bureau head Mary Anderson defended protective legislation in 1925 on the grounds that such laws were necessary to conserve the health of the nation's women.[76]

A final consequence for women was to lead them to search for jobs in non-sex-stereotyped sectors of the labor market. Employers' needs in the rapidly expanding white-collar sector led women increasingly toward secretarial and clerical work. Vocational education to train women for office jobs, teaching, and social work expanded rapidly in the early twentieth century. Working women rationalized these jobs as steps up the occupational ladder; state and local governments and employers provided financial aid; and middle-class women launched a campaign to encourage women to accept vocational training.[77] It took an astute union woman like Fannia Cohn to see what was happening. She drew a sharp line between her own function as educational director of the International Ladies Garment Workers Union and the functions of the new schools. Her hope was to train women to be better union members, not to get them out of the working class.

The parallel development of protective legislation and vocational education confirmed for many working women their marginal positions in the labor force, positions they continued to rationalize with obeisance to marriage and the family. As Alice Henry said of an earlier group of female wage-earners, "They did not realize that women were within the scope of the labor movement."[78] Fannia Cohn understood what that meant. That hard-headed and clear-sighted official of the ILGWU prefaced a call for a revolution in society's view of women with a plea for an end to competition between working women and men. Because it was destructive for all workers, she argued, "this competition must be abolished once and for all, not because it is immoral, yes inhuman, but because it is impractical, it does not pay."[79] But in the first two decades of the twentieth century, the moral arguments prevailed—releasing some women from some of the misery of toil, but simultaneously confirming their place in those jobs most conducive to exploitation.

NOTES

I wish to thank the Louis M. Rabinowitz Foundation and the American Philosophical Society for essential financial support, and Jan Shinpoch for assistance in research.

Abbreviations: WB/NA: Women's Bureau collection, Record Group no. 86, National Archives; CIR: Final Report and Testimony of the Commission on Industrial Relations, Senate Documents, vol. 21, 64th Congress, 1st session, vol. 3, 1914; *AF: American Federationist.*

1. Fannia Cohn to William Green, March 6, 1925. Fannia Cohn collection, New York Public Library, Box 4.

2. Figures are derived from John Andrews and W. D. P. Bliss, *History of Women in Trade Unions,* Report on the Condition of Women and Child Wage Earners in the U.S. (Washington, D.C.: G.P.O., 1911), vol. 10, pp. 136–39; Leo Wolman, *Ebb and Flow in Trade Unionism* (New York: National Bureau of Economic Research, 1936), pp. 74, 116; Leo Wolman, *The Growth of American Trade Unions, 1880–1923* (New York: National Bureau of Economic Research, 1923), chapter 5. Wolman estimates that about 40 percent of organized women were in the three garment industry unions: ILGWU, Amalgamated

Clothing Workers, and United Garment Workers, unions that had been either literally or virtually nonexistent before 1910. See Wolman, and Alice Henry, *Women and the Labor Movement* (New York: George Doran, 1923), chapter 4, for discussions of the difficulty of collecting trade union figures. Henry illustrates the numbers of women in specific unions.

3. The proportion of foreign-born and native-born daughters of foreign-born women declined slightly in this period and women continued to shift from manual sectors to low-level clerical sectors of the work force. See U.S. Census, *14th Census of Populations* (Washington, D.C.: G.P.O.: 1920), vol. 3, p. 15. Such occupations as taking in boarders, homework, and working on husbands' farms or in family businesses are not counted by census takers. Including these legitimate forms of labor would create drastic upward revisions in the proportion of working women, but we have no way of knowing by how much. The figures include black women, more than 40 percent of whom worked for wages, compared to about 20 percent of white women. However, about 32 percent of married black women worked, compared to less than 6 percent of married white women. Black wage-earning women are far more heavily concentrated in agricultural and domestic service jobs than their white counterparts. Figures are from Joseph Hill, *Women in Gainful Occupations: 1870–1920,* Census Monographs, no. 9 (Washington, D.C.: G.P.O., 1929), chapters 5 and 9; Janet Hooks, *Women's Occupations Through Seven Decades,* Women's Bureau Bulletin, no. 218 (Washington, D.C.: G.P.O., 1947), pp. 37, 39.

4. Andrews and Bliss, *History of Women in Trade Unions,* pp. 138–39. Even before the great uprising of 1909–1910, women, who made up 63 percent of the workers in the garment trades, represented 70 percent of the trade union members. This is all the more remarkable because their skill levels did not, by and large, match those of men. 32.5 percent of hat and cap makers were women, and 54 percent of union members were women. Women made up 50 percent of bookbinders, and 40 percent of the trade union members in that industry.

5. Ann Blankenhorn, miscellaneous notes, chapter 2, p. 12, file no. 23, box no. 1, Ann Craton Blankenhorn collection, Archives of Labor History, Wayne State University. For another example, see interview with Netti Chandler, Virginia Home visits, Bulletin no. 10, accession no. 51A101, WB/NA.

6. Interview with Faigele Shapiro, August 6, 1964. Amerikaner Yiddishe Geshichte Bel-pe, YIVO, pp. 2, 7.

7. *AF* 6 (November 1899): 228.

8. Quoted in Andrews and Bliss, *History of Women in Trade Unions,* p. 173.

9. New York Women's Trade Union League, *Report of the Proceedings,* 4th Annual Conference of Trade Union Women, October 9, 10, 1926, p. 18.

10. Vera Shlakman, *Economic History of a Factory Town: A Study of Chicopee, Massachusetts,* Smith College Studies in History, vol. 20, no. 1–4 (October 1934–July 1935), p. 216; Andrews and Bliss, *History of Women in Trade Unions,* p. 166.

11. Andrews and Bliss, *History of Women in Trade Unions,* p. 168; Massachusetts Women's Trade Union League, *The History of Trade Unionism among Women in Boston* (Boston: WTUL, n.d., but c. 1907), pp. 22, 23.

12. Theresa Wolfson, "Where are the Organized Women Workers?" *AF* 32 (June 1925): 455–57.

13. Andrews and Bliss, *History of Women in Trade Unions*, p. 151.

14. *AF* 17 (November 1911), p. 896. James Kenneally, "Women and Trade Unions," *Labor History* 14 (Winter 1973), describes, but does not explain, the A.F. of L.'s mixed feelings.

15. Eva McDonald Valesh, "Women and Labor," *AF* 3 (February 1896): 222.

16. Selig Perlman, *A History of Trade Unionism in the U.S.* (New York: Macmillan, 1923), p. 166. For illustrations of A. F. of L. policies see James Weinstein, *The Corporate Ideal in the Liberal State: 1900–1918* (Boston: Beacon Press, 1968), especially chapters 1 and 2; Ronald Radosh, *American Labor and United States Foreign Policy* (New York: Vintage, 1970); Stanley Aronowitz, *False Promises* (New York; McGraw-Hill, 1973).

17. Samuel Gompers, "Should the Wife Help Support the Family?" *AF* 13 (January 1906): 36. See also Stuart Reid, "The Joy of Labor? Plutocracy's Hypocritical Sermonizing Exposed—A Satire," *AF* 11 (November 1904): 977–78.

18. "Mainly Progressive," *AF* 3 (March 1896): 16; "What Our Organizers are Doing," *AF* 10 (April 1903): 370.

19. Editorial, *AF* 11 (July 1904): 584.

20. "Trade Union History," *AF* 9 (November 1902): 871.

21. John Safford, "The Good that Trade Unions Do," part I, *AF* 9 (July 1902): 353, 358; "Talks on Labor," *AF* 12 (November 1905): 846.

22. William Gilthorpe, "Advancement," *AF* 17 (October 1910): 847.

23. Safford, "The Good that Trade Unions Do," part 2, *AF* 9 (August 1902): 423.

24. Edward O'Donnell, "Women as Breadwinners: The Error of the Age," *AF* 4 (October 1897): 186. The article continued: "The wholesale employment of women in the various handicrafts must gradually unsex them as it most assuredly is demoralizing them, or stripping them of that modest demeanor that lends a charm to their kind, while it numerically strengthens the multitudinous army of loafers, paupers, tramps and policemen."

25. Safford, "The Good that Trade Unions Do," part 1, pp. 357–58.

26. Gompers, "Should the Wife Help Support the Family?" p. 36.

27. Ibid. See also Louis Vigoreux, "Social Results of the Labor Movement in America," *AF* 6 (April 1899): 25.

28. Women's Labor Resolution, *AF* 5 (January 1899): 220; "Talks on Labor," *AF* 10 (June 1903): 477.

29. Massachusetts, WTUL, *History of Trade Unionism Among Women in Boston*, p. 13; Elizabeth Baker, *Technology and Women's Work* (New York: Columbia University Press, 1964), p. 33.

30. Mildred Rankin to Mrs. Raymond Robins, March 30, 1919, Margaret Dreier Robins Collection, University of Florida, Gainesville, Florida. In 1918, two women members of the federation offered a resolution to the national convention urging the addition of two women to the all-male executive board. It was quietly suppressed.

31. Gompers, "Should the Wife Help Support the Family?" p. 36.

32. Alice Woodbridge, "Women's Labor," *AF* 1 (April 1894): 66–67; Valesh, "Women and Labor," p. 222; and Massachusetts WTUL, *History*, p. 32. 2.

33. WTUL Action of Policies, pp. 3, 8, box 4, accession no. 55A556, WB/NA: Proceedings of the A. F. of L. convention, 1923. See also Massachusetts WTUL, *History of Trade Unionism among Women in Boston*, p. 32.

34. Blankenhorn manuscript notes, chapter 4, p. 17, box 1, file no. 24. Such examples of family unity are not unusual in the mine/mill towns of Western Pennsylvania and the Appalachian mountains. Women helped to picket during strikes, provided essential support services, and sometimes spearheaded attacks against mine management.

35. Pauline Newman, interview, undated, Amerikaner Yiddisher Geschichte Bel-pe, p. 21, YIVO. Gladys Boone, *The Women's Trade Union League in Great Britain and the U.S.A.* (New York: Columbia University Press, 1942), p. 166, recounts a similar incident as having taken place in 1918. I suspect that it might be the same one and that her date is incorrect. Andrews and Bliss, *History of Women in Trade Unions,* p. 149, notes that women practically disappeared from this union between 1905 and 1910—a period in which master bakers were rapidly being eliminated by machinery.

36. Mildred Rankin to Mrs. Raymond Robins, March 30, 1919, Robins papers.

37. Boone, *The Women's Trade Union League,* p. 167; Alice Henry, *Women in the Labor Movement* (New York: Doran, 1923): 102.

38. Interview with Vail Ballou Press, Effects of Legislation: Night Work Schedule, New York, NA/WB.

39. See for example Rankin to Robins, March 30, 1919; and M. E. Jackson, "The Colored Woman in Industry," *Crisis* 17 (November 1918): 14.

40. New York Women's Trade Union League, *Report of the Proceedings,* 4th Conference, p. 14.

41. Undated interviews, unions, for Bulletin no. 65, NA/WB.

42. Testimony of Hilda Svenson, C.I.R., p. 2307; the testimony was taken in June 1914.

43. Florence Sanville to Rose Schneiderman, November 28, 1917, Rose Schneiderman collection, Tamiment Institute library, box A 94. For examples of union discrimination see Massachusetts WTUL, *History of Trade Unionism among Women in Boston,* p. 13; Andrews and Bliss, *History of Women in Trade Unions,* pp. 156, 157; Alice Henry, *The Trade Union Woman* (New York: Burt Franklin, 1973), p. 150.

44. Testimonies, box 15, accession no. 51A101, WB/NA. The women had been hired when the war broke out.

45. Emma Steghagen to Mary Anderson, January 15, 1919, WTUL Action on Policies, accession no. 55A556, WB/NA.

46. United States Education and Labor Committee, *Report Upon the Relations Between Capital and Labor* (Washington, D.C.: G.P.O., 1882), vol. 1, p. 453. See Andrews and Bliss, *History of Women in Trade Unions,* p. 94, for Strasser's often-quoted "We cannot drive the females out of the trade but we can restrict their daily quota of labor through factory laws," and p. 155 of the same volume for Samuel Gompers' fears of female competition as expressed in 1887.

47. Interview is with Mr. Salerno, Amalgamated Clothing Workers, interviews, unions, accession no. 51A101, WB/NA.

48. Interview with Mr. Hurley, July 1919, Women Street Car Conductors, accession no. 51A101, WB/NA.

49. Sir Lyon Playfair, "Children and Female Labor," *AF* 7 (April 1900): 103. See also Martha Moore Avery, "Boston Kitchen Help Organize," *AF* 10 (April 1903): 259, 260.

50. Ira Howerth, "The Kingdom of God in Modern Industry," *AF* 14 (August 1907): 544.

51. Mary Anderson, "The Federal Government Recognizes Problems of Women in Industry," *AF* 32 (June 1925): 453.

52. Individual interviews, Massachusetts, April 12, 1920, accession no. 5A101, WB/NA. Her preference rested on the union's ability to ask for wage raises to compensate for the reduction in hours.

53. Individual interviews, Massachusetts and New Jersey, accession no. 51A101, WB/NA. See especially interviews with A. J. Muste, Mr. Sims, Secretary of the Weavers union, and Amalgamated meeting of workers at Princeton Worsted Mills. These are undated but must have occurred in early 1921.

54. Fannia Cohn to Dr. Marion Phillips, September 13, 1827, Fannia Cohn Collection, box 4.

55. Interviews with Tony Salerno, Amalgamated Clothing Workers Union and Hat and Cap Makers Local 7, Boston, individual interviews, unions, accession no. 51A101, BW/NA. Massachusetts WTUL, *History of Trade Unionism among Women in Boston*, p. 11.

56. Lizzie Swank Holmes, "Women Workers of Chicago," *AF* 12 (August 1905): 507–10; Eva McDonald Valesh, "Women in Welfare Work," *AF* 15 (April 1908): 282–84; "Mainly Progressive," *AF* 3 (March 1896): 16.

57. Shapiro, p. 25.

58. *Justice* (April 19, 1919): 2.

59. Blankenhorn manuscript notes, chapter 13, p. 4, box 1, file 25.

60. For example, see Mary Dreier, address to New York WTUL in *Report of the Proceedings*, 4th conference, 1926, p. 14. Dreier refers in this speech to the difficulty the WTUL had getting female workers to serve on the executive board at first. See Nancy Schrom Dye, "Creating a Feminist Alliance: Sisterhood and Class Conflict in the New York WTUL, 1903–1914," *Feminist Studies* 2 (1975): 24–38. Kenneally, "Women and Trade Unions," treats the WTUL's relations with the A. F. of L. at length.

61. Individual interviews, California, effects of legislation, accession no. 51A101, WB/NA.

62. Quoted in a letter from Mary Van Kleeck to Mary Anderson, February 2, 1923, Mary Van Kleeck collection, Smith College, unsorted.

63. Breman and O'Brien, individual interviews, Massachusetts, accession no. 51A101, WB/NA. Such sentiments must, however, be treated cautiously. We know, for example, that the National Consumers' League in Philadelphia orchestrated an anti-E.R.A. letter-writing campaign by wage-earning women in 1922. The league urged women to write letters arguing that the E.R.A. would limit or eliminate protective labor legislation. See Barbara Klazcynska, "Working Women in Philadelphia: 1900–1930," (Ph.D. dissertation, Temple University, 1975). Janice Hedges and Stephen Bemis point out that most "protective" legislation has now been invalidated by EEOC decisions. "Sex Stereotyping: Its Decline in Skilled Trades," *Monthly Labor Review* 97 (May 1974): 18.

64. Sylvia Shulman, testimony, CIR, pp. 2285, 2292; Hilda Svenson, testimony, CIR, pp. 2311, 2317; Elizabeth Dutcher, testimony, CIR, p. 2392. Exceptions sometimes occurred in small western towns where workers would not patronize nonunion stores. Dutcher testified that 75 employees of Macy's were discharged in 1907 after they attended a union ball. Svenson, CIR, p. 2307; Lillian Mallach to David Dubinsky, December 18, 1964, YIVO. See also minutes of the Waistmakers Conference, January 10, 1911, ILGWU,

Ladies Waist and Dress Makers Union file, Rose Schneiderman collection, Tamiment, box A 95.

65. Rose Schneiderman with Lucy Goldthwaite, *All for One* (New York: Paul Erickson, 1967): 59; Shapiro, p. 9.

66. Elizabeth Maloney testimony, CIR, pp. 3246–47. See also M. E. Jackson, "The Colored Woman in Industry," pp. 12–17.

67. Agnes Nestor, testimony, CIR, p. 3389; Elizabeth Dutcher testimony, CIR, p. 2405.

68. Elizabeth Maloney testimony, CIR, p. 3245.

69. Leon Stein, *The Triangle Fire* (Philadelphia: J. B. Lippincott, 1952), Nestor, CIR, p. 3382.

70. Blankenhorn, manuscript notes, chapter 4, p. 17, file 24, box 1.

71. Nestor, CIR, p. 3382; Svenson, CIR, p. 3382 and Svenson, CIR, p. 2308, reveal the degree to which this was an attempt to undercut union strength; see also an unsigned typescript entitled "Personnel and Management in a Retail Store: A Study of the Personnel Policies and Practices of William Filene's Sons Co., Boston, Mass.," p. 14, in the Mary Van Kleeck collection, unsorted, Smith College; and Marie Obenauer and Charles Verrill, *Wage Earning Women in Stores and Factories*, Report on the Condition of Women and Child Wage Earners (Washington, D.C.: G.P.O., 1911), vol. 5, p. 48; Svenson, CIR, p. 2309.

72. See Cambridge Paper Box Company, Long Hour Day Schedule, accession no. 51A101, WB/NA.

73. Andrews and Bliss, *History of Women in Trade Unions*, p. 169.

74. U.S. Department of Labor, Bureau of Labor Statistics, Bulletin no. 145, 1914, p. 37.

75. *The Cotton Textile Industry*, Report on the Condition of Women and Child Wage Earners, (Washington, D.C.: G.P.O., 1910), vol. 1, p. 608.

76. Mary Anderson, "Industrial Standards for Women," *AF* 32 (July 1925): 21.

77. See Massachusetts WTUL, *History of Trade Unionism among Women in Boston*, pp. 7, 32; New York WTUL, *Report of the Proceedings*, 4th Conference, p. 21.

78. Henry, *Woman and the Labor Movement*, p. 108.

79. Typescript of "Complete Equality Between Men and Women," from the December 1917 issue of the *Ladies Garment Worker*, Fannia Cohn collection, box 7.

16

A Mother's Wages

Income Earning Among Married Italian and Black Women, 1896–1911

■

ELIZABETH H. PLECK

Since women's visible entry into the paid labor market at the start of industrialization, there have been two striking demographic changes in the female labor force: one is the growth in its numbers, the other is the shift in its age and marital status. During the nineteenth century, women who worked outside the home for wages were overwhelmingly young and single. Not until 1910 was even 10 percent of the female labor force married; and only in the post-World War II period have married women come to compose a third of paid women workers. Wives who did work outside the home during the nineteenth and early twentieth centuries were either effectively husbandless (divorced, widowed, or supporting disabled husbands), or their husbands were unemployed—with the significant exception of black women. Elizabeth Pleck begins with the fact that black wives have always shown a much higher rate of labor-force participation than have white wives. Creating a controlled comparison between black wives and Italian wives and carefully scrutinizing several theories that have been advanced to explain black wives' more frequent employment, she clarifies the economic, structural, and cultural reasons for different employment patterns among blacks and whites at similar levels of poverty. This kind of comparative study shows how group characteristics other than womanhood create cultural differentiation among women.

IN RURAL AREAS black as well as white wives were productive laborers, often working in the fields alongside their husbands. In urban areas white wives labored in their homes but did not earn wages; black wives did both. A far higher proportion of black wives were earning wages than any other group of married women: even with her husband at work, a black wife often continued to earn a living. In 1900 the rate of wage earning was 26 percent for married black women and 3.2 percent for married white women.[1] Nor does the contrast of black and immigrant wives narrow this difference. In nearly all American cities in 1900, the rate of employment for black married women was anywhere from four to fifteen times higher than for immigrant wives.[2]

A host of diverse economic, cultural, and demographic grounds have been given in accounting for the high rate of labor-force participation among black married women.[3] Many argue that slavery destroyed any vestige of domesticity and left in its place a black wife and mother hardened to back-breaking drudgery. Others refer to the menial jobs and frequent unemployment of black husbands. Because these men could not find work, it has been said, black wives had to secure jobs as domestics, laundresses, or cooks. As a result of this imbalance, many marriages broke up: husbands separated or deserted and wives were forced to support the family. Then, too, it is claimed that black mothers could easily accept paid jobs because of the availability of grandmothers or other elderly relatives as child caretakers.

Another set of explanations has been given for the absence of immigrant wives from the urban labor market. Among the immigrants Italian women have received particular attention. Italian wives rarely earned wages, despite low incomes and severe unemployment among their husbands. In her study of Italian families in early twentieth-century Buffalo, Virginia Yans-McLaughlin found very few single or married Italian women took jobs. She argued that Italian culture prohibited these women from working, even at the price of family economic well-being.[4] On the other hand, Louise Tilly suggested alternative economic and demographic explanations, such as the large number of mothers with young children or the absence of demand for women workers in Buffalo.[5]

On this subject opinions are strongly held; alas, with little empirical investigation. Survivals of peasant customs can encourage, limit or prohibit specific behavior; old cultural patterns can be enlivened by new economic circumstances or destroyed in the process.[6] Two cultures may respond in a different manner to similar economic circumstances, and a particular culture may also vary its response as economic circumstances change. Too often in recent historical writing family norms have been pitted against economic imperatives without appreciating the context of family needs and economic choices.[7] It is not a question of choosing between economic, demographic and cultural factors but of showing the interaction between these factors. A systematic comparison of groups roughly similar in economic condition is required. Because of the large body of available information and the extent of historical writing, Italians have been compared with blacks, although another European immigrant group could have been selected. Before making the comparison, some background is provided. First, special surveys of Italian and black families around the turn of the century form the basis of the comparison. A portrait of the general economic condition among blacks and Italians demonstrates that both groups lived in desperate poverty. Differences in the higher rate of wage earning for black than for Italian wives are examined in the context of similar as well as changing family conditions and economic opportunities. Finally, some of the reasons for this difference are suggested. Taken together, a black wife faced economic need and found cultural support for working; an Italian wife, often at the edge of poverty, encountered cultural barriers toward her employment which could only be offset by the offer of higher wages.

I

Several government documents permit a direct contrast of urban black and Italian wives. The U.S. Bureau of Labor in 1896 surveyed 6,773 Chicago Italians near Hull House. The same year the Bureau assigned black investigators to study living conditions among 2,748 blacks in Atlanta, Cambridge, Massachusetts, and Nashville. Fifteen years later Senate investigators conducted another survey asking similar questions. The subsequent report, issued by the Senate Committee on the Investigation of the Condition of the Immigrants, known as the Dillingham Commission, ran into forty-six volumes. Two volumes concerned black and immigrant families in seven cities: these seven differed in size, ethnic composition, and most importantly, economic opportunities for working women. Whether it was Cleveland, Boston, or any of the large cities, there was always some demand for women workers as servants. But, in addition, in four of these cities—Philadelphia, Chicago, Boston, and New York—garment industries employed many women workers. The other three—Milwaukee, Cleveland and Buffalo—dominated by aluminum and steel industries, breweries or oil refineries, offered few jobs other than service for women workers.

A comprehensive profile of women's work can be drawn from these documents. Compared with the federal census for the same period, these surveys were far more complete in delineating women's work. The federal census inquired about boarders in the household and women's paid employment but failed to inquire about wages (for women or men) and piece work performed at home.

These surveys in 1896 and 1911 included these questions and much more: data concerning hours of work, weeks of unemployment, and family income. By combining three separate pieces of information from the surveys—paid employment, taking boarders, and piece work—we are able to more accurately contrast wage earning among black and Italian wives.

One can always doubt the accuracy of this information. Surveys have rarely recorded the full range of women's work, but there is little reason to conclude that the wage earning of Italian wives was more carefully noted than for blacks. In 1896 the Bureau of Labor employed black men and women, at least one a lawyer, another a college professor, as surveyors. They asked questions similar to those in the Bureau of Labor report on Chicago's Italians the same year. Blacks have often been underenumerated in surveys, but the absent group generally consists of young black men, not married women. If, for any reason, these surveys failed to count many impoverished black wives, the percentages reported here represent conservative estimates of black women's rate of working: missing women were just as likely, if not more likely to work, as other black women.

Seen from a distance, one might have suspected that Italian wives were more tradition bound and less likely to earn a living than other immigrant women. They were raised in a Catholic, Mediterranean culture which circumscribed a woman's dress and demeanor.[8] A man's honor was a precious but fragile commodity: in her daily actions a wife had to avoid bringing shame on her husband.[9] As recent arrivals in American cities, such wives spoke no English and knew very little about finding employment. Then, too, Italian migration consisted mostly of men. Because this was so, Italian women were likely to marry, often at a young age, and if their husbands found work, it was less necessary for them to do so.

Closer scrutiny of documents for 1896 and 1911 shows that Italian wives were no more confined to the home than other immigrant wives. Peasant wives in Italy were expected to contribute to the family by field work as well as their performance of traditional female tasks. In the blistering Mediterranean sun, Italian wives picked grapes at harvest time and mowed, winnowed, bundled, and hauled sheaves of grain. In a contemporary account about women in Sicily, only the poorest wives worked alongside their husbands in the fields, yet most of the women carried heavy bags of water to the men.[10] Even in Sicily, the wives planted vegetable gardens and sold the surplus, slaughtered pigs, cut wood, dug and weeded mattock.

In American cities few married women from any immigrant

background were employed, according to the survey in 1911. Italian wives were as likely to work as German or Irish wives and more often employed than Polish or Russian Jewish married women (Table 1). Nor did Italian traditionalism prevent daughters from working in American sweatshops and factories, generally with parental approval. In depression-ridden Chicago in 1896, the one city for which information is available, about half of unmarried Italian girls between the ages of fifteen and nineteen were employed.[11] Ruth True, a New York City social reformer, recognized that Italian values, the importance of the family above individual preference, actually encouraged the employment of teenage daughters. She noted: "The girl herself is as eager to go to work as her parents are to have her. She takes it for granted that she should help in the family income. Carlotta gets a job not because she feels the need of self-support as an expression of individuality, or self-dependence, but because she feels so strongly the sense of family obligation."[12] A New York Italian daughter who quit parochial school at age twelve echoed these conclusions: "My father was a stone mason, you know how it is. He didn't have steady work and my mother used to talk all the time about how poor we were. So I had my mind on work all the time. I was thinking how I could go to work and bring money home to my mother."[13]

There are additional reasons for doubting the uniqueness of the Italian situation. Unfamiliarity with a city or with American life was never an effective barrier to employment; the level of employment rose only slightly as Italian wives became accustomed to America. For those Chicago Italian wives in 1896 residing in the city more than ten years, 16 percent were employed, only 3 percentage points higher than for wives resident in Chicago six to ten years, or 6 points higher than for wives in America less than six years.[14] Knowledge of spoken English was never a prerequisite for paid employment, at least in the kind of jobs immigrant wives were forced to accept. The typical Italian wife from any one of seven American cities in 1911 was far less likely to speak English than the Jewish, Polish, or German wife, but she was just as likely and sometimes even more likely to be employed than these women.[15] Even within the Italian community, the ability to speak English was not a necessary job qualification. Among Chicago Italian wives in 1896 the rate of labor-force participation was only 2 percentage points higher for wives speaking English compared with non-English-speaking wives (10 percent vs. 8 percent).[16] Finally, the excess of men failed to alter the rate of working women among Italians. For instance, there were 132 Italian men for every 100 New York City Italian women in 1905.[17] Nonetheless,

TABLE 1

Proportion of Black and Italian Families with Income Contributed by Wives, Children, and Lodgers[a]

Group, City and Date	% with Wives Working	% with Children Working	% with Lodgers	N
Blacks, Atlanta, 1896	65	10	8	240
Blacks, Nashville, 1896	55	12	6	199
Blacks, Cambridge, 1896	44	8	8	88
Blacks, New York, 1905	na	na	42	3014
Blacks, New York, 1911	51	10	27	145
Blacks, Philadelphia, 1911	54	13	41	71
Italians, Chicago, 1896[b]	15	36	16	1227
Italians, Chicago, 1911	19	25	17	219
Italians, Buffalo, 1905	14	19	na	na
Italians, Buffalo, 1911	0	9	37	115
Italians, New York, 1905	na	na	21	2945
Italians, New York, 1911	36	19	20	333
Italians, Philadelphia, 1911	8	23	16	195
Italians, Boston, 1911	16	25	39	210
Italians, Cleveland, 1911	10	22	41	111
Germans, New York, 1911	30	35	0	308
Germans, Chicago, 1911	8	44	11	208
Germans, Milwaukee, 1911	5	28	14	163
Poles, Chicago, 1911	7	21	43	410
Poles, Philadelphia, 1911	7	10	60	159
Poles, Boston, 1911	11	4	61	95
Poles, Cleveland, 1911	4	4	43	131
Poles, Buffalo, 1911	2	28	9	178
Poles, Milwaukee, 1911	5	24	17	150
Russian Jews, New York, 1911	1	31	56	452
Russian Jews, Chicago, 1911	8	30	38	187
Russian Jews, Boston, 1911	15	41	40	226
Irish, New York, 1911	5	18	20	272
Irish, Philadelphia, 1911	28	50	19	98
Irish, Boston, 1911	27	49	18	197
Irish, Cleveland, 1911	5	36	10	122

Sources: Computed from data in "Condition of the Negro in Various Cities," *Bulletin of the Department of Labor*, Vol. II, No. 10 (May 1897), pp. 257–360; Carroll D. Wright, *The Italians in Chicago: A Social and Economic Study* (Washington, D.C., 1897), Table 1, pp. 52–273; Virginia Yans-McLaughlin, "Patterns of Work and Family Organization: Buffalo's Italians," *Journal of Interdisciplinary History*, Vol. II, No. 2 (Autumn, 1971), pp. 111–126; U.S. Senate Reports, 62nd Cong. 1st sess., *Immigrants in Cities*, Vol. 2 (Washington, D.C., 1911), Table 401, pp. 546–548; Herbert G. Gutman, *The Black Family in Slavery and Freedom, 1750–1925* (New York, 1976), Table B-4, p. 530.

[a] Data pertains to families with both husband and wife present.

[b] All evidence for Italians is for South Italians only.

the rate of labor-force participation among Italian wives was higher there than in any other American city in 1911—almost a third of Italian wives were employed.[18] Since single women were removed as competitors for New York City jobs, it may have been slightly easier for Italian wives to find work. Or, more likely, the balance of the sexes may have had less bearing on the employment of wives than the economic demand for women in New York's garment industry.

II

Three dimensions of poverty—low family income, chronic male unemployment, and unskilled labor for men—plagued Italian as well as black families. In these conditions, Italians suffered as much as blacks from low incomes and more from severe unemployment, but they were less concentrated in dead-end and demeaning jobs. Working women from both groups were employed in low wage, low skill jobs, but black women were largely excluded from factory employment. In terms of family income, Italian poverty matched that of blacks. For Chicago Italians in 1896 the median income for a male-present family was $235 compared with black family incomes that year of $393.50 in Nashville, $374 in Atlanta, and $584 in Cambridge.[19] Fifteen years later, despite an increase in real wages, both groups continued near subsistence. Philadelphia's Italians in 1911 earned ten or twenty dollars less than blacks, and New York City's Italians earned virtually the same as blacks.[20]

Severe male unemployment was even more pronounced among Italians than blacks. During a national depression in 1896, a black father in any of eighteen northern or southern cities was out of work an average of 11.7 weeks.[21] Chicago Italian fathers, unemployed on the average thirty-six weeks during the year in 1896,[22] spent the rest of the time in "idleness and almost absolute inactivity in poorly ventilated rooms."[23] Pursuing the question of how families subsisted during hard times, the Bureau of Labor found no unemployed Italian fathers who depended on their wives' wages and only a few who relied on their children. Instead, most Italian families were living on savings or a combination of savings and credit.[24] "When no more money," one Italian father in New York City made plain, "me take out trust at grocery man."[25] An Italian daughter in New York City stated simply: "If there is no money, we eat less."[26] Asked about their means of subsistence, black families also listed savings or credit, but in addition, eleven families in Atlanta, ten in Cambridge, and seventeen in Nashville mentioned the wife's earnings.[27]

Italian as well as black husbands were heavily concentrated in unskilled labor. About one quarter of Italian husbands in Chicago or black men in Atlanta, Nashville, or Cambridge were common laborers.[28] In the other jobs available, Italians differed from blacks: they had access to jobs which in the present offered low wages and high unemployment but which held some promise for the future. Aside from unskilled labor, Italian men earned their livings as tailors, carpenters, barbers, and fruit peddlers. Among New York City Italian male workers in 1905, the racial gap is clear: almost two out of ten Italians were employed in the garment industry and another three out of ten in skilled trades; in contrast, only one out of ten employed black men was in one of these two types of work.[29] Most black husbands not employed as unskilled laborers were servants and waiters and elevator operators: in sum, low-wage jobs, paying almost half what one made in unskilled labor.

An unskilled but racially segregated labor market was even more apparent among the women. Italian daughters, not their fathers, entered factories, mostly sewing pants, shirts, dresses, and gloves, and making boxes, candy, and artificial flowers.[30] More Italian than black women found work in Philadelphia clothing factories; the few black women in this industry were confined to low-paying jobs as pressers, or they sewed the cheaper garments like middy blouses, overalls, and housedresses.[31] Most black women were excluded from factories in the North except as strike breakers or as extra laborers during wartime. Social worker Mary White Ovington summarized the difference between white and black women's work in New York City around the turn of the century:

> She [the black woman] gets the job that the white girl does not want. It may be that the white girl wants the wrong thing, and that the jute mill and tobacco shop and flower factory are more dangerous to health and right living than the mistress' kitchen, but she knows her mind and follows the business that brings her liberty of action when the six o'clock whistle blows.[32]

Two jobs were the mainstay of black women workers: laundry work and domestic service. At these two occupations eight out of ten black wives were employed in 1900. Laundry work was largely the preserve of black mothers. These women, who wanted to remain at home, worked "at their tubs or ironing boards from Monday morning until Saturday night,"[33] often at wages lower than in service. This condition, Mary White Ovington noted, "makes the tenement rooms, tiny enough at best, sadly cluttered, but it does not deprive the children of the presence of their mother, who accepts a smaller income to remain at home with them."[34] Single as well as married black women disliked service. Philadelphia black working women, interviewed in 1919, preferred their work in a rag factory to domestic service because they could enjoy free evenings, holidays, and Sundays.[35] If all else failed, a black mother entered service: five times as many black as foreign-born domestics in 1900 were married.[36] When mothers were compelled to become maids, they often left their children with "babytenders." Although some of these caretakers must have had years of experience, others were unable to properly supervise children and incapable of giving sufficient milk to infants.[37]

Despite the many similarities in economic need for both Italian and black families, there was one defining difference: black wives were far more often breadwinners than Italian wives. There is no mistaking the extent of this racial difference. First of all, the rate of black wives at work was 44 percent in Cambridge, 55 percent in Nashville, and 65 percent in Atlanta in 1896; the rate of Chicago Italian wives at work that year was 15 percent. Fifteen years later, it appears from Table 1, over half of Philadelphia and New York City black wives were employed, but just one out of six Italian wives in these cities were working.

Black mothers were also more likely to supplement the family budget by doing paid work at home.[38] The Dillingham Commission of 1911, which inquired about the number of wives working in the family's quarters, found about one in five black wives in New York City and Philadelphia working at home, usually as laundresses. The photographic record of New York City Italian mothers making artificial flowers or sewing shirts around the kitchen table harmonizes with the statistical reality. In 1911 one-third of Italian wives in New York City were earning wages at home, mostly as tailoresses. But these women were the exception for Italian immigrants: few Italian wives elsewhere were doing piece work, whether in Buffalo or Boston, Chicago or Milwaukee (Table 2).

Black and Italian wives were probably equally as likely to earn money by a third method, taking lodgers. From the percentages in Table 1, it is impossible to give the edge to blacks or Italians in this regard. The number of lodgers varied between years and between cities, perhaps coinciding with the waves of migrants reaching each locale. It is also puzzling to explain the relative absence of lodgers from black homes in Atlanta, Nashville, or Cambridge for 1896. Nevertheless, among black and Italian families in the same city, there was a tendency for blacks to house lodgers more often than Italians. Lodgers were twice as common among black than Italian New York City households in 1905,[39] although six years later the gap

TABLE 2
Percentage of All Italian and Black Wives Employed at Home, 1911

	%	N
Blacks, New York City	23	273
Blacks, Philadelphia	17	139
South Italians, New York City	22	402
South Italians, Philadelphia	3	349
South Italians, Boston	5	309
South Italians, Buffalo	1	205
South Italians, Chicago	3	349
South Italians, Milwaukee	1	145

Source: U.S. Immigration Commission, *Immigrants in Cities,* Vol. II, Tables 24, 78, 126, 290, 340, pp. 39, 83, 127–129, 239, 293–298, 350–352.

between the groups was erased. For Philadelphia in 1911, lodgers were almost three times as common in black as Italian households.

By any measure of income earning, black wives were more often breadwinners than Italian wives. They often took lodgers, earned money doing laundry in their homes, and worked as domestics or cooks. Italian wives frequently housed lodgers, avoided piece work (except in New York City), and very rarely held paid employment.

III

Common sense explanations for why black wives were so often breadwinners have rarely been subjected to systematic comparison. The idea is that some hidden difference in group composition between Italians and blacks accounted for the difference in the rate of wage earning. One by one, seven possible reasons are evaluated: that Italians differed from blacks in terms of income, male unemployment, the presence of young children at home, attitudes toward children's schooling, reliance on child labor, availability of childcare, or marital stability. Any of these seven differences may have produced the lower rate of wage earning among Italian than black wives. The research method examines differences in wage earning, holding each of these factors constant.

First of all, even with husbands earning identical incomes, a black wife was more likely to work than an Italian wife. Among the poorest families in 1896, those with husbands earning less than $200 a year, almost all black wives in Atlanta, Nashville, or Cambridge

TABLE 3
Percentage of Wives in Paid Employment According to Husband's Income, Among Chicago's Italians and Blacks in Atlanta, Nashville, and Cambridge, 1896

	$0–100 (%)	N	$101–200 (%)	N	$201–300 (%)	N	$301–400 (%)	N	$401–500 (%)	N	$501+ (%)	N
Italians, Chicago	20	334	12	379	12	178	9	89	5	55	7	43
Blacks, Cambridge	100	2	100	3	25	8	64	11	41	17	29	38
Blacks, Atlanta	80	10	77	39	66	62	40	42	36	14	28	32
Blacks, Nashville	60	15	68	19	56	43	48	48	11	19	41	27

Sources: Carroll D. Wright, *The Italians in Chicago: A Social and Economic Study* (Washington, D.C., 1897), Table 1, pp. 52–273; "Condition of the Negro in Various Cities," *Bulletin of the Department of Labor*, Vol. II, No. 10 (May 1897), pp. 257–360.

were working, whereas the same desperation sent only a fifth of Italian wives in Chicago to work. At all income levels, Table 3 demonstrates that black wives were far more likely to work than Italian wives. One also needs to include taking boarders as women's income, information which is only available for 1911 (Table 4). The inclusion of this additional income does not alter the basic difference. For every income category, black wives were still more likely to earn wages *and* admit boarders.

When her husband became unemployed, a black wife was more likely to work than an Italian wife.[40] Since the 1911 study by the Dillingham Commission did not include information on unemployment, this comparison depends on computations for 1896. Among Italian wives whose husbands were unemployed at least twenty-one weeks a year, only one in six wives earned wages. For Nashville, Cambridge, and Atlanta black wives in this predicament, the percentage of working wives was at least three times greater. The racial gap appeared whether a husband was unemployed a few weeks or most of the year; in either of these circumstances, a black wife was more likely to work than an Italian wife.

Even with young children at home, black mothers more often took paid jobs than Italian mothers.[41] It is almost a universal condition that mothers of young children find it too difficult to accept paid work; yet the presence of young children was less of a barrier to the employment of black than Italian mothers. For mothers with pre-

TABLE 4
Percentage of Wives Earning Wages or Taking in Boarders by Husband's Income for Black and Italian Families, 1911

	Husband's Income					
	0–$399	N	$400–$599	N	$600+	N
Blacks, New York City	90%	42	71%	38	61%	28
Blacks, Philadelphia	72	29	60	20	83	6
Italians, New York City	47	71	53	170	29	72
Italians, Philadelphia	25	130	16	43	8	13

Source: U.S. Senate Reports, 62nd Cong., 1st sess., *Immigrants in Cities*, Vol. 1, Table 69, p. 230, 410.

school children, probably youngsters under age six in 1896, the data in Table 5 indicates that black mothers in Atlanta, Nashville, and Cambridge were almost four times as likely to earn wages as Italian mothers of young children.

It might be thought that black mothers accepted jobs because they could depend on their kin for childcare. In *The Black Family in Slavery and Freedom*, Herbert Gutman demonstrated the importance of kin networks among slave and emancipated black families. In cities kin were not always available; the evidence suggests female kin were far more frequent in Italian than black urban households. One approximate measure of the availability of female caretakers was the residence of adult women relatives in the household. Yet the odds were one and a half times greater that an Italian household in Chicago included a female relative compared with a black household in Cambridge, Atlanta, or Nashville for 1896.[42] In 1905 the likelihood was that a New York City Italian rather than black household included relatives (23 percent for Italians, 16 percent for blacks).[43] Even when Italian kin did not occupy the same living quarters, they often lived nearby. In studying Italian families of Providence, Rhode Island, in 1915, Judith Smith found that three out of five Italian families were related to at least one other household in the city, and almost all of these kin lived less than eight blocks from their families.[44]

Another possible source of the difference might lie in parental attitudes toward schooling. There is at least substantial reason to think that black parents held more favorable attitudes toward children's education than Italians. If a black mother chose to keep her older children in school rather than sending them to work, she may have been compelled to earn the extra income for her family. To be sure, black children were more likely to attend school than Italian

TABLE 5
Relationship of Mother's Wage Earning to the Presence of Children Among Italians in Chicago, and Blacks in Atlanta, Nashville, and Cambridge, 1896

	Percentage of Mothers at Work							
	No Children at Home	N	Children at Home	N	Children at School	N	Children at Work	N
Italians, Chicago	15%	180	12%	848	18%	124	23%	75
Blacks, Cambridge	48	25	41	32	43	14	67	3
Blacks, Atlanta	49	65	60	108	61	31	50	8
Blacks, Nashville	51	51	44	89	57	37	65	17

Sources: Carroll D. Wright, *The Italians in Chicago: A Social and Economic Study* (Washington, D.C., 1897). Table I, pp. 52–273; "Conditions of the Negro in Various Cities," *Bulletin of the Department of Labor,* Vol. II, No. 10 (May 1897), pp. 257–360.

youngsters. The rate of school attendance was almost twice as great for black sons in Atlanta, Cambridge, or Nashville compared with Chicago Italian sons (aged ten to fourteen) in 1900. Similar disparities appeared in the rate of school attendance among schoolage Italian and black daughters in those cities.[45] Beyond the legal age requirements for school attendance, the pattern of difference held true. Black teenagers of both sexes in Atlanta, Cambridge, and Nashville in 1900 were more likely to attend high school than Italian adolescents. Nonetheless, there is reason to doubt that keeping children in school was the motive behind more black than Italian mothers working. If this had been the case, then one might expect such mothers to quit their jobs when their children finished school. The exact opposite situation occurred for both black and Italian mothers. Both groups of women (with the exception of black wives in Atlanta) were more inclined to work than mothers with school children.

Italian youngsters, who often dropped out of school at an early age, were contributing their wages to the family. In city after city, child labor was more common among Italians than blacks. Can we then conclude that black wives worked because the family could not rely on child labor? To test this suggestion, we can compare Italian and black mothers of child laborers. Even black mothers who could send their children to work still earned wages. Only a quarter of Chicago Italian mothers in 1896 with working children were employed, whereas between one-half and two-thirds of the black mothers of employed children in Cambridge, Atlanta, or Nashville in 1896 still earned a living.

A final explanation for black women's greater participation in the work force is rooted in the short-lived duration of many black marriages. Households with a missing (dead, deserted, or separated) husband were far more common among blacks than Italians, according to a New York City sample from the state census in 1905. In studying two Italian and black neighborhoods in New York City, one in Greenwich Village and the other in San Juan Hill, Herbert Gutman found such female-headed households were almost four times as common among blacks as Italians.[46] Given these differences, it might be argued that black wives anticipated an end to their marriages, and therefore held jobs as a form of economic insurance for the future. Evidence from my research on blacks in late-nineteenth-century Boston is relevant to this argument. The rate of marital dissolution was determined for black couples listed in the manuscript census schedules of the federal census for 1880 who were traced to the same records for Boston twenty years later. (If one or both spouses had died in the intervening period, as certified by Boston death records, they were eliminated from the trace.) Boston black wives whose husbands had left them by 1900 were no more likely to have been employed in 1880 than black wives in stable marriages lasting the two decades, but the 7 percent difference was not statistically significant. In sum, a wife's wage earning bore little connection to her husband's subsequent absence. It is still possible that taking paid employment expressed a wife's doubt about the future of her marriage, but if that was the case, her calculations were inaccurate.

To summarize these comparisons, we have seen that no single economic or demographic condition accounts for the higher rate of wage earning among black than Italian wives. Even if her husband was unemployed or earning very low wages, an Italian wife generally decided against employment, whereas her black counterpart generally took a job. More black than Italian mothers of young children went to work, despite the fact that the supply of female relatives as caretakers was greater in Italian than black households. As Italian children entered the labor force, a mother became the manager of the family finances; even after her working children contributed to the household, a black mother continued to earn an income as well as oversee family affairs. When an Italian mother could rely on the wages of her working children, she did not enter the labor market, while black mothers of working children remained in the labor force. It is true that black wives, who were more often living without husbands than Italian wives, needed to work. But there is no reason to conclude that uncertainty about the future of a marriage was the impetus behind a black wife working.

IV

Faced with similar conditions, blacks and Italian wives acted differently. Confronted with changing conditions, how did they respond? Evidence from Tables 1 through 6 illustrate the effect of changes in the economics of the family environment on the labor-force participation of Italian and black wives. Three factors—family economic need, the composition of the household, and the wage rate for women workers—led to higher rates of working among black as well as Italian wives.

As a first principle, growing immiserization was an inducement to work. The poorer her husband, the more likely that a black wife sought employment in Cambridge, Atlanta, or Nashville in 1896 or in New York City in 1911. Perhaps due to the small number of families studied, this was not true for Philadelphia black wives in 1911: there the wives of wealthier husbands were even more likely to work than more impoverished married women. The same economic squeeze compelled Italian wives to work, whether in Chicago in 1896 or New York and Philadelphia in 1911. A glance at Tables 3 and 4 demonstrates that wage earning for the Italian wife increased as her husband's wage decreased.

The evidence from Table 6 suggests a second conclusion: that chronic unemployment for either the Italian or black husband sent his wife to work. As the number of weeks a husband was unemployed mounted, the wife's rate of employment climbed. Cambridge black wives in 1896, whose incomes were higher, rarely sought work until a husband lost his job. Once that happened, they, like black wives elsewhere, entered the labor force in large numbers. Sustained unemployment for an Italian husband also increased the likelihood of a wife working. For Chicago in 1896, Italian wives with husbands unemployed at least twenty-one weeks a year were twice as likely to work as wives with fully employed husbands.

The age of her children also influenced a mother's willingness to work. All mothers of young children were more likely to remain at home before reentering the work force when their children were grown. Black mothers from Cambridge or Nashville in 1896 slightly decreased their participation in the labor market during the child-bearing years but later reentered the work force in large numbers. Atlanta black mothers never dropped out of the labor force even as young matrons. Freedom from childcare responsibilities also made it easier for Italian mothers to take paid jobs. The tendency to work

TABLE 6

Percentage of Wives Working Due to Husband's Unemployment, Among Chicago's Italians and Blacks in Atlanta, Nashville, and Cambridge, 1896

	Fully Employed	N	Unemployed for Some Time During the Year	N	Number of Weeks Husband Unemployed					
					1–10	N	11–20	N	21–52	N
Italians, Chicago	10%	370	17%	767	15%	66	9%	68	18%	633
Blacks, Cambridge	16	30	53	49	42	26	53	13	80	10
Blacks, Atlanta	50	134	64	66	58	38	63	16	83	12
Blacks, Nashville	48	127	47	53	43	21	38	16	63	16

Sources: Carroll D. Wright, *The Italians in Chicago: A Social and Economic Study* (Washington, D.C., 1897), Table 1, pp. 52–273; "Condition of the Negro in Various Cities," *Bulletin of the Department of Labor*, Vol. II, No. 10 (May 1897), pp. 257–360.

among Chicago Italian mothers was twice as strong for mothers of adult children compared with mothers of preschoolers.[47]

Outside of the family's circumstances, the offer of "higher wages" persuaded more Italian as well as black wives to work.[48] A fair comparison must exclude the black women in southern cities, working at disastrously low wages. In northern cities the offer of higher wages led to expanded levels of paid employment for both sets of wives. For instance, in Philadelphia where black women in 1911 made an average of $170 a year, about half of black wives were earning wages; in New York City that year, where the median wage was $215 a year, seven out of ten black wives worked. When offered slightly higher wages, Italian wives in 1911 were also more willing to work. At a wage of $100 a year, the average for Italian working women in Cleveland and Philadelphia, one out of ten wives worked. With a twenty-dollar increase in pay, the rate in Chicago, two out of ten wives worked. An additional sixty dollars in pay persuaded one-third of New York City Italian wives to work. Just taking the two cities where comparable information was available, Philadelphia and New York, shows that both black and Italian wives responded to economic incentives. An additional sixty-five dollars in wages increased the Italian woman's rate of working by 14 points; a slightly smaller wage increase raised the black woman's rate of working about the same level.[49]

V

A number of possible reasons often advanced to explain the higher rate of employment among black than Italian married women have been eliminated. However, no clear alternative has emerged. There remains one suggestive economic difference: that black women's wage earning was a means of coping with long-term income inadequacy. Like black husbands, Italian men suffered from low wages and chronic unemployment, but their jobs in skilled crafts, the expanding garment industry, or in retail trade offered more future promise: better pay, on-the-job training, and promotions. The jobs of black men as waiters, cooks, and elevator operators were more often dead ends. From the available evidence one can neither confirm nor deny the possibility of this kind of economic difference. However, short of this kind of proof, and having eliminated a large number of economic and demographic explanations, we are forced to consider a residual factor: cultural differences between Italians and blacks.

For Italians cultural attitudes acted as a barrier to the employment of married women. This barrer was less a high stone wall than a low chain fence. Prohibitions applied to married women, especially mothers, but did not extend to daughters. Prior to marriage, Italian daughters often earned wages: after marriage, Italian wives managed finances, cared for the home, gave birth to children, and looked after youngsters. Yet even Italian cultural prohibitions could be overcome with the offer of higher wages, especially for wives doing piece work at home or employed along with other women in neighborhood factories.

For black women the natural tendency is to trace their pattern of wage earning to the legacy of slavery. If bondage fundamentally reshaped the role of slave women, then we would expect to find nearly all of them in the labor force a generation or two after emancipation. This was clearly not the case. Nor was it true that black married women behaved in a manner similar to poverty-stricken white married women. There was a fundamental cultural difference. We need to identify the connection between the slave experience and black attitudes about the involvement of wives in productive labor and in the family. Despite the magnificent new research on slave culture, consciousness, and family life, we are still far from answering this question. What follows are suggestions about how slave culture (defined here as ways of living) related to the wage earning of black married women. It is beyond the scope of this paper to analyze the *origins* of this slave culture (in West African tradition, learning from whites, or the blending of the two experiences amidst generations of life as slaves); rather what concerns us here is to pinpoint the slave ways of life which support black women's wage earning after emancipation. More specifically, we can suggest that black women's wage earning was influenced by three patterns, husband-wife relations, child-rearing, and the emphasis on children's schooling. However, for all the cultural support favoring women's employment, black husbands and wives approached this subject with considerable ambiguity. In fact, these three cultural elements were necessary to offset strong objections to paid employment.

Among black husbands slavery left as its first legacy negative attitudes toward the employment of wives. It is true that contemporary studies, such as a 1970 survey, indicate more favorable opinions toward working wives among black than white men.[50] Another survey in 1966 also found that black husbands, even those born prior to 1911, were less opposed to the employment of mothers with school-age children than white husbands.[51] Nonetheless, contemporary surveys cannot be grafted onto the past. During Reconstruction black husbands vehemently prevented their wives from working in the fields.[52] All over the South freedmen, who demanded a man's wage to support their families, believed their wives should remain at home with the children. One Louisiana plantation mistress noted in 1865 that "Pete is still in the notion of remaining but chooses to feed his wife out of his wages rather than to get her fed for her services."[53] A cotton planter lost money because he had to support "on an average twenty-five to thirty negro (*sic*) women and children in idleness, as the freedmen will not permit their wives and children to work in the fields."[54] This idleness would continue, according to an Alabama cotton grower, because "it is a matter of pride with the men to allow exemption from labor to their wives. . . ."[55] Long after Reconstruction black husbands refused to allow their wives to work for white families. One ex-slave father in the South confessed his ambition "to support his family by his own efforts; never to allow his wife and daughters to be thrown in contact with Southern white men in their homes."[56] In the early twentieth century, an Alabama sharecropper kept his wife from doing laundry for whites. He said, "I didn't want any money comin into my house from that. My wife didn't wait on white folks for their dirty laundry. There was plenty of em would ask her and there'd be an answer ready for em."[57]

Three countervailing cultural tendencies were necessary to set aside these attitudes. The first of these was the pattern of relations between husbands and wives which arose out of slavery. These patterns of interaction were not simple character traits but rather a bundle of contradictions: belief in the husband's responsibility to support his family but doubts about his ability to do so, forthright self-assertion as well as subtle influence and crafty manipulation. The small body of evidence available indicates ex-slave wives also believed in the husband's role as family breadwinner. In the early years of emancipation, freed wives on Henry Watson's Alabama plantation refused to work. They told him "they never mean to do any more outdoor work, that white men support their wives, and they mean that their husband shall support them."[58] Throughout the South the Freedman's Bureau received complaints about black wives who "would not work at all" or others, like the freedwomen in Wharton, Texas, who "left their cabins late and quit the field early."[59] At the same time slavery also taught black women that a husband could not always provide for his family. Many slave fathers died or were sold: perhaps as many as one out of every four husbands or wives were separated by sale.[60] Even when separation did not occur, the slave family did not by itself provide for its needs. Slaves realized that the work of fathers, mothers and children contributed to food and clothing, but the master was the middleman: he not only distributed food and clothing, but also made crucial decisions about the family's future. At the same time the slave wife, who labored in the fields and often cared for her family in her husband's absence, developed more respect for her own ability to assist the family.

Given that freed women did not want to work outside their homes during Reconstruction, how do we explain their unusually high rate of wage earning by 1900? One can only speculate about how this reconciliation occurred. It appears that a black wife recognized the need for more income for the family (which probably was used to purchase food) and then identified her own responsibility for providing some of the cash for the family's needs. Even if a wife decided to seek employment, she often encountered objections from her husband. Most black wives, it appears, successfully overcame their husband's doubts. One cannot uncover this entire process of decision making in black families, except at the final stage: when a wife tried to overcome her husband's objections to her employment. Wives often defined their role in terms of "helping out." As a young girl, Hannah Shaw chopped and picked cotton and milked cows. When she married, her husband insisted she quit working in the field. But she persisted, as he recalled.

> "I'd be in the field at work and my wife—I'd look around, see her comin out there with a hoe. I'd say, "what you comin out here for."
>
> "I thought I'd come out here and help you."[61]

Years later the testimony of Hannah Shaw's husband demonstrates the success of her strategy: "Every step she took, to my knowledge, was in my favor."[62] Martha Harrison, an ex-slave mother, was equally successful in overcoming her husband's objections to her employment. She confessed her tactics:

> My husband never did like for me to work: he used to ask me how come I work; he was doing all he could to give me what I wanted. "Looks like you don't appreciate what I'm trying to do for you." But I'd say, "Yes, I do honey I just help you cause I don't want you to break down. If you put a load on a horse it will pull him down but two horses can pull it jest as easy."[63]

Since there are no parallel examples of black husbands persuading their wives to work, we can assume that black women changed their own minds about employment and then persuaded their husbands. Identifying this process may also reveal what kept Italian wives outside the labor force. To begin with, it might have been the case that they did not define a higher standard of living as a family goal or that they did so, but saw wage earning as the responsibility of the husband and children. Or they may have defined their economic responsibilities in a manner similar to black wives, but simply have been unable to overcome a husband's objection to their employment. The research task is to identify where in this process Italian wives differed from blacks, but so far no documentary material has been uncovered which makes this clear.

The pattern of child rearing in black families was a second reason black mothers found it easier to work than Italian mothers. Italians believed in close supervision of children, blacks in training for independence. Properly raised Italian children (*ben educati*) were never left alone. Mothers told their children to play with siblings and other relatives rather than with neighbors. The extent of supervision probably increased in the New World not only because of dangerous living conditions but also for fear "America . . . will take our children."[64] Far different patterns of child rearing for blacks were the result of slavery. Because mothers as well as fathers worked in the fields, elderly black nurses sometimes cared for children, but more often older siblings supervised the young. It seems plausible to suggest that slave parents rarely connected their physical presence with good parenting; an obedient youngster remained out of trouble when left alone. However, the withdrawal of women from field labor in Reconstruction again suggests that ex-slave mothers wanted to invest more time in child rearing. It seems it was with some reluctance that black families devised patterns of child rearing which taught self reliance at an early age. A working mother was forced to train her children to care for themselves and for each other. One home economist, studying the budgets of Philadelphia blacks between 1916 and 1918, observed that black children often prepared the meals and purchased food for the family at the corner store.[65] In *The Philadelphia Negro* DuBois noted that the chief employment of black children was in "helping about the house while the mother was at work."[66]

A third cultural underpinning for black women's work consisted of parental attitudes towards children's education. Even as slaves blacks desperately sought to read and write. They connected literacy with being able to read the Bible; they gave their greatest respect to fellow slaves who could read aloud passages from Scripture. Ex-slave parents reacted to their deprivations on the plantation: they wanted to read the Bible, write their names, correspond with relatives, keep accounts and much more. In the first years after emancipation, children of the slaves flocked to the newly opened missionary schools and sometimes their parents accompanied them. The belief in education persisted among black parents. We have already seen that even in 1900 the rate of school attendance was far higher among blacks than Italians. But the value of education for children operated within an economic context: because of racial discrimination in hiring, black children found it difficult to secure employment. Moreover, it is too simple to conclude that keeping children in school was the major reason a mother worked. As we have observed, mothers continued to earn wages, even when their children were grown. Instead, the importance of education for children helped a mother overcome doubts about women's wage earning.

This emphasis on children's education was imbedded within a family's plans for its survival. Both groups may have shared the same parental concern for provision in old age, but expressed the concern through different strategies: for Italians, through the continued presence of at least one adult child as a wage earner in the household; for blacks, through the education and social mobility for the children. Both groups tried to plan for the future, but a black family may have placed greater emphasis on a child's schooling as the means of meeting long-term family needs. Thus, both Italians and blacks believed in self-sacrifice, but with a difference. Whereas Italian children often submerged their needs to those of their parents, especially their mothers, black mothers deprived themselves of necessities for the sake of their children. According to a New York City social investigator, the Italian daughter was taught to "subordinate her individual desire" to family needs.[67] Such children, when they went out to work, knew their wages belonged to the family. In contrast, black mothers worked extra hours to help educate their children. Ex-slave mothers in the South "make great sacrifices to spare their own children during school-hours."[68] Mothers in demeaning jobs justified their work in terms of the dignity conferred by educating one's children. One Raleigh, North Carolina, black mother in 1869 stated proudly, "I don't care how hard I has to work if I can only send Sallie and the boys to school looking respectable."[69] We can suggest that in their relations with their husbands, their training of independent children, and their self-sacrifice for children's education, black wives and mothers found strength and support for their wage earning, but at this stage of research, these remain tentative ideas which can only be demonstrated by reexamining how black families in slavery and in the early years of emancipation made choices about women's involvement in work and in the family.

NOTES

A previous version of this paper was presented at the Newberry Library Colloquium on Family and Community History, November, 1975. The author wishes to acknowledge the helpful criticisms of this paper from Miriam Cohen, Leonore Davidoff, Douglas L. Jones, Claudia Goldin, Maurine Greenwald, Nancy Hafkin, Karen Mason, Leslie Page Moch, John Modell, Joseph Pleck, Sheila Rowbotham, and Louise Tilly.

1. U.S. Bureau of the Census, *Twelfth Census of the United States: 1900, Supplementary Analysis and Derivational Tables* (Washington, D.C., 1906).

2. U.S. Bureau of the Census, *Statistics of Women at Work* (Washington, D.C., 1900), Table 29, pp. 311, 315, 323, 325, 353–354, 359, 363–364, 373–374, 387; U.S. Bureau of the Census, *Population,* II (Washington, D.C., 1902), Table 32, pp. 311–314, 325, 337, 342.

3. Studies concerned with the higher rate of wage earning among black women include Glen C. Cain, *Married Women in the Labor Force: An Economic Analysis* (Chicago, 1966); William G. Bowen and T. Aldrich Finegan, *The Economics of Labor Force Participation* (Princeton, 1969); Duran Bell, "Why Participation Rates of Black and White Wives Differ," *Journal of Human Resources,* Vol. 9, No. 4 (Fall, 1974), pp. 465–479; Claudia Dale Goldin, "Female Labor Force Participation: The Origin of Black and White Differences, 1870 and 1880," *Journal of Economic History,* v. xxxvii, No. 1 (March, 1977), pp. 87–112; Edwin Harwood and Claire C. Hodge, "Jobs and the Negro Family: A Reappraisal, *The Public Interest,* No. 23 (Spring, 1971), pp. 125–131.

4. Virginia Yans-McLaughlin, "A Flexible Tradition: South Italian Immigrants Confront a New Work Experience," *Journal of Social History,* Vol.

7, No. 4 (Summer, 1974), pp. 442–445. See also Virginia Yans-McLaughlin, "Italian Women and Work: Experience and Perception," in *Class, Sex, and the Woman Worker,* ed. Milton Cantor and Bruce Laurie (Westport, Connecticut, 1977), pp. 101–119.

5. Louise A. Tilly, "Comments on the Yans-McLaughlin and Davidoff Papers," *Journal of Social History,* Vol. 7, No. 4 (Summer, 1974), pp. 452–459. An excellent analysis of Italian women's work that emphasizes changes in the economy is Miriam Cohen, "Italian-American Women in New York City, 1900–1950: Work and School," in *Class, Sex and the Woman Worker,* pp. 120–143.

6. John Bodnar, "Immigration and Modernization: The Case of Slavic Peasants in Industrial America," *Journal of Social History,* Vol. 10, No. 1 (Fall, 1976), pp. 44–71.

7. A more balanced approach, emphasizing family needs as well as the demands of the industrial environment, is presented in Tamara K. Hareven's "Family Time and Industrial Time: Family and Work in a Planned Corporation Town, 1900–1924," *Journal of Urban History,* Vol. 1, No. 3 (May, 1975), pp. 365–389.

8. Since Sicilian wives were more home bound than other Italian immigrants, their presence in certain cities may have accounted for the absence of Italian married women from the labor market. In point of fact, low rates of wage earning characterized Chicago and Philadelphia Italian women, despite the fact that 8 percent of Chicago's Italians and 12 percent of Philadelphia's Italians were born in Sicily, and high rates of wage earning prevailed among New York City's Italians, about half of whom were Sicilian. Carroll D. Wright, *The Italians in Chicago: A Social and Economic Study* (Washington, D.C., 1897), Table V, p. 372; U.S. Senate Reports, 62nd Cong., 1st sess., *Immigrants in Cities,* Vol. 1 (Washington, D.C., 1911), Table 13, p. 358 and Table 17, p. 175.

9. Jane Schneider, "Of Vigilance and Virgins: Honor, Shame and Access to Resources in Mediterranean Society," *Ethnology,* Vol. 10 (January, 1971), pp. 1–24. This tradition applied especially to Italian women from the South.

10. Leonard Covello, *The Social Background of the Italo-American School Child* (Totawo, New Jersey, 1972), p. 296.

11. Computed from data in Ninth Special Report of the Commissioner of Labor, *The Italians in Chicago: A Social and Economic Study* (Washington, D.C., 1897), Table I, pp. 52–273.

12. Ruth S. True, *The Neglected Girl* (New York, 1914), p. 109.

13. Louise C. Odencrantz, *Italian Women in Industry* (New York, 1919), pp. 175–176.

14. Computed from data in Commission of Labor, *Italians in Chicago,* Tables I and II, pp. 52–351.

15. U.S. Senate, *Immigrants in Cities,* Vol. 2, Table 401, pp. 546–548.

16. Computed from data in Commission of Labor, *Italians in Chicago,* Tables I and II, pp. 52–351.

17. Herbert G. Gutman, *The Black Family in Slavery and Freedom, 1750–1925* (New York, 1976), Table B-1, p. 527.

18. U.S. Senate, *Immigrants in Cities,* Vol. 2, Table 401, pp. 546–548.

19. Computed from data in Commissioner of Labor, *The Italians in Chicago,* Table I, pp. 52–273 and "Condition of the Negro in Various Cities," *Bulletin of the Department of Labor,* Vol. II, No. 10 (May, 1897), pp. 257–360.

In weekly wages Italian male laborers earned less than blacks in Cambridge, Nashville, or Atlanta. Italian wives heading households were also poorer than similar black wives.

20. U.S. Senate, *Immigrants in Cities,* Vol. I, Table 64, p. 226.

21. Computed from data in Department of Labor, "Condition of the Negro in Various Cities," pp. 257–360.

22. Computed from data in Commissioner of Labor, *Italians in Chicago,* Table I, pp. 52–273.

23. Ibid., p. 722.

24. Ibid., pp. 52–273.

25. Odencrantz, *Italian Women in Industry*, p. 163.

26. Ibid.

27. Computed from data in Department of Labor, "Condition of the Negro in Various Cities," pp. 257–360.

28. U.S. Senate, *Immigrants in Cities,* Vol. 1, Table 55, p. 216 and Table 52, p. 396; U.S. Bureau of the Census, *Occupations,* Table 43, pp. 486–489, 506–509, 618–621.

29. Gutman, *Black Family*, Table B-2, p. 527.

30. Commissioner of Labor, *Italians in Chicago*, pp. 379–380.

31. Barbara Klaczynska, "Why Women Work: A Comparison of Various Groups—Philadelphia, 1910–1930," *Labor History*, Vol. 17, No. 1 (Winter, 1976), pp. 73–87.

32. Mary White Ovington, *Half A Man: The Status of the Negro in New York* (New York, 1911; New York 1969), p. 162.

33. Ibid., p. 62.

34. Ibid.

35. Ibid.

36. U.S. Bureau of the Census, *Statistics of Women at Work,* Table 27, pp. 215–217.

37. Ovington, *Half A Man*, p. 58.

38. In New York City large numbers of Italian women were occupied earning wages, generally sewing in their apartments, and fewer wives took in lodgers. This substitution of a mother's wages for a lodger's income was true only in New York City. In other cities wives earned wages as well as taking in lodgers, and elsewhere wives did not work and did not accept lodgers.

39. Gutman, *Black Family*, Table B-4, p. 530.

40. In modern American cities male unemployment depresses the rate of female participation in the labor market, but around the turn of the century, male unemployment led to increases in the number of women working. The contemporary evidence is summarized in James Sweet, *Women in the Labor Force* (New York, 1973), p. 23.

41. Was the absence of other wage earners the reason a black wife had to work? Taking into account the number of wage earners in the family, black wives were still more likely to work than Italian wives. When an Italian family relied on one other income source, generally the husband's wage, one out of ten Chicago Italian wives worked in 1896, compared with one-third to one-half of black wives in Atlanta, Cambridge, and Nashville. With three additional incomes, about seven in ten black wives in Cambridge, Atlanta, and Nashville worked, compared with two out of ten of Chicago's Italian wives in 1896.

42. Wright, *Italians in Chicago,* Table VII, p. 374; Department of Labor, "Condition of the Negro in Various Cities," Table I, pp. 287–288.

43. Gutman, *Black Family*, Table B-4, p. 530.

44. Judith Smith, "Work and Family Patterns of Southern Italian Immigrant Women in Providence, Rhode Island, 1915," unpublished paper delivered at the Berkshire Conference on Women's History, June, 1976.

45. For school attendance figures among black children, I substituted data from the 1900 federal census, which employed a division by age unavailable in the Bureau of Labor survey. Wright, *Italians in Chicago*, Table XVI, p. 385; U.S. Bureau of the Census, *Population*, Part II, Table 54, pp. 396–397, Table 9, pp. 122–136.

46. Gutman, *Black Family*, Table B-4, p. 530.

47. The greater the number of contributors to the family's economy, the higher the rate of wives at work. If just one additional member of an Italian family was employed, then only 10 percent of the wives worked. If at least three other members of the family worked, 17 percent of Italian wives did so. Black wives also increased their rate of working as more family members entered the labor force. For Cambridge black wives, the rate of labor-force participation rose from 36 percent with one additional income earner to 60 percent in families with at least three extra incomes. The rate of working increased from 43 percent to 63 percent for Atlanta wives, and from 53 percent to 67 percent for Nashville wives.

48. A working wife could never expect to match her husband's income; hence, the availability of work for women never adequately replaced a man's wages. Nevertheless, the ratio of male to female wages was higher for blacks than Italians. In Philadelphia the wages of a black wife in 1911 were 42 percent of those of her husband, and 71 percent in New York City. By contrast, among New York and Philadelphia Italians, a wife earned one-third what her husband made. U.S. Senate, *Immigrants in Cities*, Vol. 1, Tables 66–67, pp. 228–229, 408–409.

49. U.S. Senate, *Immigrants in Cities*, Vol. 1, Table 57, p. 64; Table 65, p. 448; Table 67, p. 229; p. 409; Table 70, p. 583; Table 72, p. 746; Table 76, p. 324.

50. Karen Oppenheim Mason and Larry L. Bumpass, "U.S. Women's Sex Role Ideology, 1970," *American Journal of Sociology*, Vol. 80, No. 5, (March, 1975), pp. 1212–1219.

51. James Morgan, I. Sirageldin, and Nancy Baerwaldt, *Productive Americans: A Study of How Individuals Contribute to Economic Progress* (Ann Arbor, 1966), Figure 19-4 p. 330. Consult also John Scanzoni, "Sex Roles, Economic Factors and Marital Solidarity in Black and White Marriages," *Journal of Marriage and the Family*, Vol. 37, No. 1 (February, 1975), pp. 130–144; Leland J. Axelson, "The Working Wife: Differences in Perception Among Negro and White Males," *Journal of Marriage and the Family*, Vol. 32, No. 3 (August, 1970), pp. 457–464; D. D. Lewis, "The Black Family: Socialization and Sex Role," *Phylon*, Vol. 36, No. 3 (1975), pp. 221–237.

52. Eugene D. Genovese, *Roll, Jordan, Roll*, p. 490; Vernon Burton, "Black Household Structure in Edgefield County, South Carolina," unpublished paper, 1976; Robert Abzug, "The Black Family during Reconstruction," in *Key Issues in the Afro-American Experience*, ed. Nathan I. Huggins, Martin Kilson, and Daniel M. Fox, Vol. 2 (New York, 1971), pp. 26–41.

53. Gutman, *Black Family*, p. 168.

54. Ibid.

55. Ibid.

56. Gerda Lerner, *Black Women in White America: A Documentary History* (New York, 1973), p. 292.

57. Theodore Rosengarten, *All God's Dangers: The Life of Nate Shaw* (New York, 1974), p. 128.

58. Gutman, *Black Family*, p. 168.

59. Ibid.

60. Ibid, pp. 146–155; John Blassingame, *The Slave Community: Plantation Life in the Ante-Bellum South* (New York, 1972), p. 90; Herbert Gutman and Richard Sutch, "The Slave Family: Protected Agent of Capitalist Masters or Victim of the Slave Trade?" in Paul A. David, Herbert G. Gutman, Richard Sutch, Peter Temin, and Gavin Wright, *Reckoning with Slavery: A Critical Study in the Quantitative History of American Negro Slavery* (New York, 1976), Table 3, p. 129.

61. Rosengarten, *All God's Dangers*, p. 127.

62. Ibid., p. 475.

63. Lerner, *Black Women*, p. 15.

64. Covello, *The Social Background of the Italo American School Child*, p. 296.

65. Sadie Tanner Mossell, "The Standard of Living Among One Hundred Negro Migrant Families in Philadelphia," *Annals of the American Academy of Political and Social Science*, v. XCVIII, No. 187 (November, 1921), p. 186.

66. W. E. B. DuBois, *The Philadelphia Negro: A Social Study* (Philadelphia, 1899, New York, 1967), p. 111.

67. Mary Van Kleeck, *Artificial Flower Makers* (New York, 1913), p. 86, as quoted in Miriam J. Cohen, "The World of Work and the Family: New York City Italians, 1900–1950," unpublished paper, 1977.

68. Lerner, *Black Women*, p. 246.

69. Ibid., p. 102.

17

Our Own Kind

Family and Community Networks in Providence

■

JUDITH E. SMITH

The United States received an enormous infusion of immigrants at the end of the nineteenth century from countries such as Italy, Poland, and Russia, which had earlier yielded few. The cultural background and hence the American experience of women of these new immigrant groups were likely to differ substantially from those of American citizens. Judith E. Smith's study of Italian and Jewish families who arrived in Providence at the turn of the century depicts the double-layered web of family group and ethnic neighborhood that comprised such women's environment. Besides using newspaper accounts and social surveys, Smith draws on oral interviews with immigrants and their descendants to provide a richer and more personal view of life and work.

THE RHODE ISLAND working class has been continually reconstituted by succeeding waves of immigration in the nineteenth and twentieth centuries. First Irish, then French Canadian, then Italian, Jewish, and Portuguese: all have come from peasant communities to resettle in the mill towns and industrial cities of the state. Listening to immigrants describe their daily life in the old country and in the New World, one is repeatedly struck by their frequent references to the family. Looking more closely at the process by which thousands of immigrants found their way to Rhode Island, one sees that family ties provided the links of the chain that extended from communities in Europe to communities in Rhode Island. The family stands at the very center of their work and life. To focus on the immigrant family, then, is to begin to understand the texture of social life in immigrant communities transplanted in the New World.

Recent work in the history of the family has raised questions about the timing and character of change in family life. Standard views of this change held that the family began to lose its productive functions with the onset of industrialization and that this fundamental loss necessitated other changes: the family moved from an extended to a nuclear household, from a producer to a consumer economic unit, from a public to a private sphere.[1] New research, however, has provided examples of societies and families that defy this categorization. Nuclear families existed long before the beginnings of industrialization, just as family producer units continued to coexist with large modern industrial organization.[2] This research has generated a more flexible model of social change in which the family is seen as taking its particular form from the complex and shifting interaction of an inherited cultural tradition, the social relations of production, and the legal provisions of the state. By its challenge and adaptation to existing structures of production and social life, the family stands in a dialectical relation to its own history and to its environment.[3]

Immigrant families provide particularly rich material with which to explore the implications of this formulation. Immersed in a common cultural tradition, they moved abruptly to an alien one, where they confronted quite different structures of production. In effect, they experienced change in their own lifetimes that elsewhere required generations to unfold.

My work follows the reshaping of southern Italian and eastern European Jewish family traditions in a fast-paced, urban, industrial environment. The study is based on an analysis of the work and family histories of 160 Italian families and seventy-one Jewish families, who came to Providence between 1880 and 1914 and settled in the ethnic neighborhoods of Federal Hill and Smith Hill. These families were drawn from the 1915 Rhode Island state census and traced through state censuses, city directories, and birth, marriage and death records. The histories extend from the families' arrival in Providence to 1940, long enough in most cases to see the second generation married and settled into work. The restricted size and neighborhood setting of the group of families are at once a problem and an advantage. As the numbers are too small to be conclusive, the experiences of these immigrants can only be suggestive. But the limited scale also means that I have been able to trace these immigrants in detail, situating them in the context of their lives in family and neighborhood networks, an important dimension of immigrant history often lost or ignored. Given the limitations of these public sources which systematically under-reported women's activities, I have attempted to trace whole families: mothers and fathers, sisters and brothers, daughters as well as sons, in addition to cousins and grandparents. I have used traditional literary sources, oral history interviews, and collected family histories to give texture to the account gleaned from the public record.

The analysis of immigrant family traditions in Providence reveals neither a sharp uprooting nor a simple continuity. Italian and Jewish immigrants brought with them traditions of family and family work groups which had evolved in the particular agrarian economy of the south of Italy and in the artisan-commercial economy of Jewish communities in the Pale. Through the social and economic transformations taking place in Europe and the personal transformation undergone during migration, the family group proved to be the critical resource which facilitated both the migration to the U.S. and the reestablishment of immigrant communities here. Families migrated on the basis of kin ties and settled near relatives, recreating collective family economies and using the conditions in their new neighborhoods and workplaces to establish connections between households. The traditions of mutual support and obligations which operated inside families were embodied in the community institutions that immigrants built.

For both Italians and Jews in the different economic contexts of southern Italy and eastern Europe, the family group was the work group. Southern Italian immigrants to Providence came from towns in Abruzzi, Campania, Basilicata, Calabria, and Sicily. The economic structure of these regions depended upon the household as the primary form of economic organization. There were very few large estates in these regions still intact by the end of the nineteenth century. The break-up of the large estates did not lead to an equal land distribution, but it did increase the number of peasants who owned land. Generally, small, medium, and large holdings ranged side by side in each district. Most of the land was divided into small parcels which were cultivated independently. Partible inheritance traditions and the role of land in marriage settlements led to increasing subdivision of the land. Land changed hands frequently and ownership, rental, sharecropping, and wage labor were all common.[4]

The small size of land plots in the south limited the size of the agricultural work group to an individual family, usually parents and unmarried children, although households sometimes included aging parents who could no longer work. Even when the families owned land, the plots were too small to sustain them fully, and most families combined agricultural work with non-agricultural pursuits. Cash was usually scarce.[5] One Italian immigrant from Sicily described how her family combined work in their own fields, work in other fields for wages, and craft work for the market: "Angelina, her siblings, and her mother and father all lived with her grandmother in a small farmhouse which had been passed down to them as family land. Although they did own the house and the land around it, their annual income was just enough to sustain them. . . . The family lived from their own land and their job was to raise enough crops and produce to live on for the year. . . . In days when there was little to do on the farm, Maria, the mother, would send the children to neighboring farms to help pick the vegetables and fruits for an average 3¢ a day, while she herself would do extra weaving to sell."[6]

The survival of the family was dependent on the work of all its members; this meant mothers as well as fathers, children as well as parents. Often wages were paid to the head of the household for the labor of all family members. Usually, all worked in the fields; additionally, women cooked, cared for children, washed and patched worn clothes, and marketed extra produce. Rarely did all members of the family work in the same place, since families frequently farmed several plots at some distance from each other. In some parts of western Sicily, women worked in nearby garden plots while men worked in fields at a greater distance from their towns. Family members did not necessarily do the same kind of work, since mothers, sons, and daughters were likely to be hired out as wage laborers if the family required additional income for food, fuel, and taxes for the year.[7]

The Jewish immigrants to Providence in the late nineteenth and early twentieth centuries came from the western borders of Russia and from Poland, the area known as the Pale of Settlement. Laws in 1882 and 1891 forced the resettlement of Jews from rural villages, and from other regions of Russia, into the crowded cities of the Pale. By the census of 1897, Jews represented fifty-eight percent of the urban population in the northwestern provinces of Russia.[8] The law explicitly prohibited Jews from working on the land, and the settlement laws had the effect of keeping Jews out of the larger industrial establishments—sugar mills, mines, smelting and metal works, glass works—situated outside the towns. So Jews worked in trade, artisan crafts, and in small-scale manufacturing, disproportionately to their numbers; Jews made up only 11.6 percent of the population of the provinces which composed the Pale, but by 1898 were four-fifths of its commercial class, two-thirds of its artisan class, and one-third of its industrial class.[9] At this point, both trade and the kind of manufacture in which Jews took part were organized on a small scale, and were frequently carried on in small shops in the front of, or nearby, people's homes. Most artisans were self-employed, and according to one account, "the artisan's home is the artisan's shop."[10] Like Italians, Jews were mostly likely to work in family groups.

The settlement laws placed Jews in a marginal economic position. Even within the Pale, they were restricted to a few hundred larger and smaller towns that were not particularly well suited to either commerce or industry. Kiev, the most important commercial and industrial center, was closed to Jews. Without freedom of movement, the ability to earn a living in small trading or artisanship was limited, and Jews were forced into intense competition with each other. Seasonal unemployment and frequent periods of poverty resulted. By the 1890's, about twenty percent of the Jewish population in the Pale required charity to buy the matzoh with which to celebrate Passover; in Vilna, nearly thirty-eight percent of the Jewish population received charity for Passover.[11] These limits on their economic ability made Jewish households similarly dependent on the labor of all family members. As in Italy, women cooked, cleaned, cared for children, and produced and marketed home manufactured items. In the northwest provinces, especially, women worked as seamstresses, milliners, knit goods makers, and cigarette makers, in small shops and factories. The oldest daughter of a tailor, living in a small town not too far from Minsk, recalled the means by which her family managed to live, especially after her father was forced to leave home to avoid conscription into the Czar's army: "As soon as we were able to hold a needle, we were taught to sew. Mother taught us how to spin . . . [the mother sewed for women in the village, and the blind grandmother knitted stockings to sell]. Of course, the stockings had to be looked over, the lost stitches found and mended carefully. That was my work . . . And Grandfather . . . would go to the village to see if there were any pots to mend. Grandfather had clever hands. He could do anything with a pen knife and a piece of wood. And in mending pots he was a perfect artist."[12]

Complex social and economic changes were transforming southern Italy and eastern Europe in the late nineteenth century, unsettling ordinary family economic strategies, lending new urgency to the dependence of family members on each other, creating the conditions which prompted immigration of family groups. In southern Italy, population increases expanded the number of young men and women entering the labor market. Commercialization of agriculture in other parts of Italy made the traditional agricultural methods of the south less competitive, so that families' needs for extra, nonagricultural income were increased. But industrialization in other parts of Italy diminished the availability of the artisan work on which sons and daughters had depended to supplement the family budget. Although the broader diffusion of property rights held out the hope that families might be able to accumulate land and provide for their sons and daughters, the means of adding to family income in order to do this were diminishing.[13] One peasant from Abruzzi described both the raised hopes and the economic constraints which prompted his father's emigration to the U.S.: "The year before, my father had been trying to better our conditions. He had hired two large pieces of arable ground on which he had toiled every minute of daylight during that whole season. Having no money to make the first payment on the land, he had to borrow some at a very high rate of interest. At the end of that season, after selling the crops, he found that he had just barely enough to pay back the rest of the rent and to pay back the loan with the enormous interest. . . . That season of excessive toil made my father much older. His tall strong body was beginning to bend. He had become a little clumsy and slower. And the result of his futile attempt made him moody and silent. He would sit on our doorstep in the evening and gaze out."[14]

Jewish families experienced new instability and uncertainty in their customary way of life. The abolition of serfdom in 1861 dissolved the traditional relationship between nobles and peasants, and, with it, the place of Jews as agents and middlemen. The waves of pogroms, violent attacks on Jewish communities in the 1880's and 1900's, were brutal evidence of the new, more uncertain relationship between Jew and peasant. The introduction of modern industrial tools depressed, but did not displace, artisan craft, while the increased production of the machines, which forced manufacturers to seek wider markets, meant that artisans began to produce for stores rather than for individual customers. All through the last part of the nineteenth century, the economic position of the Jews in Russia deteriorated at the same time as their numbers increased. From 1847 to 1897, the number of Jews in the Pale tripled. The move from village to city undermined the traditional *shtetl* culture that had characterized the Jewish community for hundreds of years. But new ideas flourished in the vacuum: the religious enthusiasm of Hasidism, the modern enlightenment thought of Haskalah, the development of a secular Yiddish literature and cultural movement, *Yiddishkeit*, the political ideology of socialism, the notion of a Jewish rebirth through Zionism. Again, it was against a background of economic constraint and cultural transformation that the Jewish immigration, like the Italian immigration, took place.[15]

In the context of these shifting communities, the family economic unit was even more critical for survival in Southern Italy and Russia. Immigration was itself a family response to changing conditions. Young Italian men and women in search of new opportunities to supplement their family income came to the United States to work and start families here. Some did return to Italy, and many families continued to send money there to support family members who remained. But most families stayed in Providence, seeming evidence of a reorientation, a decision to sink roots here. Jews, in search of less circumscribed economic opportunities, and sometimes in escape from specific attacks on their communities, left their homeland when convinced that life there was hopeless, and they often pulled up stakes as family groups to resettle permanently in the United States.

The family was thus at the center of the migration process. The family economic unit was easily adaptable to migration. Migrants could look to brothers, sisters, and cousins who had gone before them to send passage money and to secure housing and jobs for the new arrivals.[16] Although migration chains were based primarily on family groups, migrants did not all arrive at the same time, and migration had its own potentially disruptive effects on traditional family expectations. Parents too old to make the journey had to die alone in the old country. Men left wives and children behind while they came to America to earn the money to bring the others over. One brother stayed behind to cultivate the family land while another made the journey across the ocean. Newcomers valued intensely whichever of their relatives were close by, as much for their connection to a familiar past as for their skills in negotiating the new environment.

Because of this structural relationship between families and migration, kinship ties connected much of the immigrant community. Over half of the Italians and one-third of the Jews lived near kin when they first appeared in the Providence city records. By 1951, three-fifths of the Italians and nearly half of the Jews had brothers, sisters, parents, cousins, and married children in their own households or nearby.

The proximity of these relatives meant that extra connections *between* households compensated in part for incomplete family groups. Most of these relatives lived near enough to each other to meet daily to exchange news, gossip, meals, and child care. Of the Italians who had kin in Providence in 1915, three-fourths lived within one block of each other, and 94 percent were within walking distance, seven to eight blocks. As one Sicilian immigrant whose family settled in Rochester, New York, explained: "Most of my relatives lived within one neighborhood, not more than five or six blocks from each other. That was as far apart as they could live without feeling that America was a desolate and lonely place. If it could have been managed, they probably would have lived under one roof."[17]

The interaction between families involved immigrants in reciprocal obligations as well as expectations of support. An Italian immigrant to Providence, Maria A., described how she and her family lived with her uncle, his wife, father, and step-mother. "As I grew up, living conditions were a bit crowded, but no one minded because we were a family." Immigrants looked to their close kin for help in times of trouble. After Maria's mother died, her aunt helped her to take care of the younger children in her family, and she felt "thankful we all lived together." A Jewish immigrant to Providence who lived in a tenement owned by his sister-in-law remembered how the children ran in and out of both families' apartments. His son recalled that the family paid no rent for several years when his father was out of work.[18]

The ethnic neighborhoods where immigrants settled provided a context in which traditional economic interdependence of family members could be recreated and new connections between families developed. The sheer concentration of immigrants in these neighborhoods made them cultural enclaves. The movement from Italy and Russia to Providence gathered momentum in the 1880's, reaching its peak for both groups around 1905. The steady stream of immigrants from regions in Southern Italy and provinces of the Pale created neighborhoods where families clustered together, surrounding themselves with familiar accents, sights, and sounds. By the 1890's, the Irish who had originally inhabited Federal Hill and Smith Hill had moved out to less densely populated sections of the city, abandoning these areas to Italian and Jewish immigrants.[19]

The needs of the crowded immigrant neighborhoods for goods and services provided a ready-made market for artisans and shopkeepers to sell their wares. Some immigrant craftsmen were able to establish themselves in their neighborhoods; by 1915, many had their own shops, or, at least, a front room in their tenements, and continued to work for themselves in or next door to their homes until they retired. Immigrants looked to their countrymen to cut a wedding suit, perhaps with a slightly more American style. Certainly one would look to a *paesan* or a *landsman* for mending shoes, sharpening knives, and buying fruit. Bakers made familiarly shaped loaves and grocers stocked favorite foods. Many kept accounts for credit, and shoppers could hear news of home and bargain in their own language. Some immigrant artisans moved beyond the world of the ethnic neighborhood; some of the tailors fitted suits in downtown department stores by 1930. But most continued to depend on the immigrant neighborhood for their livelihood. And, as in the old country, where craft skills were passed from generation to generation, artisan brothers worked with brothers, and shopkeepers looked forward to the day when their business could support a son or son-in-law.

For neighborhood artisans and their families, and for retail shopkeepers, the family continued to be the work group, as it had been in the old country. The overlap of home and workplace meant that women and children could work alongside their husbands and fathers without neglecting home duties. One Italian immigrant daughter remembered combining school and work in a family bakery: "I can remember rising as early as five o'clock to make the bread and clean the trays before going to school. At home I was given a certain amount of time to do my chores and home work, and then my father would check to see what was accomplished. I received an eighth grade education and was satisfied to work in my father's business. Both of my brothers also worked in the bakery, although it was not demanded that we do so. . . . I also managed the books at work as I was very good with figures."[20]

The immigrant neighborhood provided women and children with another way to earn money at home. They might cook, and clean for boarders and lodgers, who were likely to be new immigrants working for the passage money to bring other members of their own families to this country. The needs of newer migrants for room and board meant that women could be economically productive by extending the services they were providing for their own families. One Italian daughter remembered: "Her mother took in boarders, three at a time: everyone ate together, she [the daughter] washed and ironed their clothes, and the boarders paid accordingly." Families used their living space as a resource to extend limited incomes. A Jewish salesman's daughter remembered that her family had met hard times by renting the room her invalid grandmother had been sharing with her aunt: "My grandmother and mother got my room and Ann [her aunt] and I shared the sofa in the living room."[21]

Industrial homework provided another way for women and children to earn money at home. Various Providence industries divided and subdivided the process of manufacture, resulting in the proliferation of small tasks which could be done outside the shops. Homework provided manufacturers with a cheap reserve labor force for the busy seasons. Snaps to card, chains to link, military buttons to stamp on a foot press, rosary beads to string, artificial flowers to stem, lace threads to pull; all were widely available in Providence on a seasonal basis. Often the work was subcontracted through neighborhood networks, with one woman acting as a distributor for families within several blocks.[22]

Most immigrant families needed more than one wage earner; as one homeworker explained: "We didn't have enough money with just one man working." Clearly, homework was an important alternative to going out to work for women who had children at home: "I have two children and would rather be home to get them something to eat at mealtime." As little money as homework produced, it was a way for women to be economically productive, as this woman explained: "I like to have my own money. I like the work and would rather have $50 earned by myself than $100 saved out of my husband's pay."[23]

The Children's Bureau investigators who arrived in Providence in 1918 to report on child labor found to their dismay that children routinely helped their mothers with homework. They found homework most common in the Italian and French-Canadian neighborhoods, although they found evidence of it in most of the working-class neighborhoods of the city. One Jewish son remembered working on jewelry his father brought home from work in the busy season before Christmas. Children in the Italian neighborhood even brought chains to school to link at recess on the fine spring days, and the Children's Bureau investigators also found some teachers at those schools assigning homework at school so their classes could contribute to Liberty Bonds or Red Cross.[24] Homework provided a means of earning money which was taken for granted in the immigrant neighborhoods, part of a varied family-based economy.

Skirting the neighborhoods were the jewelry shops, machine shops, and textile mills which employed others of the immigrant generation. Where the size of fields in southern Italy and the overcrowded market competition of the cities in the Pale had discouraged the formation of work groups larger than one family, the recruitment methods of the factories lent themselves to developing connections between families. The factories were new work places for southern Italians and generally larger in scale and more modern in machinery than factories where Jews may have worked in Russia. But the immigrants made the factories more familiar by working in them with their brothers and sisters. The foreman's control over hiring made it relatively easy for immigrants to get jobs for one another. Men offered to speak to their foremen for newly arrived brothers, and if there was work, the brother usually got it. Sisters did the same for younger sisters. These kin connections at work were prominent in immigrants' descriptions of their jobs: In a rubber plant: ". . . A little later on, I was more in a position, you know what I mean, to help some of my relatives get a job. See? And so, I think I must have got at least seven or eight of them. I got Angelo a job over there, and my brother Michele the job, and my brother Albert, one time, and I think there were a couple of others on the outside, too."[25] In textiles: "It was almost a family affair there, all cousins and relatives working there, everybody."[26] In an optical shop: "My uncle was foreman there. . . . That was my first job. I worked there with my mother. . . . My sister worked there a while, too."[27]

The connections between families which ran through neighborhood and workplace were extended beyond family to the level of community in the mutual benefit societies which Italian and Jewish workers organized in their own communities in Europe, and then in Providence. Immigrants looked to these societies, which distributed sickness and death benefits, as an extension of the mutual support and obligations they experienced in their own families. The mutual benefit societies, in turn, articulated the traditions of mutual obligation on a community-wide basis, thus providing a justification for punishment through collective action of those who operated outside of community norms.

Mutual benefit societies had proliferated in southern Italy in the last part of the nineteenth century, generated by the same social and economic changes that sparked immigration. In Palermo, Sicily, there were nine such organizations by the 1860's, including groups of fruit vendors, agricultural workers, and master shoemakers. The organizations were often commune-wide, and included important local or national figures as honorary members while restricting active members to working men, men who derived their livelihood from their own labor. The division in southern Italian town life often dictated that there be two local societies, one for the town workers who saw themselves as more of an entrepreneurial group, and one for agricultural workers. These societies engaged in educational self-help activities, and organized producer and consumer cooperatives as well as providing sick and death benefits for members.[28]

Transplanted in Providence, most Italian societies were formed along provincial lines. By 1919, there were one hundred societies in Providence, seventy of which were based on provincial loyalties, a common dialect, patron saint, and social and religious customs.[29] One Providence observer remarked, "A great number of organizations such as the Societa Arcese, Societa Teanese, Circolo Frosolone, and others initially constitute provinces of their own in the community. To attend their meetings and listen to their business conducted in a characteristic dialect is like crossing from one Italian province into another."[30]

In addition to their function as a source of social and cultural roots for their members, the aid of the mutual benefit societies extended the resources of the hard-pressed immigrant families. The societies made payments if a member was sick and could not work, often providing the care of their own doctor. When a member died, the smaller societies at least insured that there would be proper ceremony at the funeral by paying the expenses of the band, and the larger and wealthier societies paid all funeral expenses. Each society also sponsored an annual feast day in honor of the patron saint of their village, and these celebrations, complete with band concerts, parades, and fireworks, were an important assertion of the Italian presence in Providence.[31]

In the Pale, mutual benefit societies called *chevrahs* had formed along trade lines as groups of men who prayed and read the Torah together. Mutual obligations of members began with night vigils with sick members and participation in the services for the dead, and naturally extended into sickness and death benefits. In the increasing economic crisis of the last half of the nineteenth century, *chevrahs* began to split along class lines. In one city, for example, there were separate *chevrahs* of independent craftsmen and workingmen of ladies' tailors, carpenters, dyers, and stove builders, and joint *chevrahs* for shoemakers, jewelers and watchmakers, tin workers, roofers, and locksmiths. The ladies' tailors' *chevrah* also acted as a union, negotiating for wages and hours. The Jewish labor movement, the *bund*, also provided organizational form to groups outside of the traditional crafts. Draymen in Pinsk and Berdichev, boatmen in Kovno, hotel attendants in Pinsk and Slonim, and domestic workers in Warsaw, Grodno, Mogilevm Bobruisk, Pinsk, and Dvinsk had organizations, which struck for higher wages and shorter hours.[32]

In Providence, *chevrahs* reappeared in different forms: as congregations based on provincial ties organized to read the Torah together and as local lodges of national Jewish organizations which provided sickness and death benefits. The first Russian *chevrah* in Providence, B'nai Zion, was started by immigrants from the northwestern provinces of the Pale in 1874; and in 1889 the Polish members split off to form their own congregation which would use their own more familiar form of ritual. Congregations from other provinces and from Austria formed in the following years.[33] Huge parades, bands, and celebrations would accompany a *chevrah* as it moved from temporary quarters to a more permanent building, as occurred in 1906 when Congregation Sons of Jacob moved into a new building on Douglas Avenue. According to the newspaper, thousands were in the streets to celebrate the transfer of the holy scriptures from one place to the other, listening to Russian music, carrying red, white and blue streamers, American flags, and Jewish flags.[34] The *chevrah* B'nai

Zion increased in size with immigration from the northwestern provinces: it grew to include a *chevrah* concerned with care for the dead in 1876, a *chevrah* responsible for care of the sick in 1890, and two *chevrahs* for study of different parts of the Talmud in 1892.[35] The local lodges included a workingman's circle and a Hebrew trades' association which organized along trade lines for self-help and collective bargaining.[36] One Jewish daughter in New York described the importance of her father's *chevrah* to him: "Father belonged to a society of which he was an active member. The men often came to our house to talk things over with him, and he felt important and often offered our front room for committee meetings. Before they opened the meeting they always assured mother that they would not keep us later than ten. But when the time came they were always so deep in discussion that they never even heard the clock strike the hour. I used to sit in the doorway of the kitchen and front room from where I could see all their faces and listen to their heated arguments. Always it was a piece of burial ground that was the subject of discussion and when a member, or anyone belonging to his family, died, whether the rest of the members should contribute an extra dollar to cover burial expenses and whether as a society they should or should not employ a doctor and pay him out of the society fund. At twelve or even later they would at last break up with the question of the burial ground and the extra dollar and the doctor still unsettled.

"Then mother and I would go into the front room, coughing and choking from the cigarette smoke and open up the folding cots and carry the sleeping children to bed. The little ones often cried at being awakened to undress. But father, if he had succeeded in carrying a point, and in the knowledge that he had served the society in giving the room, went to bed smiling."[37]

The tradition of mutual support and obligation led the immigrant communities to apply collective pressure when they felt that individuals were neglecting their responsibilities and taking advantage of the support of the community. In August 1914, Italians attended two mass meetings protesting the high price of food before they took to the streets Saturday night, August 29, to mete out special punishment to a pasta wholesaler who had raised prices. The wholesaler, Frank P. Ventrone, was a prominent businessman in the Italian community who had come to Providence in the 1880's from Isernia, a city from which many Italians had emigrated to Providence. Over a thousand people marched through Federal Hill, shattered the windows in a block of property owned by Ventrone, and then dumped his stock of macaroni and staples into the street. The participants saw this as an internal community issue and resisted the intervention of the police. According to newspaper accounts, "Jeers and catcalls greeted the police as they tried to clear the area," and "night sticks were freely used." "Every time the patrol was sent to the Knight St. station with a prisoner, it was a signal for the mob to hurl at the police anything they could grab." When the police returned to Federal Hill the next afternoon, ostensibly to make an arrest on a non-support charge, Italians again resisted the intrusion of the police in a three-hour struggle which the newspapers called "the worst riot in the annals of the city."[38]

On Monday, a meeting between the Italian Socialist Club and a representative of Ventrone negotiated an agreement which substantially lowered the price of pasta. The Italian newspaper, in its editorial the next week, articulated the basis on which community sanctions had been applied when they argued that "Signor Ventrone . . . owes everything to our colony," and thus had a responsibility to the community which he did not meet until pressure was brought to bear on him. "Our brave colony, when we all stand together, will be given justice."[39]

In 1910, women of the Jewish community in South Providence, a Jewish neighborhood similar to that on Smith Hill, took a similar action when they declared "war against the kosher butchers," because of price increases. The women planned to boycott meat sold by the kosher butchers in their community until "the meat has come down to the prices which the people could afford." The women picketed the shops, and dissuaded shoppers from buying meat. The butchers attempted to mobilize their own support by going on a house-to-house canvass to drum up business, in some cases bringing meat to families who had not ordered it. The women strikers sent delegates to the houses with an explanation of the boycott to persuade the families to rescind their orders, and "in every case, it was said, the butchers were instructed to send after the meat."[40]

More than simply prices were at stake. The strikers' demands included "respectable treatment of the customers," echoing demands of Dvinsk domestic workers for private rooms and Kishinev shop workers for "polite treatment of employees." Other demands insisted on "fresh meat wrapped in clean paper and not in newspaper as has been the custom in some of the shops," as well as a "reduction in the price of all cuts of meat." The police were called out to keep the women picketing the shops from blocking the entrances and biting prospective customers. The women won their protest when another butcher opened a shop in the neighborhood, offering meat at the prices they demanded. The other butchers reluctantly lowered their prices as well.[41]

Both Italian and Jewish immigrants actively recreated their family traditions in the process of building a new life in Providence, and in so doing, participated in the transformation of these traditions. Over time, changes in work opportunities and family residence patterns loosened the closely-woven networks of kin and community which defined daily life in the old neighborhoods. The process of change involved both the shifting of external circumstances and the reordering of individual and family priorities.

The workplaces of the immigrant generation were profoundly affected by large-scale economic shifts in the twentieth century: changes in marketing and retailing, expansion of the white-collar sector, technological and management-oriented directions of production. Small craft shops suffered from competition with department stores and ethnic food shops lost ground to supermarkets.[42] The sons and daughters of self-employed tailors, shoemakers, and peddlers became salespeople and clerks in those department stores and supermarkets, or automobile and insurance salesmen, working in English-language worlds outside the experience of their parents. Sons and daughters of factory workers who themselves worked in jewelry shops and in the dwindling number of textile mills worked on new machines which made the skills of their parents obsolete, and at speeds which would have made their parents' heads spin.

Families continued to operate as interdependent economic groups, but changing working conditions altered the responsibilities that women and children held. Families still expected every member to work, but production moved out of the home with the decline of neighborhood craft and retail shops, the immigration restriction which cut down the supply of available boarders, and the decreased availability of homework after its prohibition in the National Recovery Administration codes. It was harder for women to combine productive work with child care, and the patterns and timing of mothers' work shifted. Instead of working when their children were young, and then turning to their children for supplementary wage earning when they were old enough to work, mothers waited until all their children were in school to work.

Family economic responsibility was still shared. Even without counting the work of some married women, largely invisible in the public record, virtually all the Italian and Jewish families still in Providence in 1930 had an average of two wage earners per family, usually father and child. Sons and daughters still routinely gave their paychecks to their families, but the tradition of the children's contribution to the family began to encounter resistance. When children helped their mothers and fathers with boarders, homework, or by standing behind the counter in a shop, the income thus produced was clearly generated by family effort. But now sons and daughters were unmistakably working for their own wages. Sons and daughters had a stronger sense of their own needs, peer pressure towards certain kinds of consumption, and a feeling of entitlement to their own earnings. Some children arranged for a larger share of their wages indirectly: "Mary and her sisters resented turning over every cent they worked for and having a small allowance handed out to them to buy needed clothing, personal items, and for leisure activities. They became adept at sewing, knitting, crocheting, making do, and borrowing from mother." Other children simply withheld part of their paychecks. While an older sister dipped into her wages only to treat herself to carfare on payday, her younger sister responded differently: "I'll never forget the time I got my first pay, you know, I'm altogether different from the way she [her older sister] is. . . . I went downtown first, and I spent a lot, more than half of my money. . . . I just went hog wild, I guess. And I came home, and we used to have to hand our pays in. So I gave my father what I had left and he threw it at me. So, I just picked it up and took the rest of it. The next week he didn't throw it at me, he just kept what I gave him."[43]

Families continued to build connections between households, but the community context which had supported and extended these relationships shifted. Families continued to live near enough to each other for help and support, and when the sons and daughters of the immigrant generation married, they frequently chose to live near their parents. In 1930, sixty percent of Italian married children lived at the same address as their parents, presumably in another floor of a triple-decker, and another twelve percent lived within four blocks. Only thirty percent of Jewish married children lived in the same building as their parents, but an additional forty percent lived within four blocks. But the Italian and Jewish communities as a whole had spread out over the city. Less than half of the Italians and Jews who had lived on Federal Hill and Smith Hill still lived there in 1930. Some families left the city altogether. Italians moved with their children to two houses next door to each other on a tree-lined street in Mount Pleasant, or to two houses around the corner from each other in suburban Cranston. Jewish families moved farther west on Smith Street, and to the less crowded blocks in South Providence. Families in these less ethnically homogeneous neighborhoods were less likely to come from the same province in the old country, less likely to share a common past. The loosening of neighborhood and provincial ties combined with the provisions of social security and company insurance plans eroded the traditions of the mutual benefit societies that had extended family relationships on a community-wide basis.

Though there were differences between the Italian and Jewish experience, both groups illustrate the manner in which immigrants used the family traditions they brought with them from Europe to shape their new environment. This transformation of immigrants' lives from generation to generation illuminated a process of family change which in other circumstances took longer to develop. As the settings of work and community changed, the context in which family networks operated was altered, and old networks were loosened. But at the same time, new possibilities were created for new kinds of connections, across ethnic lines, at work in the large companies and in factories, in the new industry-wide CIO unions, in leisure activities and political clubs in the newer ethnically-mixed neighborhoods. These new kinds of community, created out of a waning immigrant consciousness, must be the focus of investigations into contemporary working-class culture.

NOTES

1. Talcott Parsons, "The Social Structure of the Family," in R. N. Anshen (ed.), *The Family: Its Function and Destiny* (New York, 1949), pp. 173–201; Neil Smelser, "The Industrial Revolution and the British Working Class," *Journal of Social History* 1 (1967), 17–35; John Demos, *A Little Commonwealth: Family Life in Plymouth Colony* (New York, 1970); Eli Zaretsky, *Capitalism, the Family and Personal Life* (New York, 1976); Barbara Laslett, "The Family as a Public and Private Institution: An Historical Perspective," *Journal of Marriage and the Family* 35 (August, 1973), 480–94.

2. Peter Laslett, *The World We Have Lost* (New York, 1965); Michael Anderson, *Family Structure in Nineteenth-Century Lancashire* (Cambridge, 1971); Elizabeth H. Pleck, "Two Worlds in One," *Journal of Social History* (Winter, 1976).

3. This critique appeared in Lutz Berkner, "The Stem Family and the Developmental Cycle: An Eighteenth-Century Austrian Example," *American Historical Review* 77 (1972), 398–418, and "The Use and Misuse of Census Data for the Historical Analysis of Family Structure," *Journal of Interdisciplinary History* 5 (Spring, 1975), 721–38. I have been particularly influenced in my own analysis by the critiques of functionalism in Pleck, "Two Worlds in One," and in Lise Vogel, "Rummaging Through the Primitive Past: A Note on Family, Industrialization, and Capitalism," *Newberry Papers in Family and Community History*, 1976.

4. J. S. MacDonald, "Agricultural Organization, Migration, and Labor Militancy in Rural Italy," *Economic History Review* 16 (August, 1963), 68–70; Sydel Silverman, "Agricultural Organization, Social Structure, and Values in Italy: Amoral Familism Reconsidered," *American Anthropologist* 70 (February 1968), 11–15; Josef Barton, *Peasants and Strangers: Italians, Roumanians, and Slovaks in an American City, 1890–1950* (Cambridge, Mass., 1975), pp. 30–35.

5. Silverman, "Agricultural Organization," 11–15.

6. GB, University of Rhode Island, New England Family History Collec-

tion, hereafter referred to as URI-NEFHC. The work of Sharon Strom, Jim Findlay and Valerie Quinney (members of the History Department at URI) in sponsoring the collection of oral and family histories has been invaluable to my research.

7. Silverman, "Agricultural Organization"; Donna Gabaccia, "Housing and Household Work: Sicily and New York, 1890–1910," paper presented at Social Science History Association, October 1977; Joan Scott and Louise Tilly, "Women's Work and the Family in Nineteenth Century Europe," Center for Research in Social Organization (October, 1973), 9–18; later published in *Comparative Studies in Society and History* 17 (January 1975).

8. I. M. Rubinow, "The Economic Condition of the Jews in Russia," U.S. Senate, *Report of the Immigration Commission: Emigration Conditions in Europe*, Senate Document 748 (Washington, 1911), 287.

9. Rubinow, "Economic Condition," 293; Ezra Mendelsohn, *Class Struggle in the Pale: The Formative Years of the Jewish Worker's Movement in Tsarist Russia* (Cambridge, 1970), 6.

10. Rubinow, "Economic Condition," 306.

11. *Ibid.*, 333–34; Henry J. Tobias, *The Jewish Bund in Russia from its Origins to 1905* (Stanford, 1972), pp. 9–10.

12. Rubinow, "Economic Condition," 305; Rose Cohen, *Out of the Shadow* (New York, 1918), pp. 23–24.

13. Barton, *Peasants and Strangers*, pp. 39–40. Frank Thistlethwaite, "Migration from Europe Overseas in the Nineteenth and Twentieth Centuries," in Katz and Kutler (eds.), *New Perspectives in the American Past*, Vol. 2 (Boston, 1969), pp. 70–76.

14. Pascal D'Angelo, *Son of Italy* (New York, 1924), pp. 48–49.

15. Tobias, *Jewish Bund*, pp. 6–7; Mendelsohn, *Class Struggle*, p. 11; Irving Howe, *The World of Our Fathers* (New York, 1976), pp. 15–24.

16. Barton, *Peasants and Strangers*, pp. 18–63; John and Leatrice MacDonald, "Chain Migration, Ethnic Neighborhood Formation, and Social Networks," *Milbank Memorial Fund Quarterly* 42 (January, 1964), 82–97; John and Leatrice MacDonald, "Urbanization, Ethnic Groups, and Social Segmentation," *Social Research* 29 (1962), 433–48; Thistlethwaite, "Migration," 66–67.

17. Jerre Mangione, *Mount Allegro* (Boston, 1943), p. 40.

18. ENC, URI-NEFHC; S. Family Interview, April, 1977; S. Family interview, September 9, 1976.

19. William Kirk (ed.), *A Modern City: Providence, Rhode Island, and Its Activities* (Chicago, 1909), pp. 33–62; John Ihlder, *The Houses of Providence, Rhode Island: A Study of Present Conditions and Tendencies* (Providence, 1916), pp. 22–25, 94–95; Bessie Bloom, "Jewish Life in Providence," *Rhode Island Jewish Historical Notes* 17 (November, 1970), 386–408.

20. ENC, URI/NEFHC.

21. MRD, URI-NEFHC; MW, URI-NEFHC.

22. Women's Bureau Bulletin No. 131, "Industrial Home Work in Rhode Island" (Washington, D.C., 1922); Children's Bureau Bulletin No. 100, "Industrial Home Work of Children: A Study Made in Providence, Pawtucket, and Central Falls" (Washington, D.C., 1922).

23. Children's Bureau Bulletin, 22, 48, 24.

24. Children's Bureau Bulletin; S. Family interview, Correspondence File, Record Group 102, Box 979, National Archives, Industrial and Social Division.

25. M. Family interview, December 1, 1975.

26. M. Family interview, December 1, 1975.

27. N. Family interview, September 2, 1976.

28. John Briggs, "Lower Class Organizational Life in Italy and America: Implications of Continuity and Change in Organizational Forms," paper presented at the Italian-American Historical Association, Jewish Historical Society Conference, March 1977, pp. 21–24. See also John Briggs, *An Italian Passage: Continuity and Change Among Immigrants 1890–1930* (Yale University Press, forthcoming).

29. "Active Fraternal Life of Little Italy," *Providence Journal*, 21 December 1919.

30. N. Ruggieri, "Societa Arcese Typical," *Providence Evening Bulletin*, 11 March 1936.

31. *Providence Evening Bulletin*, 6 March, 4 March, 11 March 1909; *Providence Journal*, 20 September 1909, 2 October 1909, 16 July 1911, 21 August 1911.

32. Rubinow, "Economic Condition," 309–10, 322–24.

33. "Chartered Organizations," *Rhode Island Jewish Historical Notes* 2 (June, 1955), 21–65.

34. *Providence Journal*, 17 September 1906.

35. Beryl Segal, "Congregation Sons of Zion of Providence, Rhode Island," *Rhode Island Jewish Historical Notes* 12 (November, 1965), 239, 248–49.

36. "Chartered Organizations," 21–65; Bessie Bloom, "Jewish Life in Providence," 403.

37. Rose Cohen, *Out of the Shadow*, pp. 196–97.

38. *Providence Journal*, 30 August, 31 August 1914.

39. *Providence Journal*, 1 September 1914; *L'Eco*, 5 September 1914. My thanks to Paul Buhle for translating this editorial for me.

40. *Providence Journal*, 22 June, 23 June 1910.

41. Rubinow, "Economic Condition," 526–62; *Providence Journal*, 23 June, 24 June 1910; personal correspondence from Beryl Segal, 8 December 1977.

42. *Providence Journal Almanac* (1935), 74–75.

43. SBS, URI-NEFHC, 44; M. Family interview, December 1, 1975.

18

Female Support Networks and Political Activism

Lillian Wald, Crystal Eastman, Emma Goldman

■

BLANCHE WIESEN COOK

Among the two generations born between 1860 and 1900 were the first American women to participate, on a large scale, in public vocations. They did so, in the main, by choosing not to marry and by avoiding the exclusive domestic vocation which late-Victorian rhetoric assigned to women. A uniquely high proportion (over 10 percent) of women born between 1860 and 1880 never married; more of those born between 1880 and 1900 married, but still not as many as among twentieth-century generations. Blanche Wiesen Cook's examination of the lives of several leading women of this period puts in a new light their choices of alternatives to typical marriage and nuclear-family living. Her evocation of the support, sensuality, and communication that women shared with one another, and the significance of these in the women's public achievements, illuminates the heterosexist bias of traditional historical writing.

IN VERA BRITTAIN'S *Testament of Friendship*, the biography of her beloved friend Winifred Holtby, the British activist and author wrote that

> From the days of Homer the friendships of men have enjoyed glory and acclamation, but the friendships of women, in spite of Ruth and Naomi, have usually been not merely unsung, but mocked, belittled and falsely interpreted. . . .[1]

Part of the problem is general in scope and involves a distorted vision of the historian's craft that is no longer operable. Historians of my generation were trained to believe that the proper study of our past should be limited to the activities of great men—the wars of kings, the hero's quest for power. We were taught that the personal was separate from the political and that emotions were irrelevant to history.

Recent history and the movements of the sixties, the decade of our professional maturing, have revealed the absurdity of that tradition. It has become clear that in history, no less than in life, our personal choices and the nature of our human relationships were and remain inseparable from our political, our public efforts. Once the personal impact of such confined historical perspective emerged, the need for revision became clear.

In my own work, ten years of work on the historical peace movement—studies that included such significant women as Lillian Wald, Jane Addams, Crystal Eastman, and Emma Goldman—I had focused entirely on women's political contributions. I wrote about their programs for social justice and their opposition to international war. Nothing else. Whenever I came across a love letter by Lillian Wald, for example, I would note "love letter," and move on.

This paper is the result of a long overdue recognition that the personal is the political: that networks of love and support are crucial to our ability as women to work in a hostile world where we are not in fact expected to survive. And it comes out of a recognition that frequently the networks of love and support that enable politically and professionally active women to function independently and intensively consist largely of other women.

LILLIAN WALD, CRYSTAL EASTMAN, EMMA GOLDMAN

Beyond their commitment to economic and social change and their opposition to America's entrance into World War I, Lillian Wald, Crystal Eastman, Emma Goldman, and Jane Addams had very little in common. They are of different generations, represent contrary political solutions, and in their private lives reflect a broad range of choice. Yet all four women expanded the narrow contours of women's role and all four left a legacy of struggle against poverty and discrimination.

Jane Addams and Lillian Wald were progressive social reformers. The most famous of the settlement-house crusaders, Wald created the Henry Street Settlement and Visiting Nurse Service in New York while Addams founded Hull House in Chicago.

Crystal Eastman, a generation younger than Addams and Wald, was an attorney and journalist who investigated labor conditions and work accidents. In 1907 she authored New York State's first workman's compensation law, which became the model for most such laws in the United States. One of the three founders of Alice Paul's Congressional Union for suffrage, Eastman was a socialist and radical feminist who believed in "free love."

More outspoken and less respectful of authority than Addams and Wald, Eastman nevertheless worked closely with them in the peace movement. Wald was president of the American Union Against Militarism, the parent organization of the American Civil Liberties Union, and Eastman was its executive secretary. Addams was president of the Women's Peace Party (renamed the Women's International League for Peace and Freedom), and Eastman, also one of its founders, was president of the New York branch. Their differences of temperament and tactics tell us much about the nature of the women's movement during the rapidly changing era of WWI.[2]

Emma Goldman was outside their company, but always in the vanguard of their activity. Addams, Wald, and Eastman worked to improve immigrant and labor conditions. Goldman, an anarchist immigrant worker, sought to recreate society. They worked within the law to modify it. Goldman worked without the law to replace it with anarchist principles of voluntary communism.

Goldman frequently visited the Nurses' Settlement on Henry Street and liked Lillian Wald and her co-workers, particularly Lavinia Dock, well enough. She thought them "women of ideals, capable of fine, generous deeds." But she disapproved of their work and feared that their activities created "snobbery among the very people they were trying to help." Although Jane Addams was influenced by anarchist writings, Goldman regarded her even more critically. She thought Addams an elitist snob.[3]

Emma Goldman's work with Crystal Eastman on behalf of birth control, the legalization of prostitution, and free speech in wartime was also dissatisfying. They agreed on more issues: but when Eastman and her circle were on the same picket line or in the same park distributing birth-control literature with Goldman and her allies, only Goldman's group would be arrested. That was the nature of class in America.

Wald, Eastman, and Addams worked to keep America out of war through the American Union Against Militarism (AUAM). They dined at the White House with Wilson and his advisors. They hired professional lobbyists to influence Congress. Goldman worked through the Antimilitarist League and spoke throughout the United States on the capitalist nature of war and the cruelties of the class system. When she was arrested, the Civil Liberties Bureau of the AUAM defended her; but the members of the AUAM were not themselves arrested. Goldman's wartime activities resulted in her deportation. Wald and Addams received commendations from the government because, in addition to their anti-war work, they allowed their settlement houses to be used as conscription centers.[4]

As different as their political visions and choice of strategies were, Addams and Wald, Eastman and Goldman were dedicated to a future society that guaranteed economic security and the full development of individual potential for women and men on the basis of absolute equality. Reformists, socialist, anarchist, all four women made contributions toward progressive change that are today being dismantled. The playgrounds, parks, and school lunch facilities they built are falling apart all over America because of lack of funding and a callous disregard for the needs of our country's children. The free-speech and human-rights issues they heralded are today facing a reawakened backlash that features the needs of "national security" and a fundamentalist Christianity that seems more appropriate to the 17th century.

The Historical Denial of Lesbianism

The vigor and strength of these four women, born daughters in a society that reared daughters to be dependent and servile, cannot be explained without an understanding of their support networks and the nature of their private lives. Their lifestyles varied as dramatically as did their public activities from the prescribed norm of "wife-mother in obedient service to husband-father" that their culture and their era valued above all.

Of the four women, only Emma Goldman relied predominantly on men for emotional sustenance and political support. Although she was close to many anarchist and radical women, there were few with whom she had intimate and lasting relations. The kind of communal and noncompetitive intimacy of the settlement houses or the younger feminist movement Crystal Eastman was associated with was never a feature of Goldman's life.

Yet throughout her life, Goldman wrote, she "longed for a friend of my own sex, a kindred spirit with whom I could share the innermost thoughts and feelings I could not express to men. . . . Instead of friendship from women I had met with much antagonism, petty envy and jealousy because men liked me." There were exceptions, and Goldman listed them in her autobiography. But basically, she concluded, "there was no personal, intimate point of contact."[5]

Like Goldman, Crystal Eastman was also surrounded by men who shared her work, her vision, and her commitment to social change. Unlike Goldman, she had a feminist support group as well. Her allies consisted of her husband (particularly her second husband, Walter Fuller), her brother Max, and the women who were her friends, many of them from childhood and Vassar until her early death in 1928. Eastman's comrades were the "new women" of Greenwich Village. Radical feminists and socialists, they considered men splendid lovers and friends, but they believed that women needed the more egalitarian support of other women. For Crystal Eastman and her associates this was not only an emotional choice, it was a political necessity.

Jane Addams and Lillian Wald were involved almost exclusively with women who remained throughout their lives a nurturing source of love and support. Henry Street and Hull House were staffed by their closest friends, who, night and day, made possible their unrelenting schedules.

In the past, historians tended to ignore the crucial role played by the networks of love and support that have been the very sources of strength that enabled political women to function. Women's friendships were obscured and trivialized. Whether heterosexual or homosexual, the private lives of political women were declared beyond the acceptable boundaries of historical inquiry. As a result, much of our history and the facts that define our heritage have been removed from our consciousness. Homophobia, a bigotry that declares woman-loving women an evil before God or a mental disease or both, has served to erase the very aspects of our history that would have enabled us to deal healthfully with what has been for most lesbians an isolating and cruel experience. Homophobia has also erased a variety of role-models whose existence would tend to obliterate crude and dehumanizing stereotypes.

The very existence of networks of women such as the creative community that flourished in France between 1880 and 1940 and beyond was unknown to us. Only recently have we begun to recover the work and correspondence of such independent women as Margaret Anderson (founder of *The Little Review*), poet and essayist Natalie Barney, artist Romaine Brooks, poet Renée Vivien, and novelist Djuna Barnes. Except for the recent and severely flawed biography of Romaine Brooks and the more recent and also flawed biography of Natalie Barney, no serious study of that generation of self-styled Amazons, the expatriate lesbians of America, has yet been attempted.[6]

This denial has persisted over time. The figures that serve as the frontispiece for Dolores Klaich's book *Woman + Woman* symbolize the problem. We see a sculpture, dated c. 200 B.C., of two women in a tender and erotic embrace. It has been called by the curators of the British Museum, "Women Gossiping."

Similarly, companionate women who have lived together all their adult lives have been branded "lonely spinsters." When their letters might reveal their love, their papers have often been rendered unavailable.* Interpreting Freud through a Victorian prism and thinking it enlightened, male historians have concluded that the settlement-house reformers were asexual women who sublimated their passionate energies into their work. Since they were not recognizably "dykes" on the order of Radclyffe Hall or Gertrude Stein, and they always functioned too successfully to be called "sick," the historical evidence was juggled to deny the meaning of their lifestyles altogether.

So, for example, William O'Neill can refer to the 40-year relationship between Mary Rozet Smith and Jane Addams as that of "spouse-surrogates" and then conclude: "Finally, one suspects, the very qualities that led [Addams] to reject the family claim prevented her from experiencing the human reality that she celebrated in her writings and defied convention to encounter. She gave her time, money, and talents entirely to the interests of the poor. . . . In a sense she rejected the personal claims upon her, . . . and remained largely untouched by the passionate currents that swirled around her. The crowning irony of Jane Addams' life, therefore, was that she compromised her intellect for the sake of human experiences which her nature prevented her from having. Life, as she meant the term, forever eluded her."[7]

Allen Davis observes a different phenomenon. "It would be easy to misunderstand," Davis writes, the friendship and affection between Jane Addams and her early companion Ellen Gates Starr. Quoting Gordon Haight, Davis concludes: " 'The Victorian conception of love between those of the same sex cannot be fairly understood by an age steeped in Freud—where they say only beautiful friendship, the modern reader suspects perversion.' "[8]

It is important to understand the language here. We are being told that, since Jane Addams was a conventional lady with pearls, her intense "romantic attachments" to other women could not possibly be suspected of "perversion." As a result, the perfectly ordinary nature of women's differing sexual preferences has been denied

* See Dolores Klaich, *Woman + Woman: Attitudes Toward Lesbianism* (Morrow, 1974). The recently successful pressure to open the Mary E. Woolley Papers at Mt. Holyoke is a case in point. The famous college president lived with the chairwoman of the English Department, Jeannette Marks, for many years. They were lovers. When that fact was discovered their papers were closed.

expression. Without information and history, we have become ignorant of the range of our choices. Repression and conformity have been fostered and an entire generation of activist and passionate women branded by historians, on no evidence whatsoever, as "asexual."

Our prejudices are such that it has been considered less critical —kinder, even—to label a woman "asexual" rather than "lesbian." Allen Reznick, for example, assures us that life did not elude Lillian Wald. His 1973 dissertation is the only study that deals with Wald's personal life, and Reznick is eager to inform us—which he does in the title of his foreword—that she was made "Not of Glazed China, But of Flesh and Blood." But Reznick is entirely unprepared to deal with the implications of women's relationships. In his view, the fact that Wald answered so many admiring letters and made no "documented effort at denial or discouragement" hints that she accepted female affection, even solicited it. Then, he concludes, she was undoubtedly too busy for social relations anyway.[9]

In their analyses, Davis and O'Neill distinguished between Victorian attitudes and our post-Freudian "enlightenment." Yet the denial of lesbianism is literally Victorian. The Queen herself was appalled by the inclusion of a paragraph on lesbianism in the 1885 Criminal Law that sought to penalize private homosexual acts by two years' imprisonment. She "expressed complete ignorance of female inversion or perversion and refused to sign the Bill, unless all reference to such practices was omitted."[10]

More sensitive than most male historians, Allen Davis notes that although the romantic words and the love letters "can be easily misinterpreted," what is important is "that many unmarried women drew warmth and strength from their supportive relationships with other women." But he concludes that "whether or not these women were actually lesbians is essentially irrelevant."[11]

If we lived in a society where individual choice and the diversity of our human rhythms were honored, the actuality of lesbianism would in fact be irrelevant. But we live in a society where children are taken away from lesbian mothers, where teachers are fired for bedroom activities, where in June 1976 the Supreme Court endorsed the imprisonment of consenting adults for homosexual relations, and where as I sit typing this paper—in June 1977—the radio announces that Dade County, Florida, by a vote of 2:1, has supported Anita Bryant's hate campaign against homosexuals.

Such legal and social manifestations of bigotry and repression have been reenforced and are validated by the historical rejection and denial of diversity in general and of independent and alternative lifestyles among women in particular. It is the very conventionality of women like Jane Addams and Lillian Wald that is significant. Not until our society fully accepts as moral and ordinary the wide range of personal choice will differences be "essentially irrelevant."

As I think about Anita Bryant's campaign to "Save Our Children" from homosexuality, my thoughts turn to Lillian Wald, who insisted that every NYC public school should have a trained nurse in residence and who established free lunch programs for the city's school children. My thoughts then turn to Jane Addams, who, in an essay called, "Women, War and Babies," wrote:

> As women we are the custodians of the life of the ages and we will not longer consent to its reckless destruction. We are particularly charged with the future of childhood, the care of the helpless and the unfortunate, and we will not longer endure without protest that added burden of maimed and invalid men and poverty-stricken women and orphans which war places on us.
>
> We have builded by the patient drudgery of the past the basic foundations of the home and of peaceful industry; we will not longer endure that hoary evil which in an hour destroys or tolerate that denial of the sovereignty of reason and justice by which war and all that makes for war today render impotent the idealism of the race.[12]

And in the wake of the first mid-20th-century American vote to discriminate against an entire group of people,[13] my thoughts turn again to Lillian Wald and Jane Addams, who campaigned for the creation of the United States Children's Bureau. That bureau set up programs throughout the United States to care for battered wives and battered children; it crusaded against child labor and for humane child care.[14] Yet Anita Bryant would demand that we save our children from Jane Addams if Anita Bryant knew that Jane Addams slept in the same house, in the same room, in the same bed with Mary Rozet Smith for 40 years. (And when they travelled, Addams even wired ahead to order a large double bed for their hotel room.)

Because difference arouses fear and condemnation, there are serious methodological problems involved in writing about women who, for political and economic reasons, kept their private lives as secret as possible. The advent of the homosexual "closet" at the end of the 19th century was not accidental. Oscar Wilde had, after all, been released from prison on 19 May 1897. In addition to the criminal stigma now attached to homosexuality, a sudden explosion of "scientific" publications on "sexual disorders" and "perversions" appeared at the turn of the century. Nancy Sahli, historian and archivist, reports that in the first series of 16 volumes of the *Index Catalogue of the Library of the Surgeon General's Office, U.S. Army*, covering the years 1740 to 1895, only one article ("A Case of Man-Impersonation") dealt specifically with lesbians. In the second series, published between 1896 and 1916, there were over 90 books and 566 articles listed that related to women's "perversions," "inversions," and "disorders."[15]

Secrecy is not a surprising response to this psychoanalytic assault. How then, male historians continually ask, do you know these women were lesbians? Even if we were to assume that Addams and Smith never in 40 years in the same bed touched each other, we can still argue that they were lesbians because they chose each other. Women who love women, who choose women to nurture and support and to create a living environment in which to work creatively and independently, are lesbians.

It may seem elementary to state here that lesbians cannot be defined simply as women who practice certain physical rites together. Unfortunately, the heterosexist image—and sometimes even the feminist image—of the lesbian is defined by sexual behavior alone, and sexual in the most limited sense. It therefore seems important to reiterate that physical love between women is one expression of a whole range of emotions and responses to each other that involves all the mysteries of our human nature. Woman-related women feel attraction, yearning, and excitement with women. Nobody and no theory has yet explained why for some women, despite all cultural conditioning and societal penalties, both intellectual and emotional excitement are aroused in response to women.

Lillian Wald

Besides, there *is* evidence of these women's lesbianism. Although Lillian Wald's two volumes of memoirs are about as personal as her entry in *Who's Who Among American Women*, her letters underscore the absurdity of a taxi conversation that Mabel Hyde Kittredge reported to Wald after a meeting at Henry Street:

> 1st man: *Those women are really lonely.*
> Second man: *Why under the sun are they lonely?*
> 1st man: *Any woman is lonely without a man.*

Unlike Jane Addams, Lillian Wald seems not to have had one particular "great friend," and the chronology of the women in her life, with their comings and goings, is impossible to follow. There are gaps and surprises throughout over 150 boxes of correspondence.

But all of Lillian Wald's companions appear to have been friends for life.

Wald's basic support group consisted of the long-term residents of Henry Street, Ysabella Waters, Anne Goodrich, Florence Kelley, Helene MacDowell, and Lavinia L. Dock. They worked together on all projects, lived and vacationed together for over 50 years, and, often in company with the women of Hull House, travelled together to Europe, Japan, Mexico, and the West Indies.

But the letters are insufficient to tell us the specifics of her life. There are turmoils that we will probably never know anything about —upheavals that result, for example, in a 10-year hiatus in Wald's correspondence with Lavinia Dock. This hiatus, combined with the fact that in November 1915, after 20 years, "Docky" moved out of the Henry Street Settlement and, in an icy and formal note of March 1916, even resigned from the Henry Street Corporation, remains unexplained. There is also the puzzling fact that Dock, the ardent suffragist, feminist and socialist, a pioneer of American nursing education and organization, appears to be R. L. Duffus' major source of information—beyond Wald herself—for his 1938 biography, *Lillian Wald: Neighbor and Crusader*. The first letter to appear in the collection after Dock's 1916 resignation is dated 1925 and implies that the two women have not had a long-term falling out at all:

> why-dear-I was imagining you radiating around the town telling about Mexico and here you are in the hospital just like any commonplace person—oh dear oh dear! . . . Dearest I would scrape up some money if you need—you have often done the same for me . . . and I am not telling anyone that you are ill and in the hospital for I know how you would dislike being thought just a mere mortal. . . .[16]

It is clear from another letter that Dock went to New York to be with Wald during her first operation. She wrote Wald's nurse that she was so relieved the tumor turned out to be benign that "for the first time my knees wobbled as I went down the steps to go to the train. . . ." The next week Dock wrote to Wald: "Dearest—I'm not sure whether to give you letters yet so I havent written before and just send this line to tell you that you do your illnesses and recoveries in the same dazzling form and with the same vivacity and originality as all your other deeds! With Love/Ever yours/Docky"

Why then did Dock leave? Was there a personal reason? A new lover? An old anger? Or was it connected with the political differences that emerged between them in 1915 when Wald became more absorbed by antimilitarist activities and Dock, also a pacifist, joined the radical suffragist movement of Alice Paul's Congressional Union? All the evidence indicates that the only significant differences between these women at this time were political. Their lives were dedicated to work each regarded as just and right. When they disagreed so intensively that they could no longer support and nurture each other's activities, they temporarily parted.

In 1914 Dock joined the Advisory Council of the Congressional Union. But she was the only member of the Henry Street community to do so. She wrote to Alice Paul that "you know I love everything you do," but "the people I live with here all have so many undertakings that they are involved up to the neck." Specifically, Lillian Wald "cannot ally herself exclusively to any suffrage group because she has close friends in all—for instance your invitation . . . was balanced by women in the National Association asking her not to [join] —this is confidential. She decided to remain independent of all and my own judgment for her is that it is best for her to do so—she has first and foremost her own immense responsibilities. . . ."

During the war, while Wald was meeting with President Wilson and being as conciliatory as possible on behalf of the peace movement, Dock and the militant suffragists were infuriating official Washington, getting themselves arrested, and generally aggravating the very people Wald was attempting to persuade—and for a different purpose.

Dock considered Paul's Congressional Union "fresh-young-glorious." She wrote to Paul in June 1915: "Pay no attention to criticism. Go right ahead with your splendid daring and resourcefulness of youth." Dock reacted furiously to criticism that the Congressional Union's confrontational tactics not only harmed the suffrage movement but threatened the peace movement. And Lillian Wald was one of the leading critics of such tactics. On this issue they disagreed utterly. Dock was adamant: "And what is this terrible burden of responsibility and anxiety now resting on the American Men's President? Is it arising from anything women have done or are going to do? Not at all. . . . I can't see it—surely there could be no more appropriate moment for women to press forward with their demand for a voice—women—who are at this moment going on errands of peace—and who are being called a national menace for doing so—followed wherever he goes, by the demand which, so long as it remains unanswered shows a painful insincerity in those rounded and sonorous paragraphs on American ideals and American freedom that he utters so eloquently. . . ."[17]

Five months after this exchange, Lavinia Dock moved permanently out of her Henry Street home of 20 years. I have not yet found one correspondence between her and Wald that deals with the event. And all Wald says about Dock in *Windows on Henry Street* is that "Everyone admired her, none feared her, though she was sometimes very fierce in her denunciations. Reputed a man-hater, we knew her as a lover of mankind."

Wald's Other Support Network

There were two other categories of women close to Wald and the settlement. The first consisted of affluent women such as Irene and Alice Lewisohn and Rita Morgenthau. Younger than Wald, they admired her and regarded her as a maternal figure. She in turn nurtured their spirits, supported their ambitions, and provided them with sustaining and secure friendship. They, together with Wald's "friend of friends" Jacob Schiff, contributed tirelessly and abundantly to Henry Street. The Lewisohns founded the Neighborhood Play House and supported the famous music and dance education projects that continue to this day. They were also coworkers in the Woman's Peace Party and the American Union Against Militarism. On occasion they travelled with Wald. And they wrote numerous letters of affection and devotion to their dear "Lady Light." Alice Lewisohn frequently signed her letters "Your Baby Alice." One letter from Irene, conveying love and gratitude after a trip the Lewisohn sisters took with Ysabella Waters and Wald, is replicated in the collection by scores of others:

> Why attempt to tell a clairvoyant all that is in one's mind? You know even better than I what those months of companionship with you and Sister Waters have meant. For way and beyond even the joys of our wanderings I have some memories that are holier by far than temples or graves or blossoms. A fireside romance and a moonlight night are among the treasures carefully guarded. . . . As an offering for such inspirations, I am making a special vow to be and to do. . . . /Much of my heart to you/

Wald's closest friend among the younger nonresidents appears to have been Rita Wallach Morgenthau, who generally signed her letters with love from "Your Daughter," "Your Foolish Daughter," or "Your Spoiled Child." However much Wald may have spoiled her "adoptive daughters," the very fact of her nurturing presence helped establish the nature of their life's work; and their work focused on social change and the education, dance, and theatre programs they created.

In 1906 Rita wrote to Wald that "everything that has stood for beauty has been inspired by you, and the thankfulness I feel for my share of you, and the dear settlement can never be whispered. . . ." During Wald's final, protracted illness in the 1930's, Rita wrote following Wald's operation:

> You always have been and always will be my "Leading Lady" and I have a feeling of deep gratitude and humility that there will spark in me that fire kindled by your flame . . .[18]

All of Wald's friends and correspondents wrote of how she inspired them, fired their imaginations, and directed their lives to greater heights of consciousness and activity. Lavinia Dock referred to this quality in a letter to Duffus for his biography of Wald: "She believed absolutely in human nature and as a result the best of it was shown to her. People just naturally turned their best natures to her scrutiny and developed what she perceived in them, when it had been dormant and unseen in them before. I remember often being greatly impressed by this inner vision that she had. . . ."[19]

The last group of women involved with Wald and the settlement differed basically from the other two. Although they also served as residents or volunteered their time to Henry Street, they were "society women" perhaps more interested in Wald than in social change. Such long-term residents as Dock, Waters, and MacDowell, and Wald's younger friends, Morgenthau and the Lewisohns, supported Wald emotionally and politically and shared collectively in all her interests. The society women, however, attempted to possess or monopolize Wald, lamented that her activities kept her from them, and were finally rebuffed in what must have been thoroughly specific terms. Generally they fell into that trap that Margaret Anderson defined so well: "In real love you want the other person's good. In romantic love you want the other person."[20]

Lillian Wald had structured her life to avoid becoming anybody's possession. While she did get involved in emotional enthusiasms, as soon as the woman involved sought to redirect her priorities Wald's enthusiasm evaporated.

The clearest representatives of the society group were Mabel Hyde Kittredge and Helen Arthur. Both women were rich "uptowners" who spent many years "downtown." Both were highly educated, hardworking, and demanding. Both devoted their time to good works, in large part because their friendship with Wald encouraged them to think politically, and not because social change was their life's commitment. But they were loyal. Kittredge, for example, evidently left Henry Street because Wald encouraged her to do so. Yet she continued to be involved in settlement activities, helped organize the free lunch program in public schools in 1908, and founded the Association of Practical Housekeeping Centers that operated as a subsidiary organization for many years.

To understand Lillian Wald fully, it is necessary to deal with her relationship with Mabel Hyde Kittredge. Kittredge's demands seem on occasion outrageous, and her biases are transparent. Yet it is clear that for a time Wald was not only smitten by this lady, but relied upon her for comfort and trusted her deeply.

A Park Avenue socialite who frequently played bridge whist all night after she had played in a golf tournament all day, Kittredge was the daughter of Reverend Abbott E. Kittredge of the prominent Madison Avenue Church. After she had lived at Henry Street for several years, she wrote to Wald on 28 April 1904 that she understood Wald's objections to what appears to have been a moment of flagrant ethnic bigotry: "I believe that I will never again say 'my people and *your* people.' It may be that even though I have no prejudice I have used words and expressions that have done something to keep the lines drawn between the two peoples. . . ."

Whatever her views, it appears that when Wald was troubled she turned for a time to Kittredge. In a long letter of tender assurance and sensible advice to Wald concerning a bereaved friend, Kittredge wrote:

> . . . I seemed to hold you in my arms and whisper all this. . . . If you want me to stay all night tomorrow night just say so when you see me. . . . Please dont feel that I keep before me the signs of sorrow that you trusted me enough to let me see—of the things of Thursday evening that are consciously with me are first the fact that in a slight degree I can share with you the pain that you suffer. Then I can hear you say 'I love you'—and again and again I can see in your eyes the strength, and the power and the truth that I love—but the confidence in yourself not there. All this I have before me—never a thought of weakness because you dared to be human. Why dear I knew that you were human before Thursday night—I think though that our love never seemed quite so real a thing before then. Good night.

But after 1904 most of Kittredge's letters became competitive—Kittredge *vs.* humanity in their claims on Wald's attentions. Wald evidently reserved one night in the week for Kittredge and then occasionally cancelled their date, infuriating her friend:

> Just because you have reformed on Tuesday night—I havent got to give you entirely to humanity. I am human too and tonight I'd keep you up until—well later than Miss McDowell would approve of—if I had you. . . .

On a similar evening Kittredge wrote that she had just done two very sensible things, not telephoned to say good night and torn up a whiny letter:

> But what business has a great grown woman like myself to sit up in her nightclothes and write nothings. . . . I am getting altogether too close to you Lady Wald—or is it . . . all those doors that you have pushed open for me? Half open-dear-just half open. And then I come up here and grow hungry for more knowledge. . . . And I feel that my strength ends and love you so. . . . I can feel your arms around me as you say I really must go.

When Wald cancelled a visit to Kittredge at Monmouth Beach, she wrote: "And so the verdict has gone forth—I cant have you. . . . But even you must want the ocean at times instead of Henry Street. . . ."

Wald did want the ocean at times. More than that, she sought the relaxation and comfort of Kittredge's friendship. During a business trip that was evidently particularly hectic, Wald wrote to Kittredge from Chattanooga that she looked forward to long, quiet, cosy evenings on the back porch. Kittredge replied that Wald's letter "was a real life-giving thing." But she no longer believed that Wald would actually make such free time possible and wrote: "When Lady Lillian is that cosy time to be? Miss McDowell says not after midnight and your humanity world would not let me have you before. 'Long evenings on the back porch'—it sounds fine—and improbable. . . ."

Eventually Kittredge's jealousy extended from humanity in general to the other residents of Henry Street in particular:

> If you think that I wasnt damned mad today it is simply that I have inherited so much self-control and sweetness from my minister parent that the fact was hidden. . . .
>
> There are times when to know that Miss Clark is standing behind one curtain, Miss MacDowell behind another and to feel an endless lot of people forever pressing the door or presenting unsigned papers makes me lack that perfect sympathy with "work for others" as exemplified by a settlement. No wonder I am called "one of your crushes." . . . It is kiss and run or run without kissing—there really isnt time for anything else. . . .

After what appears to have been for Kittredge a particularly difficult Christmas season, she gave up entirely the competition for Wald's affections:

> These may be "Merry" days but they starve one to death as far as any satisfaction in calm, every day loving and talking goes. . . . I would very much like to meet you on a desert island or a

> farm where the people cease from coming and the weary are at rest—will the day ever come? Or is that white ring, those long, lazy drives, the quiet and the yellow trees only a lost dream? And yet you love me—the plant on my table tells me so. The new coffee tray tells me so . . . and a look that I see in your eyes makes me sure. . . .

Refusing to participate, evidently for the first time, in Henry Street's Christmas festivities, Kittredge wrote that she was

> . . . not loveless nor lonely. I am free and strong and alive and awfully happy—But someway as I think back over this year, I believe that I needed you—it may be as much as the others— . . . I know that it would be a loss out of my life if my thoughts of you, my love for you and my confidence in you were taken away—I don't believe they ever could be less than they are tonight. . . .[21]

Judging from the letters, whatever gap the loss of Mabel Hyde Kittredge's friendship may have opened Wald seems to have filled by that summer. Wald vacationed through August and September 1906 with another society woman, Helen Arthur, an attorney and director of the research department of the Woman's Municipal League. Helen Arthur seems to have been more spontaneous and less complaining than Kittredge; and she had a sense of humor: ". . . I have a report to write yet tonight and read to a bunch of elegantly attired ladies who do not care a darn so long as they get home for luncheon. What a farce this old world is—remember Oliver Herford's dedication 'to the world at large,' ending up with 'why is the world at large?' "

Arthur was also more dependent on Wald, and in this relationship Wald's maternal aspects were more evident. She coaxed Arthur out of repeated depressions, encouraged her law practice, managed her finances, and kept her bankbook so that she would not overspend. This last made Arthur pout, especially during one Christmas season when she wrote to Wald that she tried to buy "exactly 28 presents for $10 worth of currency without visiting the 5 and 10 cent store which is, I regret to say, not on the Consumer's League list! If you were at 265 Henry Street—I should hold you up for my bankbook—What's vacation money compared to Christmas toys—Surely it is more blessed to give than to receive interest on deposits! Couldnt you be an old dear and let me rob it for a month? Please, mommy."

When Wald travelled, Arthur wrote long newsy letters about her law cases and activities; but they all concluded or began with a note of despair that her good mother had left her sad or naughty "son" all alone: "Such a strange feeling—no one to telephone me no 'Hello-de-e-ar' to listen for—Rainy horrid day outside and a lonesome atmosphere within. . . ." At another time she wrote "I am as near blue tonight as green can ever get and if I just had my nicest mommy to snuggle up to and talk it out straight for her son, I'd feel less like a disbarred judge. . . . Couldnt you write me a note and tell me—something?"

Eventually, Wald's busy schedule resulted in disappointments, cancelled dates, loneliness for Arthur, and what must have been for Wald familiar letters of discontent:

> Dearest, nothing could have relieved the gloom of this day except the presence of the one person her secretary notified me not to expect. . . . Now that I am being severely left alone—I have much time to spend in my own room—the walls of which formerly saw . . . me only from 2 until 7 a.m. . . . I've put you—the dear old you in your silver frame on my desk and close to me when I write and I shoved my decanter and cigarette case to the other side—If I had you, the real you instead of one-ten-thousandth part of you I might shove the unworthy things way off—Summertime has spoiled the judge who longs to get back to your comfortable lap and the delights of kicking her pajammaed legs in peace and comfort instead of being solicitously hustled from your room at 10 o'clock. . . .

In another letter, Arthur, like so many others, expressed her desire to live up to Wald's expectations of her: "If only I could pull out of my easy ways—the pleasant vices which hinder me so. . . ." But her physical longing for Wald was equally powerful. The two combined to explain Wald's magnetism: "If only August and September, 1906 were all the year round for me, but their memories stay by and perhaps some day you'll be proud of your small judge. . . . I think so often of the hundreds who remember you with affection and of the tens who openly adore you and I appreciate a little what it all means and I'm grateful to think that your arms have been close around me and that you did once upon a time, kiss me goodnight and even good morning, and I am your lonesome little/Judge."

Arthur, more than many others, was genuinely mindful of Wald's time and her emotional needs. On 30 January 1907, she wrote that "Little by little there is being brought in upon me, the presumption of my love for you—the selfishness of its demands, the triviality of its complaints—and more slowly still, is coming the realization of what it ought to bring to you and what I mean it shall. . . ."[22]

Whatever special friend came or went in Lillian Wald's life, the women of Henry Street, the residents who called themselves her "steadies," were the mainstay of her support. The women in Wald's communal family served each other as well as society. There was nothing self-sacrificing about that community: It was a positive choice. For Wald it was the essential key to her life—and the only aspect of her personal life about which she wrote clearly. On the 40th anniversary of the settlement, Wald wrote: "I came with very little program of what could or should be done. I was perhaps conscious only of a passionate desire to have people, who had been separated and who for various causes were not likely to come together, know each other that they might sympathize and understand the problems and difficulties of each other. I made no sacrifices. My friend Mary Brewster [the first coworker at Henry Street] and I were engrossed in the edifice which was taking form and in which my friends and I might dwell together."[23]

Wald and her friends lived together for over 50 years. At the end, during long years of pain and poor health, she was surrounded by love and support. After her first operation, Mabel Hyde Kittredge wrote to Wald that "at least you must feel that this is a world full of friends and love and sympathy. I hope all the bread you ever cast upon any waters has come back fresh and lovely and so much as to be a surprise. . . ." On the morning of her death, Lillian Wald turned to her nurse and said, "I'm a very happy woman . . . because I've had so many people to love, and so many to love me."[24]

The letters in the Wald collections document only a fragment of her life, and they raise as many questions as they answer. Because we can never know the intimate details of people's lives if they are censored, withheld, or destroyed, we are confined to the details we have. But the details we have make it abundantly clear that Lillian Wald lived in a homosocial world that was also erotic. Her primary emotional needs and desires were fulfilled by women. She was woman-supported, woman-allied. Once that has been established, it becomes entirely unnecessary to pursue evidence of a specific variety of genital contact. Beyond a certain point, we get into fairly small-minded questions of technique. Since society's presumption of heterosexuality stops short of any inquiry as to what the husband and wife do atop their conjugal bed, it is only to indulge our prejudices that we demand "evidence" of lesbianism from conventional or famous women. Insistence on genital evidence of proof for a lesbian identity derives from a male model that has very little to do with the love, support, and sensuality that exist between women.

Emma Goldman wrote vividly about the difficulties faced by people who attempt to express themselves in harmony with their own nature. In a 1906 essay, "The Child and Its Enemies," she wrote that society employs all its forces to mould out of all our human differences a thing of dehumanized, patterned regularity: "Every institution . . . , the family, the state, our moral codes, sees in every strong, beautiful uncompromising personality a deadly enemy." Every effort is made, from earliest infancy, "to cramp human emotion and originality of thought" in order to create "a patient work slave, professional automaton, taxpaying citizen, or righteous moralist." To that end, all the child's questions "are met with narrow, conventional, ridiculous replies mostly based on falsehoods." Thus uniformity and order, rather than "eternal change, thousandfold variation, continual innovation," have become the hallmarks of our culture.

The full implications of our brutally deforming institutions were clear to Goldman: "Since every effort in our educational life seems to be directed toward making of the child a being foreign to itself, it must of necessity produce individuals foreign to one another. . . ."[25]

Urged to deny the secrets within our natures and to reject the differences of others, we are taught to be fearful of ourselves and contemptuous of others. Separated from ourselves and isolated from each other, we are encouraged to huddle together for comfort under the socially acceptable banners of racism, sexism, classism, and homophobia. While people are called "human resources" in advanced industrial societies, we are discouraged from seeing the ways in which we are all connected. We are thus rendered powerless and immobilized by our prejudices. This is not an accident.

Emma Goldman

Ardent feminists and fiercely independent, Emma Goldman and Crystal Eastman depended on men for the comradeship and pleasure Lillian Wald and Jane Addams sought from women. Far more specific about their sexual orientation, Eastman and Goldman wrote about their private lives and their commitment to free love. They made it clear that they refused to be trapped by conventional or legal arrangements such as marriage.

Both were, in the larger sense, maternal women. Crystal Eastman considered the status of the unmarried mother and decided to get married largely for the sake of the two children she would have. Emma Goldman nurtured all her friends and associates. According to Kate Richards O'Hare, Emma Goldman while in prison was, above all, "the tender cosmic mother."

Contrary to popular notions of "free love" as promiscuous and amoral, Goldman's long-term relations with the men she loved—Sasha Berkman, Ed Brady, Ben Reitman, Max Baginsky, and Hippolyte Havel—were nurturing and tender on her part and devoted and supportive on theirs. They worked for her and cared for her. Ed Brady enabled her to go to Europe to study. Ben Reitman, her manager, served as her "advance man"; he raised money for *Mother Earth* and arranged her speaking tours. These men did not possess her, control her, dominate her, or expect from her more than she would give freely because she loved them as a free woman.

Free love, for Emma Goldman and Crystal Eastman meant simply love given freely to the lover of one's choice. Both rejected the notion that love was a limited commodity. They believed that it was an undefinable sentiment that expanded in proportion to the number of people who evoked it. Possession and jealousy were anathema to them. They rejected the notion that women were love objects to be married into the service and control of men.

Despite the clarity of their writings, their views were frequently misunderstood. The refusal of Eastman and Goldman to separate the personal from the political, their contempt for sham and hypocrisy, and their unfaltering openness about the most intimate subjects horrified their contemporaries. Among the social reformers with whom Crystal Eastman worked, she acquired a reputation as a reckless revolutionary. Her attitudes on free love and her frank affirmation of women's right to physical sexuality appeared hedonistic and horrible. A frequent contributor to feminist journals, her attitudes and behavior—notably her "affairs," divorce, and remarriage were perceived as scandalous. After years of leadership in the peace movement, as founder and president of the Woman's Peace Party of New York and as executive director of the American Union Against Militarism, she was blocked from attending the second meeting at the Hague in 1919 by a committee chaired by Jane Addams, specifically because of Eastman's radical socialism and her espousal of free love.[26]

The reaction of the older social-reform women such as Jane Addams to Crystal Eastman's lifestyle is not explained by the simple fact that the sword of bigotry is many-edged. The failure of Jane Addams and most social-reform women to analyze traditional assumptions about marriage and sexuality is another byproduct of the societal pressure that kept alternative lifestyles of any kind in the closet for so many years. The settlement-house women were supplicants to the rich on behalf of the poor. Steadfast about their priorities, they frequently made political decisions which were not in harmony with their lives and which locked them into a conservative public position regarding such issues as sexuality.

Crystal Eastman's Vision

Emma Goldman was adamant in her opposition to marriage, which she considered an economic arrangement. Since a wife's body is "capital to be exploited and manipulated, she came to look on success as the size of her husband's income." For Goldman marriage was the very antithesis of love. Why, she asked, should two people who love each other get married? Marriage is an arbitrary, mercenary, legal tie; while it does not bind, it fetters. Only love is free. Love for Emma was "the strongest and deepest element in all life; . . . love, the freest, the most powerful moulder of human destiny; how can such an all-compelling force be synonymous with that poor State-and-Church begotten weed, marriage?"[27]

Although Crystal Eastman shared Goldman's views on marriage, she married twice. But she was not limited or stifled in these marriages and arranged them to suit both her work and her emotional needs. According to one of her closest friends, Jeannette Lowe, Crystal Eastman was free—"You would not believe how free she was."[28] Vigorous and bold, Crystal Eastman discarded her first marriage with alacrity and then sought to revolutionize the institution. In her own life she extended the contours of marriage beyond recognition. During the first years of her second marriage, she and her husband, her brother Max, and several of their friends lived communally.

After the war she, her two children, and her husband, Walter Fuller, lived in England "under two roofs" as ordinary lovers. "He keeps a change of clothes and all the essentials for night and morning comfort at my house, as might a favorite and frequent guest." They phoned each other daily and often met for the theatre or dinner or at a friend's house. After the evening's entertainment they decided, "like married lovers," whether to part on the street or go home together. "Marriage under two roofs makes room for moods." As for the children, "without a scowling father around for breakfast, the entire day began cheerfully. . . ."

Crystal Eastman was, above all, a feminist. She considered the true feminist the most radical member of society. The true feminist, Eastman wrote, begins with the knowledge "that the vast majority of women as well as men are without property, and are of necessity bread and butter slaves under a system which allows the very sources of life to be privately owned by a few, and she counts herself a loyal soldier in the working-class army that is marching to overthrow that system." But she had no illusions about where men in that army placed women. "If we should graduate into communism tomorrow . . . man's attitude to his wife would not be changed." For Eastman, the creation of a communistic society based on sex equality was the task of the organized feminist movement.[29]

Unlike Emma Goldman, who lived almost exclusively among men, Crystal Eastman always had a feminist support group of considerable importance to her life. She was supported by women with whom she had deep and lasting relations: many of the ardent suffragists of the Congressional Union, her friends from Vassar who worked with her in the Woman's Peace Party of New York and who were part of her communal family in Greenwich Village. On several occasions she lived with one or more of these friends, and her experiences enabled her to write in "Now We Can Begin":

> Two business women can "make a home" together without either one being over-burdened or over-bored. It is because they both know how and both feel responsible.
>
> But it is a rare man who can marry one of them and continue the home-making partnership. Yet if there are no children, there is nothing essentially different in the combination. Two self-supporting adults decide to make a home together: if both are women it is a pleasant partnership, more fun than work; if one is a man, it is almost never a partnership—the woman simply adds running the home to her regular outside job. Unless she is very strong, it is too much for her, she gets tired and bitter over it, and finally perhaps gives up her outside work and condemns herself to the tiresome half-job of housekeeping for two.

Crystal Eastman evidently solved that problem for herself by spending her summers in the south of France with Jeannette Lowe and their children, leaving her husband under his separate roof and in his separate country.

Throughout the postwar years Eastman had planned to write a book about women. But in 1928, one year after returning to New York to look for new work, she died of a kidney ailment. She was 47 years old, and her death came as a shock to her friends. Claude McKay wrote: "Crystal Eastman was a great-hearted woman whose life was big with primitive and exceptional gestures. She never wrote that Book of Woman which was imprinted on her mind. She was poor, and fettered with a family. She had a grand idea for a group of us to go off to write in some quiet corner of the world, where living was cheap and easy. But it couldn't be realized. And so life was cheated of one contribution about women that no other woman could write." [30]

Emma Goldman and Women

Emma Goldman's lack of a feminist support group did not affect her adversely until the postwar years. Before and during the war she was surrounded by her anarchist comrades and Ben Reitman. But even then her friends found Reitman distasteful and tended to admonish Goldman for her choice of lovers. Sasha Berkman in particular hated Reitman because he was not dedicated to the revolution, anarchism, or even social change. Margaret Anderson thought that the "fantastic" Dr. Reitman was not "so bad if you could hastily drop all your ideas as to how human beings should look and act. . . ." But Emma loved him and wrote that he "gave without measure or restraint. His best years, his tremendous zest for work, he had devoted to me. It is not unusual for a woman to do as much for the man she loves. Thousands of my sex had sacrificed their own talents and ambitions for the sake of the man. But few men had done so for women. Ben was one of the few; he had dedicated himself completely to my interests."

During her last years in America, Goldman spent a good deal of time with Margaret Anderson and the women associated with *The Little Review*. In *My Thirty Years War*, Anderson described the days Emma Goldman spent in Chicago, with her and Harriet Dean, and in California, where she lived with Jane Heap. She presents a unique portrait of a gentle Emma Goldman, who was "gay, communicative, tender" and who sang Russian folk songs "in a low and husky voice" on the beach at night.

Goldman's reaction to *The Little Review* was intense: "I felt like a desert wanderer who unexpectedly discovers a stream of fresh water. At last a magazine to sound a note of rebellion in creative endeavor!" Although she was disappointed in the magazine's lack of clarity on social issues, she delighted in the fact that it was "free from the mawkish sentimentality of most American publications. Its main appeal to me lay in its strong and fearless critique of conventional standards, something I had been looking for in the United States for 25 years."

And Goldman's feelings about her generous new friends, "who were rarely away from my side for very long," were cordial:

> Harriet Dean was as much a novel type to me as Margaret, yet the two were entirely unlike. Harriet was athletic, masculine-

> looking, . . . Margaret, on the contrary, was feminine in the extreme. Constantly bubbling over with enthusiasm. . . . Underneath her apparent lightness was depth and strength of character to pursue whatever aim in life she might choose. . . . I regretted their lack of social consciousness, but as rebels for their own liberation Margaret Anderson and Harriet Dean strengthened my faith in the possibilities of my adopted country.[31]

In this case it was Emma who had been adopted. She, for herself, had emotional support only from Reitman, with whom she was to break over his vacillation concerning the war, and Berkman, who was involved with others. That lack was keenly felt during the latter years of her life in exile.

But before the war Goldman idealized heterosexual relations. In many of her writings she scorned the bourgeois American feminists whose "narrow puritanical vision banished man as a disturber and doubtful character out of their emotional life. . . ." In a March 1906 essay, "The Tragedy of Woman's Emancipation," she argued that the "greatest shortcoming" of the feminist movement was "its narrow respectabilities which produce an emptiness in woman's soul that will not let her drink from the fountain of life." In September 1915 she published a similar editorial in *Mother Earth* by one "R.A.P.," who argued that "American feminists are the exponents of a new slavery," which denied sexual activity, encouraged inhibition, and crusaded against the "sexual victimization of virtuous females by some low, vulgar male." R.A.P. judged the bourgeois feminist movement classist and hypocritical and of "no interest except as an amusing and typical instance of feminine intellectual homosexuality."[32]

This is not to imply that Emma Goldman was homophobic in any intellectual or traditional sense. On the contrary, she was the only woman in America who defended homosexuality in general and the conviction of Oscar Wilde in particular. Although she was absolute about a person's right to sexual choice, she felt a profound ambivalence about lesbianism as a lifestyle. She believed that "the body, in all its splendid sensuality, had to be reclaimed from the repressive hands of the prudes and the philistines." When she was criticized by her comrades for dealing with such "unnatural themes as homosexuality," thereby increasing the difficulties of the already misunderstood anarchist movement, she persisted. "I minded the censors of my own ranks as little as I did those in the enemy's camp." Censorship from her comrades had, she wrote, "the same effect on me as police persecution; it made me . . . more determined to plead for every victim, be it of social wrong or of moral prejudice."[33]

There is even some evidence that Goldman may have experimented with a woman herself. The 1912 letters of an anarchist worker, Almeda Sperry, to Goldman are very one-sided. They consist in part of affirmations of passionate love by Sperry and apparent rebuffs by Goldman. These do not deter Sperry, who evidently luxuriated for a time in a state of unrequited yearning: "God how I dream of you! You say that you would like to have me near you always if you were a man, or if you felt as I do. I would not if I could. . . ." In response to Goldman's queries about Sperry's feelings toward men, she replies: "If you mean have I ever loved a man I will frankly say that I never *saw* a man. No, I have never deeply loved any man." Sperry was, however, married, and several letters refer to her affection for her husband.

Then, in the summer of 1912, the letters take a different turn. Sperry thanks Goldman for addressing her with terms of endearment, and she evades Goldman's suggestion that they spend a week in the country together by noting that "I am with you in spirit, at any rate." But she tells Goldman to know, just before she sleeps, that "I kiss your body with biting kisses—I inhale the sweet pungent odor of you and you plead with me for relief." A month later Sperry refers to the week they spent together after all in the country:

> Dearest, I have been flitting about from one thing to another . . . to quell my terrible longing for you . . . I am . . . seized with a fire that races over my body in recurrent waves. My last thoughts at night are of you . . . and that hellish alarm clock is losing some of its terrors for me for my first waking thoughts are of you.
>
> Dear, that day you were so kind to me and afterwards took me in your arms, your beautiful throat, that I kissed with a reverent tenderness. . . .
>
> Do you know, sweet cherry-blossom, that my week with you has filled me with such an energy, such an eagerness to become worthy of your friendship, that I feel that I must either use my intensity towards living up to my best self or ending it all quickly in one last, grand debauch. . . .
>
> How I wish I [were] with you on the farm! You are so sweet in the mornings—your eyes are like violets and you seem to forget, for a time, the sorrows of the world. And your bosom—ah, your sweet bosom, unconfined.[34]

There is nothing simple about Goldman's attitude toward lesbianism. She never refers to Almeda Sperry, and it is impossible to know the significance of this correspondence in her life. Her absolute commitment to personal liberty and her total respect for individual choice prompted Magnus Hirschfeld, a leading homosexual rights advocate in Germany and the founder of the Scientific Humanitarian Committee, organized in 1897, to write that Goldman was the "only human being of importance in America to carry the issue of homosexual love to the broadest layers of the public."[35]

But in a long article in the 1923 Yearbook of Hirschfeld's committee, Goldman criticizes an earlier article on Louise Michel in puzzling terms. Goldman reaffirms her political commitment to free sexual choice and affirms her disinterest in "protecting" Louise Michel from the charge of lesbianism. "Louise Michel's service to humanity and her great work of social liberation are such that they can be neither enlarged nor reduced, whatever her sexual habits were." Then follows a long tirade against minorities who claim for themselves all the earth's significant people, and a longer analysis of why it would be "nonsensical" to assume that Louise Michel was a lesbian. In an ultimately vague and paradoxical paragraph, Goldman concludes: "In short, Louise Michel was a complete woman, free of all the prejudices and traditions which for centuries held women in chains and degraded them to household slaves and objects of sexual lust. The new woman celebrated her resurrection in the figure of Louise, the woman capable of heroic deeds but one who remains a woman in her passion and in her love."[36]

It appears that, in Goldman's mind, to be a lesbian was an absolute right, and nothing nasty about it. But it was also to be rendered somehow less a woman.

Emma Goldman in Exile

In the long years of Emma Goldman's exile, years made lonelier by her political isolation, she wrote a series of letters that explored the difficulties and the pain of being a free and independent woman without a support group that provided emotional nurturance as well as a shared vision of the work to be done. After two years of disappointment in Soviet Russia, Goldman travelled back and forth between England, France, and Germany, seeking to rebuild her shattered life and attempting to convince her friends on the left that her critical analysis of the Soviet experiment was correct. In these letters she revealed the toll on her spirit taken by her personal loneliness and her political isolation. Also revealed is the brutal double standard to which even advanced women in progressive anarchist circles are subjected if their friendships are limited to men. On 28 May 1925 she wrote to Berkman:

> I agree with you that both men and women need some person who really cares. The woman needs it more and finds it impossible to meet anyone when she has reached a certain age. That is her tragedy. . . . I think in the case of one who gave out so much in her life, it is doubly tragic not to have anyone, to really be quite alone. . . . I am consumed by longing for love and affection for some human being of my own. . . .

It is significant that the above passage ends a letter otherwise devoted to Goldman's visit with Edward Carpenter, one of the first British crusaders for homosexual rights, and his younger lover, Goe, who had been his companion for 35 years. Carpenter at the time was 82, and, Goldman noted, Goe had his own younger lover, the cook. But, she observed, Goe "takes good care of Ed . . . and Ed treats Goe every bit as a man treats his younger wife. It really was funny."

At this time Goldman was torn apart by her own truncated love affair with Arthur Swenson, a much younger man. There is something tragic in her dismissal of Carpenter's relationship as "screamingly comic . . . really dear, life is a circus if only one has enough sense of humor, which I do not. . . ." But the derision was possibly mixed with envy as she noted, "Well, as long as EC has a pleasant and comfortable (old) age, what is the difference?"[37]

As Goldman looked back over her life while in exile, even the good times seemed bitter. In a heartbreaking letter to Sasha she deals with the sexist double standard of her closest comrades:

> Where did you ever get the idea that I suspected you of being jealous of Ben in any sexual sense. . . . What I did suspect—more than that what I knew—was that you are a prig who constantly worries about what the comrades will say and how it will affect the movement when you yourself lived your life to suit yourself, I mean as far as women are concerned. It was painful to me, at the time, as it has been on many other occasions, to see you fly the movement in the face a hundred times and then condemn me for doing the same. . . . Do I mean to deny Ben's faults? Of course not, my dear. . . . I knew Ben inside and out two weeks after we went on tour; I not only knew but loathed his sensational ways, his bombast, his braggadocio, and his promiscuity, which lacked the least sense of selection. But above all that there was something large, primitive, unpremeditated, and simple about Ben which had terrific charm. Had you and the other friends concerned in my salvation recognized this . . . instead of writing to the university to find out about his medical degree (which the boy never could forget). . . . Ben would not have become a renegade. . . . The trouble with you was . . . as with all our comrades, you are a puritan at heart. . . .

> I have been too long in the movement not to know how narrow and moral it is, how unforgiving and lacking in understanding toward everyone different from them. . . . You will repeat your objections to Ben were because . . . "he did not belong in our ranks." All right, but what were your objections to Arthur Swenson? He never was in our ranks. Why did you treat him like a dog after he came to Berlin? Why did you fail to understand the terrific turmoil the boy created in my being? . . . Of course it is nonsense to say that the attitude of men and women in their love to younger people is the same. . . . It is nothing of the kind. . . . Hundreds of men marry women much younger than themselves; they have circles of friends; they are accepted by the world. Everybody objects, resents, in fact dislikes a woman who lives with a younger man; they think her a god-damned fool; no doubt she is that, but it is not the business or concern of friends to make her look and feel like a fool. . . .

In another letter Emma tried to console Sasha after the sudden departure of his former lover Fitzie. Secretary of the Provincetown Players, Eleanor Fitzgerald had been Sasha's companion until his arrest during World War I. In 1928 she arrived in St. Tropez to be with Djuna Barnes and to visit Berkman. Although the events are unclear, Goldman's letters of explanation for Fitzie's behavior over several years formulate her own reflections on the struggle of women to be liberated: "Here we have been worrying about who should meet Fitzie, then that crazy Djuna kidnaps her. Damned fool. . . . Really, the Lesbians are a crazy lot. Their antagonism to the male is almost a disease with them. I simply cant bear such narrowness. . . ."

By implication, Goldman denied that Fitzie's affair with Barnes might have been a positive choice. To understand Fitzie, Goldman wrote, it was necessary to understand that all her relations with men had been disastrous. Her tragedy "is the tragedy of all emancipated women, myself included. We are still rooted in the old soil, though our visions are of the future and our desire is to be free and independent. . . . It is a longing for fulfillment which very few modern women find because most men too are rooted in the old tradition. They too want the woman as wife and mother in the old sense, and the new medium has not yet been devised, I mean the way of being wife, mother, friend and yet retain one's complete freedom. Will it ever? . . ."[38]

Emma Goldman doubted it. Ultimately she even doubted that women could enjoy real satisfaction even physically with men. After a lifetime of celebrating woman's absolute right to full sexual pleasure, there is something intensively poignant about a letter to Dr. Samuel D. Schmalhausen in which she implied that all through the years the pleasure she received from the men she loved had been inadequate. Schmalhausen had written *Woman's Coming of Age,* and on 26 January 1935 Goldman wrote that ever since her "intellectual awakening" she had had the same thought. Namely,

> that the sex act of the man lasts from the moment of its dominant motivation to its climax. After that the brute has done of his share. The brute can go to sleep. Not so the woman. The climax of the embrace, far from leaving her relaxed or stupefied as it does the man, raises all her sensibilities to the highest pitch. All her yearning for love, affection, tenderness becomes more vibrant and carries her to ecstatic heights. At that moment she needs the understanding of and communion with her mate perhaps more than the physical. But the brute is asleep and she remains in her own world far removed from him. I know this from my personal experience and experiences of scores of women who have talked freely with me. I am certain that the cause for the conflict between the sexes which continues to exist regardless of woman's emancipation is due to the differences in quality of the sex embrace. Perhaps it will always be that way. Certainly I find very few men who have the same need, or who know how to minister that of the woman's. Naturally, I felt elated to read your analysis . . . which actually expresses what I have felt and voiced for well nigh 45 years. . . .[39]

Despite anger, isolation, and disappointment, Emma Goldman remained active and enthusiastic to the end of her life. After her despondent years in London, several friends presented her with a cottage on St. Tropez: "Georgette LeBlanc, Margaret Anderson, Peggy Guggenheim, Lawrence Vail and many others came for an hour or a day to discuss serious matters or in jolly company." Life in St. Tropez, Goldman wrote, restored her health and her "fighting spirit." It was there that she decided to write her memoirs, tour Canada, and cable friends in the United States for loans to continue her important work, now focused mainly in Spain.[40] But she never found the one great friend who could understand her empty places, and she never acknowledged the value of feminist alliances for active women whose very activity, depths of passion, and committed independence alienated them from the men with whom they worked and struggled.

Lillian Wald, Jane Addams, Crystal Eastman, and Emma Goldman all had visions of social change and economic justice that, 60 years later, we have yet to see fulfilled. They lived as they did at a time when, as Vera Brittain noted, women were programmed to monopolize their husbands, dominate their sons, possess their daughters, and make fetishes of their kitchens and shrines of their homes. These four women present a range of choices and affinities that were charged with courage, experiment, fulfillment, and intensity. In viewing women of the past it has been a common practice to assume that feminists, spinsters, woman-related women, and most women engaged in social reform were asexual, self-denying, and puritanical, sublimating their sexual passions in their work. Even today the myth persists that women unattached to men are lonely, bitter, and without community; that women who are political activists working with men can function effectively without a support network of women. In the lives of Wald, Addams, and Eastman, we see clearly the energy and strength they received from feminist networks. Crystal Eastman's feminism drew upon and allowed her to appreciate the woman-identification of her lesbian friends. On the other hand, despite Emma Goldman's intellectual and political identification with the oppressed, including women and homosexuals, she never did understand or identify with the feminist movement, and she never did find a friend of her own sex, "a kindred spirit with whom she could share her innermost thoughts and feelings."

For Jane Addams and Lillian Wald, service to humanity and leadership in public life were constantly refueled by their female support communities and by personal relationships with women who gave them passionate loyalty and love. The power of communities of independent women, and of the love between individual women, expressed not only sensually but in a range of ways, is part of the history that has been taken from us by heterosexist culture. To recognize this history is to recognize our own personal forces of energy and courage and the power to change.

ACKNOWLEDGMENTS

This paper would not have been possible without the encouragement of several members of my own support group. I want to thank in particular Clare Coss, Audre Lorde, Adrienne Rich, and Joan Kelly-Gadol, who read and commented and every day helped to make it all possible. I also want to thank Bernice Goodman, who helps to make it more possible.

Many friends commented generously and helpfully on this paper before and after I first presented it to the Berkshire Conference on the History of Women on 9 June 1976. I am particularly grateful to Alice Kessler Harris, Claudia Koonz, Bert Hansen, and Carroll Smith-Rosenberg. In addition to their thoughts, Richard Drinnon and Jonathan Katz shared with me some of their unpublished documents.

NOTES

1. See Vera Brittain, *Testament of Friendship: The Story of Winifred Holtby* (London: Macmillan, 1947), p. 2: "Within the framework of this biography I have tried to tell . . . the story of a friendship which continued unbroken and unspoilt for sixteen incomparable years. . . ."

2. See Blanche Wiesen Cook, "Democracy in Wartime: Antimilitarism in England and the United States, 1914–1918," *American Studies* (Spring 1972), reprinted in Charles Chatfield, ed., *Peace Movements in America* (Schocken Books, 1973), pp. 39–57; Cook, "Woodrow Wilson and the Antimilitarists, 1914–1918" (unpublished Ph.D. dissertation, The Johns Hopkins University, 1970); and Cook, ed., *Toward the Great Change: Crystal and Max Eastman on Feminism, Antimilitarism and Revolution* (Garland Publishing, 1976).

3. Emma Goldman, *Living My Life*, Vol. I (Dover Reprint, 1970), pp. 160, 375, *passim*.

4. Blanche Wiesen Cook, "The Woman's Peace Party: Collaboration and Non-Cooperation," *Peace and Change* (Fall 1972), pp. 36 ff.

5. Goldman, *op. cit.*, pp. 157–160.

6. See Margaret Anderson, *My Thirty Years' War*, *The Fiery Fountains*, and *The Strange Necessity;* Natalie Clifford Barney, *The One Who Is Legion* (London, 1930) and *Souvenirs Indiscrets* (Paris, 1960); Meryl Secrest, *Between Me and Life: A Biography of Romaine Brooks* (Doubleday, 1974); Jean Chalon, *Portrait d'une Seductrice* (Editions Stock, 1976); George Wickes, *The Amazon of Letters: The Life and Loves of Natalie Barney* (Putnam, 1976); and Gayle Rubin, introduction to Renée Vivien, *A Woman Appeared to Me* (The Naiad Press, 1976), a 1904 novel translated by Jeannette Foster. See also Jeannette Foster, *Sex Variant Women in Literature* (Diana Press, 1975 [1956]); Bertha Harris, "Lesbian Society in Paris in the 1920's," in Phyllis Birkby *et al.*, eds., *Amazon Expedition* (Times Change Press, 1973); and Dame Ethel Smythe, *Impressions That Remained*, 3 vols. (Longman's Green, 1920).

7. William O'Neill, *Everyone Was Brave: Feminism in America* (Quadrangle, 1969), p. 120.

8. Allen Davis, *American Heroine: The Life and Legend of Jane Addams* (Oxford University Press, 1973), p. 46.

9. Allen Reznick, "Lillian Wald: The Years at Henry Street" (unpublished Ph.D. dissertation, University of Wisconsin, 1973), pp. 153, 158, and foreword.

10. Vera Brittain, *Radclyffe Hall: A Case of Obscenity?* (London: A Femina Book, 1968), p. 21.

11. Davis, *op. cit.*, p. 91.

12. Jane Addams, "Women, War and Babies" (31 July 1915), reprinted in Allen Davis, ed., *Jane Addams on Peace, War and International Understanding, 1895–1932* (Garland Publishing, 1976).

13. George Will, "How Far Out of the Closet?" *Newsweek*, 3 May 1977, p. 92.

14. For information about the U.S. Children's Bureau, see Nancy P. Weiss, "The Children's Bureau: A Case Study of Women's Voluntary Networks," an unpublished paper presented at the Berkshire Conference on the History of Women, 10 June 1976, Bryn Mawr.

15. See Nancy Sahli's unpublished paper, "Changing Patterns of Sex-

uality and Female Interaction in 19th Century America," presented at the Berkshire Conference, 11 June 1976, pp. 12–13.

16. Lillian Wald's correspondence is divided between the New York Public Library and Columbia University. See Dock to Wald, 27 April 1925; 10 May 1925; 10 March 1916, Columbia University.

17. Lavinia Dock's correspondence with the Congressional Union is in the Woman's Party Papers, Library of Congress. See especially Dock to Paul, 8 September 1914, tray 1, box 6; 28 June 1915, New York, tray 1, box 6; Dock to C.U., 22 May 1915, tray 1, box 5.

18. Irene Lewisohn to Dear Lady Light, n.d., Wald Papers, Columbia. This probably refers to a round-the-world trip that lasted six months (1910). See R. L. Duffus, *Lillian Wald* (Macmillan, 1938), pp. 123 ff; Rita Morgenthau to Wald, 1 January 1905, box 14; 10 June 1906; n.d., 1930's, Wald Papers, Columbia.

19. Dock to Duffus, 28 May 1936, in Duffus, *op. cit.*, pp. 346–347.

20. Margaret Anderson, *The Fiery Fountains* (Horizon Press, 1969 [1951]), p. 84.

21. Mabel Hyde Kittredge to Wald, 28 April 1904; all Kittredge letters, Wald Papers, Columbia.

22. Helen Arthur's correspondence with Wald is generally undated between 1906 and 1908. *Ibid.*

23. Wald quoted in Duffus, *op. cit.*, p. 55.

24. Kittredge to Wald, 11 May 1925, Wald Papers, Columbia; George V. Alger, Oral History, Columbia, pp. 251–252; Reznick, *op. cit.*, p. ii.

25. Emma Goldman, "The Child and Its Enemies," *Mother Earth* (April 1906), pp. 107–109.

26. A long correspondence to block Eastman's participation at the Hague may be found in the Balch and Addams Papers at the Swarthmore College Peace Collection; see especially Lucia Ames Mead to Emily Green Balch, Balch Papers. See also Nan Bauer Maglin, "Early Feminist Fiction: The Dilemma of Personal Life," *Prospects* (1976), pp. 167 ff., for an overview of the reformists' unwillingness to deal with changing social and sexual mores.

27. See Richard Drinnon, *Rebel in Paradise: A Biography of Emma Goldman* (University of Chicago Press, 1961), pp. 149–151; and Goldman, "Marriage and Love," in Alix Shulman, ed., *Red Emma Speaks* (Vintage, 1972), pp. 158 ff. See also Shulman, *To the Barricades: The Anarchist Life of Emma Goldman* (Crowell, 1971).

28. Jeannette Lowe to author, 27 March 1973.

29. Crystal Eastman, "Marriage Under Two Roofs" (1923); "Feminists Must Fight" (1924); and "Now We Can Begin" (1920)—all reprinted in Blanche Wiesen Cook, *Toward the Great Change*.

30. Claude McKay, *A Long Way From Home* (Harcourt, 1970 [1935]), pp. 154–155.

31. Margaret Anderson, *My Thirty Years' War*, pp. 54–55; Goldman, *Living My Life*, Vol. II, pp. 530–533.

32. Goldman, "The Tragedy of Woman's Emancipation," *Mother Earth* (No. 3, 1906), pp. 9–18 (reprinted in *Red Emma Speaks*); R.A.P., "Feminism in America," *Mother Earth* (February 1915), pp. 392–394.

33. Goldman, *Living My Life*, Vol. I, p. 555.

34. See Sperry to Goldman in Jonathan Katz, *Gay American History* (Crowell, 1976), pp. 523–530.

35. John Lauritsen and David Thorstad, *The Early Homosexual Rights Movement, 1864–1935* (Times Change Press, 1974), pp. 36–37.

36. Katz, *op. cit.*, pp. 376–380.

37. Richard and Anna Maria Drinnon, eds., *Nowhere At Home: Letters From Exile of Emma Goldman and Alexander Berkman* (Schocken Books, 1975), pp. 126–128.

38. *Ibid.*, pp. 132–133, p. 86.

39. Goldman to Dr. Samuel Schmulhausen, 26 January 1935, Goldman Papers, Labadie Collection, University of Michigan.

40. Goldman, *Living My Life*, Vol. II, pp. 985–986; see also Goldman to Margaret Anderson, ed., *The Little Review Anthology* (Horizon Press, 1953), p. 363.

19

Birth Control and Social Revolution

■

LINDA GORDON

During the nineteenth century, women and men managed to limit their offspring by means such as coitus interruptus, *vaginal douching, and—most effective of all—abstinence from sexual relations. The effect of these methods can be seen in the 50-percent decline in the birth rate from 1800 to 1900. Even then (as throughout human history) sexuality was regarded as inevitably linked to reproduction. Only in our own day have the two been separated by the availability of sure contraception, vastly changing women's lives. Linda Gordon discusses the initiation of birth-control advocacy at the beginning of this century, pointing out that it was—more than a matter of medical or technical advance—a political demand, raised by feminists and left-wing radicals oriented toward a working-class constituency. Gordon's book,* Woman's Body, Woman's Right: A Social History of Birth Control in America, *from which this selection is taken, goes on to show that the union of birth-control support with left-wing politics and organized feminism was short-lived.*

THE MOVEMENT THAT first coalesced around the slogan "birth control," a phrase invented by Margaret Sanger in 1915, was a force of people fighting for their own immediate needs, and because of this it had an intensely personal dimension for its participants. The fact that the birth controllers often stood to gain immediately in their personal lives from legalization of birth control did not narrow their vision but strengthened their commitment. They united their personal experience and emotional understanding with political thought and action. They created a politics based on women's shared experience which had the potential to unite masses of women. At the same time the birth controllers transcended women's immediate needs. They were not seeking incremental improvements in their sex lives or medical care; they did not view birth control as primarily a sexual or medical reform at all, but as a social issue with broad implications. They wanted to transform the nature of women's rights—indeed, of human rights—to include free sexual expression and reproductive self-determination.

In challenging the traditional limits of people's control over their own lives, they used birth control to make a revolutionary demand, not a reform proposal. They did not want just to limit their pregnancies; they wanted to change the world. They believed that birth control could alleviate much human misery and fundamentally alter social and political power relations, thereby creating greater sexual and class equality. In this they shared the voluntary-motherhood analysis—that involuntary motherhood was a major prop of women's subjection—and added a radical version of a Neo-Malthusian analysis—that overlarge families weakened the working class in its just struggle with the capitalist class. They also demanded sexual freedom.

The birth controllers were putting forward these demands at a time when American radicalism was at one of its peaks of strength and breadth. Indeed, the birth-control movement that began in 1914 was a part of a general explosion of resistance to economic and social exploitation. Joining that resistance, birth controllers appealed for support to the powerless, particularly to women and to working-class and poor people in general, because they believed that lack of control over reproduction helped perpetuate an undemocratic distribution of power.

Strategically their analysis tried to draw together the women's movement and the working-class movement. The leading birth controllers between 1914 and 1920 were both feminists and socialists and wanted to unite their respective goals and constituencies. Many of them came to the birth-control cause from multi-issue reform or revolutionary movements, ranging from the suffrage organizations to the IWW. Few were themselves working class, although some important leaders—Margaret Sanger is only one—had working-class origins. Their experience of the common oppression of women in sexual and reproductive matters convinced them that they could transcend their class differences and create a movement that would fight for the interests of the least privileged women.

They failed in this grand intention, but that does not mean that their analysis and strategy were completely wrong or that their experiences are useless to us today. Their belief that birth control could create a new freedom and dignity for women and a new right for all people was not wrong just because it was incompletely realized.

By 1914 the radical movement in the United States was unified to a large extent in a single Socialist party. From 10,000 members in

1901 it grew to include 118,000 in 1912. Its voting strength was many times greater—almost 6 per cent of the total in 1912—and by 1912 it had elected twelve hundred public officials and regularly published over three hundred periodicals.[1] No other political party in American history has ever fought as consistently for women's rights (such as woman suffrage, employment opportunities, equal legal rights).[2] Especially after 1910 many feminists entered the Party and began agitating for more active political work by and for women. Women's committees were organized in many locals, socialist woman-suffrage societies were created, and a few women were elected to the National Executive Committee.[3]

The Socialist party's conception of what women's rights were, however, agreed in all respects with those advocated by liberal feminists. Like suffragists, most socialists accepted the conventional definition of woman's proper sphere and activities—home, motherhood, housework, and husband care. There was no general support in the Socialist party for birth control or for any reforms that threatened to alter or even to question traditional sexual roles and division of labor. In clinging to their traditional views of the family, socialists often cited as their authority the early Marxist view that drawing women out of their homes was one of the evils of capitalism that socialism would put right. The revolutionaries in the Socialist party, more inclined to reject the conventions, were concerned even more exclusively than the rest of the Party with class struggle in the workplace, and consequently had little interest in questions of domestic relations. The Party's women's journal, *Socialist Woman,* published in Girard, Kansas, did not have a single article that discussed the principle of voluntary motherhood before 1914. (Indeed, even when the journal got a letter asking them to take up the question, the editors declined to publish it.)[4] Socialist women concerned with sexual issues, even regular contributors to Party periodicals, published their writings on birth control elsewhere.[5]

Despite its great influence in the birth-control movement, the Socialist party never formally endorsed birth control. Indeed, before 1912 the issue was never the subject of major debate within the Party, so great was the disapproval of creating internal divisions. The rejection of anything but the most limited feminist goals by the Socialist-party majority reflected a larger split in the whole U.S. radical and reform community between socialism and the women's movement. That split deepened in the early twentieth century. Previously, almost all supporters of birth control had been socialists of a sort. Voluntary-motherhood advocates of the 1870s had been critical of capitalist values and social organization, as had utopian communitarians who practiced birth control; many American feminists by the end of the nineteenth century had concluded that women's emancipation would require a higher level of economic justice than capitalism could provide; most European sex radicals were socialists. But as Marxian scientific socialism began to dominate, and the organized socialist movement gained a working-class constituency, emphasis on class differences and class struggle tended to diminish the importance of sex equality as a program. Many feminists, although thoroughly anticapitalist, refused to follow socialist theory into a denial of their own experience of sex oppression.

This ideological split occurred under conditions of industrialization which deepened class differences among women as among men. A feminist analysis that in the 1870s seemed broad enough to include all women, by the early twentieth century could appeal only to upper-class women. By 1910 working-class women were more distant from the suffrage organizations in their point of view as well as in their actual political loyalties than they had been in the 1870s. On the other hand, the Marxian socialist movement in America had rejected many of the feminist and sex-radical traditions of utopian and other romantic socialisms. Furthermore, within the Marxist organizations, the tendency to emphasize unions and organizing at the workplace left men without pressing reasons to appeal to women, most of whom remained outside the labor force. The complaints of even the most antifeminist of socialist women leave no doubt that arrogance and disrespectful attitudes toward women were widespread among socialist men. Thus anyone trying to formulate a socialist *and* feminist theory about the importance of birth control faced serious difficulties: a conservative and elite woman-suffrage movement and a rather blindly antifeminist Socialist party.

Despite its limitations, however, the existence of the Socialist party was one of the most important, probably necessary, conditions for the emergence of the radical birth-control movement in the second decade of the century, in that it brought together almost all radicals and reformers in touch with the working class or concerned with working-class power. Without this opportunity to reach and to learn from working-class women, the sex radicals would have continued to pursue sterile, theoretical formulations, contributing at most to a bohemian life style among urban intellectuals. On the other hand, the sexual conservatism of the Party's male leadership could not contain the growing restlessness produced among women by their changed circumstances.

Some Midwestern socialists still cherished some of the feminist traditions of pre-Marxian socialism, for instance, Virginia Butterfield. Her book, *Parental Rights and Economic Wrongs*, published in

Chicago in 1906, argued that birth control was a form of self-defense against capitalism. In agricultural society children were a form of wealth, and therefore birth control was economically unnecessary, she argued; under conditions of industrialism birth control became necessary because capitalism's system of unjust distribution made people poor. Ideally, socialism would again make birth control unnecessary! She believed that socialism would also restore the "natural equilibrium of the sexes" by allowing men to earn enough so that all women could stay at home, and that this restoration of a natural condition would end marital unhappiness and the necessity for divorce.[6] Until then, however, women's refusal to bear children under conditions of oppression was a form of rebellion. Indeed, since procreation was one of the highest forms of human labor, birth control became, for Butterfield, a form of workers' control!* Many socialists turned their attention to the prohibition on birth control and asked: Whom does it serve? Many concluded that the ruling class kept birth control from the working class in the interest of continued exploitation. One reason was war—a large population of underlings was needed for cannon fodder.[8] Another was that a reserve army of labor was used to keep wages down.[9] To the charge that birth control might weaken the working class by decreasing its size, they pointed to historical events in which the unemployed and poor—a lumpen proletariat—had played an antirevolutionary role.[10]

The limitations of these analyses reflected the general limitations of socialist theory regarding women. The debate about whether the working class would benefit from increasing or shrinking its size implicitly left most women beyond consideration, since they were outside the wage-labor force or the armed forces.

A few U.S. radicals, Margaret Sanger and Emma Goldman among them, were able to advance beyond this partly because they were influenced by several European developments. In Protestant countries with mass working-class socialist parties, there were many birth-control clinics. In Holland a trade-union-sponsored birth-control clinic had operated since 1882. In Germany birth control had been an important issue in the Social Democratic party since early in the century, and the demands of Party rank-and-file women had forced the Party leadership to give up its opposition to endorsing birth control.[11] Even in Catholic France, socialist Paul Robin had

* Although Butterfield's identification of reproduction with production is unique, several socialist women of this period were concerned with the social importance of other aspects of women's unpaid labor in the home. Party journals sometimes discussed the economic value of housework under capitalism, suggesting that it represented perhaps the most extreme form of exploitation.[7]

organized a clandestine international Neo-Malthusian* conference in 1900. Both Goldman and Sanger, attracted more by anarchism than by the Social Democratic parties, were at first less impressed by the clinics than by the theories of sexual freedom. They transformed these ideas into an action program, a program of sex education.

In this period sex education was not merely action but militant action because it involved breaking the law. The Comstock law still barred "obscene" materials from the mails, and most noneuphemistic sex discussion—such as naming the human genitalia—was considered obscene. Defying such laws was a form of what the IWW called direct action, people acting directly against state and capitalist power, not petitioning or negotiating but taking what they needed. Women needed sex education. Feminists and sexual-freedom advocates agreed that women's ignorance of their bodies was debilitating and that deference to conventions about what was good for "ladies" to know deepened their passivity and political fearfulness.

In the United States a campaign of sex education formed a bridge between pro-birth-control ideas and an organized movement for birth control. Sex manuals had been plentiful since the mid-nineteenth century, but their style had begun to change in the 1900s. Even the conservative writers, while remaining moralistic, introduced detailed physiological descriptions and sometimes drawings of reproductive anatomy.[12] Midwestern socialists and feminists of Virginia Butterfield's tradition had been the first to appreciate the importance of sex education and had written dozens of books in the first decades of the twentieth century.[13] Somewhat later, demands for sex education appeared within the Socialist party itself. One particularly effective spokeswoman and practitioner of sex and birth-control education was Antoinette Konikow, a Russian immigrant physician. She had been one of the founding members of the Socialist party and later one of the five members of its Women's Commission. She practiced medicine in Boston after her graduation from Tufts Medical School in 1902; and although Boston was then as now an overwhelmingly Catholic city, with little support even within its radical community for sexual unconventionality, she was outspoken for birth control and probably did abortions.[14] Konikow wrote for the *New York Call*, a daily socialist newspaper, arguing that sex education was an important task for socialists.[15] Dr. William J. Robinson also wrote for the *Call* on sex hygiene; he and Konikow were the first to focus their sex-education articles on birth control.[16]

* Until several decades into the twentieth century Europeans continued to use "Neo-Malthusianism" as the generic name for birth control whether or not they accepted the social and political perspective of the Neo-Malthusian organizations and tradition.

The most notorious for her outspokenness on sexual questions was Emma Goldman. Goldman, more than any other person, fused into a single ideology the many currents that mingled in American sex radicalism. She had connections with European anarchism, syndicalism, and socialism; she knew and was influenced by American utopian anarchists and free lovers such as Moses Harman; she was also familiar with American feminism and with dissident doctors such as Robinson.[17] In 1900 she had attended the secret conference of Neo-Malthusians in Paris and had even smuggled some contraceptive devices into the United States.[18] In New York Goldman was tremendously influential on other women radicals, as a role model and a practitioner of the new morality. One woman strongly influenced by Goldman was Margaret Sanger. Sanger later tried to hide that influence. Always needing recognition and fearing rivals for power and importance, Sanger underestimated Goldman's contribution to birth control in her later writings. Sanger met Goldman when Goldman was a magnetic and dominating figure nationally and Sanger an insecure young woman lacking a cause and a political identity. Sanger still clung to more conservative sexual ideas, and Goldman must have been shocking to her, at the least.[19]

Moving to New York City in 1911 and searching for something to do, Sanger's background as a nurse made it natural for her to take an interest in sex education. She began writing articles for the *New York Call*. At about the same time she was hired as an organizer for the Women's Commission of the Socialist party (with a small salary) and elected secretary of the Harlem Socialist Suffrage Society. In both capacities she began making speeches and was so enthusiastically received when she spoke on health and sex topics that she began to specialize in these areas. Questions and responses at the meetings and letters to the *Call* gave Sanger reinforcement and a sense of appreciation.

On the other hand, Sanger was disappointed in her more "orthodox" socialist organizing, working with striking laundry workers and trying to garner support for a legislative campaign for a wages-and-hours bill. She resigned as an organizer in January 1912.[20] But her dissatisfaction with her Socialist party work did not at first push her more deeply into sex-education activities; rather she was drawn, as were so many radical intellectuals at the time, toward the greater militancy of the IWW, with its direct-action tactics. When the strike of Lawrence, Massachusetts, textile workers, supported by the IWW, broke out in January 1912, Sanger became involved in support work for the strikers, which she continued until June 1912.[21]

Sanger resumed her articles in the *Call* in November 1912 with a series, "What Every Girl Should Know." It was more daring than the first series, which had been called "What Every Mother Should Know" and had been designed to help mothers tell their children about sex and reproduction, largely through analogy to flowers and animals.[22] The second series spoke more fully of human physiology, especially the female sexual and reproductive apparatus, and argued that the "procreative act" was something natural, clean, and healthful.[23] But when Sanger turned to the problem of venereal disease, which had for decades been discussed in public only with euphemisms such as the "social problem" and "congenital taint," the Post Office could take no more. They declared the article unmailable under the Comstock law. The *Call* responded by printing the headline of the column—"What Every Girl Should Know"—and in a big, blank box underneath it, the words, "NOTHING, by order of the Post-Office Department."[24] (The Post Office ban was lifted two weeks later on orders from Washington and the article actually appeared in the *Call* on March 2. In one of the finer ironies produced by the rapid changes in attitudes of those years, this very article was reprinted—without credit to the author—by the U.S. government and distributed among troops during World War I.)[25]

Up until this time, however, Sanger had not discussed birth control in writing. Her sex-education work was again interrupted by a more urgent demand for her services—the Paterson silk-workers' strike that began in February 1913. The workers asked the IWW for help, and Big Bill Haywood sent Sanger and Jessie Ashley (a socialist, feminist lawyer later to be active in birth control) to Paterson to organize picket lines.[26] Sanger worked there until the strike's failure in the summer. She did not write anything further on sexual hygiene that year, and in October sailed for Europe with her husband and children. In Paris she began the first stage of her "research" into birth control—the sociological phase. Not yet interested in libraries and sexual theory, she spoke with her neighbors, with the French syndicalists that Bill Haywood (also then in Paris) introduced her to, with druggists, midwives, and doctors. She collected contraceptive formulas. She discovered that birth control was respectable, widely practiced, and almost traditional in France. Women told her that they had learned about contraception from their mothers.[27] In fact, birth-control advocates in the United States such as William J. Robinson had been publishing articles about the low birth rate and widespread contraceptive use in France for years.[28] Emma Goldman knew these facts about France. All this, however, was new to Sanger in 1913. For the rest of her life, birth control was to be her single, exclusive passion.

What were the sources of this decision, or conversion, of Sanger's? Years later she herself portrayed it as a rather sudden conversion and attributed it to an incident that had happened a year earlier in her work as a visiting nurse: an encounter with a poor Jewish family in which a beloved wife died from one pregnancy too many.[29] She also wrote that before going to Paris she had already spent a year in New York libraries and the Library of Congress futilely searching for contraceptive information.[30] Apparently, Bill Haywood himself urged her to go to France to learn.[31] There can be no doubt that she was hearing about birth control frequently and that it had the basic approval of people she respected. Even in the Paterson strike it was in the air. Elizabeth Gurley Flynn recalled a meeting for women strikers at which Carlo Tresca, an IWW organizer, "made some remarks about shorter hours, people being less tired, more time to spend together and jokingly he said: 'More babies.' The women did not look amused. When Haywood interrupted and said: 'No, Carlo, we believe in birth control—a few babies, well cared for!' they burst into laughter and applause."[32]

One key difference between Sanger and her radical friends who saw the importance of birth control was that she was dissatisfied with her role as a rank-and-file socialist organizer and was searching for something more like a career. Many biographers have commented on Sanger's drive for recognition. Among men in most situations that kind of drive would have seemed so commonplace that it would have gone unmentioned. Sanger instinctively understood that the recognition she needed required a special cause, a specialization. As a nurse, she felt comfortable building on expertise and experience she already had.

But the reason she chose contraception rather than venereal disease or sex education was her recognition of the potential historical and political meaning of birth control. Most American socialists at this time, primarily oriented to class relations, saw birth control in Neo-Malthusian terms, that is, in terms of economics. They were concerned to help raise the standard of living of workers and thus increase their freedom to take political control over their own lives. Measured against this goal, birth control was at most an ameliorative reform. Seen in terms of sexual politics, however, birth control was revolutionary because it could free women entirely from the major burden that differentiated them from men, and made them dependent on men. Sanger did not originally have this perspective. Although female and concerned about women's rights, her political education had been a male-defined one. She gained this perspective in Europe from the sexual-liberation theorists like Havelock Ellis. Ellis literally tutored Sanger. His idealism about the potential beauty and expressiveness of human sexuality and his rage at the damage caused by sexual repression fired Sanger with a sense of the overwhelming importance, urgency, and profundity of the issue of birth control, a sense lacking in most other American radicals.

The entire future course of birth control in the United States was influenced by Sanger's European "education" on birth control. And yet the conviction, curiosity, and drive that led her to her research in Europe would almost certainly have led someone else there if Margaret Sanger had been diverted. Sanger's European trips took place in the midst of a flurry of activity for sexual change in the United States which began before Sanger's influence was great and which would inevitably have led to a birth-control campaign before long. Sanger was stimulated by it and returned to shape it, but in all respects she was a part of a movement, not its inventor.[33]

In 1937, when the first general history of contraception was published, Benjamin Reitman, once Emma Goldman's comrade and lover, wrote a letter of protest to its author, charging that the book had suppressed the radical origins of the birth-control movement. It was a passionate and an amusing letter, and largely correct.

> My Dear Himes.
>
> You made me weep.
> Because your article
> On the history
>   Of Birth Control
> was inaccurate
>   Superficial
>   "Highschoolish"
> And you gave no evidence
> Of attempting
> To learn the facts.
>
> You delved into history.
>   But failed to get data from the living.
>   Moses Harmon*
> Was the true father of American Birth Control
> His grand Children are living
> And have lots of splendid material. . . .
>
> You "muffed" all the fine material
> In the early Socialist, Anarchist & I.W.W. literature.
> The tremendous amount of Free Love literature
> Passed you by.
> There are several hundred pamphlets
> On B.C. that you evidently know nothing about.

* Moses Harmon, free lover and anarchist from Kansas, arrested and imprisoned for birth-control advocacy.

The technique of B.C. propaganda
In America is a Mystery to you. . . .

I mean your prejudice against the RADICALS
Is so great that you COULD not give them credit.

Emma Goldman
More than any one person in America
Popularized B.C.
She was Margaret Sanger's INSPIRATION
No that ain't the word.
Margaret imitated her and denied her.
Emma was the first person in America
To lecture on Birth Control
in one hundred Cities. . . .

The physicians, Social Scientists, Clergy & etc.
Became interested in B.C.
Only after the Radicals had "broken" the ground.
And gone to jail.

The inclosed pamphlet
Was distributed by the millions.
Free.
In hundreds of Cities in America
It went through many many editions
Was copied and recopied. . . .
The decline in the Birth Rate
Was influenced by this pamphlet
More than any other one piece of literature.
Including Margaret's "Family Limitation" . . .

B.L.R.*
Was arrested
For distributing the pamphlet
In New York City (60 days)
Rochester, N.Y. (freed)
Cleveland, Ohio (six months)
He was picked up by the police in many cities
But was let go.

Big Bill Shatoff
Who was an I.W.W. Organizer
Translated the pamphlet
Into Jewish and most all
Of the Radical Jews had copies.
In the early days of the Communists' activity

* The author, Dr. Benjamin L. Reitman.

In Russia this pamphlet
Had a tremendous circulation in Russia . . .

GET THIS INTO YOUR HEAD.
This was all done as part of the radical propaganda.
ANTI WAR
ANTI MARRIAGE
ANTI CHILDREN BY ACCIDENT . . .

I see no hope for your Medical Scientific group to
make any real Contribution to history or ****

Enough for today
Ben L. Reitman[34]

Allowing for exaggeration due to nostalgia, loyalty to Goldman, and the pique of a radical who saw "his" movement taken over by conservatives, the essence of Reitman's claims is nevertheless correct. The author—Norman Himes—defended himself by pointing out that he had written a *medical* history of contraception and was primarily concerned with those who made medical and technological contributions. Nevertheless, it is true that historians and biographers have overlooked or underestimated the radical roots of the American birth-control movement. Sanger herself contributed to that distortion. She was ignorant, in the early years of her career, of the free-love and feminist roots of birth-control propaganda, and later she sought to diminish the socialist participation in the movement when she wrote and spoke about it.[35]

After about 1910 Goldman regularly included a birth-control speech on her tour offerings. In it she placed birth control in the context of women's rights and opposition to conventional legal marriage. Like all radicals of her era, she used eugenic arguments: "Woman no longer wants to be a party to the production of a race of sickly, feeble, decrepit, wretched human beings. Instead she desires fewer and better children. . . ." On the other hand, she also spoke about homosexuality, criticizing social ostracism of the "inverts," as homosexuals were commonly called at that time. Her sexual and feminist theories were not only far more radical than those of the birth controllers who followed her, but also far more systematic, integrated into her whole politics. "To me anarchism was not a mere theory for a distant future; it was a living influence to free us from inhibitions . . . and from the destructive barriers that separate man from man."[36] Reitman was himself a birth-control campaigner, not a mere companion to Goldman, and he did indeed, as he claimed, serve sixty days shoveling coal on Blackwell's Island and six months in an Ohio workhouse for distributing birth-control leaflets.[37]

Goldman and Reitman distributed a small, four-page pamphlet called *Why and How the Poor Should Not Have Many Children.* It may have been written by Goldman or Reitman, or possibly by William J. Robinson. It described condoms, instructing the user to check them for leaks by blowing them up with air; recommended rubber cervical caps, diaphragms (also called pessaries or womb veils; in the early twentieth century there was no standard nomenclature for these various devices), which could be bought in drugstores, but urged fitting by a physician for reliability. It suggested three contraceptive methods that could be homemade: suppositories, douches, a cotton ball dipped in borated vaseline. (It advised against relying on the rhythm method but unfortunately still defined the safe period as the two weeks between menstrual periods.) The political argument of the pamphlet was brief: although normal people love and want children, society today is a "wretched place" for poor children, who are not only a burden to their mothers and families, but also "glut the labor market, tend to lower wages, and are a menace to the welfare of the working class. . . . If you think that the teaching of the prevention of conception will help working men and women, spread the glad tidings."* American sex radicals, despite their militant rhetoric, had not so far defied law and convention by publishing such explicit contraceptive advice. Goldman and Reitman's ideas about birth control were not new. Their sense of the political importance of taking risks to spread it was, however.

Though Goldman and her associates were the first radicals since the free lovers to act in defiance of the law, they were not able to make birth control a mass cause. Goldman's connections made her seem the right person for that task. But Goldman was also an extremist, and as a result she was often isolated. Partly because she took outrageous positions and partly because she was personally egocentric, Goldman left most of her admirers behind. If they were feminists, they were often from the educated classes, individualist by habit and ultimately more deeply committed to professional and artistic careers than to full-time revolutionary organizing. If they were revolutionaries, they were often men, skeptical about the importance of sexual and women's rights issues.

Though she began later, Margaret Sanger was much more effective as an *organizer* for birth control. Lacking Goldman's intellectual daring and originality, she drew supporters to her, at first, through assuming a role in which she was more convincing than Goldman: that of victim. In the first years of her career, people frequently commented on Sanger's apparent fragility and vulnerability; only as they

* Note that this pamphlet was written before the term "birth control," coined by Sanger, was in use.

came to know her did her stamina, tenacity, and personal power impress them. Intellectuals repelled by the abrasive style of Goldman and her comrades could adore Margaret Sanger. Max Eastman, for example, hailed Sanger as a hero in *The Masses* but refused to speak at a Carnegie Hall meeting to welcome Goldman out of jail after she had served sixty days for distributing birth-control pamphlets, because, he said, he would not appear with Ben Reitman. "Reitman was a white-fleshed, waxy-looking doctor, who thought it was radical to shock people with crude allusions to their sexual physiology."[38] Nevertheless, Sanger's debut as a birth-control activist was tactically and substantively right within the pattern plotted out by Goldman and the IWW. Sanger began with provocative, illegal action, and, once arrested, organized support for her defense.

The key difference between Sanger's and Goldman's strategies in 1914 was that Sanger chose to act independently of any leftist organization—indeed, independently of even any close collaborators. The path that led the Sanger-inspired birth-control movement away from the Left thus began with Sanger's first actions, though they may not have been consciously intended in that direction. When Sanger's divergence from the organized Left led to total separation, it was as much because the Left had rejected birth control as because Sanger and her followers had rejected the Left. Nevertheless, the roots of the split can be found at the beginnings of the birth-control movement itself.

Sanger returned from Paris to New York in December 1913, deeply influenced by her discovery that birth control was widely accepted in Europe and by support for birth control among some French syndicalists. She did not return to Socialist-party work but decided instead to publish an independent, feminist paper. *The Woman Rebel,* which appeared seven times in 1914 until it was suppressed by the Post Office, emphasized birth control but was not a single-issue journal. It raised other problems of women's sexual liberation: "The marriage bed is the most degenerating influence of the social order, as to life, in all of its forms—biological, psychological, sociological—for man, woman and child."[39] Although concerned with the whole gamut of injustices that the capitalist system created, *The Woman Rebel* focused mainly on its effects on women. But it also sharply attacked the nonsocialist suffrage movement and various "bourgeois feminists." For example, of Katherine Bement Davis, then New York City Commissioner of Corrections (and later, ironically, a sociologist of sexual behavior who worked with Sanger on several sex-education projects), *The Woman Rebel* wrote: "We have no respect for the type of so-called 'modern' and 'advanced' woman who becomes a willing and efficient slave of the present system, the woman who curries favors of capitalists and politicians in order to gain power and the cheap and fulsome praise of cheaper and more fulsome newspapers."[40] Also characteristic of the journal was a supermilitancy, surpassing even the IWW in its rhetorical support of violence. An editorial asked women to send rifles instead of messages of solidarity to striking miners in Colorado.[41] An article in the July issue was the last straw that led the Post Office to declare the journal unmailable, although when Sanger was indicted, two counts of obscenity were also brought against her.[42]

The Woman Rebel did not represent a tendency in American feminism or socialism at this time. It was rather a singular, unrepeated attempt by Sanger to combine her IWW-influenced commitment to direct action with her deepened feminism and sense of the radical potential of birth control. At any rate, it did not last long—and its sudden demise may well have been in part Sanger's intention. She claimed that she wanted to be arrested in order to force a legal definition of what was "obscene."[43] In fact, she may have recognized the journal's lack of political viability.

But *The Woman Rebel* had given Sanger space and stimulus for further political exploration. She was able to correspond with leading European and American feminists in the name of a publication; rejected by many of them, she discovered the pro-birth-control tradition among many quasi-religious groups such as spiritualists and theosophists. She coined the phrase "birth control." When prevented from mailing the journal, Sanger drafted a detailed birth-control pamphlet, *Family Limitation,* and got IWW member Bill Shatoff to print one hundred thousand copies. She got a few hundred dollars to pay for it from a free-speech lawyer who administered a fund left by Edward Bond Foote (Sanger called him "A certain Dr. Foote," again illustrating her ignorance of the American birth-control tradition).[44] Sanger arranged that the *Family Limitation* pamphlets would be sent out by IWW comrades on receipt of a prearranged signal from her. She thought thereby to release the provocative information they contained after she was already in jail.[45] This would make an effective climax to her work, for *The Woman Rebel* was never able to print actual contraceptive information. The pamphlet not only recommended and explained a variety of contraceptive methods—douches, condoms, pessaries, sponges and vaginal suppositories—but even gave a suggestion for an abortifacient. While promising that birth control would make abortion unnecessary, she nevertheless defended women's rights to abortion, something she was never to do at any later time. In this period her attitude toward sexual issues was consistent with her general militance. Still using IWW anarcho-syndicalist rhetoric, she wrote in the pamphlet, "The working class can use direct action by refusing to supply the market with children to be exploited, by refusing to populate the earth with slaves."[46]

But when her case came to trial, Sanger changed her strategy. Fearing that she would lose publicity because of the dominance of war news, and perhaps also that juries would be unsympathetic at this time, she decided to flee and went via Canada to London under an assumed name.[47] In the United States the illegal pamphlets were mailed out as she had planned. With them went a letter asking that the pamphlets be passed on to "poor working men and women who are overburdened with large families. . . . Thousands of women in the cotton states bearing twelve to sixteen children request me to send them this pamphlet. Thousands of women facing the tortures of abortion . . . Three hundred thousand mothers who lose their babies every year from poverty and neglect . . . Are the cries of these women to be stifled? Are the old archaic laws to be respected above motherhood, womanhood! The mothers of America answer no. The women of America answer no!"[48]

Sanger remained in Europe from October 1914 to October 1915. She spent that time researching the history, philosophy, technology, and practice of birth control, working in archives and libraries and visiting clinics and doctors in Holland, France, and England. Havelock Ellis directed and encouraged her work in a relationship made only more intense and nourishing to her because it was a love affair.[49] Ellis had sympathy for neither revolution nor the working class. His influence in diminishing Sanger's attraction to the revolutionary Left was communicated to her not only through his political views, but also through the life style and charm of the British Neo-Malthusians she met through him.[50] (In Britain the sex radicals did not have connections with a revolutionary, class-conscious Left.) After she returned she herself never resumed the consistently revolutionary posture she had held until 1914. In this second trip to Europe, the basic outlines of Sanger's entire future work took shape. She became committed unwaveringly to birth control as a single issue. She would offer feminist or pro-working-class arguments for birth control when they were helpful, along with many other arguments, but she never again saw her identity as mainly within a socialist, or even a generally radical, movement. For all its rhetoric, *The Woman Rebel* had already been a step away from the radical community.

Her reputed radicalism hereafter became more specifically the sex radicalism she learned from Ellis and his circle. But this radicalism was not the hedonistic sex-for-enjoyment ideology of the mid-twentieth century. Sanger's sexual views always remained within the romantic school of thought that had reached her from the European sex radicals and American free lovers. Her orientation was always to treat sexual activity as a form of communication, expressing love through extrasensory impulses. In their desire to rescue sexuality from its degraded reputation under the reign of prudery, Sanger and the sex radicals, better called sex romantics, virtually reversed the Victorian view of sexuality: from an animal passion it became a spiritual one, at least potentially. There were degrees of the development of one's sexual nature which presumably were determined by more than technical expertise. The stages of development represented depth of communication and emotional intensity which in turn reflected men's consideration of women. (This consideration was necessary because Sanger did not argue for women's equal assertiveness in sexual encounters.) In Sanger's own sex manual, published in 1926, she entitled intercourse "sex communion," the use of a religious term revealing her tendency to spiritualize the sexual act. "At the flight, body, mind and soul are brought together into the closest unity. 'No more are they twain, but one flesh,' in the words of the Bible."

> . . . sex-communion should be considered as a true union of souls, not merely a physical function for the momentary relief of the sexual organs. Unless the psychic and spiritual desires are fulfilled, the relationship has been woefully deficient and the participants degraded and dissatisfied. . . . the sexual embrace not only satisfies but elevates both participants. The physical demands are harnessed for the expression of love.[51]

Sanger's work in sex education helped to alleviate the guilt of married couples and to give women an ideology with which to encourage—but hardly to demand—that men be considerate and proceed more slowly. But this sex education could hardly be considered radical in that it did nothing to challenge the conventional Victorian structure of sex relations, which were confined to the nuclear family and rested on male assertiveness and female passivity.

Furthermore Sanger's politics did not tend toward a socialist, and certainly not toward a Marxist, feminism but rather toward a mystique about womanliness, the successor to nineteenth-century feminist notions of the moral superiority of women (a precursor of what is known as "radical feminism" in the 1970s). Sanger believed in the "feminine spirit," the motive power of woman's nature. It was this spirit, coming from within, rather than social relations that drove women to revolt.[52] She often thought of women as fundamentally different from men. She wanted to help poor women but had no particular commitment to the working class as a class, not even to its female half, let alone its male; she simply did not see class relations, the relations of production, as fundamental to women's problems.

If any leader could have drawn Socialist party and feminist support together behind birth control, Sanger was not the one. Of course, Sanger's relative social and sexual conservatism greatly contributed to the acceptance of birth control as a specific reform. Similarly, her narrow focus and single-mindedness contributed to its legalization. But in 1914 neither the ultimate dominance of this conservative, single-issue approach nor the central role of Sanger was yet evident.

Before Sanger returned to the country, a spontaneous and decentralized movement of birth-control agitation and organization appeared in the Eastern, Midwestern and Western United States. It was stimulated by the news of Sanger's indictment, which was carried in newspapers through the country, in such distant places as Pittsfield, Massachusetts, and Reno, Nevada. Some newspapers described Sanger as an IWW editor. Local socialist groups were distributing Sanger's and other birth-control leaflets.[53] Local birth-control organizations were established in several places in 1915 long before Sanger's return to the United States and her first speaking tour.[54]

Two kinds of political groups were primarily responsible for the birth-control agitation in 1915: women's Socialist-party groups and IWW locals. In many places people had been introduced by Emma Goldman to Sanger's pamphlet, Sanger's name, and sometimes *The Woman Rebel,* just as later Goldman was to raise money for Sanger's defense on her speaking tours.[55] Elizabeth Gurley Flynn spoke about birth control in the Northwest and pledged local IWW and other anarchist support if Sanger would go on a speaking tour there.[56] Socialists saw Sanger, or adopted her, as one of their own and flooded her with letters of support and, inevitably, advice. Eugene Debs was one of the first to write and promised her the support of a "pretty good-sized bunch of revolutionists."[57] Goldman, in her motherly way, wanted to take Sanger under her wing, not only recommending a tactical plan for Sanger's trial but suggesting, "Hold out until I come back the 23rd of this month. Then go away with me for 2 weeks to Lakewood or some place . . . we'd both gain much and I would help you find yourself. . . ."[58] Others like Kate Richards O'Hare, Rose Pastor Stokes, Georgia Kotsch, Caroline Nelson, Rockwell Kent, Alexander Berkman, William J. Robinson, Jessie Ashley, and many lesser-known socialist organizers sent her messages of support and spoke on her behalf.[59] Liberals supported her too: for example, *The New Republic* published several editorials in her favor after March 1915.[60] In May 1915 birth-control supporters held a large meeting at the New York Academy of Medicine, urging public birth-control clinics. Many liberals spoke there.[61] But in March 1915, when a primarily liberal group organized the National Birth Control League (despite its name, the NBCL was never more than a New York City group), they would not support Sanger or any law-defying tactics. (They also excluded Goldman and other radicals.)[62] To the end of 1915 at least, those who supported Sanger and did local birth-control organizing everywhere except New York City were socialists.

In September 1915 William Sanger, Margaret's estranged husband, was tried for distributing her *Family Limitation* pamphlet. (He had been entrapped by a Post Office agent who requested a pamphlet.)[63] Sanger was convicted in a dramatic trial in which he defended himself. The trial was dominated by radicals, who shouted at the judge until he ordered the police to clear the courtroom. Messages of support came from various parts of the country. From Portland, Oregon, a strong IWW city that was a veritable hotbed of birth-control fervor, came a handwritten petition:

> 1. A woman has the right to control her own body even to the extent of deciding when she will become a mother.
> 2. Unwelcome or unfit children ought not to be born into the world.
> 3. Motherhood is dignified and noble only when it is desired and a joy. . . .
> 4. Scientific knowledge of sex-physiology can never be classified as impure or obscene. Those who do so classify it, proclaim only the impurity of their own minds.

The first signer added after his name: "The industrial system which needs children as food for powder or factories may desire unlimited propagation, but the masses who suffer in poverty have no right to add sufferers to the already too many competing for bread."[64] In these phrases were summarized fifty years of different birth-control arguments as they had reached the grass roots in the United States: women's rights, hereditarian social thought, social purity transformed by a faith in science and human dignity, and Neo-Malthusianism. It was such letters that made William Sanger believe his trial a great success, making "birth control a household word [*sic*]."[65]

The responses that flowed in to the Sangers showed that the concept of birth control, if not the term, was already widely known and supported. It was as if people had been waiting for leadership to ask them for help.

Margaret Sanger came home from London soon after her husband's trial. Seeking support for the trial she faced, she found that her husband's confrontational conduct at his trial had aroused many strong opinions as to how she should conduct her trial. The flurry of letters offering to tell her how to run the trial emerged from gallant but male-chauvinist assumptions that she was in need of help. Most of her friends urged her not to follow her husband's example (pleading not guilty and acting as his own lawyer) but to plead guilty and use a lawyer.[66] Goldman, on the other hand, begged her to resist those counsels, branding that line of defense cowardly.[67] One of her medical "supporters" preached to her about her duty to her children.[68] Sanger stood firm in her plan to plead not guilty.

The differences among birth-control supporters over what Sanger's trial tactics should be repeated differences that had become evident within the organization of the NBCL. In that original split it seemed that Sanger herself belonged to the ultra-left faction identified with the IWW. But Sanger's own public-relations activities in the fall of 1915 were not ultra-left at all. She had a "distinguished-guests-only" dinner at the Brevoort Hotel and in her speech gave an apologia for her militant tactics, explaining that her methods had been unorthodox merely in order to secure publicity.[69] Instead of devoting time to preparing her defense, she worked on publicity; and the steady growth of public support for her led to the government's dismissing the charges against her on February 18, 1916.[70] On April 1 Sanger left for a three-and-a-half-month speaking tour across the country. By its conclusion she was nationally famous. Newspaper coverage of her speeches was copious and often enthusiastic. Her occasional misadventures were usually transformed into successes: refused halls in Akron and Chicago, arrested and jailed in Portland, Oregon, and locked out of her hall in St. Louis by Catholic Church pressure, she responded like a seasoned political campaigner, turning always from the defense to the offense. She turned birth control into a free-speech as well as a sexual-liberation issue and won support from important liberal civil libertarians.[71] She sought to establish effective coalitions of liberal and radical groups for birth control.

Still, the grass-roots work in organizing for birth control was being done by radicals. In Cleveland (the first major city to organize a birth-control group, and a place where the birth-control campaign was later to be especially successful),[72] workers' groups sponsored Sanger's tremendously successful speeches and led the birth-control movement. In St. Paul the Women's Socialist Club led the birth-control movement,[73] and in Ann Arbor, Agnes Inglis, a socialist activist, organized a group.[74] Even the relatively staid Massachusetts Birth Control League was led by socialists.[75] In small towns as well as big cities socialists were organizing for birth control.[76] And although Sanger varied her appeals to particular audiences, she made several sharp attacks on the conservatism of privileged groups. When the snobbish Chicago Women's Club cancelled her speaking engagement, she attacked it, saying she did not care to speak to a "sophisticated" audience anyway. "I want to talk to the women of the stock yards, the women of the factories—they are the victims of a system or lack of system that cries out for corrections. I am interested in birth control among working women chiefly."[77]

In 1916 birth control in the United States was a radical movement and a large movement. Birth control as a political demand had demonstrated an ability to involve not only educated but also working-class women in a participatory social movement. Elizabeth Gurley Flynn wrote to Sanger that she found everywhere in the country the "greatest possible interest" in birth control. ". . . one girl told me the women in the stockyards District [Chicago] kissed her hands when she distributed [Sanger's birth-control pamphlet]."[78] In 1913 in Tampa, Florida, Flynn had visited a cigar factory with Spanish-speaking workers where the reader* was reading aloud a pamphlet on birth control.[79] Letters from women all over the country came pouring in not only to Sanger but also to others who were identified in newspapers as birth-control activists, letters asking for contraceptive information and thanking them for the fight they were making. Often they were fearful: "I nearly had nervous prostration after I had mailed you my letter asking for that 'information' . . ."[80] Or: "Please send me one of your Papers on birth control, I have had seven children and cannot afford any more. Please don't give my name to the Papers."[81] Usually they poured out the difficulties of their lives, with their most intimate sexual problems and most externally caused economic problems intermingled—as they indeed always are in real life.

> I was married at the age of eighteen. Now I am married for seven years and I have four children. . . . I am a little over twenty-four and already skinny, yellow and so funny looking and I want to hold my husband's love. . . . He tried to help me but somehow

* Cigar makers traditionally pooled their money to employ readers to entertain them as they worked.

> I got caught anyway and a baby came. We didn't have any money to get rid of it and now when I look on her little innocent, red face I am glad I didn't kill it. . . . When you was in Chicago I wanted to go to see you but I had no nice clothes and I knew I would make you feel ashamed if I went dressed shabbily. . . .
>
> I have six children, am forty-one years old . . . have reason to believe my husband has a venereal disease. . . . To all of my pleadings my husband turns a deaf ear. He beats me, curses me and deserts us for weeks at a time when I refuse intercourse. . . . The place we call home is only a hovel. . . . I must live with him to get his support until my youngest children are older (youngest is eighteen months . . .) but to live with him I must indulge him sexually and whatever protection I get I must provide myself.[82]

Many of the letters expressed exasperation at the class injustice behind the fact that they were deprived of birth control information. "Tell me how it is the wealthier class of people can get information like that and those that really need it, can't?"[83] And many others plunged immediately into political action, like Mrs. Lulu MacClure Clarke of St. Louis, who wrote to Sanger:

> I have been through suffrage wrangles all my adult life, in backwoods communities and [among] the vicious of a city and I know how very chivalrous indeed men can be when any new freedom is asked for by women, and this is harder for them to swallow. . . . I cannot help financially, altho I would like to. We are just working people, but I am writing to various friends about it and tonight I mailed a letter to the Post-Dispatch of my city. . . . But even if women cant help much, don't know how to speak in public or write for the press, etc., yet they are awakening up all over the nation and waiting for someone to lead the way. I think —in fact, I know—there is a well-spring of gratitude to you— that they think you are fighting for them and they wait hoping and praying. . . . I am glad you have a husband who is a help and not a hindrance. Tell him I send him my heartiest goodwill and best wishes. If there is anything that you think I could do, please let me know. And oh, Please dont give up or get discouraged. . . .[84]

Not only was there a potentially large movement here, but its people were ready for action. What they wanted personally, the *minimum* demand, was to be given information in defiance of the law. Beyond that, women in many places quickly moved to a strategy that logically followed—opening illegal birth-control clinics to give that illegal information to others. There was a practical reason for this: the best contraceptive—a vaginal diaphragm—required a private fitting. Sanger was already convinced of the efficacy of "direct action." She gained support for this plan by what she learned on her national tour.[85] In many ways that tour was as much a learning experience for Sanger as a teaching one. In Ann Arbor, Michigan, socialist Agnes Inglis had a de facto clinic functioning before Sanger returned to New York.[86] In St. Paul socialist women announced plans for a clinic in June.[87] Sanger herself dreamed of a "glorious 'chain' of clinics" throughout the country.[88]

Returning to New York City in July 1916, Sanger organized a clinic of her own in the Brownsville section of Brooklyn. Brownsville was then a Jewish and Italian immigrant neighborhood, an extremely poor slum. Sanger worked with her sister Ethel Byrne, also a nurse, and Fania Mindell, whom Sanger had recruited in Chicago. The three women rented an apartment and gave out to every family in the district a handbill printed in English, Yiddish, and Italian. They were not prepared to fit women with contraceptives, but only to "give the principles of contraception, show a cervical pessary to the women, explain that if they had had two children they should have one size and if more a larger one."[89] Women were lined up outside when the clinic opened on October 16. As many Catholics came as Jews. Sanger asked one Catholic woman what she would say to the priest at confession. "It's none of his business," she answered. "My husband has a weak heart and works only four days a week. He gets twelve dollars, and we can barely live on it now. We have enough children."[90] Most of the neighbors were friendly and supportive. The baker gave them free doughnuts and the landlady brought them tea. By the end of nine days, the clinic had 464 case histories of women on file.[91]

Then, inevitably, one of the patients turned out to be a policewoman. She seemed prosperous; Fania Mindell suspected her but did not turn her away. The next day she returned as Officer Margaret Whitehurst, arrested the three women, and confiscated all the equipment and case histories. Tried separately, Ethel Byrne was sentenced to thirty days on Blackwell's Island. Byrne immediately announced her intention to go on a hunger strike. (The hunger strikes of British suffragists were at this time an international symbol of feminist resistance.) Like the British suffragists, she was force-fed by tubes through the nose; the combination of her starvation and the brutality of the force-feeding left her so weakened she required a year to recuperate.[92] At Sanger's trial women who had visited the clinic testified. Although legally they supported the prosecution, giving evidence that they had indeed received contraceptive advice without medical indication, politically they helped the birth-control cause by their clear testimonials to the misery of involuntary pregnancy.[93] Sanger also was sentenced to thirty days but conducted herself cooperatively. When she was released on March 6 her friends met her singing "The Marseillaise."[94]

Many activists were arrested and jailed for their birth-control activities—at least twenty besides Sanger on federal charges alone. Carlo Tresca, an Italian-American anarchist, was sentenced to a year and a day for advertising a book called *L'Arte di non fare i figli* ("The Art of Not Making Children") in his radical labor paper, *Il Martello*. (American Civil Liberties Union intervention got his sentence commuted after he served four months.)[95] Emma Goldman was also jailed for giving out contraceptive information. There was, of course, class injustice in arrest, convictions, and sentences. Jessie Ashley, Ida Rauh Eastman, Bolton Hall, and Rose Pastor Stokes gave out birth-control pamphlets publicly at mass meetings at Carnegie Hall; although Ashley, Eastman and Hall were arrested, Stokes—a millionaire's wife—was not.*[96] Carl Rave, an IWW longshoreman, was jailed in San Mateo, California, for three months for selling Sanger's *Family Limitation*. He complained that Professor Holmes of the University of California (probably a eugenist) proclaimed the need for compulsory birth control on the front page of the papers with impunity.[98] Others took risks as abortionists, though none was prosecuted on such charges. In addition to Dr. Konikow in Boston these included Dr. Marie Equi in Portland, Oregon, a lesbian who later served ten months in San Quentin for making an anticonscription speech during World War I.

Police and prison guards were often hostile and violent to the birth-control prisoners, especially the women, for their advocacy of birth control seemed to violate every male fantasy about what women should be like. The detective arresting Agnes Smedley in 1918 told her that "he wished he had me in the south; that there 'I would be strung up to the first lamp post'; I would be lynched. I tried to tell him that he was on the wrong side of the trenches . . . ," Smedley recalled, but he only threatened her again.[99]

* Stokes was upset about this discrimination in her favor. Ashley wrote, reassuring her: ". . . they think you *want* to be arrested and they are loath to increase the notoriety of the b.c. propaganda. They think your trial would be as widely advertised as Margaret Sanger's or Emma Goldman's. In any case it seems to me to the advantage of all of us to keep you out of jail. While you are free you can go about doing your work, and yours is now more effective than Ida Rauh's or mine. After all, everyone knows there *is* injustice and we don't have to demonstrate that, *that* is not what we are trying to accomplish. . . ."[97]

Legal persecution always promoted publicity but sometimes also produced concrete victories. Birth-control prisoners often propagandized their sister prisoners. Agnes Smedley wrote from the Tombs, "Kitty, Mollie Steiner, and I have wonderful meetings when we can dodge in some corner or hall. Kitty is turning the place into a birth-control branch. And she has held a meeting. And her friends are writing out demanding that their parents and friends vote Socialism!"[100]

Commitment to action was strong among these birth controllers. As socialists, most of them believed that working-class strength was the key to political progress, and thus they wanted above all to reach working-class people with their message and service. As feminists, they wanted to improve the position of women. They believed that the subjugation of women supported capitalism directly by creating profit, and indirectly by weakening the socialist movement: depriving it of half its potential constituency and allowing socialist men to cling to privileges that corrupted. All of them, even the non-Marxists, shared an interest in improving the lives of poor people in the present and did not try to fob them off with promises of postrevolutionary paradise. Their work in trying to reach working-class women was made more difficult by their own class origins. Most of the leadership of this movement was from professional, even capitalist, backgrounds. Their superior confidence and articulateness often made them better talkers than listeners. But their humanitarianism, their desire to eliminate material misery, was not a symptom of elitism. Indeed it was shared by those among them of "lower" origins—like Stokes, Goldman, Equi, and Sanger. It was also a conscious tactical choice, a rejection of the myth that greater misery makes workers more revolutionary.

Similarly, the plan to agitate among working-class people, particularly women, on an issue so private and so removed from production was a conscious tactical choice, one based on political experience. Sanger had been struck by the strongly positive reaction among socialist constituencies to her writing and speaking on sexual hygiene. Flynn and Bloor had worked with women, sometimes women who were not wage workers themselves but workers' wives, in many strike situations and had perceived the deep connections between family support and workers' militancy. Robinson had been receiving for over a decade the kind of personal letters that began flooding in to Sanger and the birth-control organizations after 1915—letters attesting to the mutually reinforcing nature of sexual, economic, and political helplessness. A systematic evaluation of five thousand such letters sent to Margaret Sanger after the publication of her *Woman and the New Race* in 1920 showed that they were overwhelmingly from working-class and poor women. The most common occupation given for husbands was "laborer," the most common salary fifteen dollars per week. One-third of the women were themselves wage-earners, as compared to the over-all national average of 23 percent in 1920. Eighty percent of the writers had married before the age of twenty, and averaged five children.[101] These organizers thought birth control could improve the economic situations and family stability of the poor and give women in particular more free choice and greater alternatives. Focusing on the connection between the sexual and economic oppression of working-class women was a strategy for organizing. Its goal was to create a significant women's force within a socialist movement.

NOTES

1. David A. Shannon, *The Socialist Party of America* (New York: Macmillan, 1955), p. 76; James Weinstein, *The Decline of Socialism in America* (New York: Monthly Review, 1967), p. 27.

2. Even suffragists acknowledged this support from the Socialist party. See, for example, Ida Husted Harper in *History of Woman Suffrage*, ed. Stanton, Anthony, Gage (New York, 1881–1922), 5:362.

3. Weinstein, *Decline of Socialism*, pp. 58–59; Caroline Lowe [General Correspondent, Woman's National Committee, Socialist Party], "Socialist Women Did Much in 1911," *Chicago Evening World*, February 23, 1912, p. 4.

4. Mrs. S. I. Jenson in *Socialist Woman*, September 1913; and Helen Unterman, in ibid., October 1913.

5. For example, Caroline Nelson, "Neo-Malthusianism," *International Socialist Review* 14, no. 4 (October 1913): 228. Nelson wrote for *Socialist Woman* on other topics.

6. Virginia Butterfield, *Parental Rights and Economic Wrongs* (Chicago: Stockham, 1906), p. 87.

7. For example, Theresa Malkiel, "The Lowest Paid Workers," *Socialist Woman*, September 1908; "Woman's Work and Pay," editorial, *Chicago Evening World* [a socialist paper], June 11, 1912, p. 8.

8. For example, Jonathan Mayo Crane, in *Lucifer*, March 28, 1907; Charlotte Perkins Gilman, "Men's Babies," Gilman mss., Schlesinger Library, Folder 176, n.d. but probably after 1914; Sam Atkinson, *Science and a Priest* (Seattle: Libertarian Press, [1910]).

9. Crane, in *Lucifer;* Helen Keller, in *New York Call*, November 26, 1915; Margaret Sanger, "Comstockery in America," *International Socialist Review* 16, no. 1 (July 1915): 46; Peter E. Burrowes, "Woman and Her Masters," *The Comrade* 13, no. 8 (May 1904): 172–74; Nelson, "Neo-Malthusianism."

10. William J. Robinson, "The Prevention of Conception," *The New Review* 3, no. 4 (April 1915): 196–99.

11. Adelyne More, *Uncontrolled Breeding or Fecundity versus Civilization* (New York: Critic and Guide Co., 1917), Chapters 7 and 8; Max Hodann, *History of Modern Morals*, trans. Stella Browne (London: William Heine-

mann, 1937), passim; William J. Robinson, "The Birth Strike," *International Socialist Review* 14, no. 7 (January 1914): 404; William English Walling, in *The Masses*, October 1913, p. 20.

12. For example, Winfield Scott Hall, *The Biology, Physiology and Sociology of Reproduction* ([1906] Chicago: Wynnewood, 1913).

13. For example: Dr. Edith Belle Lowry, *Herself: Talks with Women Concerning Themselves* (Chicago: Forbes, 1911); Ida Craddock, *Advice to a Bridegroom* (Chicago, 1909); *Helps to Happy Wedlock* (Philadelphia, 1896); *Letter to a Prospective Bride* (Philadelphia, 1897); *Right Marital Living* (Chicago, 1899); and *The Wedding Night* (Denver, 1900).

14. Diane Feelley, "Antoinette Konikow, Marxist and Feminist," *International Socialist Review*, January 1972, pp. 42–46; Birth Control League of Massachusetts mss., Schlesinger Library, passim.

15. June 1, 1913, and August 16, 1914, for example.

16. Robinson in *New York Call*, for example, August 11, 1912, June 8, 1913, June 15, 1913; Konikow in ibid., August 16, 1914.

17. *Mother Earth* 6 (April 1911): 2; Richard Drinnon, *Rebel in Paradise* (Boston: Beacon, 1961), pp. 166–68.

18. Drinnon, *Rebel in Paradise*, pp. 67, 166.

19. Hapgood, *Victorian in the Modern World*, p. 170.

20. This episode is described in James Reed's dissertation, "Birth Control and the Americans 1830–1970," Harvard, 1974. I am grateful to him for allowing me to read it.

21. Margaret Sanger, *Autobiography* (New York: W. W. Norton, 1938), pp. 80–83; *New York Call*, February 18, 1912; Reed, "Birth Control," pp. 37–38.

22. For example: *New York Call*, November 5, 19, 26; December 3 and 10, 1911.

23. *New York Call*, November 7 and 27; December 1, 8, 15, 22, and 29, 1912; January 12, 19, and 26, 1913.

24. *New York Call*, February 8, 1913.

25. Peter Fryer, *The Birth Controllers* (London: Secker & Warburg, 1965), p. 202.

26. William Haywood, *Bill Haywood's Book, Autobiography* (New York: International Publishers, 1929), p. 268.

27. Sanger, *Autobiography*, pp. 103–104; Sanger, *My Fight for Birth Control* (New York: Farrar & Rinehart, 1913), pp. 68–69, 72–75.

28. For example, in *Medico-Pharmaceutical Critic and Guide* 4, no. 6 (December 1904): 163–64.

29. Sanger, *Autobiography*, pp. 89–92.

30. Ibid., pp. 93–94.

31. Ibid., p. 96.

32. Elizabeth Gurley Flynn, *The Rebel Girl* (New York: International Publishers, 1973), p. 166.

33. If we lean toward diminishing Sanger's role in this movement, it is only to correct a historical record that has exaggerated her role. At the height of the movement, between 1915 and 1918, many leading political activists worked on birth control. For example, in New York most of the socialist suffrage leaders and a few nonsocialist suffragists joined in: Jessie Ashley, wealthy lawyer, former treasurer of the National American Woman Suffrage Association (NAWSA) and Socialist-party member; Clara Gruening Stillman and Martha Gruening; Mary Ware Dennett, a right-wing socialist and former secretary of NAWSA; Martha Bensley Bruere, active in the Socialist party

and the Women's Trade Union League (WTUL); Rose Pastor Stokes, an immigrant Jewish cigar maker now active in the Socialist party and married to a socialist millionaire railroad and mining magnate; Ida Rauh Eastman and Crystal Eastman, sisters-in-law and both socialist feminists; Elsie Clews Parsons, Barnard professor; of course Dr. William J. Robinson, who brought many others from his profession into the movement; Floyd Dell and Max Eastman and other male pro-suffragists. In San Francisco, Los Angeles, and Portland, Oregon, many IWW and Socialist-party leaders organized birth-control groups. In Michigan there was Agnes Inglis, a wealthy reformer. In Cleveland Sanger found and recruited Frederick Blossom, a skilled socialist administrator and money-raiser. There were also full-time organizers, traveling, speaking, and often distributing illegal birth-control literature: Emma Goldman, Ben Reitman, Elizabeth Gurley Flynn, Ella Reeve Bloor.

34. Letter in Himes mss., Countway Library, Harvard University Medical School, February 13, 1937. I am indebted to James Reed for this reference. I have corrected spelling and punctuation.

35. For example: Sanger to T. J. Meade, September 11, 1929, in Sanger Papers, Library of Congress [hereinafter given as Sanger, LC]; Sanger, *Autobiography*, passim; and *My Fight for Birth Control*, passim.

36. Emma Goldman, "Marriage and Love," in *Red Emma Speaks*, ed. Shulman (New York: Vintage, 1972); Goldman, *Living My Life* (Garden City, N.Y.: Garden City Publ., [1931] 1934), p. 556.

37. Mary Ware Dennett, *Birth Control Laws* (New York: F. H. Hitchcock, 1926), Appendix 4.

38. Eastman, *Enjoyment of Living*, pp. 423–24.

39. Alice Groff, "The Marriage Bed," *The Woman Rebel*, no. 5 (July 1914). Groff was also a contributor to Robinson's *Critic and Guide*.

40. Ibid., no. 6 (August 1914). See also Lily Gair Wilkinson, "Sisterhood," in ibid.; and editorial in the first issue, March 1914.

41. "Watchful Waiting," ibid., no. 3 (May 1914). A similar combination of ultrarevolutionary rhetoric and feminism reappeared in the women's liberation movement at the end of the 1960s.

42. Herbert Thorpe, "A Defense of Assassination," ibid., no. 5 (July 1914). See news stories about the suppression in *New York American*, August 27, 1914, and *New York Evening Globe*, August 25, 1914, clippings in Sanger, LC. Sanger disingenuously implied that the censorship was strictly directed against the journal's advocacy of birth control: see her *Autobiography*, pp. 110–11, and *My Fight for Birth Control*, pp. 86–87.

43. Sanger to Upton Sinclair, September 23, 1914, in Sinclair, *My Lifetime in Letters* (New York: Columbia University Press, 1960), pp. 148–49; Harold Hersey, "Margaret Sanger: The Biography of the Birth Control Pioneers," ms. in New York Public Library, pp. 122 ff.

44. Sanger, *Autobiography*, pp. 108–17.

45. Sanger, *My Fight for Birth Control*, p. 87; Sanger Diary, 1914, in Sanger, LC.

46. *Family Limitation*, 1914, in Sanger, LC.

47. Sanger, *Autobiography*, pp. 119–22; and *My Fight for Birth Control*, pp. 91 ff.

48. Sanger, letter to "Friend," printed, September 1914, Sanger, LC.

49. Sanger, *My Fight for Birth Control*, pp. 102–103.

50. Ibid.: Sanger, *Autobiography*, pp. 128 ff.

51. Sanger, *Happiness in Marriage* (New York: Brentano's, 1926), pp. 142–43. For other characteristic expressions of these sexual views by Sanger,

see: Sanger to Edward Carpenter, April 13, 1918, in Carpenter Collection, Sheffield Public Library, Great Britain (I am indebted to Sheila Rowbotham for this letter); Sanger, "English Methods of Birth Control," pamphlet in Sanger, LC.

52. Sanger, *Woman and the New Race* (New York: Brentano's, 1920), pp. 239–40.

53. For example, Charles Schultz, Secretary, Oakland IWW, November 17, 1915; B. Greenberg, Devil's Lake, N.D., February 10, 1916; unsigned from Washington, D.C., August 23, 1915; and many other letters to Sanger; miscellaneous clippings; all in Sanger, LC.

54. Caroline Nelson, June 12, 1915, and Georgia Kotsch, January 18, 1916, to Sanger, in Sanger, LC.

55. For example, Alvin Heckethorn, Portland, Ore., September 9, 1914, Emma Goldman, December 16, 1915, and Caroline Nelson, June 12, 1915, to Sanger; all in Sanger, LC.

56. Elizabeth Gurley Flynn to Sanger, August 1915, in Sanger, LC.

57. Eugene Debs to Sanger, November 8, 1914 and December 16, 1914, in Sanger, LC.

58. Goldman to Sanger, from Columbus, Ohio, December 8, 1915, in Sanger, LC.

59. Various letters to Sanger, 1915, in Sanger, LC.

60. For example, March 16, 1915; April 17, 1915; December 11, 1915.

61. *New York Tribune*, May 21, 1915, p. 7, clipping in Sanger, LC. Speakers included Dr. Rosalie Slaughter Morton, professor at New York University; Dr. Emily Dunning Barringer, surgeon; Lavinia Dock, suffragist and secretary, International Council of Nurses; Dr. Lydia Allen DeVilbiss, formerly of the State Board of Health; Dr. Abraham Jacobi, president of the AMA; Dr. Ira Wile, member of the Board of Education.

62. The original call of formation of the NBCL listed Jessie Ashley, Otto Bobsien, Mary Ware Dennett, Martha Gruening, Bolton Hall, Charles Hallinan, Paul Kennaday, Helen Marot, James F. Morton, Lucy Sprague Mitchell, Lincoln Steffens, and Clara Gruening Stillman. This was published in *Survey*, April 1915, p. 5. The presence of socialist names on this list, such as Ashley and Morton, suggests that a few liberals led the organizational move —probably Dennett among them—and got the support of others who did not share equally in defining the policies of the new organization.

63. James Waldo Fawcett, ed., *Jailed for Birth Control: The Trial of William Sanger, September 10, 1915, Birth Control Review* Pamphlet (New York, 1917); Sanger, *My Fight for Birth Control*, pp. 119–21, and *Autobiography*, pp. 177–78.

64. Sanger, LC.

65. William to Margaret Sanger, September 1915, Sanger, LC. In response to the trial, many suffragists previously silent on birth control now spoke out in Sanger's defense, such as Carrie Chapman Catt, Bela Neuman Zilberman, Mrs. Norman De R. Whitehouse, and Catherine Waugh McCulloch, quoted in miscellaneous clippings from New York City newspapers, Sanger, Scrapbook no. 1, Sanger, LC.

66. James F. Morton, September 24, 1914; Bolton Hall, December 13, 1915; Max Eastman, January 11, 1916; and James Warbasse, December 7, 1915, all to Sanger, Sanger, LC.

67. Goldman, December 8, 1915 and December 16, 1915, and Alexander Berkman, December 18, 1915, to Sanger, Sanger, LC.

68. Warbasse to Sanger, December 7, 1915, Sanger, LC. See also Gold-

man's fury at Warbasse for his sexism, Goldman to Sanger, December 16, 1915, Sanger, LC.

69. Sanger, *My Fight for Birth Control,* pp. 132–34; clippings about the dinner in Sanger, LC.

70. *New York Times,* February 19, 1916.

71. Sanger, *My Fight for Birth Control,* pp. 144–49, and *Autobiography,* Chapter 16.

72. News item in *Survey,* October 21, 1916, pp. 60–61.

73. *St. Paul Dispatch,* June 12, 1916, in Sanger Scrapbook no. 3, Sanger, LC.

74. Inglis to Rose Pastor Stokes, June 2, 1916 and June 24, 1916, in Stokes mss., Tamiment Library, Tamiment, Pa.

75. Ella Westcott to Stokes, October 28, 1916, Stokes mss.

76. For example, H. P. Hough, from Fortress Monroe, Va., December 3, 1916; Joseph Rothman, Poughkeepsie, January 6, 1917; Carl Haessler, Urbana, Ill., May 25, 1916, all to Stokes, Stokes mss.; Robt. Peary, July 12, 1916, and B. Greenberg, Devil's Lake, N.D., February 10, 1916, to Sanger, all in Sanger, LC.

77. *Chicago Evening Journal,* April 25, 1916, in Sanger, LC; see also Sanger, *My Fight for Birth Control,* p. 145.

78. Flynn to Sanger in London, August 1915, Sanger, LC.

79. Flynn, *The Rebel Girl,* pp. 184–85.

80. Mrs. Elsie M. Humphries, Cincinnati, to Stokes, January 9, 1917, Stokes mss.

81. Mrs. W. R. Stevens, Swampscott, Mass., to Stokes, October 20, 1916, Stokes mss.

82. Margaret Sanger, ed., *Motherhood in Bondage* (New York: Brentano's, 1928), pp. 34, 281.

83. Mrs. K.A.B., to NBCL, n.d. (probably 1921), in Sanger, LC.

84. Letter to Sanger, February 1, 1916, in Sanger, LC.

85. Sanger, *My Fight for Birth Control,* p. 149.

86. Inglis to Stokes, June 2, 1916, Stokes mss.

87. *St. Paul Dispatch,* June 12, 1916, in Sanger Scrapbook no. 3, in Sanger, LC.

88. Sanger, *My Fight for Birth Control,* p. 144.

89. Sanger, *Autobiography,* p. 215.

90. Ibid., pp. 218–19.

91. Ibid., p. 220. Note that Sanger gives the figure as 488 in *My Fight for Birth Control,* p. 158.

92. Sanger, *Autobiography,* p. 234.

93. Ibid., for example, p. 231.

94. Ibid., p. 250.

95. Dennett, *Birth Control Laws,* Appendix 4; and Dennett, *Who's Obscene?* (New York: Vanguard Press, 1930), pp. 236–42.

96. *New York Evening Sun,* May 6, 1916, clipping in Sanger, LC; and F. M. Vreeland, "The Process of Reform with Especial Reference to Reform Groups in the Field of Population," Ph.D. dissertation, University of Michigan, 1929.

97. Jessie Ashley to Stokes, June 17, 1916, Stokes mss.

98. Rave statement, [1929], Alice Park mss., Stanford University. Carl Rave was not a representative longshoreman accidentally interested in birth control; he was married to Caroline Nelson, a birth-control activist. See

Nominations for ABCL General National Committee, May 11, 1918, American Birth Control League Papers, Houghton Library, Harvard University.

99. Agnes Smedley to Sanger, November 1, 1918, in Sanger, LC.

100. Ibid.

101. Vreeland, "Process of Reform," pp. 274–75; Sanger, *Motherhood in Bondage*, p. 439.

20

Cookbooks and Law Books

The Hidden History of Career Women in Twentieth-Century America

■

FRANK STRICKER

In The Feminine Mystique, *Betty Friedan observed that educated women of the 1940s and 1950s, in contrast to those of the two previous decades, did not think to pursue careers and sought fulfillment in the home and family only. Recent historians, revising Friedan, have asserted that disillusion with the pursuit of careers (and concomitant feminist goals) began as early as the 1920s. One buttress to their assertions is the statistical evidence that the proportion of women in various professions and professional schools peaked in 1920, but declined for the subsequent four decades. Reexamining the career history of college-educated women in the interwar years, Frank Stricker finds that their commitment to professional achievements persisted. He points out that more pessimistic observers had not carefully scrutinized the occupational statistics, which needed to be read with attention to changes in absolute numbers, rates of increase, and several different proportional relationships.*

I

A CRUCIAL PROBLEM IN the history of American women in the twentieth century involves their participation in professional and business occupations. This is but one aspect of the role of women at work outside the home. Indeed, the majority of working women in this century were employed as domestics, garment workers, clerks, typists, and in a variety of other low-level jobs—not as professionals and business-women. For most of these the job was not a career or a means of personal fulfillment but a function of sheer economic necessity.[1] Yet even in work that seemed to leave little room for creativity, organizational expertise, and human control of the tasks, the job sometimes had attributes of a career. Women wished to work not merely to support their families, but for a measure of personal economic independence, or as a byproduct of escaping from dull country life, or simply for the sociability of working with other women.[2]

This paper, however, focuses on the special group of women in professional and business occupations, roughly corresponding to the census categories of "Professional, Technical, and Kindred Workers," and "Managers, Officials, and Proprietors." The category of "Professionals" has always included large numbers of school teachers and nurses, with smaller numbers of physicians, lawyers, college teachers, and the like. The category of "Managers, Officials, and Proprietors," included government officials, managers in industry, as well as owners of small businesses. Although women with career attitudes could be found outside these occupations, and although not all women in these occupations were career minded, the general categories roughly indicate the number of women in careers.

The career woman had serious goals in mind. She wanted economic independence and a job with intrinsic satisfactions. Along with the demand for political equality, the desire for a career was a central theme in early twentieth-century feminism. Although a career was not a real possibility for the majority of women, and although the career impulse was not identical with feminism, it did express the driving impulse of many advanced middle-class women.[3]

The feminist movement had reached its high point in 1920, when, after decades of struggle, women won a federal amendment granting the right to vote. In the years that followed, the movement fell on hard times. The largest number of activist women in the 1920's were "social feminists," women involved in service to society, often animated by an ideal of selfless sacrifice, and essentially conservative about women's role in the family. A small group of women in Alice Paul's Woman's Party, at odds with the social reformers, pushed for a federal equal rights amendment. Younger women were, on the whole, disaffected from both groups of feminists. They had turned away from reform and politics. In the age of the flapper, feminism seemed unfashionable.[4]

But if the feminist movement fell into disarray in the 1920's, what was actually happening to articulate educated women? What has been their history in career positions in the twentieth century? The problem that this paper deals with is the alleged decline of women's share of professional and business occupations, which is often located in the '20's along with the difficulties of the feminist movement. The statistics do indicate a decline, although it sometimes occurs in previous or subsequent decades. For example, in

1920, one of seven doctorates was awarded to a woman; this ratio began declining in the '30's until, in 1956, only one of ten doctorates were women. Women's proportion of total college enrollment peaked in the 1920's; their percentage of total college teaching faculty in the 1930's. In some areas not only women's share but their numbers declined. There were fewer female physicians in 1930 (8,388) than there had been in 1910 (9,015), the decline beginning in the 1910's. The number of female musicians and music teachers dropped from 84,478 in 1910 to 79,611 in 1930, losing 12% in the 1910's and gaining 10% in the 1920's. Overall, women's proportion of the professional ranks reached a plateau in the 1920's and fell off in the following decade.[5]

It is, however, because of literary evidence rather than statistical facts that some historians have suggested that it was in the late 1920's that career women became disillusioned with their new role. Magazines like *Harper's, Scribner's,* and *The Forum* began publishing the confessions of professional and business-women who had apparently turned their backs on the workplace to find fulfillment at home.[6] "Feminist-New Style," as one author termed the younger generation, desired a measure of economic independence and satisfying work, but she would not sacrifice marriage and family for work. If forced to choose, she would give up her law book for the cookbook.[7]

As the 1920's came to a close, investigator Phyllis Blanchard discovered among young women "the first signs of disillusionment with the new freedom." The modern girl, "who has seen the loneliness of older unmarried friends, is beginning to discount the rewards from a material success that must be accomplished at the expense of love."[8] Even so staunch a feminist as Alice Beal Parsons had to admit that a new motto was finding its way into numerous magazines: "We are tired of our rights, give us our privileges again."[9] In short, within a decade of the high point of the woman suffrage movement, it seemed to contemporary observers that the tide had turned against woman's emancipation and that career women were going home.[10]

Having absorbed this information recent writers contend that women became disillusioned with the very ideals of economic independence and exciting work because the freer sexual morality of the period made love and marriage more attractive to women.[11]

Sociologist Jessie Bernard attaches to the 1920's the label, "Surging Flood of Disillusion," and argues that with success, the "éclat of the earlier years had spent itself." In the decade of the 1930's, academic women began "the headlong flight into maternity." Despite the lure of fellowships, "women turned their backs and ran to rock the cradle."[12] William O'Neill has argued that "the careerist myth had been deflated" and a "New Victorianism" encouraging sexual happiness for women in marriage, emerged in the 1920's.[13] The sexual revolution of the decade made romance and marriage more attractive than they had been in the Victorian period when women's sexual pleasure was discouraged. As a result, it is argued, the hardy and celibate spinster—the kind of woman who could devote herself wholeheartedly to a career—became an even rarer figure. Feminism itself was associated with flat heels and a lack of feminine charm.[14] According to this interpretation, the spread of a more sophisticated feminine mystique in the 1940's and 1950's was almost anticlimactic. Already in the 1920's, the career impulse was losing out to love and a marriage promising sexual fulfillment.[15]

In what follows I will argue against the theory of disillusionment on grounds first, that the evidence from the surveys of career intentions is inconclusive; second, that occupational statistics can be read in a nonregressive manner and that some of the explanations used for the decline are unnecessary or incorrect; third, that a woman's decision to marry was not necessarily the rejection of a career; fourth, that the public confessions of women who went home were less negative than has been supposed; and finally, that the assumptions of social scientists and psychologists must be distinguished from the complex attitudes of American women.

I will not deny that women were subject to job discrimination, the double burden of home and career, and, most of all, socialization from an early age to the domestic role. But obviously, many women received contrary pressures and went through experiences such as college education which raised opposite expectations. Women did receive strong pressures to marry, have a family, and follow a socially defined model of feminine beauty and submissiveness. But many of them also felt pressures to achieve, prepare for a career, and be intellectually alive (if only for their husbands' sakes). Our model of women's attitudes must be much more complex than the theory of disillusionment assumes, and it should view the formation of women's attitudes in the context of the varying and often contradictory social and economic forces pressing on them.[16]

II

Changes in the attitudes and aspirations of American women over the past fifty years cannot be measured with precision. In particular, the attitudes of younger women are hard to come by. They may be the most interesting, because women in their teens probably express career aspirations in a relatively pure form, before discrimination in the market place and the double burden of home and career become practical matters.

Perhaps for this reason, Lorine Pruette's 1924 survey of young women, most of them ages 15–17, shows a relatively high level of careerism. In fact, more than a third (35%) said they would choose a career even if that meant giving up the possibility of marrying and having a family.[17]

Later surveys seemed to show a decline in career sentiment. A survey completed in 1930, of women ages 18–26, found only 13% who were planning careers with no thought of marriage and who would forego marriage if it interfered with their careers. Phyllis Blanchard and Carolyn Manasses, the interviewers, concluded that young women were becoming disillusioned with the new freedom.[18] Several historians have followed their evaluation, citing similar surveys.[19]

But we must be cautious in using these surveys to demonstrate a decline of career sentiments. Each of them asks different questions of different groups. Each offers slightly different choices to the women. Even in Blanchard's group, 38% of the total wanted to combine marriage and a career, a result that is not by itself evidence of a decline in career sentiment.[20] Elsewhere the evidence is also confusing, particularly if we are interested in dating the decline and fall of career attitudes. Of Vassar women surveyed in 1923, 90% wanted to marry; yet only 70% of the graduates of New Jersey's College for Women in 1930 agreed that marriage and family took precedence over a career.[21] In 1936 a majority of Pennsylvania State College Senior Women agreed that "a young woman cannot continue her business career after her wedding . . . except in case of real financial need."[22] But half the Vassar College Seniors of 1937 would combine career and family if they could earn enough to pay for child-care and have some time for their children.[23]

The evidence of trends from the various career surveys is therefore somewhat ambiguous. One cannot feel secure in marking out long-range trends.[24] The apparently high interest of women in Pruette's 1924 survey in careers has much to do with the youth of those interviewed. Whether the lower number in Blanchard's survey who would forego marriage for a career represents a decline from previous periods among similar kinds of women is impossible to determine.

As time went on, women's career decisions grew more complex, with more and more potential career women planning some combination of vocation and domestic life. Even in the 1950's, when the feminine mystique reigned supreme, half the women in one survey of college students wanted a career, most with and some without marriage. Some 20% were determined career women. Others were willing to interrupt their work to have a family and then return to work, but some of these "would have preferred to carry on their careers without interruption" if part-time jobs and sufficient earnings for hiring domestic help were available.[25] With the spread of contraception and the lack of day-care facilities, it seems that many women made a pragmatic decision to withdraw temporarily from work, planning to return at a later date. Others, with plans for combining marriage and career, found out how difficult that was:

> I was definitely career-oriented when I was young. I had negative reactions to the thought of being tied down to housework. It seemed menial and extremely unrewarding to me. I planned to prepare for a career and, if I got married and had a family, to earn the money to hire a housekeeper. But that isn't the way it worked out. I had not gotten launched on a career by the time I was married, and we started having our family immediately . . . there was no time to give thought to a career for many years.[26]

In short, the history of career women and potential career women is much more complex than a simple story of disillusionment or the supremacy of the feminine mystique. It must be full of the twists and turns, tensions and pragmatic decisions which constituted the story of thousands of women as they worked out their desire for a career and a personal life.

III

Along with surveys of career intentions, a widely used indicator of the progress of career women is the statistical evidence of women's share of professional and business occupations. Here the evidence for a decline in the 1920's—and in some cases the 1930's—is less than convincing. In the census category of "Managers, Officials, and Proprietors," the general pattern indicates slight but real increases after 1920. [See Table 1.] The numbers of businesswomen expanded at slightly higher rates than the numbers of businessmen in most decades. The job level which these women reached is another question; they did not win seats on the New York Stock Exchange or General Motors' Board of Directors. But those historians who find a

TABLE 1
Female Managers, Officials, Proprietors (Except Farm)

Year	Number	% of Total	Decennial Increase	Male Decennial Increase
1900	77,214	4.5%	—	—
1910	216,537	8.6%	180%	43%
1920	220,797	7.8%	2%	13%
1930	304,969	8.4%	38%	27%
1940	414,472	11.0%	36%	1%
1950	699,807	13.6%	69%	33%

deflation of the career ethic in the twenties and thirties have themselves utilized the broad census categories. Moreover, women's absence from the higher ranks must have resulted as much from discrimination as from lack of desire. Simply in terms of overall statistics, there was a gradual increase in women's share of business occupations.[27]

Obviously women still gained a very small percentage of the total, but over the decades they increased their share of these and other business occupations. For example, the proportion of all real estate agents, managers, and superintendents who were women tripled from 1910 to 1920, from 2.3% to 6.1% of the total, doubled to 12.9% in 1930, and almost doubled again to 20.2% of the total in 1940.[28] Whether or not real estate work or any other business occupation expresses the highest ideals of feminism, the statistical evidence alone does not support a theory of progressive decline since the 1920's.[29]

In the other census category of significance for career women, "Professional, Technical, and Kindred Workers," the evidence indicates a decline after 1930. [See Table 2.] As suggested earlier, women increased their share steadily in the 1900's and 1910's, peaked in the 1920's, and lost ground in the 1930's and 1940's.[30]

The most drastic decline occurred in the decade of the Great Depression when the absolute number of female professionals increased by a mere 8.5%, the smallest decadal increase during the

TABLE 2
Women as a Percent of Total Professional Workers

1900	1910	1920	1930	1940	1950
35.2%	41.3%	44.1%	44.8%	41.5%	39.6%

TABLE 3
Women's Share of Total

Year	College Teaching Faculty	Doctorates Awarded
1910	18.9%	10.0%
1920	30.1%	15.1%
1930	32.5%	15.4%
1940	26.5%	13.0%
1950	23.2%	9.2%
1959-60	19.4%	10.5%

whole period.[31] Half the female professionals were school teachers and it cannot be accidental that the most substantial inroads against professional women occurred not during the sexual revolution of the 1920's but in the depression when school boards, state governments, and male teachers exerted terrific pressure against women teachers.[32] As a result, the number of female school teachers, which had risen from 635,207 in 1920 to 853,976 in 1930, actually dropped by the end of the thirties to 802,264.[33]

Other subcategories of professionals complicate the story. Not only the proportion but the number of female physicians declined, but the decline began in the 1910's, not in the 1920's.[34] The number of female editors and reporters doubled in the twenties and stabilized in the thirties—ironically the heyday of the woman reporter in American films.[35] Nurses, the second largest subcategory of female professionals after teachers, increased each decade until the 1940's. Nursing was an occupation that was highly segregated by sex, and, at least until recently, desperately underpaid. Still, as with teaching, it provided a channel for the aspirations of young women, many of them working-class and lower middle-class women whose real chances for more prestigious careers were limited for social and economic reasons.[36] In one particular area of professional endeavor, women's share quite clearly peaked in the twenties and began a long decline in the thirties.[37] [See Table 3.]

The numbers of women college presidents, professors, and instructors increased from 2,928 in 1910 to 9,974 in 1920 and 19,930 in 1930, but stagnated in the depression, reaching only 20,124 by 1940.[38] The progress of female doctorates awarded yearly was more complex. The number rose and the proportion declined in the thirties.[39] [See Table 4.]

Here, quite clearly is a basic complexity in the professional world. If we look only at the percentages, women's proportion of the total doctorates awarded peaked already in the 1920's; yet that would

TABLE 4
Women Doctorates

Year	Number Awarded	Women as % of Total	% Decennial Increase
1920	90	15.1	—
1930	311	15.4	245.5
1940	419	13.0	34.7
1950	613	9.2	46.3
1960	1090	10.5	77.8

distort the fact that more than three times as many women were receiving doctorates at the end of the decade. That women failed to keep pace with men—much less catch up to them—is clear. But that is not evidence for claiming that women became "disillusioned" with careers, or, as Bernard has argued, that women turned their backs on academe to indulge in a "reproductive mania."[40] If it is assumed that women doctorates had serious career intentions, then more of them had them in 1940 than in 1920 (more of them, it might be noted, on a per capita as well as an absolute basis).

Women's proportion of the totals is a function of two factors—the rise or fall in the number of women receiving doctorates (factor one) as a percentage of the rise or fall in the total number of doctorates awarded, that is, including men (factor two). The tremendous increase of male doctorates, which makes a rising *number* of female Ph.D.'s a *declining percentage* of the total must be considered as an independent development, shaped largely by changes in the occupational and educational structure which encouraged doctoral training for men—and not by itself a factor whose growth indicates a decline in women's aspirations.

For the question really is, decline from what? The number of women with career aspirations in 1920 was small. The number of doctorates, for example, was a mere 90 in that year. A decade later, over 300 women received their doctorates, and with several pauses, more and more women took the doctorate in each succeeding decade down to the present. Taking another perspective, the results are similar if less dramatic. If we use the census categories of "Professional, Technical, and Kindred Workers," and "Managers, Officials, and Proprietors" as rough indicators of the number of women in careers, then the proportion of adult women in careers did not decline in the 1920's, but rose, stayed the same in the 1930's, and rose in the 1940's. There were 3 career women per 100 adult women in 1920, 4 in 1930, 4 in 1940, and 5 in 1950. In short, the mere use of only certain percentages, by making it appear that fewer women were interested in careers after the 1920's, is a distortion, indeed a rather dramatic distortion of the facts.[41]

IV

It is this use of unreliable proportions that sidetracks any search for explanations of the supposed decline among professional women. Thus when Jessie Bernard suggests that the decline in women's share of doctorates and college teaching positions was due to the "reproductive mania" that American women indulged in in the 1940's and 1950's, her own evidence suggests some reason for doubting a simple relationship between birth rates and careers. The birth rate and women's share in academic life declined simultaneously in the 1930's.[42] Furthermore, consider that between 1945 and 1957, when the fertility rates climbed from 85.9 to 122.9, the height of the baby boom, *the number* of women taking their doctorates tripled.[43]

Certainly women failed to keep pace with men, yet on a per capita basis, women's movement was not downward but upward. In part because of this, the question of women's social and economic roles was a very live issue, even in the 1950's when women's lives were supposedly dominated by babies.[44]

The relationship between marriage and fertility rates on the one side and careers on the other is, then, quite complex. It has been assumed by some writers that a rise in marriage rates proves a decline in the career impulse, and that the sexual revolution of the 1920's made marriage more attractive, sapping women's desire for an independent career.[45]

Several points can be made about this line of reasoning. First, marriage rates for women in the United States did not jump sharply in the 1920's.[46] Second, even if they did rise for college women, that does not prove a decline in career aspirations. Life is complicated. People hold several apparently conflicting desires at the same time. Or they postpone the fulfillment of one desire without actually giving it up. A rise in the marriage rates for college women is not incompatible with the possibility that women have found a comfortable way to keep their childbearing years restricted to a limited period, so as to permit them to return to work at a later period. As long-range historical trends indicate, a lower age of marriage seems to follow on the possibility of controlling fertility within marriage.[47] In and of itself, marriage and child-bearing may not be an absolute indicator of disillusionment with work outside the home.

In the 1910's and 1920's, women married at a rate that was only slightly higher than in preceding decades.[48] After all, marriage had always been the occupation for which most women were trained. What was new in the 1910's and 1920's was that although a few more women married than in the past, more and more combined marriage and a professional career. The proportion of all professional women who were married rose from 12.2% in 1910 to 19.3% in 1920 and 24.7% in 1930. The proportion of school teachers who were married rose from 9.7% in 1920 to 17.9% in 1930 and 24.6% in 1940.[49] Also, as time went on, some women dropped out temporarily to start a family, and then returned later to their careers. In one study, Astin found that 91% of the women who received their doctorates in 1957–58 were employed eight years later. The older the woman, the more likely she was to be at work; "the younger woman doctorate is more likely to have children at home."[50] There is thus no reason to take the unmarried state as the main criterion of career aspirations, for marriage and childbearing do not prove a decline in the career impulse, although they may complicate its realization for a period of life.

Beginning around the turn of the century, the marrying rate for college graduates has moved from a low proportion to a very high one approaching that for the whole population. The proportion of Vassarites who married within 5½ years of graduation began a steady rise in the 1890's. By 1936, 51% of the class of 1925 at Smith married; 77% of the class of 1927 had already married.[51] A survey showed that the differences between all women and college graduates were narrowing in the 1940's, until, by 1947, 87% of all adult women had ever been married and 69% of all women college graduates.[52] By 1960, among all women, ages 30–34, almost as many college graduates as those with eight years of elementary schooling were married.[53]

There is no question that college women have married in greater numbers in each successive decade since the turn of the century. Hence, either the sexual revolution of the twenties—which O'Neill and Ryan emphasize—was not the main factor in diverting women from careers to marriage, or that revolution must be pushed back into the early 1900's or before.[54] In that case, the career disillusionment specific to the 1920's is left without an explanation. Whatever made marriage more attractive to college women or college women more attractive to men, and whatever attracted greater numbers of more "conventional women" to college was occurring by the turn of the century. No college president was a more determined feminist than M. Carey Thomas of Bryn Mawr, yet the percentage of Bryn Mawr graduates marrying rose and the percentage of childless graduates declined between the classes of 1896–1901 and 1902–1907.[55]

It seems obvious that the rising rates of marriage among women college graduates resulted in part from long-range changes in marriage patterns as well as compositional changes in and expansion of the college population. What is needed is a synthesis of the work of those who, like most historians, emphasize specific cultural and social factors in the history of career women, and the work of demographers who could fill in the long-term economic and social changes which have affected decisions to marry. On the whole, historians and demographers have ignored one another's work. Demographers probably underemphasize the significance of attitudinal changes and historians of feminism ignore the demographic factors that have shaped women's behavior regardless of the ebb and flow of career ideas.[56]

A final point: collective biographies of college women might give us hard data on the interaction of the new morality and career attitudes.[57] There is some reason to doubt that freer sexual attitudes led women to reject the independent professional life. Crystal Eastman, Vassar '03, lawyer and socialist activist, rejected Victorian sexual attitudes, yet wanted a child very badly. Although she married, she never gave up her independent career.[58] Phyllis Blanchard learned in college that sex was not "a degrading and disgusting phenomenon which men enjoyed but to which women submitted only because it was part of wifely duty," and she married. But she surrendered neither her personal autonomy nor her career.[59] Another college graduate, writing anonymously in 1927, attacked the cold, asexual atmosphere of her women's college. She had married, but she expressed no desire to give up her career.[60] Even "Feminist-New Style," the younger woman who had been touched by the sexual revolution, wanted not only a family, but a job. She knew that "there is hardly a man who will never take advantage of his wife's economic dependence upon him or who will never assume that it gives him special prerogatives."[61] In fact, it appears that the relationship between the new morality and the job could be the reverse of what we have been led to expect. Far from the freer sexual morality leading to the abandonment of the job, economic independence could nurture sexual freedom, allowing some women to avoid marriage while having sexual relationships and others to seek fulfillment in marriage while maintaining careers.[62] In short, the relationship between the sexual revolution and career aspirations was an extremely complex one. Until more case histories have been examined in detail, we will not be able to say with confidence what those relationships were, but they may have been part of the same personality development of many college-educated women.

V

The foregoing is not meant to imply that balancing a marriage, family, and a job was not extremely difficult, or to deny that some women "went home."[63] We cannot ignore the fact that in the late 1920's and through the 1930's, magazines published many reports of women who went home.[64] In light of the statistics examined earlier, it seems clear that fewer went home than stayed on the job. Perhaps the novelty of career women had worn off by the late twenties; perhaps magazine publishers welcomed the confessions as confirmations of their own prejudices. Certainly the women who went home often felt the need to defend themselves because their friends continued as career women.

It seems certain that the fugitives were given disproportionate publicity. In 1939, the "Lady in the Shoe" explained why she had given up her job. In the very same magazine, buried amidst the advertisements on the fourth-to-last page, the editors summarized the results of their informal telephone survey of ten career women. Eight of the ten were sure they would not quit their jobs and six of these eight women had children. The two who thought they might quit gave as their reasons poor pay and dull work.[65] It seems unlikely that as many readers noticed this little survey as read the confession of the "Lady in the Shoe."

An obvious reason why some women did go home, or why younger women sometimes never ventured forth into the world of work in the 1920's and 1930's was that career women faced discrimination on the job—discrimination which was intensified in the Great Depression, particularly, as we have seen, in a few career lines where women were unusually articulate (e.g., teachers, journalists). Many young women may have anticipated discrimination and stopped short of their goals. Others went home because of low pay and lack of promotion.[66]

In fact, however, many who actually announced that they had quit their jobs did not write of on-the-job discrimination. The problems they articulated were more subtle. Their attitudes toward work and independence were more complicated than they appeared on first sight. A few women gave up their careers to service the career of a husband "who had offered me the greatest opportunity for happiness in life"—love itself. Lucy Tunis did seem content applying the skills learned in law school to the mysteries of a dinner recipe.[67] There is no question that women felt the pressure to fulfill stereotypes of sweet femininity, to tend to the children, to master the domestic arts, and to service a husband's career.[68] But these women did not always go home or stay home with an undivided commitment. Rarely did they reject on principle a woman's need for an independent income or the stimulation of some exciting work besides domestic chores.[69] Wrote one woman who was stranded in a small Midwestern town: "Housework as a life job bores and enrages me. Writing even such hack work as I do, lights up windows for my soul . . . The thought of achieving even moderate success as a writer sends shivers up and down my spine."[70]

It was not so much that women repudiated the career as that many of them found it impossible to carry on. Husbands did not respect their wives' aspirations; "feminist" husbands offered no help with the housework or the children.[71] Husbands' careers necessitated moves to other cities which left the wives' careers up in the air.[72]

In several cases, women became so involved in their work that they had little time for personal life. These women experienced not a simple disillusionment with the career—in which they were in fact deeply involved—but the extra burdens of managing a family along with the normal career pressures for a high level of commitment and competitive fervor. "It was stirring work," wrote Jane Allen after quitting her job, "which at times closed in on my attention to the exclusion of everything else. I could feel myself becoming the narrow, hard, efficiency-bitten drive wheel of my department."[73] Or as another woman put it:

> Before I had a job I had been screaming for self-expression at the head of the pack. I did not stop work because I had ceased to believe in expression—self or otherwise. My reason was a deep desire to catch up with my coat tails to find out what I was expressing and to whom.[74]

These women, unlike men in the same position, were sensitive and perhaps guilty about becoming hard-bitten careerists and about neglecting their families. Some of them quit work not because they did not like their job or because they had rejected the idea of economic independence, but because they could not come home from the office rat-race to find their slippers and a warm dinner ready. And if fewer career women went home in the 1920's and 1930's than the publicity surrounding their exit would suggest, even some of these did not wholly internalize domestic values. The surrender to home life did not always mean that the appeal of economic independence and useful work had disappeared, or that the role of the happy homemaker was accepted easily. Even as the feminine mystique spread in the 1940's and 1950's, feelings of discontent and deep conflicts were bound to continue among women in careers and potential career women. More and more women went to college and many of them were touched with the possibilities of a future beyond domestic life. Hence the still small but growing number of women who took their doctorates or entered the business world.[75] Economic and social forces drew more rather than fewer women out of the home; many who stayed home had been touched by the desire for something more. As one college graduate put it, "I have needed all my philosophy courses to reconcile myself to accepting the monotony of household duties so that I will have some free time daily to express my own personality."[76] The feminine mystique did not arise in a vacuum, but to meet the real conflicts these women experienced. Domesticity had not conquered the minds of American women, even in the 1950's.

VI

What was missing all through these years was not a base of discontents or significant numbers of career women, but a feminist movement to interpret these discontents as collective phenomena, rooted in fundamentally inegalitarian social and economic structures. Nor were there many intellectuals who viewed the American social and economic structure from the outside with a critical perspective. Fervent protests about women's condition were few.[77] Some college women and academics advocated the adjustment of women to housework rather than the transformation of social and economic structures. Several alumnae agreed that college should "teach women to be household managers and mothers."[78] Yet from a feminist point of view, some of the colleges apparently strove to do a good job. As a result, the alumnae, wrote Dr. Dorothy Lee of Vassar's anthropology department, were forced to go through a long and bitter conflict before unlearning what they have learned in college, before they could find the value of office work or homemaking. The colleges had taught them that it was better to read Plato than to wash diapers, to prefer a lecture on T. S. Eliot to staying at home with the babies (indirect evidence, at least, that colleges continued to play a role in career choices and tensions). Dr. Lee urged that the colleges eliminate the tensions by training women for a domestic future. How should a wife react when her husband fumed in a traffic jam? When he came home to announce that he had been fired? These were the great questions that taxed modern woman's mind. Dr. Lee urged that she be taught "how to come out of this situation emotionally refreshed, not cross and wilted. In this way she can learn to find continuity and personal maturity in homemaking; her life as a housewife will be fulfilling and not just a series of drab chores."[79]

Obviously, if such medicine were necessary, it was clear that the domestic psychology had not been completely internalized by the alumnae themselves. Yet among academics the tide seemed to be running against feminism in the late 1940's and the 1950's, even if not all yielded to Dr. Lee's pragmatism. It is not surprising that many intellectuals—especially the Freudians in psychology and the functionalists in sociology—came forward with tools for a more efficient "adjustment" of women to the home. In the 1940's and 1950's, the United States lacked a solid core of genuinely radical intellectuals who were ready to do battle with the fundamentals of the American system. If it sometimes seemed that the feminine mystique monopolized the pages of popular magazines, it was not because of the unmitigated hold of that ideology on women themselves, but because of the absence of a loud, clear challenge from critical intellectuals and a feminist movement.

All too often American academics served the cause of adjustment rather than social change. Sociologists and psychoanalysts assumed that individuals had to adjust to roles and institutions that were conceived in fundamentally static ways. The family, with its sexual division of labor between husband and wife—each with sexually defined emotional characters—was defended as a logical and functional system.[80] It was as much this conservatism of academic thought as the alleged disillusionment among anonymous women that allowed the surge of domestic ideas in the late 1940's and 1950's.

This suggests an important general point for students of women's history. The history of the organized feminist movement and feminist thought is separable from the attitudes of women and in particular from the history of career women. In the 1920's older feminists looked with dismay on the devotion of younger women to sex and self. But the rejection of the feminist movement and of the ideal of service to society by younger women was not by itself a rejection of economic independence. As one young woman stated her credo, "We're not out to benefit society . . . We're out for Mary's job and Luella's art, and Barbara's independence and the rest of our individual careers and desires."[81] This privatized individualism naturally did not sit well with older feminists who had been animated by a broader ideal of social service and a political goal—woman suffrage. But in its way, the attitude of the younger generation may have been a necessary reaction to the feminist movement's neglect of the personal side of things and especially of self-fulfillment.

Just as feminists in the 1920's viewed the flapper as a sign of the decline of the movement, so recent writers, reading only the literary evidence or misreading the statistical evidence, have exaggerated the depth of disillusionment and actually misstated the facts of the history of career women after 1920. Moreover, no one has examined in detail the literary evidence itself. How much of the unhappiness women expressed during these transitional decades was concerned with the job and how much was simply a temporary surrender to the practical problem of running a home or to discrimination on the job? Through a synthesis of demography and traditional history, a more careful and systematic reading of the periodical literature, and the collection of oral histories and biographies of women who lived through the 1920's, '30's, '40's, and '50's, we may be able to show a gradual progression in the spread of career impulses, proceeding despite many obstacles and finally erupting in one segment of the women's liberation movement of the 1960's.

In constructing this history, our models of economic and social trends as well as individual psychology must be dynamic and complex. The American economic and social system transformed the roles of American women, even as it limited women, denied them equal opportunity, and perpetuated the idea that their primary role was that of wife and mother. American capitalism profited from sexual discrimination in the workplace and women's unpaid labor at home. Yet the system also sent hundreds of thousands of women into the workplace or college. Formally, the American system promised equality; in actuality, women were faced with discrimination and painful role conflicts. But the important point is that there were conflicts, having two sides to them. The minds of working career women and potential career women were not monopolized by conservative ideologies. Indeed, the feminine mystique of the 1940's and 1950's arose in part to smooth over the contradictions which the American system itself created. As more and more women entered careers or came in touch with the possibility of economic independence, the strains intensified. In each succeeding decade since 1920, some women who were out in the world did "go home." Many more were in touch with the possibility of a permanent place in the world outside the home, often trying to combine this place with the home, in an unprecedented mixture of roles and identities.

NOTES

1. For a brief survey, see Robert W. Smuts, *Women and Work in America* (New York, 1971). William Chafe, *The American Woman: Her Changing Social, Economic, and Political Roles, 1920–1970* (New York, 1972), is a useful analysis, especially of career women. For the flavor of women's work at the turn of the century, read Dorothy Richardson, *The Long Day* (1905), in William O'Neill, ed., *Women at Work* (Chicago, 1972).

2. See Frances Donovan, *The Woman Who Waits* (Boston, 1920), especially pp. 9–11, 223–227. Also Alice Beal Parsons, *Woman's Dilemma* (New York, 1926), pp. 272 ff.

3. For three feminist statements on work from three different periods, see Charlotte Perkins Gilman, *Women and Economics* (New York, 1966); Parsons, *Woman's Dilemma;* and Betty Friedan, *The Feminine Mystique* (New York, 1963).

4. The term "social feminism" is used by William L. O'Neill throughout his *Everyone Was Brave: The Rise and Fall of Feminism in America* (Chicago, 1969). For comments on the twenties, see *ibid.*, pp. 304 ff. On the battle over the Equal Rights Amendment, see Chafe, *The American Woman*, pp. 112–132. Also see Sophonisba P. Breckinridge, *Women in the Twentieth Century: A Study of Their Political, Social and Economic Activities* (New York, 1933), for a survey of women's organizations, and especially pp. 93–95, for an insight into the way reform activities absorbed women who might otherwise have had careers. R. Le Clerc Phillips, "The Real Rights of Women," *Harper's Monthly Magazine*, October, 1926, pp. 609–614, is important as a warning against feminine self-sacrifice.

5. O'Neill, *Everyone Was Brave*, pp. 304–305; Jessie Bernard, *Academic Women* (University Park, Pennsylvania, 1964), p. 40; Breckinridge, *Women in the Twentieth Century*, p. 188; Chafe, *The American Woman*, pp. 48–65; and U.S. Department of Labor, *Women's Occupations Through Seven Decades*, by Janet M. Hooks, Women's Bureau Bulletin No. 218 (Washington, D.C., 1947), pp. 154–189.

6. See for example, Lucy R. Tunis, "I Gave Up My Law Books for a Cook Book," *American Magazine*, July, 1927, pp. 34–35, 172–177; and Jane Allen, "You May Have My Job, A Feminist Discovers Her Home," *The Forum*, April, 1932, pp. 228–231.

7. Dorothy Dunbar Bromley, "Feminist-New Style," *Harper's Monthly Magazine*, October, 1927, pp. 552–560.

8. Phyllis Blanchard and Carolyn Manasses, *New Girls For Old* (New York, 1937), p. 237. See also, with a different slant, Nancy Evans, "Good-by, Bohemia," *Scribner's Magazine*, June, 1931, pp. 643–646.

9. Alice Beal Parsons, "Man-Made Illusions About Woman," in Samuel D. Schmalhausen and V. F. Calverton, eds., *Woman's Coming of Age: A Symposium* (New York, 1931), pp. 20–34. Quotation on p. 23.

10. Evidence from the films of the period is mixed. In some ways the 1930's offered a more positive image of the career woman than the 1920's. See Marjorie Rosen, *Popcorn Venus* (New York, 1973), pp. 144, 147, 154. Rosen argues that the positive image of women reporters in films of the depression decade insulated women from the reality of declines in profes-

sional occupations. See also Joseph Kirk Folsom and Marion Bassett, *The Family and Democratic Society* (London, 1948), pp. 616 ff., especially p. 623 for remarks on the negative image of career women in films of the period.

11. O'Neill, *Everyone Was Brave*, pp. 304 ff. Bernard, *Academic Women*, consistently dismisses discrimination and anticipated discrimination as important factors in women's declining proportion of academic positions.

12. Bernard, *Academic Women*, pp. 36–37, 61–62, 215.

13. O'Neill, *Everyone Was Brave*, p. 308.

14. Mary P. Ryan, *Womanhood in America: From Colonial Times to the Present* (New York, 1975), pp. 235, 255–57, 287–293. Also Bernard, *Academic Women*, pp. 209–210, and Chafe, *The American Woman*, pp. 92–93. Historical treatments of Victorian sexual morality can be sampled in Andrew Sinclair, *The Emancipation of the American Woman* (New York, 1966), pp. 127–136, and Daniel Scott Smith, "Family Limitation, Sexual Control, and Domestic Feminism in Victorian America," *Feminist Studies*, I (1973), pp. 40–57.

15. On the feminine mystique, Friedan, *The Feminine Mystique*.

16. Useful research in this connection includes Matina Horner, "The Motive to Avoid Success and Changing Aspirations of College Women," and Mirra Komarovsky, "Cultural Contradictions and Sex Roles," in Judith M. Bardwick, ed., *Readings on the Psychology of Women* (New York, 1972), pp. 58–67. Both show the conflicting pressures on college women. A fictional treatment of a young woman and the beauty ideal is Alix Kates Shulman, *Memoirs of an Ex-Prom Queen* (New York, 1973).

17. Lorine Pruette, *Women and Leisure: A Study of Social Waste* (New York, 1924), pp. 116 ff., 122 ff., 131 ff., and 199. Pruette remarked that the career goals of the girls were somewhat unrealistic. Nearly half hoped to make a career in the arts. See pp. 125–126. O'Neill makes the same point in *Everyone Was Brave*, pp. 322–323.

18. Blanchard and Manasses, *New Girls for Old*, pp. 175–177. The authors had no data from an earlier period as the basis for their discovery of a "disillusionment."

19. O'Neill, *Everyone Was Brave*, pp. 307–309; Ryan, *Womanhood in America*, p. 255; and Chafe, *The American Woman*, pp. 102–103.

20. Blanchard and Manasses, *New Girls for Old*, pp. 175–177.

21. Chafe, *The American Woman*, p. 102.

22. Folsom and Bassett, *The Family and Democratic Society*, p. 617.

23. *Ibid.*, p. 616.

24. Mirra Komarovsky, "Cultural Contradictions and Sex Roles: The Masculine Case," *American Journal of Sociology*, 78 (1973), pp. 873–884, is an exception in that it includes, p. 883, comparisons of similar college groups in 1943 and 1971.

25. Mirra Komarovsky, *Woman in the Modern World: Their Education and Their Dilemmas* (Boston, 1953), pp. 92–99; quotation from p. 97.

26. Quoted in Bernard, *Academic Women*, p. 228.

27. Table 1 is based on the numbers in Gertrude Bancroft, *The American Labor Force: Its Growth and Changing Composition* (New York, 1958), Table D-2, p. 209. I calculated the percentages and rounded off the last digit.

28. Hooks, *Women's Occupations Through Seven Decades*, p. 89; and Breckinridge, *Women in the Twentieth Century*, pp. 172, 174. Generally on businesswomen, see Hooks, pp. 180–189.

29. However, it was proof against any who were naive enough to expect that the achievement of woman suffrage in 1920 would bring equality with

men in all occupations. See also Anne W. Armstrong, "Seven Deadly Sins of Woman in Business," *Harper's Monthly Magazine*, August, 1926, pp. 295–303, which describes and in some ways surrenders to the pressures on businesswomen.

30. Table 2 based on figures in Bancroft, *The American Labor Force*, p. 209.

31. In the same decade, male professionals increased their numbers by about 24%. Based on figures in *ibid.*

32. On discrimination during the depression, see Chafe, *The American Woman*, pp. 107 ff.; Helen Buckler, "Shall Married Women Be Fired," *Scribner's Magazine*, March, 1932, pp. 166–168; and J. Stanley Lemons, *The Woman Citizen: Social Feminism in the 1920's* (Urbana, 1973), pp. 230 ff.

33. Cynthia Fuchs Epstein, *Woman's Place: Options and Limits in Professional Careers* (Berkeley, 1971), Table II, pp. 200–201.

34. Breckinridge, *Women in the Twentieth Century*, pp. 188–190.

35. Epstein, *Woman's Place*, Table II, pp. 200–201.

36. *Ibid.*, and p. 64, for signs that even in the "female" occupation of nursing women experience anxieties about sex roles.

37. Table 3 is taken from Table 2/2.B, and Table 4/5 in Bernard, *Academic Women*, pp. 40, 70.

38. Epstein, *Woman's Place*, Table II, pp. 200–201.

39. Columns 1 and 2 of Table 4 are from Bernard, *Academic Women*, pp. 70–71. I calculated the decennial increases. It should be noted that the distribution of subject areas changed dramatically. Of five subject areas, the fewest doctorates in 1920 and the most in 1961 were awarded in education. Women showed the smallest numerical increase in the physical and biological sciences.

40. Bernard, *Academic Women*, p. 215.

41. Calculations based on the figures for adult women and women in career occupations in Bancroft, *The American Labor Force*, pp. 203, 209.

42. Bernard, *Academic Women*, p. 74.

43. The general fertility rates (births per 1000 women, ages 15–44) are given in George Grier, *The Baby Bust* (Washington, D.C., 1971), p. 73. Female doctorates awarded yearly from Bernard, *Academic Women*, p. 71.

44. Chafe, *The American Woman*, pp. 199–225.

45. See above, notes 11–14, on Ryan and O'Neill.

46. Paul H. Jacobson and Pauline F. Jacobson, *American Marriage and Divorce* (New York, 1959), Table 2, p. 21.

47. See Geoffrey Hawthorn, *The Sociology of Fertility* (London, 1970), pp. 25–26.

48. Jacobson and Jacobson, *American Marriage and Divorce*, p. 21, Table 2.

49. Figures for all professional women from Elizabeth Nottingham, "Toward an Analysis of the Effects of Two World Wars on the Role and Status of Middle-Class Women in the English-Speaking World," *American Sociological Review*, XII (1947), pp. 666–675, especially p. 670. Figures for school teachers from U.S. Bureau of the Census, *Census of Population, 1930*, Vol. V, *General Report on Occupations*, pp. 276–280, and U.S. Bureau of the Census, *Census of Population, 1940*, Vol. III, *The Labor Force, Occupation, Industry, Employment, and Income*, Part 1, U.S. Summary, p. 115.

50. Helen S. Astin, "Factors Associated with the Participation of Women Doctorates in the Labor Force," in Athena Theodore, ed., *The Profes-*

sional Woman (Cambridge, Mass., 1971), pp. 441–452. Quotation from pp. 444–445. See also Valerie Kincade Oppenheimer, *The Female Labor Force in the United States: Demographic and Economic Factors Governing Its Growth and Changing Composition*, Population Monograph Series, No. 5 (Berkeley, 1970), especially pp. 8–15.

51. Mable Newcomer and Evelyn S. Gibson, "Vital Statistics from Vassar College," *The American Journal of Sociology*, XXIX (1924), pp. 430–442; Mable Newcomer, *A Century of Higher Education for American Women* (New York, 1959), pp. 212–214; Rosewell H. Johnson, "Marriage and Birth Rates at Bryn Mawr," *Eugenics*, II (1929), p. 30.

52. Ernest Havemann and Patricia Salter West, *They Went to College: The College Graduate in America Today* (New York, 1952), pp. 61–62.

53. Clyde V. Kiser, Wilson H. Grabill, and Arthur A. Campbell, *Trends and Variations in Fertility in the United States* (Cambridge, Mass., 1968), pp. 148–149. The percentages were 90% for the college graduates and 95% for those women with an eighth grade education.

54. James R. McGovern has already pushed the sexual revolution back to the 1910's in his "The American Woman's Pre-World War I Freedom in Manners and Morals," *Journal of American History*, LV (1968), pp. 315–333. For evidence of a more positive view of women's sexuality in the late nineteenth century, see Carl N. Degler, "What Ought To Be and What Was: Women's Sexuality in the Nineteenth Century," *American Historical Review*, LXXIX (1974), pp. 1467–1490.

55. Johnson, "Marriage and Birth Rates at Bryn Mawr," and Newcomer, *A Century of Higher Education for American Women*, pp. 30–31. On Carey Thomas, see O'Neill, *Everyone Was Brave*, pp. 110–114; and on the success of Bryn Mawr graduates, Newcomer, *A Century*, pp. 196–197.

56. An excellent example of demographic work relevant to students of women's history is Richard Easterlin, *The American Baby Boom in Historical Perspective*, Occasional Paper 79 (New York, 1962). Easterlin offers an economic and demographic explanation of the baby boom.

57. Ryan and O'Neill may rely too much on the fears of older feminists for their picture of the effects of the new morality on younger women. See, for example, Ryan, *Womanhood in America*, pp. 255–256.

58. June Sochen, *Movers and Shakers: American Women Thinkers and Activists, 1900–1970* (New York, 1973), pp. 45 ff., and Vassar Alumnae Collection, 1903, in Vassar College Library.

59. Phyllis Blanchard, "The Long Journey," *Nation*, 124 (1927), pp. 472–473, reprinted in Anne Firor Scott, ed., *The American Woman: Who Was She?* (Englewood Cliffs, N.J., 1971), pp. 164–166.

60. Anonymous, "The Harm My Education Did Me," *Outlook*, November 30, 1927, pp. 396–397, 405.

61. Bromley, "Feminist-New Style," p. 555.

62. Ryan, *Womanhood in America*, p. 270. On a broader scale, seeking to explain the surge in European illegitimacy in the eighteenth century, Edward Shorter has linked women's sexual autonomy to their involvement in a wage economy and their freedom from patriarchal controls. As their sense of self increased, young women engaged in sex more frequently and demanded greater fulfillment. See Shorter, "Female Emancipation, Birth Control, and Fertility in European History," *American Historical Review*, LXXVIII (1973), pp. 605–640. How economic activity affected career women in modern America is not clear, but Shorter's frankly speculative article suggests how complex is the relationship between work and sexual behavior.

63. For a contrasting view, see Bernard, *Academic Women*, p. 311, n.14, which reveals Bernard's curious view that career-home conflicts are hardly more onerous for women than for men.

64. See Tunis, "I Gave Up My Law Books for a Cook Book"; Allen, "You May Have My Job"; Anonymous, "Lady in the Shoe," *Harper's Monthly Magazine* (1939), pp. 629–634; Judith Lambert, "I Quit My Job," *The Forum*, July, 1937, pp. 9–15; Katherine Gauss Jackson, "Must Married Women Work," *Scribner's Magazine* (1935), pp. 240–242; Harriet Bradley Fitt, "In Praise of Domesticity," in Herbert Elmer Mills and His Former Students, *College Women and the Social Sciences* (New York, 1934), pp. 265–279; and Chafe, *The American Woman*, pp. 99–106.

65. Anonymous, "Lady in the Shoe." Folsom and Bassett, *The Family and Democratic Society*, p. 623, offer an interesting example of slanted publicity. In 1938 a photo of the "Ideal American College Girl" appeared in the press with the caption, "Ideal College Girl Puts Marriage Before Career." Only in small print was it revealed that putting marriage first was a requirement for entering the "Ideal Girl" contest.

66. On discrimination, see, for example, Breckinridge, *Women in the Twentieth Century*, pp. 238–241; Chafe, *The American Woman*, pp. 60, 107 ff., 271, n.23; Nottingham, "Toward an Analysis," pp. 671–672; Marion O. Hawthorne, "Women as College Teachers," *The Annals*, CXLIII (1929), pp. 146–153; Alice I. Bryan and Edwin G. Boring, "Women in American Psychology: Factors Affecting Their Professional Careers," *The American Psychologist*, 2 (1947), pp. 3–20, especially pp. 8 ff. In addition to on-the-job discrimination, there were the usual anti-feminist attacks, such as John Macy, "Equality of Woman with Man: A Myth," *Harper's Monthly Magazine*, (1926), pp. 705–713; and harsh attacks on women's colleges and college women from men who worried that the "best" people were not reproducing in sufficient numbers. See Henry Carey, "Career or Maternity: The Dilemma of the College Girl," *North American Review* (1929), pp. 737–744; and Willis J. Ballinger, "Spinster Factories: Why I Would Not Send a Daughter to College," *The Forum* (1932), pp. 301–305. See also n. 32 above for additional references on discrimination during the depression. On the anticipation of discrimination, see Bernard, *Academic Women*, pp. 174, 181–184.

67. Tunis, "I Gave Up My Law Books," p. 174.

68. *Ibid.*; Jackson, "Must Married Women Work," by a career woman who would have felt "more a woman" if she could have turned out a proper soufflé; and Eva Von B. Hansl, "What About the Children? The Question of Mothers and Careers," *Harper's Monthly Magazine* (1927), pp. 220–227.

69. It should be mentioned that some of these women might have found home life more attractive because they were of a class that could afford a nice house in the country.

70. Edith Clark, "Trying To Be Modern," *Nation*, 125 (1927), pp. 153–155, in Scott, ed., *The American Woman*, pp. 141–146. Quotation on p. 146.

71. Anonymous, "Lady in the Shoe"; Lambert, "I Quit My Job"; and Caroline Ware, *Greenwich Village, 1920–1930, A Comment on American Civilization* (New York, 1965), p. 260. The avant-garde men of Greenwich Village were more backward in practice than in theory when it came to helping around the house.

72. The necessity to relocate for the husband's job damaged the careers of Fitts, Tunis, and Clark.

73. Jane Allen, "You May Have My Job," p. 229.

74. Anonymous, "Lady in the Shoe," p. 634.

75. To information given earlier about women in the professions and business might be added the figures on college women. The total number of women in college was as follows:

1920	282,942
1930	480,802
1940	600,953
1950	805,953

Women as a proportion of total enrollment declined for the same years as follows: 47.3%, 43.7%, 42.1%, and 30.3%. These percentages show how women were losing ground to men. But another way of looking at the same figures is to use college women as a proportion of young women. Taking the age group of women 20–24 as a rough base, the proportion of women in college rose, from 60 per 1000 women 20–24 in 1920, to 87 in 1930, 102 in 1940, and 137 in 1950. This does not negate the fact that women were denied equal opportunities in college. It does suggest that more and more women were put in touch with the possibilities of a future broader than homemaking. Sources for college enrollments: Bernard, *Academic Women*, pp. 68–70; for females' aged 20–24, Bancroft, *The American Labor Force*, p. 203.

76. Havemann and West, *They Went to College*, p. 64.

77. But see Della D. Cyrus, "Why Mothers Fail," *Atlantic Monthly* (1947), pp. 57–60; and Edith M. Stern, "Women Are Household Slaves," *American Mercury* (1949), pp. 71–76, reprinted in Aileen S. Kraditor, ed., *Up From the Pedestal: Selected Writings in the History of American Feminism* (Chicago, 1970), pp. 346–353.

78. Havemann and West, *They Went to College*, pp. 64–65.

79. Dorothy D. Lee, "What Shall We Teach Women?" *Mademoiselle*, August, 1947, pp. 213, 354, 356, 358.

80. See for example, Friedan, *The Feminine Mystique*, pp. 117–141. An early document that mixed psychoanalysis and an adjustive approach against feminism was Floyd Dell, *Love in the Machine Age: A Psychological Study of the Transition from Patriarchal Society* (New York, 1930). For more recent examples, see Bernard, *Academic Women*, pp. 200–201, 305–306, n. 27, which accepts as "functional" the sexual and emotional division of labor in the family; and Chafe, *The American Woman*, pp. 212–216, on role theory.

81. Anne O'Hagan, "The Serious-minded Young—If Any," *The Woman's Journal*, XIII (1928), p. 7, quoted in O'Neill, *Everyone Was Brave*, p. 307.

21

Time Spent in Housework

JOANN VANEK

It has become increasingly plain that technological innovation takes place much faster than change in people's longheld beliefs and habits. In the household, there have been vast technological changes during the past hundred years and much less obvious alteration in the responsibilities and time commitment assumed by women. Comparing surveys of time spent in housework from the 1920s to the 1960s, in urban and rural areas, by employed and nonemployed women, Joann Vanek swiftly delineates a picture of remarkable stasis. Her findings provoke further thought about the relative strength of technology, ideology, and politics in allowing or causing social change.

ONE WOULD SUPPOSE, in view of all the household appliances that have been introduced over the past 50 years, that American women must spend considerably less time in housework now than their mothers and grandmothers did in the 1920's. I have investigated the matter and found that the generalization is not altogether true. Nonemployed women, meaning women who are not in the labor force, in fact devote as much time to housework as their forebears did. The expectation of spending less time in housework applies only to employed women.

Certainly the reasons for thinking that the time spent doing housework must have diminished are abundant. Most of the household appliances that have come on the market since the 1920's have been marketed as (and have generally been regarded as) laborsaving devices. Many other products and services designed to ease the homemaker's task have been put on the market during the past 50 years. In addition to these technological changes one can cite several other factors that would seem to indicate a shorter work week in the household. They include the movement of families from the farm; the decline in boarding; changes in the birth rate that cause women to spend fewer years in the direct care of children; the fact that fewer members of the family come home for lunch, and the pronounced increase in the number of married women in the labor force.

Fortunately information is available about time spent in housework. It is not as complete as an investigator might wish or as readily comparable from one period of time to another, but it does provide data on how women budget time for their daily activities.

In 1925 the Federal Government made money available (under the Purnell Act) for research in home economics. One of the results was a series of studies of how women budgeted their time. My analysis is based on about 20 of these studies. They are reasonably comparable because they were conducted under a set of guidelines developed by the U.S. Bureau of Home Economics. Although most of the studies were made in the 1920's and 1930's, the guidelines were also applied to a few studies conducted in the 1940's, 1950's and 1960's. For detailed analysis of the contemporary period I have employed the *United States Time Use Survey*, a study made in 1965 and 1966 by John P. Robinson and Philip E. Converse of the Survey Research Center at the University of Michigan. In this study women were asked to keep a diary of activities at 15-minute intervals for a full day. In the earlier studies women kept a diary of activities at five-minute intervals for at least a week.

Only the Robinson-Converse survey is based on a national sample. The studies made under the aegis of the Bureau of Home Economics involved certain localities and tabulated primarily the activities of rural women. To infer national averages from such limited studies is open to question. It is significant, however, that the findings of the earlier studies were much the same, which lends support to the supposition that they reflect national patterns.

At first the primarily rural composition of the early samples appears to be a limitation. Actually it is an advantage. During the 50 years under consideration the scene of household activity—in terms of the preponderance of women—shifted from the farm to the city. Thus one comparison I want to make is between time spent in homemaking by rural homemakers 50 years ago and time spent by urban homemakers today. Several of the early studies included town and city samples, so that it is also possible to make comparisons between rural and urban women in the 1920's.

Let us turn first to nonemployed women. In 1924 such women spent about 52 hours per week in housework. The figure differs little (and in an unexpected direction) from the 55 hours per week for nonemployed women in the 1960's. It is remarkable that the amount of time devoted to household work by such women has been so stable, varying only within the range from 51 to 56 hours. It is also noteworthy that the work week of homemakers is longer than the work week of the average person in the labor force.

A comparison of rural and urban women yields another unexpected finding: Rural homemakers spend no more time in household work than urban ones. At least in part this consistency may be due to the way the early researchers distinguished between housework and farm work. Farm work included all tasks connected with the home that were not commonly carried on by both rural and urban women. Among the tasks defined as farm work were gardening, dairy activity and the care of poultry. In this way rural and urban women were compared on the same set of tasks.

Notwithstanding the distinction between household work and farm work, one would suppose that at least in the early period urban women would have spent less time on the job than rural women, inasmuch as a number of differences in working conditions remained between them. For example, urban homes were more likely than rural ones to have electricity, running water and laborsaving machines. In addition urban women could make more use of markets and commercial services, simply because they lived closer to them. Another factor was that the farm household produced a larger proportion of the family's material needs than the urban household. (A study in 1924 showed that rural families produced about 70 percent of their own food, compared with 2 percent for urban families.) In spite of all these differences urban and rural women have spent about the same amount of time in household work throughout the 50-year period. Urbanization reduced women's work only by eliminating the 10 hours per week spent in farm tasks.

Perhaps trends affecting the household have created as much work as they have saved. If less time is required for producing food and clothing, time must be added for shopping. It is not difficult to think of a number of other time-consuming household tasks that must be done now but that were nonexistent or rare 50 years ago. Therefore the figure for time spent on housework probably conceals a shift in the amount of time devoted to various tasks.

The data do show that the nature of household work has changed. The time spent in the tasks classified as shopping and managerial has increased. So has time devoted to family care. Less time is spent preparing food and cleaning up after meals, although together these activities continue to be the most time-consuming aspect of housework. No change has occurred in general tasks of home care such as cleaning.

Probably no aspect of housework has been lightened so much by technological change as laundry. In the 1920's a great many houses lacked hot and cold running water. A large variety of soaps and detergents and automatic appliances have come on the scene, and the once burdensome requirement of ironing has been greatly reduced by wash-and-wear fabrics. Nonetheless, the amount of time spent doing laundry has increased. Presumably people have more clothes now than they did in the past and they wash them more often.

Time spent on child care has also increased. The change reflects postwar modifications in standards of child care. Today's mother is cautioned to care for the child's social and mental development in addition to the traditional concerns of health, discipline and cleanliness.

More time is spent today in the tasks associated with consumption. They include shopping, household management and travel connected with the household. Contemporary women spend about one full working day per week on the road and in stores compared with less than two hours per week for women in the 1920's.

Although technological change has created new time demands in homemaking, this factor alone does not explain the consistently large amount of time devoted to housework. If it did, all women would spend long hours in housework. The data I have analyzed show that they do not. Employed women spend considerably less time in housework than nonemployed women.

In contrast to the 55 hours per week that nonemployed women spend in housework, employed women spend only 26 hours. In other words, employed women devote about half as much time to household tasks as nonemployed women. Technological change has in fact liberated some women from a certain amount of household work.

The time patterns of employed women become more significant when trends in the employment of women are taken into account. During the past 50 years women have entered the labor force in increasing numbers. Moreover, since World War II the increase has been caused primarily by the dramatic rise in the employment of married women. In 1920 it was rare to find married women working outside the home; today about 40 percent of them are in the labor force. Proportionately fewer women are full-time homemakers. Notwithstanding the stability of housework time for nonemployed women, therefore, the shift in the proportion of women employed signifies a reduction over the years in the amount of time women spend in housework.

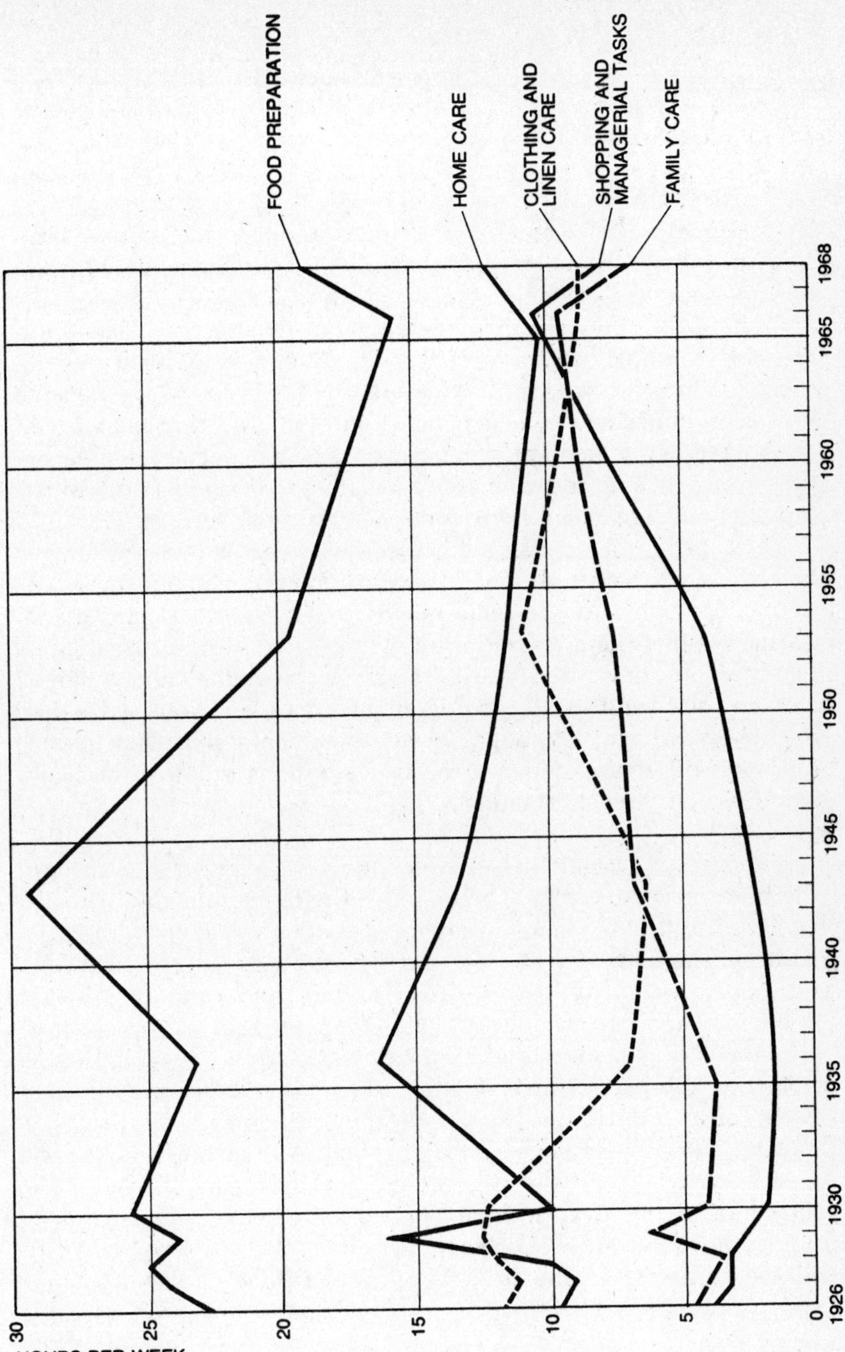

Distribution of time among various kinds of household work is traced from 1926 to 1968. The data relate only to nonemployed women, meaning women who did not have full-time jobs outside the household. Top curve includes cleaning up after meals.

Although the impact of social change on time spent in housework is thus clarified, the question remains of why nonemployed women spend so much time in homemaking. It is possible that this finding can also be explained in a fairly straightforward way. Perhaps nonemployed women have larger families and younger children and therefore more work than employed women. In addition the nonemployed women may have less household assistance.

It has been shown by other investigators that a woman's decision to work is limited by the presence of children, particularly young children. In other words, women are less likely to work when the burden of household tasks is greatest. I tested this argument with an analysis drawing on employment, marital status, socioeconomic status (family income and woman's education) and family composition (number and age of children) as points of comparison.

The technique enables one to see whether or not a difference between employed and nonemployed women remains if the distribution of women is the same on the other points of comparison. Assuming that the distribution of women according to social class, family composition and marital status is the same, nonemployed women would still spend considerably more time in housework than employed women. Although these adjustments somewhat reduce the time differences between the two groups of women, the major amount of difference remains.

Another explanation is a reflection of the amount of assistance the homemaker receives. The employed wife may be able with her earnings to buy laborsaving devices and the services of others. In addition she may have another, perhaps subtler resource: help from other members of the family. The fact that she works outside the home may give her leverage to call on them for help.

However plausible this explanation appears to be, information from the Robinson-Converse study shows that differences in help with housework do not explain the time differences between employed and nonemployed women. Employed women made no greater use of paid help than nonemployed women. Furthermore, husbands of employed women gave no more help than husbands of nonemployed women. Contrary to popular belief, American husbands do not share the responsibilities of household work. They spend only a few hours a week at it, and most of what they do is shopping.

Other factors could explain the puzzle. Perhaps employed women receive more help from children, live in smaller dwelling units or rely more on commercial services and laborsaving devices. Unfortunately the Robinson-Converse survey did not cover these matters. Other studies, however, contain little evidence that such factors would explain the time differences between the two categories of women.

Apparently one must look deeper for the explanation. One clear contrast between employed and nonemployed women is that work in the labor market earns a paycheck whereas housework does not. In the families of nonemployed women this contrast underscores an imbalance in the economic roles of husband and wife.

This kind of imbalance was not always embedded in marriage. In the farm household of earlier decades there was little separation of domestic and productive roles. Both the husband and the wife contributed to the family's production, and their contributions were probably regarded as being equal. It seems unlikely that anyone would regard the bread, butter and clothing made by the woman as any less valuable than the man's work in the fields.

In modern society the homemaker's contribution to the family economy is less clear. Although cooking, cleaning and shopping for bargains are important to the family, one cannot find much evidence that they are regarded as contributions equal to the wage earner's. As S. Ferge of the Sociological Research Institute in Budapest has written: "The results of housework do not serve this [economic] justification in a satisfactory manner because they are accepted as natural and are only noticed when they are absent. It is therefore the work itself whose existence must be felt and acknowledged; working long hours and working on Sunday can serve to demonstrate this. (These considerations are not conscious to those who are doing it; on the contrary, they are convinced of the functional necessity of this work.)"

Ferge suggests comparing women's housework schedules for weekdays and weekend days. I have done this and found that nonemployed women outdo employed women in housework on both types of day. Employed women "catch up" on housework on weekends. Nonetheless, they spend less time at it then than full-time homemakers who have all week to accomplish their work.

Perhaps the composition of the family has something to do with this finding; the presence of children, particularly young children, creates time demands that do not fit into a five-day week. I examined weekend time expenditures for women without children. Again nonemployed women spent about half an hour more per weekend day than employed women. The pattern is consistent with the view that nonemployed women schedule work so that it is visible to others as well as to themselves.

Since the value of household work is not clear, nonemployed

women feel pressure to spend long hours at it. Time spent in work, rather than the results of the work, serves to express to the homemaker and others that an equal contribution is being made. Women who work in the labor force contribute income to the family and so do not feel the same pressure.

There are, to be sure, additional factors that give rise to such high expenditures of time in housework. For example, in a consumption-oriented society the time involved in obtaining and taking care of household goods is far from negligible, although it is often assumed to be. Such tasks fall to the homemaker. Moreover, a large amount of time devoted to homemaking probably reflects a family's tastes and its preference for a particular quality of life.

Thus I am not suggesting that a homemaker's work is merely a matter of keeping busy, with no effect on the quality of the work performed. The enormous technological improvements affecting the household, together with the continued large amounts of time spent in housework, make it reasonable to assume that qualitative improvements have taken place. The example of laundry indicates that in this activity at least standards today are higher than they were in an earlier era.

It appears that modern life has not shortened the woman's work day. Farm work has been greatly reduced, but it has been replaced by work in the labor force. Indeed, for married women in full-time jobs the work day is probably longer than it was for their grandmothers.

22

Women's Work and the Economic Crisis

Some Lessons from the Great Depression

■

RUTH MILKMAN

The conditions of wage work in the 1930s and 1940s were shaped by the Great Depression, which brought vast unemployment, and World War II, which created great demand for production workers. Ruth Milkman examines these succeeding events in order to test the Marxist thesis that women workers are used as a "reserve army of labor," called on when demand for workers is high, and cavalierly discarded to return to their homes when production-demand slumps. In her analysis of the effects of the Great Depression on women's labor-force participation, Milkman also uses to good effect the Marxist-feminist emphasis on the reciprocal functioning of the productive relations of the workplace and the social relations of the home. A sociologist, Milkman employs the perspective of Marxist theory to draw new insights from familiar published sources, Labor Department employment statistics, and social surveys of family life. In the epilogue to her essay, omitted here, she goes on to apply lessons from the Great Depression to the economic recession of the 1970s.

THE FAMILY IS . . . an important component of our economic system, and this is the material basis of the cultural definition of women as primarily wives and mothers. And yet, with economic development and growth, increasing numbers of women have entered the paid labor force, in a wide range of occupations. This, in women's real lives, has meant greater opportunity to receive pay for their labor, a development which clearly threatens the culturally prescribed sexual division of labor assigning them the responsibility to work without pay to maintain their families.

There is, then, a real contradiction between the economy's need for women as unpaid family workers and its tendency to draw all available labor power, regardless of sex, into the sphere of production for profit. This creates a disjuncture between the ideology about sex roles, which continues to define women with reference to their family role, and the material reality of their increasing participation in the "male" sphere of paid production. As a result, as Juliet Mitchell has pointed out, women who work for pay tend nevertheless to view themselves as wives and mothers, not as "workers."

> Because the economic role of women is obscured (its cheapness obscures it) women workers do not have the pre-conditions of class consciousness. Their exploitation is invisible behind an ideology that masks the fact that they work at all—their work appears inessential.[1]

Because of this lack of class consciousness, Mitchell argues, the labor market behavior of women is easily manipulated with changing economic conditions. She and other Marxist-feminists have argued that women function as a "reserve army" of labor power, to be drawn on in periods when labor is scarce and expelled in periods of labor surplus. Ideology, in this view, plays a crucial role, both perpetuating women's lack of class consciousness over the long term and propelling them in and out of the labor force in response to changing economic conditions.

Exponents of this "reserve army" theory agree, and the historical evidence is fairly clear, that in periods of economic expansion women do tend to enter the paid workforce. In periods of contraction, however, the situation of women is more problematic. On the one hand, as Mitchell suggests, "in times of economic recession and forced labour redundancy, women form a pool of cheap labour."[2] Since women work for lower wages than men, one might expect them to be the last to lose their jobs in a slump. On the other hand, this would violate the basic cultural prescription which, as Mitchell so strongly emphasizes, dictates that "woman's place" is in the home, that men are the "breadwinners." Reasoning from this basis, Margaret Benston, who also characterizes women as a "reserve army," suggests that women leave the labor market in a period of contraction.

> When there is less demand for labor . . . women become a surplus labor force—but one for which their husbands and not society are economically responsible. The "cult of the home" makes its reappearance during times of labor surplus and is used to channel women out of the market economy. This is relatively easy since the pervading ideology ensures that no one, man or woman, takes woman's participation in the labor force very seriously.[3]

This notion has gained wide currency—indeed, it has risen to the level of dogma—both in the women's movement and on the Left.

There are, then, contradictory arguments about women's labor force behavior in an economic contraction. If the Marxist concept of a "reserve army" of labor power is useful for analyzing the entrance of women into the paid workforce over the long term, Marxist-feminist applications of its converse do not tell us very much about their economic roles in a period of crisis. Those theoretical applications, moreover, are somewhat mechanistic, and are insufficiently grounded in knowledge of history. This paper is an effort to remedy that through an analysis of the experience of women, both in the labor market and as unpaid family workers, during the Great Depression, the most severe economic crisis of the twentieth century. The experience of women during the period immediately following World War II will be considered also, as a contrasting case in which the "reserve army" theory is of some use. . . .

The first part of the paper consists of a discussion of the changes in women's paid employment patterns which resulted from the 1929 crash, in which I hope to demonstrate that the sex-typing of occupations created an inflexibility in the structure of the labor market which prevented the expulsion of women from it in the manner Benston suggests. It was not because of the fact that women's labor power is cheaper than men's, but rather because women's work is so rigidly sex-typed, that women enjoyed a measure of protection from unemployment in the Great Depression. It was the case, however, that women were urged to leave the paid labor force during the 1930s. That most of them did not suggests that ideological sex role prescriptions must be viewed not as determinant of, but rather in constant interaction with behavior in analyzing women's experience during periods of economic crisis.

In the next part of the paper, the focus of the discussion shifts to the impact of the economic crisis of the 1930s on women's economic role in the family—their unpaid work in the home. It is ironic that the Marxist-feminist discussion of women and economic crises has so far ignored this dimension of their experience, for it is a basic insight of Marxist-feminist theory as a whole that both paid work outside the home and unpaid work in it are crucial to women's experience in capitalist society. I will argue that in fact it was the work of women in the home, rather than their labor market participation, which was forced to "take up the slack" in the economy during this period of contraction.

After having considered the economic behavior of women in the 1930s, both in the labor market and in the home, and on this basis having rejected the "reserve army" theory, I will turn to a counterexample. The manner in which large numbers of women were drawn into the paid labor force during World War II, and their expulsion from it during the period of demobilization which followed, certainly seems to suggest that the "reserve army" theory does in fact have some explanatory power. I will argue, however, that the circumstances under which this occurred were highly peculiar and did not really constitute a "crisis," so that this case is by no means an adequate basis from which to generalize. . . .

UNEMPLOYMENT OF WOMEN IN THE GREAT DEPRESSION

The Great Depression of the 1930s was the most severe economic contraction Americans have experienced in the twentieth century to date. The official estimate of unemployment for 1933 is 25 percent[4] (and the actual proportion of people who experienced economic deprivation was probably much larger). Unfortunately, the only national unemployment data available for this period which are disaggregated by sex are those collected by the U.S. Census Bureau in 1930, when the percentage of all workers who had been laid off or fired and were seeking work was only 6.5.* These early data are in several respects highly problematic, and can by no means be assumed to be an accurate representation of the extent to which the nation's available labor power was unutilized in 1930. Nevertheless, for our purposes they are quite instructive.[7]

The April 1930 census found an unemployment rate of 4.7 percent for women, while that enumerated for men was 7.1 percent.

* In fact, the only reliable national data of any sort which exist for the entire period are those in the 1930 and 1940 censuses. The 1933 figure cited here and the other official annual unemployment statistics are interpolations made using the decennial census figures as "benchmarks."[4] Moreover, unemployment is calculated as a residual, that is, the difference between the estimated size of the civilian labor force and that of the employed population. Nor were data for these items collected directly in the decade of the 1930s. Rather, they were estimated later with the use of a variety of sources.[5] (Adjustments were made in the 1930 Census data to make them comparable with those collected on a monthly basis by the Bureau of Labor Statistics beginning in the 1940s; the official revised figure for 1930 is 8.7 percent.)

The situation in regard to data on sex differences in unemployment is even worse. Because the nature of the relationship of female labor force participation to economic fluctuations is even today only dimly understood, it is impossible to interpolate from the decennial census data that are available. This is of course a severe limitation to the present study.

Annual data on sex differences in unemployment was collected for a small number of states. Most of this information is unpublished, however, although it is described in a few published sources[6] and will be used to support the argument made here.

There is some evidence that as the Depression deepened the relative position of women grew somewhat worse, but the available data clearly indicate that, *insofar as their paid labor-force participation was concerned, women were less affected than men by the contraction.*

This is precisely the opposite of what the "reserve army" theory about the relationship of women to economic fluctuations would lead one to expect. One might turn to an alternative hypothesis, reasoning that since women's labor power is sold at a cheaper price than that of men, they are the last to be fired during a period of worsening business conditions. While this interpretation may seem satisfactory for purposes of explaining the *aggregated* unemployment figures, an examination of the statistics on joblessness across the occupational structure suggests an altogether different explanation.

Table 1 shows sex differences in the 1930 unemployment rates for the broad set of occupational groups used by the Census Bureau at the time, and for a small selection of specific occupational groups characterized by high concentrations of workers of one sex. The table suggests that the female unemployment rate was lower than the male rate in 1930 *because the occupations in which women were concentrated, occupations sex-typed "female," contracted less than those in which men were concentrated.*

Indeed, there is substantial evidence that, accompanying the dramatic increases in the proportion of women in the paid workforce over the course of the twentieth century,* there has been a consistent pattern of labor market segregation by sex. Everyone "knows," of course, that typists and nurses are women, while steelworkers and truckdrivers—and bosses—are men. Statistically, sexual segregation is an extraordinarily stable feature of the occupational structure. An analysis of the detailed occupational data in the decennial censuses taken between 1900 and 1960 has shown that the amount of job segregation by sex varies remarkably little, showing no fluctuations related to the fact that decennial censuses occurred at many different points in the business cycle. In any of these seven census years, about two-thirds of the women in the paid labor force would have had to change their occupation in order for their distribution in the paid-labor force to approximate that of men.[8]

This extraordinary phenomenon results from the fact that the increasing participation of women in the "male" sphere of paid work outside the home has been carefully delimited by an ideology linking

* Twenty percent of all women 14 years and older were in the paid labor force in 1900, and by 1970 this figure had risen to 40 percent. Increasing female labor force participation is a secular trend, which registered little variation in response to the contraction of the 1930s.

TABLE 1

Employment and Unemployment, by Sex and Occupational Group, U.S., 1930

Occupational Group	Size[a] (Thousands)	% of Total	% of All Female Workers	% of All Male Workers	Females As % of Total	Unemployment Rate[b] Total	Female	Male
General Division of Occupations (U.S. Census Series)								
All occupations	48,830	100.0	100.0	100.0	22.0	6.5	4.7	7.1
Agriculture	10,472	21.4	8.5	25.1	8.7	1.4	1.2	1.4
Forestry & fishing	250	0.5	0.0	0.7	0.1	10.4	10.3	10.4
Extraction of minerals	984	2.0	0.0	2.6	0.1	17.8	13.8	17.8
Manufacturing & mechanical industry	14,111	28.9	17.5	32.1	13.4	12.8	9.7	13.2
Transportation and communication	3,843	7.9	2.6	9.4	7.3	7.3	2.5	7.7
Trade	6,081	12.5	9.0	13.4	15.8	3.7	4.4	3.6
Public service	856	1.8	0.2	2.2	2.1	3.5	1.6	3.5
Professional service	2,254	6.7	14.2	4.5	46.9	2.8	2.4	3.1
Domestic & personal services	4,952	10.1	29.6	4.7	64.2	4.9	4.6	5.5
Clerical occupations	4,025	8.2	18.5	5.4	49.4	4.3	3.8	4.7
Selected "pure" sex-typed occupational groups[c]								
Stenographers & typists	811	1.7	7.2	0.1	95.6	4.7	4.6	7.2
Laundresses & launderers[d]	361	0.7	3.3	0.0+	98.7	3.0	2.9	8.0
Trained nurses	294	0.6	2.7	0.0+	98.1	4.2	4.1	8.9
Housekeepers & stewards	257	0.5	2.2	0.1	92.1	3.1	2.8	7.1

Telephone operators	249	0.5	2.2	0.0+	94.6	2.5	2.5	2.7
Dressmakers & seamstresses[e]	158	0.3	1.5	0.0+	99.7	3.6	3.6	8.2
Midwives & nurses (not trained)	157	0.3	1.3	0.0+	91.2	12.0	12.4	7.4
Iron and steel industries[f]	1,314	2.7	0.7	3.3	5.4	12.9	8.9	13.1
Chauffeurs & truck & tractor drivers	972	2.0	0.0+	2.5	0.2	8.5	7.7	8.5
Carpenters	929	1.9	0.0+	2.4	0.0+	18.9	12.0	18.9
Machinists, millwrights & toolmakers	761	1.6	0.0+	2.0	0.0+	9.0	5.0	9.0
Laborers, railroad	481	1.0	0.0+	1.3	0.7	8.9	4.0	8.9
Laborers, road & street	307	0.6	0.0+	0.8	0.0	13.4	12.8	13.5
Technical engineers	226	0.5	0.0+	0.6	0.0	3.6	2.7	3.6

[a] These data on the number of gainful workers in each occupational group, although collected after the onset of the Depression, approximate conditions before its onset, since people were asked to report their "normal" occupations to the Census taker.

[b] This includes those workers enumerated in Unemployment Classes A and B as defined by the U.S. Census Bureau. Class A includes "Persons out of a job, able to work, and looking for a job." Class B includes "Persons having jobs but on layoff without pay, excluding those sick or voluntarily idle." These two classes include almost all of the people counted as unemployed in the 1930 Census.

[c] These occupational groups were selected by the author from those in the most detailed occupational breakdown used in the 1930 Census of Unemployment, a breakdown comprised of approximately 300 occupational groups. The selection was made according to two criteria: (1) a high degree (90 percent or more) of concentration of workers in the occupational group were members of one sex; (2) the occupational group included at least one percent of all workers of that sex which predominated in it. All of the occupational groups sex-typed female and meeting these criteria are included in the table, and the seven largest of those sex-typed male were selected from a slightly larger set of occupational groups meeting these criteria.

[d] This occupational group *excludes* laundresses and launderers working in commercial laundries.

[e] This occupational group *excludes* dressmakers and seamstresses working in factories.

[f] Operatives and laborers (in iron and steel industries) have been aggregated here, although they are listed separately in the Census table from which this one was made. This is appropriate since both occupational groups are overwhelmingly male in composition and both were similarly affected by the contraction.

Source: *15th Census of the U.S.*, 1930. Unemployment, Vol. II, pp. 13-18. (Totals and percentages were computed by the author.)

that activity to their sex. The vast majority of women work in "women's jobs," occupations which frequently have some structural resemblance to their family role. They work in industries which produce commodities formerly manufactured by women in the home, such as clothing and processed food. In white collar occupations, as secretaries, teachers, waitresses, nurses, and so forth, women perform such wifely and motherly functions as schedule management, ego-building, child socialization, cleaning up, caring for the ill, and serving as a sexual object. Even in instances where such structural resemblance to the traditional female role is absent, more often than not women's paid labor activity is sex-typed and set apart from that of men. The mere fact that a woman traditionally does a certain job is usually sufficient to stigmatize it as "women's work," to which members of the female sex are supposed to be "naturally" suited.* Occupations in the "female labor market" are also characterized by low status and pay relative to men's jobs,[9] reflecting the sexual inequality rooted in the family and basic to the organization of American society.†

* It is virtually impossible to determine precisely what proportion of the jobs women hold are sex-typed in this manner. It seems reasonable to assume that occupations with extremely high concentrations of workers of one sex (such as those in the lower half of Table 1) are of this character. But since the government's occupational statistics are not designed for the purpose of facilitating analysis of this dimension of the occupational structure, even the most detailed breakdowns offered by them frequently group together two or more occupations which are sex-typed differently. Thus while it is likely that the degree to which the labor market is sexually segregated is even greater than the study of the 1900–1960 decennial census data cited above indicates, it is not possible to gauge the actual extent of sex-typing from currently available data.

† Even in the relatively infrequent cases where women do the same jobs as men, they almost invariably receive less pay. A study by the U.S. Bureau of Labor found only 800 cases, in a 1895–96 sample of 150,000 workers, in which men and women were in the same job classifications. In 600 of these cases the men earned more, by an average of about a third.[10] Cases of "equal work" are still quite rare, but the most cursory examination of earnings by sex across the decennial Census' detailed occupational classification shows that women still earn much less than men when they do equivalent work. Male sociologists, for example, earned 65 percent more than their female counterparts in 1970.[11] The gap in status and pay between men and women has actually been widening in recent decades.[12]

It is often suggested that economic discrimination of this type and differential treatment generally (including sex-typing) are justifiable because of differences in the "costs" of hiring men and women. Studies which control for such cost differentials, however, clearly show that only a fraction of the earnings gap can be so accounted for.[13] There are some sex differences in absenteeism and turnover rates in aggregated data, but if one examines instead the rates for men and women with similar occupational characteristics, the differences almost completely disappear.[14] Absenteeism seems to be a result of discrimination and not a cause. It is closely associated with lack of qualifications, which in turn is related to lack of responsibilities at work, absence of promotion prospects and low wages.[15] These are typical characteristics of occupations which are sex-typed "female." A skilled woman worker with responsibility on the job, however, does not stay away from it any more often than a man in a similar position.

The sex-typing of occupations does, in part, represent a cultural acknowledgement of the existence of wage-earning "*women* workers," and yet "workers" are clearly distinguished as a separate, male species. This helps to mediate the contradiction between the continuing need for women's unpaid work in the family and the tendency for women's work to be increasingly integrated into the sphere of paid production for profit. Sex-typing is an ideological mechanism which denies the existence of any conflict between women's family role and their role in paid labor, blithely labelling both "women's work."

But the contradiction has been reproduced in a new form in the workplace as more and more women have entered paid employment: occupational segregation along sex lines conflicts with the ideal of a fluid labor market which can be "rationally" shaped by the laws of supply and demand. It is this caste-like character of the female labor force which, ironically enough, prevented the automatic expulsion of women from the labor market during the economic contraction of the 1930s—despite the emergence of an ideology prescribing precisely that to ameliorate the unemployment situation. This dimension of women's role in paid labor, sex as caste, is a twist in the interaction of capitalism and patriarchy which the "reserve army" fails to capture in its full significance. And yet, sex-typing is the very essence of the blunting of women's consciousness of themselves as workers which is the starting point of the "reserve army" theory.

Because of the rigidity of sex-typing, the occupational distribution of women before the 1929 crash (shown in the upper left portion of Table 1) proved to be of great importance in determining the impact on women workers of the severe unemployment which followed. The "white collar" clerical, trade, and service occupations provided employment to more than half of all the women in the paid labor force at this time, while men predominated in the manufacturing sector. The "white collar" group was comprised of the very occupations whose rapid expansion in the early part of the twentieth century had drawn many women into the paid labor force; their growth accounted for 85 percent of the rise in female labor force participation during the period between 1890 and 1930.[16] As women entered them, the new clerical, trade, and service occupations were typed "women's work," and became an essentially permanent part of the *female* labor market.[17] During the Great Depression, for reasons outside the scope of the present study, these predominantly "female" occupations declined less, and later, than the predominantly male manufacturing occupations. As a result, women suffered less than men from unemployment.

The examples of "pure" sex-typed occupational groups in the

lower half of the table further illustrate the way in which sex-typing protected women from differential unemployment. Although these occupations are in no way strictly representative of the labor market as a whole, they do hint at the structure of sexual segregation at a somewhat greater level of detail than that offered in the broad occupational groupings, and offer further support for the argument being made here.

It should be observed, however, that even in occupational groups sex-typed male, the unemployment rates of women are lower than those of men in the same occupation. This suggests that the overall gap between the male and female rates may have been somewhat less wide in actuality than the data indicate. One reason for this is that women were probably undercounted in the Census of Unemployment. To be counted as "unemployed" one must either have been temporarily laid off or have lost her/his job and be actively seeking another one. Young single women and, even more so, widows and divorced women would be those most likely to be self-supporting, and therefore most likely to continue seeking work in spite of any difficulties. This would also be true of the majority of men in the labor force. Married women, in contrast, might be more easily discouraged if their husbands were employed, and as a result undercounted in the official unemployment statistics. Indeed, those data indicate that women under twenty suffered the highest unemployment rates, and that there was a general decrease in frequency of unemployment with increasing age.[18] Furthermore, the recorded unemployment rate of married women was slightly lower than that of single women, while that of widowed and divorced women was highest of all.[19]

There are other factors as well which suggest that the gap in male and female unemployment rates may have been somewhat less wide than the data indicate. Women workers, both in hard times and in the best of times, suffer various forms of discrimination which increase the likelihood that they will be underemployed. They frequently work in highly seasonal industries, and therefore have only irregular employment, being hired and fired in response to *short-term* industrial fluctuations.[20] Also, women work part-time more frequently than men.* Thus there is characteristically a substantial amount of unrecorded underemployment among women, even in

* The extent to which this may have been ignored in unemployment statistics is phenomenal. One study found that, in 1932, only 4 percent of the women surveyed in South Bend, Indiana—95 percent of whom were "normally" employed full time in manufacturing jobs—had full-time work. However, almost three-fifths of them were reported as "employed" in the Indiana unemployment statistics.[21]

good times, and under depressed industrial conditions one would expect some increase in its frequency. To the extent that this was true in the 1930s, one might conclude that the "reserve army" theory is applicable to some sectors of the female labor market, but this was the case only because the "women's jobs" involved were volatile, *not because men replaced women in them.**

There does seem to have been a gradual deterioration of women's situation relative to men's as the depression deepened, however. Data collected in some states on an annual basis clearly indicate a relative worsening of women's position,[23] although when this change occurred and what its implications were for women in particular occupations cannot be gauged with any precision, since the federal government did not regularly collect unemployment data by sex in the 1930s.

The earliest set of reliable national data on sex differences in unemployment after 1930 is that in the U.S. Census of 1940.† The recovery that would accompany World War II had only begun, and 8.3 percent of the experienced labor force were still seeking work.‡

* It is possible that in some "mixed" occupations men actually did replace women to some extent. Given the high degree of sex-typing evident even in the poor data that are available (as discussed above), however, it seems likely that such replacement was the exception rather than the rule. A few studies of the question done during the 1930s reflected an understanding of this.[22]

We can understand this intuitively by noting that even unemployed men would tend to be extremely reluctant to take a job as a secretary—"that's women's work." Nor will the average secretary be likely to voluntarily give up her job in a time of economic hardship.

† The U.S. Census Bureau did conduct a *Census of Partial Employment, Unemployment and Occupations* in 1937. It found a *higher* unemployment rate for women than for men, 14.9 percent and 13.9 percent respectively. Registration of unemployment status was voluntary in this enumeration, intensifying the general tendency for women to be undercounted. A special "Enumerative Check Census" was conducted by the U.S. Census Bureau in the same year for a smaller sample in an effort to correct for this. It found that actually the unemployment rates of both men and women were much higher than the original data indicated, although women were undercounted to a greater extent than men. The revised figures were 18.6 percent for men and 24.6 percent for women.

However, both the first enumeration and the revisions have been widely discredited. Stanley Lebergott of the U.S. Bureau of Labor Statistics, in an extensive retrospective analysis of all the available data on unemployment in the 1930s (the analysis upon which the current official government figures are based), found that the 1937 Census data were methodologically unsound and noted that they were inconsistent with virtually all other available evidence in their findings on sex differences in unemployment.[24]

‡ This differs from what is now the official unemployment figure for 1940, which is 14.6 percent (including public emergency workers). As in the case of the 1930 census data, adjustments were made in the 1940 Census data to render them comparable with the unemployment statistics collected on a monthly basis by the U.S. Bureau of Labor Statistics beginning in the mid-1940s.[25]

Another 4.9 percent were employed in public emergency work. The female unemployment rate was still lower than that of men, but the gap had narrowed somewhat. 8.6 percent of the experienced male labor force were unemployed in 1940, and 7.5 percent of the experienced female labor force were seeking work. The male unemployment rate was thus only 15 percent greater than the female unemployment rate, as compared with a differential of 49 percent in 1930. This is partly explained by the sex differential in public emergency work, which occupied 5.2 percent of the experienced male labor force but only 3.6 percent of the experienced female labor force in 1940. But even if persons doing public emergency work are counted as unemployed, the resulting male unemployment rate is only 24 percent above the female rate.[26]

One explanation for the deterioration of women's relative position in the unemployment rolls might be that large numbers of women previously engaged only in unpaid housework were forced to seek paid work during the depression, in efforts to compensate for the decline in family income resulting from the unemployment of male family members. Indeed, total female labor force participation rose in the period from 1930 to 1940 more than in any previous decade in the twentieth century. There were, moreover, declines in the participation of teenaged females and older women during this period so that the increased participation of women between 20 and 65 years old was even greater than the aggregated figures suggest.* There is also a vast amount of qualitative evidence supporting the hypothesis that many married women sought paid employment to compensate for their husbands' unemployment.[28]

If correct, this suggests that the fact that the unemployment rate of men was higher than that of women had only an indirect effect on the unemployment rate of women, insofar as the wives and daughters of unemployed men could find jobs more easily than they, and were thus drawn into the labor market because of their declining family income. There is no evidence of any mobility from the male to the female labor market in the course of the depression decade,† and the deterioration of women's relative position in the labor mar-

* Male labor force participation declined between 1930 and 1940, but this was largely due to decreases in the participation of teenaged and retirement-aged males. The labor force participation rate of males aged 25 to 64 changed insignificantly.[27]

† There is substantial evidence, on the other hand, of widespread downward mobility *within* the female labor market. Women who were unemployed were evidently willing, after a certain point, to seek work in an occupation different from their former one, even when this meant a cut in status and/or pay.[29] Men probably experienced a similar pattern of downward mobility in the 1930s, and in light of this it is all the more surprising that they did not replace women to any significant extent.

ket seems to have been due primarily to increased competition among women for jobs in the female labor market. In fact, the degree of sex segregation within the occupational structure actually increased slightly between 1930 and 1940.[30]

Because the data on unemployment are so poor and so problematic, it is not possible to learn from them exactly what the relation of women to the labor market was in the Great Depression. But it is clear that the "reserve army" theory is not very useful for this purpose, and that sex-typing is an extremely important factor.

Perhaps one reason that the "reserve army" theory has so seldom been questioned is that on the ideological level, it was in fact the case that women were urged to return to the home during the 1930s. Male unionists and others frequently suggested that women were taking "men's jobs." Their entrance into the paid labor force in the previous years, these men argued, had produced a scarcity of jobs for men.[31] Disapproval of married women who worked was particularly fervent. The executive council of the A.F. of L. urged that "married women whose husbands have permanent positions . . . should be discriminated against in the hiring of employees."[32] A 1936 Gallup poll indicated that most Americans agreed, 82 percent of those polled.[33]

Nor were these totally idle arguments. Discriminatory practices against married women were actually instituted in a number of cases. Many states reactivated old laws by means of which teachers and other female civil servants were dismissed upon marrying.[34] And yet, more and more married women were being forced into the labor market as unemployment struck their families. It was clearly better, in spite of the cultural sanctions which had emerged, to have what little income a woman could earn than no income at all in a household in which the male "breadwinner" was unemployed. As a result, it was not possible for ideological forces to successfully push women out of the labor market. Such behavior was in direct opposition to their material interests.

Nevertheless, the ideological condemnation of women's paid work did serve to diffuse people's discontent in the early 1930s. To the extent that women could be blamed for the economic crisis, attention was distracted from analyses which found its roots in the workings of capitalism. The number of people who actually thought that women had "caused" the crisis was in any case quite small, and yet women were not considered equally entitled to paid employment by large numbers of people. This was a less effective outlet for discontent, but not altogether unlike what might have occurred if women had in fact transferred their jobs to men. Had that been the case, as the "reserve army" theory suggests, women would have "taken up the slack" in the economy quite directly. As it was, they generally retained their jobs, while on the cultural level some anger was directed at them rather than at those who controlled the society that now could not provide jobs for those who sought them.

MAKING ENDS MEET: THE UNPAID WORK OF WOMEN IN THE GREAT DEPRESSION

Perhaps the most important reason for the inadequacy of the "reserve army" theory is its failure to comprehend the primary importance of women's economic role in the family. Indeed, it is the economic need for their unpaid work in the home from which the caste-like structure of the female labor force, which is so basic to the experience of women during a crisis in their role as paid workers, first emerges. Even for this reason alone, it would be foolhardy to overlook the impact of economic crises on women's family role.

The productive activity of women in the home is accorded lower social status than any other occupation:* housework is a "labor of love" in a society whose universal standard of value is money. Because it is not remunerated with a wage, housework does not directly produce surplus value. However, it does maintain and reproduce the ability of family members to work productively, their labor power, which they sell in the labor market for a wage.

The work involved in providing personal services has been greatly influenced by technological developments in the course of capitalist expansion, just as various productive activities which once engaged housewives—food processing, clothing manufacture, and so forth, have been increasingly integrated into the sphere of paid labor. Paralleling this process of the socialization of production is the transformation of the family from a unit of production into a unit of consumption. At the same time, other institutions have taken over some of the functions the family used to perform, like vocational training and the care of the aged. As this occurs, there is also a tendency toward nuclearization of the institution. All of these changes were well underway by 1930.

Within this general tendency for housework to become increasingly dependent on commodity production, at any one point in time there is a great deal of flexibility in the allocation of work between

* The status of a housewife is, of course, partly dependent on the occupational and social status of her husband. A ruling class housewife has more status than a garbage collector in most contexts.

the home and the industrial workplace. During the Great Depression, the long-term trends reversed themselves, and women's unpaid household production became more important than it had been in earlier years. In a sense, the family "took up the slack" in the economy during the 1930s.

People who were unemployed naturally turned to their families for support. The work of women in physically and psychologically maintaining their families became tremendously difficult as family incomes declined and the psychological stresses attending unemployment took their toll. Women showed amazing resourcefulness in coping with the crisis on the family level. They used a wide variety of strategies, generally turning back toward "traditional" forms of family organization.

The most immediate problem facing the family struck by unemployment was the material hardship created by their lowered income. Women cut back family expenditures in many areas. Typical strategies were moving to quarters with lower rent, having telephones removed, and denying themselves many purchased goods and services to which they had become accustomed in the prosperity of earlier years.[35] Clothing, prepared meals, domestic service, automobiles, magazine subscriptions and amusements were among the many products and services which suffered declines in sales as optimists heralded the "live at home movement."[36]

Many women managed to approximate their families' prior standard of living despite lowered incomes by substituting their own labor for goods and services they had formerly purchased in the marketplace, reversing the trend toward increased consumption in the preceding decades. Home canning was so widespread that glass jar sales were greater in 1931 than at any other point in the preceding eleven years. There was a corresponding drop in sales of canned goods, which had doubled in the decade from 1919–29.[37] Similarly, the 1930s saw a revival of home sewing. People who had never sewed before attended night school classes to learn how to sew and remodel garments.[38]

Women's efforts to cut back family expenses by substituting their own labor for purchasable commodities represented only one set of alternatives in the struggle to make ends meet.* Many women

* Another strategy was that of going back to the land. Actually, most farmers had lived in poverty even during the "prosperous" 1920s, but this fact was evidently not widely appreciated, for in the early 1930s, the flow of people from farms to cities slowed and then actually reversed itself for the first time since records of internal migration had been kept. By 1935, 2 million people were living on farms who had not been there five years before.[39] This strategy had an understandable appeal at a time when fear of starvation was realistic and widespread.

engaged themselves in paid work in attempts to compensate for a reduction in family income. There was a revival of domestic industry: women took in laundry, ironing, and dressmaking; they baked cakes to sell; they took in boarders.[40] Everywhere there were signs in yards advertising household beauty parlors, cleaning and pressing enterprises, grocery stores, and the like.[41]

Women also sought paid jobs outside their home to increase the family income. They did this despite the strong cultural sanctions against married women working, sanctions which were strongly reinforced with the onset of mass unemployment. Women who thus defied the cultural prescription frequently justified their behavior as a response to the family emergency created by the unemployment of their husbands, and they generally planned to stop working for pay as soon as the situation improved.[42] The following case is representative:

> Until 1930 Mr. Fetter was able to support the family. After that date his earnings from irregular work were supplemented by his wife's earnings of $9.00 per week in a restaurant. Both husband and wife disliked to have the wife work, but there seemed no other solution of the economic problem.[43]

The last resort of families for whom none of these strategies succeeded—and there were many—was to go "on relief." Accepting this alternative, however, was widely viewed as an admission of failure of the family. Mr. Fetter's "reaction to the idea of relief was violent."[44] In another case study, a husband and wife expressed their reluctance to accept any government assistance: "We are able people; we must keep on our feet."[45] And in cases where the relief strategy was pursued, a great deal of resentment toward the social service agencies was expressed. Experienced wives and mothers often felt, not without reason, that the social workers they dealt with were too young and naive to understand the costs involved in raising a large family.[46]

Added to the difficulties in maintaining families on a reduced income were the demands placed on the institution to reabsorb members who had been independent during the better times before the crash. Not only did unemployed husbands spend more time around the house, but old people, who frequently suffered from discrimination in employment, tended to "double up" with their sons' and daughters' families.[47] The younger generation was likely to be relatively better off in terms of employment, but were less likely to have a securely owned dwelling. This strategy of pooling the resources of two generations represented a clear break with the long-term trend toward nuclearization.

Youth, who also faced discrimination in the labor market, returned home during the Depression.* The dependence of this generation on the previous one caused delays, sometimes permanent ones, in new family formation. The marriage rate dropped sharply, from 10.1 marriages per thousand people in 1929 to 7.9, the low point in 1932.[49] In 1938 it was estimated that 1.5 million people had been forced to postpone marriage because of the economic depression.[50] Cohort data on ever-married rates reveals that many of these "postponements" were permanent. The proportion of single women (never married by 1970) aged 25–30 in 1935 is about 30 percent higher than the proportion in the cohort five years younger.[51] One spinster of this generation recalls:

> There were young men around when we were young. But they were supporting mothers.
>
> It wasn't that we didn't have a chance. I was going with someone when the Depression hit. We probably would have gotten married. He was a commercial artist and had been doing very well. I remember the night he said, "They just laid off quite a few of the boys." It never occurred to him that he would be next. He was older than most of the others and very sure of himself. This was not the sort of thing that was going to happen to him. Suddenly he was laid off. It hit him like a ton of bricks. And he just disappeared.[52]

The material tasks of family maintenance became extraordinarily challenging during the 1930s, as women struggled to stretch a decreased income to maintain the members of their nuclear family and, in many cases, the younger and older generations as well. However, this was but one aspect of the increased importance of women's unpaid labor in the home during the depression. The task of psychological maintenance was also made much more difficult in families affected by unemployment. The concrete fact of idleness, the declassment in the community which generally accompanied it, and a multitude of side effects associated with the various strategies pursued to maintain the family materially placed enormous strains on the family as an emotional support system, and on women's role in its maintenance.

* As far as I am aware, data on school retention rates for the 1930s are not available by sex. However, a recent study based on data on the postwar business cycles, found that teenage boys accelerate their school-leaving in times of prosperity, while girls tend to do so in times of depression. Since girls are more productive at home in hard times, the logic runs, they leave school and devote their energy to helping their mothers to carry the increased burden of housework in depressions. Boys, in contrast, decide when to leave school according to their opportunities for paid employment, and thus go to school longer during hard times. It seems plausible that this would hold for the 1930s also.[48]

Since his role as wage-earner is often the basis of the father's status within the family, that status tends to be lowered by his unemployment. The man without a job in the 1930s often felt superfluous and frustrated, "because in his own estimation he fails to fulfill what is the central duty of his life, the very touchstone of his manhood—the role of family provider."[53] The strain attending unemployment was exacerbated in cases where other family members were earning money. A woman who replaced her husband as the "breadwinner" during the Depression recalls:

> In 1930, it was slack time. He didn't have a job, my husband. Even now, the painter's work is seasonal. So I went to work those times when he wasn't working, and he took care of the boy.
>
> Yah. He said he's walking upside down, if you know what that means. (Laughs.) You start walking on the floor, and then you put yourself upside down, how you feel. Because he couldn't provide for his family. Because when we got married, he actually said, "You're not gonna work."[54]

To say that the unemployed father lost status in the family would seem to imply that women who assumed the role of "provider" gained somehow. But such a role reversal was not a simple exchange of power. Women's responsibility for providing emotional support to family members was not diminished during this period. On the contrary, the reversal roles made this task much more difficult, for an unemployed husband demanded more support than ever before. If there was any increased recognition of woman's economic role in the family, it did not represent a gain in status, for no one was comfortable with the new state of affairs, and the reversal of roles was resented by everyone involved.

The tension unemployment produced within the family was intensified by the general declassment accompanying lowered family income. As the status of the family in the community dropped there appeared alongside the tendency for families to strengthen their ties with relatives a general decrease in social contacts outside the family circle. Lacking appropriate clothing and money for dues or donations, many families stopped attending church and dropped their club memberships. In addition, many had sacrificed their telephones and there was little money for carfare, so it was more difficult to socialize with friends.[55] People were ashamed of their lowered standard of living and hence reluctant to invite guests into their homes.[56]

Further pressures on the psychological balance of the family were exerted by the various strategies women pursued to maintain its members materially. The simple fact of decreased income increased family discord over financial matters,[57] and the crowding resulting from "doubling up," moving to less expensive quarters, or being unable to heat all the rooms in a house during the winter, produced much friction among family members.[58] Moreover, they saw much more of each other than before, whether they wished to or not, simply because they were unemployed and spent more time at home.

Women in families affected by unemployment, then, were under incredible pressure from all sides. Their responsibility to maintain their families materially and psychologically became much more difficult to fulfill. Sociologists who studied the impact of the depression on families at the time noted that these strains generally resulted in an initial period of disorientation, which was ultimately resolved either through adjustment or "disintegration" of the family.[59] Whether or not a family was able to adjust to the new situation depended on a variety of factors, but on the whole, these studies showed that the impact of the crisis was to exaggerate previous family patterns. "Well-organized" families became more unified, while the problems of unstable families were accentuated.

Families which survived the crisis intact certainly were more "unified" in the sense that they spent more time together than before, but it is not clear that this choice was freely made or that families were newly prized by their members. Indeed, the Lynds reported that "Each family seems to wish wistfully that the depression had not happened to *it*, while at the same time feeling that the depression has in a vague general way 'been good for family life.' "[60] Families which broke under the strain did not always fall apart visibly. Although the frequency of desertion, the "poor man's divorce," rose, legal divorce was expensive, and its rate declined.[61]

There is scattered evidence that in some families the strain was manifested in a decline in sexual activity. The most common reason given for such declines was fear of unwanted pregnancy.* In a number of instances, however, women reported that they had lost respect for their unemployed husbands, and could no longer love them as before.[63] A psychiatrist observed of a group of long-term unemployed miners:

> They hung around street corners and in groups. They gave each other solace. They were loath to go home because they were indicted, as if it were their fault for being unemployed. A jobless man was a lazy good-for-nothing. The women punished the men

* The birth rate dropped from 21.3 live births per thousand population in 1930 to 18.4 in 1933.[62]

> for not bringing home the bacon, by withholding themselves sexually. . . . These men suffered from depression. They felt despised, they were ashamed of themselves. They cringed, they comforted one another. They avoided home.[64]

There must have been many cases like these, in which the family simply could not cope with all the strains which converged on it. The emergence of social services on a large scale during the later 1930s probably represented, at least in part, a response to these family failures, and supplied a bolster to the institution. But what is really more remarkable than the record of failures is the amazing extent to which families were able to successfully absorb all the new strains placed upon them.

In some cases there was organized resistance to the agents of dispossession. In the country, there were "ten cent sales" in which neighbors would bid ridiculously low prices for a farmer's property that was being auctioned off by creditors trying to collect on a mortgage, and then return it all to the original owner.[65] In the city, people would move the furniture of an evicted family back into the tenement as soon as it had been put out in the street, to the despair of the landlord.[66]

While actions like these must often have represented the difference between survival and disintegration of a family, most families seem to have depended even more on their internal strengths. It was, to a great extent, women who took up the increased burdens involved in maintaining the family—indeed, this was their traditional responsibility. The importance of their contribution to family maintenance during the crisis was probably only seldom recognized. In Tillie Olsen's fictional portrayal of a family's efforts to cope with the crisis, for example, the husband only appreciates his wife's contribution after she is taken sick. "You useta be so smart with money—make it stretch like rubber. Now it's rent week and not a red cent in the house. I tell you we gotta make what I'm getting do. . . ."[67]

Some women were revitalized by the increased responsibility they acquired during the Depression. One woman's hypochondria disappeared with the crisis: "Now her mind is taken up with the problems of stretching her kitchen dollar further than ever and keeping the home up-to-date and clean without new furnishings and the help of a cleaning woman."[68] Another woman, a daughter, who would never have looked for paid work if not for the decline in her once wealthy family's income, developed a whole new sense of self-respect from her experience as a wage-earner. She recalls:

> Now it was necessary for me to make some money because the stepfather was drunk all the time and the father was pretending

> it hadn't happened. Having gone to a proper lady's finishing school, I didn't know how to do anything. I spoke a little bad French, and I knew enough to stand up when an older person came into the room. As far as anything else was concerned, I was unequipped.
>
> I heard there was a call for swimmers for a picture called *Footlight Parade*. At Warner Brothers. The first big aquacade picture. I went, terrified, tried out on the high diving thing and won. I couldn't have been more stunned. I truly think this is where I got a lifelong point of view: respect for those who *did*, no respect for those who *had* . . . just because their father had done something and they were sitting around.
>
> I loved the chorus girls who worked. I hated the extras who sat around and were paid while we were endangering our lives. I had a ball. It was the first time I was better than anybody at something. I gained a self-respect I'd never had.[69]

This kind of depression experience was, of course, limited to women of privileged social groups, those who would otherwise have spent their lives as more or less leisured symbols of their father's or husband's status. Hard work was nothing new to working class women, and their increased responsibilities could not have been welcomed so eagerly. For these women and their families, the experience of sex-role-reversal—either a complete shifting of responsibility for earning money from husband to wife, or simply an increased reliance on the wife's unpaid work and her strategies for survival—was a part of a very painful period in the family's history. The deviation from traditional sex roles was thus, to say the least, negatively reinforced by the accompanying experience of economic deprivation for most families.* It did not generally mean that the husband-wife relationship became more egalitarian in the long run, rather the impact of the crisis was to define women in terms of the traditional female role even more rigidly than before.

Women "took up the slack" in the economy during the Great Depression, then, not by withdrawing from the paid labor force, as the "reserve army" theory suggests, but in their family role. There was an increased economic dependence on their unpaid household labor, reversing the pre-Depression trend toward increased use of consumer goods. The process of nuclearization, similarly, reversed

* This inference is supported by Elder's finding that females who were adolescents during the depression years (born 1920–21) were more likely to marry early if their families of orientation experienced deprivation (defined as a 35 percent or greater loss in family income) during the 1930s. These women also showed a marked preference for the domestic role over any alternative one.[70] Aggregate cohort data shows that daughters born in the late depression years—roughly parallel to the daughters of the women in Elder's cohort—have the highest proportion "ever married" on record.[71]

itself, as the unemployed turned to their kin for help. The family's role in maintaining people psychologically also became more difficult for women to fulfill.

The traditional family role of women was reinforced because of its increased material importance during the 1930s, then, although women did not "return to the home" in the way the "reserve army" theory suggests. On the contrary, role reversals between husband and wife were common, and precisely because of the *negative* reinforcement given to sex role reversal which resulted from its origin in economic deprivation, traditional sex roles were reinforced.

WOMAN'S PLACE IN THE WORLD WAR II EMERGENCY

The Great Depression ended with a boom in the early 1940s, when U.S. involvement in the Second World War stimulated a tremendous amount of investment in war-related industrial production. The labor surplus of the Depression years rapidly disappeared, and soon the problem of unemployment was replaced by a severe shortage of labor power. All of this happened very fast, so that it is appropriate to describe the situation as a "crisis of expansion," a truly extraordinary kind of economic recovery.

Huge numbers of women were drawn out of their homes and into the paid labor force to meet the demand for workers. Many of them took "war jobs" in industries which produced military equipment or other war-related items, so that when the war ended, so did their jobs. Thus the "reserve army" theory, which, as we have seen, is quite inadequate for analyzing the experience of women during the contraction of the 1930s, fits their situation during the period of demobilization in the late 1940s rather well. Women were drawn into war production "for the duration," in many cases losing their jobs immediately upon the conclusion of hostilities. Most of them eventually found employment in the postwar years in traditional "women's jobs," so that their expulsion from the paid labor force was only temporary. Nevertheless, the war experience did demonstrate that women could, albeit under rather peculiar circumstances, function as a "reserve army" which was pulled in and then pushed out of the labor force in the way the usual formulation of the concept suggests.

The demand for female labor power created by the expansion of the American economy during World War II was of unprecedented magnitude. Between 1940 and the peak of war employment in 1944, the number of women in the paid labor force increased by more than

6 million, or 50 percent. The largest demand came from manufacturing industries, in which the number of women workers increased by 140 percent from 1940 to 1944, as can be seen in Table 2. In industries producing directly for war purposes it rose by 460 percent. The female clerical labor force experienced a doubling in the same period. The only occupational group to experience a decrease in the number of women workers was domestic service.*

Sixty percent of the women who entered the labor market between 1940 and 1944 were 35 years old or more, and more than half of them were or had been married.[76] Although many of these women worked full time, the labor shortage also stimulated substantial efforts to provide part-time employment for women with heavy family responsibilities.[77] The first large scale child care programs were set up (although these never met the huge demand). Lighting and other workplace amenities were improved in many plants as well, and employers redesigned the work process of many industrial jobs with women in mind, eliminating the need to lift heavy weights, for example. The motivation for all of this was, unmistakably, the need to maximize the efficiency of the new workers, who were difficult to recruit. Thus one government pamphlet distributed widely to employers, entitled *When You Hire Women*, pointed out that efficiency decreased after a point with longer hours, and that "Harassed mothers make poor workers."[78]

Employers who offered women "men's" wages and working conditions could be assured of a labor supply, and during the war it was common for the government to assume the costs incurred in paying women high wages in war industries. Ostensibly because of the difficulties in estimating the costs of producing military items,

* This was due to the unfavorable comparison between domestic work and other occupations in which there were openings. There was a great deal of upward occupational mobility during the 1940s. Women left occupations with low status and pay like service and sales jobs for new opportunities in war industries which offered better pay and working conditions. Movement out of service employment was so pronounced that there were many shortages in provision of services. In 1942, for example, 600 laundries closed because of their inability to recruit workers.[72]

There was also a great deal of geographical mobility, for war production was not evenly distributed across the country but, on the contrary, centered in a relatively small number of urban areas. Many women migrated from areas outlying the war production centers in response to the spectacular demand for their labor power.[73]

These mobility patterns completely reversed those which had characterized the Depression years, when most occupational mobility had been forced and in a downward direction, and geographical mobility had been from urban to rural areas.[74] The mobility that was possible for women, moreover, was no longer limited to the female labor market, for the heavy industrial "war jobs" which accounted for the largest single part of the increased employment of women—jobs in aircraft assembly, shipbuilding, ammunition manufacturing, and steel—had traditionally been sex-typed male.[75]

TABLE 2
Changes in Women's Employment, 1940–1944

Occupational Group	Women Employed (thousands)		
	1940	1944	% change
All occupations[a]	11,140[b]	16,480	+48.0[b]
Professional and semiprofessional	1,470	1,490	+1.2
Proprietors, managers and officials	420	650	+53.3
Clerical and kindred	2,370	4,380	+84.5
Sales	780	1,240	+58.4
Craftsmen, foremen (sic), operatives and laborers	2,250	4,920	+118.7
Domestic service	1,970	1,570	−20.4
Other service	1,260	1,650	+30.9
Farm workers	470	560	+18.6
Manufacturing, total[c]	2,320	5,590	+140.7
War industries—metal, chemicals, rubber	480	2,690	+462.7
Consumer industries—food, clothing, textiles, leathers	1,330	2,160	+62.6
Other industries	510	730	+42.6

[a] Totals do not add due to the failure to record the occupations of some workers.
[b] This takes no account of the women who in 1940 were unemployed or on emergency work, and who were thus technically part of the labor force. Their inclusion reduces the increase to about 36%.
[c] This classification is *part* of a Census breakdown by *industry*, altogether separate from the *occupational* breakdown given in its entirety in the first half of the table.
Source: Adapted from tables in U.S. Dept. of Labor, Women's Bureau, Special Bulletin No. 20, *Changes in Women's Employment During the War* (1944), pp. 9, 15.

which often underwent changes in design, government contracts often stipulated that the manufacturer would be reimbursed for all the costs of production plus a "fixed fee." The government thus took on all the risks of war production and capitalists were guaranteed a profit.[79]

Even where the beginning wages for women and men were equal, however, women rarely had equal opportunities for advancement.[80] Similarly, although women war workers often became members of unions, they frequently experienced differential treatment within the union structure. Many contracts provided that women and men be listed on separate seniority lists, and some stated outright that women's tenure in jobs previously held by men would be theirs "for the duration" only.[81]

This definition of women's war employment as temporary was

not limited to unions, but had been explicit in all of the propaganda issued by government and industry urging women to enter the paid labor force. The thrust of the appeal, indeed, was that women could do "their part" in the war effort by taking industrial jobs. The expectation that they would gracefully withdraw from "men's jobs" when the war ended and the rightful owners reappeared on the scene was clear from the first.

Moreover, during World War II, suddenly jobs which had previously had all the attributes of "men's work" acquired a new femininity and glamour. There was an unrelenting effort to reconcile the traditional image of women with their new role. It was suggested, for example, that an overhead crane operated "just like a gigantic clothes wringer" and that the winding of wire spools was very much like crocheting.[82] A pamphlet emphasizing the importance of safety caps for women machine operators to prevent industrial accidents showed pictures of pretty women dressed in the twelve available styles of head covering.[83] A 1943 advertisement in *Fortune* for an iron works company showed a photograph of a woman worker operating a steel-cutting machine with this caption:

> Tailor-made suit cut to Axis size! . . . Skillful Van Dorn Seamstress, with scissors of oxyacetylene, cloth of bullet-proof steel, and pattern shaped to our enemy's downfall! . . .[84]

The women who took war jobs were not allowed to forget their sex for a moment. They were not to be viewed as war workers, but as *women* war workers in "men's jobs" "for the duration" of the war emergency. Media images of these women almost invariably contained allusions to their sexuality. An article on "Girl Pilots" in *Life,* for example, quips:

> Girls are very serious about their chance to fly for the Army at Avenger Field, even when it means giving up nail polish, beauty parlors and dates for a regimented 22½ weeks. . . . They each have on the G.I. coveralls, called zoot suits in Avenger Field lingo, that are regulation uniform for all working hours. Though suits are not very glamourous, the girls like their comfort and freedom.[85]

Many women war workers reported similar attitudes being expressed by their male co-workers. One personal account, for example, noted:

> At times it gets to be a pain in the neck when the man who is supposed to show you work stops showing it to you because you have nicely but firmly asked him to keep his hands on his own

> knees; or when you have refused a date with someone and ever since then he has done everything in his power to make your work more difficult. . . . Somehow we'll have to make them understand that we are not very much interested in their strapping virility. That the display of their physique and the lure of their prowess leaves us cold. That although they have certainly convinced us that they are men and we are women, we'd really rather get on with our work.[86]

Women were laid off in huge numbers immediately after the war ended. As industrial plants reconverted to consumer-oriented production they returned to their pre-war male work force. In January 1946 the number of women in the labor force was 4 million less than at the 1944 peak, and only 2 million more than in 1940.[87] The most dramatic decline was in durable goods manufacturing, the sector where most of the high-paying "war jobs" had been located. The employment of women in these industries declined by 1.5 million between the 1944 peak and January 1946.[88]

Despite the fact that the nation had been well prepared for this eventuality ideologically, women themselves resisted the notion that they were working only "for the duration." Most insisted that they would remain in the paid labor force after the war. Although at the beginning of the war polls had indicated that 95 percent of the women who were new entrants to the labor force expected to quit after the war,[89] the Women's Bureau's survey of 13,000 women war workers in 1944–45 found that three out of every four wanted to continue working after the war ended.[90] Moreover, the older women who had made up so large a portion of the new recruits to the labor force planned to stay there: 81 percent of the women who were 45 or older said that they intended to remain in the paid work force.[91]

Women clearly enjoyed working, and they had strong material incentives to continue to do so in a period of high inflation. The case of Alma is perhaps representative of the general feeling of women at the close of hostilities:

> Alma goes to work because she wants to go to work. She wants to go now and she wants to keep going when the war is over. Alma's had a taste of LIFE. She's poked her head out into the once-man's world. . . . Of course, all the Almas haven't thought through why they want to work after the war or how it's going to be possible. But they have gone far enough to know that they can do whatever is required in a machine shop. They've had the pleasure of feeling money in their pockets—money they've earned themselves.[92]

And yet, the material fact of "reconversion" to peacetime production would force the withdrawal of many women from the labor force. They were eventually reintegrated into it, not in the heavy industry "war jobs" but rather in the white collar and service occupations which had been part of the female labor force before the war and which continued to expand in the postwar years. While women's penetration into "men's jobs" with high status and pay during the war years proved ephemeral, then, their increased presence in the paid labor force would be duplicated in later years.

The experience of World War II clearly demonstrated that women could function as a "reserve army" to meet the economy's needs in a crisis of expansion. Had a depression followed the war—an eventuality widely feared at the time—women would almost certainly not have re-entered the paid labor force as easily as they did in the period of expansion that followed the initial postwar contraction. And yet, the war-induced labor shortage that drew women into paid employment was of an extraordinary type. The jobs created by the boom in industrial production for military purposes were, by definition, temporary ones, whereas in other periods of expansion the jobs women took became integral parts of the occupational structure. This difference was crucial, for it meant that in the contraction of "reconversion" which followed the war boom, the jobs women had were essentially eliminated from the occupational structure. This was most unlikely to occur in a depression following a "normal" period of economic growth, so that the demobilization experience can only be regarded as atypical. . . .

In 1940, 26 percent of American women of working age were in the paid labor force. By 1970, that figure had risen to 40 percent. Accompanying this dramatic increase in the size of the female labor force has been an important change in its composition. The labor force participation rate of married women rose from 15 percent to 39 percent during the same period, and that of women between 25 and 44 rose from 31 to 48 percent.[93] This represents a major change in the typical life cycle pattern of female labor force participation, and a new relationship between women's family role and their role in paid labor. While in the early part of the twentieth century, the normal pattern for middle class women was to leave the labor force when they became wives and mothers, in the 1970s it is common for women of both the middle and working classes to work for pay at virtually every point in their life cycles.

Accompanying this development has been a remarkable change in the *male* labor force participation rate. As Table 3 shows, while the labor market participation of women rose in the postwar de-

TABLE 3

Labor Force Participation Rates,[a] by Sex and Age, for Persons 16 Years and Over, Selected Years, 1950–1973

Year	Males				Females				Female/ Male x 100	
	Total	16–24	25–64	65+	Total	16–24	25–64	65+	Total	25–64
1950	86.8	79.3	94.8	45.8	33.9	44.0	35.1	9.7	39.1	37.0
1953	86.9	80.2	95.8	41.6	34.5	42.9	40.1	10.0	39.7	41.9
1956	86.3	78.9	95.8	40.0	36.9	44.5	39.9	10.9	42.8	41.6
1959	84.5	75.5	95.4	34.2	37.2	41.9	41.3	10.2	44.0	43.3
1962	82.8	73.8	94.9	30.3	38.0	43.4	42.4	9.9	45.9	44.7
1965	81.5	72.3	94.5	27.9	39.3	44.1	44.4	10.0	48.2	47.0
1968	81.2	73.0	94.0	27.3	41.6	48.6	46.8	9.6	51.2	49.8
1970	80.6	73.4	93.4	26.8	43.4	51.3	48.6	9.7	53.8	52.0
1973	79.5	74.5	91.8	22.8	44.7	55.0	49.9	8.9	56.2	54.3

[a] Defined as "percent of noninstitutional population in the labor force."

Source: Computed from U.S. Departments of Labor and H.E.W., *Manpower Report of the President* (1974), pp. 254–255. This data is from the Current Population Survey, a series which has somewhat different statistics than the decennial censuses for the years involved.

cades, there was a major *decline* in that of men. Until the late 1960s, the decline in the male rate was at least partly due to the fact that men went to school longer, but the fact that the rate for men aged between 25 and 64 also decreased, although less rapidly, indicates that this is really a more basic trend.* Indeed, this is the age group of men most likely to be in the labor force if employment is available to them. Since this is also the age group in which female labor force participation has expanded most rapidly, the ratio of women to men in the labor force, within that age bracket alone, has increased steadily from .37 in 1950 to .54 in 1973. This is almost exactly parallel to the changes in the ratio of women to men among labor force participants of all ages, suggesting that the trend among the "hard core" of the male labor force is representative of the overall situation.

The explanation for this seems to be that the economic expansion of the post-war period has been in occupational groups that were early sex-typed "female": clerical, service and sales jobs. Once these

* Ginzberg pointed out the salience of the "elongation of the educational cycle" in 1968, just before the labor force participation of males aged 16 to 24 began to rise again. He also suggests that part of the decline is due to the buildup of the armed forces in the postwar period, since this would reduce the number of men in the labor force. However, the data in Table 3 include persons in the armed forces, and yet the labor force participation of men clearly decreases quite persistently.[94] In any case, even if the decline in male participation can be "explained" by external factors, the change in the relationship between male and female rates is a highly significant one.

jobs were established as "women's work," employers had little motivation to hire men to fill them. Thus the demand for labor in the postwar period was largely a demand for *female* labor power and older and married women responded to the demand.[95]

Rough indicators of the demand for male and female labor power can be derived from the broad occupational groupings used by the Census bureau. Throughout the period since World War II, nearly half of all male workers were blue collar workers, while only about 15 percent of female workers were in this group. Similarly, about half of all female workers during this period were in clerical or service (other than private household) jobs, and only about 15 percent of all male workers were in these groups. Between 1958 and 1973, the proportion blue-collar workers formed of all gainfully employed persons dropped slightly, from 37 to 35 percent, while the proportion of clerical and service workers grew from 23 to 29 percent.[96]

Female labor force participation, for reasons that are not altogether clear, has been increasing faster than the number of available "women's jobs," so that the female labor market is "overcrowded."[97] The unemployment rate of women has been higher than that of men throughout the postwar period, and the gap was widening until the onset of the current crisis. In 1950 the unemployment rate of men was 5.1 percent and that of women 5.8 percent. In 1973, that of men was 4.1 percent and women's 6.0 percent.[98]

The accelerating integration of female labor power into paid production in the years since World War II has not left the family unaffected. Wives and mothers who work for pay have increasingly come to depend upon consumer goods and services in maintaining their families. While the much-vaunted affluence of this period has doubtless been disproportionately enjoyed by those women whose husbands earn enough to allow them to remain outside the labor force for most of their lives, clearly many mass-produced household "conveniences" have become widely available.

Even more striking in its effect on women's home responsibilities is the drop in the birth rate since 1957, and the tendency for women to stop bearing children at a much younger age than formerly.[99] The period of their lifetime devoted to maternity in relation to their life expectancy is rapidly shrinking. More than half of all American mothers have had their *last* child by the time they reach their thirtieth birthday. This is a very important change: the maternal role by which women have traditionally been defined now takes up less than a seventh of their average life-span, and presently the longest phase of the female life cycle is that which follows family completion.[100]

Thus as women's role in the paid labor force has come to take up a longer period of their lives, their family role has yielded more and more of its direct production functions to the sphere of commodity production, while the reproduction of children, the one commodity which this society still inevitably depends on women to produce, now takes up a much shorter period of their lives.

All of these changes, combined with the increase in female labor force participation, have made it somewhat easier for women to exist outside the institution of marriage. It is true that the family as an institution and women's work within it continues to be economically essential, as has been emphasized repeatedly here. Also, women continue to experience discrimination in wages, and this still makes it very difficult for them to survive without having the additional source of income that accompanies marriage. And yet, the situation of women is significantly different in this regard today from what it was in the early part of the century, when the vast majority of women who worked for pay left the labor force when they married and had children, never to return. The woman in a dual-worker family, even though her contribution to family income is much less than her husband's, can, simply because she has some independent income, more easily choose to strike out on her own than her grandmother, who was totally dependent on her husband's support.

Indeed, there has been a dramatic increase in the number of women who have established single person households in recent years.[101] The divorce rate (per thousand women under age 45) increased by a dramatic two-thirds between the mid-1950s and 1970, while the remarriage rate (per thousand divorced or widowed women under aged 55) rose by about one-third during the same period.[102] Clearly the family is experiencing real pressures as a result of women's dramatically increased role in paid labor, and the subordination of women to men is thus threatened.

Yet, the degree to which traditional sexually stratified family patterns have persisted is as remarkable as the signs of pressure on the family as an institution. Because women's paid employment continues to be so sex-typed, so thoroughly linked to their sexuality and to their family role in its cultural definition, their increased labor force participation has made only a slight difference in their family role. Sex-typing, based on the assumption that women's labor force role is "secondary," insures that they will earn less than men, which renders marriage to a man with greater earning power more attractive. It also tends to suppress women's consciousness of their actual power as wage workers.

It is not surprising, then, that in the years after World War II, the rapid increase in female labor force participation which represented such an unprecedented threat to the perpetuation of a family structure in which women have heavy unpaid responsibilities was accompanied by an intensification of the ideology that said that their "place" was in the home. This cultural current, which Betty Friedan called "the feminine mystique" in the 1960s,[103] was nothing new in the history of America, but the extent to which it diverged from the reality and the possibility of women's lives was much greater than at any previous point. Women were working outside of their homes, and they could choose not to live the "mystique" to a greater degree than ever before.

NOTES

1. Juliet Mitchell, *Women's Estate* (New York: Vintage Books, 1971), p. 139.
2. *Ibid.*, p. 124.
3. Margaret Benston, "The Political Economy of Women's Liberation," *Monthly Review*, 21 (1969), reprinted in Edith Hoshino Altbach, ed., *From Feminism to Liberation* (Cambridge, Mass.: Schenkman Publishing Co., 1971), p. 206.
4. U.S. Census Bureau, *Historical Statistics of the U.S.* (1960), p. 73.
5. For details see Stanley Lebergott, "Labor Force, Employment, and Unemployment, 1929–39: Estimating Methods," *Monthly Labor Review*, Vol. 67, No. 1 (July 1948), pp. 50–53.
6. R. R. Lutz and Louise Patterson, *Women Workers and Labor Supply* (New York: National Industrial Conference Board Studies, No. 220, 1936); U.S. Women's Bureau Bulletin No. 159, *Trends in the Employment of Women, 1928–1936* (1938).
7. *Historical Statistics, op. cit.*, pp. 71–72. Also see Chapter One of Valerie Kincade Oppenheimer, *The Female Labor Force in the U.S.* (Berkeley: University of California Population Monograph Series, No. 5, 1970) for an excellent discussion.
8. Edward Gross, "Plus Ca Change . . . The Sexual Structure of Occupations Over Time," *Social Problems*, Vol. 16, No. 2 (Fall 1968), pp. 198–208.
9. For discussion see Chapter 3 of Oppenheimer, *op. cit.* Data on sex differentials in pay are fragmentary. Some good collections of tables can be found in: U.S. Women's Bureau Bulletin No. 155, *Women in the Economy of the U.S.A.* (1937), pp. 46–76, and U.S. Women's Bureau Bulletin no. 294, *1969 Handbook on Women Workers*, pp. 132–138.
10. Robert W. Smuts, *Women and Work in America* (New York: Schocken Books, 1959), p. 91.
11. Computed from U.S. Census Bureau, *1970 Census of Population*, Vol. PC(2)-7A, p. 1.
12. Albert Szymanski, "Race, Sex, and the U.S. Working Class," *Social Problems*, Vol. 21, No. 4 (June 1974), pp. 706–725.
13. For a review of this literature, see Beth Niemi and Cynthia Lloyd, "Sex Differentials in Earnings and Unemployment Rates," *Feminist Studies*. Vol. 2, No. 2/3 (1975), pp. 194–201.
14. U.S. Women's Bureau, "Facts About Women's Absenteeism and

Labor Turnover" (August 1969), reprinted in *Woman in a Man-Made World: A Socio-Economic Handbook,* ed. Nona Glazer-Malbin and Helen Youngelson Waehrer (New York: Rand McNally and Co., 1972), pp. 265–271.

15. Evelyne Sullerot, *Woman, Society and Change* (New York: McGraw-Hill World University Library, 1971), p. 183.

16. Lutz and Patterson, *op. cit.*, p. 19.

17. For an excellent discussion of this process as it affected clerical workers, see Margery Davies, "Woman's Place is at the Typewriter: The Feminization of the Clerical Labor Force," *Radical America,* Vol. 8, No. 4 (August 1974).

18. Computed from U.S. Census Bureau, *15th Census of the U.S.*, 1930, *Unemployment,* Vol. II, pp. 280–281.

19. Computed from *ibid.*, p. 344 and *15th Census of the U.S.*, 1930, *Population,* Vol. V, p. 276.

20. For data on this phenomenon in the early 1930s see U.S. Women's Bureau Bulletin No. 113, *Employment Fluctuations and Unemployment of Women, Certain Indications From Various Sources,* 1928–31 (1933).

21. U.S. Women's Bureau, Bulletin No. 108, *The Effects of the Depression on Wage Earners' Families: A Second Survey of South Bend* (1936), p. 19.

22. Lutz and Patterson, *op. cit.*; Women's Bureau Bulletin No. 159, *op. cit.*; and Marguerite Thibert, "The Economic Depression and the Employment of Women," *International Labor Review,* Vol. XXVII, Nos. 4 and 5, (April and May 1933), pp. 443–470; 620-630.

23. Lutz and Patterson, *op. cit.*; Women's Bureau Bulletin No. 159, *op. cit.*; Also see William H. Chafe, *The American Woman: Her Changing Social, Economic and Political Role, 1920–1970.* (New York: Oxford University Press, 1972), p. 270.

24. U.S. Bureau of the Census, *Census of Partial Employment, Unemployment and Occupations,* 1937; Vol. I, p. 17, has the data from the first voluntary registration enumeration; Vol. IV, p. 9, has those for the enumerative check census. Reasons for the official rejection of the 1937 Census are mentioned in Lebergott, *op. cit.*, p. 52.

25. For details, see Lebergott, *op. cit.*

26. All statistics in this paragraph are from U.S. Census Bureau, *16th Census of the U.S.*, 1940, *Population,* Vol. III, p. 10.

27. *Historical Statistics, op. cit.*, p. 71.

28. See for examples the case studies in: Ruth S. Cavan and Katherine H. Ranck, *The Family and the Depression: A Study of One Hundred Chicago Families* (Chicago: University of Chicago Press, 1938); Mirra Komarovsky, *The Unemployed Man and His Family: The Effect of Unemployment upon the Status of the Man in Fifty-nine Families* (New York: The Dryden Press, Inc., 1940).

29. Data on this point are scattered. Figures from a Pennsylvania employment office show that the proportion of women seeking jobs as service workers and in sales occupations in 1936 was substantially larger than the proportion of women in those occupational groups in 1930. See U.S. Women's Bureau Bulletin No. 155, *op. cit.*, p. 37. Another interesting study with data on downward mobility is: Pennsylvania Department of Labor and Industry, Bureau of Women and Children, *Women Workers After A Plant Shutdown* (Special Bulletin No. 36, Harrisburg, 1933). For discussion of the upgrading of educational requirements of teachers and nurses which displaced women into occupations of lower status see Smuts, *op. cit.*, pp. 103–4.

30. Gross, *op. cit.*

31. Caroline Bird, *The Invisible Scar* (New York: David McKay Company, Inc. 1966), pp. 56–58.

32. Chafe, *op. cit.*, p. 108.

33. Oppenheimer, *op. cit.*, p. 44.

34. Smuts, *op. cit.*, p. 145.

35. Cavan and Ranck, *op. cit.*, p. 1.

36. Dixon Wecter, *The Age of the Great Depression, 1929–41* (Chicago: Quadrangle Books, 1948), p. 26; Winona L. Morgan, *The Family Meets the Depression: A Study of a Group of Highly Selected Families* (Minneapolis: The University of Minnesota Press, 1939), p. 22.

37. Cecile Tipton LaFollette, *A Study of the Problems of 652 Gainfully Employed Married Women Homemakers* (New York: Teachers College, Columbia University, Contributions to Education No. 619) 1934, pp. 95–96.

38. *Ibid.*, p. 102.

39. Wecter, *op. cit.*, p. 133.

40. Cavan and Ranck, *op. cit.*, p. 82, Wecter, *op. cit.*, p. 26.

41. Robert S. Lynd and Helen Merrill Lynd, *Middletown in Transition: A Study in Cultural Conflicts* (New York: Harcourt Brace Jovanovich, 1937).

42. Cavan and Ranck, *op. cit.*, p. 83.

43. *Ibid.*, p. 57.

44. *Ibid.*, p. 57.

45. *Ibid.*, p. 56.

46. *Ibid.*, p. 159.

47. Wecter, *op. cit.*, p. 29; Glen H. Elder, *Children of the Great Depression: Social Change in Life Experience* (Chicago: University of Chicago Press, 1974).

48. Linda Nasif Edwards, "School Retention of Teenage Males and Females over the Business Cycle," 1971, unpublished manuscript. Wecter, *op. cit.*, p. 29, argues that youth returned home during the 1930s.

49. *Historical Statistics, op. cit.*, p. 30.

50. Wecter, *op. cit.*, p. 199.

51. Paul C. Glick and Arthur J. Norton, "Perspectives on the Recent Upturn in Divorce and Remarriage," *Demography*, Vol. 10, No. 3 (August 1973), p. 305.

52. Studs Terkel, ed., *Hard Times: An Oral History of the Great Depression* (New York: Avon Books, 1970), p. 447.

53. Komarovsky, *op. cit.*, p. 74.

54. *Hard Times*, p. 191.

55. Cavan and Ranck, *op. cit.*, p. 86.

56. Morgan, *op. cit.*, p. 46.

57. *Ibid.*, p. 21.

58. Cavan and Ranck, *op. cit.*, p. 86.

59. See Cavan and Ranck, *op. cit.*, Komarovsky, *op. cit.*, and Robert Cooley Angell, *The Family Encounters the Depression* (Charles Scribner's Sons, 1936).

60. *Middletown in Transition*, p. 146.

61. Wecter, *op. cit.*, p. 198.

62. *Historical Statistics*, p. 23.

63. Komarovsky, *op. cit.*, p. 130.

64. *Hard Times*, p. 229.

65. *Ibid.*, p. 248.

66. *Ibid.*, p. 248; also see Gladys L. Palmer and Andria Taylor Hourwich, *A Scrapbook of the American Labor Movement* (New York: Affiliated Summer Schools for Women Workers in Industry, 1931–32), passim.
67. Tillie Olsen, *Yonnondio: From the Thirties* (Delacorte Press/Seymour Lawrence, 1974), p. 81.
68. Angell, *op. cit.*, pp. 124–125.
69. *Hard Times*, p. 127.
70. Elder, *op. cit.*, pp. 214–215.
71. Glick and Norton, *op. cit.*, p. 305.
72. International Labor Office, *The War and Women's Employment: The Experience of the United Kingdom and the United States* (Montreal, 1946), p. 212.
73. See Women's Bureau Bulletin No. 209, *Women Workers in Ten War Production Areas and their Postwar Employment Plans* (1946).
74. Wecter, *op. cit.*, p. 130.
75. See Women's Bureau Special Bulletin No. 20, *Changes in Women's Employment During the War* (1944) for discussion.
76. U.S. Women's Bureau Bulletin No. 211, *Employment of Women in the Early Postwar Period, with Background of Prewar and War Data* (1946), pp. 7, 10.
77. U.S. Women's Bureau Special Bulletin No. 13, *Part-Time Employment of Women in Wartime* (June 1943).
78. U.S. Women's Bureau Special Bulletin No. 14, *When You Hire Women* (1944), p. 18.
79. Richard Polenberg, *War and Society: The United States, 1941–1945.* (Philadelphia: J. B. Lippincott Co., 1972), pp. 12–13.
80. International Labour Office, *op. cit.*, p. 214.
81. US Women's Bureau Special Bulletin No. 18, *A Preview As To Women Workers in Transition From War to Peace* (1944), p. 13.
82. Chafe, *op. cit.*, pp. 138–139.
83. US Women's Bureau Special Bulletin No. 9, *Safety Caps for Women Machine Operators*, supplementary folder.
84. *Fortune*, Vol. 27, No. 2 (February 1943), p. 37.
85. "Girl Pilots: Air Force Trains Them at Avenger Field, Texas," *Life*, Vol. 15, No. 3 (July 19, 1943), pp. 75–76.
86. Josephine von Miklos, *I Took A War Job* (New York: Simon and Schuster, 1943), pp. 188–189.
87. U.S. Women's Bureau Bulletin No. 211, p. 2.
88. Sheila Tobias and Lisa Anderson, "What Really Happened to Rosie the Riveter? Demobilization and the Female Labor Force, 1944–47," MSS Modular Publications, Inc. (New York: Module 9, 1974), p. 9.
89. J. E. Trey, "Women in the War Economy—World War II," *Review of Radical Political Economics*, Vol. 4 (July 1972), p. 47.
90. U.S. Women's Bureau Bulletin No. 209, p. 4.
91. U.S. Women's Bureau Bulletin No. 211, p. 8.
92. Elizabeth Hawes, "Woman War Worker: A Case History," *New York Times Magazine* (December 26, 1943), p. 21.
93. *Historical Statistics*, pp. 71–72; *1970 Census of Population*, pp. 68–69.
94. Eli Ginzburg, "Paycheck and Apron—Revolution in Womanpower," *Industrial Relations: A Journal of Economy and Society*, Vol. 7, No. 3 (May 1968), p. 196.
95. Oppenheimer, *op. cit.*, pp. 97, 102.

96. U.S. Departments of H.E.W. and Labor, *Manpower Report of the President* (1974), p. 268.

97. See Barbara Bergmann, "Labor Turnover, Segmentation, and Rates of Unemployment: A Simulation-Theoretic Approach," University of Maryland Project on the Economics of Discrimination, mimeo, August 1973.

98. A full set of data on this topic can be found in the table in Beth Niemi and Cynthia Lloyd, "Sex Differentials in Earnings and Unemployment Rates," *Feminist Studies*, Vol. 2, No. 2/3 (1975), pp. 194–201.

99. Ginzberg, *op. cit.*, p. 198.

100. Evelyne Sullerot, *Woman, Society, and Change* (McGraw-Hill World University Library, 1971), pp. 74–75.

101. Frances E. Kobrin, "Women and a Room of One's Own: Sex Differences in Living Arrangements, 1940–1970," unpublished paper, presented at the Berkshire Conference on Women's History, Cambridge, Mass., 1974.

102. Glick and Norton, *op. cit.*

103. Betty Friedan, *The Feminine Mystique* (New York: Dell Books, 1963).

23

The Kindred of Viola Jackson

Residence and Family Organization of an Urban Black American Family

■

CAROL B. STACK

Black women today are much more likely than white women to live in husbandless households; and black children more often grow up without fathers at home, even when compared with whites at similar income levels. In his controversial "The Negro-American Family: The Case for National Action" (1965), Daniel Moynihan considered such arrangements a "tangle of pathology" underlying social problems such as black unemployment. Carol B. Stack, an anthropologist, disputes his assertions by rejecting the use of "household" as the meaningful unit in lower-class urban black family life and offering an alternative perspective. She focuses on the kinship network, a family system which links several households and operates in crisis situations. Her essay suggests the importance of understanding the family and kinship context in order to compare black and white women's history.

INTRODUCTION

Concepts can become so widely accepted and seem so obvious that they block the way to further understanding. Descriptions of black American domestic life (Frazier 1939; Drake and Cayton 1945; Abrahams 1964; Moynihan 1965; Rainwater 1966a) are almost always couched in terms of the nuclear family and in terms of the fashionable notion of a matrifocal complex. But in many societies the nuclear family is not always a unit of domestic cooperation, and the "universal functions" of family life can be provided by other social units (Spiro 1954; Gough 1959; Levy and Fallers 1959; Reiss 1965). And matrifocal thinking, while it may bring out the importance of women in family life, fails to account for the great variety of domestic strategies one can find on the scene in urban black America. The following study suggests that if we shed concepts such as matrifocality we can see that black Americans have evolved a repertoire of domestic units that serve as flexible adaptive strategies for coping with the everyday human demands of ghetto life.

In the fall of 1966 I began to investigate black family organization in midwestern cities. I concentrated upon one domestic family unit —the household of Viola and Leo Jackson—and their network of kinsmen, which proved to number over 100 persons. My immediate aim was to discover when and why each of these people had changed residence, and what kind of domestic unit they joined during the half-century since they had begun moving north from Arkansas.

The data show that during the process of migration and the adjustment of individuals to urban living, clusters of kin align together for various domestic purposes. It soon became clear that matrifocal thinking provided little insight into the organization of domestic units of cooperation, for example, those groups of kin and non-kin which carry out domestic functions but do not always reside together (Bender 1967). In certain situations such as the death or desertion of a parent, the loss of a job, or in the process of migration it was found that an individual almost always changed residence. But matrifocality proved to be a poor predictor of the kind of domestic unit the individual might subsequently enter. Among Mrs. Jackson's kin one can find various assortments of adults and children cooperating in domestic units: children living with relatives other than their parents, and also clusters of kin (often involving the father) who do not reside together but who provide some of the domestic functions for a mother-and-child unit in another location. Not only does matrifocal thinking fail here, but also little or nothing in the current writing on black American family life helps deal with questions such as the following that arise when we examine Mrs. Jackson's kin: Which relatives can a person expect will help him? Which relatives will care for parentless or abandoned children? And who will look after the ill and elderly? I will discuss these questions, and the challenge that Mrs. Jackson's kin and their lifeways put to our powers of explanation. First, however, I will deal briefly with the nature of matrifocal thinking.

THE MATRIFOCAL COMPLEX

Matrifocality has become a popular replacement for the discarded nineteenth-century concept of matriarchy. Some would argue that matrifocality is more sophisticated, but I suggest that it is no more useful than matriarchy for characterizing urban Negro households.

When the rules for reckoning kinship are not explicit, then it is difficult to determine the basis upon which households are formed. As so, as M. G. Smith (1962b:7) has pointed out, by necessity the anthropologist then must rely on data on household composition. It is in this context that the term "matrifocality" is most widely used. However, it also has been used to refer to at least three units of information: (1) the composition of a household, (2) the type of kinship bond linking its members, and (3) the relationship between males and females in the household. In fact, matrifocality tells us little about the actual composition of the household, and the relational link upon which the household is formed. Schneider (1961) points out that in the past the terms "matrifocal marriage" and "matriliny" were used interchangeably (see Bachofen 1861) and that the matriarchal complex referred to a household which did not include the husband or father. Both González (1965) and Smith (1962b) use matrifocality to refer to the composition of households. These and similar formulations ignore the developmental history of domestic groups (Goody 1958). In addition, they supply no information on the age and circumstances in which individuals join households, the alternatives open to them, the relational links they have with other members, or who the members are. *Matrifocality is not a residence rule, and in particular, it is not a rule for post-marital residence.* Residence, one of the dynamics of social organization, can be understood only if the basis for the active formation of households is known.

A further complication is that notions such as matrifocality, maternal family (King 1945), and matriarchy inadvertently are associated with unilineal descent. It was Bachofen's contention (1861) that matriliny (descent through women) and matriarchy (rule by women) were but two aspects of the same institution (Schneider 1961; Lowie 1947). This claim had to be discarded when observers failed to find any generalized authority of women over men in matrilineal societies. This controversy is well known. What is less widely appreciated is that there is a close parallel between matriarchal and matrifocal thinking, in that both imply descent through women. For example, M. G. Smith (1962b) defines Caribbean matrifocal households as ones which are composed of blood-related women plus all their unmarried children. González (1965:1542) defines consanguineal households in terms of the type of kinship bond linking adult men and women in the households such that no two members are bound together in an affinal relationship. She suggests that consanguineal households may also be matrifocal (1965:1548) and that there is evidence that consanguineal households exist among lower class Negro American groups (DuBois 1908; Frazier

1939; King 1945). The tentative classification that emerges from studies of black American households as consanguineal or as both consanguineal and matrifocal is confusing. In this confusion the use of the notion of matrifocality roughly coincides with Schneider's (1961:3) definition of matrilineal descent units in which he states that the "individual's initial relationship is to his mother and through her to other kinsmen, both male and female, but continuing only through females." *Matrifocality is not necessarily a correlate of matrilineal descent, nor does it imply a structure for linking families in the same community.*

The term "matrifocality" may have value as an indication of the woman's role within the domestic group, but it tells us little about authority, decision-making, and male-female relationships within the household, among extended kin, and in the community. Used in this context to refer to a dominant female role, and as a designate of residence classification, reference to the matrifocal household may lead to confusion between residence and role behavior. Analysis of role relationships and interactional patterns which is limited to their classification as matrifocal is at best uninteresting. The role organization of urban Negro households exists in a dynamic system which can be illustrated by the life histories of individuals in households as they adapt to the urban environment. This adaptation comes out dramatically when one examines Viola Jackson's kin and their many ways of forming a domestic unit.

Frequently, discussions of matrifocality and consanguineal households ignore crucial aspects of family organization. Some of the matrifocal thinkers seem to assume that children derive nothing of sociological importance from their father, that households are equivalent to the nuclear family, and that resident husband-fathers are marginal members of their own homes (M. G. Smith 1957b). A look at Viola Jackson's kindred raises doubts about many of these assumptions.

URBAN FAMILY ORGANIZATION

Clusters of Kin

The past fifty years have witnessed a massive migration of rural, southern blacks to urban centers in the United States. The kindred of Viola Jackson are a part of this movement. Ninety-six of them left the South between 1916 and 1967. Some of them first moved from rural Arkansas to live and work harvesting fruit in areas around

Grand Rapids and Benton Harbor, Michigan, and Racine, Wisconsin; eventually they settled in the urban North. Two major patterns emerge from their life histories: (1) relatives tend to cluster in the same areas during similar periods; and (2) the most frequent and consistent alignment and cooperation appears to occur between siblings.

During the process of moving, Viola Jackson's kin maintained communication with relatives in the South. They frequently moved back to the South for short periods, or from Chicago and other midwestern cities to fruit harvesting areas on a seasonal basis. Therefore it is difficult to separate the data in terms of phases such as "migration" and subsequent "urban adaptation." During some seasons bus loads of rural blacks were brought to the North to harvest fruit. Many families worked their way back South only to repeat the process in order to avoid the poverty and unemployment there. This circulatory migration mainly involved the younger families and individuals.

Frequently, migrant workers follow their relatives and large urban neighborhoods reflect the geographical boundaries of the hinterland. Once these facts are established it is important to find out who made the original move, his age at the time of the move, which relatives joined one another to form households, and the context of each move.

Between 1916 and 1967 Mrs. Jackson's kin lived in five states, and groups of 10 to 15 individuals tended to cluster in the same areas during the same time periods. An example of this can be seen in the Table, which shows where Viola's mother and siblings were living during that time period.

The basis for the active formation of households during migration and urban settlement can only be understood if material developing out of life histories is related to the realities of kinship and non-kinship factors. During this period of migratory wage labor in the young adult's life, the data show that the strongest alignment is of cooperation and mutual aid among siblings of both sexes (after the age of thirteen). Siblings left the South together, or shortly followed one another, for seasonal jobs. They often lived together in the North with their dependents and spouses, or lived near one another, providing mutual aid such as cooking and child care.

Domestic Arrangements

Case 1 In 1945 *C* left her husband and daughter in the South with his parents and moved to Racine, Wisconsin, to harvest fruit. At the

TABLE
Residence and Kin Clusters

Area and Time Period	Ego's Mother (Magnolia)	Ego (Viola)	B	Z	Z	Z	B
Arkansas 1916–1917	X	X	X				
Arkansas 1928–1944	X	X		X	X	X	X
Blythe, Calif. 1927–1928	X	X	X				
Grand Rapids, Mich. 1944–1946			X		X		
Racine, Wisc. 1947–1948		X		X			X
Benton Harbor, Mich. 1946–1948		X	X	X			X
Decatur, Ark. 1948–1952	X	X			X		X
Chicago, Ill. 1950–1953				X			
Champaign, Ill. 1952–1954	X	X	X				
Gary, Ind. 1954–1955			X				
Champaign, Ill. 1955–1967	X	X	X		X	X	X
Chicago Heights, Ill. 1959–1967				X			
Chicago, Ill. 1965–1967			X				

same time *C*'s brother's wife died leaving him, *J*, with two young sons. *J* decided to move north and join *C* in Racine. He and his two sons took a bus to Racine where he got a job in a catsup factory. The company furnished trailers which *C* and *J* placed next to each other. *C* cooked for *J* and his two sons and cared for the children. They were cooperating as a single domestic unit. This situation continued for about a year and a half and then they all returned to the South.

Case 2 By 1946 Viola and Leo had four children and Leo was picking cotton. They were anxious to leave the South in order to find better wages and living conditions. Viola, Leo, and their children joined a bus load of people and moved to join Viola's brother, *L*, in Benton Harbor, Michigan. In Benton Harbor all the adults and the older children worked harvesting fruit. At the same time Leo's twin brother and Viola's brother, *J*, and his two sons moved to Benton Harbor. Leo's twin brother moved into Viola's and Leo's household. *J* and his sons moved into the household of *J*'s brother, *L*, and *L*'s wife.

Case 3 In 1948 *C* decided to move north again. This time she took her daughter with her. She moved to Benton Harbor where Viola and her family, their two brothers, *L* and *J*, and Leo's twin brother were all living. *C* and *J* and their children began cooperating as a single domestic unit as they had in Racine.

The pattern described above of cooperation and mutual aid among siblings becomes even more apparent as these individuals move to urban areas. Sibling alignment in the urban context will be discussed in the next section.

SIBLING ALIGNMENT AND KIN COOPERATION IN URBAN AREAS

Understanding residence and family organization for people whose economic situation is constantly changing, and who therefore frequently change households, is not easy. Aside from the common observations of household composition based upon where people sleep, there are many other important patterns to be observed, such as which situations lead to a change in residence, which adults share households, and with which adult relatives are children frequently living.

One pattern, a continuation of a pattern formed during the early stages of migratory labor, is the cooperative alignment of siblings. By the time the majority of Viola Jackson's relatives had established permanent residence and jobs in the North there were numerous examples of siblings forming co-residential and/or domestic units of cooperation. These sibling-based units, apparently motivated by situations such as death, sickness, desertion, abandonment, and unemployment, most often focused around the need for child-care arrangements. Here are two examples:

1. Sister/Brother

In 1956 Viola and Leo were living in Champaign, Illinois. Viola's brother, *J*, took the train from the South to visit them. After the visit he decided to move to Champaign with his two sons and look for work. *J* rented a house near Viola's and got a construction job. When he brought his sons to Champaign Viola cooked for them and cared for them during the day.

2. Sister/Sister

In 1959 Viola's sister, *E,* was suffering from a nervous breakdown. *E*'s husband took their four youngest children to his mother in Arkansas. *E*'s sister, *C,* was living in Chicago and she cared for *E*'s oldest daughter. After *E*'s husband deserted her, *E*'s twin sister, *M,* moved into *E*'s house. The household was composed of *E,* her oldest daughter who had been in Chicago, *M,* and *M*'s two youngest daughters.

These alignments may be largely attributed to adaptation to urban socioeconomic conditions. One such urban pattern is a minimum of emphasis on the inheritance of property. For obvious social and economic reasons, poor and highly mobile urban apartment dwellers do not develop strong ties to a homestead or a particular piece of land, even though they may express strong regional and even neighborhood loyalty or identification. This contrasts with the rural South and with Young's and Willmott's (1957) observations that apartments in Bethnal Green were kept in the family. The high frequency of moving from one apartment to another in economically depressed urban areas is related to the degree of overcrowding, the shortage of apartments, urban renewal, and the changing employment situation. Another situation causing these alignments to form is the arrival of a new migrant to the urban area wherein he lives with siblings. With time, if he successfully establishes himself in a job in the urban area he may move out of his sibling's household.

CRISIS SITUATIONS AND THE RESIDENCE OF CHILDREN

It has already been pointed out that migration, unemployment, sickness, and desertion by necessity often lead to a change in residence. Most often these changes are closely related to the need for child-care arrangements. The choices and expectations involved in placing children in a relative's home largely focus around which adult female relatives are available. In selecting the specific relative, the following criteria are considered: the geographical locations of these adult female relatives; their source of financial support, their age, their marital status, the composition of their household, and the ability of the people making the decision to get along with these females. At the same time, due to the flexibility and mobility of urban individuals, decisions frequently center around the relational link the child has with female members of a particular household. This means that the distance and location of a household, for example, are not a great deterrent, and that in fact the economic, distance, and other decisions are made after the kin criteria are met.

Children in the extended kin network of Viola Jackson frequently live with relatives other than their biological parents. The child-female links which most often are the basis of new or expanded households are clearly those links with close adult females such as the child's mother, mother's mother, mother's sister, mother's brother's wife, father's mother, father's sister, father's brother's wife.

Here are some examples.

RELATIONAL LINK	DOMESTIC UNIT
Mother	Viola's brother married his first wife when he was sixteen. When *she* left him, she kept her daughter.
Mother's mother	Viola's sister, *M*, never was able to care for her children. In between husbands, her mother kept her two oldest children, and after *M*'s death, her mother kept all three of the children. Her brother offered to keep the oldest girl.
Mother's mother	Viola's daughter (age 20) was living at home and gave birth to a son. The daughter and her son remained in the Jackson household. The daughter expressed the desire to set up a separate household.
Mother's sister	*M* moved to Chicago into her sister's household. The household consisted of the two sisters and four of their children.
Father's mother	Viola's sister, *E*, had four daughters and one son. When *E* was suffering from a nervous breakdown her husband took three daughters and his son to live with his mother in Arkansas. After his wife's death he also took the oldest daughter to his mother's household in Arkansas.
Father's mother	When Viola's younger sister, *C*, left her husband in order to harvest fruit in Wisconsin she left her two daughters with his mother in Arkansas.
Father's sister	When Viola's brother's wife died, he decided to raise his two sons himself. He kept the two boys

and never remarried. His residence has consistently been close to one or another of his sisters who have fed and cared for his two sons.

These examples do indeed indicate the important role of the black female. But the difference between matrifocal thinking and thinking about household composition in terms of where children live is that the latter can bring to light the dynamics of household formation, and the criteria, rules, and decisions that the process entails.

The summaries of the social context in which children changed households indicates which adult female relatives are frequently called upon for service. The alignment and cooperation between siblings, such as mother's sister and father's sister, has already been noted. This has been underestimated by workers who select the grandmother household (especially mother's mother) as the only significant domestic unit. It must be noted that the crucial role which paternal as well as maternal grandmothers assume in socialization is a frequent, but definitely not a unique, alternative.

Since social scientists have stressed the existence of female-centered, woman-headed, matrifocal black families, it is of particular interest to look at the formation of grandmother households in Viola's kin. Here is a summary of the households in which Viola's mother, Magnolia, has lived.

MAGNOLIA

AGE	CONTEXT OF DOMESTIC UNIT OR HOUSEHOLD
60	In 1958 Magnolia's second husband died and she was left alone with her daughter's (*M*) two oldest children. Viola sent her two oldest sons to care for Magnolia and the two children.
62	In 1960 Magnolia moved to Champaign and joined the household of her twin daughters, *E* and *M*, bringing *M*'s children with her.
65	After *E*'s death, Magnolia and her daughter moved to Danville, Illinois, with *M*'s two children, whom Magnolia raised in the South, and *M*'s two youngest children.
67	After *M*'s death, Magnolia joined her daughter Viola's household for a short time.
67	Soon afterward, Viola and her husband rented a nearby house for Magnolia and the four grandchildren. Magnolia is on welfare, cares for the four children, and constantly receives help from the Jacksons and from her children living in Chicago.

When a grandmother household is characterized as matrifocal we get little insight into the dynamics of its formation. At best, it suggests a mother hen who gathers her chicks about her. After age sixty, Magnolia's residence was determined by her children, who decided to bring her to the urban North to care for her. Her move North was prompted by her children's concern for her health and well-being.

We find that Magnolia has frequently shared households with her children and grandchildren. In fact, she has consistently moved to join her daughters' households to be cared for, or to care for her grandchildren. Instead of simply gathering her flock, each move and new household in which Magnolia lived after age sixty was formed on a different basis.

By the time Magnolia was elderly she was living in the urban North in a grandmother household caring for her grandchildren. This was the result of the illness and subsequent death of one of her daughters. At this time a house was rented and maintained for Magnolia and the four grandchildren by Viola and her husband, Leo. The rented house was one block from Viola's home and the two households functioned primarily as a single domestic unit of cooperation. The cluster of relatives consisted of four generations: Magnolia, the four grandchildren, Viola and Leo Jackson, ten of their children, and their grandchild, the son of Viola Jackson's oldest daughter.

This four-generational kin cluster is not a co-residential unit, but a domestic unit of cooperation. The main source of financial support consisted of Leo's seasonal construction work, welfare payments to both Magnolia and Viola's daughter (for her son), and the part-time jobs of some of the teenage children. These individuals used Viola's house as home base where they shared the evening meal, cared for all the small children, and exchanged special skills and services. Frequently, Viola's brother (whose wife had died) ate with the group and participated in the exchange of money, food, care for the sick, and household duties. The exchange of clothes, appliances, and services in crisis situations extended beyond this kin cluster to relatives in Chicago and St. Louis. This group is an example of an urban kinship based domestic unit which formed to handle the basic family functions.

CONCLUDING REMARKS

The examples from the preceding sections support the suggestion that domestic functions are carried out for urban blacks by clusters of kin who may or may not reside together. Individuals who are members of households and domestic units of cooperation align to provide the basic functions often attributed to nuclear family units. The flexibility of the blacks' adaptation to the daily social and economic problems of urban living is evidenced in these kinship-based units which form to handle the daily demands of urban life. In particular, new or expanded households and/or domestic units are created to care for children. The basis of these cooperative units is co-generational sibling alignment, the domestic cooperation of close adult females, and the exchange of goods and services between the male and female relatives of these females. To conclude, it is suggested that these households and domestic units provide the assurance that all the children will be cared for.

NOTES

ABRAHAMS, ROGER D.
1964 Deep down in the jungle . . . Negro narrative folklore from the streets of Philadelphia. Hatboro, Pa.: Folklore Associates.

BACHOFEN, J. J.
1861 Das Mutterrecht. Basel: Benno Schwabe.

BENDER, D. R.
1967 A refinement of the concept of household: families, co-residence, and domestic functions. American Anthropologist 69: 493–504.

DRAKE, ST. CLAIR, AND HORACE R. CAYTON
1945 Black metropolis, a study of Negro life in a northern city. New York: Harcourt, Brace.

DUBOIS, W. E. B.
1908 The Negro family. Atlanta: Atlanta University Press.

FRAZIER, E. FRANKLIN
1939 The Negro family in the United States. Chicago: University of Chicago Press. Revised and abridged edition 1948. New York: Dryden. Paperback edition of 1948 edition 1966, Chicago: University of Chicago Press.

GONZÁLEZ, NANCIE L.
1965 The consanguineal household and matrifocality. American Anthropologist 67: 1541–49.

GOODY, JACK, ED.
1958 The developmental cycle in domestic groups. Cambridge Papers in Social Anthropology No. 1. London: Cambridge University Press.

GOUGH, KATHLEEN
1959 The Nayars and the definition of marriage. Journal of the Royal Anthropological Institute of Great Britain and Ireland 89: 23–34.

KING, CHARLES E.
1945 The Negro maternal family: a product of an economic and a cultural system. Social Forces 24: 100–04.

LEVY, M. J., JR., AND LLOYD A. FALLERS
1959 The family: some comparative considerations. American Anthropologist 61: 647–51.
LOWIE, ROBERT H.
1947 Primitive society. New York: Boni and Liveright.
MOYNIHAN, DANIEL PATRICK
1965 The Negro family: the case for national action. Washington, D.C.: Government Printing Office. Prepared for the Office of Policy Planning and Research of the Department of Labor.
RAINWATER, LEE
1966a Crucible of identity: the Negro lower-class family. Daedalus 95 (2): 172–216.
REISS, I. L.
1965 The universality of the family: a conceptual analysis. Journal of Marriage and the Family 27:443–53.
SMITH, M. G.
1957b Introduction. *In* My mother who fathered me, Edith Clarke. London: George Allen and Unwin.
1962b West Indian family structure. Seattle: University of Washington Press.
SPIRO, MELFORD E.
1954 Is the family universal? American Anthropologist 56:839–46.

24

Feminism and the Contemporary Family

BARBARA EASTON

Before the recent development of social history, historians tended to see organized activity for women's rights as a strictly political phenomenon, originating in women's objection to their exclusion from public arenas such as education, employment, and electoral participation, or generated by the momentum of other social movements. More recently, historians have recognized that feminist protest arises from more deep-seated changes in women's lives. Using the latter approach, Barbara Easton analyzes the forms and motivations of feminism since the early nineteenth century and puts the current women's movement in historical perspective. Her premise, that the balance of power between the sexes (especially as manifest within the family) has not been static, leads her to place current feminism in a unique context.

MOST CONTEMPORARY American feminists see the nuclear family as patriarchal, based on male dominance and female subordination. Furthermore, feminists tend to see these family relations and the patriarchal system that they support as largely unchanging, impervious to political change and the rise and fall of social systems. Most feminist literature implies that patriarchy is static, by describing it as a uniform system, failing to point to any change within it. Some feminists make this point explicit by arguing that men have kept the realm of family life out of the arena of social struggle, acting upon a tacit agreement that whatever conflicts they engage in among themselves shall not be allowed to impinge upon the power of each man over his wife and children. If patriarchy were historically constant, then the task of feminism, the destruction of patriarchy, would also be fundamentally unchanging. Feminists might differ over the strategy to be employed in attacking patriarchy, or over the form that social relations should take after a feminist revolution, but these would be differences in approach rather than in fundamental aim.

But in fact the aims of feminism have shifted quite markedly, at least in the United States. The American women's movement of the nineteenth and early twentieth centuries took not the patriarchal family but the exclusion of women from public life as its main target. In this period of American feminism, women's oppression in the family was a subordinate theme of feminist discussion, and the term patriarchy was used little if at all. The critique of family relations has moved to the center of feminism only in the contemporary women's movement, in the 1960s and 1970s. Surely such a shift must point to some change in the structures that oppress women. Not that each new target necessarily represents what at the time constitutes the center of male power over women. In fact, I will argue, at each stage the women's movement has wisely chosen to attack the weakest, not the strongest, area of male dominance. The point is that the form of feminist activity, and the theoretical formulations accompanying that activity, have shifted in response to women's changing situation. When, in the mid-nineteenth century, the growth of capitalism and the emergence of an ideology of equality of rights and opportunity made it difficult to defend the exclusion of particular groups from the public realm, feminists demanded equal rights for women in public life. Now, as women's increased political and legal rights and their entry into the labor force begin to undermine traditional male power in the family, the critique of patriarchy comes to the fore.*

The central purpose of this article is to argue that the twentieth-century feminist attack on patriarchy has accompanied an actual weakening of patriarchy, and the emergence of new forms of male dominance. We do not yet have a name for these new forms, nor do we understand very much about them, but it is necessary to begin trying to identify them. It is always the first task of a movement to attack oppressive institutions that are in decline. To the extent that they are anachronistic they can be shown to be illegitimate; it is possible to turn public sentiment against them with relative ease. But then it is necessary to begin to identify and attack forms of social control that are on the rise.

* This article is about the history of white women and the white family in the United States. The discussion of the relationship of black women and the black family to feminism would require another article. I use the term "patriarchy" to mean male dominance and female dependence, based on men's ownership of property, ability to earn money, and legal rights over women. In this sense the American slave family was not patriarchal. The fact that since emancipation large numbers of black women have routinely worked outside the home places the issue of patriarchy in a different light in black than in white families. Because of these and other differences, it is necessary to discuss the histories of black and white women in the United States separately. Because American feminism has been shaped largely by white women, I restrict my discussion to their history.

In the twentieth century, the virtually absolute economic and legal power that men once held over their families has been eroded; as men lose these formal rights it becomes easier to attack the ideas of female inferiority and the division of labor between the sexes that were shaped by patriarchy. But as men lose formal, socially recognized forms of control over women, they are likely, consciously or unconsciously, to turn to forms that are more subtle or less legitimate. If the women's movement and the left cannot address the new problems that women face in a post-patriarchal period, we will be in the position of those sections of the left that continue to describe capitalism as it appeared in the late nineteenth century, and so lose their audience and their relevance to popular concerns. One way to begin the task of identifying new forms of male dominance is to ask how feminist concerns have shifted in the past, and to look at the present women's movement with an eye to the places where significant concerns are not explained by present theory.

Nineteenth-Century Feminism

The feminists of the mid-nineteenth century regarded the winning of equal rights for women as their central task. The first women's rights convention, held in Seneca Falls, New York, in 1848, issued a list of women's grievances that reflected this perspective. Women's disfranchisement was placed at the top of the list, in spite of some trepidation; the demand for suffrage had nearly been voted down as opponents argued that such a demand was too controversial and would discredit the movement. This grievance was followed by a list of women's legal and political disabilities: women's obligation to obey laws that they had no part in framing, the refusal of the courts to recognize the interests of married women apart from their husbands', the legal right of husbands to their wives' property and earnings, and women's legal disadvantages in case of divorce. Social issues such as women's exclusion from colleges and second-class status in the church, and the separate standards of morality for men and women, were lower on the list. At no point did the statement question marriage itself, the nuclear family, or the primary responsibility of women for children.[1]

In the years between Seneca Falls and the outbreak of the Civil War, women's rights conventions were held almost every year to discuss women's position, arrive at demands, and formulate strategies for achieving those demands. The protest against the inequality of power between men and women, and the demand for female autonomy, were at the heart of these discussions. Many feminists understood that the roots of this power imbalance and of women's dependence lay in the family, but the family itself was never the central issue for early feminism that it is for the contemporary women's movement. In the movement of the mid-nineteenth century, the topics of marriage and the family were more likely to come up in the context of discussions of women's legal rights or public role than to be raised as issues in themselves. For instance, Elizabeth Cady Stanton in her autobiography described a women's rights convention held in 1861 at which she argued that the movement should protest the legal biases against women in divorce proceedings. Wendell Phillips, an abolitionist who usually supported women's rights, opposed her motion. (Men who were sympathetic to feminism often attended these meetings.) Phillips proposed that the question of divorce be dropped, arguing that "as marriage concerned man and woman alike . . . woman had no special ground for complaint."

Susan B. Anthony rose to support Stanton's motion. She challenged the idea that men and women were equal in marriage:

> Marriage has always been a one-sided affair, resting most unequally upon the sexes. By it man gains all; woman loses all; tyrant law and lust reign supreme with him; meek submission and ready obedience alone befit her. Woman has never been consulted; her wish has never been taken into consideration as regards the terms of the marriage contract. By law, public sentiment, and religion . . . woman has never been thought of other than as a piece of property, to be disposed of at the will and pleasure of man.[2]

The early feminists could use strong language when speaking of women's role in marriage and family; a critique of Victorian marriage was a sub-theme of the feminist discussion of women's status. Many feminists pointed out that it was unhealthy for women's activities to be confined to the home. Antoinette Brown Blackwell pointed out that no one would consider urging that men stay at their places of work twenty-four hours a day, and that the importance of fresh air, exercise, and change of scene to mental and physical health was common knowledge. The high incidence of illness among women confined to their homes should be no surprise, she wrote.[3]

Other feminists, in discussing women's position in the family, emphasized the deleterious moral effects of women's subordination. Susan B. Anthony wrote that though women were much less given to drunkenness and sexual licentiousness than men, women suffered most from these evils. She pointed out that women had little protection against the violence of a drunken husband or the corruption of a man who visited prostitutes. By virtue of men's power over women's subsistence, Anthony wrote, they were able to dictate to women a moral code much higher than the code to which men themselves adhered. At the same time, men deprived women of the power to insist on a higher standard of behavior from men.[4] Elizabeth Cady Stanton wrote of the damage this did to female self-respect. Women, she wrote, were "stripped of all . . . virtue, dignity and nobility" by pervasive female inequality. She asked, "How can women endure our present marriage relations, by which woman's life, health and happiness are held so cheap, that she herself feels . . . no individuality of her own?"[5]

These early feminist discussions of marriage and family give us a picture of virtually unlimited male power; lucky women were treated well by their husbands, but the unlucky ones had little recourse. In 1848 Emily Collins described a woman she had known as a child whose husband whipped her "because she scolded."

She wrote,

> And pray, why should he not have chastised her? The laws made it his privilege—and the Bible, as interpreted, made it his duty. It is true, women repined at their hard lot; but it was thought to be fixed by a divine decree, for "The man shall rule over thee," and "Wives submit to your husbands," and "Wives, submit yourselves to your husbands as to the Lord," caused them to consider their fate inevitable.[6]

Though many early feminists condemned the subordination of women within marriage, no leader of the women's movement was willing to reject the institution of marriage itself. Many went out of their way to voice support for marriage, and for the sexual division of labor in the family, with women's responsibility for child rearing, and men's for economic support of the family. . . .

Nineteenth-century women were trapped in domesticity not only because the economy was not open to them as it was to men, but also because in the nineteenth century marriage meant childbirth which meant domesticity, whereas failing to marry meant a lonely life. It was virtually impossible for a woman to choose not to have children once she married, not only because birth control information was relatively unavailable, but also because everyone, including the woman herself, expected that once she married she would have children. A woman who did not have children was pitied, and was likely to regard herself as a failure. And in a society in which men took no responsibility for child care and there was no provision for child care outside the home, continual childbirth meant that motherhood was a full-time job. Childcare had always been mainly women's responsibility, but in previous centuries it had been only one among many female tasks. In the nineteenth century motherhood was women's work, their main role in society; few women were able to carve out satisfying lives that did not involve having children.

Nineteenth-century American women were trapped into subservience to men within the family not only because they were largely excluded from the economy and, once they married, absorbed by childbirth and child care, but also because the power that men held over women in this situation was reinforced by the law. In the nineteenth century married women possessed few legal rights, and virtually none in relation to their husbands. In the rare event of divorce, custody of children was ordinarily granted to the father. Not only in divorce but in marriage as well women's rights were severely restricted; any inheritance or earnings that a woman might bring to a marriage or accrue once married were legally considered the property of the husband.[7]

Circumvention of these codes required elaborate legal work. As long as women did not have the vote, it was difficult for them to challenge such laws successfully. In the second half of the nineteenth century some progress was made, in some states, in women's legal position; this was in part due to feminist protest, but probably was more the result of pressure from wealthy and powerful families. Such reforms were only the first step towards any real weakening of men's power in the family. Through the nineteenth century, few cracks appeared in the patriarchal structure of the American family. Feminists would have been foolish to challenge men's power in the family head on.

It was possible for nineteenth-century feminists to challenge the exclusion of women from the public arena. It was not too difficult to stretch the definition of the domestic role to include nurturant, humanitarian activity outside the home; women could teach in Sunday Schools, raise money for missionaries, and even engage in campaigns for temperance or other reforms without stepping too far outside the accepted female role. Some women stretched at least their own understanding of their role far enough to become involved in the abolitionist movement, and here they confronted the question of actual inequality in a society that proclaimed equality for all. Feminism first arose in the United States out of women's involvement in this movement, in part because abolitionist women began to extend their principles of human rights to themselves, and in part because in their activity on behalf of equal rights for blacks they were forced to confront their own lack of rights as women, especially the prohibitions against women engaging in public activity.[8]

While activity in the abolitionist movement helped to shape the outlook of the early women's movement, in a larger sense the early feminist focus on women's exclusion from the public arena was determined by the shape of American society in the mid-nineteenth century. The traditional restrictions on women's activity were by this time in contradiction with the norm of equal opportunity that was held to govern public life; this blatant contradiction impelled nineteenth-century feminists to demand for women the rights that were promised to men. In the seventeenth and eighteenth centuries a movement for female equality would not have arisen because the promise of equal rights was not held out in any arena, for either sex. Outside the family as well as within it, people expected to defer to their superiors and be deferred to by their inferiors. In the nineteenth century, in the oldest and most populated areas of the country, the same areas in which feminism arose first, the competitive relations of the market were replacing the deferential relations of the earlier, more agrarian and less commercial society, and the ideology of competitive individualism was replacing the older ideology of hierarchical, corporate order.

The family, however, remained exempt from these developments. In the context of a society rapidly moving away from traditionalism, the patriarchal restrictions on women's activities appeared increasingly anachronistic. It was possible for women to demand equality in the public arena for the same reason that it was possible for freed black males to demand the vote: a capitalist system that promised equality of opportunity to all was vulnerable to protest from groups excluded from these opportunities.

Gilman and the Early Critique of the Family

Over the second half of the nineteenth century, women gained confidence and some measure of power through their increasing activity in the public arena, not only in the feminist movement but also in the other reform and humanitarian movements of the time. It was on the basis of these gains that it began to be possible for a few women to raise the issue of power relations within the family. In the late nineteenth century Charlotte Perkins Gilman made an extended feminist analysis of the position of women in marriage and the family, criticizing sex roles for the first time without apologies. In *Women and Economics*, published in 1898, she described women's economic dependence upon men in marriage as the central problem facing women. Sexual attractiveness and childlike helplessness, Gilman wrote, were a woman's main assets in achieving marriage and the economic support that it brought; therefore women cultivated these qualities while their personal and intellectual growth were stunted. Gilman urged women to work outside the home, arguing that only economic independence could bring women a sense of integrity and true equality with men. She did not reject marriage or the family; she argued that in the long run they would be strengthened when women gained economic independence, for then women could marry without giving up the rest of their lives. But Gilman did believe that marriage would be tainted so long as within it men could buy sex with a promise of financial support.[9]

Gilman had a following within the women's movement, but the movement as a whole did not adopt her outlook or even consider her ideas to any great extent. This was partly because by the early twentieth century the struggle for suffrage was claiming most of the energies of the women's movement, and prospects of success were improving. A critique of marriage and the family would have been not only a distraction from that struggle but a real threat; raising such controversial issues might have lost the women's movement male support that it needed in order to win electoral victories.

Gilman's ideas were ignored primarily because for most women the situation that feminists had faced at mid-century still obtained. Opportunities for work outside the home, if slightly expanded by this time, were still limited, and women's power inside the home was still negligible. The main checks on men's power over women were men's own moral scruples, social pressure, and whatever leverage a woman could gain due to her husband's feelings for her. Physical abuse of wives took place, but it was not nearly as widespread as the damage done to women's self-respect by their dependency. Male power in the family was still too great for feminism to be able to confront it directly.[10] . . .

The New Feminism of the 1960s

The women's movement of the early twentieth century did not pursue the issues that Gilman had raised in *Women and Economics* and *The Yellow Wallpaper*. These issues remained the concerns of a small section of the movement, while the majority of feminists focused their attention upon the campaign for woman suffrage. When suffrage was won in 1920, the women's movement died. But over the four decades that followed it became increasingly evident that suffrage had been only the first step. When feminism ultimately re-emerged in the 1960s, the new movement was shaped by the fact that formal equality, having been at least partially achieved, was no longer as pressing an issue for women as it had once been, and also by the recognition that in any case equal rights in the public arena were not enough. The new feminists reversed the priorities of their predecessors: while they recognized the importance of continuing to fight for equality in the public arena, their central concern was the question of women's subordination within the family.

Like the early feminist movement, the feminism of the mid-sixties emerged out of women's experience in non-feminist political movements, and was shaped by that experience. In the early sixties young women were drawn to the civil rights and anti-war movements for much the same reasons as were their male contemporaries, out of outrage at a society that professed democratic and humanitarian principles while practicing racism and military aggression. Within these movements and the new left as a whole, it was men who took on leadership roles while women for the most part found themselves in the role of followers. At first this was tolerable: it was subtle, and it was no more than women expected. But as women's confidence and political awareness grew, so did authoritarianism within the movement. The seemingly unstoppable escalation of the war in Vietnam drove the left to increasing levels of desperation, a mood that allowed leaders to treat followers, especially women, in an increasingly high-handed manner. In the name of fighting for the liberation of black people at home and the Vietnamese abroad, women were now being asked to subordinate themselves to the authority of male leaders of their own movement.

Confronted with such hypocrisy, women began to leave the new left to form women's groups. The process was much the same as it had been over a century earlier, when abolitionist women had turned to feminism as obstacles to their activity in behalf of the abolition of slavery had made them aware of their own lack of rights as women. The difference was that while the abolitionist women had confronted the constraints on the public, political role of women, for the women of the new left, a primary issue was the discrepancy between the formal accordance of equality and the informal and private treatment of women as men's inferiors.

The feminism of the mid-sixties, again like early feminism, arose not only out of women's experience of discrimination within a movement for democracy, but also out of changes in the situation of women, especially those of the social strata that formed the base of the new left. In the fifties and sixties women of these strata were attending college in numbers greater than ever before. Like men, they were being trained for professional careers; unlike men, when they left college they were likely to face the choice between family life and no careers, or careers and no family life. There were few models for combining the two, and few men who were sympathetic to such an effort.

Because contradictions of this nature affected much larger numbers of women than those in the new left, a liberal feminist movement began to emerge at roughly the same time that new left women were forming the first women's groups. And the liberal wing of feminism quickly came to predominate in numbers. But it was the radical wing of feminism that gave the movement most of its impetus and direction, and that not only in the sixties but in the seventies as well has produced the main body of influential feminist literature.

The radical wing of feminism in the mid-sixties was united by its militant opposition to sexism, not by a coherent or shared analysis of the sources of sexism. And as such analyses began to be put forward, this wing of the women's movement began to split into two camps. One, which came to be called radical feminism, was made up of women who saw the oppression of women by men as the basis for all forms of oppression. These women also believed that it was necessary to build a women's culture and women's institutions, to make it possible for women to live as far as possible in a female world. They argued that the women's movement should be autonomous of all other movements, and they tended to see that movement as holding out a new way of life for women rather than as a short-term strategy for overcoming women's oppression within a society that included men. Radical feminists, of all feminist tendencies, most sharply rejected marriage and the nuclear family. The theory that they produced criticized these institutions and their impact on women's lives, often without understanding the historical and social origins of these institutions. The most influential radical feminist writings linked family and society, but often described social roles outside the family as products of sex roles within the family rather than placing the family within a social context.[11]

The second tendency within the radical women's movement called itself anti-imperialist or Marxist feminist; part of this tendency evolved into socialist feminism. These women saw female oppression as one of many kinds of oppression, and sought to link the women's movement with others, especially the anti-war and black liberation movements. The Marxist feminists took issue with the radical feminist assertion that the oppression of women had formed the historical basis of class divisions, and that sex oppression continued to be of greater social significance than class oppression. Instead, the Marxist feminists placed the oppression of women within what they saw as the more basic framework of class relations.[12]

The third tendency in the women's movement was liberal feminism. In 1966, at the same time that radical women were leaving the new left, a group of women who had been involved in liberal and Democratic politics also came to the conclusion that there was a need for a women's movement, that mainstream liberal organizations would not take women's rights seriously. These women founded the National Organization for Women, which worked to complete the struggle for women's equality, especially in education, hiring, and the law. Since then a large number of women's organizations have emerged with the same goal of improving women's status; this is the largest section of the women's movement. But this section of the women's movement has been less interested in the origins of women's oppression than in practical activity, and has added relatively little to feminist theory.[13]

In the late sixties and early seventies, radical feminist writings dominated discussion in the radical wing of the women's movement and were influential in liberal feminist circles as well. The two most widely read statements of this outlook were Kate Millett's *Sexual Politics*, especially the chapter entitled "Theory of Sexual Politics," and Shulamith Firestone's *The Dialectic of Sex*. Both contributed to developing the theory, hinted at by so many early feminists, that the oppression of women had its origin in women's role in the family.

Kate Millett described both the family and society as patriarchal, characterized by men's domination of women and children. She distinguished between "traditional patriarchy," in which women had no legal standing or economic existence, as they could not own or earn in their own right, and "modern patriarchy," in which women are formally accorded equal or nearly equal rights with men, but in which most women do unpaid labor in the home rather than working for wages outside it.

Millett recognized that some women work outside the home in present-day America, but argued that these women have only a temporary relation to the labor force, constituting a reserve labor force "enlisted in times of war and expansion and discharged in times of peace and recession." She saw women's position as fundamentally defined by their dependence upon men rather than by their class position. "In general," she wrote, "the position of women in patriarchy is a continuous function of their economic dependence. Just as their social position is vicarious and achieved (often on a temporary or marginal basis) through males, their relation to the economy is also typically vicarious or tangential."[14]

Kate Millett described a male-dominated society based on a male-dominated family, but she did not discuss the workings of that family, or the link between it and society, in any detail. Shulamith Firestone, in *The Dialectic of Sex,* published the same year, developed these ideas further. She described the hierarchy of power in the nuclear family. Children, she wrote, are at the mercy of their parents, but ultimate authority rests with the father:

> In the prototypical patriarchal nuclear family . . . the father is the breadwinner; all other members of his family are his dependents. He agrees to support a wife in return for her services: housekeeping, sex, and reproduction. The children whom she bears for him are even more dependent. . . . His rights over them are complete. If he is not a kind master/father, tough luck. They cannot escape his clutches until they are grown, and by then the psychological molding has been accomplished: they are now ready to repeat his performance.[15]

Firestone argued that children of both sexes initially feel closest to the mother because she nurtures them and because they identify with her powerlessness. They fear the father and may secretly feel contempt for him. Firestone understood the oedipus complex as the father's intervention in this early mother-child relationship, his way of insuring that the nuclear family on which his power rests will be reproduced. He promises his son male status and power in return for the son's renunciation of loyalty to and identification with the mother. All the father holds out to his daughter, as a reward for shifting her love and loyalty from her mother to him, is that eventually she will marry and partake of male power through association with it. The daughter may envy her brother's privileges; she may even wish that she had a penis, out of a desire for the status associated with it. But eventually she must recognize that the male role is closed to her, and accept femininity and subordination to men.

Firestone saw male domination in the family as the historical origin of class systems, and the patriarchal family as the basic unit of societies—all historical societies—in which men hold power over women and a dominant class holds power over subordinate classes. She pointed out that the first division of labor was that between men and women, and was based on women's pregnancy and their responsibility for child care. She argued that a biological family in which women are dependent upon men creates a psychology that makes possible hierarchical relations throughout society. She wrote:

> Marxian analysis itself was insufficient: it did not dig deep enough to the psychosocial roots of class. Marx was onto something more profound than he knew when he observed that the family contained within itself in embryo all the antagonisms that later develop on a wide scale within the society and the state. For unless the revolution uproots the basic social organization, the biological family—the vinculum through which the psychology of power can always be smuggled—the tapeworm of exploitation will never be annihilated. We shall need a sexual revolution much larger than—inclusive of—a socialist one to truly eradicate all class systems.[16]

Firestone's rewriting of the Freudian account of the family was mechanical in its substitution of power relations for sexuality, and her social theory did not provide the basis for understanding the history of either women or the family, much less class relations in general. Firestone did not explain how hierarchies are transposed from family to society. Furthermore, women's mothering has thus far been a constant through history; in order to explain the changes in women's role in the family and in society it is necessary to look to economic and social forces outside the family and their impact upon it, not to an unchanging element of family structure.

The importance of Firestone's book lay not in her social theory or the specifics of her psychology, but in the fact that she linked sex roles with power relations in the family, and linked feminism with a protest not only against women's subordination, but against social hierarchies in general. Charlotte Perkins Gilman had said seventy years earlier that femininity was a product of women's economic dependence upon men; Firestone's presentation of this point was more psychologically sophisticated than Gilman's, but the main difference was that in 1970 the women's movement was ready to listen, while in 1898 it had not been.

Why was the women's movement now ready to hear this message? In 1970 the radical wing of the women's movement—the section that was most responsive to these issues—was made up largely of college-educated young women, often from professional families. These women were able to criticize the family in a way that their feminist forebears could not because in the social milieu of the new feminists patriarchy was rapidly breaking down. Many of them were unmarried and quite able to support themselves; if they married, it was likely to be more out of choice than necessity, and they were likely to retain the ability to leave marriage if necessary. More importantly, these young women moved in a world in which the old patriarchal values were beginning to falter. A man whose education was in no way superior to his wife's, and whose work was, by his own standards, no more valuable than hers, might lack the old male self-confidence in proclaiming his superiority. A cultural vacuum had been created, and it was possible for the new feminism to walk into it and create a new set of values.

Although feminism appeared first among college-educated women who felt the changes in women's status most sharply, neither the changes nor the concerns were confined to this stratum. For about a century, an expanding American economy had been slowly drawing American women out of the domesticity of the nineteenth century and into increasingly full participation in the labor force.

At all times in American history some women had worked outside the home, and from the late nineteenth century on, the poorest women, blacks, and many immigrants had routinely worked outside the home when young, and often continued to work after marriage. But it was in the twenties and more dramatically in the forties and fifties that new groups of women began to join the labor force in large numbers: young white women who were needed to help support their families or who wanted the independence that their own incomes made possible, and, increasingly, white married women who needed to help support their families, and who may have wanted some life outside the home as well.[17]

Conveniently for capitalists, it was widely believed that women worked only temporarily, and that their work was not central to their lives in the way that men's was to theirs. Such ideas helped to keep women workers unorganized and highly exploited. Many unions excused their failure to organize women workers on grounds that they were marginal members of the work force, and many women failed to join unions out of the hope that they would stop working soon.[18] But though women's work has often been regarded as temporary and incidental, in fact in the middle decades of the twentieth century there has been a steady growth in the numbers of women who work outside the home, and in the number of years that women do such work. Furthermore, women are increasingly likely to work at points in their life cycles during which they once would have remained in the home. At the turn of the century, working women were almost invariably unmarried, and usually young. Now the majority of married women, and a large proportion of women with children, hold jobs. At the turn of the century, for most white women marriage involved the expectation that one would be supported by one's husband for the rest of one's life, and remain in the home raising children and doing housework. Now most American women can expect that they will work outside the home for much of their adult lives, including the period when their children are growing up.[19]

Women's increasing employment outside the home has increased women's options, in particular their ability to leave an unsatisfactory marriage, or to back up demands for improvement with the threat of leaving. A woman's ability to leave her marriage is of course affected by the wages that she can earn and the number of children that she would find herself supporting after a divorce. Clearly women of the poorer sections of the working class, who are likely to have less training, to marry earlier, and to have more children, have fewer options than women from more privileged sections of the working class, or the middle classes. But since the turn of the century there has been a general expansion of women's options that has affected women throughout American society, even though unequally. In the 1970s there are not only many more jobs available to women than there were at the turn of the century; the incomes that these jobs bring in have risen, making it much more likely that a working woman will be able to support not only herself, but perhaps children as well. At the turn of the century most women's jobs were so poorly paid that it took great ingenuity for a woman to support herself on her wages; prostitution constituted a major source of income to working women, who turned to it because it was the only alternative to starvation wages. There are no overall statistics on the relationship between men's and women's wages in this period, but it has been estimated that among factory workers, women generally earned less than fifty percent of what men earned.[20] In the economy as a whole the income of working women was probably an even lower percentage than this of the income of working men. Roughly a quarter of all working women were employed as domestics or servants at the turn of the century, and these women ordinarily earned even less than female factory workers, while the median income of working men was raised by the fact that men occupied the higher-paid clerical and white-collar jobs.

At the turn of the century, it was largely black, first-generation immigrant, and single women who worked outside the home. These women had little bargaining power: their desperate economic situation, their lack of organization and of political power forced them to accept virtually whatever wages were offered them. Thus it was possible for employers to pay women workers wages that were quite minimal. In the middle decades of the century employers faced the necessity of drawing new groups of women into the labor force, including women whose greater economic resources and social leverage enabled them to demand better wages. No doubt partly as a result, women's wages during these decades were slightly upgraded in relation to men's. In 1956, for instance, white women earned 63 percent of what white men earned. In the sixties and seventies this trend has again reversed, and the gap between men's and women's incomes has widened; in 1973, white women earned only 56.3 percent of what white men earned. Perhaps this shift reflects women's increasing need for jobs, and the fact that once women have been drawn into the labor force their labor can be treated as cheap and expendable.

But in spite of the current widening gap between men's and women's incomes, over the twentieth century as a whole women's ability to support themselves has improved. The United States is now considerably more prosperous than it was at the turn of the century. The growth of trade unionism, with union struggles for higher wages, has raised the standard of living not only of union members but to some extent of unorganized workers as well. A woman's 56 percent of a man's income in the 1970s brings her considerably closer to self-sufficiency than did her roughly 40 percent of her male counterpart's pittance at the turn of the century. Working women are still much more likely to be poor than working men. The difference is that now a woman is especially likely to fall below the poverty line if she is supporting a family by herself; seventy years ago virtually all working women in the United States were poor, and it was near-impossible for them to support families on their incomes alone. In 1973 the median income of a family headed by a woman who worked full-time was $8,795. While this is hardly a comfortable income, it does place self-sufficiency and the support of one or two children within the realm of possibility.[21]

Women's entry into the labor force and the overall rise in women's wages have increased women's chances for attaining economic independence, and increased their leverage within their families. The breakdown of patriarchy has been hastened by these changes, but it has also proceeded according to a rhythm of its own. As the social and economic basis for the old notions of male superiority has crumbled, new ideas have begun to take hold even in families in which women are still in fact economically dependent. In 1900 the vast majority of white American husbands, if asked, would have proudly announced that they would never allow their wives to work. In the 1970s, even in blue-collar families where women's economic dependence is most pronounced, husbands would be less likely to make such statements; those who did would be aware that they were going against the tide.[22]

Over the twentieth century women's legal and political gains and women's entry into the labor force have weakened the traditional sources of male power in the family, and it has become possible for the women's movement to make a direct attack upon patriarchy. Though it is the weakness of the institution that makes such an assault possible, the need to focus energies on this task has led feminism to emphasize the strength of patriarchy. But the women's movement is concerned with the immediate problems of women, especially those of the women closest to the movement itself, as well as with problems of theory. And the problems faced by women today, especially women of the professional families or milieus who are likely to be close to the women's movement, are more often those associated with the breakdown of traditional relations between men and women than those emanating from a strong and viable patriarchal structure. There is a discontinuity in feminist literature: while it presents a theory of patriarchy, it describes the problems associated with the breakdown of patriarchy. These problems cannot be fully understood in the context of that theory. In part, the theory of patriarchy is maintained because patriarchy tends to be seen as synonymous with male dominance, and it is clear that male dominance has not disappeared. But in fact patriarchy is only one possible form of male dominance. Feminist literature itself documents the emergence of a new form, one for which we do not yet have a name.

A central theme in contemporary feminist literature is that of the difficulties that women confront in trying to establish satisfying personal relations with men. Men are likely to be unable or unwilling to express deep emotions, to maintain the level of intimacy that women want in personal relations. Men are described as pulling away from such intimacy, either because they cannot tolerate it or because withdrawal itself can become a weapon in their struggles with women. In *The Dialectic of Sex,* Shulamith Firestone devotes several chapters to this theme. She quotes from the remarks of patients in clinical studies: women who complain of men who are emotionally distant or who withhold commitment, men who seem at pains to show how cool and cynical they are, how emotionally uninvolved. Firestone concludes that women need love and that men can't love; she writes, "love, perhaps, even more than child-bearing, is the pivot of women's oppression today."[23]

Firestone's presentation of the contradiction between men's and women's emotional needs is extreme, but the theme itself is common in feminist literature, though much more in fiction and in discussions of women's experience than in theoretical pieces. Women's sharp awareness of emotional needs and men's emotional withdrawal is a central theme of Doris Lessing's writing, especially *The Golden Notebook*, a book that was widely read in the radical section of the American women's movement.[24] Lesbians point out that one of the advantages of loving women is that both partners are capable of emotional expressiveness.[25] Marge Piercy, in a discussion of sexism in the left, points to the ability of men to use sexual relationships for short-term gratification or political advantage, and the vulnerability of women, through their greater emotional involvement.[26] Firestone tries to explain the emotional contradictions between men and women in the framework of patriarchy: it is the imbalance of power that corrupts love, she writes, for in love both partners must be vulnerable, and man's greater power erases his consciousness of need. But this is inadequate. . . .

The problem that Firestone and Lessing point to is a problem not of patriarchy but of its collapse. In the nineteenth century, women knew what marriage entailed and knew that there was no alternative. From everything that we know of marriage in this period, it seems that women were resigned to a certain emotional distance between themselves and their husbands, and that they routinely turned to other women, and perhaps to children, for the emotional contact that marriage so often lacked. What has changed over the twentieth century is less male behavior than women's expectations. As the traditional sources of male power in the family begin to slip away, men may be more prone to use emotional withdrawal as a weapon; but the unemotional male style itself is not new. What has changed is women's demands. With the geographical mobility and breakdown of communities of the twentieth century, women's support networks outside the family have weakened, and they are likely to turn to their husbands for intimacy that earlier generations would have found elsewhere. And increasingly women can back up these demands with the threat of leaving.

Another issue of contemporary feminism that is better understood in the context of the breakdown than the viability of patriarchy is that of women's difficulties in constructing new identities for themselves, finding a bridge between traditional domestic femininity and their new roles in work and social involvement outside the home. Most women, even if they work outside the home, are expected to take the main responsibility for children and housework. Like nineteenth-century women, women today are likely not to have families if they are not willing to do this. Women who work outside the home must do two jobs at once; this is alleviated only to the extent that they can induce their husbands to help them. Pat Mainardi's "The Politics of Housework"[27] was immensely popular in the women's movement of the late sixties because it outlined strategies for involving men in work in the home. Work outside the home often brings a new sense of independence, and it may bring greater leverage within the family, but it also entails new struggles.[28]

Women who work outside the home are under pressure not only to take on two sets of responsibilities, but also to behave according to two sets of standards. "Femininity" still means compliance, submission to men, and childlike helplessness, while women's work requires the competence and often the aggressive self-assertion that have been associated with masculinity. The transition from housewife to working woman involves finding a new way of looking at oneself and one's place in the world, often in the face of male resistance to what men understand as encroachment on their territory. . . .

The problems of establishing satisfying personal relations with men, of constructing a new female identity, may be emotionally wrenching, but at least they can be seen as part of a welcome process of reconstructing the roles of the sexes. But there are aspects of the decline of patriarchy that are much grimmer. As the old mechanisms of male control over women break down, the blatant efforts of some men to retain that control, through rape and other forms of violence, intensify. Recently, statistics indicate that rape has increased faster than any other violent crime. Over the past five years reported rapes have increased by 62 percent; other violent crimes, murder, aggravated assault, robbery, have together risen by 45 percent.[29]

It can be argued that this rise reflects nothing more than the impact of the women's movement, which by opening up public discussion of rape and beginning to remove the blame from the victim has enabled more women to report assaults.[30] But it seems likely that two other factors are also at work: women are readier to report rapes, and rape is also more widespread. Rape has been closely associated with periods of social breakdown, such as war. Invading soldiers are likely to treat women of an enemy population in a manner in which they would not treat their countrywomen. In a stable society in which there are established notions of how women should behave, and women generally adhere to those standards, rape is not likely to be a major problem. Male control is asserted in more subtle, less disruptive ways, and men's anger at and contempt of women is for the most part kept within certain bounds.

In the United States of the 1970s, as women begin to take the freedom to carry themselves with new confidence, to behave in ways that many men consider outside the bounds of femininity, male anger can become volatile. Stretching the boundaries of acceptable female behavior is often described as inviting attack from men; but women who live alone, or walk alone at night, are doing no more than what would be taken for granted in a man. With the breakdown of patriarchy women who are without the old male protections become more vulnerable, and men, as they lose familiar avenues of control, may respond with violence.

The emphasis on the strength of patriarchy and the parallel demand for female autonomy have had and continue to have a place in feminist strategy. Though the development of capitalism has drawn large numbers of women out of domesticity and enabled them to exert greater leverage within their families, as long as women are mainly responsible for children it remains possible for men to play a role in the family that contains some elements of patriarchal power. The sexual division of labor will not be overcome by the workings of capitalism but by the concerted efforts of people, especially women. And until there is real equality between the sexes in the family and elsewhere, patriarchy cannot be forgotten and demands for female autonomy cannot be entirely put aside.

But as patriarchy weakens, old demands begin to recede, old issues lose their force; new issues come to the fore. We are witnessing the emergence of a new form of male dominance, one that is much less clearly defined than patriarchy and that cannot claim the social acceptance that patriarchy once possessed. For these reasons it is more difficult for us to confront. . . .

Feminism has at least by reputation often been associated with a female strategy of independence and with a rejection of the family, of marriage and monogamy. According to this popular view, a feminist would urge a woman who was unhappy with her marriage to leave it, and would probably regard the marriage as having been dishonorable in the first place. But most women want to establish and maintain relations with men, and want the security that marriage suggests.

It is a tricky business to construct a critique of marriage and the family that presents a vision of a future in which equality between the sexes makes possible new forms of personal life, and at the same time is responsive to the immediate interests of women in a male-dominated society. . . . Anita Bryant's attack on homosexuality as a threat to the family, or Marabel Morgan's Fascinating Womanhood movement which purports to teach women to hold onto their husbands through seduction, feed on fears of social isolation that have a basis in reality. The anti-abortion movement speaks to women's fears that motherhood is being devalued; this is a legitimate concern at a time when, for most women, there are no adequate alternatives to it.

The solutions that right-wing movements pose to these problems are not only anti-feminist but inadequate. Seducing one's husband will not alleviate the growing pressures on marriage, suppressing homosexuality will not hold families together, and preventing abortions will not improve the status of mothers. These movements attract women not because they point to any viable solutions, but because they bring into the open problems associated with the breakdown of traditional family structure and roles. They provide arenas in which women can voice real concerns. It is time for feminism and the left to address these questions.

NOTES

1. Elizabeth Cady Stanton, Susan B. Anthony, and Matilda Joslyn Gage, eds., *History of Woman Suffrage*, vol. 1 (New York, 1881), "Declaration of Sentiments," pp. 70–74.

2. Elizabeth Cady Stanton, *Eighty Years and More Reminiscences, 1815–1897* (New York: T. Fisher Unwin, 1898; Schocken, 1973).

3. Antoinette Blackwell Brown, "The Relation of Women's Work in the Household to the Work Outside," quoted in Aileen S. Kraditor, ed., *Up from the Pedestal: Selected Writings in the History of American Feminism* (Chicago: Quadrangle, 1970), pp. 150–59.

4. Ida Husted Harper, *The Life and Work of Susan B. Anthony* (Indianapolis, 1898), pp. 104–12, quoted in Kraditor, pp. 159–67.

5. Elizabeth Cady Stanton, in a letter to Lucy Stone, quoted in Leslie B. Tanner, ed., *Voices from Women's Liberation* (New York: Signet, 1970), p. 77.

6. *History of Woman Suffrage*, vol. 1, p. 88.

7. For a description of the legal status of women in nineteenth-century America, see Eleanor Flexner, *Century of Struggle* (Cambridge: Harvard University Press, 1959), ch. 4; and Leo Kanowitz, *Women and the Law: The Unfinished Revolution* (Albuquerque: University of New Mexico Press, 1969).

8. On the role of women in the abolitionist movement, see Gerda Lerner, *The Grimké Sisters from South Carolina: Rebels against Slavery* (Boston: Houghton Mifflin, 1969). On the impact of abolitionism on early feminism, see Flexner, ch. 3.

9. Charlotte Perkins Gilman, *Women and Economics* (Boston: Small, Maynard & Co., 1899; New York: Harper & Row, 1966).

10. The patriarchal father and husband, austere, emotionally distant from mother and children, and the ultimate power in the family, appears in biographies, autobiographies, and novels of the nineteenth century, as well as in guides to family life for women. See, for instance, Lucy Larcom, *A New England Girlhood* (Boston: 1889), Kathryn Kish Sklar, *Catharine Beecher: A Study in American Domesticity* (New Haven, Conn.: Yale University Press, 1973); Louisa May Alcott, *Little Women* (Boston: 1868). For an example of a

nineteenth-century marriage guide, see William A. Alcott, *The Young Wife, or Duties of Woman in the Married Relation* (Boston: 1837).

11. Central pieces of radical feminist literature include the following: Kate Millett, *Sexual Politics* (New York: Avon, 1969); Shulamith Firestone, *The Dialectic of Sex: The Case for Feminist Revolution* (New York: Bantam, 1970); articles in Anne Koedt, Ellen Levine, and Anita Rapone, eds., *Radical Feminism* (New York: Quadrangle, 1972); and the journal *Notes.*

12. Central pieces of socialist-feminist literature include the following: Juliet Mitchell, "The Longest Revolution," *New Left Review* 40 (November–December 1960), pp. 11–37; Eli Zaretsky, "Capitalism, the Family, and Personal Life," *Socialist Revolution* 13/14, 15 (January–June 1973); Sheila Rowbotham, *Woman's Consciousness, Man's World* (London: Penguin, 1973); and articles in Leslie B. Tanner, ed., *Voices from Women's Liberation* (New York: Signet, 1970); in Robin Morgan, ed., *Sisterhood Is Powerful: An Anthology of Writings from the Women's Liberation Movement* (New York: Vintage, 1970); and from Edith Hoshino Altbach, *From Feminism to Liberation* (Cambridge, Mass.: Schenkman, 1971).

13. Judith Hole and Ellen Levine, *Rebirth of Feminism* (New York: Quadrangle, 1973) is a good history of the contemporary women's movement, with an emphasis on liberal feminism.

14. Millett, p. 38.

15. Firestone, p. 48.

16. Ibid., pp. 11–12.

17. William Chafe, *The American Woman: Her Changing Social, Economic, and Political Role,* 1920–1970 (New York: Oxford, 1972).

18. See Heidi Hartmann, "Capitalism, Patriarchy, and Job Segregation by Sex," *Signs,* vol. 1, no. 3, part 2 (Spring 1976), pp. 137–70, for an account of the exclusion of women from unions and from higher-paying jobs, and an argument that this is the work of male trade unionists, acting in what they see as their own self-interest.

19. Chafe, pp. 144–46, 218–20.

20. Robert W. Smuts, *Women and Work in America* (New York: Schocken, 1971), p. 91.

21. These statistics are from the following sources: U.S. Dept. of Commerce, Bureau of the Census, *Historical Statistics of the United States, Colonial Times to the Present;* U.S. Dept. of Labor, Employment Standards Administration, Women's Bureau, *Bulletin* 297, 1975 *Handbook on Women Workers;* U.S. Dept. of Commerce, Bureau of the Census, *Statistical Abstract of the United States,* 1976.

22. See Lillian Rubin, *Worlds of Pain: Life in the Working-Class Family* (New York: Basic Books, 1976), ch. 9.

23. Firestone, p. 126.

24. Doris Lessing, *The Golden Notebook* (New York: McGraw-Hill, 1962).

25. "Loving Another Woman—Interview," in Koedt, Levine, and Rapone, pp. 85–94.

26. Marge Piercy, "The Grand Coolie Damn," in Morgan, pp. 421–38.

27. Pat Mainardi, "The Politics of Housework," in Morgan, pp. 447–54.

28. There is a large sociological literature on how marriage is affected when a woman works outside the home, most of it arguing that when women go to work their decision-making power within the family is enhanced. See Robert O. Blood and Donald M. Wolfe, *Husbands and Wives* (Glencoe, Ill.: Free Press, 1960), ch. 2; David Heer, "The Measurement and

Bases of Family Power: An Overview," *Journal of Marriage and Family Living*, vol. 25, no. 2 (May, 1963), pp. 133–38; David Heer, "Dominance and the Working Wife," *Social Forces* 36 (May 1958), pp. 341–47; and Janice Neipert Hedges and Jeanne K. Barnett, "Working Women and the Division of Household Tasks," *Monthly Labor Review* (April 1972), pp. 9–14. Dair Gillespie, in "Who Has the Power? The Marriage Struggle," *Journal of Marriage and the Family*, vol. 33, no. 3 (August 1971), pp. 445–58, criticizes this literature for failing to recognize the sources of male dominance that persist regardless of women's employment and income.

29. Susan Brownmiller, *Against Our Will: Men, Women and Rape* (New York: Bantam, 1975), pp. 190–91.

30. Brownmiller, for instance, makes this argument.

SUGGESTIONS FOR FURTHER READING

Banner, Lois W. *Women in Modern America: A Brief History*. New York: Harcourt Brace, 1974.

Barker-Benfield, G. J. *The Horrors of the Half-known Life: Male Attitudes Toward Women and Sexuality in Nineteenth-Century America*. New York: Harper and Row, 1976.

Baxandall, Rosalyn; Gordon, Linda; and Reverby, Susan, eds. *America's Working Women: A Documentary History, 1600 to the Present*. New York: Vintage, 1976.

Berg, Barbara. *The Remembered Gate: Origins of American Feminism—The Woman and the City, 1800–1860*. New York: Oxford University Press, 1978.

Brownlee, W. Elliot, and Brownlee, Mary M., eds. *Women in the American Economy: A Documentary History, 1675 to 1927*. New Haven, Conn.: Yale, 1976.

Brownmiller, Susan. *Against Our Will: Men, Women and Rape*. New York: Simon and Schuster, 1975.

Buhle, Mari Jo, and Buhle, Paul, eds. *The Concise History of Woman Suffrage: Selections from the Classic Work of Stanton, Anthony, Gage, and Harper*. Urbana: University of Illinois Press, 1978.

Cantor, Milton, and Laurie, Bruce, eds. *Class, Sex, and the Woman Worker*. Westport, Conn.: Greenwood Press, 1977.

Carden, Maren Lockwood. *The New Feminist Movement*. New York: Russell Sage, 1974.

Carroll, Berenice A., ed. *Liberating Women's History: Theoretical and Critical Essays*. Urbana: University of Illinois Press, 1974.

Chafe, William H. *The American Woman: Her Changing Social, Economic, and Political Roles, 1920–1970*. New York: Oxford University Press, 1972.

Chafe, William H. *Women and Equality: Changing Patterns in American Culture*. New York: Oxford University Press, 1977.

Chevigny, Bell Gale. *The Woman and the Myth: Margaret Fuller's Life and Writings*. Old Westbury, N.Y.: Feminist Press, 1976.

Conrad, Susan P. *Perish the Thought: Intellectual Women in Romantic America, 1830–1860*. New York: Oxford University Press, 1976.

Cook, Blanche Wiesen, ed. *Crystal Eastman on Women and Revolution*. New York: Oxford, 1978.

Cott, Nancy F. *The Bonds of Womanhood: "Woman's Sphere" in New England, 1780–1835*. New Haven, Conn.: Yale University Press, 1977.

Cott, Nancy F., ed. *Root of Bitterness: Documents of the Social History of American Women*. New York: E. P. Dutton, 1972.

Demos, John, and Boocock, Sarane Spence, eds. *Turning Points: Historical and Sociological Essays on the Family*. Chicago: University of Chicago Press, 1978.

Donegan, Jane B. *Women and Men Midwives: Medicine, Morality, and Misogyny in Early America*. Westport, Conn.: Greenwood Press, 1978.

Douglas, Ann. *The Feminization of American Culture*. New York: Knopf, 1977.

Dublin, Thomas. *Women at Work: The Transformation of Work and Community in Lowell, Massachusetts, 1826–1869.* New York: Columbia University Press, 1979.

DuBois, Ellen Carol. *Feminism and Suffrage: The Emergence of an Independent Women's Movement in America, 1848–1869.* Ithaca, N.Y.: Cornell University Press, 1978.

Ehrenreich, Barbara, and English, Deirdre. *Complaints and Disorders: The Sexual Politics of Sickness.* Old Westbury, N.Y.: Feminist Press, 1974.

Ehrenreich, Barbara, and English, Deirdre. *Witches, Midwives and Nurses: A History of Women Healers.* Old Westbury, N.Y.: Feminist Press, 1972.

Evans, Sara. *Personal Politics: The Roots of Women's Liberation in the Civil Rights Movement and the New Left.* New York: Knopf, 1978.

Faragher, John Mack. *Women and Men on the Overland Trail.* New Haven, Conn.: Yale University Press, 1979.

Filene, Peter Gabriel. *Him/Her/Self: Sex Roles in Modern America.* New York: Harcourt Brace, 1975.

Firestone, Shulamith. *The Dialectic of Sex.* New York: Bantam Books, 1971.

Fischer, Christiane, ed. *Let Them Speak for Themselves: Women in the American West, 1849–1900.* Hamden, Conn.: Archon Books, 1977.

Flexner, Eleanor. *Century of Struggle: The Woman's Rights Movement in the United States.* Cambridge, Mass.: Harvard University Press, 1959.

Frankfort, Roberta. *Collegiate Women: Domesticity and Career in Turn-of-the-century America.* New York: New York University Press, 1978.

Freeman, Jo. *The Politics of Women's Liberation: A Case Study of an Emerging Social Movement and its Relation to the Social Policy Process.* New York: McKay, 1975.

Friedan, Betty. *The Feminine Mystique.* New York: Norton, 1963.

Friedman, Jean E., and Shade, William O., eds. *Our American Sisters: Women in American Life and Thought.* 2d ed. Boston: Allyn and Bacon, 1976.

Fryer, Judith. *The Faces of Eve: Women in the Nineteenth-Century American Novel.* New York: Oxford University Press, 1976.

Gluck, Sherna, ed. *From Parlor to Prison: Five American Suffragists Talk About Their Lives.* New York: Random House, 1976.

Gordon, Linda. *Woman's Body, Woman's Right: A Social History of Birth Control in America.* New York: Grossman, 1976.

Gordon, Michael, ed. *The American Family in Social-Historical Perspective.* 2d ed. New York: St. Martin's, 1978.

Gornick, Vivian, and Moran, Barbara K., eds. *Woman in Sexist Society: Studies in Power and Powerlessness.* New York: Basic Books, 1971.

Haber, Barbara, ed. *Women in America: A Guide to Books, 1963–1975.* Boston: G. K. Hall, 1978.

Hall, Jacquelyn Dowd. *Revolt Against Chivalry: Jessie Daniel Ames and the Women's Campaign Against Lynching.* New York: Columbia University Press, 1974.

Hareven, Tamara, ed. *Transitions: The Family and the Life Course in Historical Perspective.* New York: Academic Press, 1978.

Hareven, Tamara, and Vinovskis, Maris A., eds. *Family and Population in Nineteenth-Century America.* Princeton, N.J.: Princeton University Press, 1979.

Harley, Sharon, and Terborg-Penn, Rosalyn, eds. *The Afro-American Woman: Struggles and Images.* Port Washington, N.Y.: Kennikat Press, 1978.

Harris, Barbara J. *Beyond Her Sphere: Women and the Professions in American History*. Westport, Conn.: Greenwood Press, 1978.
Hartman, Mary, and Banner, Lois W., eds. *Clio's Consciousness Raised: New Perspectives on the History of Women*. New York: Harper and Row, 1974.
Hersh, Blanche Glassman. *The Slavery of Sex: Feminist-Abolitionists in America*. Urbana: University of Illinois Press, 1978.
Hole, Judith, and Levine, Ellen, eds. *Rebirth of Feminism*. New York: Quadrangle Press, 1971.

James, Edward T., and James, Janet W., eds. *Notable American Women, 1607–1950: A Biographical Dictionary*. 3 vols. Cambridge, Mass.: Harvard University Press, 1971.
Johnston, Jill. *Lesbian Nation: The Feminist Solution*. New York: Simon and Schuster, 1974.

Kahn, Kathy. *Hillbilly Women*. Garden City, N.Y.: Doubleday, 1973.
Katz, Jonathan, ed. *Gay American History: Lesbians and Gay Men in the U.S.A.* New York: Thomas Y. Crowell, 1976.
Katzman, David M. *Seven Days a Week: Women and Domestic Service in Industrializing America*. New York: Oxford University Press, 1978.
Kenneally, James J. *Women and American Trade Unions*. St. Albans, Vt.: Eden Press, 1978.
Kraditor, Aileen. *Ideas of the Woman Suffrage Movement, 1890–1920*. New York: Atheneum, 1965.
Kraditor, Aileen, ed. *Up from the Pedestal: Selected Writings in the History of American Feminism*. Chicago: Quadrangle, 1968.

Lane, Ann J., ed. *Mary Ritter Beard: A Sourcebook*. New York: Schocken Books, 1977.
Lemons, J. Stanley. *The Woman Citizen: Social Feminism in the 1920s*. Urbana: University of Illinois Press, 1973.
Lerner, Gerda. *The Majority Finds Its Past: Placing Women in History*. New York: Oxford University Press, 1979.
Lerner, Gerda, ed. *Black Women in White America: A Documentary History*. New York: Pantheon, 1972.
Lerner, Gerda, ed. *The Female Experience: An American Documentary*. Indianapolis: Bobbs-Merrill, 1977.
Litoff, Judy Barrett. *American Midwives: 1860 to the Present*. Westport, Conn.: Greenwood Press, 1978.
Loewenberg, Bert James, and Bogin, Ruth, eds. *Black Women in Nineteenth-Century American Life: Their Words, Their Thoughts, Their Feelings*. University Park: Pennsylvania State University Press, 1976.
Lurie, Nancy O., ed. *Mountain Wolf Woman, Sister of Crashing Thunder: Autobiography of a Winnebago Indian*. Ann Arbor: University of Michigan Press, 1961.

Melder, Keith E. *Beginnings of Sisterhood: The American Woman's Rights Movement, 1800–1850*. New York: Schocken Books, 1977.
Millett, Kate. *Sexual Politics*. Garden City, N.Y.: Doubleday, 1970.
Mohr, James C. *Abortion in America: The Origins and Evolution of National Policy*. New York: Oxford University Press, 1978.
Morgan, Robin, ed. *Sisterhood is Powerful: An Anthology of Writings from the Women's Liberation Movement*. New York: Vintage, 1970.

Neithammer, Carolyn. *Daughters of the Earth: The Lives and Legends of American Indian Women.* New York: Macmillan, 1977.

Oakley, Ann. *Woman's Work: The Housewife, Past and Present.* New York: Pantheon, 1974.

O'Neill, William L. *Everyone was Brave: A History of Feminism in America.* Chicago: Quadrangle, 1971.

O'Neill, William L., ed. *The Woman Movement: Feminism in the United States and England.* Chicago: Quadrangle, 1969.

Oppenheimer, Valerie Kincade. *The Female Labor Force in the United States: Demographic and Economic Factors Governing Its Growth and Changing Composition.* Berkeley: Institute of International Studies, University of California Press, 1970.

Pleck, Elizabeth H., and Pleck, Joseph H., eds. *The American Man.* Englewood Cliffs, N.J.: Prentice-Hall, 1980.

Reiter, Rayna, ed. *Toward an Anthropology of Women.* New York: Monthly Review Press, 1975.

Rich, Adrienne. *Of Woman Born: Motherhood as Experience and Institution.* New York: Norton, 1976.

Robinson, Paul A. *The Modernization of Sex: Havelock Ellis, Alfred Kinsey, William Masters, and Virginia Johnson.* New York: Harper and Row, 1976.

Rosaldo, Michelle Zimbalist, and Lamphere, Louise, eds. *Woman, Culture, and Society.* Stanford, Calif.: Stanford University Press, 1974.

Rosen, Ruth, ed. *The Maimie Papers.* Old Westbury, N.Y.: Feminist Press, 1977.

Rossi, Alice, ed. *The Feminist Papers: From Adams to de Beauvoir.* New York: Columbia University Press, 1973.

Rothman, Sheila. *Woman's Proper Place: A History of Changing Ideals and Practices, 1870 to the Present.* New York: Basic Books, 1978.

Ryan, Mary P. *Womanhood in America, from Colonial Times to the Present.* New York: New Viewpoints, 1975.

Scott, Anne Firor. *The Southern Lady: From Pedestal to Politics, 1830–1930.* Chicago: University of Chicago Press, 1970.

Seifer, Nancy. *Nobody Speaks for Me! Self-portraits of American Working Class Women.* New York: Simon and Schuster, 1976.

Showalter, Elaine. *These Modern Women.* Old Westbury, N.Y.: Feminist Press, 1978.

Sklar, Kathryn Kish. *Catharine Beecher: A Study in American Domesticity.* New Haven, Conn.: Yale University Press, 1973.

Smuts, Robert. *Women and Work in America.* New York: Columbia University Press, 1959.

Sochen, June. *The New Woman: Feminism in Greenwich Village, 1910–1920.* New York: Quadrangle Press, 1972.

Walsh, Mary Roth. *Doctors Wanted: No Women Need Apply—Sexual Barriers in the Medical Profession, 1835–1975.* New Haven: Yale University Press, 1977.

Welter, Barbara, ed. *Dimity Convictions: The American Woman in the Nineteenth Century.* Columbus: Ohio University Press, 1975.

Wertheimer, Barbara. *We Were There: The Story of Working Women in America.* New York: Praeger, 1975.

Yans-McLaughlin, Virginia. *Family and Community: Italian Immigrants in Buffalo, 1880–1930*. Ithaca, N.Y.: Cornell University Press, 1977.

Zaretsky, Eli. *Capitalism, the Family and Personal Life*. New York: Harper and Row, 1976.

NOTES ON CONTRIBUTORS

LOIS GREEN CARR is Historian, St. Mary's City Commission, State of Maryland. Her publications include a book, *Maryland's Revolution of Government, 1689–1692* (with David W. Jordan) and several articles on colonial Maryland. She is currently preparing a study of the early development of the Maryland county courts and their function in the society.

BLANCHE WIESEN COOK is Associate Professor of History at the John Jay College of Criminal Justice, City University of New York. She has written extensively on the peace movement of the World War I era; her most recent publication is *Crystal Eastman: On Women and Revolution*.

NANCY F. COTT teaches history and American Studies at Yale University. She is the author of several articles and books in women's history, including *The Bonds of Womanhood: "Woman's Sphere" in New England, 1780–1835*, and is currently researching feminism after 1920.

BARBARA EASTON teaches American history at the University of California at Santa Cruz and is an editor of *Socialist Review*. Her forthcoming book is a study of women's religious movements and their role in the formation of women's consciousness in nineteenth-century America.

JOHN MACK FARAGHER is a member of the History Department of Mount Holyoke College, and the author of *Women and Men on the Overland Trail*. He is currently working on an ethnographic and social history of women and men in antebellum rural Illinois.

EUGENE GENOVESE is a past president of the Organization of American Historians, and the author of numerous articles and books on theory and practice in history and on antebellum Southern society. His most recent book, *Roll, Jordan, Roll: The World the Slaves Made*, won the Bancroft Prize. He is Editor of the newly-established journal *Marxist Perspectives*, and teaches history at the University of Rochester.

LAURENCE A. GLASCO is Associate Professor of History at the University of Pittsburgh. His several published articles reflect his interest in ethnic relations, family, and class and color differences among Americans.

LINDA GORDON, author of *Woman's Body, Woman's Right: A Social History of Birth Control in America* and an editor of *America's Working Women: A Documentary History*, is Associate Professor of History at the University of Massachusetts in Boston.

HERBERT G. GUTMAN is Professor in the Ph.D. program in History at the Graduate Center, City University of New York. His published works include *Work, Culture and Society in Industrializing America; Slavery and the Numbers Game: A Critique of "Time on the Cross"*; and *The Black Family in Slavery and Freedom, 1750–1925*.

ALICE KESSLER-HARRIS is Associate Professor of History at Hofstra University, where she co-directs the Center for the Study of Work and Leisure. She is the author of *Women Have Always Worked,* and scholarly articles on wage-earning women.

GERDA LERNER teaches history at Sarah Lawrence College, and has been director and co-director of the M.A. program in Women's History there, which she founded in 1972. Among her books are *Black Women in White America: A Documentary History; The Female Experience: An American Documentary;* and, most recently, *The Majority Finds Its Past: Placing Women in History.*

RUTH MILKMAN is a graduate student in Sociology at the University of California, Berkeley, where she is writing a dissertation on women workers and trade unions during the period of the independent C.I.O., 1935–1955. She has been active in the women's movement for many years and is a member of the editorial board of *Socialist Review.*

MARY BETH NORTON is a member of the History Department of Cornell University. Her special interests are the study of the American Revolution, and women's history. Her first book, *The British-Americans: The Loyalist Exiles in England, 1774–1789,* won the Allan Nevins Prize. Her second, *Liberty's Daughters: The Revolutionary Experience of American Women,* will be published in 1980. She has also written a number of scholarly articles and is co-editor (with Carol Berkin) of *Women of America: A History.*

ELIZABETH H. PLECK is a Fellow at the Bunting Institute, Radcliffe College. She is the author of *Black Migration and Poverty: Boston, 1865–1900,* and co-editor (with Joseph Pleck) of *The American Man.* Her current research concerns the history of wife and child abuse in the American family.

DANIEL SCOTT SMITH teaches history at the University of Illinois, Chicago Circle, and is the author of several articles on demographic and family history. At present he is researching the history of old people in America.

JUDITH E. SMITH has taught at Brown University and at the University of Rhode Island. She is a graduate student in the American Civilization Department at Brown University, completing her dissertation on immigrant families and work traditions.

CARROLL SMITH-ROSENBERG is Associate Professor in the Departments of History and Psychiatry at the University of Pennsylvania. The author of *Religion and the Rise of the American City* and numerous articles in women's history, she is currently engaged in a study of gender roles in America, 1785–1895.

CAROL B. STACK is Associate Professor of Anthropology and Public Policy, and Director of the Center for the Study of the Family and the State, at Duke University. She is the author of *All Our Kin: Strategies for Survival in a Black Community* and many articles on the black family and on the impact of welfare, child custody policies, and urban renewal on low-income families and communities. Her current research combines the study of culture, ideology, and family policy.

CHRISTINE STANSELL teaches American social and cultural history at Bard College. She is a Ph.D. candidate in the American Studies Program at Yale University, completing her dissertation on "Woman of the Laboring Poor in New York City, 1815–1860."

FRANK STRICKER is Associate Professor of History at California State University, Dominguez Hills. Interested in social and economic history, he is currently writing an analysis of Frank Capra's films, and a primer on the causes of the Great Depression.

LAUREL THATCHER ULRICH is a doctoral candidate in American history at the University of New Hampshire. She recently received a Woodrow Wilson research grant to complete her dissertation, "Good Wives: A Study in Role Definition in Northern New England, 1650–1750."

JOANN VANEK, formerly at Queens College, is now working at the National Science Foundation in a program which is concerned with the adequacy and accessibility of social science data. She has published "Housewives as Workers" in the collection *Women and Their Work* edited by A. Yates and S. Harkness.

LORENA S. WALSH is Assistant Historian, St. Mary's City Commission, State of Maryland. She is the author of several articles on the social and demographic history of the colonial Chesapeake region and is presently preparing a book on the social, political and economic development of Charles County, Maryland, in the colonial period.

ROBERT V. WELLS is Associate Professor of History at Union College in Schenectady, New York. He is the author of *The Population of the British Colonies in America before 1776* and numerous articles in American demographic and family history.

Index